CHURCHILL AND S

Christopher M. Bell is Professor of History at Dalhousie University in Halifax, Nova Scotia. He has published widely on twentieth century naval history, and is the author of *The Royal Navy, Seapower and Strategy between the Wars* (2000) and co-editor of *At the Crossroads between Peace and War: The London Naval Conference of 1930* (2014), and *Naval Mutinies of the Twentieth Century: An International Perspective* (2003).

Praise for Churchill and Sea Power

'Illuminating'

Publishers Weekly

'A very well argued defence of Winston Churchill against those who rebelled against his immense post-World War II prestige...it is authoritative and rigorous, and a good read for naval history buffs.

Standpoint

'Even Churchill's greatest critics will have to make some revisions of their opinions after reading this important book.'

Eric Grove, author of The Royal Navy Since 1815

'What makes this book so readable and rewarding is its taut, paced development of Churchill as thinker, politician and Whitehall servant—we see his strategic world-view developing and we read his remarkably incisive, beautifully wrought appreciations of strategic dilemmas and problems. He was a vivid writer and clear thinker, and Bell has done the profession (and Churchill fans everywhere) a great service with this captivating text.'

Geoffrey Wawro, author of Quicksand: America's Pursuit of Power in the Middle East

CHURCHILL AND SEA POWER

CHRISTOPHER M. BELL

OXFORD
UNIVERSITY PRESS

OXFORD
UNIVERSITY PRESS

Great Clarendon Street, Oxford, OX2 6DP,
United Kingdom

Oxford University Press is a department of the University of Oxford.
It furthers the University's objective of excellence in research, scholarship,
and education by publishing worldwide. Oxford is a registered trade mark of
Oxford University Press in the UK and in certain other countries

First Edition published in 2013
First published in paperback 2014
Impression: 1

Published in the United States of America by Oxford University Press
198 Madison Avenue, New York, NY 10016, United States of America

British Library Cataloguing in Publication Data
Data available

ISBN 978–0–19–969357–3 (Hbk.)
ISBN 978–0–19–967850–1 (Pbk.)

Printed in Great Britain by
Clays Ltd, St Ives plc

For Rae

Preface

It seems almost obligatory these days for new books about Winston Churchill to begin with a rationalization for their existence, and this strikes me as a healthy trend. The field is already a crowded one, and some justification is surely needed for cluttering it further. Bookshops today teem with Churchill biographies of all shapes and sizes aimed at every conceivable audience, in addition to specialized studies that promise, among other things, to debunk long-established myths, reveal the 'true story' behind some controversial episode, or examine a hitherto neglected aspect of his long and diverse career. Some of these works cater unashamedly to Churchill's legion of admirers, and some to his smaller, but no less fervent, army of detractors; most aim, with varying degrees of success, to achieve a degree of impartiality. Confronted with the sheer volume of writing on Churchill, the reader is justified in questioning whether there is anything new left to say.

What is remarkable, however, is not the amount that has been written about Churchill, but how much still needs to be done. There are, of course, facets of his life that have not yet been subjected to thorough study; and new documents will undoubtedly emerge from time to time to cast fresh light on old controversies. But where Churchill is concerned, the biggest challenge for historians of the twenty-first century will be to question what we think we already know—to go back into documents long available to us, test our underlying assumptions, and if necessary reject well-worn and time-honoured arguments that do not hold up to scrutiny. Many talented historians are already doing these things, but for every new study that makes a genuine contribution to our knowledge about Churchill (or, for that matter, the Royal Navy or British history generally), many others appear that only reinforce outdated and inaccurate views.

This book emerged out of my own long-standing fascination with Winston Churchill, and my desire to understand his contribution to the maintenance, exercise, and decline of Britain's sea power during the first half of the twentieth century. This is not a subject that has ever been systematically addressed. Part of the reason undoubtedly lies in the inward focus of much traditional naval history, which naturally tends to concentrate on the actual conduct of warfare at sea. But the history of a nation's sea power is only partly told in terms of the outcome of great battles, the skill of its officers and sailors in uniform, and the fighting power of its ships. One of the most astute observations in Alfred Thayer Mahan's classic study, *The Influence of Sea Power upon History*, first published in 1890, is that a nation's sea power—that is, its ability to use the seas, in times of peace and war alike, to further its ends—also depends on the actions of its civilian statesmen and politicians. They are the ones, after all, who decide how much of the nation's wealth to allocate to navies and the other elements of sea power, who determine broad priorities in wartime, and who have the final word in matters of peace and war.

This is a book about the history of British sea power in the twentieth century as seen from the very top. It takes the perspective of civilian decision-makers in Whitehall, and in particular the politician and statesman who had the greatest influence on the Royal Navy's fortunes in the modern era. Limitations of space prevent me from examining all facets of Churchill's relationship with the Royal Navy, or providing detailed accounts of naval operations during the whole of this period. To keep the book to a manageable length, it has been necessary to stay focused on Churchill's influence on, and exercise of, the nation's sea power in the broadest sense. On one level the book is intended to provide a sort of intellectual history of Churchill's development as a maritime strategist, and to chart the evolution of his views on the utility of sea power and its relationship to the other elements of British grand strategy. At the same time, I have sought to explore, in more concrete terms, Churchill's record as a naval strategist and his role in the critical events that shaped the fortunes of the Royal Navy during this eventful period.

Parts of this story have often been told before, but not always well, and never as a coherent subject in its own right. Churchill's ideas about sea power and maritime strategy are too often treated as being rigid and unchanging, and different periods of his career are typically viewed in isolation from one another. His record as a naval strategist is often reduced to the simplest black-and-white terms—he was either brilliant or incompetent, a hero or a villain. And while specialist historians have treated the subject in more nuanced terms, the various shades of grey they offer still seem to fall short of what is needed. Churchill may have started his military education in the British Army in the reign of Queen Victoria, but over the next sixty years he adjusted effortlessly to major geopolitical shifts and the unprecedented pace of technological development, culminating in the development of nuclear weapons. His views were constantly evolving, and his motives were seldom simple or straightforward. These aspects of Churchill's career, like so many, need to be painted on a broad canvas. My hope here is to move beyond shades of grey and apply the bright swathes of colour that are necessary to understand this complex and important subject.

A great many debts have been incurred in the course of producing this book. I have been consistently impressed by the helpfulness and knowledge of the staffs at the many archives and libraries I have used. Particular thanks are due to Allen Packwood and the staff of the Churchill College Archives Centre in Cambridge; Warren Hollrah and others at the Churchill Memorial and Library, Westminster College; The National Archives (formerly the Public Record Office) in Kew; the Imperial War Museum; the National Maritime Museum; the Brass Foundry, Woolwich; the British Library; the Naval War College Library; the Sir Basil Liddell Hart Archives Centre at King's College London; George A. Malcolmson at the Royal Navy Submarine Museum; Barbara Gilbert at the Fleet Air Arm Museum; and the University of Southampton Library. Closer to home, Marlyn McCann at Dalhousie University's Killam Library has gone above and beyond the call of duty to meet my endless requests for inter-library loans.

I am indebted to these institutions for permission to examine and quote from papers in their possession. Documents in The National Archives and all other material under Crown copyright are cited by permission of the Controller of Her Majesty's Stationery Office. I am grateful to the Countess of Avon for permission to quote from the papers of the first Earl of Avon.

Research for this book was assisted at an early stage by the Churchill Memorial and Library, Westminster College, which awarded me a Tyler Research Fellowship and provided a very congenial setting for research. The Social Studies and Humanities Research Council of Canada granted me a postdoctoral fellowship at a critical juncture in my academic career, and made it possible for me to embark on this project. During my two and a half years at the Naval War College in Newport, Rhode Island, I benefited greatly from the support of my colleagues and superiors, and in particular Alberto Coll, whose interest in this project ensured that it did not founder. The book could not have been finished without the generous financial support provided by Dalhousie University. I am especially grateful to the

Faculty of Arts and Social Sciences for a Burgess Research Award during the final stages of writing.

Many others have provided advice, assistance, and encouragement over the years, and I especially wish to thank John Beeler, Trevor Checkley, Graham Clews, Ronald I. Cohen, Richard Gimblett, Richard Goette, John B. Hattendorf, Holger H. Herwig, Rafe Heydel-Mankoo, Edward Ingram, Andrew Lambert, Nicholas Lambert, Richard Langworth, Michael Leach, Todd McCallum, Geoffrey Miller, David Morgan-Owen, Keith Neilson, Cynthia Neville, and Donald Stoker. I am grateful to Eric Grove and the anonymous reviewers who offered many helpful suggestions, and to colleagues who have generously agreed to look over drafts of the book, in whole or in part. Their suggestions have been of inestimable value. Thanks to Shawn Grimes, James Levy, John H. Maurer, Matthew Seligmann, and Kevin E. Smith. John R. Ferris once again provided a detailed, insightful, and blunt critique that has made this a far better book. Needless to say, any shortcomings that remain are entirely my own responsibility.

The people at Oxford University Press have been a pleasure to work with, and I am particularly indebted to Matthew Cotton, Luciana O'Flaherty, Deborah Protheroe, and Emma Barber for their advice, assistance, and enthusiasm. The copy-editing was completed with precision, efficiency, and speed by Richard Mason, who made many valuable suggestions and saved me from more errors than I care to admit.

Finally, my greatest debt is to my family, who put up with a great deal so that I might finish this book. My wife Rae and our two sons, Alex and Matthew, have been a constant source of joy and inspiration. I could not have done any of this without them.

Contents

List of Plates	xiii
List of Maps	xiv
List of Abbreviations	xv
Introduction: Sea Power in the Age of Churchill	1
1. Apprenticeship, 1900–14	11
2. Learning Curve: The First World War	49
3. Adjusting to the Post-War World, 1919–24	85
4. The Treasury Years: The Ten-Year Rule, Japanese 'Bogey', and 'Yankee Menace'	103
5. Disarmament, Rearmament, and the Path to War: The 1930s	135
6. First Lord of the Admiralty, 1939–40: The Phoney War and the Norwegian Campaign	160
7. The War Against Germany and Italy, 1940–1	195
8. 'Courting Disaster': The Deterrence of Japan and the Dispatch of Force Z	230
9. The Battle of the Atlantic, the Imports Crisis, and the Closing of the 'Air Gap'	254
10. The Defeat of the Axis Powers	283
11. Churchill's Last Naval Battle	308
Epilogue: The Verdict of History	321

Notes   342
Select Bibliography   396
Photographic Acknowledgements   417
Index   419

List of Plates

1. Churchill and Lord Fisher

2. Churchill on submarine D2

3. Churchill boarding a Maurice Farman seaplane

4. Churchill and Sir Robert Borden

5. Churchill at the Yarrow shipyard

6. Churchill, Jellicoe, and Madden

7. The Board of Admiralty, December 1939

8. Churchill and Admiral Pound

9. Churchill addressing the company of HMS *Exeter*

10. Churchill signs autographs for men of HMS *Ajax* and HMS *Exeter*

11. Churchill inspecting RAF personnel, Reykjavik

12. The sinking of HMS *Prince of Wales*

13. Churchill on deck of the aircraft carrier HMS *Victorious* during a visit to the Royal Navy's Home Fleet on 11 October 1942. Left to right: Captain Henry Bovell, Churchill, Rear-Admiral Arthur Lumley Lyster, Sir Stafford Cripps

14. Churchill, Fraser, Tovey, and Randolph Churchill

15. Churchill with members of the Board of the Admiralty and US government and naval officials

16. A Hawker Sea Hurricane being catapulted from a Catapult Armed Merchant Ship

17. Churchill and Brooke crossing to France on HMS *Kelvin*

18. Protagonists in the 'Battle of the Air'

19. Churchill crossing the Rhine River

List of Maps

1. The North Sea in the First World War   55
2. The Dardanelles Campaign   60
3. The North Sea and the Baltic in the Second World War   172
4. The Mediterranean   198
5. The Battle of the Atlantic   223
6. The Indian Ocean   234
7. South East Asia Command   288

List of Abbreviations

ABC	American-British-Canadian
ACNS	Assistant Chief of the Naval Staff
ADB	American-Dutch-British
ASV	air-to-surface vessel radar
ASW	anti-submarine warfare
BA	Battle of the Atlantic Committee
BAD	British Admiralty Delegation, Washington
BEF	British Expeditionary Force
CAM	Catapult Aircraft Merchantmen
CAS	Chief of the Air Staff
CID	Committee of Imperial Defence
CIGS	Chief of the Imperial General Staff
C-in-C	Commander-in-Chief
CNS	Chief of the Naval Staff
COS	Chiefs of Staff Committee
CP	Cabinet Paper
CVE	Escort Aircraft Carrier
DCNS	Deputy Chief of the Naval Staff
DCO	Director of Combined Operations
DNC	Director of Naval Construction
DNI	Director of Naval Intelligence
DNO	Director of Naval Ordnance
D of C	Director of Contracts
D of P	Director of Plans
D of T	Director of Training
DRC	Defence Requirements Committee
DTSD	Director of Training and Staff Duties
E in C	Engineer in Chief
FAA	Fleet Air Arm

FO	Foreign Office
GRT	gross registered tons
HMG	His Majesty's Government
HMS	His Majesty's Ship
IIC	Industrial Intelligence Centre
IJN	Imperial Japanese Navy
JPC	Joint Planning Committee
MAC	Merchant Aircraft Carrier
MCC	Military Coordination Committee
MEW	Ministry of Economic Warfare
NID	Naval Intelligence Division
PD	Plans Division
RAF	Royal Air Force
RN	Royal Navy
RNAS	Royal Naval Air Service
SWC	Supreme War Council
USN	United States Navy
VCNS	Vice Chief of the Naval Staff
WO	War Office
WSA	War Shipping Administration (USA)

Introduction: Sea Power in the Age of Churchill

Winston Churchill enjoyed a longer and closer relationship with the Royal Navy than any British politician of the twentieth century. In 1911, at the relatively young age of thirty-six, Churchill was appointed First Lord of the Admiralty, the political head of the British navy. He threw himself into the task of preparing the service for war, and presided over its fortunes until May 1915, when a political crisis, partly of his own making, drove him from office in disgrace. His reputation as a strategist and war leader was badly damaged by his prominent role in the ill-fated Dardanelles campaign, although his political career soon revived. Churchill's part in the Dardanelles was eventually overshadowed in the public mind by his warnings about Adolf Hitler and high-profile fight for rearmament during the 1930s. Churchill became First Lord of the Admiralty again on 3 September 1939, the day Britain declared war on Nazi Germany, but he remained at this post less than a year, during which time he presided over a second failed campaign, this time in Norway. This new disaster evoked memories of the Dardanelles and sparked another political crisis, but rather than being cast back into the political wilderness, as some observers hoped, Churchill emerged as prime minister. Acting as his own Minister of Defence, he shaped British grand strategy and oversaw all three fighting services for the duration of the Second World War.

Churchill's influence over the Royal Navy was not limited to his time in these offices. He helped to guide its fortunes in every Cabinet post he held over the course of his long career, and could claim some influence even when out of office. The navy felt the effects of Churchill in many areas over the years. Prior to the First World War, for example, he was responsible for completing the fleet's conversion from coal to oil; he oversaw the creation of the Admiralty's first fully fledged naval staff; he worked to improve conditions for seamen and non-commissioned officers (i.e. the 'Lower Deck');

and he opened up opportunities for naval ratings to become commissioned officers. There was no area that Churchill regarded as off-limits. As one officer recalled, Churchill's 'curiosity about the service for which he was responsible seemed to many of the older officers almost indecent'.[1] The famous quip that naval tradition amounted to nothing but 'rum, sodomy, and the lash' may not have been uttered by Churchill, but it nicely captures his impatient and irreverent attitude towards the service.[2] As First Lord, and even as prime minister, he did not hesitate to voice strong opinions on professional matters that civilian leaders typically steered clear of, such as warship design and naval strategy. Admiral Sir Reginald 'Blinker' Hall, the legendary Director of Naval Intelligence, observed that 'Even in matters of the extremest technicality [Churchill] would insist on elaborate presentation of his own views, and his powers of argument were so extraordinary that again and again tired Admiralty officials were hypnotised—I can think of no better word—into accepting opinions which differed vastly from those they normally held.'[3]

There are few aspects of Churchill's career that have not generated controversy, and his relationship with the navy is no exception. Inside the service, opinion on Churchill was invariably divided. Within months of arriving at the Admiralty in 1911, his forceful and sometimes unorthodox methods were already beginning to raise concerns. One officer, Captain Osmond de Beauvoir Brock, then the Assistant Director of Naval Mobilisation, observed at the time that 'the new 1st Lord is a young man in a hurry & what is more he is—in his opinion—a heaven born strategist both military & naval; whether all his schemes are quite sound I shouldn't like to say, but I do know that those which have come this way bear traces of great haste & little thought.'[4] In both world wars Churchill gained a reputation for pressing reckless and impractical schemes on his naval advisers, for demanding constant action, and for dealing harshly with officers who failed to meet his expectations. He also took a far more active role in shaping strategy and directing operations at sea than was normal for civilian leaders.

Given the force of Churchill's personality and propensity to intervene in all aspects of naval business, it is not surprising that naval leaders were often agitated. 'Mr Churchill proved himself to be a very clever and able First Lord in some directions,' wrote Admiral Sir John Jellicoe after the First World War, 'but his fatal error was his inability to realize his own limitations as a civilian with, it is true, some early experience of military service but quite ignorant of naval affairs.'[5] Similar views were expressed during the

Second World War. Admiral Sir Dudley Pound, Britain's First Sea Lord—i.e. the professional head of the navy—during the first four years of the conflict, confided to a colleague in 1940 that Churchill was 'quite impervious to arguments and sweeps them aside as if they did not exist'. His successor, Admiral Sir Andrew Cunningham, complained the following year that Churchill was 'a bad strategist but doesn't know it and no one has the courage to stand up to him'. Admiral John Tovey, commander of Britain's Home Fleet, remarked that 'as a strategist and tactician' Churchill was 'liable to be most dangerous. He loves the dramatic and public acclimation. He has, to my knowledge, put up some wild schemes.' Looking back after the war, Admiral Sir William Davis concluded that Churchill 'thought he had a special knowledge and flair for handling matters maritime—alas many of his suggestions & ideas were juvenile & ill judged in the extreme'.[6]

But Britain's naval leaders of the Second World War were also quick to acknowledge Churchill's positive attributes, and invariably concluded that these outweighed his defects. Admiral Pound, for example, maintained that Churchill was 'so magnificent in many ways and the ideal leader of the Nation in these times that I must put up with his idiosyncrasies'. As First Sea Lord, Cunningham confided to his diary in 1944 that 'It would be a tragedy if anything should happen to him now. With all his faults (& he is the most infuriating man) he has done a great job for the country & besides there is no one else.'[7] Admiral Tovey conceded that Churchill 'as Prime Minister is magnificent and unique'. Davis insisted that his criticisms 'must not detract from the greatness and grandeur of the old man', while Admiral Sir Reginald Drax concluded that the 'greatest commanders all make some mistakes in war and Churchill made fewer than most. His greatest quality however, which we all admired immensely, was his splendid leadership, his daunting courage and his inflexible determination that nothing could or should prevent us from winning the War.'[8]

As might be expected, Churchill has usually been judged according to the success or failure of his actions in wartime. However, no consensus has emerged on his record as a naval strategist. To his harshest critics, Churchill was a dismal failure. The inability of the navy to force the Dardanelles and the subsequent deadlock on the Gallipoli Peninsula are often treated as the first manifestation of an incompetence that led directly to the embarrassing defeat in Norway in 1940 and the needless loss of the battleship *Prince of Wales* and battlecruiser *Repulse* to Japanese aircraft in December 1941. If not for the resistance of his professional advisers, Churchill, it is argued, would have forced even more wild and reckless schemes on the navy, with inevitably disastrous results. This school of thought holds that Churchill also exercised a destructive influence in peacetime. His efforts as Chancellor of the Exchequer during the 1920s to reduce naval expenditure have been treated as evidence of a dangerous inconsistency, a blindness to emerging threats, and a fundamentally poor grasp of strategy. Not only did he emasculate the navy, his critics claim, he was also responsible, through the propagation of the infamous 'Ten Year Rule', for the poor state of Britain's defences during the 1930s and the early stages of the Second World War.

Churchill's admirers, on the other hand, have no difficulty painting a more flattering portrait. In their version of events, Gallipoli was the one brilliant and original strategic initiative of the First World War. If it had succeeded, Britain might have avoided the stagnation and bloodshed of the Western Front and dramatically shortened the war. Its failure, they argue, was not Churchill's fault: his vision was undermined by less capable colleagues and inept subordinates. Churchill's attacks on defence expenditure during the 1920s are easily dismissed as an unfortunate by-product of the single-minded determination that would save Britain from disaster in 1940. After all, Chancellors of the Exchequer are *supposed* to reduce defence expenditure: Churchill's only fault was to do his job too well. Any negative effects of his cost-cutting in the 1920s were more than offset by his early recognition of the German danger and campaign to rearm Britain. As First Lord of the Admiralty in the Second World War, Churchill's boldness is contrasted with the hesitation and indecisiveness of Neville Chamberlain and other members of the War Cabinet. And, while Churchill may have made mistakes in Norway and other campaigns, they pale in comparison with his inspiring leadership after the fall of France in the summer of 1940, and the overall soundness of his strategic vision.

The truth lies somewhere between these two extremes. This book aims to reach a balanced verdict on Churchill's record as a naval strategist and the most influential custodian of Britain's sea power during the modern era. To do so, it is necessary first to strip away much of the baggage that has accumulated over the last eighty years, beginning with Churchill's own highly influential accounts of the two world wars.[9] Recent scholarship has shown how effectively Churchill established the case for his own defence and set the parameters for much of the subsequent debate over the origins and course of the Second World War.[10] But the early publication of his memoirs did not always work to his advantage. In the case of the war at sea, Churchill failed to anticipate many of the criticisms that would be raised, leaving his detractors with a relatively open field. The main outlines of the case against him were firmly established during the 1950s by Captain Stephen Roskill, a recently retired naval officer who was chosen to prepare the British official history of naval operations in the Second World War.[11] Roskill's *The War at Sea* was unusually critical for an official publication, especially considering that Churchill was again prime minister when the first volume appeared in 1954. Roskill grudgingly submitted to pressure from the Cabinet Office to tone down his criticisms, but there were limits to how far he would go. As a result, volume one of the navy's official history contained two explicit criticisms of Churchill: that he intervened excessively in naval operations during the Norwegian campaign; and that he overruled his naval advisers and despatched the *Prince of Wales* and *Repulse* to Singapore on the eve of war because he did not grasp the principles of naval strategy.

Roskill's work on the navy's official history established his reputation as a formidable naval historian. His credentials were seemingly unassailable: he could draw on his unrivalled access to official documents, an extensive post-war correspondence with leading naval personalities, and his own experience on the naval staff during the Second World War. His criticisms of Churchill, written at a time when the British government's archives were closed to researchers, were highly influential. In a later book, *Churchill and the Admirals*, Roskill developed a more elaborate indictment of Britain's wartime leader. This work focused on Churchill's sometimes turbulent relationships with his leading naval advisers, and detailed controversial episodes that could not be fully treated in the official history. The list of mistakes attributed to Churchill is a long one. In addition to the Norwegian fiasco and the loss of the *Prince of Wales* and *Repulse*, Roskill maintained that Churchill's obsession with offensive operations led him to divert critical resources from the Battle of the Atlantic to the strategic bombing campaign against Germany. The book was not designed to give a balanced assessment of Churchill's relationship with the navy, however; Roskill saw it as an opportunity to address subjects that he had not been free to treat in his earlier work, and to correct what he saw as an overly favourable popular perception of Churchill as a war leader. The emphasis was therefore on controversial subjects, and he largely glossed over or ignored areas where Churchill's influence was either harmless or positive.

Roskill's criticisms of Churchill have been widely regarded as authoritative—so much so, in fact, that they have seldom been subjected to rigorous analysis. But historians have not just accepted Roskill's interpretations: they have embellished them and, in many cases, amplified and distorted them. Thus, what began in the 1950s as relatively moderate criticism of Churchill for exceeding his authority during the Norwegian campaign, has gradually transformed into charges that his meddling and poor strategic judgement were largely, if not solely, responsible for Britain's defeat there. Virtually every misstep and miscalculation during this campaign has been attributed directly to Churchill at one time or another, even when unsupported by the documentary evidence.

This same trend is evident in recent writing on all aspects of Churchill's career. The passage of time has only served to heighten the prominence assigned to the greatest wartime prime minister in modern British history. While other politicians, statesmen, and warriors—many of them prominent figures in their own time—have virtually disappeared from the public's memory, Churchill's stock has steadily risen. The temptation always to place him at the centre of events—and to push other decision-makers to the sidelines—seems to be overwhelming. British strategic foreign policy during the 1930s is sometimes reduced to little more than a struggle between Churchill and Neville Chamberlain, and the summer of 1940 to a personal duel between Churchill and Hitler. Even during the war Churchill was widely viewed abroad as the personification of Britain's heroic resistance to Nazism, and this close association of the nation's collective war effort with its famous leader has only grown stronger over time. The popular narrative of this period has become highly personalized: the nation's history and Churchill's personal history are now more closely intertwined than ever.

Churchill himself is partly responsible for this. Through his memoirs and journalistic writings he constructed a simple and compelling narrative of critical events in the nation's history, with himself always at centre stage. He painted himself as a bold, dynamic leader, a far-sighted statesman, and a skilled strategist. In the summer of 1940, Churchill's self-image seemed almost to match reality. He became, for a time, the heroic figure he had always longed to be. And because of this, his view of British history and his role in it have been accorded a privileged place by both the public and historians for generations. This has been good for Churchill's reputation, but it has seldom made for good history. The romantic and personalized narrative Churchill constructed was never going to survive close examination, and historians have been chipping away at it for years. Churchill's almost mythical status continues to find fervent supporters, but it has also generated a strong, often exaggerated, backlash. Those who would defend Churchill's every action are increasingly confronted by debunkers and iconoclasts just as eager to find fault. But both sides of this debate seem implicitly to agree on one thing: that Churchill was *the* driving force in British policy- and strategy-making during the periods he was in office.

Demythologizing Churchill is no easy task. The Churchillian view of British history is now firmly entrenched, and much cherished. It also contains more than a kernel of truth. Churchill *was* often present at critical moments, and he wielded a great deal of power and influence throughout his long and remarkable career. At times, his impact on the course of events was tremendous, and the role he played was unique. It would be just as wrong to write him out of the story as it is to give him undue prominence. The challenge, then, is to strip away the myths, to give other historical actors their due, and to recognize that Churchill was sometimes a supporting character rather than the lead. The figure that emerges from this process is more human, more fallible, and less influential, but hardly less impressive.

A re-examination of Churchill's record as a naval strategist serves several purposes. To begin with, it provides an opportunity to reconsider his role in a number of important and controversial episodes, to resolve conflicting interpretations, and to debunk a variety of myths that have gained currency. This book offers a new interpretation of Churchill's tenure as Chancellor of the Exchequer during the 1920s, of his influence during the Norwegian campaign, and of his direction of British strategy as prime minister during the Second World War, particularly his policies relating to the Far East and the Battle of the Atlantic. Churchill made many mistakes over the course of his career, some of them costly and avoidable. The goal here is not to absolve him of blame, but to understand his motives, assess the extent of his responsibility, and evaluate the soundness of charges that have been levelled against him.

Churchill emerges from this process with his reputation generally enhanced. In part this is because some criticisms have been exaggerated or distorted, and some are simply not supported by the evidence. As long as Churchill is treated as the only decision-maker who mattered, it is easy to assume that he was solely to blame when things went wrong, or that any mistakes he made must have had momentous results. There is also a tendency to oversimplify Churchill's motives, which were usually more complex than historians have recognized. By reconstructing his views and taking into consideration the decision-making process as a whole, a more sympathetic picture usually emerges. However, there are exceptions. Some of Churchill's mistakes have attracted little attention. This is particularly true of the Battle of the Atlantic. Churchill's post-war claims that he was constantly worried about the U-boat threat and gave it his full attention are both inaccurate and misleading, yet they have been widely accepted as fact. Churchill's interest in the German attack on British trade actually fluctuated considerably. He consistently kept the navy short of air support in order to bolster the strategic bomber offensive against Germany, and he was perfectly willing to accept heavy losses to merchant shipping—and consequently a severe reduction in imports—so that he might maximize Britain's immediate offensive capabilities. Churchill clung to this policy despite mounting evidence that the Royal Air Force was not inflicting decisive damage on Germany. It was only when this strategy threatened to reduce British imports to critical levels and disrupt Anglo-American strategic plans that Churchill finally gave the anti-U-boat campaign his full attention and ensured that the necessary resources were allocated to it. Curiously, however, little blame has been directed at Churchill for prolonging the Battle of the Atlantic.

This study also addresses claims that Churchill attempted to initiate a 'naval revolution' prior to the First World War. Revisionist naval historians have argued that Churchill, inspired by Admiral Sir John ('Jacky') Fisher's radical views on submarines, secretly decided in 1914 to abandon Britain's battleship standard in favour of 'flotilla defence'.[12] This policy would have seen Britain protected from invasion by submarines and other flotilla vessels, while capital ships were freed up for the protection of British trade and overseas possessions. These claims do not withstand close scrutiny, however. Churchill was undoubtedly enthusiastic about the future of the submarine, as the revisionists have shown, and he was even willing to consider 'flotilla defence' as a means to protect British interests in a subsidiary theatre like the Mediterranean. But this study will show that he was not prepared in 1914 to abandon the capital ship as the Royal Navy's ultimate defence against the naval challenge from Wilhelmine Germany.

A critical examination of Churchill's role as a steward of the Royal Navy also makes it possible to measure his long-term impact on British sea power. Navies are particularly expensive institutions to build and maintain. They rely on a large and technologically advanced industrial infrastructure to provide warships and weapons systems. They require a network of bases and extensive logistical capabilities to project their power globally. And they need to be supplied with highly skilled personnel. As a rule, none of these things can be improvised in a hurry; they required then, as they do now, a deliberate and long-term commitment by the state. This, in turn, requires that the nation's leaders recognize the value of sea power and possess both the resources and the will to maintain it. The need to invest continually in the industrial underpinnings of British sea power largely escaped Churchill, as it did most British politicians of this era. When he left office in 1945, Britain's resources were no longer adequate to the task. The explanation most commonly offered for the country's demise as the world's dominant maritime power is economic decline, but this does not fully explain the erosion of Britain's sea power over the first half of the twentieth century.[13] British leaders also took deliberate decisions during the period that gradually but steadily undermined the nation's strength at sea.

Churchill took a leading role in this process, although the part he played has attracted little attention. It was not, of course, something that he wished to call attention to. He was conscious, like other politicians of this period, that the Royal Navy was not only popular, but also occupied a prominent place in British national mythology. He also had a genuine affection for the Royal Navy. But for all his romantic rhetoric about Britain's glorious naval past, Churchill's views on the utility of sea power in the modern era were unsentimental and pragmatic. They also evolved continuously over the course of his career in response to shifting geopolitical and technological developments. Churchill's early faith in the navy as a potent and decisive weapon was badly shaken by the navy's inability to strike a decisive blow against Britain's enemies during the First World War. After that conflict, he developed doubts about Britain's ability to protect its interests in the Far East against Japan through sea power alone. The rise of Nazi Germany during the 1930s began to reorient his strategic thinking towards air power as the foundation of Britain's future security.

Churchill came to view the navy as a predominantly defensive weapon. This was confirmed by his experiences during the early stages of the Second World War, when he was frustrated in his efforts to find an offensive role for the navy. After the fall of France in 1940, it was clear that Germany was immune to economic pressure exercised through maritime blockade. By the end of 1941, it was equally clear that amphibious raids could do little to challenge Germany's domination of Europe, and that the navy alone could not exert decisive pressure against even a second-tier power like Italy. Churchill concluded that the navy should only be maintained at the lowest level necessary to fulfil its essential defensive functions, and that national resources should be channelled as far as possible towards the other services, and particularly the air force, to enhance Britain's offensive power. As prime minister during the Second World War, Churchill did not just neglect the foundations of Britain's sea power: he willingly sacrificed the nation's maritime interests in the pursuit of victory over Nazi Germany, and in so doing hastened the process by which the United States replaced Britain as the world's greatest maritime power.

I

Apprenticeship, 1900–14

On 12 May 1901, in one of his first speeches to the House of Commons, the young Winston Churchill proclaimed that 'The honour and security of the British Empire do not depend, and can never depend, on the British Army.' The Admiralty,' he remarked, 'is the only Office strong enough to insure the British Empire'. His audience may have been surprised to hear this sentiment from a politician who had recently been an active army officer, but what undoubtedly caught their attention was his brash attack on his own party's plans to expand the British army. Churchill made no attempt to conceal that his position owed much to the memory of his late father, Lord Randolph Churchill, who had resigned as Chancellor of the Exchequer in 1886 over his inability to force economies on the army and navy. This had destroyed Lord Randolph's political career, and Churchill, eager to vindicate his father's actions, now announced his intention to 'lift again the tattered flag of retrenchment and economy'.[1] Over the next two years, the young backbencher poured scorn on his Conservative government's schemes. The British army needed to be more efficient, he argued, not larger. The desire to maintain more troops than was strictly necessary for the needs of imperial defence was 'unhealthy', he charged. 'It betrays immoral yearnings, and cannot fail to multiply suspicion and hatred against us.'[2] Moreover, army expansion would do nothing to make Britain safer. On the contrary, it threatened to drain resources from the one service that *could* guarantee Britain's security—the Royal Navy.

Churchill's early public statements on defence show that he was largely immune to the militarism that swept Britain in the aftermath of the Boer War. While continental states relied on large conscript armies for their security, Churchill maintained that ships must be the main protection for an island power like Britain. 'It is the Navy which alone can secure the food and commerce on which the crowded population of England depends,' he asserted in a speech of February 1903, 'and which alone can keep this island itself free from the mighty hosts of Europe.'[3] As long as Britain maintained its supremacy at sea, Churchill was confident it had little to fear from other Powers. The navy protected Britain's trade and empire; it ensured that Britain's factories received the raw materials they needed and that the British people were fed; and it provided a shield behind which the nation could mobilize its resources in wartime and even, if necessary, raise great armies. Naval supremacy also allowed Britain to project its power abroad. 'It does not mean merely the command of the [English] Channel,' Churchill continued in the same speech, 'or of the Mediterranean, or of the Atlantic or of the Persian Gulf—it means something much wider than that—it means the power to send our ships wherever the waters roll, to fly our flag on every sea, to land our troops on any shore.'[4] But Britain's professional army was too small to threaten other Powers. This, in Churchill's view, gave Britain the moral high ground: the Royal Navy, in his opinion, was strictly a defensive force. 'Our position is highly artificial,' he told the House of Commons in March 1912. 'We are fed from the sea; we are an unarmed people; we possess a very small Army . . . We cannot menace the independence or the vital interest of any great Continental State.'[5]

Churchill also shared the popular view that Britain could be trusted not to abuse its privileged position on the seas.[6] 'For more than 300 years,' he proclaimed in March 1913, 'we alone amongst the nations have wielded that mysterious and decisive force which is called sea-power. What have we done with it? We have suppressed the slaver. We have charted the seas. We have made them a safe highway for all.' Britain's naval supremacy, he declared, was 'part of the common treasure of mankind'.[7] This view rested on a highly selective reading of history, and Churchill himself was well aware that the Royal Navy had not always been used for altruistic purposes. 'We have got all we want in territory,' he remarked in a speech in March 1914, 'but our claim to be left in undisputed enjoyment of vast and splendid possessions, largely acquired by war and largely maintained by force, is one which often seems less reasonable to others than to us.'[8] But this does not appear to have diminished his underlying conviction that the Royal Navy was a stabilizing force in world affairs. Britain, in his view, had a right, if not a duty, to maintain its naval supremacy against any challenger.

Churchill's attacks on the Conservative government's plans for army expansion came at a time when the Royal Navy's dominant position was not in question, but by 1908, when he was drawn for the first time into high-level debates over naval policy, this could no longer be taken as certain. Churchill's political career had, by this time, taken off. He moved to the Liberal Party in early 1904 and received his first Cabinet post, as President of the Board of Trade, in 1908. Even though he was the most junior minister in the Cabinet, Churchill did not hesitate to plunge into the controversy over the emerging German challenge to Britain's naval supremacy. Germany had embarked on a programme of naval expansion in 1898, but the Royal Navy's numerical superiority over the new German fleet was so great that British leaders and the public did not immediately take alarm.[9] This had changed, however, by the time Britain launched the first all big-gun battle-ship, HMS *Dreadnought*, in 1906. *Dreadnought* marked such an advance in firepower and speed that earlier battleships were soon regarded as virtually obsolete. This new class of battleship, known generically as dreadnoughts, quickly became the principal means of measuring a state's naval power. Britain gained an early lead over rivals by initiating this technological advance, but its huge numerical advantage in pre-dreadnought battleships immediately became a wasting asset. Germany now had an opportunity to compete with Britain on a relatively level playing field.

The Germans were quick to take advantage of this unexpected opportunity. When the Admiralty's annual budget estimates came up for consideration by the Cabinet in 1909, Germany had no fewer than thirteen dreadnoughts under construction. Against this, Britain possessed seven ships of this class, including three of the new battlecruiser type, which possessed nearly the same armament as a dreadnought but sacrificed armour for increased speed. Britain also had an additional five dreadnoughts being built. To prevent Germany stealing a lead, the Admiralty and its supporters demanded the inclusion of six, and later eight, dreadnoughts in the new construction programme for 1909. Churchill, however, was strongly committed to the Liberal government's costly new social programs, and immediately aligned himself with the economizers within the Cabinet, led by the Chancellor of the Exchequer, David Lloyd George, who opposed a large naval program. In public, Churchill derided the idea that Britain was in any real danger. In his opinion, the international situation had, if anything, improved in recent years. The Russian fleet had been destroyed during the Russo-Japanese War, and Anglo-French relations had improved with the conclusion of the Entente Cordiale in 1904. He dismissed the idea of war with Germany as far-fetched: there was nothing for the two nations to fight over, he argued in a speech in August 1908, 'except perhaps a few tropical plantations and small coaling stations scattered about the world'.[10] Churchill also tried to persuade his Cabinet colleagues that Germany's ability to menace Britain should not be exaggerated. Even if the Germans temporarily gained a slight lead in dreadnoughts, Britain's huge advantage in predreadnought battleships would still secure its commanding position at sea.[11]

A compromise was eventually worked out by which the navy was guaranteed four new dreadnoughts and promised an additional four in the event that Germany's allies, Austria-Hungary and Italy, also began to lay down ships of this class. This was a minor setback for Churchill and the economists, but the promise of eight dreadnoughts satisfied the government's critics and soothed public fears. Churchill soon threw himself back into his ministerial duties and only took a sporadic interest in Germany and naval matters before the summer of 1911, when the arrival of a German gunboat at the Moroccan port of Agadir sparked an international crisis. Like other ministers, Churchill, now promoted to Home Secretary, was alarmed by Germany's aggressive actions, which seemed designed to bully France into making colonial concessions. In recent years, British foreign policy had undergone a major reorientation. Britain's relations with long-standing rivals France and Russia had steadily improved, while Germany, now a major competitor at sea, was regarded as the main threat to the European balance of power. The Foreign Secretary, Sir Edward Grey, and other leading policy-makers distrusted Germany's long-term intentions in Europe and believed Britain must use its influence to maintain French independence as a counterweight to German power. The threat of a Franco-German war in 1911 seems to have dispelled any optimism Churchill may have had about the improbability of conflict between Britain and Germany. If the Agadir crisis escalated into war, he was certain Britain must support France.[12]

The form that British support would take was a controversial subject. Army leaders believed that Britain could contribute most effectively to the common cause by dispatching an expeditionary force to the Continent to operate alongside the French army. Secret staff talks had opened up with the French in 1905 to work out the details. This strategy was rejected by the Royal Navy, however. Admiral Sir John ('Jacky') Fisher, the First Sea Lord from 1904 until 1910, did not want the navy tied down safeguarding communications with France, and believed British troops would be more profitably employed in amphibious operations against the German coast. The Admiralty made no preparations to transport an expeditionary force to France during Fisher's tenure as First Sea Lord. Admiral of the Fleet Sir

Arthur Wilson, Fisher's successor, also refused to fall in with the army's plans. The issue was not formally addressed until it appeared Britain might actually have to act. The Committee of Imperial Defence (CID), the Cabinet subcommittee charged with the oversight of strategic issues, met on 23 August 1911 to consider how Britain would support France in the event of war. The army's case for direct military assistance was ably presented by Sir Henry Wilson, the War Office's Director of Military Operations, who maintained that the presence of four to six British divisions alongside the much larger French army might play a decisive role in halting a German advance into France. The navy's proposals were presented, albeit with considerably less skill, by the First Sea Lord, Sir Arthur Wilson, who outlined a scheme for a close blockade of the German coast and the use of soldiers and Royal Marines to seize the German island of Heligoland.[13] These plans had been formulated in great secrecy by the First Sea Lord himself, and without the benefit of advice from a formal naval staff, which did not yet exist. The impracticability of the navy's scheme was immediately evident to committee members, including Churchill.

The Admiralty's poor showing at this important meeting led directly to a change in leadership. The prime minister, Henry Asquith, concluded that a new hand was needed to bring about the creation of a fully developed naval staff. This task fell to Churchill, who was moved from the Home Office to become First Lord of the Admiralty in October 1911.

Churchill threw himself into this new position with all his characteristic energy and enthusiasm. As an advocate for the navy in Parliament and the Cabinet, he proved to be remarkably effective. Admiral Sir John Jellicoe, then the Second Sea Lord, later wrote that he 'admired very much [Churchill's] wonderful argumentative powers when putting a case before the Cabinet or the CID. He surpassed the ablest of lawyers and would make a weak case appear exceedingly strong.'[14] The service was well provided for in the years leading up to the First World War. Churchill repeatedly wrung heavy expenditure out of his Cabinet colleagues, ensured the navy's numerical lead over its rivals, and encouraged the construction of ever larger and more powerful capital ships. The navy was also fortunate that its new leader held progressive views on technology and innovation, and was particularly receptive to the idea that submarines and aircraft had the potential to revolutionize naval warfare. As First Lord, Churchill was eager to ensure that the navy was at the cutting edge of technological developments, and enthusiastically fostered the growth of the new naval air service.[15] In addition, he supported a variety of reforms within the navy, the most important of which was the development of a formal naval staff to improve the Admiralty's organizational and planning capabilities. Churchill also had progressive ideas about personnel issues. He obtained much-needed pay increases for the men of the Lower Deck, and, when it became necessary to increase the navy's supply of officers to keep pace with heavy pre-war construction, he instituted a scheme for naval ratings to obtain commissions.

But Churchill was not easy to work for. Naval officers, accustomed to considerable freedom in strictly professional matters, did not welcome intrusions by politicians. Most civilian service leaders during this period were content to defer to their uniformed advisers on technical questions. Churchill was not typical: he not only intruded where he was not welcome, he pressed his views on subordinates with confidence and vigour. The average naval officer was not well equipped to stand up to him. Churchill's eloquence 'became a positive danger', Jellicoe lamented, 'when the First Lord started to exercise his powers of argument on his colleagues on the Board [of Admiralty]. Naval officers are not brought up to argue a case, and but few of them can make a good show in this direction.'[16] Even such a powerful personality as Lord Fisher would complain during the First World War that 'on purely technical naval matters he is frequently over-ruled ("he [i.e. Churchill] out-argues me")'.[17] To make matters worse, Churchill could be overbearing and tactless, and he was not especially adept at handling naval officers' particular susceptibilities. One of the most serious causes of friction during these early years was the First Lord's propensity to invite junior officers to air their views directly to him, thereby subverting the established (and much cherished) chain of command. One such incident in 1913 nearly led to the resignation of the entire Board of Admiralty.[18]

The first challenge facing Churchill when he took up his new post was to satisfy powerful factions within his own party demanding that he control naval expenditure, which had risen rapidly in recent years and showed no sign of slowing down. Churchill's own instincts were still in favour of economy. In his first public speech as First Lord in November 1911, he expressed his hope that 'the high-water mark' of naval expenditure had now been reached.[19] During his first months in office, he considered a variety of schemes for saving money. One of the first ideas he floated was to replace the four battleships planned for the following year's estimates with an equal number of less expensive battlecruisers.[20] This was an idea that had been pressed on him by his friend and unofficial adviser, 'Jacky' Fisher, the former First Sea Lord. Churchill had admired Fisher since their first meeting in 1907, and briefly considered bringing the controversial admiral out of retirement after taking up the post of First Lord.[21] He decided against this, but nevertheless listened sympathetically to Fisher's advice on a range of service matters. Fisher was an enthusiastic proponent of the battlecruiser, whose high speed and endurance made it, in his view, the type of capital ship best suited to protecting Britain's global interests. He had attempted to impose this view on the Admiralty during his tenure as First Sea Lord, but the Board of Admiralty preferred a more conservative policy and consistently gave priority to battleship construction.[22] Churchill, however, was evidently persuaded by Fisher's arguments.

The new First Lord also considered dropping one of the four capital ships from the new construction programme planned for 1912. To ensure the Germans did not gain any relative advantage as a result of this reduction, he proposed to retain in home waters a battlecruiser earmarked for dispatch to the Pacific.[23] However, the naval members of the Board of Admiralty rejected both this idea and the substitution scheme. Churchill's plans for economy received another setback in January 1912 when he learned that Germany intended to build additional dreadnoughts over and above those already provided for in its most recent navy law. With German naval strength likely to increase, there was little choice but to prepare for corresponding increases to the British programme.[24] Churchill was eager, however, to avoid a new and even costlier phase of naval competition. He therefore began to explore the possibility of a diplomatic agreement with Germany to reduce the pace of naval construction.

In his speech of 18 March 1912 presenting the annual navy estimates to Parliament, Churchill explicitly linked the size of Britain's naval programme to Germany's, and declared that the Liberal government would meet any increase in German building with additional British construction. But he also proposed that the two nations might agree to take a 'naval holiday', during which they would both drop new dreadnoughts from their programmes for a given year.[25] This would result in large savings for both sides without altering their relative strength in modern capital ships. Churchill realized that this would be a difficult proposition to sell, but he believed the Germans should be receptive to the idea, since they could not hope to overtake the British in new construction. And if they were not willing to go along, at least the offer had been made—Churchill would be in a stronger position to deflect criticism from the 'radical' wing of the Liberal party, which traditionally opposed heavy expenditure on armaments.[26]

Germany's leaders had no interest in Churchill's proposed naval holiday, but he was reluctant to drop the idea and revived it several times over the next couple of years, although never with any great prospect of success. In the absence of an agreement to curtail competitive building, Churchill accepted that Germany's additional construction would have to be matched. The new German navy law of 1912 represented a formidable challenge, however. The Germans not only intended to build more dreadnoughts, but also to keep a higher percentage of their warships in full commission at all times, which would significantly increase the immediate striking power of the German fleet.[27] To meet this new construction, and as a deterrent to further German increases, the annual Navy Estimates for 1912 called for the construction of two additional British capital ships for every one added to the German programme. Churchill announced to Parliament that in 1909 the Admiralty had abandoned the traditional 'two-power standard', by which Britain's naval strength was measured against its two strongest competitors (typically France and Russia), and that the Liberal government was now committed to maintaining a 60 per cent superiority over Germany alone. But additional new construction would not solve all Churchill's problems. To ensure that the ships were properly positioned to meet the German challenge, he announced that Britain would also begin moving battleships from the Mediterranean into home waters.[28]

The foundation of Churchill's naval strategy prior to the First World War was the primacy of British home waters over all other theatres and requirements. He therefore insisted that Britain must retain at all times a pronounced numerical superiority over the German fleet in the North Sea, which he regarded as the decisive theatre in any future war. If risks had to be run, they would be run in other theatres: the navy could not be strong everywhere. '[M]astery on the seas,' he noted in January 1912, did not depend 'on the simultaneous occupation of every sea':

> On the contrary it depends upon the ability to defeat the strongest battlefleet or combination wh[ich] can be brought to bear. This ability cannot be maintained by a policy of dispersion. The sea is all one, and war is all one. The supreme strategic principle of concentration of superior force in the decisive theatre…must govern all naval dispositions….Dispersion of strength, frittering of money, empty parades of foolish little ships 'displaying the flag' in unfrequented seas, are the certain features of a policy leading through extravagance to defeat.[29]

The 'first of all the laws of war,' he later explained to the Secretary of State for War, is 'overpowering strength at the decisive point'. As desirable as it was to maintain strong forces everywhere, Churchill rightly judged that his Liberal colleagues would build no more capital ships than were needed to maintain the 60 per cent margin over Germany. The nation simply could not afford to maintain a crushing numerical superiority over Germany in the North Sea while also matching the fleets of Germany's allies, Austria-Hungary and Italy, in the Mediterranean, and keeping powerful squadrons in more distant waters to deal with enemy raiders. The only solution, Churchill argued, was to concentrate on the most important theatre. As long as Britain won the decisive battle against the German fleet 'we can put everything else straight afterwards,' he observed. But if Britain lost that battle, 'there will not be any afterwards'. 'It w[oul]d be very foolish,' he concluded in May 1912, 'to lose England in safeguarding Egypt.'[30]

Churchill was not oblivious to the risks in stripping the Mediterranean of capital ships, but he believed these would have to be accepted. To minimize the danger to British interests in the region in the absence of a full battle fleet, he proposed to concentrate submarines, destroyers, and other flotilla vessels at Gibraltar and Alexandria.[31] This expedient of 'flotilla defence' was another controversial idea that Churchill had picked up from Admiral Fisher, who believed that modern torpedo craft presented such a formidable threat to large surface ships that they could be relied upon to deter or defeat an invasion of Britain.[32] Churchill now proposed to adopt this strategy in the Mediterranean. This, in his view, offered a viable means to safeguard British interests in the region at a bearable cost.

These proposals met with strong opposition, however. Within the Admiralty, there were doubts about whether the strategy would in fact provide adequate protection for Britain's extensive trade and imperial possessions in the Mediterranean. Admiral Troubridge, the head of the navy's new war staff, conceded that light craft might deter attacks on British bases in the short term, but he pointed out that they were little use for protecting trade passing through the Mediterranean, and that they would be vulnerable to an enemy's heavy ships.[33] Churchill's redistribution plans also drew a storm of protest from other quarters, much of which was aired in Parliament and the press. Even within the Liberal government, there were many who feared that the complete withdrawal of capital ships from the Mediterranean would badly damage British prestige and leave vital interests vulnerable in wartime.

In May 1912, Churchill tried to satisfy his critics by agreeing to station two modern battlecruisers at Gibraltar, where, he argued, they would be immediately available for service in the Mediterranean if required. But this did little to satisfy the widespread concern that the Mediterranean was being 'abandoned', and he continued to face strong pressure in Cabinet to maintain a full squadron of capital ships there. Fearing that this would mean a reduction of capital ship strength in the critical North Sea theatre, Churchill appealed to his colleagues to reconsider. The pre-dreadnought battleships Britain currently maintained in the Mediterranean were simply no match for new Austrian and Italian dreadnoughts, he warned in June 1912. In war-time, the older British ships 'would only be a cheap and certain spoil'. He was therefore opposed to leaving these ships at Malta solely to '*keep up appearances*. It would be a bluff,' he warned, 'which would deceive nobody.'[34] Only the most modern warships would be any use in the Mediterranean, and Britain could not afford to maintain a two-power standard in the Medi-terranean against Italy and Austria while preserving a 60 per cent margin over Germany in the North Sea. 'This would be a very extravagant policy,' he remarked, 'and is not necessary to the fundamental safety of the British Empire or to our ultimate victory and supremacy at sea.'

Flotilla defence in the Mediterranean was not an ideal solution, but Churchill insisted that there was no other realistic choice. 'It must be plainly recognised that we must adopt the *rôle* in this minor theatre appropriate to the weaker naval Power, and while in the North Sea we rely on the gun as our first weapon, we must in the Mediterranean fall back mainly on the torpedo.' To make this idea more attractive, he pointed out that these flotil-las would probably never be tested, as Britain could expect support from the French navy in the event of war with Germany and its allies. British and French forces in the Mediterranean would easily match the combined forces of Italy and Austria-Hungary, and Churchill advocated 'a definite naval arrangement' with France to secure British interests in the region.[35]

None of this satisfied Churchill's critics, however, and the Mediterranean question was examined by the Committee of Imperial Defence (CID) on 4 July 1912. Churchill, with the support of his naval advisers, continued to insist that the first priority must be to maintain Britain's 60 per cent margin of superiority over Germany in the North Sea. '[A]ll other objects,' he argued, 'however precious, must, if necessary, be sacrificed to secure this end.' To meet his colleagues' concerns about the security of British interests in the Mediterranean, he proposed that Britain and France together should aim to maintain superior strength over the combined strength of Austria-Hungary and Italy. Britain would then require just four battlecruisers at Malta in peacetime, which was sufficient, he insisted, to maintain British prestige in the region. The committee, following the lead of the Foreign Secretary, Sir Edward Grey, rejected this advice. It was decided that Britain must maintain rough equality in capital ships with the strongest power in the region (excluding France)—i.e. a regional 'one-power standard'—so as to give weight to British diplomacy in the area. The CID also ruled that the Admiralty's first priority must be to retain a 'reasonable margin' of superiority over Germany, but as the margin was not defined, Churchill and the Admiralty were not guaranteed the 60 per cent superiority they wanted.[36]

This decision, later ratified by the full Cabinet, marked a significant setback for Churchill and the Admiralty. In taking this step, the Liberal government effectively transformed Britain's naval race with Germany into a naval race with Germany *and* Austria-Hungary. The former competition was certain to be expensive, but the latter threatened to be ruinous. The 60 per cent margin Churchill had announced to Parliament had made no allowances for matching construction by another great power, but the Admiralty was now expected to counter Austrian strength in the Mediterranean. Because Churchill was determined, for strategic reasons, not to denude the North Sea of capital ships, he would spend much of the next two years scrambling to find the ships he needed to meet the new Mediterranean one-power standard.

As an interim measure, he persuaded the Cabinet that it would be sufficient to station four British battlecruisers at Malta.[37] But in the long term, as Austrian and Italian dreadnoughts were completed, more modern heavy ships would be required. Churchill calculated that by mid-1915 he would need a squadron of eight capital ships in the Mediterranean to maintain the one-power standard. On 10 July 1912 he appealed to the Cabinet to agree to the construction of three extra dreadnoughts to ensure the standard could be preserved from 1916 onward. According to one of the ministers present, Churchill now proposed to abandon the policy of maintaining a 60 per cent superiority over the German navy in favour of 'something like 40 per cent over the next two strongest fleets combined'.[38] This formula would have tied British strength directly to its two principal rivals, so that Austrian dreadnought construction would automatically trigger corresponding increases in British strength, thereby ensuring that enough ships would always be available to maintain a large margin over Germany in the North Sea and a one-power standard in the Mediterranean.

This expensive proposal was promptly rejected by the Cabinet, but Churchill never gave up his belief that some modification of British policy would eventually be required. In a speech to the House of Commons on 22 July 1912, he pointedly omitted any reference to the new Mediterranean standard, which he probably hoped would be abandoned, and he hinted that more dreadnoughts might eventually have to be built to meet Britain's commitments in this region.[39] But one other possibility soon presented itself. Churchill began to explore the idea that the burden of additional new construction could be shifted to Britain's self-governing Dominions. Australia was already building a battlecruiser in British shipyards for the newly established Royal Australian Navy, and New Zealand was financing the construction of another for use by the Royal Navy. The Canadian government was also showing an interest in building dreadnoughts for Britain. In early July, Churchill outlined the naval situation at length to Sir Robert Borden, the prime minister of Canada, at a meeting of the CID in London. The First Lord explained that Britain needed to lay down three extra capital ships to ensure that it maintained its minimum standards of strength in both the Mediterranean and the North Sea. This would be difficult, he stated, for financial reasons, but also because additional construction by Britain might increase the strain on Anglo-German relations. However, he suggested that diplomatic complications could be avoided if Canada undertook to build these ships.[40]

Churchill's idea of using Dominion capital ships to fulfil the new one-power standard in the Mediterranean conflicted with a previous Admiralty commitment to begin establishing a stronger British naval presence in the Pacific. At the Imperial Conference of 1909, the Admiralty had recommended that Dominion governments interested in developing their own navies should each construct a distinct 'fleet unit', consisting of a battle-cruiser, three unarmoured cruisers, six destroyers, and three submarines. Such a force would be capable of catching and destroying an enemy's detached commerce raiders on the high seas, and could take over some of the burden of trade protection in distant waters. They could also, if necessary, be integrated into a larger fleet. The Conference had concluded with an agreement that a new Pacific Fleet would be established consisting of three such fleet units. Two of these would be provided by Britain; the third would be Australian. Churchill was willing to go along with these plans in his first months at the Admiralty, but he was hardly enthusiastic: it made little sense, in his opinion, to dispatch modern warships—especially the newest and most powerful capital ships—to distant stations at a time when Britain faced a major threat from Germany in its own home waters.[41]

When the Canadian government first expressed an interest in building capital ships, Churchill thought he saw an opportunity to improve on the 1909 arrangements. In April 1912 he had outlined plans for a 'Dominion Squadron' to Asquith. This force would combine the battlecruisers being built by Australia and New Zealand with two new—and still speculative— Canadian battlecruisers. He also hoped that South Africa and India might contribute to the squadron, which would be responsible for protecting imperial communications in distant waters. The advantage of this arrangement from the Admiralty's perspective was that Britain could withdraw its modern ships from the Pacific without recriminations from the dominions. 'Here then,' Churchill wrote in April 1912, 'is the fundamental division of labour wh[ich] the mother country should make with her Colonies:—We will cope with the strongest combination in the decisive theatre, you shall patrol the Empire.'[42]

Churchill outlined this plan publicly in May 1912, but he promptly abandoned it when the Cabinet decided on the one-power standard against Austria-Hungary. Imperial defence would now take second place to the principle of concentration in the decisive theatre: Churchill wanted all the empire's capital ships available for service in Britain's home waters and the Mediterranean. This redistribution began in July, when two battlecruisers, *Indomitable* and *New Zealand*, which had been allocated to Britain's fleet units in the Pacific, were reassigned to home waters. But the only way to ensure that Britain maintained its essential margin over Germany without increasing its own shipbuilding programme was to rely on the Dominions for the additional ships needed in the Mediterranean. There was little prospect of Australia releasing its new battlecruiser, HMAS *Australia*, which would form an integral part of the new Royal Australian Navy, so it was Canada that Churchill looked to for support. To everyone's relief, Borden appeared eager to cooperate. He asked Churchill to outline the arguments for a contribution of dreadnoughts for the Royal Navy in two separate documents, one suitable for presentation to the Canadian Parliament and another, 'confidential and in detail', that he could share with his Cabinet.[43]

To overcome domestic opposition, Borden believed he must have a clear and unequivocal statement from the Admiralty that Britain faced an emergency. But this created problems for Churchill, who did not want to suggest that the Admiralty might conceivably fail to meet its defence obligations to the Dominions. He informed Borden privately that without Canadian assistance, Britain would have to take additional measures 'over and above the very great exertions they are already making' to provide for the safety of both Britain and the empire. But he confided in August 1912 that he was wary about presenting the situation 'so nakedly, even in a confidential document'.[44] After two weeks working on the document, he confided to the Colonial Secretary, Sir Lewis Harcourt, in September that it was proving difficult 'to make a case for an emergency policy in Canada without admitting that we have not provided adequately for the safety of the Country here, and without unduly dwelling on the facts regarding the German naval development or committing ourselves to a position which would not leave us any choice but to make additional provision if Canada does not'.[45]

The memorandum Churchill provided to Borden in September studiously avoided any hint of a crisis. Britain, it affirmed, would not 'in any circumstances fail in her duty to the Oversea Dominions of the Crown'. The British Parliament would take whatever measures were necessary to safeguard the vital interests of the empire. But Canada's aid, it maintained, would have a tremendous moral value:

> Any action on the part of Canada to increase the power and mobility of the Imperial Navy, and thus widen the margin of our common safety, would be recognised everywhere as a most significant witness to the united strength of the Empire, and to the renewed resolve of the Oversea Dominions to take their part in maintaining its integrity.[46]

Churchill was also quick to reassure Borden that the Admiralty was receptive to proposals that would support the Canadian shipbuilding industry by building some new warships—other than dreadnoughts themselves—in Canada.[47] His efforts were rewarded in December 1912 when Borden introduced a Naval Aid Bill to the Canadian Parliament calling for the financing of three dreadnoughts for the Royal Navy.

Churchill initially had no reason to doubt that the ships would be approved, but it soon became apparent that Borden's Conservative government was unlikely to obtain the support of Canada's Liberal-dominated upper chamber. To strengthen Borden's hand, and secure the dreadnoughts he needed for the Mediterranean, Churchill decided that he must after all endorse the Canadian leader's claims that Britain was facing an emergency. When presenting the Royal Navy's annual estimates to Parliament in March 1913, the First Lord declared that while Britain's margins relative to Germany were not in danger, the proposed Canadian dreadnoughts were 'absolutely necessary for the whole-world defence of the British Empire from the end of 1915, or from the beginning of 1916 onwards'.[48]

The potential loss of the Canadian dreadnoughts was partially offset by increased naval cooperation with France. In July 1912, Churchill had accepted a French request to consider arrangements for joint naval action in the event the two powers became embroiled in war with Germany. While taking care to ensure that a naval agreement did not entail any binding political commitments, he encouraged the French to maintain enough ships in the Mediterranean to match the forces of Austria-Hungary and Italy combined.[49] Over the next several months, an agreement was hammered out between the two governments that gave the French navy responsibility for protecting British interests in the western Mediterranean, while Britain agreed, under certain conditions, to protect French interests in the North Sea and English Channel. When a formal convention was concluded in February 1913, the British were not committed to supporting France automatically in the event of a Franco-German conflict. However, if Britain remained neutral in such a war, France's Atlantic coast would be exposed to German assault. Churchill himself was confident that France was well advised to concentrate its forces in the Mediterranean no matter what Britain did, but the French were undeniably running a risk at Britain's behest and, whether Churchill and his colleagues liked it or not, Britain incurred a moral obligation to France.

The naval convention eased some of the government's concerns about the situation in the Mediterranean, but Churchill was still no closer to having the ships necessary to maintain the one-power Mediterranean standard. His difficulties increased in May 1913 when Borden's naval aid bill was rejected outright by the Canadian Senate. Churchill had to scramble again to find ships for the Mediterranean, despite his clear lack of enthusiasm. He still disliked the idea of tying up modern capital ships in a secondary theatre, and he assumed that the naval agreement with France made it strategically unnecessary for Britain to match Austrian strength. It was 'extremely improbable', he argued in September 1913, that Britain would have to face Germany and one or both of its allies without French support. And since France alone could be expected to match both Austria-Hungary and Italy, Britain could afford to remove some, if not all, of its capital ships from the Mediterranean in wartime. If Britain were at war with Germany alone, Churchill proposed to bring home the *entire* Mediterranean fleet.[50] He continued to plan for a full squadron of capital ships in the Mediterranean in peacetime as the Cabinet had stipulated, but he seems to have regarded these ships as a sort of reserve force available for redeployment to home waters in wartime.

Churchill was also prepared to revert to his earlier idea of relying on 'flotilla defence' in the Mediterranean if it proved impossible to secure enough capital ships for the one-power standard. In the autumn of 1912 he had considered reducing the number of battleships in the estimates for 1913–14 in order to divert resources to the expansion of the submarine fleet. There is no indication of how the additional submarines were to be deployed, but Churchill clearly saw a use for them in the Mediterranean. 'There is no doubt that Austria intends to have a great Mediterranean Fleet,' he had told Grey and Asquith in October 1912. 'Our best and cheapest— perhaps our only—way of meeting this will be a large submarine and tor-pedo development supported by a fast squadron.'[51] At that time, his naval advisers were receptive to this idea. A study by the Naval Staff's operations division in November 1912 concluded that the Austrian fleet would be vul-nerable to British submarines and destroyers as it exited the Adriatic Sea through the Strait of Otranto, which was only 40 miles wide. Captain George Ballard, the division's director, believed that a 'force of 80 sea-going Submarines' could 'make the Adriatic entrance practically impossible [for the Austrians] if properly disposed and manoeuvred'. This would allow Brit-ain to reduce its capital-ship requirements in the Mediterranean.[52]

But Churchill was still bound by the Cabinet's decision to maintain a one-power standard in the Mediterranean, and he continued to view flotilla defence as an inferior means of protecting British interests. Since the Cabi-net had created the need for capital ships in the Mediterranean, he naturally looked to this body for relief. In June 1913 he explained again to his col-leagues that without the three Canadian dreadnoughts Britain would fall behind Austrian capital-ship strength in the Mediterranean by the autumn of 1915. To prevent this, he recommended moving ahead the start date of three British dreadnoughts already authorized in the Admiralty's 1913–14 estimates. This boost would enable Britain to maintain the approved stand-ards in both home waters and the Mediterranean until the autumn of 1916. But he warned that the acceleration of the current programme would only provide a temporary solution. If the Canadian government did not con-struct any of the proposed dreadnoughts, Britain would have to consider adding ships to its 1914–15 programme to be sure of maintaining the one-power standard beyond 1916.[53]

After obtaining Cabinet sanction for the accelerated delivery of the Brit-ish ships, Churchill wrote privately to Borden stressing the importance of the Canadian dreadnoughts to imperial security. The Cabinet had already rejected a proposal from the Canadian prime minister that the British government should order three additional dreadnoughts, which would eventually be taken over and paid for by Canada.[54] Churchill now suggested that a declaration from the Canadian government that it intended to build these vessels might be sufficient to induce one of Britain's shipbuilding firms to begin work on the dreadnoughts 'as a speculation'. This was an unconventional and indeed improper step, but the important thing from Churchill's perspective was to find some way to get the necessary ships into production. Even if the Canadian government ultimately decided not to pay for them, he was optimistic that the British government would take them over rather than risk seeing them sold to another power.[55]

The situation was complicated, however, by Churchill's contingency plans for Britain's 1914 programme of new construction. The Naval Staff was investigating means to increase the number of submarines in the annual estimates the following year without increasing the overall cost of its new construction programme.[56] Churchill had no desire to see these plans wrecked for the sake of laying down additional battleships for the Mediterranean. He therefore explained to Borden that if the Canadian dreadnoughts were not approved by the following spring, when the annual estimates were submitted to Parliament, the Admiralty would probably expand its submarine fleet rather than build additional capital ships of its own. 'My naval colleagues,' he informed Borden, 'consider that for less money than 3 capital ships would cost, we could by a greatly increased flotilla construction in the narrow seas liberate [sic] 3 ships for general service.' The difficulty with this course is that Churchill—with the consent of the Cabinet—had publicly stated that the Canadian dreadnoughts were needed to meet an emergency. Building submarines rather than additional battleships would appear to contradict the Admiralty's earlier advice that Canada should build dreadnoughts, and belie Churchill's assurances that the Canadian ships were urgently needed to meet the Admiralty's global requirements.[57]

The Mediterranean one-power standard continued to complicate Churchill's plans during the autumn of 1913. Borden remained committed to financing dreadnoughts for the Royal Navy, but he clearly faced enormous obstacles to securing the necessary political support. Churchill calculated that further delays in the construction of the Canadian ships could only be covered by moving forward the start date of the battleships in the Admiralty's 1914–15 programme. This would allow Britain to continue meeting its Mediterranean standard for another year, but it was another short-term solution. If Canada ultimately did not build the additional dreadnoughts, Churchill assumed he would have to ask the Cabinet for three capital ships beyond those already projected. He explained his difficulties in a Cabinet memorandum in early December 1913, outlining the Admiralty's proposed estimates for 1914−15. Britain could have a one-power standard fleet in the Mediterranean at the end of 1916 or by early 1917, he advised, but *only* if the Austrians did not add to their current building plans *and* if Canada financed three dreadnoughts. In the meantime, four battlecruisers would be based at Malta to support British diplomacy. If Canada did not begin building dreadnoughts, Britain would have to make good this shortfall. He also warned that Austria-Hungary was contemplating an additional four capital ships in its programme, and those ships would have to be matched as well.

A request for more capital ships was hardly unreasonable in the circumstances, but Churchill probably assumed that his colleagues, faced with the tremendous expense of building three or more additional dreadnoughts, would quietly abandon the Mediterranean standard and rely on the understanding with France to safeguard British interests there.[58] If he expected debate over the 1914 naval estimates to revolve around the question of expanding Britain's building programme, he was mistaken. A strong faction within the Cabinet favored a *reduction* in the estimates. This group, which included Lloyd George, proposed to drop two of the four dreadnoughts included in the following year's new construction programme. Their reasons were mainly financial. The navy estimates for 1911, the year Churchill arrived at the Admiralty, had been £42.4 million. Since then, naval expenses had increased drastically. Britain was building more ships than before, at a greater individual cost, and keeping more vessels in commission. The number and pay of naval personnel was also increasing, and a new naval air service had been created. Churchill's proposed estimates for 1914 came to nearly £50.7 million, and he warned that an additional £2 million might become necessary if shipyards made more rapid progress than expected on vessels already under construction. This represented an increase of nearly 25 per cent in naval expenditure in just four years. The Chancellor of the Exchequer, who was faced with the prospect of raising taxes in the coming year (an election year), was alarmed by the size of Churchill's estimates, and did not believe that a small reduction in the capital-ship programme would jeopardize British security. To his colleagues, he argued that four dreadnoughts were not needed that year to maintain 60 per cent superiority over Germany, and that such a large programme would be 'distinctly provocative' at a time when Anglo-German relations seemed to be improving.[59]

Sir Edward Grey proposed to the Cabinet in mid-December that reductions in the shipbuilding programme might be possible if Britain withdrew some of its capital ships from the Mediterranean.[60] This would have gone a long way towards solving Churchill's difficulties, and he probably would have been happy to reduce the Mediterranean commitments if this were not linked to a reduction in the shipbuilding programme. But Churchill had publicly committed himself in March 1912 to building four capital ships in 1914, and to the preservation of 60 per cent superiority over Germany. If the Cabinet—which had not protested against these commitments—now repudiated them, Churchill's position would be untenable and he was prepared to resign. The situation was further complicated by his public declarations that the Canadian dreadnoughts were required to meet a naval emergency. It would be highly damaging to Churchill personally if the government demonstrated that there was no emergency, and that the situation was in fact so secure that it could afford to reduce Britain's own programme. Any chance of obtaining the Canadian ships would likely be wrecked. Churchill was also alarmed about the repercussions in Germany. The construction programme outlined in 1912 had been the stick with which he hoped to induce the Germans to accept his proposals for a naval holiday. He feared that a major change in British policy would signal a weakening of British resolve and encourage the Germans to renew their efforts.[61]

On 18 December Churchill appealed to Asquith for patience. There still appeared to be a chance that Borden would obtain funds for the new dreadnoughts, in which event Britain could maintain both the 60 per cent margin over Germany and the one-power standard against Austria-Hungary. In other words, by approving all four battleships in the current program, Britain ultimately stood to obtain seven new dreadnoughts. Cutting the programme to two, on the other hand, would ensure that two were the most Britain could hope for. By 'hold[ing] firm now', Churchill insisted, there were still 'good chances of a complete success'. But if Borden failed, Churchill did not see any insuperable obstacle to reducing Britain's commitments in the Mediterranean. He suggested to Asquith in December 1913 that he could if necessary 'develop an argument ab[ou]t submarines in that sea wh[ich] will obviate a further constr[uctio]n of battleships for this 2dary theatre'.[62] In other words, flotilla defence might still provide an alternative to a one-power standard in capital ships in the Mediterranean.

An unpublished memorandum dating from around this time illustrates Churchill's thoughts on this subject. Matching Austrian dreadnoughts with

British dreadnoughts represented 'no more than a plain and simple interpretation' of the one-power standard, he argued. Britain, in his opinion, would have to rely on what would now be called an 'asymmetric strategy':

> The obvious method of meeting like with like [i.e. battleships with battleships] would impose an unbearable strain on our resources. We must therefore seek safety in some disconcerting variation. To do the same thing as your enemy but on a smaller scale is futile. If you cannot be superior, you must be different. We are justified in adopting less direct methods of maintaining our position in a secondary theatre than are required in the North Sea.

Rather than build three additional British dreadnoughts to maintain a precise one-power standard, Churchill suggested that Mediterranean requirements be met by building additional vessels in other classes, including twelve submarines and eight fast destroyers, which could then be used to augment British capital-ship strength. It would then be possible to get by with just five fast capital ships in the Mediterranean by 1915. Such a 'force is not directly comparable to the Italian or Austrian fleets', he conceded:

> but we consider that its speed and quality would enable it, if well handled, to seize any opportunity of striking a heavy blow which a temporary weakness of the enemy might offer, and to avoid being brought to action in unfavourable circumstances. It is peculiarly well adapted to protecting British trade in the Mediterranean, and could continually harass and injure the enemy. We are of opinion that such a force would in fact though not in form meet the requirements of the 'One Power Standard' prescribed.[63]

To strengthen his position in Cabinet, Churchill enlisted Borden's support. On 19 December he warned the Canadian prime minister that the Admiralty was being pressed to reduce its battleship programme for the coming year. He invited Borden to send him a letter stating that such a reduction 'would be disastrous to your Government & its naval policy, & that you w[oul]d consider you had been ill-used'. Such a letter, he predicted, would have a strong impact on his colleagues. 'The claim of obligation & good faith is one wh[ich] no British Cabinet will reject; & an argument on these lines makes it easy for persons who do not agree on the merits of particular proposals to bow to what they can regard as past commitments.'[64] Borden promptly replied along the lines requested. If Britain cut its capital-ship programme for 1914 by half, he warned that it 'would be quite impossible for us to persevere in proposals which were based upon considerations of an urgency which we vigorously proclaimed and in which we fully believed'.

At the same time, he reassured Churchill of his determination to obtain funding for the Canadian dreadnoughts, although he admitted that until the composition of the senate was altered to favour his party there was no point in introducing a new naval-aid bill.[65]

When the debate over the naval estimates resumed in January 1914, Churchill produced a new memorandum for the Cabinet clearly laying out the full implications of the decision in July 1912 to maintain a one-power standard in the Mediterranean. If the government did not accelerate more of its own ships in 1914–15 temporarily to fill the gap left by the Canadian dreadnoughts, the Opposition would have every right to demand that Britain build an additional three capital ships to fill the gap permanently, making a total of seven new dreadnoughts that year. By accelerating three capital ships in the previous year's estimates, Churchill maintained that his colleagues had publicly committed themselves to providing enough ships to maintain a one-power Mediterranean standard. The only alternative to building three additional ships, he argued, was to accelerate work on two of the new ships in the 1914–15 programme. This would provide another temporary solution. If that course were rejected, he insisted that the Cabinet would have to consider revoking the one-power Mediterranean standard entirely. And if it wished to retain the standard, it would also have to consider its response if either Austria-Hungary or Italy increased its building programme, as appeared likely.

Churchill made his own position on these issues clear in a draft minute to Admiral Prince Louis of Battenberg, the First Sea Lord, and Admiral Sir Henry Jackson, the Chief of the Admiralty's War Staff. All four battleships must be approved, he stated, in order to maintain the 60 per cent standard, and two of these vessels should be laid down as soon as possible to cover temporarily the expected shortfall in the Mediterranean. He also proposed that the government should continue to 'Adhere to the Mediterranean decision [i.e. the one-power standard]: but keep it secret.' This would make it easier to drop the standard later if the Canadian dreadnoughts fell through. Finally, Churchill suggested that Britain should simply ignore future building by Italy, while matching new Austrian battleships with submarines.[66]

After a protracted and sometimes acrimonious debate, Churchill and Lloyd George reached a compromise at the end of January 1914. The First Lord obtained approval for the construction of four new dreadnoughts, which would entail estimates of £52.8 million. In return, Lloyd George was assured that the estimates for 1915–16 would be kept below £50 million.[67]

The only outstanding question now was the fate of the Mediterranean standard. In early February, Churchill took the question of acceleration back to the Cabinet. If the start date of two ships of the new programme were not moved forward, he warned again that it would be necessary to abandon either the existing margin of 50 percent over Germany in home waters or the one-power Mediterranean standard. The latter course would destroy any chance of obtaining dreadnoughts from Canada, and Churchill was still eager not to take this step unless absolutely necessary. To make an acceleration more attractive, he proposed that offsetting economies could be obtained by delaying the start of a number of smaller warships and the other two dreadnoughts in the 1914 estimates. If Borden obtained authorization for the Canadian dreadnoughts, Churchill suggested it might even be possible to delay some of the battleships in the 1915 programme. But if the Canadian ships were definitely abandoned, it would be necessary to accelerate part of the 1915 programme in order to maintain the Mediterranean standard for another year. Churchill suggested, however, that by the time such a decision had to be taken, 'the progress of naval science, especially in regard to submarine construction, may enable a new view to be taken of the naval situation as a whole'. The Cabinet would therefore not necessarily be committed to building additional battleships if the Canadian contribution did not materialize.[68]

The accelerated production of two ships from the 1914 programme was approved in February, despite strong opposition from some ministers. But the Cabinet was not willing to commit to any future increase in Britain's capital-ship programme for the sake of the Mediterranean. According to Asquith's account, the Cabinet agreed 'that Parliament should be clearly informed that in the event of Mr Borden's continued default, the British government was under no obligation to supply the 3 missing Canadian ships, and that our standard of construction is to be maintained at 60 per cent'.[69] This amounted to a tacit repudiation of the one-power Mediterranean standard. The details of the Cabinet's discussion about naval standards are not recorded, but ministers were by now well aware that by adopting the Mediterranean standard alongside the 60 per cent standard over Germany, the government had inflated its battleship requirements beyond what the Admiralty considered necessary and what the Cabinet was willing to pay for. As Churchill noted shortly afterwards, in a minute to the Director of the Admiralty's Intelligence Division, the existing battleship standards 'would carry us to an individual strength superior to the whole Triple Alliance'. In other words, Britain had unintentionally created a de facto three-power standard. 'Such a position,' Churchill remarked, could not be defended.' He noted, however, that the Cabinet was inclined to limit its obligations by adopting a new formula by which Britain would maintain either a 60 per cent standard against the next strongest power, or a two-power standard measured against the next two strongest powers excluding the United States, 'whichever alternative is the greater'.[70]

A new formula along these lines would have reduced the government's obligations in battleships to a more manageable and realistic level. Numbers were only a problem from Churchill's perspective if he had to maintain *both* the 60 per cent standard against Germany and the one-power standard in the Mediterranean. If Britain abandoned the latter, there would be enough ships on hand to maintain the Admiralty's 'irreducible' requirement of 50 per cent superiority over Germany in the North Sea and still provide a small but fast squadron for the Mediterranean. No formal decision was taken to abandon the one-power standard, but it had clearly became untenable by April 1914, when it was learned that Austria-Hungary and Italy intended to increase their existing programmes by an additional four dreadnoughts each.[71] Neither the 'acceleration' of British ships nor Canadian construction would suffice any longer to maintain the one-power standard. This development appears to have convinced Churchill that the time had come to rely more heavily on submarines as a substitute for capital ships in the Mediterranean.

At the time, the First Lord regarded Britain's position in the North Sea with considerable confidence. British shipyards were able to build capital ships more rapidly than their German counterparts, and in the spring of 1914 Churchill was optimistic that the navy could maintain its 60 per cent margin over Germany alone. Writing to Battenberg on 13 May, he noted that Britain could expect to complete thirteen new capital ships between the fourth quarter of 1914 and the first quarter of 1916, while Germany would complete only two. This 'great military fact', he remarked, altered 'the whole proportion of battle strength between the fleets'. In his opinion, this development was 'one of the strongest justifications for a general review of types [for construction]'.[72] Not long afterwards, he observed to his private secretary that 'the European situation has so greatly improved and the German increase has been so largely overhauled by our exertions' that it would now be safe to begin scrapping a large number of obsolescent warships, a policy he had planned to pursue when he came to the Admiralty but which had been shelved following the German naval increases in 1912.[73]

The worsening situation in the Mediterranean, on the other hand, bolstered Churchill's resolve to reduce Britain's commitments in this secondary theatre.[74] There is no record of the Mediterranean standard being formally dropped, but an informal understanding appears to have been reached. On 4 July 1914, Churchill informed the prime minister that he was 'looking to the development of flotilla defence in the Mediterranean as a partial substitute for battleship strength, which would entail such heavy new construction charges'.[75] Preparations were, in fact, already under way to increase the British submarine force at Malta. But there was no desire to publicize any of this. On the contrary, Churchill attempted to conceal what was under way. On 7 July, just three days after informing Asquith of the plan to substitute flotilla vessels for battleships in the Mediterranean, the First Lord informed the House of Commons that Britain would 'have a battle-squadron of eight battleships in the Mediterranean, which is a very powerful squadron'.[76]

This would maintain the appearance that British policy had not changed. Altering or abandoning a naval standard was always a significant step, and the Liberal government had good reason to worry that its domestic critics would seize on any change to claim that Britain's naval security and interests in the Mediterranean were not being adequately protected. More seriously, British prestige abroad would be damaged and potential enemies warned of the changes in Britain's naval force structure in the Mediterranean. It was therefore more convenient in 1914 not to announce any change in policy. When the eight capital ships failed to appear in the Mediterranean as promised, Churchill presumably intended to fall back on the argument he later outlined in an unpublished draft chapter of *The World Crisis*—that dreadnoughts could be treated 'not as capital ships but as units of power which could, if desirable, be expressed in any other form'.[77] By this sleight of hand, the one-power *battleship* standard in the Mediterranean could be transformed into a something that could still be described as a one-power standard, thus reassuring the public that no significant change was taking place.

Churchill was willing to run risks in the Mediterranean because of the overriding importance of maintaining a large margin of superiority over Germany in the main and decisive theatre, and because he was confident that British interests in the Mediterranean could be adequately protected by the powerful French navy. But while financial considerations forced

Churchill to accept a sharply reduced role for battleships in the Mediterranean, he does not appear to have lost faith in the battleship as the ultimate
guarantee of British security in the North Sea. The strong preference of
Churchill and his advisers for keeping these ships concentrated in what was
regarded as the most important theatre represents a clear affirmation of their
faith in the battleship.

Churchill's views on the *future* of the battleship were complex, however.
He was fully aware of the claims being made in some quarters that submarines and aircraft would one day make modern capital ships obsolete; he
believed this outcome would probably be realized as new technologies were
developed; and he was eager that the Royal Navy should be at the forefront
of progress in these areas. But at the same time he was conscious of the limitations of the existing technology, and he was instinctively cautious about
abandoning a proven type of warship prematurely. On 10 November 1913
he told an audience at the Guildhall in London that the 'question has often
been raised whether the great ships of the Dreadnought era will some day
follow the mammoth and the mastodon into a convenient and highly desirable extinction':

> Those who believe that that time will come—and they are a considerable
> school—point with a warning finger to the ever-growing power of the sub-
> marine, and to the new and expanding possibilities of the air, and they ask
> whether the day will not come when, guided by information out of the sky,
> a blow may not be struck beneath the water which will be fatal to the pre-
> dominance of great capital ships, at any rate in the narrow seas.

'That time,' he assured his audience, 'has not yet come, and the ultimate
decision of naval war still rests with those who can place in the line of battle
fleets and squadrons which in numbers and quality…are superior to anything they may be called upon to meet'.[78]

His views on submarines were also complicated. In August 1913 he
drafted a detailed minute outlining the roles these vessels could be expected
to play. In his opinion, there were three distinct types to consider. The first
were 'coastal' vessels with limited range suitable for protecting the narrow
waters around Britain itself. The second were 'overseas' vessels with considerably greater range and capable of operating near the enemy's shores. The
third were 'ocean' submarines, which he described as a 'decisive weapon of
battle; and as such must count in partial substitution of battleship strength.'
No submarine of this class—later known as 'fleet' submarines—had yet
been developed, but Churchill believed these must possess a surface speed

of around 24 knots, which would allow them to 'overhaul a battle fleet so as to make sure of being able to anticipate it at any point, or to get ahead of it in order to dive and attack. Such vessels attack by getting there and being overtaken.' Churchill suggested that three or four of these vessels could be grouped together into a submarine flotilla along with two fast light cruisers. Each flotilla would be 'considered equal as a decisive fighting unit to a first class battleship or battle cruiser'.[79] The submarine would thus be capable of supplanting the battleship when a new class had been developed capable of achieving the necessary surface speed.

Until new technology or improved designs produced a submarine with the necessary capabilities, Churchill was not prepared to experiment with anything as radical as flotilla defence as Britain's main defence in the North Sea. The stakes there were simply too great. He was determined to maintain a powerful fleet in home waters superior to its German counterpart in all classes of ship, but most importantly in modern capital ships. This force had to be ready at all times to engage the enemy's main fleet if a favourable opportunity arose. As long as Britain maintained a clear quantitative advantage, there were no doubts as to the outcome of a fleet action. The German High Seas Fleet would be either destroyed or, if it did not accept battle, neutralized.

Churchill was confident that these arrangements would enable the navy to fulfil its main duties in wartime with relative ease. The first and most obvious of its tasks was to deter or defeat an invasion of the British Isles. Churchill's views on this threat were fairly consistent. Even before arriving at the Admiralty, he assumed that Britain's naval predominance effectively ruled out a full-scale invasion. No enemy would be prepared to risk such an undertaking in the face of an undefeated British fleet. The army, therefore, only had to be large enough to deal with raiding forces, which might conceivably elude the fleet, but which would also be too small to achieve decisive results.[80] The possibility of invasion was a controversial subject in the decade before the First World War, however. The view of some, particularly within the army, was that Britain had to maintain large forces at home in the event an enemy evaded the British fleet and successfully landed a large body of troops on Britain's shores. The idea of a full-scale invasion coming as a 'bolt-from-the-blue' was consistently rejected by the navy and its supporters who, like Churchill, believed the navy would detect and intercept any invasion force large enough to achieve decisive results.

An investigation by the CID in 1907–8 accepted the Admiralty's view that invasion was unlikely as long as Britain retained command of the sea. It recommended that the army keep enough strength at home to deal with an enemy force around seventy thousand strong, the most that could be expected to land in the face of British naval superiority.[81] This conclusion accorded with Churchill's own views, although his optimism was shaken by the navy's large-scale fleet manoeuvres in 1912, which were specifically designed to test its ability to prevent an invasion. On this occasion, the 'red' force, representing an enemy fleet and transports, was able to evade the 'blue' fleet and theoretically get troops ashore. Churchill subsequently put a positive spin on the manoeuvres in his report to Asquith. It was reasonable, he claimed, to conclude that real enemy landings 'would be interrupted; and that the forces landed would have their oversea communications immediately severed.' He conceded, however, that 'a determined enemy, not afraid of risking the loss of 15,000 or 20,000 men', might make 'a series of simultaneous or successive descents upon different portions of the British coast'.[82]

The navy's ability to detect and intercept an enemy invasion was also threatened by major changes in its war plans. Developments in submarines, aircraft, mines, and torpedoes made it increasingly dangerous for the navy to maintain a close watch on the enemy's coastline in wartime, the scheme Admiral Wilson had outlined to the CID in the summer of 1911. Plans for a close blockade were dropped early in 1912, and the Admiralty's new war staff initially contemplated its replacement with an 'intermediate' or 'observational' blockade, which involved keeping the main British fleet in its own northern waters while cruisers and destroyers patrolled a line extending midway through the North Sea between Britain and Germany. Churchill was never enthusiastic about this plan, however, and it was dropped after the 1912 manoeuvres demonstrated that it was not practicable.[83] Towards the end of the year, the naval staff began to outline new plans for a 'distant blockade' of Germany. This called for British cruisers to patrol a line from the Shetlands and Orkneys to the Norwegian coast, with the goal of exercising 'economic pressure upon Germany by cutting off German shipping from oceanic trade'. The British fleet would now be retained in Scottish waters to support the blockading cruisers, intercept an invasion force, and engage the enemy's main fleet if a suitable opportunity occurred.[84]

This was an improvement on earlier schemes, but Churchill continued to worry that the fleet would be too far north to cover the transportation of a

British army to France, or to be certain of intercepting German forces assaulting Britain's east coast. The main defence against such attacks would be Britain's light coastal vessels and shore defences, and Churchill, who would bear the brunt of any backlash if the Germans succeeded in landing troops or bombarding the coast, harboured serious misgivings about this new strategy.[85] And he was not the only one concerned about the vulnerability of Britain's shores. In early 1913 the CID set up another subcommittee to investigate anew the danger of invasion.

While this body deliberated, Churchill cast around for an alternative to the naval staff's distant blockade strategy. 'It is impossible,' he complained to Battenberg in February 1913, 'by a purely passive defensive to guard against all the dangers which may be threatened by an enterprising enemy':

> When one menace has been provided against, another appears. Along the whole line from the Shetlands to the Straits of Dover we shall be dispersed, anxious, weak and waiting: the only question being where are we going to be hit. Whatever may be said in favour of distant blockade as the guiding policy of a long war, and I agree with what is said, such a policy can only be effectively maintained on a basis of moral superiority. Unless and until our enemy has felt and learned to fear our teeth, it is impracticable. We must so conduct ourselves that the sea is full of nameless terrors for him—instead of for us.

The solution, he proposed, was to project British naval power more aggressively into the North Sea. The great mass of the navy's light vessels should therefore establish an 'overwhelming flotilla superiority' off the German coast during the first week of war. This would provide cover for the transport of the British Expeditionary Force (BEF) to France and allow the Royal Navy to establish an early moral ascendancy over its foes, which would reduce the likelihood of a German assault on the British coast.[86] Around this same time, Churchill also attempted to revive Admiral Wilson's idea of seizing an island near the German coast to serve as a forward base from which British flotilla vessels could establish a powerful and continuous presence in German home waters. To circumvent the naval staff, which disliked the idea, he established an informal planning body under Rear Admiral Sir Lewis Bayly to investigate the feasibility of occupying a German or Dutch island. Churchill's efforts were not well received by the naval staff, however, which raised legitimate concerns about the practicability of his proposals. Churchill was not prepared to press the matter at this time, and the Admiralty's official war plans continued to embody the distant-blockade policy favoured by staff officers.[87]

The vulnerability of Britain's east coast was an ongoing source of concern, however, and Churchill developed doubts about the wisdom of the War Office's plan to dispatch to France at the beginning of a war the entire BEF, a force of around six regular army divisions that had been designated for service on the Continent. In April 1913 he prepared a memorandum for the CID's subcommittee on invasion entitled 'The Time Table of a Nightmare', which described in considerable detail a hypothetical descent by the Germans on the British coast at the outset of war. In this document, the Germans, after using naval guns to silence the local defences at Harwich, land forty-five thousand troops, along with artillery and ammunition.[88] Churchill intended this memorandum to show that it would be a grave mistake 'to send away or promise to send away the whole regular army' at the outset of war.[89] His concerns about the vulnerability of the British coast would have been increased by the navy's 1913 manoeuvres. Once again, the 'red' force managed to evade its pursuers and land troops on 'blue' (i.e. British) territory. Churchill was sufficiently alarmed by the success of the theoretical invasion that the manoeuvres were terminated early, 'for fear', as Admiral Jellicoe put it, 'of giving useful information to the Germans'.[90] By mid-1913, the navy's inability to prevent attacks on the British coast had convinced Churchill that a portion of the regular army must be kept in Britain to deal with large raids.[91] The CID's invasion inquiry reached the same conclusion. Its final report, issued in April 1914, recommended that two divisions of regular troops be held back from France to supplement the forces of the Territorial Army.

The defence of British trade—the navy's other main defensive task— seemingly presented fewer problems. Churchill and his advisers were confident that the sheer size of the British merchant fleet would be sufficient in itself to ensure a steady and adequate flow of food and raw materials into the British Isles, even if German raiders were not immediately hunted down. 'We must rely on numbers and averages,' the First Lord wrote in a comprehensive overview of trade protection in August 1913. The most serious danger from Churchill's perspective was not that British merchant ships would be destroyed or captured in large numbers, but that they would be 'frightened out of putting to sea' by the threat of enemy commerce raiders.[92] The interruption of imports on a large scale could have serious consequences for the British war effort, especially, Churchill feared, if disruption to the nation's food supply led to a breakdown of public order. The solution to this, he believed, was for the state to underwrite the risk to merchant shipping in wartime. A national insurance scheme would ensure that merchant ships were not deterred from sailing by sharp increases in commercial insurance rates due to fears of enemy action. Churchill first recommended this scheme to the Admiralty in 1911, while he was still Home Secretary, and gave it his enthusiastic backing after becoming First Lord. These measures met with strong opposition within the government before the war, but were nevertheless put into place with little delay in August 1914.[93]

The Admiralty assumed at this time that the main threat to British merchant ships would be enemy surface raiders, a problem Churchill regarded as easily manageable. If the Germans diverted cruisers from their main fleet and employed them on the trade routes, Britain's detached cruiser squadrons could, if necessary, be augmented by cruisers from the British fleet. Churchill was confident that German warships on the trade routes would be systematically hunted down and destroyed by superior numbers of British warships. The situation would be more complicated, however, if the Germans kept their cruisers with the High Seas Fleet and relied on armed merchant ships for attacks on British trade. In this event, Churchill was not prepared to withdraw cruisers from the fleet for trade-protection duties. It was more important, he believed, to ensure superiority over the Germans in this class of vessel in a fleet action. He also doubted whether a handful of additional British cruisers on the trade routes would really be much use in suppressing this threat. 'It is no use,' he wrote, 'distributing isolated cruisers about the vast ocean spaces. To produce any result from such a method would require hundreds of cruisers.... We must recognize that we cannot specifically protect trade routes; we can only protect confluences.'[94]

The scale of the threat from armed German merchant ships was difficult to gauge. When he arrived at the Admiralty in 1911, Churchill was immediately alarmed by reports from the Naval Intelligence Division that the Germans were supplying large numbers of their merchant ships with guns and ammunition so they could be immediately converted into commerce raiders at the outbreak of war.[95] Churchill was willing to use some of the navy's fast older cruisers in focal points as a deterrent to enemy merchant cruisers, but he believed that the best defence against this form of attack would be the defensive arming of Britain's own merchant ships.[96] This idea was enthusiastically supported by Admiralty officials, and in early 1912 the first steps were taken to begin mounting 4.7-inch guns on suitable British merchant vessels. This, as Matthew Seligmann has shown, was an important departure in British trade defence policy, involving 'complex negotiations with shipping companies, careful consideration of international law, and the institution of a new naval [reserve] training scheme and a range of other measures in the diplomatic sphere'.[97]

Churchill publicly announced the Admiralty's new policy in March 1913, but his naval advisers were concerned that the defensive arming of merchant ships would not by itself provide adequate protection to British trade.[98] The problem with arming British merchantmen, they pointed out, was that only the fifty or sixty vessels equipped with guns would actually be protected; the vast majority of merchant ships would remain unarmed and vulnerable. In September 1913, Churchill was dismayed to learn that Admiralty officials wanted to increase the number of cruisers on the trade routes to provide additional security.[99] Up to this time, he had assumed that Britain's armed merchantmen would actively protect unarmed merchant vessels from Germany's converted mercantile cruisers. 'British armed merchantmen,' he had written only a month before, 'stand in the same relation to British ships of war or ...auxiliary cruisers, as the special constable sworn in in times of emergency bears to the regular members of the police or military forces'.[100]

There were serious objections, however, to using these ships, whose guns were mounted on the stern so as to emphasize their defensive role, in a policing capacity. Churchill soon dropped the idea, but he continued to block requests from his naval advisers for more cruisers to protect the trade routes. This policy would not only require heavy new construction, which the navy could not afford, it would also be ineffective.[101] In a sharp rebuke to the First Sea Lord in September 1913, Churchill again denounced 'the policy of dotting the British cruisers' at intervals of 800 miles or more along the trade routes. These dispositions, he argued, would only 'induce British trade to follow the usual trade routes without affording compensating protection', thereby making the task easier for German raiders. Safety could only be provided, he insisted, by encouraging 'British trade to scatter widely and to follow unfrequented sea routes'.[102] The sole additional measure that Churchill was willing to accept were preparations to arm suitable merchant ships for use by the Royal Navy in wartime as commissioned auxiliary cruisers.[103]

Neither Churchill nor his naval advisers gave much consideration at this time to placing British merchant ships into convoy for protection. This practice had been effective during the age of sail, but it was now generally thought to be outdated and unnecessary.[104] Churchill's 1913 memorandum on trade defence had allowed that 'In exceptional cases convoys will, if necessary, be organized under escort', but he also expressed his hope that 'this cumbrous and inconvenient measure will not be required'.[105] There was also little concern about the submarine threat to British trade. As long as enemy submarines adhered to international law they appeared to pose little danger to merchant shipping. When Admiral Fisher predicted in 1913 that the Germans would disregard the law and use their submarines to sink British merchant ships, Churchill dismissed the idea out of hand. 'I do not believe this would ever be done by a civilised power,' he told Fisher in January 1914. 'If there were a nation vile enough to adopt systematically such methods it would be justified and indeed necessary, to employ the extreme resources of science against them: to spread pestilence, poison the water of great cities, and, if convenient, proceed by the assassination of individuals.' But he did not pursue these ideas, as he considered them 'frankly unthinkable propositions'.[106] To the Board of Admiralty, he wrote that Fisher's ideas could be rejected, 'and certainly we have no need to construct submarines for attack or defence of commerce'.[107]

Churchill gave less thought than might be expected during these years to how sea power could contribute directly to the defeat of Germany. In the decade before the outbreak of the war, naval leaders, including Fisher, and key naval supporters in Whitehall, such as Sir Charles Ottley, Maurice Hankey (successive secretaries of the CID), and Lord Esher (one of its most prominent members), had embraced the idea that Germany could ultimately be defeated by economic pressure. The navy was expected by many to play a central role in this process by destroying the German merchant marine and implementing a commercial maritime blockade to deprive Germany of essential imports.[108] British naval preponderance promised to make it relatively easy to sweep German merchant ships from the seas. The only snag in the plan, and a serious one, was that Germany could not be completely cut off from global trade without also blocking its imports through neutral states.

This would be complicated by legal restrictions on Britain's ability to interfere with neutral trade. Some of these dated back to the Declaration of Paris in 1856, but in 1909 the Liberal government had taken a leading role in formulating the Declaration of London, an international agreement to regulate the rights of neutrals and belligerents at sea in wartime. Although never ratified by Britain, this agreement tacitly accepted important limitations on Britain's ability to intercept cargoes bound for Germany through neutral ports. British leaders understood that the complete elimination of the German merchant fleet would not prevent contraband reaching

Germany through contiguous neutrals, particularly Belgium and the Netherlands. As Churchill noted when the problem was discussed by the CID in December 1912, if 'these countries were neutral, the efficacy of our blockade would be halved'.[109] The difficulty in interfering with neutral trade was the risk of alienating neutral powers, and in particular the United States. One possible solution, suggested by Lloyd George, was to limit wartime imports to Belgium and the Netherlands to their normal peacetime levels. Churchill also saw the value in this, but he proposed a more radical solution. The only way to plug this hole entirely would be if these states were *forced* to take sides. Neutrality, he advised, 'was out of the question. They must either be friends or foes.' If the latter, Britain could legally extend its blockade to their coasts and block all imports bound for Germany.

Ministers were clearly attracted to this idea. The draft minutes for the CID meeting on 6 December 1912, where these problems were discussed, stated that 'In order to bring the greatest possible economic pressure upon Germany', it was 'essential that the Netherlands and Belgium should be compelled to declare at the outset to which side in the struggle they would adhere'.[110] Asquith, however, was clearly troubled with the phrase 'should be compelled to declare', which implied a commitment to a definite—and certainly controversial—course of action upon the outbreak of war. When the CID reconvened on 7 January 1913, the prime minister indicated that the draft minutes for the previous meeting 'in some ways went rather further than he thought the Committee meant to go', and he proposed a new conclusion. This stated only that it was 'essential' that the Netherlands and Belgium 'should either be entirely friendly to this country, in which case we should limit their oversea trade, or that they should be definitely hostile, in which case we should extend the blockade to their ports'. This new formula continued to acknowledge the desirability of these states taking sides in a conflict, but did not commit ministers to any particular course of action, or to taking any action at all.[111]

From December 1912 onward, naval planners assumed that the maritime blockade would be just one part, albeit a critical one, of a wider effort to wage economic warfare against Germany. At this time, the CID accepted in principle the report of a major subcommittee recommending sweeping measures on the outbreak of war to prevent all forms of direct trade between Britain and Germany (including insurance and banking services), restricting British exports that might fall into enemy hands, and forbidding British ships from carrying contraband between neutral ports without assurances that it would not make its way to Germany.[112] Besides inducing Germany to take risks with its fleet, the Admiralty predicted that its commercial blockade would, 'as time passes inflict a steadily increasing degree of injury on German interests and credit sufficient to cause serious economic and social consequences'.[113] A strong current of opinion held that these measures might achieve decisive results, although recent claims that the Admiralty and some members of the Liberal government expected them to produce a rapid victory are unconvincing.[114] Churchill certainly does not appear to have expected economic pressure to end a war quickly. As already noted, he looked upon blockade 'as the guiding policy of a *long* war'.[115] He also appreciated that adherence to the Declaration of London, whose terms were directly incorporated into the navy's prize manual, would make it virtually impossible to prevent contraband reaching Germany through neutral ports.[116] To circumvent this problem Admiralty planners began developing plans to place minefields in the North Sea to prevent neutral shipping from reaching German and neutral ports, but these measures were not ready to implement when war broke out in 1914, and there could have been little certainty that such drastic steps would have been endorsed by the government.[117]

Given the lack of reliable data available to planners, and the inherent uncertainty about the effects of economic warfare, expectations of a rapid victory through economic pressure would have required a tremendous leap of faith. As the first historian of the British blockade wrote in 1937, 'if it has to be admitted that economic coercion was recognised to be a powerful engine of war, it must be added, by way of qualification, that the recognition was no more than the recognition of a distant object: its outlines were faintly discernible through a mist of conjecture, which made all measurement of its mass impossible.'[118] But Churchill was no less committed to blockade because its effects were uncertain. As long as the potential existed to disrupt Germany's war effort, he favoured the most vigorous action possible against the enemy's trade. He was confident that the 'distant blockade' of the enemy's coast would ensure German merchant ships were swept from the high seas, and that contraband destined for German ports in neutral vessels was intercepted or deterred. This outcome seemed so certain, in fact, that he saw no need to divert resources from other objectives to ensure its success. 'British attacks on German trade are a comparatively unimportant feature in our operations,' he concluded in 1913, 'and British cruisers should not engage in them to the prejudice of other duties.'[119]

Churchill's pre-war interest in blockade was thus largely directed towards its military rather than its commercial aspects. The greatest disadvantage of the Admiralty's proposed distant blockade was that it provided too much scope for German warships and transports to slip out of their bases undetected and inflict periodic blows against Britain and France in the North Sea and English Channel. The solution Churchill was repeatedly drawn to was that the navy must adopt a more offensive posture. In late 1913 he and his naval advisers generally agreed that the best means to prevent an unexpected blow by the German fleet would be to strengthen Britain's force of 'overseas' submarines in order to maintain a close and continuous watch on German ports. Submarines were very much on Churchill's mind at his time. He was also eager in late 1913 to press on with efforts to develop an efficient 'ocean' submarine capable of performing some of the roles traditionally assigned to the battleship. He therefore supported the construction of experimental boats that promised to meet his technical requirements.

Developing these new vessels while simultaneously expanding Britain's fleet of 'overseas' submarines was prohibitively expensive, however. At an Admiralty conference on submarine policy in early December 1913, Churchill and his advisers agreed that priority should be given to the construction of 'overseas' submarines for blockading purposes. But the First Lord still hoped for a breakthrough in the development of an effective 'ocean' submarine, which would allow him to achieve long-term economies in the capital-ship budget without sacrificing any of the navy's essential capabilities, especially its ability to overpower the main German fleet. The Director of Naval Construction produced a design in December 1913 for a 24-knot 'ocean' submarine using steam propulsion, and Churchill was eager to proceed with the construction of more than one of these vessels. His professional advisers were more cautious, however. Britain already had two experimental steam submarines under construction at the time, HMS *Swordfish* and HMS *Nautilus*, and they felt that these should be completed and tested before any commitment was taken to producing a new and untried design. Churchill secured agreement to the construction of one experimental 24-knot submarine, but agreed to shelve the question of building more until late 1914.[120]

Churchill was impatient, however, and was soon under pressure from the Cabinet to effect reductions in the 1914 estimates. He therefore informed the Sea Lords on Christmas Day 1913 that they must press ahead with the development of the new design that might 'supply us with ocean submarines of the required speed and sea-going qualities'.[121] Churchill was evidently confident that the Royal Navy was on the verge of building a successful 'ocean' submarine, and, desperate to rehabilitate himself in the eyes of his Cabinet colleagues and economists within the Liberal Party, he was prepared to rush preparations along. With the future of the Mediterranean one-power standard looking increasingly uncertain at this time, the need for additional flotilla vessels for the Mediterranean also had to be considered. These concerns, together with the possibility that an expansion of Britain's 'overseas' submarine force would allow the navy to attempt a close blockade of the German coast, all pointed in the same direction: an immediate expansion of the British submarine fleet. In late December 1913, Churchill and the naval staff began exploring the possibility of replacing one or possibly two of the four battleships in the 1914–15 new construction programme with submarines and other light torpedo craft.[122]

Churchill was clearly the driving force behind this idea. Not only would it reduce some of the financial pressure on the Admiralty, it would also help meet the navy's immediate operational needs in the North Sea and the Mediterranean. By May 1914, Churchill would have been confident that one or two battleships could be dropped from the current programme without endangering Britain's margins in the North Sea. And by strengthening the submarine presence in the Mediterranean, even more capital ships would be available for home waters. There was thus little risk involved in this course. In an unpublished draft chapter of *The World Crisis*, Churchill later described how he explained the rationale for his policy to Lloyd George and worked out an agreement, later endorsed by Asquith, allowing the Admiralty to replace two of its capital ships for that year with flotilla vessels of equivalent value.[123]

The timing of this agreement is uncertain. Churchill only began to press the naval members of the Board of Admiralty for a final decision on the substitution programme in July 1914. The new 'ocean' submarines that Churchill had hoped for were evidently not yet sufficiently developed at this time to proceed with, but his hopes for an immediate technological breakthrough had not disappeared. In June he had instructed Sir Eustace Tennyson d'Eyncourt, the Admiralty's Director of Naval Construction, to draw up plans for a new Polyphemus-class warship, a semi-submerged and armoured 'torpedo cruiser' capable of launching up to eight torpedoes against an enemy fleet. Designs for this new ship were well advanced by July.[124] Churchill now proposed to substitute fifteen submarines for one of the approved new battleships, and six of the new Polyphemus-class 'torpedo cruisers' for another. He also considered substituting either cruisers, flotilla leaders, or submarines for ten of the approved programme of destroyers.[125]

There is no doubt that Churchill was eager to proceed. 'I am convinced that the time has come for action,' he told Battenberg in July, 'and although the steps are serious I do not feel any anxiety about taking them.'[126]

There was general support within the Admiralty for a substitution policy at this time, although no consensus emerged as to precisely what form it should take. Senior naval leaders tended to be more cautious than the First Lord and deprecated any radical departure from existing policies. The new Polyphemus-class threatened to be particularly controversial. Admiral Sir Doveton Sturdee, the Chief of the Admiralty's War Staff, prepared two memoranda on 24 July outlining his strong reservations. These ships were relatively expensive to build, he warned, but they offered no clear advantage over existing types of warship. Like other surface vessels, they would be no substitute for submarines in a blockade; and with their low freeboard, they would be little use for defending or attacking trade on the high seas. They were fast enough to accompany a battle fleet, but in a fleet action they would be particularly vulnerable to the enemy's destroyers, which presented a smaller target for torpedoes. Most importantly from Churchill's perspective, Sturdee maintained that battleships could not 'be replaced by any number of Polyphemus's'. The best course at this time, in his opinion, was to 'develop the Submarine for oversea attack and maintain our Battleship strength by Battleships to overpower those of the enemy'.[127]

While Churchill would have been happy to introduce a new type of warship that could reduce Britain's battleship requirements, a revolutionary transformation of the navy's force structure depended on innovative designs or new technology that were clearly still not ready in July 1914. His naval advisers were even less adventurous when it came to committing scarce funds to untested designs. Despite claims to the contrary by some revisionist historians, no final decision on the substitution programme was taken before the outbreak of the First World War.[128]

The final months of peace also found Churchill intensifying his efforts to achieve a more offensive posture in the North Sea in order to strengthen Britain's defensive position. The revision of the Home Fleet's war orders in May 1914 offered an opportunity to implement some of the ideas he had outlined the year before. Battenberg informed the Chief of the War Staff on 11 May that it was 'essential' on the outbreak of war to launch a large 'reconnaissance-in-force' including capital ships towards the enemy's coast. The object, according to the First Sea Lord, was 'to bring home to the enemy how hazardous it would be for him to dispatch any raiding expedition or other relatively weak detachments of his main fleet across the North Sea towards the British Coasts'. He proceeded to explain the advantages of this course in terms virtually identical to those Churchill had employed:

> Uncertainty as to the whereabouts of a large powerful fleet, known to be at sea within a relatively-speaking restricted area must have a disheartening effect on the enemy…and should go a long way toward depriving him of the advantages attached to initiative & offensive. This should therefore in itself be the most effective defence against hostile raids on the coast, provided the enemy will everywhere find an adequate military to deal with him, if he should effect a landing.[129]

The following month, Churchill revived the idea of seizing an island as a forward base for a close blockade. He instructed the Commander-in-Chief (C.-in-C.) of the Home Fleet, Sir George Callaghan, and his designated successor, Sir John Jellicoe, to draw up plans, 'subsidiary & incidental to the main [war] plans', for a close blockade of the Heligoland Bight, either with or without a forward base to operate from. He also requested plans for a cruiser and flotilla base near Stavangar, Norway. Churchill suggested that the plans drawn up the previous year by Bayly's planning group, which considered the seizure of an island feasible, would be helpful to the admirals in their work.[130] In late July he approved a proposal by the Admiralty war staff to revive the CID subcommittee charged with overseeing the development of combined army-navy war plans.[131]

The outbreak of the First World War undoubtedly caught Churchill and the Admiralty in a transitional period, although the changes under way at the time should not be exaggerated. Some revisionist scholars have argued that Churchill and his advisers were on the verge of implementing a 'naval revolution' based on Fisher's plans to adopt flotilla defence in home waters. But Churchill's plans in July 1914 were relatively conservative. He did not have sufficient faith in flotilla defence, given the technology then available, to gamble Britain's survival on it. The Royal Navy would therefore continue to maintain a large preponderance in capital ships over Germany in home waters. This powerful force, concentrated in the Grand Fleet, would provide cover for the detached squadrons and other warships enforcing the commercial blockade of Germany and guarding British trade, the British coast, and communications with France. All that remained, from Churchill's perspective, was to find the means to ensure that the navy's numerical advantage in heavy warships was not neutralized by the fleet's distance from the German coast.

2

Learning Curve:
The First World War

The outbreak of war between the Dual Alliance (France and Russia) and members of the Triple Alliance (Germany and Austria-Hungary) at the end of July 1914 initially left decision-makers in London divided over British intervention. The 'Hawks' within the Cabinet, including Churchill, the Foreign Secretary Sir Edward Grey, and Asquith, believed that Britain had, quite apart from any moral obligation, a vested interest in preserving France from German domination; the 'Doves', including David Lloyd George, Chancellor of the Exchequer, were just as strongly convinced that Britain had no vital interests at stake and should remain neutral. The British fleet, which had undertaken a trial mobilization in mid-July, was kept together throughout the crisis, but as long as the Cabinet was split no clear warning of British intentions could be sent that might deter German aggression.[1] Opinion within the government only shifted decisively towards intervention after Germany's invasion of neutral Belgium, which finally brought Britain into the conflict on 4 August 1914.

'Now we have our war,' Churchill commented the next day to Captain Herbert Richmond, the Assistant Director of the Naval Staff's Operations Division. 'The next thing is to decide how we are going to carry it on.' Richmond, one of the most gifted thinkers produced by the Royal Navy during this period, was appalled by this 'damning confession of inadequate preparation for war', he recorded in his diary.[2] But this criticism was not entirely fair: there were many details still to be worked out, but the government *was* prepared to exert economic pressure on Germany and to provide direct military support to France on the Continent. The British Grand Fleet immediately took up its war stations, and detached cruiser squadrons began the commercial blockade of Germany. On 5 August royal proclamations were issued forbidding trade between Britain and Germany.[3] And the following day, after much debate, the decision was taken to dispatch four divisions of the British Expeditionary Force to France.

Nevertheless, some important questions still had to be settled. Within the navy, opinion was divided over the relative merits of relying on a distant blockade and of adopting a forward strategy that would take the war to the German coast. Inside the government, ministers could not agree on how rigidly the blockade of Germany should be enforced. But in broad terms, there was a consensus among Liberal leaders at the outset of war about the main outlines of British grand strategy. The natural inclination of most was to leave the heavy fighting on land to France and Russia, continental states that, unlike Britain, possessed large conscript armies. Britain's contribution to the Allied cause, in their opinion, should be mainly financial and naval. As one cabinet minister remarked:

> We decided that we could win through by holding the sea, maintaining our credit, keeping our people employed & our own industries going—By economic pressure, destroying Germany's trade cutting off her supplies—we would gradually secure victory. This policy is steadily pursued—We never thought we could successfully afford to compete with her [i.e. Germany] by maintaining also a continental army on her scale—Our Navy, finance and trade was our life's blood, & we must see to it that these are maintained.[4]

The consensus behind this policy of 'business as usual', as it was dubbed, did not last long.[5] Churchill, who as First Lord of the Admiralty might have been expected to favour a strategy that privileged his service, was one of the first to question whether a token contribution of British forces to the war on land would be sufficient to preserve allied unity and ensure Germany's defeat. He undoubtedly shared the view, popular within the Admiralty, that the navy's main contribution to victory would be economic pressure, but it is probably going too far to suggest that he entered the war expecting this pressure to achieve either rapid or decisive results.[6] He was not, at any rate, prepared to rely on economic measures as Britain's sole contribution to the common cause. During the first weeks of war, the limitations of economic warfare would have become painfully evident to the First Lord. The German merchant fleet was quickly captured on the high seas or driven into port by the Royal Navy, but, as pre-war planners had foreseen, the problem of preventing cargoes reaching Germany on neutral ships through neutral ports was not easily overcome.

Within the government, Churchill was consistently among the strongest advocates of vigorous measures to tighten the economic blockade of Germany.

His advice to the CID in 1912 about the necessity of forcing neutral states to take sides was clearly fresh in his mind on 3 August 1914, before war had even begun, when he and his top advisers urged the prime minister and the Foreign Secretary to bring Belgium, the Netherlands, and Norway into the war as allies to ensure that their ports would be closed to German trade.[7] When it became clear that this was unlikely, the First Lord considered whether his goals could be achieved by violating Dutch neutrality. On 8 August he directed the First Sea Lord and the Chief of the Naval Staff to develop plans for the seizure of a Dutch island near the German coast. This, he suggested, would likely provoke a German invasion of the Netherlands, which would be a more serious violation of Dutch neutrality than Britain's actions.[8] The Netherlands would thus be drawn into the conflict and, like Norway in 1940, could be expected to remain friendly to Britain.

The possibility that British actions might bring the Netherlands into the war as an enemy did not seem to alarm Churchill, however. On 7 September he explained to Asquith, Grey, and Field Marshall Lord Kitchener, the Liberal government's new Secretary of State for War, that 'From a purely naval point of view, war with Holland would be better for us than neutrality. Their reinforcement of German naval forces would be puny, and the closing of the Rhine which we could accomplish without the slightest additional effort, is almost vital to the efficiency of the naval blockade.'[9] Churchill acknowledged—probably without much conviction—the strength of concerns within the government that it was not in Britain's best interest to provoke Dutch hostility, but he was nevertheless willing to run this risk if there was good cause. The Dutch decision to obstruct British access to Antwerp via the Scheldt in August 1914 was ample provocation in Churchill's eyes. In Cabinet, he argued that Britain should 'take the Dutch Govt. "by the throat", and force them to allow us to use the Scheldt to revictual and rearm Antwerp'.[10]

Churchill's efforts in the first six weeks of war to tighten the blockade were uniformly unsuccessful, as the government was unwilling to take strong action against the Netherlands. Opinion within the Cabinet and Foreign Office also shied away from tough measures to interfere with neutral trade, or even placing strict controls on Britain's own trade with neutrals. There were many reasons to question whether the vigorous conduct of economic warfare would really be in the Allies' best interests. Some feared that this would do more damage to Britain's economic and financial strength than to Germany's; others were determined not to alienate neutral powers, particularly the United States.

The matter was debated at length during mid-August.[11] The Foreign Office hoped to preserve the neutral rights embodied in the unratified Declaration of London, even though this would allow neutral states considerable freedom to import cargoes intended for re-export to Germany. To avoid the legal restrictions imposed by this agreement, ministers discussed a variety of options, including the possibility of limiting the Netherlands to pre-war levels of imports, laying minefields in the North Sea to close neutral ports to unauthorized trade, or chartering all available neutral shipping so that none was available to supply Germany. Despite Churchill's strong support for the rigid enforcement of the blockade, the Cabinet-level debate ended with only a slight modification of the restrictions contained in the Declaration of London. The list of items classified as contraband was expanded by an order-in-council on 20 August, and many goods, including food, that fell into the 'conditional contraband' category (i.e. items that could be seized if intended for military rather than civilian use by the enemy), would now be subjected to the doctrine of 'continuous voyage', but this did little to hinder Germany's access to global trade. The problem was that Britain still had to prove that any goods it intercepted bound for neutral ports were ultimately intended for German use, which proved extremely difficult. Efforts by the Foreign Office to obtain agreements from neutral states not to re-export contraband to Germany were also ineffective at this stage of the war.

The obvious shortcomings of the British blockade would have confirmed Churchill's natural preference for other, more direct, means to strike at the enemy. By the end of the first month of war, the First Lord's attention seems to have become fixed on the great clash of armies on the Continent. He correctly assumed that an Allied victory depended on the defeat of the powerful German army, and, unlike many of his Liberal colleagues, he was eager to see Britain take its full share in this fighting. At the urging of Kitchener, Britain began preparing to raise a mass volunteer army, even though most members of the Cabinet remained committed in principle to a 'business as usual' strategy. In his memoirs, Churchill records how Kitchener 'proclaimed a series of inspiring and prophetic truths' in the early days of the war. Britain, Kitchener asserted, 'must prepare for a long struggle. Such a conflict could not be ended on the sea or by sea power alone. It could only be ended by great battles on the Continent. In these the British Empire must bear its part on a scale proportionate to its magnitude and power.'[12] Churchill was an early convert to Kitchener's outlook. The navy was not, in his opinion, capable of winning the war single-handed: its main role, he predicted, would be to provide 'the cover and shield' that would allow Britain to create an army 'strong enough to enable our country to play its full part in the decision of this terrible struggle'. Speaking to the National Liberal Club on 11 September, Churchill declared that 'The sure way—the only way—to bring this war to an end is for the British Empire to put on the Continent and keep on the Continent an army of at least one million men.'[13]

The Royal Navy was well placed to provide 'cover and shield' for the empire's mobilization. The Grand Fleet, commanded by Admiral Sir John Jellicoe, heavily outgunned its German counterpart. In August 1914, Britain possessed thirty-three dreadnoughts (battleships and battlecruisers), and had another twelve under construction; Germany had nineteen, with another six being built. The British public entered the war expecting the Royal Navy to smash its rival in a magnificent Trafalgar-like battle, but the Germans, conscious of their numerical inferiority, were not eager to play the part assigned to them by the British. The German High Seas Fleet declined to engage superior British forces and waited instead for opportunities to whittle down Britain's numerical advantage. But even without a great clash in the North Sea, the Royal Navy found itself in a commanding position: the BEF was transported to France without incident; German trade rapidly disappeared from the high seas; and British merchant ships continued to use the sea lanes with only slight losses. Despite some minor setbacks and lost opportunities, 1914 was a good year for the Royal Navy. The Germans initially observed international law and did not use submarines to sink merchant ships without warning. The destruction of Admiral Graf von Spee's powerful cruiser squadron in the South Atlantic in December 1914 eliminated the last serious threat to British trade from German surface raiders.

Churchill took some satisfaction from these successes, but he chafed at what he saw as the passivity of the British fleet. In public, he put a positive spin on the situation. Economic pressure could not achieve results quickly, he informed an audience in November 1914. Nor was the inactivity of the British fleet an abnormal development. In Britain's earlier wars, blockades had sometimes lasted years before a fleet action took place. 'We are only just beginning,' he proclaimed. 'We must not be impatient. Our turn will come.'[14] Privately, however, Churchill was deeply frustrated by the navy's inability to strike a telling blow at the enemy. His wife Clementine chided him in September 1914 for being 'gloomy & dissatisfied' with his current position. 'It is really wicked of you not to be swelling with pride at being 1st Lord of the Admiralty during the greatest War since the beginning of the World.'[15]

Captain Richmond noted the following month that his chief was 'in low spirits…oppressed with the impossibility of *doing* anything':

> The attitude of waiting, threatened all the time by submarines, unable to strike back at their Fleet, which lies behind the dock-gates of the [Kiel] Canal, Emden or Wilhemshaven, and the inability of the [Naval] Staff to make any suggestions seem to bother him. I have not seen him so despondent before.[16]

After taking personal control of the Allied defences at Antwerp earlier that month, Churchill confided to Asquith that he would not be sorry to leave the Admiralty altogether and be 'put in some kind of military command'. The 'naval part of the business is practically over,' he lamented, 'as our superiority will grow greater & greater every month'.[17] Churchill's naval secretary, Commodore Charles de Bartolomé, observed the following month that his chief seemed 'bored with the Admiralty', and 'could talk of nothing else but army operations'.[18]

Churchill was temperamentally ill-suited to preside over a naval strategy that relied entirely on economic pressure to achieve results, but his pre-war efforts to stimulate offensive planning within the navy were slow to bear fruit. In June 1914 he had asked Jellicoe to review the plans Rear Admiral Bayly had drawn up the previous year to seize an island near the German coast, but the admiral was unimpressed by the project. Churchill nevertheless broached the idea with the prime minister at the end of July 1914, when it began to look like Britain might be drawn into the war.[19] The outbreak of hostilities only strengthened Churchill's determination to take the offensive. 'It is necessary,' he wrote to Battenberg in early August, 'to sustain and relieve our general strategic defensive by active minor operations.' Churchill recommended the occupation of one of the Dutch Frisian islands (Ameland) near the German coast (Map 1). This would provide a forward base for British submarines and other light forces to keep a close watch on the approaches to the Elbe, and create opportunities to wear down German naval strength. Aircraft might also be employed from this location to observe German naval movements in the Heligoland Bight and to attack the Kiel Canal. The most important thing, Churchill charged, was to 'maintain in lively vigour the spirit of enterprise & attack wh[ich] when excluded from warlike operations, means that you are only waiting and wondering where you will be hit'.[20]

While this essentially amounted to action for action's sake, Churchill soon began to develop more ambitious ideas. If the seizure of a forward base allowed the Kiel Canal to be blocked, he predicted that a British fleet and

Map 1. The North Sea in the First World War

transports could be sent into the Baltic Sea, which would enable Russian troops to land on the German coast. Britain's ally could then turn the flank of the German army on the Eastern Front, or attack either Berlin or the Kiel Canal.[21] Churchill even attempted to enlist Russian support for this project in August, although the rapidly deteriorating situation on the Eastern Front made such cooperation unlikely. A more active naval strategy was also being advocated by Admiral Arthur K. Wilson, the former First Sea Lord, who was brought to the Admiralty as an unofficial adviser at the beginning of the war. Wilson drew up detailed plans for the capture of the German island of Heligoland, but his proposals, like Churchill's, were not well received by the naval staff.[22] Richmond, a perceptive but critical observer, judged that Churchill's schemes were 'an amateur piece of work of a mediaeval type'. In his opinion, Britain had nothing to gain by running unnecessary risks with the fleet. 'We have the game in our hands if we sit tight,' he wrote in August, 'but this Churchill cannot see. He must see something tangible & can't understand that naval warfare acts in a wholly different way from war on shore.'[23]

This view was generally shared by senior naval officers. Churchill's and Wilson's schemes were considered on 17 September at a conference on Jellicoe's flagship at Loch Ewe, attended by Churchill, leading members of the naval staff, and senior officers of the Grand Fleet. Naval opinion was solidly against major operations along the German coast or an expedition into the Baltic, which seemed to run the risk of serious losses for little corresponding gain.[24] For any other First Lord this would have been the end of the matter, but Churchill was not easily deterred. He wrote to Jellicoe the following month urging him to give his schemes further consideration, and noting the advantages Germany gained from its undisputed command of the Baltic, particularly access to critical supplies, such as iron ore, from Sweden and Norway. By October 1914, Churchill had clearly decided that the ultimate objective of British naval strategy would be securing command of the Baltic. On the 8th he instructed Jellicoe to begin considering how a British fleet could be introduced into the region once the High Seas Fleet had been neutralized.[25] Writing to Asquith in late December, Churchill explained that he saw the naval war developing in three stages:

> first the clearance of the [outer] seas and the recall of the foreign squadrons, that is nearly completed; second, the closing of the Elbe—that we have now to do; and third, the domination of the Baltic—that would be decisive.[26]

The First Lord repeated this advice to his colleagues on the War Council in late January 1915, noting that the 'ultimate object of the Navy was to obtain access to the Baltic'.[27]

The difficult part of this plan, of course, was the second phase, which entailed neutralizing a powerful German fleet that remained unwilling to accept battle. Churchill considered a variety of means to accomplish this. One possibility was that Britain might create two separate fleets, one for the Baltic and one for the North Sea, each superior to the German High Seas Fleet. In 1914 this seemed possible if Italy entered the war on the Allied side, as French ships could then be moved from the Mediterranean to form part of an Anglo-Franco-Russian fleet in the Baltic. Thus, the 'effective command of the Baltic could be secured without prejudice to that of the North Sea either before, or still more after, the destruction of the Austrian fleet in the Adriatic'.[28] This idea was rejected, however, by Arthur Wilson, who maintained in December 1914 that such a scheme would reduce 'the North Sea fleet below a safe limit until we have found some means of partly reducing the danger from submarines or else of completely blocking the canal'.[29]

Churchill was willing to set this idea aside, but he continued to explore other possibilities. The most efficient and satisfying solution to the problem was to find some means to get at the German fleet in harbour and destroy it there. On 21 September 1914 he boasted to an audience in Liverpool that if the enemy 'do not come out and fight in time of war they will be dug out like rats in a hole'.[30] To make this possible, Churchill contemplated the use of custom-built big-gunned monitors. These warships would be designed with a shallow draught and large 'bulges', which it was hoped would render them virtually immune to torpedoes and mines. Such a force, once constructed, could do what the Grand Fleet could not: 'go close in shore and attack the German fleet in its harbours'. In December 1914, Churchill told Fisher, who had replaced Battenberg as First Sea Lord in late October, that 'in default of a general [fleet] action', these 'special vessels' would give the navy 'the power of forcing a naval decision at the latest in the autumn of 1915'.[31]

The other possibility was that the German fleet could be neutralized by seizing an island near the German coast to serve as a forward base for British flotilla forces. This would ideally draw out the German fleet for battle, and at the very least would expose it to heavy losses from British light craft. Failing that, the German fleet could be blocked in with minefields, which would be continuously maintained by flotilla forces. On 1 December, Churchill presented his scheme to the Cabinet's War Council, a new ministerial committee charged with the central direction of the war effort. On this occasion, he chose to emphasize the defensive advantages of his plan. The German fleet, he maintained, could be kept constantly under observation by light forces, making it virtually impossible to launch an invasion of Britain. According to the minutes, Fisher, who was also present, did not actively support the proposal, but agreed that some offensive naval action was desirable to keep up morale in the fleet. Kitchener was opposed to diverting any large body of British troops from the Western Front, but there was enough interest in the scheme for ministers to agree that it should be investigated by the Admiralty.[32]

Churchill's efforts to move this scheme forward were frustrated by the continued opposition—and, he would later complain, 'apathy'—of the naval staff.[33] He eventually appealed to Fisher for support. 'The key to the naval situation is an oversea base,' he wrote, 'taken by force and held by force'. With naval opinion solidly against Wilson's plans to seize Heligoland, Churchill's attention now settled on another German island, Borkum, which was identified by Admiral Henry Oliver, the new Chief of the Naval War Staff, as the most promising target.[34] But he complained to Fisher in December that he could not 'find anyone to make such a plan alive and dominant; & till then our situation is…that of waiting to be kicked, & wondering when and where'.[35] The First Lord had good reason to think that Fisher would be supportive, as the admiral had long been attracted to employing a British fleet in the Baltic, and continued to promote the idea in 1914.[36]

Fisher was instinctively more cautious than Churchill, however. The First Sea Lord continued to hope that the blockade would eventually produce decisive results, and after his recall he lobbied for measures to increase the economic pressure on Germany by laying minefields in the North Sea so that Britain could regulate neutral trade.[37] Even when these plans foundered for lack of support within the Admiralty, not least from Churchill himself, Fisher was reluctant to contemplate a Baltic expedition if it endangered the navy's superiority over the German fleet.[38] It was only if Britain's economic blockade proved ineffective that Fisher was willing to contemplate a bolder strategy. But if it did become necessary to move British ships into the Baltic, Fisher hoped that the German fleet could be safely blocked into harbour with minefields.[39] His views therefore diverged significantly from Churchill's. The admiral had no interest in seizing an island near the German coast, while the politician doubted that mines alone would be sufficient to neutralize the German fleet.[40]

With professional support for his scheme wanting, Churchill redoubled his efforts to obtain political backing. On 29 December he wrote directly to the prime minister to argue that greater advantage should be taken of Britain's sea power. By this time it was clear that a stalemate had emerged on the Western Front. Neither side could penetrate the other's defensive lines, and any attempt to do so invariably produced heavy casualties. This situation seemed unlikely to change, and Churchill maintained that it would be foolish to commit more British resources than necessary to this theatre. 'Are there not other alternatives,' he asked, 'than sending our armies to chew barbed wire in Flanders?' There were other theatres to wear down German strength, he argued, and at a lower cost. If the German fleet could be neutralized, Churchill foresaw enticing, if not entirely realistic, new opportunities: Britain could land forces in Schleswig-Holstein, which would bring Denmark into the war, threaten the Kiel Canal, and secure British domination of the Baltic. And the possibility remained that Russian armies could be transported to the German coast only 90 miles from Berlin. The 'first indispensable step to all these possibilities', he advised, was to secure an oversea base from which the navy could either provoke a fleet action or drive the German fleet permanently into its harbours. Churchill insisted that action could be taken as early as April or May 1915, but only if Asquith threw his weight behind the scheme.[41]

Churchill was not the only one dismayed by the prospect of sending the large new armies being raised by Kitchener to the Western Front. In late December both the Chancellor of the Exchequer, Lloyd George, and Maurice Hankey, the Secretary to the War Council, proposed to divert British resources into new theatres. Unlike Churchill, however, they favoured an attack on Germany's allies. Germany would be defeated, Lloyd George proposed, by 'the process of knocking the props under her'. The Chancellor outlined two ideas: an attack on Turkish forces in Syria, and the dispatch of British forces to support a coalition of Balkan states—Greece, Serbia, Roumania—against Austria-Hungary. Hankey also liked the idea of a British-backed Balkan coalition (Greece and Bulgaria), although he preferred to concentrate on Turkey, with the goal of occupying Constantinople, the Dardanelles, and the Bosphorus (Map 2).[42] By the beginning of 1915 a consensus was forming around the idea of using the strategic mobility conferred by sea power to strike a blow in some new theatre. Fisher was particularly enthused about Hankey's proposed operations in the Near East. 'I CON-

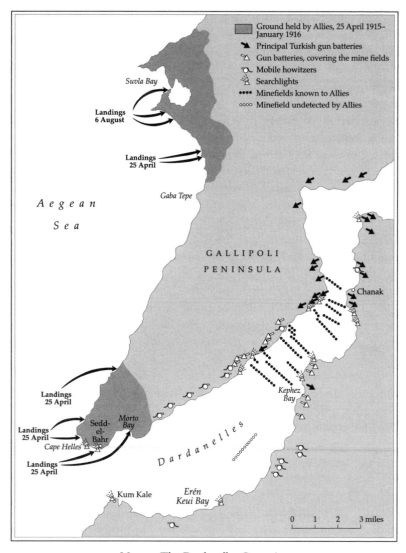

Map 2. The Dardanelles Campaign

SIDER THE ATTACK ON TURKEY HOLDS THE FIELD,' he wrote to Churchill on 3 January, 'but ONLY if it's IMMEDIATE!'[43]

The idea of attacking Turkey, which had entered the war in late October, was not new. Churchill had himself expressed an interest in striking this new enemy on several occasions. In August 1914 he had wanted to send a torpedo flotilla through the Dardanelles to sink the German battlecruiser *Goeben*, which had eluded British warships in the Mediterranean and taken refuge there at the beginning of the war. A month later, Churchill proposed to Grey that Britain could easily defeat Turkey by transporting fifty thousand Russian or Greek troops to attack the Gallipoli Peninsula. In October he suggested that if Turkey entered the war, it was desirable to bombard the forts guarding the Dardanelles at the earliest opportunity.[44] But he was hardly obsessed with the Dardanelles, as some accounts suggest: at the end of 1914 his attention was still fixed firmly on the North Sea and the Baltic.[45] When Hankey raised the possibility of an attack on Turkey at the end of 1914, Churchill initially rejected the idea. '[I]t's too far from the main theatre of war,' he told Fisher on 2 January 1915.[46] When the First Sea Lord continued to press the scheme, Churchill again discouraged him. 'Germany is the foe,' he wrote on 4 January, '& it is bad war to seek cheaper victories and easier antagonists.'[47]

The popular image of Churchill as a committed 'Easterner', determined to win the war by scoring easy victories against Germany's weaker allies, is difficult to sustain.[48] He preferred to avoid a bloody attritional strategy on the Western Front, to be sure, but his first instinct was to concentrate British resources against Germany, Britain's most powerful and dangerous enemy. The most pressing need, as he saw it, was to stimulate offensive operations in the main theatre. During the first week of January, Churchill intensified his efforts to motivate his subordinates and, more importantly, to push his own ideas on future operations, an area that many believed should be left to the First Sea Lord and the appropriate sections of the naval staff. He now instructed Fisher to begin preparations for the capture of Borkum, and resumed his efforts to win Jellicoe over to the idea.[49] On 7 January he took the project to the War Council, which approved an attack on Borkum in principle, subject to the Admiralty producing an acceptable plan.[50]

As late as 11 January, Churchill was still expressing reservations about 'deserting the decisive theatre & the most formidable antagonist to win cheaper laurels in easier fields'.[51] But an attack on Turkey continued to appeal to Fisher and members of the War Council. A request from the Russians on 1 January for a military or naval demonstration against Turkey prompted an admission from Kitchener that the army could not take any significant action in this theatre 'for some months', although he raised the possibility of a purely naval action against the Dardanelles.[52] Fisher had suggested that a naval assault using old battleships would have to be supported by British and Indian troops, and coordinated with attacks by Greece and Bulgaria. But if no troops were immediately available, Churchill was willing to explore the possibility of launching a strictly naval attack. This course had several obvious attractions: it would only employ older battleships of no use in the North Sea; it could be launched at short notice; and it would provide an offensive outlet to keep the navy occupied while new monitors were built to support the assault on Borkum, which could not take place until May.[53]

Churchill's initial conception of a Dardanelles offensive as a minor and subsidiary operation has largely been overlooked. Churchill himself was not eager to publicize this after the war, and in *The World Crisis* he concealed his strong preference for operations in the North Sea. But in a passage excised before publication, he was candid about his real priorities in early 1915. The difficulty with the Borkum scheme, Churchill explained, was that 'many months would be required before any decision other than preparation and study need be taken':

> Meanwhile the naval operation at the Dardanelles, which was a far smaller and less formidable business, would either fail or succeed....If it succeeded, we should gain the prestige, which alone would enable so terrific and deadly a business as the storming of Borkum...to be carried out....[E]ven while the Dardanelles was on I always regarded it as [long] as I was in power only as an interim operation, and all the plans for the Borkum-Baltic project were going forward.[54]

On 3 January, Churchill wrote to Vice Admiral Sir Sackville Carden, commander of the navy's Eastern Mediterranean Squadron, for his views on the prospect of forcing the Dardanelles by ships alone. Carden replied that the Dardanelles probably could not be rushed, but that they might be forced by extended operations.[55] In other words, a fleet would have to proceed slowly and methodically, taking care to neutralize the Turkish shore defences and minefields as it advanced through the straits. A more optimistic view was provided a few days later by Admiral Bayly, now Vice Admiral commanding the Channel Fleet, who was eager to command such an operation. Bayly submitted a proposal to the Admiralty on 8 January to rush a squadron of pre-dreadnought battleships through the Dardanelles. Such a force would be sufficient, he concluded, to destroy the Turkish navy, sever Turkish communications between Europe and Asia, clear the Dardanelles of mines, and transport Russian troops through the Black Sea. No attempt would be made, however, to land British troops and occupy Constantinople.[56]

Opinion within the Admiralty was far from enthusiastic. Admiral Henry Jackson, a senior member of the naval staff and future First Sea Lord, agreed with Carden's opinion that the Dardanelles could probably be forced by ships alone in extended operations, but he was pessimistic about the prospects of a purely naval assault. He prepared a memorandum on 5 January predicting heavy losses for the attacking squadron, emphasizing the precarious position of a British fleet once it had passed through the Dardanelles, and questioning what ships alone could accomplish if they reached Constantinople. They 'might dominate the city and inflict enormous damage', he remarked, but they could not actually capture it without a large military force. A naval bombardment of the city, he concluded, 'would probably result in indiscriminate massacres'.[57]

A week later Carden submitted detailed proposals for an attack on the Dardanelles, which called for the systematic destruction of the forts along the straits by battleships preceded by minesweepers. This would require a large expenditure of ammunition, but the admiral estimated that the operation might be successfully concluded within a month.[58] The proposal for a methodical attack on the Turkish forts appealed strongly to Churchill. His principal advisers at the Admiralty clearly had some reservations, but they nevertheless voiced cautious support for the scheme at this early stage. Fisher, Jackson, and Oliver even proposed to bolster the attacking squadron with Britain's newest super-dreadnought, HMS *Queen Elizabeth*, which was then due to begin her gunnery trials.[59] Churchill did not regard any of the concerns raised so far by his professional advisers as decisive obstacles. Like many others, he had been impressed by the ability of German heavy artillery to overcome Belgian fortresses in the opening months of the war, and he assumed that British naval guns would be as effective against the Turkish forts lining the straits. The absence of British troops was clearly regrettable, but Churchill was confident that the fleet's passage through the straits would lead immediately to attacks on Turkey by Russia and some Balkan states, and that Turkish resistance would collapse long before a fleet reached Constantinople.[60] The fleet therefore did not need to worry about its communications or the return passage through the straits, and it would not have to bombard the capital to compel the Turks to surrender. Churchill also had a clear 'exit strategy': if the naval attack stalled, it could simply be called off and the fleet would withdraw.

When the War Council met on 13 January, Churchill still regarded the capture of an island near the German coast as the ideal objective for the navy. '[W]e ought not to go South [i.e. into the eastern Mediterranean] until we are satisfied that we can do nothing in the North,' he advised his colleagues. But he had clearly warmed to the idea of a naval assault on the Dardanelles. Here was an operation that seemed to offer the prospect of a major victory at little risk—one that would not tie down British troops in a protracted campaign in a secondary theatre, and, most importantly, one that could be wrapped up quickly so that naval resources could be transferred back to the North Sea in time for an assault on Borkum. Churchill presented the operation to his ministerial colleagues in the best possible light. Carden, he informed them, was confident that a naval squadron could systematically silence the Turkish forts and reach Constantinople. One of the chief attractions of the project was that no troops would need to be diverted from the Western Front, and decision-makers were particularly impressed by the idea that a naval bombardment could easily be broken off if it failed to achieve results. As Grey later recorded, 'the attack on the Dardanelles was agreed to on the express condition that it should be a naval operation only; it was under no circumstances to involve the use of troops...If the attack on the Dardanelles did not succeed, it was to be treated as a naval demonstration and abandoned. It was on this condition only that Kitchener agreed to it.'[61]

Members of the War Council shared Churchill's low opinion of Turkish fighting ability, and assumed that resistance was likely to collapse quickly and completely at the first sign of defeat.[62] Significantly, however, the risks involved in the operation were not discussed. Churchill did not mention Jackson's doubts about the utility of a purely naval assault, or his prediction of heavy losses. Fisher, who had reservations about attacking with ships alone, was present at the meeting, but he was not asked for his opinion and did not feel it was appropriate to offer one.

The idea of sending ships through the Dardanelles was well received by the War Council. 'The idea caught on at once,' Hankey recalled. 'The whole atmosphere changed. Fatigue was forgotten. The War Council turned eagerly from the dreary vista of a "slogging match" on the Western Front to brighter prospects, as they seemed, in the Mediterranean.'[63] After a relatively brief discussion, the War Council decided that the Admiralty should begin preparing '*for a naval expedition in February to bombard and take the Gallipoli penin-*

sula, with Constantinople as its objective.[64] The full Cabinet was given a very optimistic account of the forthcoming operation a few weeks later. Sir Charles Hobhouse, the Postmaster General, recorded in his diary for 16 February that the *Queen Elizabeth*:

> and a large squadron of old battleships armed with new guns are to lie off the town, well beyond the range of the forts' guns, and to batter to pieces at their leisure each fort in turn, until the way through to the Black Sea is clear. No risks are to be run, and the operation may take a fortnight or 3 weeks....We are promised a military rising and ultimate revolution on the fall of the first fort. W.S.C. said policy was decided at War Council and he would take all responsibility.[65]

Having obtained explicit political backing for the scheme, Churchill was in a strong position to sweep aside his subordinates' concerns at the Admiralty. Opposition to the project was slow to develop, however. On 15 January, Admiral Jackson reported to the Chief of the War Staff that he concurred generally with the plan proposed by Carden. He recognized that the fleet would have to destroy both the heavy guns in the Turkish fortresses and the large number of mobile, concealed guns that would also line the straits, but he was optimistic that this could be accomplished provided large quantities of ammunition were available, and that the loss of some vessels was accepted. He was therefore prepared to support a bombardment of the outer defences of the Dardanelles in order to gain experience before committing the fleet to operations within the straits.[66] Churchill was also inclined at this stage of the planning to bring the assault to an early conclusion if Turkish defences proved stronger than expected. In this event, he suggested launching another assault immediately on Alexandretta, a port in the Ottoman province of Syria, to create the impression that the Dardanelles attack was only a feint.[67]

Fisher had other reservations about the navy-only plan. He feared exposing a fleet to heavy losses, which would threaten the navy's margins in the crucial North Sea theatre. On 25 January the First Sea Lord prepared a lengthy memorandum outlining his concerns. The navy's first obligation, he argued, was to maintain its superiority over Germany in the decisive theatre. Subsidiary operations that endangered British ships 'play[ed] into Germany's hands' by reducing Britain's strength in the North Sea. Fisher also defended the navy's inactivity, which so dismayed Churchill. 'The pressure of sea power to-day is probably not less but greater and more rapid in action than in the past,' he wrote, 'but it is still a slow process and requires great patience':

Ours is the supreme necessity and difficulty of remaining passive, except in so far as we can force the enemy to abandon his defensive and expose his fleet to a general action....

Being already in possession of all that a powerful fleet can give a country we should continue quietly to enjoy the advantages without dissipating our strength in operations that cannot improve the position.[68]

Churchill insisted that he was in complete agreement with these principles, and in a broad sense he was—but he also felt that Fisher overestimated the Grand Fleet's requirements. It had to be strong enough to ensure a British victory over Germany's naval forces at any time, but Britain did not necessarily need the overwhelming margin of superiority that both Fisher and Jellicoe demanded. Churchill was prepared to get by with less than his advisers wanted, and believed that even numerical equality with the Germans would be sufficient to ensure a decisive British victory.[69] He was therefore quick to designate ships—especially older battleships unsuited for North Sea Operations—as 'surplus' to the fleet's needs, and therefore available to 'be used for the general cause'.[70] In short, they were expendable.

Fisher's growing opposition to the Dardanelles project prompted Asquith to intervene. The prime minister was an enthusiastic supporter of the operation, and was particularly eager in late January to reduce bread prices in Britain by opening up the Black Sea for the export of Russian wheat. Fisher bowed to this additional pressure and agreed to support the Dardanelles operation, although his heart was clearly not in it.[71] Nor was he the only one anxious about the venture. By late January, naval concerns about the absence of soldiers were beginning to mount. The operational orders sent to Carden in early February allowed for the temporary landing of small detachments of Royal Marines under the cover of ships' guns, but only two battalions were to be made available for this purpose. Naval leaders wanted more. On 13 February, Jackson submitted a memorandum outlining his growing concerns. The proposed naval bombardment was not, he now declared, 'a sound military operation, unless a strong military force is ready to assist in the operation, or, at least, follow it up immediately the forts are silenced'. His concerns were twofold. First, that a large body of troops might be needed to complete the destruction of the Turkish defences. Second, that the Gallipoli Peninsula must be occupied to protect Allied communications through the straits once a fleet had penetrated to the Sea of Marmara. The presence of a Turkish army on the peninsula, he warned, would mean that only armoured ships could be sent through the straits, even after the permanent fortifications had been destroyed.[72]

The prime minister learned of naval leaders' concerns through Hankey, who also wished to see the army support the Dardanelles operation.[73] At first, nothing came of it. The War Council was more interested at the time in the possibility of sending troops to Salonica, where it was hoped they could assist Serbia and help induce the Balkan states to enter the conflict against Austria-Hungary. This idea was popular with ministers, including Churchill, who made no effort to divert troops to the Dardanelles expedition. Kitchener also favoured the dispatch of forces to the Balkans, and even proposed to send the British 29th Division, a regular formation previously intended for service on the Western Front. Behind the scenes, Hankey lobbied for the dispatch of these troops to the Dardanelles instead. When the Greek government refused to support an expedition to Salonica, the idea of opening a new Balkan front had to be abandoned. But an important development had taken place: a large body of troops had been earmarked for service in the Mediterranean theatre. Asquith was receptive to the idea being pushed by Hankey that these forces should back up the Dardanelles operation.[74] An informal meeting of the War Council on 16 February concluded that British and Commonwealth troops, including the 29th Division, would be assembled in the Mediterranean to support the upcoming naval attack.[75]

This marked a major turning point in the conception of the Dardanelles campaign. With the naval assault set to begin in just three days, there was clearly no possibility that the offensive could be mounted from the outset as a combined operation. But the War Council, at the urging of senior officers at the Admiralty, now ensured that troops were available to support the naval assault, which made it virtually inevitable that troops *would* eventually be employed for this purpose—although not until after the Turks had been alerted by the naval assault. The purely naval nature of the Dardanelles offensive was thus tacitly abandoned by most members of the War Council. However, there was no clear idea as to when and how troops would be employed. More seriously, both Churchill and Kitchener continued to adhere to the original plan to force passage through the Dardanelles by ships alone. The Field Marshal assumed that the arrival of the fleet in the Sea of Marmara would induce the Turks to abandon the Gallipoli Peninsula without a fight. Churchill, still confident of a Turkish collapse, was also convinced that amphibious operations would not be required. However, he accepted the idea that troops should be assembled in the theatre to exploit the navy's eventual success. Writing to Kitchener two days after the decision was taken, Churchill proposed that fifty thousand soldiers should be kept in readiness to occupy the Gallipoli Peninsula and Constantinople. 'We shd never forgive ourselves,' he wrote on 18 February, 'if the naval operations succeeded & the fruits were lost through the Army being absent.'[76] A week later Churchill revised this figure to one hundred thousand. With such a force available, he optimistically predicted that Constantinople could be taken by the end of March.[77] But this was not, as many accounts suggest, an acknowledgement by Churchill that the naval scheme was impracticable. On the contrary, the First Lord promptly informed Admiral Carden that his original orders to force the Dardanelles without military assistance had not changed. 'It is not proposed at this stage,' Churchill wrote, 'to use military force other than parties of Marines landed to destroy particular guns or torpedo tubes.'[78]

While the War Council agreed on the desirability of sending troops to the theatre, controversy emerged over the necessity of including the 29th Division. Kitchener had second thoughts about diverting a regular army division that might be required in France.[79] Churchill, however, believed that a leavening of regular troops would ensure that operations against Turkey were wrapped up quickly. While the employment of the 29th division was hotly debated in London, the naval assault was already under way. On the morning of 19 February Carden's fleet had opened fire on the outer forts guarding the entrance to the Dardanelles. By 3 March the forts' heavy guns had been silenced, and a combined Anglo-French fleet had entered the straits.[80] These early successes produced a wave of optimism among decision-makers in London. The naval assault seemed to be going according to the original plan. Churchill informed Kitchener on 4 March that Carden expected to need only fourteen days of good weather to force a passage through the straits and into the Sea of Marmara.[81]

In London it appeared that Britain was on the verge of an early and decisive success. Hopes ran high that the arrival of the fleet at Constantinople would lead to an immediate Turkish collapse. The War Council accordingly began to consider how to follow these anticipated successes. Attention focused on the possibility of drawing the Balkan states into the war in order to open up a new offensive, with British support, against Austria-Hungary. Churchill's attention, however, had shifted back to his plans for the North Sea. With victory against the Turks seemingly within reach, he wanted British forces in the Mediterranean theatre kept to a minimum; further offensives in the region should be left to new Balkan allies, who would soon fall on the defeated Turks. Only token British support seemed necessary to secure a coalition of Balkan states on the Allied side. Churchill informed the War Council on 3 March that the 'proper line of strategy was an advance in the north through Holland and the Baltic. This might become feasible later on when our new monitors were completed. The operation in the East should be regarded merely as an interlude.'[82] He informed Jellicoe on 9 March that additional monitors should soon be ready, and that he hoped to launch an assault on Borkum in mid-May.[83]

Churchill's plans were soon upset by a lack of progress in the Dardanelles. The fleet's initial successes, which had raised such high hopes, were largely illusory. The destruction of the guns in the outer Turkish forts had mostly been the work of small landing parties, and not, as expected, the heavy guns of the fleet. Naval gunfire had, in fact, been largely ineffective. The Turks had not interfered with the demolition parties at first, but after the Allied fleet entered the straits it became virtually impossible to land marines. The fleet's gunnery also continued to be ineffective. Direct hits on the Turkish guns were difficult to obtain, and nothing less would neutralize the forts. To make matters worse, British minesweepers—actually converted North Sea trawlers with civilian crews—had difficulty clearing Turkish minefields owing to strong currents and the heavy fire they encountered from concealed guns on shore.

With characteristic impatience, Churchill on 11 March urged Carden to press on, even if it meant accepting heavier risks: 'The results to be gained are…great enough to justify loss of ships and men if success cannot be obtained without'.[84] The possibility that the naval assault could be called off was becoming increasingly remote. Once operations started, decision-makers began to worry that British prestige would suffer a massive blow if forces were withdrawn. Kitchener informed the War Council on 24 February that if the naval offensive stalled, there would be no choice but to commit the army. 'The effect of a defeat in the Orient would be very serious,' he warned. 'There could be no going back.' Grey also feared that a failure to force the Dardanelles 'would be morally equivalent to a great defeat on land'. Churchill himself was disinclined, once the naval attack had begun, to consider calling it off. The War Council, he remarked, 'were now absolutely committed to seeing through the attack on the Dardanelles'.[85]

On 18 March, Vice Admiral John de Robeck, who had replaced the ailing Carden two days earlier, mounted a major operation to clear the straits. The entire fleet, including all sixteen capital ships, was employed to bombard the enemy forts and provide cover for minesweeping operations. Nothing went according to plan. Three battleships—two British and one

French—were sunk by mines, and another three were badly damaged. There was virtually nothing to show for these losses. No mines had been swept, and only one heavy gun was put permanently out of action.[86] It was now clear that troops would be needed to ensure the navy's passage through the straits or, at the very least, to protect the fleet's communications once it had passed into the Sea of Marmara. Even Churchill now accepted that military operations would be necessary, but he was nevertheless determined to resume the naval attack immediately so as to keep up the pressure on the Turks. A naval breakthrough still seemed possible. Admiral de Robeck took a different view, however. He had had doubts about the feasibility of advancing without military support even before the setbacks on 18 March, and he now concluded that troops would have to be landed before the naval advance could resume. After meeting with General Sir Ian Hamilton, who had been dispatched by Kitchener to command the British and Commonwealth troops gathering in the region, de Robeck informed the Admiralty on 23 March that further operations would be delayed until mid-April so that the army could participate.[87]

Churchill was incensed. He correctly noted that de Robeck's proposal meant the complete abandonment of the War Council's original plan. The following day he drafted an order to the admiral to resume the naval attack, but Fisher and other senior naval officers forced him to back down.[88] Members of the War Council, including the prime minister, also hoped for the immediate resumption of the naval assault, but the decision of the commanders on the spot was decisive. The Dardanelles campaign was thus transformed into a major combined operation. The navy's role was now to support operations by the army to seize the Gallipoli Peninsula, which in turn would allow the resumption of the naval advance through the straits.

Churchill had no choice but to accept these changes. But even at this stage, he was reluctant to abandon his hopes for the capture of an island near the German coast. On 24 March, with the Dardanelles operations now suspended, he drafted a lengthy memorandum outlining operations to seize Borkum sometime after 15 May. The assault he envisaged would open with a massive bombardment of the island's defences by the navy's new monitors and other ships, supported by a vast flotilla of submarines and destroyers. Up to twelve thousand troops would subsequently be landed to overcome the German defences. Once in British hands, he proposed that Borkum be transformed into a base from which monitors, submarines, destroyers, light cruisers, and aircraft could dominate the Jade and Elbe estuaries. The High

Seas Fleet could then be bottled up with minefields.[89] But the Borkum scheme continued to run into opposition within the Admiralty, and even Churchill was forced to admit that nothing could be contemplated in the North Sea until the Dardanelles operation had been wrapped up.

The landing of Allied forces on the Gallipoli Peninsula on 25 April did nothing to improve the situation, however. The Turks put up a much stronger defence than the British expected, and within two weeks a stalemate had emerged in this theatre just as it had on the Western Front. De Robeck reported to the Admiralty on 9 May that the army was unable to make further progress. Faced with this fresh setback, Churchill urged a renewal of the naval assault. This led to more friction with Fisher, who was convinced that a new offensive would lead to the loss of additional ships without any offsetting gains. By the time the War Council met on 14 May, Churchill would have been well aware that his political position was closely linked to the outcome of the Dardanelles campaign. He was determined to bring it to a successful conclusion, and proposed to pour in enough resources to ensure victory within three months. On the naval side, he reported that the *Queen Elizabeth* would be withdrawn to home waters and replaced with newly built monitors, which had previously been earmarked for the Borkum expedition.[90]

Churchill probably hoped this concession would placate Fisher, who was concerned about the appearance of German submarines in the region, but relations between the two men, which had been under increasing strain for months, was now near the breaking point. The admiral was convinced that his chief's commitment to the Dardanelles operation would continue to drain vital resources from the Grand Fleet. On 15 May, therefore, Fisher sent Asquith his resignation. From Churchill's perspective the timing could not have been worse. The Liberal government was already under attack for not providing the BEF with an adequate supply of munitions. This new crisis at the Admiralty convinced Asquith that he would have to broaden the basis of the government by bringing in members of the opposition. Churchill was one of the chief casualties of the resulting reorganization. As part of their price for participation in a coalition, the Conservatives demanded his removal from the Admiralty. When Asquith's new government was settled, Churchill had been relegated to a sinecure, the Chancellorship of the Duchy of Lancaster.

Although he remained a member of the government's War Council (now renamed the Dardanelles Committee), Churchill's influence on the direction of the war was sharply reduced. The most frustrating aspect of the new situation was that his reputation was more than ever linked to the outcome of the Gallipoli campaign, but he was now little more than a bystander. 'It is a horrible experience,' he wrote on 30 July to a friend, Sir Archibald Sinclair, 'remaining here in the midst of things knowing everything, caring passionately, conscious of capacity for service, yet paralysed nearly always. It is like being in a cataleptic trance while all you value is being hazarded.'[91]

Churchill initially hoped that the stalemate on the Gallipoli Peninsula could be broken by a fresh landing behind the Turkish lines near Bulair. This, he calculated, would enable the British to get astride the neck of the peninsula and sever the enemy's supply lines.[92] His colleagues also believed that some new initiative was needed to break the deadlock, and another landing took place in early August at Suvla Bay, much further south than Churchill had wanted. This offensive also failed to achieve decisive results. With no end in sight to the stalemate on land, Churchill again pressed for a renewal of the naval offensive. He tried to persuade members of the Dardanelles Committee that the naval losses of 18 March were really quite light. Britain had suffered little more than one hundred casualties, he noted, and lost only obsolete battleships of no use against the Germans in the North Sea. The naval advance should therefore 'be resumed,' he argued on 21 August, 'pressed to a decision, and fought out, as it has never yet been'.[93]

This proposal generated little enthusiasm, and in October Churchill suggested to Asquith that Anglo-French forces might be used to open up an entirely new land front against Turkey in conjunction with Greece.[94] But by this time decision-makers were beginning to discuss the possibility of evacuating Allied troops from the Gallipoli Peninsula altogether. Churchill struggled in vain to resist this development.[95] The decision to withdraw Allied troops was finally taken in December, by which time Churchill was no longer a member of the government. In early November he had been excluded from the new War Committee, which replaced the Dardanelles Committee as the main body for managing the war effort. Churchill found himself completely removed from the executive direction of the war. Rather than remain on the sidelines, he decided to seek active service with the army in France.

The fighting on the Gallipoli Peninsula dragged on until the final soldiers were evacuated in January 1916. Over the course of the campaign, Allied battle casualties (killed and wounded) exceeded 132,000. British, French, and imperial troops (Australian, New Zealand, and Indian) also suffered heavily from disease and other causes. In the British army, non-battle casualties were around double the rate of combat casualties. When these additional losses are taken into consideration, one authority estimates that the overall casualty figures for the campaign may rise as high as 390,000.[96] As an alternative to 'chewing barbed wire' in Flanders, the attempt to force the Dardanelles was a remarkable failure.

As the originator of the navy-only scheme to force the Dardanelles, the operation's most forceful advocate, and later its foremost apologist, it is only to be expected that Churchill has borne the brunt of the blame for its failure, and, in some eyes, for subsequent losses in the Gallipoli campaign as well. Even now, nearly a century later, no simple verdict on these events is possible. The Dardanelles campaign undoubtedly demonstrates Churchill's shortcomings as a war manager and strategist, and brings into sharp relief traits that would continue to frustrate his uniformed advisers during the Second World War. But this episode also highlights many of his strengths, which were hardly less formidable than his weaknesses. The Liberal government was in most respects fortunate to have Churchill among its ranks at the outset of the First World War. His boldness, imagination, and strategic insights clearly distinguished him from other civilian ministers. 'Winston Churchill was a man of a totally different type from all his colleagues,' Hankey observed. 'He had a zest for war. If war there must needs be, he at least could enjoy it. The sound of guns quickened his pulses, and he was one of those rare people who could, at the outset of the war at any rate, feel something of the *joie-de-bataille*.'[97] Churchill was one of the first to grasp the nature of the First World War and recognize the futility of frontal assaults on the Western Front, and he aggressively sought out more creative and advantageous opportunities to wear down the enemy's strength. He also possessed the knowledge and the confidence to question the advice of generals and admirals, a trait that was often in short supply.

There is a great deal of truth in Churchill's later description of the Dardanelles campaign, in its original form, as a 'legitimate war gamble'.[98] The pay-off was potentially enormous, while the risks seemed relatively low. Britain *could* afford to lose the older capital ships employed on this assault without endangering its security in the North Sea against Germany. And as long as the assault was limited to ships alone, and decision-makers were willing to bring it to an early conclusion if it did not prosper, Churchill and the War Council can perhaps be forgiven for not dwelling on worst-case scenarios that seemed easily avoidable. But there is no doubt that Churchill was too quick to ignore or sweep aside inconvenient obstacles and advice that might hamper his plans, and that his professional advisers provided early warning of some of the difficulties that might be encountered. Churchill gave insufficient weight to these and, more seriously, failed to convey the full range of Admiralty opinion to the War Council. As a result, the Dardanelles scheme that Churchill pitched to his colleagues in January 1915 rested on an overly optimistic assessment. To succeed, the fleet's heavy guns had to be able to destroy Turkish guns along the straits, minesweepers had to be able to clear a path, and Turkish resistance would have to collapse before the fleet reached Constantinople. The first two assumptions proved to be mistaken, and the third, although never tested, now seems doubtful.

None of this would have mattered if the assault had been called off after the naval advance began to stall. Churchill overestimated how easily this could be done once Britain's prestige seemed to be on the line, although he was not the only one to do so: his colleagues were guilty of the same self-deception. Once the campaign began, the pressures towards escalation were difficult to resist. Churchill was by temperament probably the least likely member of the War Council to contemplate withdrawal. He never seems to have lost his optimism that victory was possible, and with his career and reputation on the line, he had a far greater personal stake in the operation than any of his colleagues. This clearly affected his judgement. It is difficult to justify his determination to press on with the naval assault after the disastrous events of 18 March. The claim, later popularized by Churchill, that the Turkish guns were by then critically short of ammunition, and that another determined push would have succeeded, is not supported by Turkish sources.[99] The naval attack had failed and the time had come for Britain to cut its losses.

The situation was complicated, however, by the decision, taken almost casually by the War Council the previous month, to send troops to support the naval operation. The military operation was, as Churchill later noted, something 'far more momentous and far reaching in its scope' than the naval operation, '& irrevocable in its character'.[100] Churchill was not responsible for this particular act of escalation—he continued to adhere to the navy-only scheme long after his colleagues had decided to make soldiers available. The common perception that Churchill was the driving force behind the Dardanelles campaign right until he was driven from office is inaccurate: in reality, he was one voice among many on the War Council, and he did not always have the final say. From mid-February 1915 onward, Churchill's original plan for a naval assault was continually modified by others until, by late March, it had been transformed into something he never intended—a major land campaign on the Gallipoli Peninsula to secure the passage of an Anglo-French fleet through the straits. Churchill was increasingly swept up in events he could not control. The losses incurred on the peninsula after 25 April are often blamed on him alone, although in this instance responsibility properly rests with the War Council as a whole.

Churchill's contribution to the planning of the Dardanelles campaign must be recognized as part of a decision-making process that was characterized to a remarkable degree by improvisation and amateurism. The bureaucratic machinery for coordinating Britain's war effort would only be developed in stages. During this phase of the war, the War Council met irregularly and the views of its professional advisers were too often filtered through their ministerial masters. This allowed considerable scope for Churchill and Kitchener to dominate proceedings early in the war by virtue of their greater experience and their positions as heads of the fighting services. In early 1915 Churchill could advocate schemes that did not have the unreserved backing of his professional advisers, and the War Council remained largely ignorant of the naval staff's concerns. This suited Churchill's purpose when it came to obtaining backing for his more ambitious projects, but it also proved fatal when Asquith and others began to participate more actively in the strategy-making process. Churchill, who probably understood the implications of committing troops to the theatre better than anyone, could not prevent his colleagues remaking his plan. His inability to control British strategy after his design had been adopted made a deep and lasting impression. 'If I have erred,' he wrote in June 1915, 'it has been in seeking to attempt an initiative without being sure that all the means & powers to make it successful were at my disposal.'[101] This lesson was still fresh in his mind over thirty years later. 'I was ruined for the time being in 1915 over the Dardanelles,' he reflected in his Second World War memoirs, 'and a supreme enterprise was cast away, through my trying to carry out a major and cardinal operation of war from a subordinate position. Men are ill-advised to try such ventures. This lesson had sunk into my nature.'[102]

After resigning from the Asquith coalition, Churchill obtained command of a battalion and spent several months on the Western Front. He had little prospect of rising to high command, however, and by May 1916 the lure of politics had drawn him back to London. His brief time in the trenches did nothing to alter the strategic priorities he had accepted at the beginning of the war. He remained convinced that Germany was the main enemy, that the outcome of the war would ultimately be decided on land, and that Britain must contribute a vast army to the common cause. Writing in the *Sunday Pictorial* in July 1916—the same month Kitchener's new mass armies were committed to their first major offensive on the Western Front—Churchill, now a backbench MP, noted with satisfaction that Britain had the remarkable ability to transform itself into a land power without sacrificing its position at sea. Britain, he wrote, was 'The Great Amphibian', whose natural home was 'in the broad seas':

> If need be, she can crawl or even dart ashore—first, a scaly arm with sharp claws; then, if time and circumstances warrant it, a head with teeth, and shoulders that grow ever broader; and then she can draw out convolution after convolution of muscular body till one cannot tell where the end of her may be found. Or she can return again to the deep, and strike anew, now here, now there, and no one can guess where the next attack will fall.

'The Great Amphibian is going ashore,' Churchill proclaimed. 'She must transform the larger part of her body. Armies of millions must be raised—one, two, three, four millions, or more.'[103] But Churchill was never an uncritical 'Westerner', like so many of Britain's top generals—his commitment to a continental strategy was tempered by a conviction that Britain and France should remain on the defensive along the Western Front. Modern firepower conferred such a clear advantage to the defender that taking the initiative would only lead to an unfavourable attrition rate. He was happy to see the Germans wear themselves out in the West while the Allies conserved their strength and mobilized their superior resources. If the 'Germans are to be beaten decisively,' he told the House of Commons in May 1916, 'they will be beaten like Napoleon was beaten and like the Confederates were beaten—that is to say, by being opposed by superior numbers along fronts so extensive that they cannot maintain them or replace the losses incurred along them.'[104]

The navy enjoyed a more uncertain place in Churchill's strategic outlook at this time. Britain's ability to project its power onto the Continent rested upon its maritime predominance and could not under any circumstances be jeopardized. As Churchill had predicted to Asquith in 1914, the Grand Fleet's commanding position in the North Sea only became more secure as the war progressed. But a naval victory remained elusive: the long-awaited clash of the British and German fleets on 31 May 1916 at the Battle of Jutland produced no clear decision. The British lost more heavily in the engagement—115,000 tons, including three battlecruisers, as against 62,000 tons and one battlecruiser for the Germans. But while the battle could be considered a tactical success for the Germans, the hasty retreat of the High Seas Fleet to its bases confirmed Britain's strategic dominance at sea. Churchill, who was invited to write a communiqué on the battle by Arthur Balfour, his successor as First Lord of the Admiralty, accurately noted that Britain's margin of superiority in capital ships was 'in no way impaired' by the losses at Jutland, and that Germany remained in a position of 'definite inferiority'.[105]

Churchill elaborated on this theme in the *London Magazine* a few months later. Britain had not won a great victory at Jutland, he noted, but it nevertheless continued to exercise the 'full and unquestioned command of the sea', as it had from the outset of the war. Churchill now deployed the same arguments Fisher had used the previous year to dismiss complaints that the navy was not being sufficiently aggressive. 'We are entitled to be quite satisfied with [the current] situation,' he wrote. 'The war function of the British Navy is being discharged with absolute thoroughness and success. Without a battle we have all that the most victorious of battles could give us':

> Consideration of these simple facts will reveal to the lay mind what is so often overlooked or not understood—namely, that the action of the British Navy is essentially offensive and aggressive. We have seized the initiative and gathered all the advantages, and our silent attack upon the vital interests of the enemy proceeds without cessation winter and summer, night and day, year in, year out. No obligation of war requires us to go further. The next move is with the Germans. It is a perfectly simple and obvious move. If they do not take it, it is because they are not strong enough to take it, and do not dare to take it.[106]

Churchill clearly still felt—as he had when First Lord—that there was no need to jeopardize Britain's maritime predominance by running unnecessary risks with the Grand Fleet. But he was nonetheless dismayed by the navy's unwillingness to undertake offensive measures with its 'surplus' forces. 'The Admiralty dozes placidly,' he complained to Sinclair in August 1916.[107] He was probably surprised, therefore, when his opinions were denounced in the press. Lord Sydenham of Combe, a former Secretary of the CID, and Sir Reginald Custance, a retired admiral, complained in October 1916 in letters to *The Times* that Churchill's views were fundamentally flawed in that they disregarded the importance of engaging and destroying the German High Seas Fleet in battle. Sydenham and Custance were both long-standing critics of Sir Julian Corbett, a naval historian, Naval War College lecturer, and close associate of Lord Fisher. Corbett had angered many naval officers before the war by teaching that battle was not an end in itself: the navy's job, he insisted, was to protect the nation's maritime communications, and battle was only necessary if the enemy was in a position to challenge them. In other words, battle was only a means to an end.[108] Sydenham and Custance regarded these ideas, which they thought had been taken up by Churchill, as a dangerous heresy that would fatally undermine the navy's fighting spirit. 'If ever Boards of Admiralty and naval commanders afloat become imbued with ideas of this kind,' Sydenham warned, 'we may bid farewell to the dominion of the sea.'[109]

These criticisms were both simplistic and misplaced. Churchill fully shared their desire to take the offensive and gain the initiative at sea, but he was not about to side with those who demanded reckless offensive measures that would endanger Britain's superiority in modern capital ships. In December 1916 he defended his position in an article in the *London Magazine*, where he explained again that Britain's distant blockade *was* an offensive action. If the Germans declined to accept a decisive battle with the British fleet, even near their own coast, there was little more the Admiralty could do. He conceded that 'other methods' of forcing the enemy to action 'must be sought'. But he reiterated his belief that 'in pursuing this quest nothing must be done which would jeopardize the solid advantages of our main and primary position; for it is on these that our whole existence depends.'[110]

He returned to the attack again the following month, writing that those who believed the navy could easily get at the enemy's fleet were 'ignorant of the physical conditions of modern naval war':

> They are also singularly unmindful of the teachings of naval history. Even in Nelson's time the most he could do until the enemy put to sea voluntarily was to blockade him in his ports. Under present conditions we achieve this blockade almost as effectively from a distant strategic base, and in addition we exert a control over the oceans never dreamed of in the old wars, even after the most dazzling victories.

'The man who would jeopardize these primary advantages,' he charged, 'is a maniac.'[111]

At the Admiralty, Admiral Sturdee, the former Chief of the Naval Staff, complained that the strategy espoused by Churchill was 'the exact reverse of what he advocated when in office and expressed in public speeches', but this is not fair either.[112] Churchill had always accepted that the superiority of the Grand Fleet must not be jeopardized recklessly. He differed from naval leaders only in his willingness to endanger 'surplus' ships if some advantage could be secured thereby, even if it was only to help the navy maintain its moral ascendancy over the German fleet. Churchill made his position clear to Jellicoe when the latter became First Sea Lord in late 1916. 'You may be able,' Churchill wrote, 'to win for the Navy, without jeopardising its main strength, those opportunities of *minor* offensive action without which neither glory nor in the long run safety can be achieved.'[113] During the final years of the war, the overriding naval concern for Churchill was whether Britain's 'surplus' forces should be allowed to remain idle. His own belief was that the Grand Fleet's margin of superiority was so great that a more aggressive strategy at sea was both possible and desirable.

During the first half of 1917, Churchill began to think seriously about how the navy might be used to increase the pressure on Germany. He was by now convinced that economic pressure was unlikely to have a decisive impact on the course of the war. 'It is clear,' he wrote in January, 'that by itself the naval blockade, however stringent, will not effect the ruin of Germany within any period which we can at present foresee.'[114] If the Admiralty and the government were content simply to maintain the blockade, Churchill suggested that the navy should be maintained at the lowest level necessary to perform this task, with all additional resources redistributed to support the army. But Churchill believed that the navy still had a contribution to make, and that it could safely commit some of its resources to offensive measures. 'An aggressive spirit is the soul of successful war,' he wrote:

> The feeling is widespread that the enterprise and audacity of our seamen have not been accorded the outlet and scope which they require. This feeling would be mischievous if it led to vague demands that the Grand Fleet should abandon the sure and sound strategic policy it has hitherto followed. It would be wholly beneficial if it led to the encouragement of a naval offensive which did not compromise the vital elements of our strength.

'For a year and a half,' he complained, 'no aggressive action of this character has been taken by the Admiralty.'[115]

Churchill was not alone in deprecating the Admiralty's lack of initiative. Similar views were being expressed in varying degrees in political circles, the press, and even within the navy itself. Confidence in the Admiralty reached a low point in 1917 with the intensification of German submarine attacks on British seaborne trade. Shipping losses increased sharply with Germany's decision in February to adopt a policy of unrestricted submarine warfare, which had been tried and abandoned earlier in the war. German submarines were now authorized to sink merchant ships without warning or making provision for the safety of their crews, just as Fisher had predicted before the war. Over 328,000 tons of shipping were lost to submarines in January. The following month losses jumped to over 520,000. In April 1917, the worst month of the war, the figure exceeded 830,000 tons.[116] The Admiralty was initially at a complete loss as to how to solve this problem, and Jellicoe did little to conceal his pessimism.

The solution to the submarine threat was eventually found in the adoption of a convoy system for merchant ships, an essentially defensive measure that had been successfully employed in Britain's earlier wars. Admiralty officials were initially reluctant to take this step during the First World War, however, fearing that convoys would only make British ships easier targets by conveniently grouping them together. Churchill had not been an advocate of convoy before the war, and he did not consider it now. His sole contribution to the discussion over defensive measures was a proposal in March 1917 that British merchant shipping should be organized so as to arrive in the danger zones around British shores at four-day intervals. German submarines would thus be deprived of targets for three continuous days, and then be overwhelmed on the fourth day. The enemy, he predicted, would not be able to inflict proportionately heavy damage during this period, and British losses overall would be reduced.[117]

The Admiralty began experimenting with convoy at the end of April 1917, and was still in the process of implementing a comprehensive system in June when Churchill renewed his pleas for a naval offensive in the *Sunday Pictorial*. His patience with the Admiralty was clearly waning. The navy, he complained, was content merely to 'keep the ring' while the outcome of the war was determined by land operations. The entry of the United States into the war in April had added still more capital ships to the Grand Fleet, and Churchill insisted that the margin of superiority over Germany was now so great that Britain and its allies had more reason than ever to undertake offensive operations.[118] This was not a repudiation of Churchill's earlier views, as some historians have suggested.[119] Churchill still proposed to employ only 'surplus' ships in German waters. The difference now was that the size of the Allies' surplus was so great that bolder and more ambitious schemes could be contemplated.

In early July, Churchill, although still a backbench MP, prepared a memorandum for the War Cabinet outlining specific proposals for action. He now revived the scheme he had set aside in 1914 to create two distinct fleets, both capable of meeting the German fleet on favourable terms. The first, which would closely resemble the existing Grand Fleet, would be a 'fast blue water fleet' ready at all times to engage the German fleet if it emerged to challenge Britain's command of the seas. The second would be comprised of older vessels fitted with special 'bulges' around their sides to render them relatively safe from torpedoes and mines. These modifications would greatly reduce their speed, but would enable them to operate as an 'Inshore Aggressive Fleet' near the German coast, where they could restore Britain's traditional policy of close blockade. Churchill maintained that this fleet would also require an island such as Borkum as a forward base. If one could not be seized, he suggested that it might be possible to create an artificial island. Britain could then stifle the submarine offensive, send ships into the Baltic, win Denmark and the Netherlands to the Allied cause, and open up the prospect of invading northern Germany. But he warned that if the navy was not willing to use its 'surplus' forces for this purpose, it could afford to do without them. 'We do not want,' he wrote, 'upwards of 200 battleships continually manned in full commission to "keep the ring".' If these ships were not making a positive contribution to winning the war, the men and resources needed to maintain them 'should be released for other purposes. The guns and ammunition should go to the front,' he proposed, and 'officers and expert ratings should go to the Tanks or to the air, where they are greatly needed.'[120]

The severity of the submarine threat in mid-1917 ensured that Churchill's proposals were not rejected out of hand. With pressure on the Admiralty and the First Sea Lord mounting, the naval staff could not afford to appear complacent. Churchill's memorandum was studied by Admiralty officials, including Captain Dudley Pound, who would later serve as First Sea Lord under Churchill during the Second World War. But once again, the conclusion was that there were insurmountable practical difficulties to operations near the German coast. Jellicoe also had strong doubts about the desirability of seizing an island like Borkum or Heligoland, and he questioned whether Churchill's scheme, even if it could be implemented, would eliminate the submarine threat, since it would not block Germany's exits from the Baltic.[121] The First Sea Lord kept staff officers busy over the next two months investigating a variety of offensive schemes in the Heligoland Bight, most notably a massive blocking operation to seal German ships and submarines into their ports. Jellicoe's expectations were not high. Indeed, he only seemed to want a concrete plan so as to demonstrate that the concept was unworkable. In this he was not disappointed. A proposal was drawn up for blocking Germany's ports using approximately forty old battleships and forty-three old cruisers, which would be supplied by Britain, the United States, France, Italy, and Japan. The scheme was considered by Allied naval leaders in September 1917, and promptly rejected. The only measure approved was the creation of a massive mine barrage from the Orkneys to Norway intended to hold German submarines in the North Sea.[122]

The success of the convoy system in containing the submarine threat reduced the pressure on the Admiralty to take drastic measures, although there were still widespread concerns that the navy was not being sufficiently aggressive. Churchill's own conviction that this was so was only strengthened after he was appointed Minister of Munitions in July 1917 by Lloyd George, who had succeeded Asquith as prime minister the previous year. Churchill's appointment provoked a storm of protest that caught even him by surprise. His judgement was widely distrusted, and leading Tories in particular had no desire to see him return to a position of power. Not surprisingly, the new minister was denied a seat on the War Cabinet. This was an arrangement that suited Lloyd George well: it enabled him to exploit Churchill's drive and administrative talents for the sake of the war effort, and kept an unpopular and controversial colleague at a safe distance from the central direction of the war effort.

Churchill now became responsible for munitions production for the army and, the following year, for the new independent Royal Air Force (RAF) as well. He immediately threw himself into this task and, as his opponents had feared, found it difficult not to interfere in all aspects of war direction. His views on grand strategy were carefully thought out, however. Churchill understood the requirements of modern industrialized warfare better than most of his colleagues, and he offered a realistic prescription for winning the war.[123] Britain, he insisted, must remain on the defensive against Germany until overwhelming force could be gathered for an Allied offensive in 1919 or 1920. Costly battles like the Somme and Passchendaele in 1916 and 1917 respectively, which had taken a heavier toll on Britain than Germany, were to be avoided at all costs. Britain should conserve its manpower while massive American armies were transported to the Western Front to ensure a large margin of superiority over the German army. Most importantly, every opportunity should be seized to exploit mechanical means of waging war. Lives would be saved by capitalizing on and increasing the Allies' superiority in new weapons like the tank and aeroplane. Even before his return to office, Churchill had embraced mechanization as the key to fighting the war at an acceptable cost. 'Machines save life,' he told the House of Commons in March 1917, 'machine-power is a substitute for man-power, brains will save blood, manoeuvre is a great diluting agent to slaughter, and can be made to reduce the quantity of slaughter required to effect any particular object.'[124]

The Admiralty, which continued to manage its own supply organization, was directly in competition with Churchill and the Ministry of Munitions for resources. Conflict was inevitable. Churchill gave the Admiralty full credit for mastering the submarine threat, and applauded the daring raid in April 1918 on the Belgian port of Zeebrugge, which was being used as a submarine base by the Germans. The latter, he remarked, gave the navy 'back the "*panache*" that was lost at Jutland'. But he continued to view the service's passivity with misgiving, and was particularly frustrated by the high priority the government accorded to the Admiralty in the allocation of resources. He generally supported the construction of escort vessels and merchant ships to replace losses, but he was not prepared to go any further. In November 1917, Churchill estimated that the Admiralty was employing between 35 and 40 per cent of the country's supply of munitions workers.[125] This was not the right balance to strike between the services at this stage of the war. The navy already possessed more than enough ships to meet its essential requirements. If anything, in Churchill's opinion, it had too many ships. The navy, he remarked to Fisher in May 1918, 'does not render a full return for the drain it makes on our resources'.[126]

Churchill had a strong case that much of the manpower, steel, and other resources controlled by the Admiralty would be better employed in supplying the guns, tanks, and aeroplanes needed on the Western Front. During the final months of the war he struggled, with little success, to weaken the Admiralty's privileged position. In an unsent letter drafted in December 1917 to Sir Eric Geddes, the new First Lord, he had claimed that it was 'shocking beyond words, knowing what I do of the relative strength of the British and German Navies, and indeed, of the Allied and enemy Navies, that we should be actually robbing our Army of shell and other vital equipment for the sake of still further piling up an enormous surplus of Blue Water craft that will be left on our hands at the close of the war. We have reached a point,' he concluded, 'where every ton taken by the Navy directly reduces the battery which protects the British troops in the field.'[127]

The rapid collapse of the German war effort in late 1918 caught Allied leaders by surprise, and Churchill was no exception. In the autumn of 1918 he was preparing British industry to support a major Allied offensive in 1919. The possibility that the war might drag on into 1920 did not seem far-fetched at the time. When the fighting abruptly ended in November 1918, Churchill's attention was fastened more firmly than ever on the Western Front. His learning curve over the course of the war had been a sharp one. As First Lord in 1914–15, Churchill had sought to use sea power to strike a major blow against Britain's enemies, and his efforts had met with nothing but frustration. Amphibious operations had failed against Turkey, widely regarded as a second-rate power, and had not even been attempted against Germany. The British were denied the satisfaction of destroying the German fleet, and even if an overwhelming victory could have been achieved, Britain's strategic position would not necessarily have been much stronger. Germany was not dependent, like Britain, on its access to the sea lanes, and Churchill—who always preferred instant and tangible results—never seems to have taken the economic blockade entirely seriously, even in the latter stages of the war when it finally started to become effective. At best he saw the blockade as an inconvenience to the Germans, but he did not expect it to win the war on its own. Germany was a modern, industrialized state with the greatest army in Europe and vast resources to draw upon, and Churchill quickly realized that it could only be defeated on land, and only then through a drawn-out process of attrition.

Churchill never doubted that the Royal Navy was essential to the Allied victory. If Britain had lost command of the seas, its war effort would have collapsed. And, despite the perception in some quarters that he was prepared to run huge and unacceptable risks, Churchill did fully appreciate the importance of maintaining a comfortable margin of superiority over the main German fleet, the only force capable of destroying Britain's maritime security. But by the end of the war, Churchill had no reason to doubt what he had intuitively grasped at the start of the conflict: that the navy's contribution to the defeat of Germany would be largely indirect. It would enable Britain to draw on the resources of the world, to transport armies from around the empire and the United States into Europe, to feed the British people and keep Britain and its allies supplied with munitions. The dominant lesson for Churchill insofar as sea power was concerned, was how little it could achieve by itself against a major continental power. The Royal Navy successfully provided the 'cover and shield' that Britain and its allies needed to achieve victory, but in Churchill's eyes it had done little more.

3

Adjusting to the Post-War World, 1919–24

.

After the 1918 general election returned Lloyd George's coalition government to power, Churchill expressed his interest in returning to the Admiralty. Rumours that this appointment was being considered caused some alarm in naval circles. Admiral Sir Rossyln Wemyss, the current First Sea Lord, told one senior admiral that he would resign immediately if Churchill were made First Lord, 'on the grounds that I could not work with a man whose presence at the Admiralty I should consider a national danger'.[1] In the event, Churchill was sent to the War Office and the new Air Ministry. As Secretary of State for War and Air from 1919 to 1921, he exerted a strong influence over the development of the post-war policies of both the army and the Royal Air Force (RAF).

Despite taking responsibility in 1919 for the largest army in British history, Churchill assumed that the nation would eventually revert to something like its 'normal' peacetime defence priorities, with the navy enjoying predominance and the army reduced to a small volunteer force for imperial policing. But he was not looking simply to turn the clock back to 1914: the application of modern technology and new weapons to the battlefield during the war had made a deep impression on Churchill, and he continued to hold progressive views long after the fighting ceased. The best path forward for the army, he felt, was to substitute aircraft and mechanized ground forces for traditional cavalry and infantry formations.[2]

Churchill had always taken a romantic view of air power, and it is hardly surprising that he became an enthusiastic supporter of the RAF. He assumed that the new service could immediately take over some of the duties traditionally assigned to the army and the navy, and that in time it would overshadow the other services altogether. With 'superior thinking power & knowledge,' he predicted in January 1919, the air force would one day 'obtain the primary place in the general conception of war policy'.[3] But in the short term, Churchill was well aware of the RAF's limitations. In 1919–20 he hoped to lay the foundation for a thoroughly modern peacetime army that would be supported by the RAF, not replaced by it. Army modernization was difficult to accomplish in the early post-war years, however. The demand for British troops at home and abroad did not immediately disappear with the Armistice. Occupation forces were required in both Germany and Turkey, and troops were needed for service in a variety of new theatres—in Russia, where Britain initially supported 'White' forces in the civil war; in Ireland, to quell the escalating nationalist unrest; and in the Middle East, to assert British control over new possessions. Army leaders shared Churchill's interest in mechanization, but were slow to embrace a policy of substitution. They wanted large and modern forces suitable for routine imperial policing but also capable of meeting an emerging major threat. This ultimately worked to the advantage of the RAF, which increased its share of defence funding by promising politicians a more cost-effective means to maintain order within the empire.[4]

While Churchill believed that the RAF could take over some of the duties performed by the navy, he did not attack naval expenditure simply to obtain additional funds for the air service.[5] Nor did he question the wisdom of maintaining a powerful fleet. The navy may have contributed less to the Allied victory in the First World War than he had hoped, and the air force might have a dazzling future before it, but maritime power was clearly still essential to Britain's security. In his first major speech after the war, Churchill paid generous tribute to the navy's wartime work and denied that a League of Nations could ever eliminate the need for a powerful fleet. 'This is a matter on which you have to stand on your guard,' he warned his constituents in November 1918. 'Nothing in the world, nothing that you may think of, or dream of, or anyone may tell you, no arguments, however specious, no appeals, however seductive, must lead you to abandon that naval supremacy on which the life of our country depends.'[6] Privately, almost a year later, he wrote to Walter Long, the new First Lord of the Admiralty, that 'There really is nothing to be ashamed of in the record of the Navy during the great war. I do not admire the writers who are making huge sums of money by running down their own profession and each other.'[7]

The fact remained, however, that a large reduction in naval expenditure would deflect some of the pressure on Churchill to reduce spending on his departments. The Royal Navy emerged from the First World War in a remarkably strong position. The German High Seas Fleet was interned at Scapa Flow as one of the Armistice terms, and after the German ships were scuttled in June 1919 Britain possessed numerical superiority in capital ships over all the other major navies of the world combined. Moreover, there were no clear or imminent naval threats on the horizon: the other great maritime powers—the United States, France, Italy, and Japan—had been Britain's wartime allies and posed no immediate threat to British interests. Writing to Lloyd George on 1 May 1919, Churchill insisted that it would be impossible to solve the problem of inflated defence expenditure without a large reduction in the navy estimates. There was no compelling reason, he asserted, to expand the fleet beyond its present strength. The only serious competitor to Britain's naval position on the horizon was the United States, which had authorized large battleship programs in 1916 and 1918. However, Churchill did not regard the United States as a likely antagonist, and he was confident that naval competition could be avoided. To this end, he suggested that the Americans might be given some of the interned (but not yet scuttled) German battleships. 'It would be a mark of great confidence and trust,' he claimed, 'and would do more to lay naval competition to rest than anything else.' The only foreseeable danger to Britain's maritime position, he remarked, would be a *qualitative* naval challenge. If the new American capital ships significantly outmatched their British counterparts, he conceded that Britain would eventually have to respond in kind. But for the time being, he believed that Britain did not need to build any new warships 'except of a minor character'.[8]

Churchill made his views public in a June 1919 article in *The Weekly Dispatch*, although he now argued that a qualitative naval challenge would not require an immediate response. On the contrary, he maintained that Britain only stood to gain by postponing its reaction to new American construction. 'The longer you can delay the building of new ships without letting your margin fall too low,' he wrote, 'the better and more powerful is the ship you can build when the time comes.' This was a theme Churchill would frequently return to over the next decade: that in the absence of an imminent threat, Britain should avoid building expensive warships that might soon be outclassed by the new constructions of potential enemies. Britain had this luxury, in his view, because of its margin of superiority over its rivals, the strength of its armaments industry, and the excellence of its naval architects. The Admiralty, therefore, he wrote in June 1919, 'could afford to study new developments and delay its response to foreign construction'.[9]

In August 1919, with defence expenditure forecast at a staggering £500 million for the coming financial year (nearly one-third of total government spending), Churchill mounted another attack on the navy estimates, which then stood at £170 million. Britain's position at sea was so secure, he argued in a Cabinet memorandum on 1 August, that it did not need to build *any* new ships for the next three to four years, and should not complete any vessel less than 80 per cent finished already. Further economies could be achieved by reducing the number of ships in full commission. And as an expedient to reduce total defence expenditure, he suggested that the Cabinet should instruct the fighting services to rule out 'the possibility of another great war occurring in the next five years, and that they are to consider it only remotely possible in the five years following that'. This, he claimed 'would wipe out a whole series of obligations and anxieties which the military and naval authorities have at present to reckon with'.[10] Three days later he drove these points home in a letter to the prime minister. 'The army has definite additions to its responsibilities & the Air Force is a new arm,' he wrote. 'But the Navy must be reduced in accordance with the altered state of the world & of other maritime powers.'[11]

This advice dovetailed with recommendations the prime minister had received from Hankey, a few weeks earlier. The Cabinet Secretary had provided Lloyd George with a detailed memorandum arguing that post-war economic imperatives dictated a reduction of 'non-productive' expenditure on the armed services. The navy, in Hankey's view, could control expenses by excluding the United States from any new naval standard.[12] The Treasury also dismissed suggestions that expensive naval preparations were required by any imminent threat to British interests. The Chancellor of the Exchequer, Austen Chamberlain, pressed the Cabinet through July 1919 to cut expenditure on the armed services in general, and infuriated the Admiralty by recommending a reduction in capital ships with full crews to a number below that maintained by the United States.[13] This proposal come as a rude shock to naval leaders. At the time, the navy planned to keep twenty-one capital ships in full commission, but the Treasury wanted this figure decreased immediately to fifteen, with larger reductions to follow in 1920. With the United States expected to maintain eighteen dreadnoughts and eleven pre-dreadnoughts in full commission, the Admiralty denounced this proposal, which it warned would 'be regarded generally as the handing over of sea-supremacy by the British Empire to the United States of America'.[14]

Naval leaders were horrified by the prospect of Britain sinking to the position of the world's second naval power. Fears of an American challenge were also fostered by the widespread 'big-navy' agitation in the United States and a perceived attempt to build up a mercantile marine capable of challenging Britain's domination of the world-carrying trade.[15] The likelihood of an Anglo-American war was regarded as remote, but even pro-American naval officers were reluctant to entrust Britain's vital interests to American goodwill. Besides leaving Britain vulnerable to American pressure, it was feared that the loss of maritime supremacy would undermine British prestige, weaken the bonds between Britain and its Dominions, and hinder the recovery of Britain's international trade. The American challenge to Britain's maritime supremacy was therefore too serious to be ignored. The United States had authorized eight new capital ships in 1916, and two years later proposed to lay down another sixteen. The Admiralty was alarmed not just by the size of these programs, but also by the fighting power of the proposed vessels compared to Britain's capital ships, all but one of which was of pre-Jutland design. Faced with this emerging challenge, the navy abandoned its delusions of securing government support for a new two-power standard against the next strongest naval powers, the United States and France. It now began to concentrate on a more realistic goal: ensuring Britain's continued superiority over the United States alone.[16]

Lloyd George had no intention of being forced down this costly and, in his mind, unnecessary path. On 15 October the War Cabinet accepted a recommendation from the ministerial Finance Committee to reduce defence spending to approximate pre-war levels, which would mean estimates for all three services totalling £135 million. The fighting services were formally instructed to assume 'for framing revised Estimates, that the British Empire will not be engaged in any great war during the next ten years, and that no Expeditionary Force is required for this purpose'. The navy was allocated only £60 million for the following year's estimates, a sharp drop from the £170 million that had been approved in July. It was also instructed to revert to the naval standard in place before the war—60 per cent superiority over the next strongest naval power *excluding* the United States.[17] Churchill has sometimes been identified as the primary instigator of the so-called 'ten-year rule' in 1919, but he played only a peripheral role in the process—the real driving force behind the decision was Lloyd George.[18]

However, the prime minister was only partially successful in reining in naval spending, as the Admiralty was not prepared to relinquish its lead over the United States without a fight. Over the next several months naval leaders struggled unsuccessfully to overturn the Cabinet's ruling. In the end, they had to admit defeat, although their fallback position was still ambitious: they now lobbied for a naval standard based on parity with the United States.

Britain could expect to maintain equality only through an accommodation with the United States or by launching an expensive new construction programme.[19] In February 1920, as the Admiralty prepared its estimates for the coming fiscal year, Walter Long approached the Cabinet for fresh guidance on the question of the USN. If a naval agreement could not be reached with the United States, he warned that it would be 'necessary definitely to lay down that a one-power standard against the strongest naval power is the minimum standard compatible with our vast sea requirements, and that the building programme in all types of vessels must be such that this one-power standard is fully maintained.'[20] The Cabinet agreed, and Long announced to the House of Commons that the government adhered to the principle 'that our Navy should not be inferior in strength to the Navy of any other Power'.[21]

This announcement of a one-power standard was, in the circumstances, a substantial victory for the Admiralty: it now possessed a naval standard relative to the United States—a power Britain was unlikely ever to face in war—and one that might permit the resumption of capital- ship construction in the near future. The Naval Staff soon shocked the government by proposing a large construction programme designed to maintain the standard. The full financial implications of the new policy were now apparent.[22] Hoping to reassert control over the size of naval estimates, the prime minister initiated an inquiry by the Committee of Imperial Defence into the question of whether the navy should make preparations for war with the United States.

When this inquiry commenced on 14 December 1920, Lloyd George warned his colleagues that entering into naval competition 'would be the biggest decision they had taken since 1914, and conceivably greater than that taken in 1914'. In his view, Britain could neither afford to compete nor expect to prevail if the United States were really determined to achieve naval superiority. He therefore suggested that the USN simply be eliminated as a point of reference. The government had ruled out war with the United States before 1914, he argued, and it could do so again without jeopardizing Britain's vital interests. American naval construction would

have to be curtailed through diplomatic means. He suggested an agreement
with the United States 'on the following basis':

> that we had no intention of embarking on a rivalry in respect of general
> supremacy at sea, but we propose that each nation should be superior in her
> own seas. We, for instance, in the North Sea, the Mediterranean, the Indian
> Seas, &c., while the United States should be conceded unchallenged superi-
> ority in her special seas. This was not challenging American supremacy. If, on
> the other hand, Great Britain claimed complete supremacy in all seas, the
> United States would undoubtedly accept the challenge, and this would even-
> tually lead to a fight.

In the event that any genuine naval threat emerged from across the Atlantic,
the prime minister suggested that Britain might rely on its alliance with
Japan for security.[23]

The CID naturally hoped for a diplomatic solution, but if this could not
be achieved most members preferred competitive building to reliance on
the Anglo-Japanese Alliance. Churchill was one of those who strongly
opposed the latter course. 'Great Britain must remain the strongest naval
Power,' he insisted:

> It would be a terrible day for the country when she ceased to be this. Great
> Britain, since the most remote time, had always been supreme at sea. The life
> of the nation, its culture, its prosperity, had rested on that basis, and he would
> most profoundly regret having to abandon this position.

In his opinion, Britain's efforts to maintain a favourable position relative to
the United States would not inevitably lead to conflict. Moreover, the prime
minister's suggestion that the United States and Britain could 'divide the
seas' between them was unrealistic. 'The seas were all one,' Churchill argued,
'and the fleets, however dispersed, could rapidly link up':

> Indeed, the mobility of fleets to-day was vastly greater than it had ever been,
> and oil-burning vessels could almost compass the world without replenishing
> fuel. Naval power, therefore, must be regarded *generally* and not as an agglom-
> eration of dispersed units.[24]

Churchill was especially critical of the idea that the alliance with Japan
might compensate for any shortfalls in British strength in the event of a
clash with the United States. There was 'no more fatal policy,' he argued,
'than that of basing our naval policy on a possible combination with Japan
against the United States'[25] Lloyd George countered that 'there was one

more fatal policy, namely, one whereby we would be at the mercy of the United States'. Churchill, however, represented the dominant view within the Cabinet. The one-power standard was upheld.

Having failed to reduce naval expenditure by removing the United States as a basis for comparison, Lloyd George attacked the problem from a different direction. A CID subcommittee was set up under the chairmanship of Bonar Law, the Lord Privy Seal and leader of the Conservative Party, to examine the future of the capital ship itself.[26] If air power or submarines were about to render battleships obsolete, as some prominent figures continued to argue, the government could safely reject the navy's plans to build more of these vessels. Churchill was appointed to this committee along with Walter Long, Robert Horne (President of the Board of Trade), Admiral Beatty (the new First Sea Lord), and another former First Lord, Sir Eric Geddes.

The hearings of the capital-ship subcommittee began on 30 December 1920 and lasted nearly a month. Serving naval officers, who provided the majority of the subcommittee's witnesses, maintained a solid front: they acknowledged that capital ships were vulnerable to mines and torpedoes, but insisted that the Grand Fleet had been essential to the Britain's maritime dominance during the recent war, and that modern battleships continued to be indispensable. Even Herbert Richmond, one of the navy's most progressive thinkers, pronounced firmly in favour of the capital ship. The 'experiences of the past war,' he declared, 'lead to only one possible conclusion—that the battle fleet played the same vital part, in the same manner and with the same results, as battlefleets have played in the past; and that without battleships on our side the [Great] war would have been lost by the Entente; without them on the German side we could have not merely held the Submarines as we eventually did, but have crushed the submarine campaign at a comparatively early stage.'[27] The only real dispute amongst the admirals was whether Britain needed to build more of these ships immediately. Admiralty opinion strongly favoured construction of new vessels, although two naval witnesses, Richmond and Rear Admiral Bartolomé, recommended a delay.

The Admiralty was fortunate that there were few effective critics of the capital ship among the witnesses. The testimony of Admiral S. S. Hall, a former Commodore of the submarine service who had recently written articles for *The Times* attacking the battleship, was too muddled to make much of an impression.[28] The most dangerous criticism came from the Royal Air Force. The Air Staff submitted a paper in January 1921 claiming that the future value of the capital ship 'must be greatly reduced and will become an insurance for which we cannot afford to pay the premiums....Just as in the past we concentrated on the Navy, so in the future, if air power should be as decisive a factor as the Air Staff confidently anticipate, we shall have to concentrate on the air even at the expense of the Navy.'[29] The Air Ministry's attack was blunted, however, by the relatively moderate views expressed by General Hugh Trenchard, the Chief of the Air Staff (CAS). Trenchard acknowledged that military aircraft still had many limitations and could not yet expect to sink a battleship. He maintained that the air force could take over some of the roles assigned to the navy, but not all of them. 'I do not want it to be thought that I am a whole-hogger for the Air,' he told the subcommittee, 'or that we can do all the Navy does, because we do not. We cannot.'[30]

Major General Sir Frederick Sykes, a former CAS, argued that the only factor which might justify the immediate construction of capital ships was 'that very big and intangible one—world prestige'. He maintained, however, that the right course for Britain over the next few years was 'to put money into the development of the air service to do all it can to assist and relieve the Fleet, rather than put it directly into the Fleet'. Only in this way, he maintained, could the RAF begin to develop the resources that would enable it to take over duties traditionally performed by the Royal Navy.[31] Admiralty representatives were considerably irritated by the Air Force's vague and ambitious claims about the future importance of air power. 'The point,' Beatty countered, 'is that the Navy has to consider these questions of new forms of attack to provide the antidote. It is no use making our flesh creep with what may be done in ten years' time. We want to know what is being done today.' Admiral Osmond Brock, the Deputy Chief of the Naval Staff (DCNS), also took time during his testimony to attack critics whose claims were based on things that 'may happen a few years hence':

They imagine that ships may fly, that aeroplanes will be able to cover 1,500 miles...and back, and fire torpedoes from guns. All I wish to say is that imagination is a good servant but an extremely bad master....It is a fatal thing for those in responsibility to let their imagination run away with them and say well we may produce something in five years' time that will wipe out everything that has gone before. It is easy enough for those who have no responsibility but for those who have to advise the policy to be carried out, surely they can only base their advice on what they know and visionary things cannot be admitted.[32]

Churchill had long been receptive to the idea that the days of the battleship were numbered, but the experiences of the First World War seemed to show that its time was not yet up. Not only were capital ships still indispensable to the exercise of sea power, they remained the basis on which a nation's maritime strength was measured. Britain therefore could not afford to be seen to be deficient in this area. 'We are in danger of sinking to the position not only of second but of third naval power in a few years' time,' he warned a colleague, Arthur Balfour, in February 1921:

> I consider that the Adm[iral]ty have made out an overwhelming case for the Capital Ship as the foundation & ultimate sanction of sea-power in the period with wh[ich] we are immediately concerned. I am sure that we will be judged all over the world in peacetime on the numbers of Capital ships available. I do not see how the foreign or Colonial policy of our Empire can be carried on on the basis that we have ceased to be the leading naval power.[33]

Despite his enthusiasm for 'substitution', Churchill was also sceptical of the RAF's ability to step immediately into the void left by a greatly diminished navy.

Taking all this into consideration, Churchill was prepared to recommend the construction of four capital ships annually for the next four or five years. Not all subcommittee members were prepared to go this far, however. There was a consensus that no evidence had been presented showing that the capital ship was obsolete, but no agreement on the need for new construction in this class. In the event of an Anglo-American war in 1924–5, by which time the Royal Navy would be inferior in post-Jutland capital ships, Bonar Law, Horne, and Geddes maintained that Britain would still be strong enough at sea to withstand a 'knock-out blow' even without new naval construction. Conversely, more ships would not substantially increase Britain's ability to apply pressure to the United States in the event of armed conflict. The result of any trans-Atlantic war, they concluded, would be 'a stalemate in which neither side could obtain a decisive victory'.[34]

A minority report by Beatty, Churchill, and Long took the danger of an Anglo-American war more seriously, if only because the consequences of a decisive naval defeat would be grave. A 'knock-out blow against the United States Fleet would not necessarily constitute a knock-out blow against the United States as a nation,' they noted, but 'a knock-out blow against the British fleet would mean the inevitable defeat of the British Empire'. Moreover, in any such conflict the United States navy could adopt a defensive strategy and gain an advantage from the proximity of its bases. The report also warned that falling behind the US in modern battleships would reduce 'our prestige in the Dominions and throughout the world' and harm 'our maritime trade and foreign and imperial policy'. Britain would also be unwise, they felt, to enter into 'a conference with the United States on the limitation of armaments with empty hands, that is, with an obsolescent fleet, while the United States possess a large fleet of modern ships in process of construction'. These factors seemed to point clearly towards the need to maintain a one-power standard and to lay down new capital ships immediately.[35]

The Admiralty's failure to achieve firm backing for new construction did not prove to be a serious setback. As long as the one-power standard was not formally renounced, the Admiralty's building programme was kept alive. And because the subcommittee endorsed the navy's views on the future utility of battleships, the door was not shut on new construction. But with Britain and the United States now preparing for a naval arms-limitation conference, there was little likelihood of a large building programme actually being launched. The possibility of naval competition with the United States nevertheless haunted British decision-makers throughout 1921. One of the most serious obstacles to an agreement was Britain's long-standing alliance with Japan. The unpopularity of the Anglo-Japanese Alliance in the United States gave British leaders good reason to fear that its continuation would block an Anglo-American accord on naval armaments. Failure to renew the Alliance, however, would offend Japan and weaken Britain's strategic position in the Far East. There was no easy solution. In May 1921 Churchill hoped that US-Japanese relations could be improved by holding a conference of Pacific powers. If successful, Britain might conceivably keep the Alliance, maintain American goodwill, and avoid a costly naval arms race. But if the United States and Japan could not be reconciled, he somewhat naïvely suggested that a modified Anglo-Japanese Alliance could be negotiated and the United States reconciled by explaining that it 'was not in any way directed against American interests'.[36]

Renewal of the Anglo-Japanese Alliance, a course generally favoured by the British government, was endorsed by the Australian and New Zealand representatives at the 1921 Imperial Conference. The Canadian government, however, fearing a decline in its relations with the United States, came out strongly against renewal.[37] Churchill, now Colonial Secretary, entered the debate in early July with a lengthy Cabinet memorandum. While still reluctant to offend Japan by terminating the Alliance, he was increasingly disinclined to take any course that might endanger Anglo-American relations. Most importantly, he insisted that Britain's position in the Far East would be better protected in the long run by alignment with the United States than by alliance with Japan. The only real danger to Australia and New Zealand, he warned, was posed by Japan. There was, in Churchill's view, no reason to suppose that the continuation of the Anglo-Japanese Alliance would act as a restraint upon Japanese behaviour. 'An alliance between the British Empire and Japan for the purpose of protecting Australia and New Zealand against Japan is meaningless,' he argued:

> We should stand entirely on the basis of Japanese goodwill and good faith. They would fulfil their bargain by the simple process of holding themselves in check. So long as they did not molest us we should be their debtors and we should have to pay our dues, but if at any time we were not punctual in our payments or if they changed their minds, our security would vanish and it would vanish simultaneously with the apparition of the very danger against which it was devised. Getting Japan to protect you against Japan is like drinking salt water to slake thirst.

The right course for Britain in the long term, Churchill held, was to establish a 'great unity of interests' with the United States, which would leave Japan 'so hopelessly outmatched that there can be no war, and the rivalries in armaments which are the precursors of war would have no purpose. The combatants will be too unequal for the question even to arise.' In a statement that he might just as easily have written twenty years later, he asserted in July 1921 that war with both the United States and Britain would be a 'hopeless proposition for Japan. A giant and a boy may fight a bigger giant, but if the two giants get together the boy has got to be content with innocent pleasures.'[38]

Throughout the summer of 1921 Churchill was one of the strongest advocates in the government of an agreement with the United States. When preparations for the conference on naval armaments began to stall in July, he worked to remove the obstacles, warning his colleagues that Britain had nothing to gain from a naval competition 'and everything to lose'. If the United States chose 'to put up the money and persevere', it would have 'a good chance of becoming the strongest Naval Power in the world and thus obtaining the complete mastery of the Pacific'.[39] These warnings were unnecessary, however, as British leaders were already well aware of the United States' ability to challenge Britain's naval position. A multilateral conference was duly convened in Washington in November 1921 to consider the inter-connected problems of naval arms limitations and stability in East Asia.

Over the next two and a half months several agreements were hammered out in Washington. The Anglo-Japanese Alliance was superseded by a new four-power treaty in which Britain, the United States, Japan, and France agreed to respect each other's 'insular possessions and insular dominions' in the Pacific. A nine-power treaty, to which Italy, Holland, Belgium, Portugal, and China also adhered, pledged to preserve the independence and integrity of China and maintain an 'open door' there for all trading nations. Naval limitations were imposed by a five-power treaty, which established a ratio of 5:5:3:1.75:1.75 in capital ships and aircraft carriers between the United States, Britain, Japan, France, and Italy. The maximum tonnage allowed to each power in these classes was laid down, while qualitative limits were imposed on battleships, aircraft carriers, and cruisers. Furthermore, the replacement of older battleships was to be abandoned for a period of ten years, despite the Admiralty's warnings about the impact of such a course on the health of the naval shipbuilding industry. Britain, however, was allowed to construct two new battleships of 35,000 tons to balance recent construc-tion by the United States and Japan.

The British government was well satisfied with the results of the Wash-ington Conference. As Churchill observed in January 1922, Britain had suc-cessfully removed 'the Anglo-Japanese Alliance from the path of American friendship, without subjecting Japan to anything like desertion or ill-usage at our hands'.[40] Britain also secured parity with the United States and avoided a costly building race. Back in London, however, the one-power standard was under attack. In October 1921 the Cabinet had appointed an economy committee under Sir Eric Geddes to examine means of reducing national expenditure. Its first report, issued in December 1921, recom-mended drastic reductions to all three fighting services. If its proposals were implemented, navy estimates would be reduced from £81 million to £60 million. Under strong pressure from the fighting services, the government appointed a separate committee under Churchill to review the Geddes Committee's conclusions.[41]

The Admiralty defended its position by arguing that Geddes' proposals would threaten the maintenance of a one-power standard even if the agree-ments in Washington were ratified.[42] A decision was required, therefore, as to whether the one-power standard must be maintained regardless of the cost, or whether the ten-year rule and the need for economy took precedence. Also at issue was the precise meaning of the one-power standard. It was generally assumed before the Washington Conference that the standard fixed Britain's capital-ship requirements. The most recent statement on the standard, issued by the 1921 Imperial Conference, stated that 'the minimum standard of naval ship construction necessary for the maintenance of the position of the British Empire among the nations of the world is an equality in fighting strength with any other Naval Power'.[43] But this could be interpreted to mean different things. Did the standard apply to all classes of warship, or only to capital ships? Did equality mean numerical equality on paper or parity in fighting power? And if war-fighting capabilities were considered, should the navy calculate its requirements on the basis of an offensive or defensive strategy?

The Admiralty naturally had strong views on these questions. It argued that the one-power standard meant that the navy must be maintained 'at sufficient strength to ensure the safety of the British Empire and its sea communications as against any other Naval Power'.[44] This required a clear margin of numerical superiority over the USN, as Britain could not hope otherwise to meet all its worldwide commitments and simultaneously challenge a strong enemy fleet operating near its own bases.[45] But the Admiralty case assumed that an Anglo-American war was a reasonable possibility, which was not widely accepted. The only compelling need to match American strength, therefore, was prestige. The Treasury insisted that as long as the United States did not actually threaten Britain's maritime security, Britain did not need a navy capable of defeating the USN in its own waters. Politicians also had no intention of allowing the navy to calculate its requirements on the basis of a forward strategy in American waters. On the other hand, Churchill was not prepared to support Treasury claims that the ten-year rule must always take precedence over the one-power standard. It certainly did not mean, in his view, expressed in January 1922, that 'we should not maintain a Navy':

> On the contrary it was necessary that we should make provision to enable us to defend ourselves until we were able to bring the whole of the fighting resources of the Empire to bear against an enemy. The fundamental elements of naval strength which could not be improvised must, therefore, be maintained at such a cost as the country could bear.[46]

Churchill's committee outlined a compromise between the positions of the Admiralty and the Treasury. It was not necessary, they concluded in February, that 'the British and United States Navies should be exactly matched in every particular, or that a fair allowance should not be made in estimating personnel for the great reserves which these Islands possess in their seafaring population':

> But we consider that, not only in our own judgment but in that of foreign nations, the standard at which the British Navy is maintained should not be definitely inferior to that of the United States. Any such condition of inferiority would undoubtedly affect our whole position and influence in the world, and indicate to our Dominions that a new centre had been created for the Anglo-Saxon world. We have felt that the Cabinet, and indeed Parliament, would expect us to regard the maintenance of the one-Power standard as an imperative condition.[47]

The two navies need not be precisely matched in every class of ship, therefore, as long as their overall strength remained approximately equal on paper. Treasury officials were not pleased. Sir George Barstow, the Controller of Supply Services, complained that Britain's political leaders were 'in serious danger of making themselves slaves to a formula'.[48] But the Treasury's opposition ensured that the standard would be interpreted in a relatively conservative fashion. Given the government's determination to reduce defence expenditure, the Admiralty probably did as well as it could have hoped for. Its position had, in any event, been eased considerably by the results of the Washington Conference. Churchill was confident that the navy could easily trim its estimates to £62 million now that a large battleship programme had been avoided. 'I consider this is a very remarkable achievement,' he told the Chancellor of the Exchequer in February, 'and I only hope it has not been secured by any endangering of our vital naval position.'[49]

By February 1922, therefore, the most complicated post-war naval questions had apparently been resolved: the one-power standard was established on a firm basis; a consensus had been achieved over its definition; the future of the battleship had been affirmed; naval rivalry with the United States had been averted; and the contentious Anglo-Japanese Alliance had been terminated. Attention now began to shift to the strategic situation in the Far East. Concern about this region had been growing since the First World War. Japan was clearly a rising power, and many naval officers viewed its contribution to the Allied war effort as perfunctory and self-serving.[50] The Admiralty assumed that Japan would pursue an expansionist course if favourable opportunities arose, and that this would come at the expense of Britain and other Western powers. The principal restraint on Japan appeared to be the ability of the United States and Britain to defend their positions in the Far East. Prior to the Washington Conference, the Admiralty had derived some comfort from the belief that Japan was more likely to fight the United States than Britain. But naval leaders had no wish to take Japan's side in such a conflict, and spoke out strongly against renewal of the Anglo-Japanese Alliance.[51]

If Japan could not be trusted, Britain would require other means to protect its Eastern interests. In 1919 Jellicoe had recommended the permanent stationing of a large battle fleet in the Far East to deter Japanese encroachments on British interests. This was judged to be prohibitively expensive, however, and the decision was taken instead to retain the bulk of the British navy in European waters and only transfer a fleet to the Far East in the event of a crisis. As long as Britain possessed sufficient warships and suitable bases, the Admiralty was confident that the threat of force would not need to be carried out. As Admiral Keyes stated in March 1925, it would not actually be 'necessary to fight a great war in the Pacific, or "to put a battle fleet in the Pacific," but it is necessary that we should be able to send a fleet to the East capable of defeating or neutralising the Japanese fleet should the occasion arise, and this fact being known to the Japanese would at least make them discreet and check their forward policy'.[52] To make this possible, the Admiralty lobbied for the construction of a major naval base at Singapore and the accumulation of the oil fuel reserves required for large-scale fleet movements. These programmes were endorsed by the CID in June 1921 and later approved by the Cabinet.[53]

In early 1922, Churchill professed to be 'deeply impressed' by the navy's warnings about the Far East. His Cabinet committee observed that the 'position of Japan during the next few years will be formidable', particularly as the United States now appeared incapable of projecting its power effectively into the western Pacific. In the event of war, the committee maintained that Britain would be in an unfavourable position:

> Unless Singapore is adequately protected before it is attacked, we cannot hold Singapore. Until oil-fuelling stations have been established there and on the route to the East at Aden and Colombo, we cannot base a fleet capable of fighting Japan on Singapore. If Singapore fell in the first two or three months of a war, the whole of the Pacific would fall under the complete supremacy of Japan, and many years might elapse before either Britain or the United States could re-enter that ocean in effective strength.

The Churchill committee supported the expensive programmes required by the navy to wage a campaign in the Far East, calling for 'the discreet building up of the fuelling stations and of the base at Singapore which alone can enable our fleet to offer some protection to all our interests in the Pacific, including Australia and New Zealand'.[54]

This policy was reversed by Ramsay MacDonald's Labour government when it came to power in January 1924. Committed to the cause of international disarmament, MacDonald ignored the Admiralty's objections and cancelled work on the Singapore naval base. Churchill, now out of office and, temporarily, without even a seat in Parliament, immediately joined in the Conservative Party's attacks on Labour's naval policies. Writing in the *Sunday Chronicle* in March, he lamented that the British navy, for the first time in its history, was powerless to protect Australia and New Zealand, 'and that the Mother Country has deliberately resolved to put it out of her power to come to their aid, whatever their need might be'.[55] Churchill repeated this message in March when he spoke at a public meeting at Winchester House under the auspices of the Navy League, a popular organization dedicated to supporting the navy.[56] Britain's moral obligation to defend Australia and New Zealand was his paramount concern. 'Disguise it as you will,' he remarked, 'wrap it up in cloaks of smooth pretence, cover it with layers of excuses, hide it in a fog of technicalities, the stubborn brutal fact remains that the decision to abandon the Singapore base leaves Australia and New Zealand to whatever fate an anxious and inscrutable future may have in store.' Britain's Far Eastern Dominions, which had so recently 'sent their hearts' blood in our salvation', deserved better than to be abandoned 'even before the last dead have been gathered from the battlefields of France and Flanders into the National Cemeteries'. This, in his view, was an 'act of ungrateful desertion, it is a plain refusal without precedent in our history on the part of the Mother Country to discharge an Imperial duty.'[57]

The Conservative victory in the October 1924 general election gave the Singapore naval base a new lease on life. The same is true for Churchill, who not only returned to the Conservative Party in 1924 but was offered the position of Chancellor of the Exchequer by Stanley Baldwin, the new prime minister. The Admiralty undoubtedly expected its fortunes to improve under the new government, and had reason to expect an easier ride from the Treasury than they had become accustomed to in recent years. Churchill, after all, had been one of the navy's keenest supporters in the Lloyd

George coalition. Although critical of heavy naval expenditure in the first year of peace, his enthusiasm for economies had soon subsided as new global challenges began to emerge. From 1921 to 1924 he had consistently backed the Admiralty's most expensive programs, supported its views on the capital ship, and generously praised its leaders on numerous occasions. The Treasury's relationship with the Admiralty proved, however, to be nearly as adversarial during Churchill's tenure as Chancellor as it had been under his predecessors.

4

The Treasury Years: The Ten-Year Rule, Japanese 'Bogey', and 'Yankee Menace'

Churchill arrived at the Treasury in November 1924 eager to make his mark on Britain's struggling economy by lowering taxes, reviving industry, and stimulating trade. Success in these areas would confound his many critics and secure his future within the Conservative Party, which never entirely forgave his defection to the Liberals in 1904. One of the first challenges facing the new Chancellor was the escalating cost of defence. As usual, the Admiralty was the worst offender: it planned to increase expenditure in the coming year by nearly £10 million. Treasury officials forecast naval estimates for 1927–8 as high as £80 million (as against £55.8 million in 1924–5), and Churchill immediately determined to resist. Naval expenditure on this scale threatened to drive up taxes, divert money from social programmes, and alienate the electorate. And with the Labour Party a rising force in British politics, Churchill questioned whether the navy would even benefit from the increased spending. 'If the Socialists win [the next election] in a tremendous economy wave,' he warned the prime minister, Stanley Baldwin, in December, 'they will cut down and blot out all these Naval preparations so that in the end the Admiralty will not get the Navy programme for the sake of which your Government will have broken itself.'[1]

The Admiralty's most expensive policies were closely linked to its preparations for war with Japan. Naval leaders believed that Britain's former ally presented a real threat to the security of the British Empire; that this threat necessitated both immediate and long-term preparations; and that Britain must be capable of waging an offensive, and likely protracted, naval campaign in Japan's home waters.[2] This, in turn, translated into demands for enough new construction to maintain a clear margin of superiority over the Japanese navy, a large oil fuel reserve to ensure the mobility of the British fleet, and the completion of a major naval base at Singapore. With capital-ship strength regulated by the Washington naval treaty of 1922, the most expensive warships demanded by the Admiralty during this period were cruisers. In 1924 the Naval Staff set out a ten-year construction programme to meet Britain's needs in this class of ship, which it calculated as forty-five for trade defence and twenty-five for work with the main fleet. In 1925 Britain possessed only fifty-one cruisers, with another five being built. With thirty-two of these ships due to be scrapped over the next decade, the Admiralty claimed that an additional forty-six cruisers must be built by 1936 to achieve its minimum requirements.[3]

As Chancellor, Churchill sought to undermine the justification for the navy's most expensive programmes by challenging the idea that Japan posed an immediate threat to vital British interests. His opening salvo was fired in a letter of 15 December 1924 to Baldwin, which dismissed the possibility of war in the Far East. 'I do not believe there is the slightest chance of it in our lifetime,' he insisted:

> The Japanese are our allies. The Pacific is dominated by the Washington Agreement. America is far more likely to have a quarrel with Japan than we are. What question is pending between England and Japan? To what diplomatic combination do either of us belong which could involve us against each other?

There was, he asserted, 'absolutely no resemblance between our relations with Japan and those we had with Germany before the war'.

While this was a reasonable characterization of Anglo-Japanese relations as they stood in the mid-1920s, it was a notoriously poor prediction of Japan's long-term intentions. However, Churchill's attacks on the navy's programmes were also based on the soundness of its war plans. He was on firmer ground here. The Admiralty's belief that it could inflict a decisive defeat on Japan was never realistic: sea power alone would not be sufficient for the task, and Britain did not possess the resources for an extended campaign in the Far East comparable to the one the United States would conduct in 1942–5. Such a war, Churchill predicted in the same letter, 'would last for years. It would cost Japan very little. It would reduce us to bankruptcy.'[4] Nor, in his opinion, was there any need to contemplate such an offensive, as no truly vital British interests were at stake in the region. 'Japan is at the other end of the world,' he reminded the prime minister. 'She cannot menace our vital security in any way.' Britain could afford, if necessary, to sacrifice its position in China. The only action that would justify the mobilization of British and imperial resources for a major war on the other side of the world would be a Japanese invasion of Australia, a possibility he was quick to dismiss. 'Does anybody imagine she is going to do so?', he asked:

> Would she not be mad to do so? How could she put an army into Australia, over 5,000 miles across the ocean and maintain it at war with the Australians and the whole British Empire[?] Nothing less than half a million Japanese would be any good, and these would have to be continually supplied and maintained. It is an absolute absurdity. Even if America stood inactive Japan would be ruined. She would never attempt it.[5]

Churchill therefore preferred a much less ambitious strategy for protecting British interests in the Far East. From the mid-1920s until December 1941 he contemplated an essentially defensive response to Japanese aggression. Britain would hold Singapore as a means to project its power into the region, to contain Japanese expansion, and, if necessary, to ensure the defence of Australia and New Zealand.

The Treasury could only reduce the navy's programmes by obtaining explicit Cabinet support for its policies. Churchill wanted to give the Admiralty clear guidelines on which to base its programmes, and in November 1924 he suggested that his colleagues revive the decision of August 1919 that the fighting services should assume there would be no great war within the next ten years.[6] Rather than risk a confrontation with all three fighting services, Churchill decided to focus on the navy's programmes. A few weeks later, he suggested to Baldwin that naval leaders should be 'made to recast all their plans and scales and standards on the basis that no naval war against a first class Navy is likely to take place in the next *twenty* years'.[7] In January 1925 he took his case for reduced naval expenditure to the CID, where his optimistic views about Japan were endorsed by the Foreign Office. Austen Chamberlain, the Foreign Secretary, advised the committee that the likelihood of war was 'very remote'. Moreover, if the 'danger of a struggle ever materialises', he predicted that the government would have 'plenty of warning'. It would therefore be 'a great mistake', he concluded, 'to disquiet the Japanese and render them more nervous than they are'.[8]

The Admiralty contested these views, arguing that Japan did pose a serious threat to British interests, at least in the long term; that Britain could not necessarily count on a long warning period; and that the government must still make provision for the defence of British interests in the Far East.[9] When the navy refused to fall into line, Churchill insisted that the navy estimates for 1925–6 would have to be settled by the Cabinet.[10] If the government cancelled all new construction other than a handful of submarines, it could save approximately £1.8 million in the coming financial year, and as much as £8 million in the following one. Treasury officials also recommended freezing personnel levels and adopting later completion dates for both the Singapore naval base and the accumulation of oil reserves, which would keep naval expenditure down to £57,650,000, a figure nearly £2 million *above* the previous year's estimates. 'No one,' Churchill claimed, 'can say this is not an ample supply.'[11]

Churchill hoped to avoid a bitter struggle with the navy. After a series of 'very amicable and friendly' discussions with Beatty, the First Sea Lord, he proposed a compromise by which the Admiralty would give up some of its future expenses in return for Treasury support for annual estimates of £60 million for the next few years. Churchill insisted that this figure, which was 'more than £4 millions above this year in a period when everyone was looking for reductions', was the 'absolute limit' on which he could agree.[12] This was, in fact, a generous offer, and would have provided more money for the navy than it actually received over the life of Baldwin's government. In making the offer, Churchill was effectively abandoning the idea of restricting naval expenditure on the basis of Cabinet-imposed policy guidelines. This would have allowed the navy considerable freedom to allocate funds as it saw fit within the total figure available. In return, Churchill would obtain his immediate goal, holding overall naval expenditure to a level the Treasury considered manageable.

Before the Admiralty could respond to his offer, Churchill circulated another lengthy Cabinet memorandum criticizing the Admiralty's position. This included a pre-emptive strike against its efforts to link its cruiser programme to the one-power standard. Britain, he insisted, should not attempt to match the United States Navy *and* maintain sufficient strength to wage war 'upon Japan in her own quarter of the globe'. The latter would involve virtually unlimited expenses, and Churchill wanted the standard interpreted along the lines laid down by his Cabinet committee in 1922, with navies compared solely by their strength on paper. Most members of the Cabinet shared Churchill's views, and supported his plan to maintain the navy estimates at £60 million for several years. However, when William Bridgeman, the First

Lord, took the proposal to the Board of Admiralty on 11 February, it was rejected. The Board was adamant that anything less than £62.5 million would critically undermine its long-term building programme. Naval leaders were apparently confident that their construction programme could be defended on the basis of the one-power standard, and expected this to give them leverage in their battle with the Treasury.[13] But their most effective weapon was the threat of resignations. Bridgeman warned Baldwin that the entire Board would step down if the Cabinet did not immediately approve four new cruisers for the 1925 construction programme. If this happened, Bridgeman predicted that 'a very large proportion of our party will sympathise with their attitude'.[14]

The Admiralty found little support inside the government, however. Lord Cecil was the only minister to vote with Bridgeman at the next day's Cabinet, and he did so, he claimed, only because the First Lord was 'a very old friend' and there was 'no danger of his views being adopted'.[15] The threat of resignations was a potent weapon, but the Admiralty's obvious isolation induced Bridgeman to agree to estimates of £60.5 million for the year 1925, excluding new construction. To placate the Admiralty and avert a crisis, Baldwin referred the cruiser question in February 1925 to an ad hoc Cabinet committee under Lord Birkenhead, the Secretary of State for India and a close friend of the Chancellor.[16] This body began its deliberations in early March. The outcome depended on the navy's ability to link its cruiser programme to the one-power standard. The Admiralty insisted that since cruisers were required both for work with the fleet and for trade protection, it would need at least seventy of these vessels to meet all the navy's requirements in wartime. It also claimed that this figure was essential to maintain equality in fighting strength with Japan in eastern waters. Hence, these programmes were essential for the maintenance of a one-power standard relative to Japan.[17] The Admiralty also broadened its definition of the standard to encompass not only warships but all aspects of the navy's fighting strength. Thus, the navy claimed that it must maintain not only a clear margin of naval superiority over Japan, but also docking and repair facilities at Singapore and a large oil fuel reserve.

Throughout these deliberations Churchill continued to insist Japan was unlikely to attack British interests and that the cruiser situation was not urgent.[18] He also sought to undermine the navy's case by pointing out that the Singapore naval base was so far from completion that there was no prospect of basing a large fleet there for at least another ten or eleven years. 'We might as well make a virtue of necessity,' he suggested, and abandon preparations for a major war in the Far East for the next decade. If this were done, 'there would fall to the ground the whole expense of building and victualing ships, the submarines and destroyers and depot ships which are required to carry the main British Fleet into Far Eastern waters'. The Admiralty might then only require fifty cruisers to meets its obligations.[19] But the navy was unwilling either to exclude the possibility of war with Japan or abandon its interpretation of the one-power standard, and both issues had to be referred to the CID for a decision.[20]

When these matters were considered on 2 April 1925, Austen Chamberlain reaffirmed the Foreign Office's view that 'aggressive action by Japan against the British Empire on the part of Japan within the next ten years is not a contingency seriously to be apprehended', but he was unwilling to go so far as to advise that no preparations for a Far Eastern war were needed in this period. After a lengthy deliberation, the committee ruled that for the next decade the Admiralty did not need to prepare to dispatch to Singapore a 'battle fleet, with cruisers, flotillas, and all ancillary vessels superior in strength, or at least equal, to the sea-going Navy of Japan'.[21] This effectively established a new 'ten-year rule', but only, it should be noted, to cover naval preparations for war with Japan before 1935. The CID was not prepared, however, to leave Britain's Far Eastern interests undefended indefinitely, and allowed the Admiralty to continue its long-term projects as insurance against a Japanese threat in the more distant future. It therefore approved a new definition of the one-power standard including the provision that arrangements should be made 'from time to time in different parts of the world, according as the international situation requires, to enable the local naval forces to maintain the situation against vital and irreparable damage pending the arrival of the main fleet, and to give the main fleet on arrival sufficient mobility'. The Singapore naval base and the oil fuel programme were thus enshrined as an integral part of the one-power standard.[22]

In view of the prevailing opinion in Whitehall regarding the possibility of war against Japan, this was a significant accomplishment for the navy. The compromise was also acceptable to Churchill, who did not wish to cancel the Singapore naval base and oil fuel programmes outright. Where he hoped to achieve substantial economies was by reducing the navy's new construction programmes. The Admiralty was unwilling to concede defeat on this issue, however, and continued to defend its long-term building programme vigorously before Birkenhead's committee. The limitations of the new ten-year rule soon became apparent. In the absence of an unambiguous Cabinet declaration that the rule took precedence over the one-power standard, Beatty continued to defend the navy's construction programme on the grounds that the Admiralty had a duty to maintain the latter, and that Churchill's proposals could not be reconciled with it. The government, he maintained in June 1925, must therefore either renounce the standard, build the ships the navy demanded, or 'tell the Admiralty that they are incapable of doing their job and get someone else to do it for them'.[23]

Churchill complained that Beatty was taking an unreasonable position. The Admiralty should not tell the government that it 'must raise from Parliament whatever money you require, or else you must recognise that your British Empire cannot be defended'. It was absurd, he suggested, to claim that 'the question whether the British Empire is to be adequately defended or not' depends 'upon whether there are 4 cruisers in this year or whether you drop one year behind':

> In these matters, when you come to deal with this great mass of cruisers and the great problem attaching to it, it is admittedly a question of degree—with the 4 cruisers the Admiralty profoundly say 'Britannia rules the waves'; without 4 cruisers 'We are at the mercy of Japan'. I am sure that is not a true picture of the case.[24]

The committee's final report sided with Churchill and the Treasury. When the Cabinet met on 15 July, only a handful of ministers supported the navy. With neither side willing to make substantial concessions, the Admiralty fully expected the government to decide against it, in which event Beatty and the rest of the Board were prepared to resign. Eager once more to avert a crisis, Baldwin proposed a compromise on 22 July that both sides were willing to accept.[25] Four new cruisers were to be laid down in the current year, but substantial savings would be achieved by starting work on these ships as late as possible. Another three cruisers were approved for the following year. In return, the Admiralty agreed to search for offsetting economies.

This was a clear setback for Churchill and the Treasury. Despite the consensus within the Cabinet over the lack of any immediate danger from Japan *and* the establishment of a fresh ten-year rule aimed explicitly at the navy's preparations for a Far Eastern war, they failed either to control naval expenditure or eliminate a shipbuilding programme that had been rejected by a major Cabinet subcommittee. Still, the Admiralty's position was considerably weaker than it appeared. It had only been able to outmanoeuvre Churchill over the cruiser question by exploiting backbench Conservative support for the navy and threatening mass resignations. These heavy-handed tactics alienated not only the Treasury but also many of the navy's potential supporters.[26] As long as the government was broadly in agreement with Churchill's assessment of the international situation, of Britain's naval requirements, and of the mood of the electorate, the Treasury was in a strong position to dominate the formulation of British strategic policy.

If Treasury officials were pleased by the force and skill that the new Chancellor had deployed against the Admiralty, they were likely disappointed over his unwillingness to adopt their position on all defence issues. P. J. Grigg, Churchill's principal private secretary at the Treasury, observed in May 1925 that his chief was not as 'malleable' as either Sir Robert Horne or Philip Snowden, two recent chancellors.[27] The most obvious disagreement between Churchill and his advisers was over the Singapore naval base. Treasury officials shared Churchill's optimistic views about Japan and his doubts about the feasibility of the Admiralty's war plans, but they were more willing to sacrifice British interests in the Far East if the cost of defending them seemed prohibitively high.[28] Officials had opposed the construction of a naval base at Singapore when the idea was first raised, and repeatedly pressed for its cancellation after the Cabinet approved it.[29] Churchill, on the other hand, remained committed in principle to the project, although he insisted that it was 'a purely defensive measure from the point of view of the British Empire'. It would be a link 'in Britain's inter-Imperial communications, and one of the great guarantees we can give to our Australasian Dominions', but he had warned the navy in January 1925 not to expect it to serve 'as a jumping off ground to attack Japan in her own home waters'.[30]

It was the Admiralty's determination to use the Singapore naval base as the cornerstone of an offensive strategy against Japan, not its desire to possess such a base, that increasingly frustrated Churchill. He complained to the CID in July 1926 that 'If he had foreseen that the decision to develop a base at Singapore would be used as a gigantic excuse for building up armaments and that this country would then be invited to pour out money with a view to conducting war at the other end of the world, he would never have agreed to the development of this base.'[31] But he never sought to cancel it, as some historians have claimed.[32] When one of his officials suggested in 1927 that Japan might be persuaded to reduce its fleet significantly in return for the termination of the Singapore base, Churchill immediately dismissed the idea. 'I am sure that [such an offer] would be met with a blank refusal,' he wrote in May of that year. 'The Australasian position wd be considered decisive. We must link the Empire together. The public declarations are explicit. None more than mine.'[33]

Churchill and his officials did agree, however, that no opportunity should be lost to economize on this massive project. When the Singapore naval base came up for discussion at the CID in January 1925, Churchill pushed for the establishment of a new subcommittee, with himself as a member, to look into the site of the base, its defences, and the timetable for completion.[34] The resulting committee rejected Churchill's proposal to relocate the base in order to take advantage of existing commercial facilities at Singapore's Keppel Harbour, but its deliberations soon stalled due to inter-service disagreement over the base's defences. Churchill and the Treasury sided with the Air Ministry in the ensuing 'guns-*vs*-planes' debate, believing that an enlarged role for the RAF would ultimately lead to significant savings.[35]

Discussion of Singapore's defences dragged on until the following year, when an offer from the Federated Malay States to contribute £2 million towards the cost of the naval base facilitated a compromise. This prompted the Admiralty to begin lobbying for a decision on the facilities to be provided at Singapore. The Admiralty's plans division estimated the cost of a fully equipped base at £11 million, plus an additional £3.25 million for defences. Realizing that this scheme had little chance of obtaining approval in the current economic climate, the Sea Lords proposed instead a 'truncated scheme' in July 1926, with an estimated cost of £7.75 million, excluding defences.[36] The Admiralty's modified proposals were approved by the CID in July 1926, with no opposition from Churchill being recorded.[37]

By rejecting Churchill's offer to stabilize naval spending at £60 million per annum, the Admiralty ensured that no part of its annual estimates would be safe from Treasury scrutiny. One area in which the navy was vulnerable was the oil reserve programme, which could only be justified by the threat of war with a first-class power. The Admiralty had been building up fuel supplies for several years in order to obtain a reserve equal to one year's consumption in wartime. This objective was first approved by the Cabinet in 1919, and had been enshrined in the one-power standard adopted in 1925. The government's Oil Fuel Board estimated that over 7 million tons of fuel would be required to meet this goal, and the Admiralty intended to accumulate this amount by 1935, when the ten-year ruling of the previous year would no longer apply. Churchill, intent on securing some savings, maintained that a six-month supply of fuel would be sufficient, and could be accumulated at a slower pace than the Admiralty proposed. With the international situation becoming, 'if anything, more favourable', the navy found itself isolated once again. The prime minister suggested a reduction in the service's annual fuel programme from 330,000 tons to 100,000 tons. Beatty insisted that this would threaten the mobility of the fleet in wartime and was inconsistent with the one-power standard, but the committee was intent on economy and the proposal was accepted.[38]

The navy estimates for 1926 were settled at £58 million, and Churchill hoped that the following year's estimates could be kept down by once again delaying new construction until the end of the fiscal year. He was also becoming concerned about the effect of the Admiralty's cruiser programmes on Britain's rivals. In December 1926 he suggested to the First Lord that slowing down new construction in 1927 would 'have a beneficial effect in chilling off Japanese, and still more American, competition':

> It is a profound interest of Britain to keep the naval temperature low. The damnable thing is that they [foreign powers] all want to have navies now, instead of leaving it to us who managed so well and behaved so well for a hundred years of supremacy. The smallest turn on the side of diminution and retardation will, I am sure, bring about favourable reactions.[39]

The Chancellor, well aware of the persistent agitation for greater naval construction on the other side of the Atlantic, was especially concerned about sparking a costly and acrimonious arms race with the United States. He admitted that the Americans possessed a strong case for building up their cruiser strength, given the higher levels of British and Japanese construction since the First World War. But he did not believe that the Coolidge administration really wished to adopt a large construction programme, and he worried that it might use the *threat* of a naval race to wring concessions from the British. 'I am not prepared to accept dictation from the United States,' Churchill declared to Bridgeman, 'and if they attempt to bully us by threatening a large programme, I shall hope to be able to range myself with you and Beatty as to the manner in which such a threat should be dealt with.'[40]

The Treasury and the Admiralty had no difficulty settling the Navy Estimates for 1927 at £58 million, and the government would probably not have taken much further notice of naval matters that year if a new naval disarmament conference had not been set to open in Geneva in June.[41] It was hoped that this tripartite conference between Britain, Japan, and the United States would lead to an agreement to limit naval armaments not already covered by the Washington Treaty. New opportunities to reduce naval expenditure seemed to beckon, and Churchill was initially impressed by the Admiralty's arms-control proposals. Naval leaders were genuinely interested in securing a deal to limit naval armaments. They appreciated better than anyone that heavy increases in naval spending would face strong opposition from the government; international arms control presented a means to reduce expenditure without undermining Britain's strategic position.[42] It was also clear to many that if things were bad under Churchill, they would be much worse if Labour returned to power. As Rear Admiral Dudley Pound, the Assistant Chief of the Naval Staff (ACNS), noted at the time, the navy estimates 'will automatically in a few years reach a total which it does not seem within the bounds of possibility that we should be able to screw out of any Gov^t'. The Naval Staff hoped that by getting 'something concrete out of this conference it may make things considerably easier for the Admiralty when the next non-Conservative Government comes in'.[43]

The Admiralty's proposals for the conference were outlined by Bridgeman and Beatty at the CID on 20 May 1927.[44] With battleship construction expected to resume in 1931 under the terms of the Washington Treaty, naval leaders hoped to secure long-term economies by extending the life of capital ships beyond the existing limits; by reducing the tonnage and armament of capital ships below the Washington Treaty levels; and by imposing a variety of restrictions on smaller classes of warships. The future of the 10,000 ton, 8-inch-gun cruisers permitted by the Washington Treaty was a matter of particular concern. These ships were so expensive that they appeared to threaten Britain's ability to maintain a total cruiser force of seventy ships. The Naval Staff concluded that smaller cruisers, which could be built in greater numbers, would better serve Britain's interests. The Admiralty opposed quantitative restrictions to this type of ship, but it was willing to accept parity with the United States in the more expensive 'Washington Treaty' cruisers. At the same time, it recommended quantitative limits for these vessels, which it hoped eventually to phase out entirely.

Churchill considered these proposals 'more admirably broadminded than those put forward by any previous Board of Admiralty', and hoped that they would mark real progress towards 'economy and world peace'.[45] However, shortly after the Geneva Conference opened on 20 June, it became clear that the United States' representatives were determined to achieve parity with Britain in all classes of warships on terms favourable to themselves. Cruisers quickly became the most serious obstacle to an agreement.

The Americans proposed to limit this class by total tonnage, but the figures they suggested were so low (250,000–400,000 tons) that Britain would have been left far short of the seventy cruisers the Admiralty considered essential for British security.

Churchill watched carefully as the Geneva Conference began to unfold and was alarmed by both the British and American bargaining positions. In an uncirculated Cabinet memorandum of 25 June, he denounced what he termed 'three monstrous fallacies' underlying the negotiations at Geneva.[46] The first was the 'Anglo-Japanese "War Scare"', on which,' he asserted, 'the Admiralty extorted the last four annual cruiser programmes'. Another fallacy, he maintained, was the 'Admiralty 70 cruiser guarantee for our food supply':

> 70 cruisers are not an absolute standard for the British Empire. If others have none, they are too much. If others have equal, or even half as many, they are too few. The largest part of the problem is relative. Lines of communication cannot be guaranteed in terms of cruisers. Not five to one superiority would master in the fox and geese game. Convoy for merchant ships would be imperative, and for convoy guards quite different types of ships than these costly cruisers would be required.

The Treasury had always disputed the Admiralty's claim for seventy cruisers, and Churchill was clearly worried that if this figure gained general acceptance as a result of the Geneva Conference he would have a harder time limiting future construction programmes.

Churchill's third 'fallacy' was potentially the most serious: the American desire to secure by treaty numerical parity with Britain in all classes of warship. For this development Churchill held the Admiralty ultimately to blame: Britain's large cruiser programmes, justified 'on the fictitious Anglo-Japanese war scare,' had naturally 'roused the Americans to their present attitude'. He derided the idea that the United States was entitled to 'absolute numerical parity' in cruisers, but he recognized that if the Americans ever decided 'to build up to it', Britain would be condemned 'to permanent naval inferiority'.

Parity quickly became the main point of contention at Geneva. The American government and public suspected that the British were attempting to force them to accept continued inferiority in cruisers. Concerned that the conference might break down over this question, the government instructed Bridgeman and Lord Cecil, Britain's delegates, that it was desirable on diplomatic grounds to make a public statement that 'while we mean to build cruisers up to our needs, we lay down no conditions limiting [US] cruisers to a similar number'.[47] This was not done without serious misgiving in some quarters. Naval leaders held that numerical parity between Britain and the United States in auxiliary warships would put the latter in a superior strategic position since Britain relied on access to the sea lanes for its survival and the United States did not. In wartime, most of Britain's cruisers would have to be dispersed for the protection of essential maritime communications, but the majority of American cruisers could be concentrated for offensive operations.

Churchill agreed with this assessment: there could 'really be no parity,' he declared in a Cabinet memorandum, 'between a Power whose Navy is its life and a Power whose Navy is only for prestige. Parity for the former is supremacy for the latter.' He also expressed a less conciliatory attitude towards the United States than he had in 1921, urging his colleagues 'not to be disturbed by unjust American irritation, nor let them feel that we shall make haste to obey their will'. Britain, he noted, had conceded parity in capital ships at Washington, sacrificed the Anglo-Japanese Alliance, and given in to the United States over the settlement of war debts, but these concessions 'have only resulted in new assertions and demands on their part. It always seems that it is our duty to humour the United States and minister to their vanity. They do nothing for us in return, but exact their last pound of flesh.'[48]

These sentiments were widely shared. By 1927 many leading figures in Whitehall had become frustrated by the steady demands from the United States for concessions, and the continuing anti-British sentiment emanating from there despite repeated gestures of British goodwill. Hankey, for example, concluded that Britain was 'less popular and more abused in America than ever before, because they think us weak....I would refuse either to be blackmailed or browbeaten.' Similarly, Bridgeman complained in 1928 that it was a 'fatal policy to be running after the U.S.A. It makes them despise us, and ask for more. I wish there was a little more of the Palmerston touch at the F.O. He at any rate knew how to behave to a bully.' Even the prime minister, in Beatty's opinion, was 'imbued with a total distrust of the United States'.[49]

A further pronouncement on parity, this time delivered to the US State Department, was initially blocked by the Admiralty, with Churchill's support, but in the end the British ambassador in Washington was instructed to restate Britain's commitment to parity.[50] These declarations did not improve the situation in Geneva, however. The American delegates insisted that they would not accept a figure greater than 400,000 tons for cruisers, which would prevent Britain coming anywhere near its ambitions for seventy cruisers. To make matters worse, the delegates indicated that the United

States wanted to build twenty-five of the large 'treaty cruisers', which the British were hoping to phase out, and that the balance of their cruisers would be armed with 8-inch guns even if they were of lower displacement than the 10,000 tons permitted by the Washington Treaty.[51] In this case, even small American cruisers would outgun their British counterparts.

These proposals were discussed by the CID on 7 July.[52] Beatty doubted that any agreement would be possible on terms acceptable to Britain 'in the present temper of the United States'. Limiting cruisers by tonnage, he warned, would force Britain to restructure its cruiser force completely. Large numbers of small cruisers would have to be scrapped in order to 'build bigger and better ships, so as to ensure a measure of equality with the Fleets of the other two principal Naval Powers'. As Britain possessed only fourteen 'treaty cruisers', the American proposals would also mean the construction of eleven more of these expensive and unwanted ships. 'In this way,' he concluded, 'the needs of economy would not only be disserved, but considerable additional expenditure would be incurred.'[53]

Churchill came down firmly against any agreement along the lines proposed by the United States. 'To become entangled in an undesirable set of conditions and limitations would be much worse,' he insisted, 'than a breakdown of the Conference.' In this event, the United States might embark on a large cruiser programme, although this was not certain, given the domestic opposition such a programme would generate. Furthermore, as the Japanese would feel threatened by any large American naval programme, Britain and Japan might find themselves drawing closer together. Churchill had rejected the idea of relying on Japan as a substitute for competitive building with the United States in 1921 when Lloyd George had proposed it, but he now reversed his position. '[T]he fact that relations between Japan and Great Britain were becoming closer would cause America to reflect,' he predicted. Britain could therefore afford to view a large American cruiser programme 'with outward equanimity'. And if the Anglo-Japanese Alliance could be renewed, there would be no need to match new United States construction. Churchill therefore argued that Britain should 'resolutely refuse to accept any binding limitations' on smaller cruisers: 'We should publicly announce our intention of building as few of these cruisers as possible, having regard to our commitments for the protection of our trade, and that we would never consent to any conditions which fettered our freedom in this direction.'

Austen Chamberlain, the Foreign Secretary, disagreed with Churchill's predictions. He feared that the American public would blame Britain for the breakdown of the conference and unite behind a large building programme. In this event, Britain must either match American construction or abandon the one-power standard. 'Either alternative,' he remarked, 'would be deplorable.' There was a general consensus within the committee, however, that the American proposals could not be accepted as they stood, and that the risk of offending American opinion would have to be run. The CID therefore united behind an Admiralty scheme to distinguish between the large treaty cruisers and the smaller ones required for protecting imperial communications. In the former class, Bridgeman was instructed to 'assent to a basis of equality with the United States'. In the latter, committee members insisted that they could not 'surrender our freedom of action, and we do not question the right of other countries to decide at their discretion upon their own requirements'. Thus, Britain would not deny the *right* of the United States to numerical parity in smaller cruisers, but would not voluntarily reduce its strength to a level convenient to its rival.[54]

Churchill, like the Admiralty, consistently advocated a firm line. 'Parity in cruisers for us meant supremacy for the United States,' he insisted later in July, 'and they should not be allowed to obtain this supremacy so easily.' If the United States really wanted to become the leading naval power, it should be made to do so by its own exertions rather than through British concessions. But he still did not think the Americans would be prepared to pay the bill:

> I believe they would blow off steam in a few programmes of aggressive cruisers, and that if we lay quiet and calm and studied scientific improvements we should find in a few years a strong reaction in the United States against unnecessary expenditure and a strong revival of Anglo-Japanese association. Anyhow, it is a very long business. Supreme Navies cannot be made at a stroke of a wand or the signing of a cheque … Why should we sacrifice our title-deeds to save them the embarrassments which properly attend a wrongful national assertion?[55]

Churchill was thus perfectly willing to *reduce* British naval building in the event that the conference failed so as to give the Americans no additional reason to lay down new ships. This would be difficult to accomplish, however, if the Admiralty's claim to possess seventy cruisers by 1936 gained currency. Churchill had noted his opposition to this figure on several occasions, but had not pressed for a decision on the issue. On 14 July he reminded the CID that the Cabinet had not yet approved any cruisers for the period after

1929, and insisted that the question of construction in subsequent years would have to be carefully considered. 'Our naval policy for future years should have a most searching examination,' he suggested, 'not across the table in that room [in Geneva], but in a manner similar to that adopted in 1925 when the Naval Programme Committee was set up.'

In the same meeting Beatty, hoping to avoid a debate in which the Admiralty stood only to lose ground, noted that the seventy-cruiser programme had in fact been tacitly accepted by the government as part of the Admiralty's original proposals for the Geneva Conference.[56] The next day Barstow confirmed for Churchill that this was in fact the case.[57] From Churchill's perspective, therefore, the Geneva Conference was fast becoming a no-win situation. The American proposals for naval limitation might ultimately threaten Britain's security, and would undoubtedly involve increased expenditure rather than economies; the British proposals, on the other hand, probably would secure some long-term economies, but would bind Britain to a large programme of new cruiser construction. In these circumstances, the breakdown of the conference seemed increasingly desirable. Churchill believed this would be preferable to further negotiations, which could only result, he predicted a few days later, in 'large programmes, naval inferiority, and handcuffs'.[58]

His was not the only voice expressing reservations. At a special Cabinet committee formed on 15 July to consider the treaty negotiations, Chamberlain stated that the government 'did not admit a moral right to parity in small Cruisers', but had only recognized that if the United States 'insisted in building to parity we could not prevent it.' Similarly, Balfour noted that 'We did not in our hearts think that we could prevent the Americans building to parity if they insisted, but we were not willing to embody the doctrine in a Treaty.'[59] The government was thus determined to remain firm on the question of cruiser parity. New instructions from Baldwin to the British delegates in Geneva, dispatched on 15 July, insisted that Britain could not 'admit by treaty that in regard to small cruisers the case of the British Empire resembles other Powers; or that parity of numbers means parity of strength.' Bridgeman was told not to bind Britain 'to any arrangement which placed us in a position of permanent inferiority'.[60] In other words, Britain must retain the right to build as many small cruisers as were necessary to ensure its security.

The British delegates in Geneva were 'rather surprised and not a little perturbed' by this telegram, feeling that the government was attempting to go back on its assurances that Britain did not dispute the United States' right to parity. Churchill and Balfour insisted, however, that the delegates had misunderstood their instructions.[61] In a lengthy memorandum of 20 July, Churchill charged that the British delegates at Geneva had unwisely committed Britain 'to the principle of absolute parity by treaty, although such a principle is fatal to British naval security'. He also outlined for the first time the strategic dangers of accepting full parity with the United States:

> No doubt it is quite right in the interests of peace to go on talking about war with the United States being 'unthinkable'. Everyone knows that this is not true. However foolish and disastrous such a war would be, it is in fact, the only basis upon which the Naval discussions at Geneva are proceeding. We do not wish to put ourselves in the power of the United States. We cannot tell what they might do if at some future date they were in a position to give us orders about our policy, say, in India, or Egypt, or Canada, or on any other behind which their electioneering forces were marshalled. Moreover, tonnage parity means Britain can be starved into obedience to any American decree. I would neither trust America to command, nor England to submit. Evidently on the basis of American Naval superiority speciously disguised as parity immense dangers overhang the future of the world.

On 19 June Bridgeman and Cecil were recalled to London for consultation.[62] Inside the Cabinet, Churchill's hardline position found broad support. With the exception of Cecil, ministers saw no compelling reason to compromise British security in order to appease the United States. The two delegates returned to Geneva armed with a modified set of proposals, but as these set a high total tonnage figure for cruisers and restricted smaller cruisers to 6-inch guns, they were unlikely to appeal to the Americans.[63]

The different strategic requirements of the United States and Britain in cruisers proved to be a fatal obstacle: the Geneva Conference broke up on 4 August 1927 without any agreement being reached. Cecil, frustrated by his colleagues' unwillingness to compromise on the cruiser issue, resigned from the Cabinet in protest. Churchill was sorry to see him depart, but must have been satisfied in all other respects.[64] The Admiralty certainly had no regrets. Bridgeman professed to be happy to have avoided 'an agreement which might not be wholly to our advantage. I am pretty sure that the Americans never meant to agree to anything unless it gave them parity on the cheap or was humiliation to us.' Beatty, who retired as First Sea Lord shortly before the conference concluded, was also delighted that the United States had been unable to achieve 'command of the sea at no cost. Every nation in the history of the world,' he reflected, 'has only obtained Sea Power as the result of great achievements and the price of many lives and much money. The D – – – – D Yanks thought they could get it for nothing!!'[65]

The navy had little time to enjoy its victory. The failure of the disarmament conference meant that serious thought had to be given to Churchill's idea of curtailing cruiser construction so that tempers in the United States could cool down. On 4 August, while the First Lord was still in Geneva, the Cabinet assented to a new inquiry into future naval construction.[66] Churchill hoped to eliminate the three cruisers authorized for the 1927–8 programme and the three projected for the subsequent year. Treasury officials believed their chief should go further and seek additional reductions in other classes of ship, but Churchill would only agree to reopen the question of the navy's oil fuel reserves.[67] Bridgeman was incensed when he learned how far Churchill proposed to go and refused to consider dropping ships from a programme that had been approved by the Cabinet in 1925.[68] When no agreement could be reached in inter-departmental discussions, Churchill insisted in November 1927 that the matter be referred to a new Naval Programme Committee.[69]

This body, which was chaired, like its predecessor in 1925, by Lord Birkenhead, began its deliberations on 10 November.[70] Churchill wisely emphasized the impact that dropping cruisers from each of the 1927 and 1928 construction programmes would have on the United States. 'If anything could soothe down the American attitude; if anything could have the effect of removing the pressure on the President and give him a chance to follow a sane policy, it would be that,' he insisted. Churchill buttressed his case with assurances that his proposals would not endanger British interests. By 1931, he noted, Britain would possess more than a 25 per cent superiority over the United States and Japan *combined* in cruiser strength even if no new construction were undertaken. He also attacked the Admiralty's claims that Britain must build cruisers in large numbers prior to the resumption of capital-ship construction after 1931 so as to moderate the navy estimates during later years. As in 1919 and 1925, Churchill insisted that new warships should not be built when there was no clear threat on the horizon. The cruisers the Admiralty wanted would be 'wasting from the moment of construction,' he warned, 'because they would be obsolete or half obsolete before the time arrived when they would be really needed'.[71]

The Admiralty's defence of its cruiser programme avoided most of the issues raised by the Chancellor. Admiral Sir Charles Madden, Beatty's successor as First Sea Lord, insisted that Britain had an exceptionally large need for cruisers; that its requirements in this class could not be measured strictly in relation to the strength of other powers; that a minimum of seventy cruisers was essential; and that the Treasury's proposals would put Britain's security at risk. Churchill vigorously challenged the last two assertions. He reminded the committee that he was not proposing to cease new cruiser construction altogether. 'No one in their senses would ever suggest that,' he insisted. The only issue was how Britain could replace its existing fleet 'with the least possible cost and burden to the taxpayer'. The choice was not 'between letting the bottom fall out of the British Navy, on the one hand, and building excessive strength, on the other. The proposal is to arrive at a just rate of building new ships to replace the old ones.'[72] Britain, he argued, was far enough ahead of its rivals in cruisers that it could afford to reduce its programme for two years without incurring any risks.

Churchill also refused to accept the Admiralty's claim to seventy cruisers. The Admiralty strongly disagreed, but could only point to Britain's clear need for a large number of these ships to protect trade in the event of a Far Eastern war. These requirements were virtually impossible to quantify, however.[73] Churchill maintained that Britain's present superiority over Japan was sufficient for all purposes. Madden, on the other hand, insisted that Japan would be a more difficult adversary than Germany because it had easier access to British trade routes. Hence, a greater margin of superiority in cruisers was necessary. To reinforce this point, the First Sea Lord referred to Churchill's *World Crisis*, noting that a relatively small force of eight or nine German cruisers had tied down seventy British and Allied cruisers during the First World War.[74]

This did not have the desired effect. Madden now appeared to be contradicting his claims that the number of cruisers required for trade defence could be measured in absolute terms. Churchill immediately denounced his 'completely false argument':

At the present time, he tells us, we have 54 cruisers, while Japan has 30. If it takes 70 cruisers to hunt down 9, 54 seems a very small allowance for hunting down 30. As a matter of fact, this comparable figure, which I have worked out here, is 233 ⅓. If we assume that we require such an enormous superiority in

cruisers to hunt down the raiding cruisers of Japan, which we found necessary
in the war, then the Admiralty should not ask for 50 or 60 or 70, but for nearly
250 cruisers.

The Chancellor insisted that the solution to Japanese raiders was not to
build a virtually unlimited number of cruisers, but to adopt a policy of convoy, for which different ships were required.

When the committee met on 1 December to reach a decision, its members unanimously backed Churchill. The only part of the Admiralty's case
that made any impression was the need to minimize disruption in the British shipbuilding industry. It was essential, Birkenhead stated, that Britain
maintain its ability to build ships better and faster than its rivals in an emergency. As long as Britain's 'dockyards and other establishments were kept up
to date we should always be in a position to prepare any time for any danger
which might arise'. Neville Chamberlain, the Minister of Health, agreed.
Without a steady shipbuilding programme, he warned, the dockyards would
become inefficient and skilled workers 'would drift off elsewhere'. If the
United States decided to compete with Britain, there would 'be a big
demand for skilled craftsmen in America, and our best dockyard hands
would migrate there and would not return. If this happened our boasted
supremacy would have vanished for good.'[75]

The committee's report on cruisers was a clear victory for the Chancellor. It recommended dropping two of these vessels from the current year's
programme and one more the following year. The three cruisers approved
for 1929 would not be affected. On the question of seventy cruisers, the
committee lamented that this figure 'has become public property in consequence of the course of events at the Geneva Naval Conference', but was
not prepared to disavow it entirely, advising only that it should be 'referred
to as little as possible'.[76]

Having soundly defeated the navy on the cruiser question, Churchill
immediately took aim at its 1928 estimates. The Admiralty had proposed a
figure of £58,330,000, but the Chancellor insisted on no more than £56
million, claiming that the Admiralty had not taken full account of the
favourable international situation, 'especially as regards Japan', or the government's decision that no great war 'need be anticipated for at least ten
years'.[77] Bridgeman denied this charge, but there was much truth in it.[78]
The Admiralty continued to prepare as best it could for a major war with
Japan, despite repeated instructions not to do so. The ten-year rule was

simply ignored by Admiralty officials, who, when challenged, interpreted it to mean that the navy must complete its preparations for a Far Eastern conflict by 1935, when the ten-year period laid down in 1925 would expire.[79]

The Chancellor's frustration over Japan's continuing prominence in the navy's calculations was shared by his subordinates. Treasury officials' minutes on the proposed navy estimates for 1928 showed their exasperation with what they regarded as the navy's 'stubborn unhelpfulness' and 'unstinted lavishness'.[80] The navy's attitude was also contrasted unfavourably with that of the army.[81] The War Office had requested a Cabinet declaration in July 1927 that the ten-year rule should be extended to cover a European war, 'and that the immediate plans of the Army should be based upon prepared-ness for an extra-European war'.[82] The army's willingness to abide by this Cabinet decision fuelled the Treasury's irritation with what it correctly saw as the Admiralty's 'refusal to acknowledge the government policy of "peace for 10 years"'[83] According to A. C. Waterfield of the Treasury's supply depart-ment, it was 'simply perversion of facts' for Bridgeman to claim that the 1928 estimates conformed to the ten-year rule. 'The Admiralty,' he com-plained in January of that year, 'are not talking the same language as the Government.'[84]

When the Naval Programme Committee discussed the oil fuel reserve in February 1928, the Chancellor again denounced 'the great Japanese war bogey', which, he claimed, had been created by Beatty in 1920–1 'with a view to supplying the necessary stimulus on which naval estimates, naval expansion and naval supplies could be based'. Everything, he insisted, 'excludes a war between England and Japan from the sphere of reasonable probability'.[85] The Naval Programme Committee rejected the Admiralty's plans to purchase 330,000 tons of oil fuel for the navy's annual reserve in 1928, and for the third consecutive year the figure was reduced to 100,000 tons.[86] Other economies were worked out by Admiralty and Treasury offi-cials, who finally settled on a sum of £57.3 million for the upcoming year.

Even so, Churchill and his advisers were not pleased with the outcome and immediately determined to bring future naval expenditure more firmly under control by enforcing their interpretation of the ten-year rule. Before the 1928 navy estimates had even been submitted to Parliament, Churchill informed Bridgeman that he hoped to create a new Cabinet committee to examine the 1929 estimates.[87] The main point of contention was the Admiralty's insistence that the ten-year rule of 1925 required it to be ready for a major war by 1935.

In inter-departmental discussions over the 1928 estimates, Captain Ernle Chatfield, the navy's Controller (responsible for naval materiel), maintained that the Admiralty had never been told anything different. Churchill's view, however, was that 'the end of the 10 years was continually receding'.[88] The Treasury informed the Admiralty in March 1928 that the Admiralty's interpretation was 'out of harmony with repeated decisions of His Majesty's Government under which the "ten years period" is renewed from year to year, and should now be regarded as running until 1938 at least'.[89]

This question was taken up by the CID on 5 July 1928. Austen Chamberlain was Churchill's strongest supporter. He warned that the Foreign Office could not guarantee its prediction about the possibility of war, but nevertheless accepted that the ten-year rule could be a useful tool. '[I]n framing defence policies,' he stated, 'a compromise always had to be adopted':

> The desirability of certain measures as represented by the Service Departments stood on the one hand, and the need for husbanding our resources in peace so that we might be in a position to meet the difficulties of war lay on the other. It rested with the Cabinet to decide where that compromise should be drawn.

Chamberlain did not oppose a renewal of the rule, provided that it was merely a guide for framing the service estimates. As a safeguard, he suggested that the hypothesis should be reconsidered each year, and that the fighting services should have the opportunity of raising any concerns about the ten-year period at any time. This opinion was generally shared by the committee.

Bridgeman and Madden did not attempt to defend either the Admiralty's interpretation of the ten-year rule or its assessment of the Japanese threat. Instead, they fell back on the old argument that the rule could not be allowed to interfere with the maintenance of the one-power standard. This prompted a rebuke from Chamberlain, who declared that the Cabinet, rather than the Board of Admiralty, was ultimately responsible for determining whether the standard was being jeopardized. A short time later, the Foreign Secretary struck the final blow to the Admiralty's hopes by providing another optimistic survey of international affairs, which identified the Soviet Union as the only likely threat to British interests over the next decade. The prime minister supported Chamberlain's recommendations, and the committee recommended in July that 'it should be assumed, for the purpose of framing the Estimates of the Fighting Services, that at any given date there will be no major war for ten years'. This decision was to be reviewed annually by the CID, and could be challenged at any time by any department or dominion.[90]

Churchill had every reason to be pleased with this outcome. His interpretation of the ten-year rule obtained official endorsement at the highest level, and in the process was extended to cover all three services and all potential major conflicts. Treasury officials expected more naval reductions to follow. Sir Warren Fisher, the Permanent Secretary, remarked optimistically in November that 'Our margin in naval strength, the absence of anyone to fight at sea, the Cabinet instruction about no "major" war, the Kellog[-Briand] Pact [for the renunciation of war], & our financial situation seem to me to provide in the aggregate an overwhelming argument for a drastic cut in naval expenditure.'[91] For once, all factors seemed to be aligned in the Treasury's favour. Churchill resumed his pressure on the Admiralty in late July 1928, calling for cuts to reserves of armaments and naval stores.[92]

The First Lord was justifiably irritated by what he regarded as the Treasury's propensity 'to try to put off indefinitely even the most inevitable naval expenditure, vaguely imagining that we could redeem our position by a great intensive effort at some future time'. This policy, in his view, was 'open to strong practical objections', as it would 'inevitably lead to the disappearance of the very organisations, skilled designers and workmen whose assistance we should require in order to recover ourselves when the need arose'.[93] The Treasury, however, was unmoved. After months of bargaining, the 1929 estimates were finally settled at £55,865,000—a figure nearly £1.5 million below the previous year, and over £4.5 million lower than 1925.[94]

Throughout these deliberations, Churchill kept a close watch on the state of Anglo-American relations. In January 1928, as the Treasury's attack on that year's navy estimates was intensifying, he instructed Treasury officials to be ready to compromise with the Admiralty at any moment. 'I am worried,' he stated, 'about the Navy in view of the Yankee menace.'[95] The surge in American animosity towards Britain following the breakup of the Geneva Conference also demanded the attention of the Foreign Office and the Cabinet. The former rejected Churchill's view that no dramatic action was required and that Anglo-American relations would gradually improve on their own accord. The Foreign Secretary and his advisers were particularly eager to avert any further deterioration in relations during upcoming negotiations for a new arbitration treaty with the United States, which would raise the touchy subject of maritime belligerent rights. Britain's interference with American trade during the First World War had caused considerable bitterness in the United States, but President Woodrow Wilson's efforts to establish 'freedom of the seas' for neutral shipping in wartime had been blocked by the British during the Paris Peace Conference in 1919. The Foreign Secretary, hoping that concessions to the United States on the question of belligerent rights would lead to an improvement in Anglo-American relations, convinced the prime minister to set up a CID Belligerent Rights subcommittee to examine this question.

Opinion within the subcommittee was sharply divided.[96] When meetings began in January 1928, the Admiralty and Hankey strongly opposed any concessions that might limit Britain's ability in wartime to apprehend and search neutral ships and seize contraband cargoes. This insistence on 'high' belligerent rights stemmed from a conviction within the navy that economic pressure exercised through maritime blockade had historically been one of the most powerful weapons in Britain's arsenal; that it had been a decisive factor in securing Germany's defeat in the First World War; and that it would continue to be a valuable offensive weapon in future conflicts, especially against Japan.[97] Foreign Office officials, on the other hand, believed that because Britain could not hope to impose any future blockade in the face of American opposition, some concessions to the United States' position were unavoidable and desirable.

Churchill, who was not a member of the Belligerent Rights subcommittee, was also inclined to think that Britain would be sacrificing little by making concessions to the Americans in this area. Unlike naval leaders of this period, the Chancellor was unimpressed by the impact of the economic blockade in the last war. In a long memorandum to Hankey in February 1928, he argued that the primary offensive role of sea power was not economic pressure, but rather the 'transport of invading armies and their maintenance overseas'.[98] Looking back on the experiences of the First World War, Churchill maintained that Britain's first concern in any future conflict would be keeping its own essential trade routes open. This, in his opinion, 'far outweighs the importance of harrying the routes of other people'. Because Britain no longer possessed unchallenged naval supremacy and faced new threats to its commerce from the submarine, it had more to gain than to lose by an agreement limiting belligerent rights. 'In a war between Great Britain and the United States, a convention protecting sea-borne commerce from attack would be of priceless help to a small over-crowded island and scattered Empire, and of equal disadvantage to a self-contained half-continent.' Nor could Britain afford to alienate a neutral United States by enforcing high belligerent rights. 'We must recognise,' Churchill stated:

> that in any future war between Great Britain and a European power, the United States will be the arbiter of the law of the sea. To fight the United States alone, or even with a powerful combination of allies on our side, is a bleak prospect and one that policy should avoid; but to bring them in against us after we had for some time been engaged in a war with a first-class power would be fatal.

The Chancellor also hoped that a compromise on belligerent rights might lessen the United States' desire to build a large navy, although he maintained that Britain's security ultimately depended upon maintaining 'the best and strongest Navy'. This would not be easy to accomplish, he warned Hankey, and Britain must not reduce its naval strength to a level dictated by the United States. The situation would not be hopeless, though, if the US attempted to build a superior navy. 'Although their wealth is greater,' he remarked, 'our needs for a navy are so much more real than theirs that we should probably make far greater sacrifices for sea-power over a long period of time':

> The addition of 20 or even 30 millions a year, which we could easily afford if we had to, would soon carry our fleet to dimensions which the United States could not surpass without encountering the gravest internal problems. At any time when we conceived ourselves to be in danger in consequence of their naval programme, the mere suspension of our debt-payments would subtract 35 millions from their revenues and add it to our own. Even quite a moderate building-programme maintained independently year by year would keep us comfortably ahead for a long time. A stern chase is a long chase; and we ought neither to court it nor to fear it.

But, while confident of the outcome, Churchill still believed that all Britain could hope for 'is just to be a little stronger and a little better at sea than any other country, and to possess only a small fraction of the Fleets of the world'.[99]

Hankey, who took a leading role in the debate over belligerent rights, disagreed with most of these arguments. He shared the Admiralty's overly optimistic view that the blockade of the Central Powers during the First World War had proven the efficacy of economic pressure exercised through sea power. 'Remove the fear of a repetition of that action,' he warned in February 1928, 'and you remove the greatest deterrent to a breach of the peace. Deprive the British Empire of her own peculiar weapon, and—without an army—you reduce her at one stroke to a lower level in the estimation of the world.' The Cabinet Secretary predicted that the United States would probably not be so antagonized by the exercise of Britain's belligerent rights in a future conflict that it would be drawn into hostilities against Britain. It would only be if the United States did 'show herself screwed up to the point of intervention against us' that Britain should 'pipe down and waive some of our rights', but only, he argued, 'for that particular occasion; not today and for all time.'[100]

The deliberations of the Belligerent Rights Subcommittee dragged on for months, during which time the Foreign Office pressed for concessions as the best means to improve Anglo-American relations and pave the way for a settlement of the contentious cruiser question. The Admiralty, Hankey, and Leo Amery, the Secretary of State for Dominion Affairs and a former First Lord, firmly opposed any lessening of Britain's traditional belligerent rights, but the majority of the committee tended to be sympathetic to the Foreign Office's arguments. Before any final decision was reached, Anglo-American relations declined still further as a result of naval arms-control discussions at the League of Nation's Preparatory Commission for the General Disarmament Conference. In the summer of 1928, France agreed to support Britain's position on cruiser limitations—the same position rejected by the Americans at Geneva in 1927—in return for British support on other issues.[101] This agreement, known as the 'Anglo-French compromise', provoked a fresh crisis in Anglo-American relations.

Opinion again divided over the proper British response. While the Foreign Office continued to hope that an agreement with the Americans on belligerent rights would remove the main obstacle to better relations, Churchill disliked giving in to pressure and instinctively sided with hardliners like Bridgeman and Hankey who preferred to take a firm stance. 'It seems to me this is a turning point in our history,' he wrote to Baldwin in September 1928. 'Of course it would be so much easier to "give in" and follow along meekly in the wake of the new English-speaking authority. But I hope we shall try to keep the flag flying.'[102] He sent the prime minister a lengthy note that he hoped might serve as the basis of Britain's formal reply to criticisms from the United States. In this document, Churchill restated Britain's position on cruisers, defended the Anglo-French compromise as a reasonable attempt by Britain and France to further the work of the disarmament conference, and urged that the cause of naval disarmament would be best served by the discontinuation of arms-control negotiations.[103]

When President Coolidge threw his support behind an ambitious new US cruiser programme, the British government became even more alarmed. Churchill, however, refused to panic. He still expected the United States to lose interest in competitive building after a few years; and he felt that the American president-elect, Herbert Hoover, would be easier to deal with than his predecessor. Churchill advised his colleagues against making any immediate concessions on the question of belligerent rights, which he feared might divide 'the Conservative Party from end to end on the eve of the Election'. These recommendations were tied to Churchill's irritation at a recent speech by Coolidge calling for US superiority in cruisers. Coolidge's views, Churchill complained, were those of 'a New England backwoodsman'; and Coolidge himself, he predicted, would soon 'sink back into the obscurity from which only accident extracted him'.

Churchill was still convinced that American 'ill-temper' would eventually disappear if Britain did nothing provocative, and that there was little to gain by making concessions on naval issues. He noted again that Britain had made other sacrifices in the last decade that might have been expected to improve Anglo-American relations, including 'the abrogation of the Anglo-Japanese Alliance, the settlement of the Irish question, the Washington Treaty and the Anglo-American debt settlement'. However, if the failure to reach an agreement at Geneva was enough to destroy American goodwill, it only showed:

> how little advantage is to be gained by making such efforts to conciliate American opinion. Whatever may have been done at enormous cost and sacrifice to keep up friendship is apparently swept away by the smallest little tiff or misunderstanding, and you have to start again and placate the Americans by another batch of substantial or even vital concessions.

He therefore urged a firm stand. 'The great mass of the British public do not desire to see England obsequious to the United States,' he claimed, 'and would be deeply anxious if it were thought the Government were ready to palter with our Naval security.'[104]

Churchill was willing, however, to exploit his colleagues' concerns about the United States to launch one final assault on the navy's cruiser programme. In December 1928 he asked the Cabinet to consider dropping the two ships to be laid down late in the 1928–9 fiscal year, arguing that such a gesture would help to improve Anglo-American relations and reduce defence expenditure on the eve of a general election, a measure that would be popular with voters.[105] The Foreign Office agreed that this action might be desirable, but the majority of the Cabinet supported Baldwin's view that such a move might be regarded in the United States 'as a calculated political manoeuvre on our part with the object of influencing the situation in America, and that consequently it might have the very opposite effect that we desired'.[106]

Churchill accepted this decision, but returned to the attack in early February 1929 after learning details of the new 'pocket battleships' being planned by Germany. These ships, which combined high speed and endurance with a powerful 11-inch armament, threatened to outclass Britain's existing treaty cruisers by a wide margin. Churchill feared that future American cruisers would more closely resemble the new German ships than the treaty cruisers Britain already possessed and, more importantly, the new cruisers that the Admiralty planned to lay down that year. This new development confirmed for Churchill the wisdom of not building new warships prematurely. The right course, he insisted, was to postpone the 1928–9 cruisers 'so as to incorporate all the most recent technical improvements'. This would ensure that Britain 'should get the advantage not only of better ships but also we should show to the world a more pacific policy'. Bridgeman protested strongly that the new German ships had no bearing on the British programme. The Cabinet agreed not to disturb the Admiralty's plans to begin two new heavy cruisers in the current year.[107]

With the cruiser programme finally settled, the Baldwin government turned its attention to the final reports of the Belligerent Rights Subcommittee.[108] In March 1929 this body recommended, with only one member dissenting, that Britain should endeavour to maintain its belligerent rights as high as possible. The majority, however, were prepared to include these rights in any new arbitration treaty with the United States. A minority, which included Bridgeman, Amery, and Lord Peel, claimed that this was 'too great a risk'. Like Churchill, they were 'profoundly sceptical' that 'one more great concession' would secure any permanent improvement in Anglo-American relations or reduce the American naval programme.[109] Despite these reservations, the reports represented a modest victory for the Foreign Office view. Austen Chamberlain's efforts to conciliate American opinion were soon frustrated, however, by the May 1929 general election, which resulted in the formation of a new Labour government. The Conservative Party now moved into opposition, forcing Churchill and his colleagues to watch from the sidelines as the management of British sea power was taken over by men with a very different strategic outlook.

Historians have struggled to explain Churchill's position on defence spending as Chancellor of the Exchequer. How could the prophet who foresaw the dangers from Nazi Germany and, later, the Soviet Union have openly ridiculed the idea of war with Japan? How could the architect of the Anglo-American 'special relationship' during the Second World War have taken such a hard line towards the United States? And, most perplexing of all, how could Churchill's reputation as the champion of the armed forces prior to both world wars be reconciled with his aggressive pursuit of economy and fierce attacks on service policies during the 1920s?

The most common explanation for these apparent contradictions is that Churchill invariably threw himself wholeheartedly into the pursuit of his departmental objectives.[110] Thus, Churchill assailed the spending proposals of the fighting services during the 1920s because that is what chancellors of the exchequer were *supposed* to do. His forceful attacks on the service departments—and the navy in particular—are often treated as a regrettable side effect of the resolve and drive that Churchill demonstrated during his wartime leadership. But to some observers, Churchill's record as Chancellor points to more serious shortcomings. It has been argued that by cutting defence expenditure during this period, he actually created many of the deficiencies in Britain's defences that he decried during the 1930s; that he demonstrated poor strategic judgement and recklessness; and that his influential account of British policies during the 1920s was both self-serving and inaccurate.[111]

These explanations are problematic. There is little basis for the argument that Churchill was incapable of looking beyond the narrow needs of the department he headed at any particular moment. As Chancellor, he pursued the Treasury's objectives with all his characteristic vigour, but he always insisted on a strong voice in determining what those objectives would be. He also did not hesitate to overrule his departmental advisers when he disagreed with them, as he did over critical issues like the Singapore base, naval competition with the United States, and the use of 'liberal' means such as arms control to protect British interests. For the most part, however, their goals coincided. Churchill's determination to reduce government spending ultimately stemmed from a mixture of political, economic, and financial considerations. The pursuit of economies at the expense of the fighting services offered significant political dividends, and appeared justified by the prevailing assessment of the international situation. And, whereas all three services could claim to be underfunded during the life of the Baldwin government, the navy repeatedly bore the brunt of the Treasury's attacks because Churchill and his colleagues rejected the strategic rationale for its most expensive programmes.

The navy was singled out for attack because its demands seemed more extravagant than those of the other services, being based primarily on the distant and seemingly remote threat from Japan. The navy had ample strength during the 1920s to meet any potential naval threat in Europe. If Japan was not an immediate danger, as many outside the navy believed, the only other conceivable challenge on the seas would come from an American bid for maritime supremacy. When that possibility emerged in 1927, Churchill did not hesitate to reject the Treasury line and back the Admiralty. Paradoxically, however, protecting Britain's naval position in this instance seemed to require not more but less naval construction. This was more than just opportunism, although Churchill was undoubtedly pleased to have an excuse to put the cruiser programme back on the chopping block in 1927 and later.

The widespread view that Churchill's actions as Chancellor were fundamentally inconsistent with his stance prior to the two world wars also needs to be qualified. The policies that he adopted during the 1920s arose from balanced assessments of Britain's strategic requirements, and were essentially rational responses to major changes in the international environment following the First World War. To be sure, Churchill made mistakes. His predictions about the likelihood of war in the Far East make for uncomfortable reading today and can only detract from his reputation as a prophet. His attacks on naval construction programmes contributed to the deterioration of the naval shipbuilding industry during the 1920s, a problem later compounded by the restrictions accepted by the Labour government at the 1930 London Naval Conference.[112] Churchill did not appreciate, either at the time or later, the precarious state of this sector of the British economy. But even in these matters, his actions were, if nothing else, generally consistent. His optimistic reading of the international situation did not change as soon as he left the Treasury. Even when Churchill began to perceive a threat from a resurgent Germany, his views on Japan, Singapore, and naval strategy altered little, as subsequent chapters will show. And, while he was consistently prone to underestimate the likelihood of an Anglo-Japanese war, his doubts about the feasibility of the navy's plans to inflict a decisive defeat on Japan in its home waters were fully borne out by events during the Second World War.[113]

The long-term impact of Churchill's policies is more difficult to judge. His unrelenting pursuit of economy during the 1920s certainly contributed something to the navy's difficulties during the early 1930s, as Churchill himself was willing to concede. But the severity of his cuts should not be exaggerated. Baldwin's government spent more on the navy than the Labour governments that followed or preceded it, and authorized more new construction than any of Britain's rivals during the same period. The argument that Churchill was one of the leading causes of the services' deficiencies during the 1930s and the early years of the Second World War are generally linked to claims that he was responsible not just for the cuts implemented while he was Chancellor but also for those imposed by his successors, who continued to utilize the ten-year rule as a means to limit defence expenditure.[114] This sleight of hand makes it possible to blame Churchill for the deficiencies accumulated by the services during the period 1929–32, when the deepest cuts were made in Britain's interwar defence budgets.

Some critics have gone further, suggesting that Churchill was the principal instigator of the original ten-year rule in 1919, and consequently responsible for virtually all the problems accumulated by the armed services during the period from 1919 until at least 1932, if not later.[115] These claims need to be examined carefully. To begin with, they rest on the mistaken assumption that the revival and extension of the ten-year rule are nothing more than the by-product of Churchill's fanatical pursuit of economy and disregard of potential risks. But this exaggerates his influence during the 1920s. His position as Chancellor and the force of his personality ensured that he often played a leading role in the formulation of Britain's strategic policies, but the Treasury could only dominate defence policy as long as its priorities were endorsed by the Cabinet as a whole. The service departments and the Foreign Office continued to exert a strong influence on the decision-making process, and the navy in particular retained significant power to thwart the Treasury. Strategic policies were never simply dictated by Churchill; they emerged out of the dynamic process of competition, negotiation, and compromise among the various actors involved.

Similarly, the significance of the ten-year rule must be kept in perspective. The Treasury had little difficulty under Churchill in controlling expenditure on both the army and the air force without invoking the rule, while the Admiralty openly flouted it prior to 1928 (and continued to evade it afterwards). Lloyd George had been able to use the rule in 1919 to impose sweeping economies on the Admiralty, but Churchill could not do the same from a subordinate position, even one as powerful as the Chancellorship. Instead, he had to rely on his powers of persuasion. He did not resurrect the ten-year rule in 1924–5 in order to control spending by all three defence departments, but as a means to a more limited end: reducing costly preparations for a specific conflict that the government and most of Whitehall regarded as unlikely. Similar guidelines were embraced by the army, but the navy never accepted the Treasury's opinions on the likelihood of war with Japan or the means of waging such a conflict. As long as the Admiralty refused to be bound by the spirit of the Cabinet's earlier rulings on this subject, the Treasury was unable to enforce the priorities established by the government in 1925.

The extension of the ten-year rule in July 1928 resulted from Churchill's need to consolidate his previous bureaucratic victories, not a desire to achieve new ones. It proved to be a milestone in the lengthy struggle between the Treasury and the Admiralty over the basis of the naval estimates, but even then the rule's limitations were considerable. It did not give the Treasury unlimited power, as is often implied. This is amply demonstrated by the fact that Churchill's attacks on the navy's cruiser programme during the final months of the Baldwin government both failed: he actually had greater success in cutting naval expenditure before the rule was made permanent than after. There was no reason, therefore, for Churchill to assume that the rule would be abused by his successors. Churchill's influence over service policies effectively ended when he left office in 1929. MacDonald's governments, like Baldwin's and Lloyd George's, would spend only as much on defence as they wished to, whether the ten-year rule existed or not.

5

Disarmament, Rearmament, and the Path to War: The 1930s

Churchill's views on naval arms control and imperial defence did not suddenly change when he left office. In a series of speeches delivered in Canada in August 1929, he repeated the arguments he had developed as Chancellor: that the naval requirements of the British Empire and the United States were fundamentally different, and that an agreement between them establishing numerical parity in all classes of warship would relegate Britain to a position of 'permanent inferiority on the seas'. In his opinion, there was no way for Britain to gain from naval negotiations with the United States. Another round of failed talks would further harm Anglo-American relations, while an agreement, even on terms advantageous to Britain, might set in motion a 'perilous train of mutual suspicion and distrust'. In these circumstances, Churchill maintained that the whole question of naval arms limitation should simply be shelved. Britain and the United States, he argued, should 'make a friendly agreement to go our ways in peace and in friendship, acting in a sober, reasonable, and neighbourly fashion, and building no more vessels than we each think we require for our own purposes and at our own discretion'.[1]

There was much to be said for this proposal, but the new Labour government intended to chart a different course. Ramsay MacDonald, the prime minister, had been a harsh critic of the Baldwin government's foreign policy. He came to power in June 1929 determined to improve Anglo-American relations, which he regarded both as a desirable end in itself and a means to further the cause of international disarmament.[2] The Foreign Office was also eager to take the initiative in mending relations with the United States, but the strong opposition it encountered from the Admiralty to any weakening of maritime belligerent rights made it clear that this issue could not be resolved quickly or easily. However, the new American president, Herbert Hoover, was more interested in a naval limitation agreement than arbitration treaties or belligerent rights, prompting the Foreign Office to turn its attention back to arms control as early as March 1929, while the Conservatives were still in power.[3] The prospects for a naval settlement appeared to improve dramatically the following month when the United States indicated that it was prepared to develop a formula that made allowances for age, displacement, and armament of warships in calculating relative strength in any class of vessel. This apparent concession promised to break the deadlock over cruisers by allowing the United States to equate its relatively small fleet of predominantly large, 8-inch-gun cruisers with the much larger fleet of smaller 6-inch-gun cruisers that the British wanted. Both sides might therefore emerge from an agreement with the cruiser force it needed, while claiming that overall parity existed, even though there would be a difference in numbers of ships and overall tonnage.

MacDonald and the Foreign Office moved quickly to take advantage of these new opportunities, but settlement of the cruiser question proved more difficult than initially thought.[4] High-level negotiations over the summer of 1929 demonstrated that the United States' position had actually altered very little since the Geneva Conference in 1927. The Americans continued to demand parity, but also hoped to secure a reduction of cruiser strength. To obtain an agreement, MacDonald dropped Britain's cruiser requirements from seventy ships of about 450,000 tons to fifty ships totalling only 339,000 tons, a figure the United States would agree to. He obtained the consent of the naval staff by promising them a steady annual programme of new cruisers for the duration of the treaty.[5] At the time, Britain possessed only fifty-three cruisers, many of which had been built during the war. With a large number of these ships soon to become overage, the promise of new construction was more important to the Admiralty than a nominal commitment to a strength of seventy (or even sixty) cruisers that naval leaders knew could not be achieved for the foreseeable future. Indeed, with the full impact of the Great Depression now starting to be felt, the navy would be hard pressed to obtain funds for new construction from any government, not just a Labour one.

Once the navy had agreed to this deal, MacDonald moved to pre-empt criticism by reassuring the Conservatives, who had previously supported the Admiralty's claim to seventy cruisers, that no vital interests were being sacrificed. Thomas Jones, the deputy secretary to the Cabinet, writing on

MacDonald's behalf, informed Baldwin in September that the 'Admiralty are behind the P.M. without reserve, and that if there is any opposition, the Admiralty support will be publicly announced.' Jones also appealed to Baldwin to use his influence to restrain Churchill. This was motivated, he wrote, by MacDonald's 'fear that at the last moment the agreement with Hoover may be imperilled, if not wrecked, by some speech by, or interview with, Winston', who was touring the United States at the time.[6]

With the Anglo-American cruiser dispute effectively resolved, a naval conference was convened in London in January 1930. Three months later, the United States, Britain, and Japan concluded a new agreement. The London Treaty allowed Britain to construct fourteen new 6-inch cruisers by 1936, but this was virtually the only bright spot for the Admiralty.[7] In all other respects, the treaty was a disappointment. MacDonald had supported the Admiralty's plans to resume capital-ship construction until just a few days before the conference opened, when he suddenly reversed his position. Admiralty officials were caught off guard, but their protests had no effect. The treaty formally extended the capital-ship building holiday for another five years. The earlier restrictions imposed by the Washington Treaty and the reluctance of the governments of the 1920s to construct auxiliary warships had devastated the naval arms industry in Britain even before the London Conference opened. The decision not to resume capital-ship construction after 1931 would result in the further decline of Britain's industrial capacity for building warships.[8] The treaty also ensured that Britain's naval strength would diminish in both absolute and relative terms. No fewer than five existing capital ships were to be scrapped rather than replaced during the years 1931–6, so that when naval rearmament began in 1937, British shipyards would be fully occupied with the replacement of obsolete ships and could not immediately make up lost ground. The treaty also meant that new naval construction in Europe by powers outside the agreement would erode Britain's ability to defend its interests in the Far East against Japan by tying down more British ships in European waters.

Churchill instinctively disliked the treaty. His criticisms in the House of Commons focused on the impact of the agreement on British prestige. In May 1930 he charged that the Labour government had effectively abandoned the one-power standard and accepted de facto naval inferiority to the United States. It was difficult to press this argument, however, without seeming to overrate the dangers of an Anglo-American war. Churchill therefore attempted to embarrass the government by suggesting that the Admiralty was unhappy with the treaty and that Britain had made more concessions than other powers. There was considerable truth in both claims, but Churchill was unable to demonstrate that any tangible British interests had been jeopardized. When he resumed his attack on the treaty in June, he insisted that the agreement threatened Britain's ability to defend its essential imports in wartime. Neither the United States nor Japan could hope to send a fleet to European waters to challenge the main British fleet, he argued, but both could threaten Britain's seaborne trade. The same was true of European powers, and France in particular. Even though Churchill had considered fifty cruisers adequate to defend British interests while he was at the Treasury, he now claimed—probably less from conviction than the desire to score points off the government—that the new restrictions on this class of ship would render Britain weaker than at any time 'since the reign of Charles II'.

Britain, he argued, could not afford to leave itself vulnerable in this area. 'The purpose of our Navy is to secure the arrival of our daily bread,' he told the House of Commons. 'We cannot and we ought not to let ourselves get into a position in which any Power, even the most friendly, has undoubted means of putting irresistible pressure upon us by threatening to starve us out.' But even here, his criticism was blunted by the absence of any obvious or imminent threat:

> If trouble comes—I do not believe that trouble will come; I believe that wars are over for our day—it is indispensable that we should be able to survive for two years, and to feed ourselves for two years, so that we could rebuild, as we could in these Islands, with our unequalled resources, the naval power necessary to secure victorious escape from that trouble.[9]

Churchill also repeated his argument that it was a mistake to measure Britain's naval strength against that of the United States. Privately, he wrote to Baldwin that the wisest course would be to scrap the one-power standard entirely and develop a new standard relative to the next two or even three strongest powers excluding the United States.[10] The important thing, he later remarked to Admiral Richmond, was to put the new standard high enough to 'get at least the same size of fleet as we are going to have now'. The advantage of this course, according to Churchill, was that it would give the British a standard 'related to our own needs and actual dangers, which we are entirely free to build up to in any form of craft as we may think fit. This would not necessarily be more expensive than the present proposed system,' he told Baldwin, and 'it might well be less so, because it would give our naval designers free play for their unmatched knowledge.'This last point was an important one. Given the difficulties Britain would face in maintaining its traditional numerical superiority in warships, Churchill hoped that qualitative factors would enable Britain to maintain an advantage over its maritime rivals. One of the worst things about arms-control agreements, he complained, 'is that they deprive us of all that flexibility and authority in variants of design which are our birthright'.[11]

This criticism failed to deflect the Labour government from its course, or even cause it serious discomfort. Over the next three years, Churchill's opposition to arms-limitation agreements hardened as Britain participated in the Conference on Limitation and Reduction of Armaments held at Geneva under the auspices of the League of Nations. The most important issue during the early 1930s was whether Germany would be allowed to rearm. Weimar Germany was insisting that other states must recognize its right to equality of armaments. Churchill maintained, however, that disarmament would be neither practical nor safe until the underlying causes of hostility between states had been removed. Moreover, he was suspicious of Germany's goals even before Hitler came to power in January 1933. In November 1932, for example, he warned MacDonald's 'National' government—a coalition formed in August 1931, including Conservatives, Liberals, and a small number of former Labour Party members—that it should not be deluded into thinking that 'all Germany is asking for is equal status':

> That is not what Germany is seeking. All these bands of sturdy, Teutonic youths, marching through the streets and roads of Germany, with the light of desire in their eyes to suffer for their Fatherland, are not looking for status. They are looking for weapons, and, when they have the weapons, believe me they will then ask for the return of lost territories and lost colonies, and when that demand is made it cannot fail to shake and possibly shatter to their foundations every one of the countries I have mentioned [i.e. France and its Eastern European allies], and some other countries I have not mentioned.[12]

France, on the other hand,'though armed to the teeth is pacifist to the core'. Churchill was confident that Britain's recent ally was committed to maintaining the status quo, and he was not concerned by France's dominant military position on the Continent. The French army, in his view, was a stabilizing force in Europe, and one that would relieve Britain of the need to become too closely involved in European affairs. Placing Germany on an equal military footing with France, Churchill warned in May 1932, 'would bring us to within practical distance of almost measureless calamity'.[13]

A resurgent Germany was not the only threat to the relatively stable world order that had emerged by the end of the 1920s. Over a year before Hitler came to power, the authority and prestige of the League of Nations was undermined by developments in the Far East. In September 1931, Japan's Kwantung army initiated hostilities against Chinese troops in Manchuria and quickly overran the province. This act of blatant aggression vindicated the navy's warnings about Japan, but Churchill was not unduly alarmed. He continued to regard Japan as a distant power unable to threaten any vital British interests. In February 1933 he even expressed some sympathy towards the Japanese, who were faced on one side, he noted, by 'the dark menace of the Soviet Union' and on the other by 'the chaos of China, four or five provinces of which are now being tortured under Communist rule'.[14] With China seemingly torn between anarchy and communism, it was, he suggested, 'in the interests of the whole world' that Japan should establish law and order in China's northern provinces. At all events, there was little that could be done to reverse Japan's conquests. The League of Nations was virtually powerless to intervene. Two of the most important powers with interests in the region—the United States and the Soviet Union—were not even members. Churchill insisted that the League should avoid tasks 'beyond its strength and absolutely outside its scope' and that Britain should maintain a position of strict neutrality in the Sino-Japanese conflict.

After Hitler came to power in January 1933, Churchill began to press for British rearmament. His influence was considerably constrained, however. In 1931 he had broken with Baldwin and the leaders of the Conservative Party over the question of granting greater freedom to India. When the 'National' government was formed in the autumn of 1931, Churchill was not offered a seat in the Cabinet. Though still a member of the Conservative Party, he was now relegated to the back benches by the party's leaders, and he would remain there for most of the decade.

Churchill's views on foreign policy and defence frequently diverged from those of the new government, despite the growing dominance of the Conservative Party within its ranks. At first, he was confident that France and its continental allies in Eastern Europe could contain Germany, and that close Anglo-French collaboration would not be necessary. And by building up Britain's military strength, he hoped that the country could avoid being drawn into European entanglements.[15] The most serious potential threat at this time to Britain's security appeared to be a powerful German air force. Like most British leaders of this period, Churchill assumed that British cities would be bombed in wartime, and with devastating results. In November 1934, for example, he predicted that after seven to ten days of bombing, between thirty thousand and forty thousand people would have been killed or injured, while 3 or 4 million more would have been driven out of London into the surrounding countryside.[16] But he rejected Baldwin's famous assertion that there was no adequate defence against bombers, and that the only effective response was a counter-bombing campaign against the enemy's cities. To begin with, he predicted that military targets would ultimately be more valuable than purely civilian objectives. The enemy's bombers, he suggested, could inflict the greatest damage by attacking Britain's manufacturing centres and the dockyards and oil-storage facilities on which the navy depended.[17] British bombing efforts, in turn, should be concentrated on enemy communications, troop concentrations, munition depots, and war industry. Churchill also favoured an active defence against enemy bombers. This would involve the continuous harassment of enemy aircraft by British fighters, and other measures such as aerial mines—another attempt to counter emerging threats by developing new technologies.

Churchill's efforts to strengthen the nation's defences during the early and mid-1930s concentrated on improving Britain's strength in the air. He was not concerned at this time about the state of the navy. The Treaty of Versailles had given Britain a crushing superiority over Germany at sea, and there was no possibility the Germans could overcome this weakness quickly. If Hitler wanted a great navy, he would have to build it virtually from scratch. An air force could be created far more quickly. Speaking in the House of Commons in March 1933, Churchill emphasized that the defence of Britain in the air was now every bit as important as its defence at sea.[18] His preoccupation with Germany was not shared by the Admiralty, however, which continued to regard Japan as the most immediate danger to imperial security. The other services also viewed the situation in the Far East with considerably more alarm than Churchill.[19] In 1932 the Chiefs of Staff Committee (COS), comprising the professional heads of the three services, persuaded the government to strengthen Britain's position in this region by resuming work on the Singapore naval base—which had been suspended by the Labour government in 1929—and by formally abandoning the ten-year rule. However, this did not lead to the rapid improvement of Britain's position, as the harsh economic climate prevented the government from diverting additional funds to defence.

Only ten months after Hitler came to power was serious attention given to strengthening the armed services. In November 1933 the Cabinet formed a Defence Requirements Committee (DRC) consisting of the professional heads of the three fighting services, the Treasury, and the Foreign Office. This body was charged with recommending a programme for making good the worst deficiencies accumulated by the armed services over the previous decade. The committee's first report, completed in January 1934, attempted to strike a balance between the requirements of home and imperial defence. Nazi Germany, which might one day pose a mortal threat to Britain itself, was identified as the 'ultimate potential enemy against whom all our "long range" defence policy must be directed'.[20] But Germany would require time to rearm, and could not become a critical threat for approximately five more years. Japan, on the other hand, was in a position to threaten important British interests immediately, even if it could not menace Britain itself.[21] The committee hoped to prepare against both threats by meeting the most pressing needs of all three services. This translated into additional expenditure of nearly £40 million on the army, around £20 million for the navy, and just over £10 million on the air force.[22]

These priorities did not survive Cabinet scrutiny. Britain's political leaders accepted the need to rearm, but they were also determined to keep defence spending to the lowest level possible so as not to damage Britain's economic strength, on which its strategic position ultimately rested. And like Churchill, they were preoccupied with the physical proximity of Germany and the vulnerability of British cities to a terror-bombing campaign. Germany potentially had the power both to dominate Europe and to strike a crippling blow directly at Britain. The Japanese threat was far less serious. In June 1934 Neville Chamberlain, the Chancellor of the Exchequer, informed the Cabinet committee examining the DRC's report that it could 'hardly be disputed that the anxieties of the British people are concentrated on Europe rather than on the Far East, and that if we have to make a choice we must prepare our defence against possible hostilities from Germany rather than from Japan'. Britain, in his opinion, could not undertake 'simultaneous preparation against war with Germany and war with Japan'.[23]

Nor could it afford to lavish funds on all three services: defence spending would have to be carefully tailored to the government's strategic priorities. Chamberlain's recommendations and the logic underlying them were accepted by his colleagues. The German threat was to be met primarily in the air rather than on the battlefields of western Europe. The War Office could begin preparing to dispatch a modest force for the defence of the Low Countries, but the sum recommended by the DRC for the army was cut by half. The navy's share of new expenditure was similarly reduced by around 38 per cent. Chamberlain accepted that the naval base at Singapore must be completed—'if only out of good faith to the Dominions'—but, in language reminiscent of Churchill's a few years earlier, he insisted that the Admiralty 'must postpone the idea of sending out to it a fleet of capital ships capable of containing the Japanese fleet or meeting it in battle'.[24] The main beneficiary of these new priorities was the RAF, whose allocation of new expenditure increased by a massive 94 per cent.[25]

Churchill was broadly in agreement with Chamberlain and the National governments of the 1930s on spending priorities: Britain should concentrate on bolstering its air force in order to deter a German attack. The only substantial difference between them was over how fast Britain should rearm.[26] As a backbencher, Churchill was much less inclined than the government to worry about the economic implications of rearmament. Financial concerns, in his opinion, should not be allowed to hinder Britain's preparations. Churchill's differences with the government in this respect were clear by 1936, when his alarm about the widening gap between British and German arms production prompted him to begin campaigning for a Ministry of Supply and government interference with industry in order to shift resources from civilian to military production. But these measures were intended to benefit only two of Britain's fighting services, the army and the air force. There was no urgency over the navy, Churchill maintained, because its needs could easily be met by its own arsenals and dockyards, supplemented by a large and, in his mind, still-thriving network of naval armament firms. Consequently, there was 'no difficulty in maintaining the Navy, and even in expanding it very considerably, without doing more than open out its existing sources of supply. The maintenance or increase of British naval power is therefore solely a question of money, and the House of Commons is eager to vote for this purpose any sum.'[27] The government, however, did not share Churchill's sense of alarm and rejected measures that might undermine Britain's economic recovery.[28]

The other area of disagreement between Churchill and the National governments of the 1930s, especially after Neville Chamberlain became prime minister in May 1937, was the appeasement of Germany. As is well known, Churchill was increasingly critical of British efforts to conciliate the Nazis. Unlike Chamberlain, he appreciated that Hitler intended to pursue an ambitious programme of territorial expansion. Peaceful coexistence was therefore not an option. Following the Munich Conference of late September 1938, for example, he warned that there could:

> never be friendship between the British democracy and the Nazi Power, that Power which spurns Christian ethics, which cheers its onward course by a barbarous paganism, which vaunts the spirit of aggression and conquest, which derives strength and perverted pleasure from persecution, and uses, as we have seen, with pitiless brutality the threat of murderous force. That Power cannot ever be the trusted friend of the British democracy.[29]

Back in 1936, Churchill had concluded that the rapid growth of German power made close Anglo-French collaboration essential. Germany could ultimately be deterred from aggression only by the threat of overwhelming force. The best means to contain Germany, Churchill argued, would be for the states of Europe to rally behind the leadership of Britain and France in the name of collective security and under the banner of the League of Nations. In 1938 he went further and called for the creation of a 'Grand Alliance' of Britain, France, and the Soviet Union. These views were rejected by Chamberlain, however. Churchill's vigorous advocacy of a firm and united front against Germany, more than his views on rearmament, ensured that he remained out of office until war broke out.

The first sign that Britain's maritime security might become endangered was the conclusion of the Anglo-German Naval Agreement in June 1935. This treaty allowed Germany to build a navy up to 35 per cent the size of Britain's in all classes of warships except submarines, where the figure was set at 45 per cent (with an option to increase to 100 per cent). When the Germans approached the British for an agreement on these terms, naval leaders were happy to accept. With German naval rearmament seemingly inevitable, the Admiralty was concerned about the size and composition of the new German navy. This agreement had several things to be said in its favour. First, the ratio accepted by Germany was low enough that Britain might still hope to maintain a rough two-power standard relative to Germany and Japan, its two most likely enemies. Second, it prevented a qualitative challenge to the naval status quo by ensuring that Germany would not build bigger and more heavily armed warships than those already possessed by Britain and the other major naval powers. Third, it ensured that Germany would create a 'balanced' fleet rather than concentrate its resources on U-boats and other commerce raiders, a potentially more dangerous course for the British.[30]

Churchill took a different perspective and promptly denounced the agreement in two speeches made in July. It was a serious mistake, he insisted, for Britain to condone *any* violation of the Treaty of Versailles. The rebuilding of the German fleet might be unavoidable, he maintained, but the question should have been referred to the League of Nations for resolution. Doing otherwise only weakened Britain's commitment to collective security and the League of Nations.[31] Churchill also appreciated that German naval rearmament would ultimately threaten the balance of naval power in both Europe and the Pacific. Even if Germany adhered to the figures set out in the treaty, it was clear that Britain could expect increased naval construction by other European powers threatened by Germany's new navy. And as the navies of Europe expanded, fewer British ships would be available for dispatch to the Far East. 'What a windfall this has been to Japan!' Churchill remarked. 'The British fleet, when this [German] programme is completed, will be largely anchored to the North Sea. That means to say the whole position in the Far East has been very gravely altered, to the detriment of the United States and of Great Britain and to the detriment of China.'[32]

Churchill had little faith in Hitler to live up to these new commitments. He warned that there was nothing to stop the Germans from adopting unrestricted submarine warfare in a future conflict or from continuing naval construction when they reached the 35 per cent limit, which he believed might occur as early as 1938–9. Germany's warships would also be much newer than their British counterparts. As Churchill reminded the House of Commons in May 1935, twelve of Britain's fifteen capital ships had been 'constructed in the days when I was at the Admiralty more than twenty years ago'.[33] Britain could not immediately match Germany's new capital ships, however, because of the restrictions imposed by the 1930 London Treaty. This agreement would expire only at the end of 1936. A second London Naval Conference was held early that year to decide what would replace it. It was clear from the outset that the quantitative limitation of warships was no longer feasible. Japan was unwilling to accept anything less than parity with Britain and the United States, and its delegates left the conference when it became clear that this concession would not be granted.

A new treaty—the Second London Naval Treaty—was signed by Britain, the United States, France, and Italy. This agreement placed qualitative restrictions on various classes of warship, but without Japan as a signatory it was uncertain how long these limits would survive. Churchill was one of those who welcomed this outcome. Like the Admiralty, he was convinced that Britain must begin rebuilding its battle fleet the moment it was free to do so. But he was irritated during the life of the treaty by the restrictions that continued to be placed on Britain's freedom to design and build warships according to its own interests.[34]

Churchill's concerns about the emerging maritime threat from Germany were exacerbated by growing alarm over developments in the Far East. By 1936 it was evident that Japan was dominated by nationalist and militarist extremists determined to expand Japanese influence in East Asia. This was not a development that Churchill or most westerners had predicted during the 1920s. But Churchill's opinion of the Japanese had changed sharply. He noted in February 1937 that in earlier years they had shown themselves to be 'steady, grave and mature people; that they can be trusted to measure forces and factors with great care, and that they do not lose their heads, or plunge into mad, uncalculated adventures'. More recently, however, Japan's 'elder statesmen and their sagacious power seem to have dispersed'.[35] Japan, he claimed back in November 1936, had become a 'nation imbued with dreams of war and conquest'.[36]

The 'Mikado's government has only an imperfect authority over the naval and military warriors of Japan,' he charged in January 1938, 'and still less over their aviators':

> The secret societies in the Japanese army and navy have very largely taken charge of the policy of their country. They have murdered so many politicians who were thought to be weaklings and backsliders that they have terrified the rest. It is painful to say it, but there are moments when we must feel ourselves in the presence of an army and navy which are running amok.[37]

With Japan now assigned to the ranks of the 'predatory military dictatorship nations', Churchill began to take the Far Eastern situation more seriously.[38] The greatest danger now appeared to be that Japan would take advantage of Britain's difficulties in Europe to challenge its position in the east. But Churchill remained optimistic, in part because he assumed that Japanese expansion would bring Britain and the United States closer. Churchill increasingly regarded the United States as a valuable potential ally rather than an inconvenient naval competitor. His parliamentary speech on the

1936 navy estimates, for example, not only denounced the idea of competition between the US and British navies, as he had frequently done in the past, but also acknowledged that both parties had an interest in seeing the other as strong as possible. This was a clear recognition that the world had fundamentally changed since 1929. It was 'no exaggeration,' Churchill claimed in March 1936, to say 'that the stronger the United States Navy becomes, the surer are the foundations of peace throughout the world'.[39]

But he did not yet discount the possibility that a large British naval building programme might cause friction with the United States. He therefore sought to disarm American critics by insisting that Britain did not deny the *right* of the United States to naval parity. On the contrary, he claimed that Britain was perfectly content to see the United States build whatever it felt was necessary for its own security, even if that gave it, at least temporarily, a stronger battle fleet. But as it would clearly be Britain forcing the pace in naval construction for the next few years, he probably did not think that was likely to happen. The important thing was to bury for good any question of naval rivalry with the United States. By 1938 Churchill was even willing to concede that the first London Treaty had, whatever its defects, been beneficial in bringing about an improvement in Anglo-American relations.[40] In the event, there was little to worry about. With the international situation deteriorating steadily, both sides realized that Anglo-American naval competition no longer served any useful purpose.

Churchill warmly supported the government's decision in 1936 to begin building new battleships when treaty restrictions lapsed at the end of the year. He informed the House of Commons in the spring of 1937 that this measure constituted 'the most decisive assertion of the British will to live that has been made public since the end of the Great War'.[41] At the same time, he publicly endorsed the Admiralty's view that the battleship was still a critical element of British sea power.[42] The future of the capital ship was more controversial than ever, but the Admiralty remained confident that innovative designs and efficient anti-aircraft defences would render battleships *relatively* safe from modern forms of attack. Admiral Ernle Chatfield, the First Sea Lord, wrote to Churchill in May 1936 to outline the navy's case. It would be 'a great mistake,' he asserted, 'for Parliament to imagine that we believe that battleships can or should, be made unsinkable or invulnerable':

We are far from having any such crude idea. Ships, on the contrary, are meant to be sunk and unless battleships could be sunk no naval victory could ever be won. Our policy is not to build ships that cannot be sunk but to build ships so efficient and so strong, and with such highly trained personnel, that we shall sink the enemy battlefleet, whether by shell or torpedo or bombs, more rapidly than he will be able to destroy ours. That is the only fighting policy on which the Navy can rest.[43]

Churchill was impressed by the Admiralty's arguments, which were confirmed later that year by the investigations of a CID subcommittee (the Vulnerability of Capital Ships committee) set up to consider this problem.[44] The ability of modern ships to withstand aerial attack also appeared to be confirmed by the experiences of the Spanish Civil War.[45] As Churchill noted in September 1938, 'The extravagant claims of a certain school of air experts have not been fulfilled':

> We were assured some time ago that navies were obsolete and that great bat-tleships costing seven or eight million pounds, would be easily destroyed by aeroplanes costing only a few thousands. I asked in the House of Com-mons...why it was that no Spanish warships on either side had been sunk by aircraft. The Spanish fleets are not well equipped with anti-aircraft artillery. Their vessels have no special armour against overhead attack. Yet we see them cruising about the coast, often in full view from the shore, apparently as free from danger as if aeroplanes had never been invented.[46]

Moreover, the anti-aircraft defences of British warships would be 'the most dangerous to aeroplanes in the whole world'. Churchill boasted that the 'two square miles over the British Fleet' will contain 'a greater concentra-tion of anti-aircraft fire and highly-skilled gunners than has ever been known'.[47] All this made it seem reasonable to assume that 'great ships of war can be constructed which can exercise their full influence and efficiency under modern conditions, and that the air menace, however seriously it may operate in other directions, will not destroy the validity of sea power'.[48]

Churchill also backed the Admiralty's campaign in 1936–7 to regain con-trol over the Fleet Air Arm (FAA), which had been part of the Royal Air Force since 1918. The arrangements by which the navy enjoyed operational but not administrative control of its aircraft and personnel had steadily undermined Britain's once-commanding lead in naval aviation.[49] As Churchill noted in 1936, the FAA was well behind the United States in both numbers and quality of naval aircraft and personnel. Even Japan possessed a large lead over Britain.[50] Churchill agreed with naval leaders that aircraft had an essential role to play in modern naval operations, and that the navy was greatly hampered by the present arrangements. 'It is impossible,' he asserted, 'to resist an Admiral's claim that he must have complete control of and confidence in the aircraft of the battle fleet, whether used for reconnaissance, gun-fire or air attack on a hostile fleet. These are his very eyes.' He therefore insisted, both in his public speeches and private communications with members of the government, that 'the Admiralty view must prevail'.[51] This would not only increase the efficiency of the fleet, he felt, but also free the Air Staff to concentrate its efforts on Britain's critical air rearmament program.[52]

The Admiralty appreciated Churchill's prominent intervention on its behalf. In 1937 their efforts were rewarded when the government returned the FAA to navy control. While this debate was under way, both the First Sea Lord and the Controller corresponded with Churchill on a variety of other naval issues, most notably the threat posed by submarines in a future conflict. On this question the Admiralty proved to be unduly optimistic. Chatfield informed Churchill in May 1936 that the navy's 'anti-submarine methods are now so efficient, not of course 100 per cent efficiency, but I do not think that 80 per cent is too high an efficiency safely to place it at, that the number of destroyers and such like vessels that we shall require in a future war...is greatly reduced'.[53] In an effort to convince Churchill that the submarine was nearly mastered, the First Sea Lord took him to see a demonstration of the navy's Asdic (i.e. sonar) equipment in a mock 'submarine hunt' at Portland in June 1938.[54] Churchill was clearly impressed. Asdic, he remarked, was 'a marvellous system and achievement'.[55] But while he accepted that the submarine menace had diminished, he continued to regard it as a serious danger for which a large programme of destroyers was an essential counter.[56]

The main difference between Churchill and the Admiralty during the final years of peace was over the design of Britain's new battleships. The navy's 1936–7 estimates included two 35,000-ton battleships armed with 14-inch guns. These ships, which would become the *King George V* and *Prince of Wales*, were followed by three ships of the same class in the 1937–8 estimates. Churchill believed at the time that it was a serious mistake not to arm them with 16-inch guns, particularly as it appeared likely that both the United States and Japan would adopt larger armaments for their new capital ships.[57] The Admiralty was in a difficult position, however. In 1936–7 Britain was still bound by qualitative treaty limits. The naval staff hoped that all powers would adhere to these restrictions, as it was Britain that stood to lose the most from a qualitative arms race, which would rapidly make Britain's large fleet of capital ships obsolete. They were reluctant, therefore, to build larger and more heavily armed ships as long as the London treaty limits stood any chance of gaining general acceptance. At the same time, they were conscious that European shipyards were busy building new ships, and that Britain could not afford to delay its rebuilding program.[58] The decision was thus taken to adopt the lower displacement for the navy's first new battleships and, if necessary, move to larger ships and 16-inch guns in the 1938 program. This was a difficult decision, but, as Sir Samuel Hoare, the First Lord, told Churchill in July 1936, 'we shall be much better off with our very fine 14-inch 35,000 ton ships than if we did not have the new ships at all'.[59]

Churchill was also critical of the Admiralty for not including any destroyers in its 1938 new construction programme, but again he did not fully understand the reasons. The navy had laid down no fewer than thirty-six destroyers in the years 1936–7, which represented a drastic acceleration of its previously authorized programs. This figure was double what had been approved for the years 1936–8, and was only two short of the new construction authorized for the entire 1936–44 period. The Treasury was on strong ground, therefore, when it insisted in 1938 that the navy forego any destroyers in the current year's programme so as not to disrupt the long-term building programme laid down by the government. The Cabinet, rather than the Admiralty, was responsible for dropping destroyers from the navy's 1938 programme.[60] But other than these concerns, Churchill was generally satisfied with Britain's naval rearmament programme. His speeches in the late 1930s frequently note with satisfaction how favourable the naval balance was relative to Germany, especially compared to the years leading up to the First World War.[61] In January 1939, for example, he declared that there was 'no fear of Germany overtaking Great Britain on the sea. The immense fleets now under construction in the British dockyards leave Germany running along far behind.'[62]

Hitler's denunciation of the Anglo-German Naval Agreement in April 1939 was therefore not regarded as a serious cause for alarm. Britain clearly possessed, and was likely to maintain, a comfortable superiority in surface ships over Hitler's nascent navy. There was no possibility of Germany challenging Britain directly for command of the sea. At the same time, Germany's still relatively small U-boat force did not appear to pose any insurmountable threat to Britain's maritime communications. German submarines would, Churchill predicted, be 'a serious inconvenience and injury to British commerce', but he was confident that the threat would be manageable so long as Britain began to mass produce escort vessels on the outbreak of war.[63]

Churchill therefore had grounds to think that Britain was doing enough to ensure its strength at sea. Even with German naval building proceeding at full speed, he was confident that Britain's numerical lead over Germany was secure and that any threat from this quarter would ultimately be manageable. Moreover, he had doubts as to whether the greatest threat to Britain's sea-borne imports would necessarily be the German navy. Like the Admiralty, he was worried about the dislocation that would be caused by 'continuous air attack upon our commercial ports, warehouses, and landing stages'.[64] And, because he was still inclined to regard the navy primarily as a defensive weapon against Germany, he did not see additional rearmament in this sphere contributing much to Britain's deterrent strength. His attention therefore remain focused on the threat from the air, although he never doubted that Britain needed a strong navy. 'Nothing can be a substitute for naval strength,' he wrote in 1938. 'That alone can bring in our food and trade across the seas. That alone can prevent the swarming legions of the Continent being landed on our shores.'[65] These facts had not changed. But it was equally clear to Churchill that the navy was no longer sufficient to protect the British Isles from direct attack. 'If we are to continue to enjoy our old envied position as an island,' he remarked, 'we must have an Air Force which, both in size and quality, will be a heavy deterrent against hostile attack.'

The addition of Italy to the Royal Navy's potential opponents did little to disturb Churchill's calculations. In his opinion, the Italian navy was simply too weak to challenge Britain's position in the Mediterranean. 'I do not consider that the Navy should have any difficulty in discharging its duties in that Sea,' he confidently predicted in March 1938.[66] Like Japan, Italy did not pose a mortal threat to the British Empire. This confidence was shared by the Admiralty, which never had any doubt as to the outcome of a purely Anglo-Italian naval war. The problem that increasingly worried decision-makers was that Britain's enemies would combine. They had to assume that war with one of the Axis powers would lead to war with one or both of the others. Naval leaders refused to write off Britain's eastern interests and prepared as best they could to fight both Nazi Germany and imperial Japan simultaneously.[67] To accomplish this, they insisted that Britain must complete work on the Singapore naval base and build up to a full two power standard of naval strength measured against Japan and the strongest European naval power. This would allow Britain to dispatch a substantial battle fleet to the Far East while retaining sufficient naval forces in home waters to neutralize the German navy.

The DRC endorsed this plan in November 1935, recommending, as Churchill had suggested in 1930, that Britain replace its outdated one-power standard with a '*new* standard of naval strength' equivalent to a two-power standard.[68] This programme would be expensive, however. The five new battleships authorized in the navy's 1936–8 programmes would replace older vessels as they passed out of service, but it was only by continuing to build new ships at the same rate in 1939 and later that the navy could hope to expand the fleet beyond its current strength of fifteen capital ships to the twenty required for its proposed 'new standard'. In 1937 naval planners calculated that a two-power standard would entail annual estimates of £97–104 million.[69] The government rejected this proposal on financial grounds, but the Admiralty refused to abandon its campaign for a 'new standard'.[70] Naval leaders warned that even this would be inadequate in the event that Britain found itself confronted by three major enemies simultaneously, as appeared increasingly likely. 'If we must include Italy as well as Germany and Japan among our potential enemies,' the Admiralty cautioned, 'our naval strength must either be still further increased or we must rely on a naval combination with another power.'[71]

The Treasury and the government opposed this expense. Neville Chamberlain, who became prime minister in May 1937, remained committed to the strategic priorities he had championed as Chancellor of the Exchequer in 1934, when the DRC's first report had come up for consideration. At the same time his government was reluctant to reject the navy's 'new standard' outright because that would mean a tacit admission that Britain's eastern interests were considered expendable. It was also unwilling to take the politically unpopular move of cutting back on naval rearmament at a time when the international situation was clearly worsening. Consequently, the navy fared better than it might have expected in the competition for funds. In the short term, the Admiralty played its hand skilfully and managed to build warships to the limits of Britain's industrial capacity. In 1938 the government even agreed that the Admiralty could build as close to the 'new standard' as it could with the funds available. But this did not represent a genuine commitment by Chamberlain's government either to naval expansion or a forward strategy in the Far East.

The Admiralty nevertheless enjoyed considerable freedom during the 1930s to develop its plans for a war in the Far East.[72] Its strategy continued to depend on the dispatch of a fleet to Singapore at the beginning of a conflict, but by mid-decade its plans to move this force to Hong Kong and other forward bases along the Chinese coast were becoming impracticable. As the dangers facing Britain in Europe increased, the Admiralty lost confidence that an advance from Hong Kong would be feasible, or that capital ships could operate from this base except under the most ideal circumstances. It was also increasingly plain that the British fleet might face a Japanese force of equal or even greater strength. In 1937 the Admiralty recast its plans to account for these changing conditions. A new Eastern War Memorandum assumed that the fleet might be able to operate from Hong Kong, but that it was more likely to remain based at Singapore. Planners hoped, however, that it could still inflict decisive pressure on Japan from this location. They calculated that Japan could not make up all its deficiencies in essential raw materials from the Asian mainland, and that its war economy would be fatally crippled if its trans-Pacific trade were severed.[73] This assessment was wildly optimistic, but it seemed to reduce the problems facing Britain in the Far East to manageable proportions. The Admiralty now began to prepare for a protracted campaign in which economic pressure applied through a distant maritime blockade would compel Japan's leaders to accept British terms.[74]

Churchill's thoughts on the dynamics of a Far Eastern war continued to diverge from the Admiralty's. He did not have great faith in the value of economic blockade, and assumed that distance would be the dominating factor in an Anglo-Japanese war. A British fleet could be sent to Singapore, he admitted, but this was still a very long way from Japan. To deliver a decisive blow, he assumed that British forces would have to move into the enemy's home waters. But this posed potentially insurmountable problems, as the strength and effectiveness of a British fleet would steadily decline the further it advanced from Singapore. Japan's strength, on the other hand, would increase with proximity to its bases. Thus, even if Britain could dispatch a numerically equal or superior fleet to the Far East, it could only engage Japan's main force in its home waters at a disadvantage. The enemy's defensive position appeared therefore to be virtually unassailable. Japan would 'always have complete supremacy in the yellow seas,' Churchill concluded in December 1936. 'To challenge this supremacy would be impossible and futile.'[75]

This logic cut both ways, however. Singapore's distance from Japan also appeared to render it relatively safe from attack. 'Consider how vain is the menace that Japan will send a fleet and army to conquer Singapore,' Churchill wrote in March 1939. 'It is as far from Japan as Southampton from New York. Over these two thousand miles of salt water, Japan would have to send the bulk of her fleet, escort at least sixty thousand men in transports in order to effect a landing, and begin a siege which would only end in disaster if the Japanese sea-communications were cut at any stage.'[76] By this reasoning Australia was even more secure. 'Can one suppose that Japan, enjoying herself in the mastery of the Yellow Sea, would send afloat a conquering and colonizing expedition to Australia?' Churchill asked. 'It is ludicrous. More than one hundred thousand men would be needed to make any impression upon Australian manhood.'[77] Japan would never undertake such a major attack, he concluded, as long as Britain held Singapore and possessed a fleet capable of moving to the Far East.

Churchill was therefore still thinking in terms of an essentially defensive strategy in the Far East. A British fleet, operating from Singapore, would concentrate on keeping open communications with Britain's Pacific dominions. Like most British leaders, Churchill had a tendency to overestimate Britain's ability to dispatch strong forces to the region. He also systematically underestimated Japan's ability and willingness to project its power into South East Asia and beyond. The image of the Japanese as an instinctively cautious race was still well entrenched. Churchill assumed that Japan's new leaders would hesitate to attack Britain unless it had suffered crippling defeats at the hands of Germany or Italy.[78] In the meantime, Japan seemed to have more than enough to keep its hands full. After July 1937 it was embroiled in an inconclusive and costly war in China and had to worry about a hostile Soviet Union on its northern flank.

Churchill noted with satisfaction in May 1938 that large Russian armies along the Siberian frontier were tying down nearly half a million of Japan's 'finest troops'. It was, he remarked, 'a daring adventure for Japan to try to ward off the Russian masses with her right hand while strangling this voluminous China with the other':

> On the one side, a great bear growling low; on the other, an enormous jelly-fish stinging poisonously. Altogether a nasty job for an over-strained, none-too-contented nation to tackle. Japan is sprawled in China; Russia is crouched ready to spring in the North.

The Soviet air force, he observed, could 'inflict frightful damage upon Tokyo and other Japanese cities any fine night'.[79] The roles Churchill had assigned to the USSR and Japan in 1933 were therefore reversed: it was now the USSR that was rendering a valuable service 'in the Far East to civilisation and also to British and United States interests'.[80]

Japan also had to take into account the attitude of the United States, which was opposed to Japanese expansion and could place a powerful fleet on Japan's eastern flank. Churchill was encouraged by the increasingly close cooperation between Britain and the United States in the Far East during the late 1930s. And even at this early date he was prepared to allow the Americans the leading role in this area. When the possibility of applying sanctions against Japan was raised in October 1937, for example, Churchill emphasized the importance of acting in support of any action taken by the United States:

> If they are prepared to act you are quite safe in working with that great branch of English-speaking people. If our two countries go together in this matter, I doubt whether any harm could come to either of us. Alone we cannot intervene effectively. It is too far off and we are not strong enough. Our rule must be to give more support to the United States. As far as they will go we will go.[81]

One of Churchill's main concerns in the final year of peace was that Britain's naval position in European waters might be jeopardized by the premature dispatch of a large British fleet to the Far East. By 1938 his hopes that Italy would realign itself with Britain and France against Germany had faded: Mussolini's increasingly close ties to Nazi Germany made it clear that Italy had to be considered a potential enemy. In 1937 the COS and the government concluded that if confronted with war against Germany, Italy, and Japan simultaneously, the Far Eastern theatre rather than the Mediterranean would have top priority after the defence of Britain itself.[82] Under Chatfield, who served as First Sea Lord until November 1938, the navy not only accepted but embraced these priorities. His successor, Admiral Sir Roger Backhouse, was less certain. By early 1939, with Britain's new battleships still under construction and some older capital ships undergoing extensive modernization programs, the Admiralty acknowledged that the fleet Britain could send to the Far East might not only be weaker than Japan's, but significantly weaker.

Backhouse calculated that Britain must retain a force of at least six capital ships in European waters to contain the German and Italian navies. This would leave only five or six capital ships available for the Far East, and

Backhouse asserted that a force this size 'against a Japanese Fleet of 10 ships plus her full strength in other classes of ships is not adequate in the proper meaning of that word'.[83] With the support of Admiral Reginald Drax, who had been brought to the Admiralty to develop offensive war plans, Backhouse proposed a new strategy for a three-front war.[84] Rather than abandoning the Mediterranean for the Far East, Britain would concentrate its forces there first in order to knock out Italy, the weakest of Britain's enemies. British interests in the Far East would be protected at first by a small 'flying squadron' comprised of two fast battleships, two aircraft carriers, and various auxiliary vessels. It was hoped that such a force could protect British trade and territory in the Indian Ocean, prevent Japan from establishing a base in the region, destroy Japanese raiders, and pose a threat to Japan's communications with China.[85]

Although this scheme was received with apprehension in the navy, British politicians were enthused about the idea of concentrating British naval forces in the Mediterranean for a 'knock-out blow' against Italy.[86] The Strategic Appreciation Committee of the Cabinet concluded that a small covering force *could* defend British interests in the Far East for a prolonged period. It decided in April 1939 that 'Offensive operations in the Mediterranean against Italy offered the best prospects for speedy results and should not, therefore, be lightly broken off.'[87] There was opposition, however. Chatfield, now serving in Chamberlain's Cabinet as Minister for Coordination of Defence, warned that failure to send a strong fleet immediately to the Far East would have serious political repercussions, and might ultimately drive Australia and New Zealand to look to the United States for their protection. The right course, he maintained, was to rely on French support to deal with the combined German–Italian naval threat in Europe, abandon the eastern Mediterranean if necessary, and dispatch a fleet of at least seven capital ships to Singapore. This force would, he maintained in March, 'adopt the normal strategy of the weaker fleet, a strategy which was well defined in history and which had been employed by the German Fleet in the last war'.[88]

Churchill entered into this debate later in March with a lengthy memorandum on sea power. Although still only a backbench MP, his stature was such that he did not hesitate to send a copy directly to both the prime minister and Lord Halifax, the Foreign Secretary. In this document he warned against diverting forces to the Far East before Britain's position in Europe was secure.[89] Britain, he insisted, 'must not be drawn from our main theme by any effort to protect' minor interests in China. 'Only if the United States comes in against Japan could we supply even a squadron of cruisers to operate with them. On this tableau we must bear the losses and punishment, awaiting the final result of the struggle.' There was little doubt in his mind that Singapore could hold out long enough for the Royal Navy to 'liquidate' the Italian fleet. The government should therefore make its case to the Australians, who could be expected to 'play the game by us as they have always done. Tell them the whole story,' he advised, 'and they will come along. In the first year of a world war they would be in no danger whatever in their homeland, and by the end of the first year we may hope to have cleared up the seas and oceans.' British sea power should be employed at the beginning of a war to inflict a decisive blow against Italy. In his opinion, British forces could achieve 'a series of swift and striking victories in this theatre', especially if Britain's ample naval superiority were further augmented by the French navy. Control of the Mediterranean might be achieved, he predicted, 'certainly within two months, possibly sooner'. This would effectively isolate Italian forces in North Africa and might easily force Italy out of the war.[90]

Notably, the naval threat from Germany was still not a serious concern for Churchill, even in the spring of 1939. It would be years before the German navy could 'form a line of battle for a general engagement', he informed Parliament in March. And because the Germans would be reluctant to jeopardize their command of the Baltic by risking important ships in attacks against British trade, there would be little for the Admiralty to worry about from Germany except 'submarines and raiding cruisers, or perhaps one pocket-battleship'.[91] It was only after Britain had secured command of the Mediterranean, and assuming no expedition had been launched against Singapore or Australia, that Churchill recommended a 'great naval offensive' against Germany. As in the First World War, his long-term ambitions were focused on the Baltic, an area that continued to be critical to the Germans. 'Scandinavian supplies, Swedish ore, and above all, protection against Russian descents on the long, undefended coast-line of Germany (in one place little more than a hundred miles from Berlin) make it imperative,' Churchill concluded, 'for Germany to dominate the Baltic.'[92] He therefore recommended that 'Ardent officers should be set to work for a year upon the problems of entering the Baltic and living there in indefinite ascendancy.' To General Sir Edmund Ironside, soon to be appointed Chief of the Imperial General Staff (CIGS), he proclaimed in July 1939 that a squadron of battleships in the Baltic would 'paralyse the Germans and immobilize many German divisions'.[93]

Churchill's memorandum received a warm welcome at the Foreign Office. Sir Alexander Cadogan, the permanent undersecretary, forwarded a copy to the British ambassador to the United States, noting that Churchill's views on the importance of concentrating first on Italy 'accord very closely with our own'.[94] Chamberlain sent his copy of the memorandum to Chatfield, who reported that Churchill's ideas were generally sound and, with respect to the Mediterranean, that his recommendations had recently been accepted by the Strategic Appreciation Committee. Chatfield continued to have doubts about this policy, however, and took this opportunity to warn Chamberlain that it would mean running considerable risks in the Far East, especially if, as he thought, the Italians could not be knocked out within two or three months. Chatfield was non-committal about Churchill's idea of sending British forces into the Baltic. 'This,' he concluded, 'is a problem for the Admiralty.'[95]

In the event, the debate over strategic priorities remained unresolved. Despite the enthusiasm of politicians for a 'knock-out blow' against Italy, Admiralty support for this policy suddenly disappeared in mid-1939 when poor health forced Backhouse out of office. He was succeeded as First Sea Lord by Admiral Dudley Pound, and the Admiralty quickly reverted to a more orthodox strategy. In July 1939 all references to the dispatch of a 'flying squadron' were dropped from the Admiralty's war plans.[96] A revised Eastern War Memorandum asserted that any fleet sent to the Far East 'must be capable of engaging the main Japanese Fleet under conditions favourable to ourselves. In September 1939, this force must include 7 capital ships.'[97] If the Cabinet chose instead to concentrate British ships in the Mediterranean rather than the Far East, Pound believed a small covering force could do no more than secure communications in the Indian Ocean and deter the Japanese from major operations in the South China Seas or Australasian waters. If the Japanese fleet moved south in strength, he expected British naval forces to retire from Singapore and operate from another base, probably Trincomalee in Ceylon.[98]

Thus, on the eve of the Second World War, Churchill's strategic views diverged from those of the Admiralty in several important areas: on the order of priorities in a three-front war, on the likelihood of delivering a knock-out blow against Italy, and on whether Britain should adopt an offensive or defensive strategy against Japan. But in most other respects, Churchill was substantially in agreement with naval leaders. Like Chamberlain, he had increasingly looked towards the air force rather than the navy to ensure Britain's security and deter Germany from war. But he nevertheless remained committed in principle to the maintenance of British sea power, and continued to view the navy as essential to the survival of the British Empire. Moreover, he had publicly sided with the Admiralty in the battles most important to it: the rebuilding of the battle fleet, the primacy of the capital ship, and navy control of the Fleet Air Arm. When Churchill became First Lord of the Admiralty in September 1939, Japanese and Italian neutrality meant that the most potentially divisive strategic questions could be avoided. The issue that would soon plague Churchill's relationship with his naval advisers was one that he devoted little attention to during the 1930s: how to use the navy offensively against Germany.

6

First Lord of the Admiralty, 1939–40: The Phoney War and the Norwegian Campaign

Winston Churchill's banishment to the political wilderness ended on the day Britain and France declared war on Germany, 3 September 1939. As war approached and Hitler's true nature became more evident, Churchill's stock with the British public increased. When hostilities finally broke out, Prime Minister Neville Chamberlain accepted, although without any enthusiasm, that Churchill would have to be given a place in the government. The renegade Conservative was offered the same post he had left in disgrace almost twenty-five years earlier: First Lord of the Admiralty. Like the other two service ministers, Churchill also became a member of the War Cabinet, a small group of ministers who, together with the prime minister, oversaw the central direction of the war effort.

The main outlines of Anglo-French grand strategy had been decided well before the outbreak of war.[1] Germany's rapid rearmament during the 1930s meant that Hitler entered the conflict with the advantage in both land and air forces, but British leaders assumed that the superior resources of the British and French empires would ensure their ultimate victory in a protracted conflict. The Allies therefore adopted a defensive posture at the outset: as long as they could hold off strong German attacks early in the war, they could begin mobilizing their economies for a lengthy attritional struggle in which they would have the advantage. Meanwhile, Allied superiority at sea would be exploited to impose an economic blockade and begin wearing down German strength and resolve. Once the balance of forces on land and in the air had tipped in the Allies' favour—a process that was likely to take several years—they would shift to the strategic offensive and take the war to Germany.

British governments of the 1930s had been reluctant to commit themselves to the dispatch of ground forces to operate on the Continent, but by early 1939 it had been accepted that a 'continental commitment' of British troops to fight alongside the French was both politically and militarily necessary, as it had been in the First World War. Britain's contribution to the Allied cause therefore included a large army. Churchill was less enthusiastic about this course than he had been in 1914, but he accepted that it was unavoidable. 'I doubt whether the French would acquiesce in a division of effort which gave us the sea and air and left them to pay almost the whole blood-tax on land,' he remarked to Chamberlain not long after the outbreak of war. 'Such an arrangement would certainly be agreeable to us; but I do not like the idea of our having to continue the war single-handed.'[2] In March 1939 the government had authorized the expansion of the army to a force of thirty-two divisions, twenty-six of which would belong to the Territorial Army. Shortly after the outbreak of war, the War Cabinet established a special Land Forces Committee to consider the future size of the army. This body proposed that Britain should prepare to support an army of fifty-five divisions by the end of the second year of war. This figure would include Britain's thirty-two divisions, plus another fourteen from the Dominions, four from India, and five belonging to allies.[3]

There was no concern that this ambitious programme would draw resources away from the navy. 'Our naval demands would probably be less than in the last war,' Churchill assured the War Cabinet.[4] Chamberlain and other ministers were in fact more worried that the army's programme might interfere with the expansion of the Royal Air Force, which was their top priority.[5] Germany's continuing superiority over the Allies in the air and the devastating impact of German air power in the rapid conquest of Poland made a strong impression on British leaders. Lord Halifax, the Foreign Secretary and an influential member of the War Cabinet, was stating the prevalent view when he remarked that 'the air would probably prove the decisive factor [in the War]. Sufficient strength in the air might make German victory on land an impossibility.'[6] Churchill shared this sentiment. Writing to Chamberlain on 18 September, he professed to be 'entirely with you in believing that Air Power stands foremost in our requirements, and indeed I sometimes think that it may be the ultimate path by which victory will be gained'.[7] But he did not feel Britain could afford to reduce its commitment to support an army of fifty-five divisions. This figure was not formally approved, however, until the Land Forces Committee reassured the War Cabinet that the Air Ministry's requirements could still be met.[8]

The navy occupied a more uncertain place in Allied grand strategy. No one, least of all Churchill, questioned the need to maintain a large fleet to protect Britain's essential maritime communications from surface raiders and U-boats. But this task was essentially defensive, and Britain seemed to possess ample forces to secure the sea lanes. Germany was incapable of challenging Britain directly for command of the sea. The German navy's two battlecruisers (*Scharnhorst* and *Gneisenau*) and three 'pocket battleships' (large armoured cruisers with 11-inch guns) were potentially formidable commerce raiders, but they were significantly outgunned by the thirteen capital ships immediately available to Britain on the outbreak of war. Moreover, two additional battleships were expected to rejoin the fleet once their modernization programmes were completed in 1940, and the five new King George V-class battleships would be ready in 1940–2. The two German battleships then under construction, *Bismarck* and *Tirpitz*, would be a serious menace once completed, but they were unlikely to upset the overall balance at sea. Nor was there reason to question the navy's ability to fulfil its offensive role. Allied planners entered the war with high expectations for economic warfare, but with Germany able to draw on the resources of the Soviet Union, Italy, and most of Eastern Europe, blockade was unlikely to have a significant impact in the short term. There was thus little incentive for the War Cabinet to invest heavily in expanding a fleet that was already capable of meeting its immediate offensive and defensive obligations.

As First Lord of the Admiralty, Churchill might have been expected to press the navy's case for a greater share of the national resources, but he was reluctant to do so. The Admiralty, he explained to Chamberlain in September, had used its position 'arbitrarily and selfishly' during the First World War to the detriment of the other services. This was especially true, he felt, during the final year of the conflict, 'when they were overwhelmingly strong, and had the American Navy added to them. I am every day restraining such tendencies in the common interest.'[9] To ensure that the navy did not claim more than its fair share of resources, Churchill carefully scrutinized its building plans. A week after taking office, he proposed to suspend work on heavy ships that would not be ready before 1942, including one or possibly two of the King George V-class battleships. He also wanted to delay the start of the four Lion-class battleships, which had been authorized (but not started) before the war. He hoped these measures would free up resources for army expansion and the construction of smaller ships for trade-protection duties. Germany, he predicted, would be building submarines 'day and night', and might have a fleet of two to three hundred by the summer of 1940.[10] To counter this threat, Churchill hoped to increase the production of destroyers and other escort vessels.[11]

Admiral Sir Dudley Pound, the First Sea Lord, and his advisers took a different view. With Japan and Italy both still potential enemies, the Naval Staff continued to aspire to a two-power standard in capital ships. They calculated that failure to complete all five King George Vs and the first two Lion-class battleships would leave Britain as many as five capital ships behind Germany and Japan by 1943. The navy could maintain a margin of superiority over these two powers only if it completed all its authorized construction *and* if Germany did not complete any battleships, including *Bismarck* and *Tirpitz*. This, Pound remarked, was not a possibility 'on which we should be wise to gamble'. Britain's battlefleet was, he warned Churchill, 'the foundation of our maritime power....Once we have delayed these ships, we cannot retrieve the situation.' Naval leaders were therefore alarmed by Churchill's single-minded focus on the war with Germany. 'There may be a time,' Pound wrote, 'when, in order to win this war, we may have to divert labour to other purposes and run the risk of naval inferiority at its end, but in my opinion that time has not yet come.'[12] On 12 September he warned his chief that 'It would be fatal to the Empire to emerge from this war only with old battleships, when we might be faced with sending a fleet to the Far East.'[13]

A collision between Churchill and his advisers was avoided only because of delays in the production of 16-inch gun mountings for the Lion-class battleships. The Board of Admiralty agreed on 28 September that the hulls for these ships could be 'deferred for a year without materially prejudicing the ultimate date of completion'.[14] This delay would allow the navy to build additional destroyers and cruisers. Churchill remained unhappy, however, about delays in the completion of battleships, aircraft carriers, and cruisers already under construction. 'We have at this moment to distinguish carefully,' he admonished Pound in October, 'between running an industry or a profession, and winning the war.' Above all, he considered it essential to transfer workers to ships that could be finished the soonest. 'All ships finishing in 1941 fall into the shade,' he wrote, 'and those of 1942 into the darkness. We must keep the superiority in 1940.'[15]

Churchill's assumption that Britain's capital-ship position was secure began to appear less certain as evidence mounted of heavy Japanese naval construction.[16] In January 1940 the Naval Intelligence Division (NID) estimated that Japan was building four new battleships, three aircraft carriers, and as many as five heavy armoured cruisers.[17] When the 1940–1 navy estimates came up for consideration at the Admiralty in February, Churchill agreed to match this capital-ship construction by proceeding with all four of the Lions and authorizing one new 15-inch battlecruiser. He was not convinced, however, that the navy's intelligence was accurate. In a minute to Pound, Rear Admiral Tom Phillips (the Vice Chief of the Naval Staff), and Rear Admiral John Godfrey (the Director of Naval Intelligence), Churchill demanded a careful examination of Japan's shipbuilding capabilities before he took his new building programme to the Cabinet. In his opinion, the NID had not made sufficient allowances for a drastic deterioration in Japan's finances due to its protracted war in China. Moreover, he doubted whether Japan could produce sufficient steel for such a large programme of new construction. 'I do not feel,' he concluded, 'that mere rumours of ships they are said to have laid down' were sufficient justification for a large British capital-ship programme.[18]

The problem for the intelligence services, as Godfrey readily admitted, was that Japanese secrecy was virtually impossible to penetrate. '[W]e do not know for certain what their Naval Programme is,' he reported in February, 'and the information we have given is based on meagre reports from Secret Sources, Naval Attaches' reports and C.-in-C. China's conclusions.'[19] The government's Industrial Intelligence Centre (IIC), which had been incorporated into the Ministry of Economic Warfare (MEW) at the outset of war, shared many of Churchill's views on Japan's economic limitations, but its chief, Desmond Morton, generally supported the NID's conclusions. Morton, a close pre-war associate of Churchill, calculated that Japan might be building up to six battleships, two 'pocket' battleships, six heavy cruisers, and four aircraft carriers.[20] Godfrey therefore stood by his earlier estimate, and cautioned Churchill not to underestimate Japan's ability to pursue a large armaments programme. Germany's financial problems had not apparently hampered its armaments efforts, he noted, and Japan's might not do so either.[21]

The Admiralty's case for capital-ship construction was thus based on a 'worst-case' analysis of Japanese shipbuilding capabilities, rather than on reliable intelligence about Japan's actual construction programmes. Churchill was sufficiently concerned about the long-term naval balance that he endorsed most of the Admiralty's proposals, although he ultimately decided to delay work on the final two Lion-class battleships (*Conqueror* and *Thunderer*), a decision the Sea Lords accepted only with 'great reluctance'.[22] The estimates presented to the Cabinet in March 1940 authorized work on three new capital ships, the *Lion* and *Temeraire* (originally included in the 1938/39 estimates), and a new 15-inch-gun battlecruiser, *Vanguard*, whose construction would be hastened by using spare gun turrets already on hand.[23] According to the Naval Staff's projections, this programme would provide rough equality in capital ships between the Japanese navy and a British Far Eastern fleet up to 1944.[24] The new estimates also called for additional deck armour to be fitted to Britain's four old 'R'-class battleships, to strengthen them against air attack, the construction of a monitor, 'which may be needed for inshore work', and a large programme of escort vessels. There was no room left, however, for other classes of warships, and no new aircraft carriers or cruisers were authorized for the fiscal year 1940–1.

This programme reflects Churchill's overriding concern with the war against Germany. Potential threats from Italy and Japan were as yet secondary considerations. And if the war went according to plan, these dangers might never materialize at all. The Naval Staff shared Churchill's belief that the naval challenge from Germany alone was manageable. A massive naval expansion programme authorized by Hitler in early 1939 was still in its early stages when Germany invaded Poland on 1 September, and the Royal Navy, its strength bolstered by the French fleet, possessed an overwhelming superiority over the German navy. The Germans were themselves pessimistic about their prospects in the coming naval war. Admiral Erich Raeder, the head of the German navy, recorded in September 1939 that his forces were 'in no way very adequately equipped for the great struggle with Great Britain'. The submarine arm was too small, in his opinion, 'to have any decisive effect on the war', and the surface fleet was 'so inferior in number and strength' that 'they can do no more than show that they know how to die gallantly and thus are willing to create the foundations for later reconstruction'.[25]

In September 1939 Britain's Home Fleet, under the command of Admiral Sir Charles Forbes, contained five battleships, three battlecruisers, and two aircraft carriers. This force, based primarily at Scapa Flow in the Orkney Islands, was positioned to block German surface ships from the Atlantic, and provide 'cover' for British forces in the North Sea.[26] Given the imbalance between the two fleets in surface forces, nobody expected Germany to concentrate its heavy ships in home waters, a strategy that had failed in the First World War. The greatest threat to Britain's maritime communications now appeared to be the dispersal of Germany's relatively small force of modern warships to prey on British shipping. As Pound remarked, 'Nothing would paralyse our supply system and seaborne trade so successfully as attack by surface raiders.'[27] These raiders came in a variety of forms, the most dangerous of which were Germany's three 'pocket battleships'. These warships, conceived under the restrictions of the Treaty of Versailles, were formidable commerce raiders. Built for high endurance and armed with 11-inch guns, they significantly outgunned the 6- and 8-inch armament carried by the British cruisers that normally protected the far-flung sea lanes. With a speed of 26 knots, the German raiders could expect to outrun more heavily armed vessels.

Germany's U-boats did not yet pose the same level of threat. Germany had only fifty-seven submarines in service at the beginning of the war, and only about half were capable of operations in the Atlantic. Hitler, moreover, initially avoided unrestricted submarine warfare: U-boat commanders were instructed to adhere to prize regulations. These restrictions were gradually relaxed in the coming months, but not formally abandoned until August 1940. All this considerably reduced the dangers for British shipping, and appeared to justify the Admiralty's pre-war predictions that the combination of convoy and asdic (sonar) would reduce the U-boat problem to manageable proportions. Churchill, for his part, recognized that the Germans would not neglect this form of warfare indefinitely. His enthusiasm for building escort vessels in large numbers was driven by the need to meet future threats as much as current ones. He was right to do so. The head of the U-boat service, Commodore Karl Dönitz, hoped eventually to expand his force to at least three hundred vessels. Fortunately for the British, German resources were not allocated to this programme until after the fall of France in the summer of 1940.

As First Lord, Churchill strove to contain the U-boat threat to the North Sea. He hoped to block German access to the Atlantic by laying minefields in the English Channel and across the North Sea from the Orkney Islands to Norway. The former were completed by October 1939, although the latter—known as the 'northern barrage'—were only approved the following month, and not started until after the fall of France. Air and sea patrols were also established to cover the area between the Orkney Islands and Norway.[28] These measures, along with the establishment of a partial convoy system, proved effective. During the first four months of war, U-boats sank an average of approximately 105,000 tons of merchant shipping per month. However, most of their successes came against vessels sailing independently. Of the 114 ships lost in this period, only four were sailing in convoy. During the first four months of 1940, 115 ships were lost, of which eight were in convoy. Though significant, these losses were far from crippling—and they came at a heavy price for the Germans: twenty-two U-boats were sunk in the same eight-month period.[29]

Churchill, who tended to measure success in the U-boat war by the number of enemy vessels destroyed, had good reason to be satisfied with these results. But he hoped to inflict even greater losses on the U-boats by actively hunting them down rather than relying on counter-attacks by convoy escorts. The use of the navy's large ('fleet') aircraft carriers to protect trade in the Western Approaches was not a success, and had to be discontinued after the loss of HMS *Courageous* to a U-boat in September 1939. Churchill remained committed, however, to developing the means to seize the initiative. 'Nothing can be more important in the anti-submarine war,' he wrote to Pound in November, 'than to try to obtain an independent flotilla which could work like a cavalry division on the approaches without worrying about the traffic or U-boat sinkings, but could systematically search large areas over a wide front.'[30] Naval leaders were sympathetic to this idea, although the general shortage of escort vessels for convoy work in this phase of the war ruled against it.[31]

The navy enjoyed similar successes against German surface raiders. In September 1939 two pocket battleships, *Graf Spee* and *Deutschland*, were already in the Atlantic awaiting the commencement of hostilities. The *Graf Spee* was the more aggressive of the two raiders. Its first victim was sunk off the coast of Brazil on 30 September. The Admiralty responded to this news by forming nine separate 'hunting groups' to locate and destroy the ship and any other German raiders. These groups were a significant commitment of Allied naval forces, including five aircraft carriers, four capital ships, and fourteen cruisers, many of which were drawn from the Home and Mediterranean fleets. In addition, three battleships and two cruisers were diverted for convoy-protection work in the north Atlantic.[32] The *Graf Spee* sank nine more ships in the coming weeks, but was located and engaged by three British cruisers (*Exeter*, *Ajax*, and *Achilles*) on the morning of 13 December. The German ship soon broke off the action and retired to Montevideo harbour in Uruguay, a neutral port. Four days later, believing that the British had amassed superior forces outside the harbour, the *Graf Spee*'s captain scuttled the ship.

The *Deutschland*, less enterprising than its sister ship, returned to Germany in mid-November after destroying just two ships. The only other significant threat to British shipping during this period came from air attacks and mines.

The German air force accounted for thirty-seven ships in the first eight months of the war. Mines were a more serious problem, destroying 140 ships in these months and damaging many others, including the fleet flagship *Nelson*. Germany's new magnetic mines were a particular concern for the Admiralty, although their impact was significantly reduced when effective countermeasures were developed in early 1940.

The navy's primary offensive task was to weaken Germany's war economy by cutting off its imports of essential raw materials by sea. As in the First World War, the navy intercepted contraband cargoes destined for enemy ports, while diplomatic measures were employed to limit Germany's trade with European neutrals. Blockade was an inherently slow method of wearing down an enemy's war-making ability, but Britain's leaders entered the war confident that it had been effective in the First World War, and that Germany would be susceptible to this form of pressure again. Even though the Nazi-Soviet pact of August 1939 would undermine the effectiveness of the Allied blockade, the Ministry of Economic Warfare still believed that Germany would have trouble making good its deficiencies in imported raw materials. Churchill, whose faith in blockade was never strong, was not as optimistic. He was also temperamentally incapable of waiting patiently for blockade to produce tangible results. Shortly after arriving at the Admiralty in September 1939, he had begun looking for opportunities whereby the navy could strike directly at the enemy. The 'search for a naval offensive,' he asserted, 'must be incessant'.[33]

Churchill's attention was once again drawn to the Baltic. On 12 September 1939 he prepared a detailed memorandum outlining the potential benefits of operations in this region. The Scandinavian states, he argued, could be brought into the war on the Allied side, which in turn might have a 'far-reaching' impact on the attitude of the Soviet Union. A powerful British squadron in the Baltic would isolate Germany from Scandinavia and deprive it of supplies of iron ore and food. It would also force the Germans to keep their limited naval forces concentrated in the Baltic and to divert resources to defend their coastline 'against bombardment, or possibly even, if the alliance of the Scandinavian Powers was obtained, military descents'.[34] It is notable, however, that Churchill no longer regarded the occupation of an island near the German North Sea coast as an essential precondition for the movement of ships into the Baltic. The solidity of naval opinion against the scheme during the First World War had made an impression on Churchill, although not, it seems, until after the war was over. In 1926, while completing the final volume of his wartime memoirs, Churchill had sufficient doubts about the feasibility of the Borkum plan to ask Admiral Keyes, an aggressive admiral whose professional opinion he respected, for his views. Keyes advised that the scheme had been carefully studied and rejected during the war by the Admiralty's Plans Division. Churchill was evidently convinced that the idea was unworkable, as he dropped from his memoirs a chapter outlining the offensive naval plans he had advocated in 1917.[35]

This was the end of Churchill's enthusiasm for seizing an island base in the North Sea. In 1939 his Baltic schemes depended, much as Fisher's had, on the employment of specially designed or modified vessels. Churchill was optimistic that ships' anti-aircraft batteries could neutralize the danger from air attack once a squadron had reached the Baltic. To provide additional security, he proposed increasing the deck armour of two or three of the old 'R'-class battleships. Caissons—large watertight chambers—would be attached to the sides of these ships to offer protection against mines. These modified battleships would provide the firepower to drive away the enemy's heavy surface ships. Churchill proposed that they be accompanied by a supporting force of cruisers, destroyers, submarines, and a variety of ancillary craft, including specially prepared tankers capable of supplying the squadron with oil for at least three months. An aircraft carrier might also be employed. In the event that Britain gained allies in the region, suitable bases would become available, considerably easing the fleet's problems. And if bases did not materialize, Churchill did not see 'why the Fleet should not return as it came'.[36]

Churchill dubbed this project 'Catherine', after Empress Catherine the Great of Russia, and instructed the Naval Staff to give it further consideration. Developments in air power made the idea of a Baltic expedition completely impractical, although this was not yet evident to Churchill or all of his professional advisers. Anticipating opposition from the Naval Staff, Churchill also created his own ad hoc committee to study the scheme. The officer in charge was the recently retired Admiral of the Fleet the Earl of Cork and Orrery. Cork was an offensively minded commander who could be counted on to produce the sort of optimistic assessment Churchill wanted, and he did not disappoint. As a 'military undertaking,' Cork wrote on 26 September, an expedition into the Baltic was 'perfectly feasible—hazardous no doubt but, for that very reason, containing the germ of a great triumph'.[37]

Pound and Phillips disliked the scheme from the outset, however. Like most naval leaders, they were instinctively opposed to exposing warships to destruction by mines or aerial attacks in operations where they would not have an opportunity to inflict comparable damage on enemy warships. They also had justifiable doubts about what such an expedition might achieve. The First Sea Lord reminded Churchill that even if a strong naval force were placed in the Baltic, Germany would still have access to the Soviet Union through their common border in Poland. There would also be little impact on Germany's supplies of Scandinavian iron ore, which only came through the Baltic during the months it was ice-free, approximately April through November. Pound insisted that such an operation could only be contemplated if the Soviet Union remained neutral and if Britain had the active cooperation of Sweden. Moreover, he stipulated that any force dispatched to 'the Baltic must be such that we can with our Allies at that time win the war without them in spite of any probable combination against us'.[38] Churchill tended to view the R-class battleships as expendable because they were not essential for maintaining naval superiority over Germany, but the First Sea Lord and his advisers were naturally eager to preserve these ships in the event that Italy or Japan entered the conflict. Even old battleships would still have a role to play in these circumstances. In any event, Pound did not feel that he could afford to take two or three capital ships out of service long enough to make the necessary modifications, at least until it was certain that Italy and Japan would remain neutral.

By late November 1939, Churchill admitted that there was no possibility of assembling the necessary forces until the end of March 1940 at the earliest. He instructed that planning be continued on that basis, but little progress was in fact made.[39] By early December 1939, Pound had decided that the Baltic project should be formally abandoned. He wrote to Churchill that there appeared to be 'no possibility whatever' that the Soviet Union would welcome a British presence in the region, and that this, rather than the attitude of Sweden, must be the determining factor. The First Sea Lord proposed to suspend preparations indefinitely and disband Cork's independent planning committee.[40] These proposals immediately drew fire from Churchill. He informed Pound and Phillips that he was not prepared to rule out the possibility that 'Catherine' might be feasible under certain conditions, and he requested that preparations for this operation 'should be pressed in so far as they do not impede daily operations'.[41]

Three months into this new war, Churchill was once again becoming frustrated by the Admiralty's inability to generate plans for striking at the enemy. Rather than disbanding Cork's committee, Churchill decided that its functions needed to be broadened. It now became responsible for examining the offensive schemes being developed by the Plans Division of the Admiralty and for reviewing proposals put forward by another offensively minded senior officer, Admiral Sir Reginald Drax.[42] Churchill concluded his minute by lecturing the First Sea Lord on the importance of seizing the initiative at sea. 'Our dominant strategy,' he wrote on 11 December 1939, 'must be shaped by events':

> The entry of the Baltic, for instance, would soon bring the raiders home and give us measureless relief. If we allow ourselves indefinitely to be confined to an absolute defensive by far weaker forces, we shall simply be worried and worn down while making huge demands upon the national resources. I could never become responsible for a naval strategy which excluded the offensive principle and relegated us to keeping open the lines of communication and maintaining the blockade. Presently we may find the U-boats in the outer sea, and what is to happen then?[43]

With resistance to a Baltic expedition mounting, Churchill's attention shifted to other offensive projects. The first, conceived as retaliation for Germany's indiscriminate use of mines in British waters, was to launch floating mines into the Rhine to paralyze German traffic on the river. In mid-November Churchill instructed the Naval Staff to investigate whether mines could be fed into the river from French territory, and constructed either to sink or explode before reaching neutral waters.[44] The plan was soon expanded to include air-dropped mines and a wider range of targets within Germany's internal waterway system. The Air Ministry raised concerns about German retaliation and the legality of the scheme, but the War Cabinet agreed with Churchill in early December that Germany's disregard for international law justified British countermeasures.[45] With the French army also favourably disposed to the project, the British began preparing to lay mines in March or April 1940.

Churchill was also drawn to offensive measures in the North Sea that would tighten the British blockade. The navy had little trouble denying German merchant ships access to the Atlantic sea lanes once war broke out, but preventing Swedish iron ore from reaching Germany was a more difficult proposition. There were strong incentives to interfere with this trade. During the late 1930s the intelligence services had concluded that the German economy was particularly vulnerable in two areas: imports of iron ore from Sweden and oil from Romania and the Soviet Union.[46] According to one optimistic IIC assessment, the denial of Swedish iron ore would not only dislocate the German economy but might bring German industry 'to a stop in a very short time, possibly measurable in weeks'.[47] The Gulf of Bothnia in the Baltic Sea was normally frozen over during the winter months, which forced the Germans to import Swedish ore through Oxelösund in the Baltic or Narvik in northern Norway during that part of the year (Map 3). Various schemes had been considered in Whitehall in 1937–9 to interfere with this trade in wartime, including military action or sabotage to destroy Sweden's mines, or similar action against the Norwegian port of Narvik and the railway lines connecting it to Sweden.[48]

Churchill turned his attention to this problem in September 1939. At this time, he hoped diplomatic efforts would be sufficient to reduce Swedish

Map 3. The North Sea and the Baltic in the Second World War

exports to Germany, but he reminded the War Cabinet that Britain's sea power would allow them to ration Sweden if it did not cooperate. In the event that large quantities of iron ore reached Germany through Norwegian ports, he warned his colleagues that 'more drastic action' would eventually be needed.[49] To prepare for this eventuality, Churchill instructed the Naval Staff to begin planning for the laying of a minefield in Norwegian territorial waters.[50] His attention returned to Narvik in November, just prior to ice rendering the Baltic supply route unusable. Ronald Cross, the Minister of Economic Warfare, sent new intelligence on Swedish iron-ore shipments to Churchill on the 9th, noting that it was 'of the utmost importance that everything possible should be done' to prevent these supplies being shipped from Narvik.[51] Churchill asked Desmond Morton at the MEW for additional information on Swedish iron-ore exports to Germany, and received an optimistic report highlighting Germany's vulnerability.[52] Three days later, when the War Cabinet discussed plans for the northern barrage, Churchill raised the idea of extending the minefield into Norwegian waters in order to block iron-ore shipments from Narvik.

The idea initially met with little enthusiasm, but a report subsequently prepared by the MEW seemed to justify Churchill's enthusiasm.[53] This document concluded that cutting off the flow of iron ore to Germany through Narvik would probably not produce decisive results, but would nevertheless 'have an extremely serious repercussion on German industrial output' by the spring of 1940. If Germany's iron-ore imports via the Swedish port of Luleå, in the northern end of the Gulf of Bothnia, could also be stopped, the MEW predicted that it 'might well bring German industry to a standstill and would in any case have a profound effect on the duration of the War'.[54] Thus encouraged, Churchill laid out two courses of action open to the British in the short term. First, a minefield could be placed in Norwegian waters to force ships travelling along the coast to move beyond the three-mile limit, where they could legally be seized. Second, British warships might enter these waters to capture as prizes all ships carrying iron ore to Germany.[55]

These proposals were less ambitious than a large-scale naval movement into the Baltic, but they were also less dangerous and seemed to hold out the possibility of significant gains. The War Cabinet invited Churchill to prepare a memorandum outlining his ideas, and the First Lord pressed the scheme with his usual vigour. 'The effectual stoppage of the Norwegian iron ore to Germany ranks as a major offensive operation of war,' he wrote on 16 December:

No other measure is open to us for many months to come which gives so good a chance of abridging the waste and destruction of the conflict, or of perhaps preventing the vast slaughters which will attend the grapple of the main armies....

If Germany can be cut from all Swedish iron ore supplies from now onwards till the end of 1940, a blow will have been struck at her war-making capacity equal to a first-class victory in the field or from the air, and without any serious sacrifice of life. It might, indeed, be immediately decisive.

Churchill was confident that the Norwegians would not retaliate against Britain, either militarily or economically, and he *welcomed* the possibility that British actions might provoke a German invasion of Scandinavia. Britain's mastery of the sea would allow the Allies to meet the Germans on advantageous terms in the region, he predicted.[56] 'If Germany attempted an overlordship of Scandinavia,' he claimed, 'it would give us the opportunity to take what we wanted, and this, with our sea power, we could do.' In his view, the Allies would have little difficulty establishing sea and air bases on islands in the region, and if necessary they could dispatch troops to the mainland, where the mountainous terrain would nullify Germany's superiority in armoured and mechanized forces. Ultimately, Britain might establish air bases far enough south to support naval operations in the Baltic. When the War Cabinet met on 18 December, Churchill insisted that Britain 'had everything to gain and nothing to lose by the drawing of Norway and Sweden into the war'.[57]

Churchill also took his arguments to the Military Coordination Committee (MCC), an important committee that included both the professional and political heads of the three armed services. Chaired by the Minister for Coordination of Defence, Lord Chatfield, this body was responsible for advising the War Cabinet on questions of strategy. Churchill found a valuable ally here in General Ironside, the Chief of the Imperial General Staff (CIGS), who shared Churchill's frustration with Allied passivity. Ironside was also impressed by the MEW's assessments of German vulnerability. Scandinavian operations, in his view, offered 'a legitimate side-show': the Allies appeared to have an opportunity to seize the strategic initiative and divert German forces into a theatre where they would be forced to operate at a disadvantage. The MCC was receptive to the idea of sending Allied forces into Sweden to seize control of its minefields.[58]

The outbreak of hostilities between Finland and the Soviet Union on 30 November 1939 also focussed attention on Scandinavia. Churchill was quick to exploit the general outpouring of sympathy for the beleaguered Finns to gather support for his Scandinavian plans. On 22 December he proposed to the War Cabinet that Sweden and Norway be urged to go to the aid of Finland in return for an Anglo-French guarantee of assistance in the event of a Soviet or German invasion.[59] This would be accompanied by a declaration to Norway and Sweden that Britain intended to take active measures if necessary to stop the flow of iron ore to Germany. In the event that Germany attempted to use force to secure these supplies, Britain should be ready to send forces into the region and secure the ore fields.

Chamberlain and Halifax, the Foreign Secretary, who generally dominated discussion within the War Cabinet, were both impressed by the economic arguments for interrupting Sweden's exports to Germany.[60] In the prime minister's opinion, 'it certainly seemed as if there was a chance of dealing a mortal blow to Germany'. Halifax was concerned, however, that Churchill's plans would only interrupt supplies from Narvik, which could not achieve decisive results by itself but would alienate Norway and Sweden and make it impossible to cut off the more important iron-ore trade through the Baltic. The War Cabinet therefore delayed action over Narvik while the Chiefs of Staff (COS) investigated the military implications of Churchill's proposals.

The possibility of action in Norwegian waters did not diminish the First Lord's enthusiasm for a Baltic expedition, rather the opposite. He now viewed the two schemes as complementary. In a memorandum written on Christmas Day 1939, Churchill urged Pound to continue the modification of ships for 'Catherine'. What mattered most, he argued, was to begin wearing down Germany's strength as soon as possible.[61] But Pound remained firmly opposed to 'Catherine'.[62] On 31 December the First Sea Lord protested to Churchill that the dispatch of a fleet into the region would be 'courting disaster' without strong fighter protection and the active support of Russia. In his opinion, the navy should plan to send only submarines into the Baltic. Even these forces would probably suffer heavy losses from air attack, he claimed, but at least they would 'not be pitting our ships against forts'—a remark probably intended to evoke memories of the Dardanelles.[63] Churchill insisted that planning should continue, although he conceded that there was little prospect of carrying out the endeavour with the forces that would be available in the first half of 1940.[64] He therefore encouraged the First Sea Lord in early January 1940 to explore the idea of sending a strong force of submarines into the Baltic, 'a much less serious, but at the same time quite hopeful, operation'.

This marked a significant retreat, but Pound would not be content until the scheme was scrapped altogether. He warned Churchill again that the capital ships he had earmarked for the operation could not be considered expendable:

> The one sure method in which we can be defeated is by the destruction of our sea power, and I cannot conceive of anything which would be more agreeable to the Germans and also the Italians, Russians and Japanese in the near future than to see this operation attempted in the existing conditions. The loss of such a large proportion of our Fleet would be the surest inducement to either Italy or Japan to come in against us.

'Our first object must be to win this war,' he concluded, 'but it is important that we should if possible end the war with our sea supremacy unchallenged. Even if we lost the whole of the submarines we sent into the Baltic it would not really matter, whilst if we lost a considerable part of our surface fleet the story would be a very different one.'[65] This produced another retreat by Churchill, who replied in mid-January that he had 'reluctantly but quite definitely' concluded that 'Catherine' could not be launched that year. However, he still hoped that the scheme might become practicable if the war continued into 1941, and he instructed Pound to continue modifying warships as suitable opportunities arose.[66]

The First Sea Lord was more sympathetic to the idea of cutting off German supplies of iron ore by dispatching Allied troops to occupy the Swedish minefields.[67] By late December attention was becoming fixed on Scandinavia. Ironside in particular was enthusiastic about prospects for action in this region. 'I believe we have stumbled upon the one great stroke which is open to us to turn the tables upon the Russians and Germans,' he recorded in his diary on 28 December. But unlike Churchill, the CIGS considered the cooperation of Norway and Sweden to be vital to the success of any scheme to disrupt Germany's iron ore imports. The COS's investigation into Scandinavian operations, completed on 31 December, concluded that the Allies would be justified in diverting resources into this region. The service chiefs rightly observed such a course would represent a 'fundamental change' in Allied strategy, but they believed that the risks were worth accepting if the MEW's appreciation of the enemy's economy was accurate. The Germans would need approximately twenty divisions to invade Scandinavia, they calculated, which compared favourably to the five to six divisions that the

Allies would have to dispatch to the region. Most importantly, this diversion of forces into a peripheral theatre would leave the Germans too weak, they predicted, to launch a successful offensive into France. The greatest danger for the Allies, they warned, was that Germany might establish naval and air bases in southern Norway and Sweden from which to intensify attacks on Britain's maritime communications and to launch a major air offensive against either Britain or France. This danger, like the possibility of Soviet intervention, was considered small, however, 'compared with the opportunity now offered of achieving the early defeat of Germany'.[68]

The Chiefs of Staff submitted an additional report to the War Cabinet emphasizing the importance of Norwegian and Swedish goodwill to the success of the project and advising *against* the use of naval measures to stop the export of iron ore through Narvik alone. This action would alienate the Norwegians, they warned, but could not in itself produce decisive results. Moreover, it might provoke a German invasion of Scandinavia before the Allies were ready to counter it.[69] None of this was to Churchill's liking. He complained to the War Cabinet that the COS report would lead to a 'purely negative conclusion, and that nothing will be done'. Norway and Sweden would never voluntarily agree to any course that would ensure a German invasion, he observed. It was therefore in Britain's interest to provoke a German attack by interfering with the iron-ore traffic. Only this, he argued, would induce the Scandinavian neutrals to seek British aid.[70]

Chamberlain was impressed by the COS's report on the military aspects of the iron-ore problem, and when the War Cabinet discussed the subject on 2 and 3 January he gave the Narvik project his cautious support.[71] The prime minister was not convinced that the Germans would respond to a stoppage of this trade by invading Norway. Ironside, moreover, now retreated somewhat from his earlier opposition to the Narvik scheme and reassured the War Cabinet that the weather at that time of year would work against German intervention in Norway. Churchill suggested that Britain should nevertheless be prepared to send British forces to occupy the Norwegian ports of Stavanger and Bergen. 'There was no reason why this small diversion should develop into a large commitment, unless we wished it to,' he claimed. While this sounded alarmingly similar to his reassurances in 1915 that naval operations in the Dardanelles could easily be broken off, ministers nevertheless decided that detailed plans should be worked out for the occupation of these two ports and a third, Trondheim. The Foreign Secretary, in the meantime, would approach the Norwegian government to determine its reaction to British actions to disrupt the flow of iron ore through Narvik.[72]

Churchill's project appeared to be off to a promising start, but when the Norwegian and Swedish governments vigorously protested against any attempt by the Allies to interfere with their neutrality, the War Cabinet backed off. When the project was considered again on 10 January, ministers were hopeful that the mere threat of Allied intervention might be sufficient to induce Norway and Sweden to restrict their trade with Germany. Churchill, however, was not convinced. He insisted that since Britain's goal must be the complete stoppage of Swedish iron-ore exports to Germany, any agreement by which that trade was simply curtailed would be insufficient. Nor could the Swedish and Norwegian governments be relied upon to adhere to any agreement in the face of German pressure. He therefore urged his colleagues to send a flotilla immediately to stop the Narvik traffic and only then to seek a diplomatic arrangement with the Scandinavian powers. The best means to obtain their cooperation, he asserted, 'would be to face these countries with a choice of two evils. We should have to make them more frightened of us than they were of Germany.'[73] But when discussion continued the following day, ministers were hesitant to jeopardize their broader goal of stopping all ore exports by causing a rift with Sweden. The desirability of a cautious approach was reinforced by Anthony Eden, Secretary of State for Dominion Affairs, who informed the War Cabinet that the Dominion High Commissioners were opposed to any course that might alienate the Swedes.[74]

On 12 January Halifax reported that his discussions with the head of the Swedish trade delegation had convinced him that 'the Narvik project by itself was not worth the risk involved to the success of the larger project'. Churchill renewed his appeal for naval action, but Chamberlain and Halifax insisted instead on the dispatch of a diplomatic mission to Sweden. When the War Cabinet met on the 17th, Churchill urged that the mission should threaten naval or military action to stop the flow of essential supplies to Germany. But this was too much for Chamberlain, who insisted that the Swedes would have to be persuaded that it was ultimately in their best interest to support the Allies. Halifax, however, was now having doubts about the dispatch of a high-level diplomatic mission. After a lengthy discussion, the War Cabinet opted for discrete conversations between the Foreign Secretary and the Norwegian and Swedish ministers in London.[75]

Churchill agreed to drop his proposal for immediate measures against the Narvik iron-ore traffic, but he was clearly unhappy about it. As a concession to the First Lord, the War Cabinet agreed that the COS could continue investigating the possibility of seizing Sweden's Gällivare ore fields in the face of Swedish and Norwegian opposition.[76] The idea of opening up a new theatre of operations in Scandinavia continued to hold a strong appeal for the COS. On 28 January, the service chiefs issued a report predicting that the Germans would attempt to secure their supplies of iron ore and oil prior to launching a major offensive in the West. Germany was expected, therefore, to move into Sweden and the Balkans. Like Churchill, the COS believed that it was important for the Allies to seize the initiative from the enemy. It would be a mistake, they warned, to 'leave Germany undisturbed to prepare the long-term plans which would enable her to build up her resources for an ultimate major offensive against Great Britain and France'. In their view, intervention in Scandinavia remained the 'first and best chance of wresting the initiative' from Germany, 'and, in fact, of shortening the war'. With the French High Command also in favour of action in Scandinavia, the COS proposed to send an initial force of two brigades to seize the Gällivare ore fields and the port of Luleå, and approximately five divisions to operate in southern Sweden. This would be a difficult operation, they admitted, but the potential rewards appeared to be great enough to justify the risk.[77]

The continuing hostilities between Finland and the Soviet Union soon emerged as a possible pretext for dispatching Allied forces into northern Sweden. Meeting in Paris on 5 February, the Anglo-French Supreme War Council agreed to begin preparations for intervention in the region under the cover of aid to Finland. Once an expeditionary force was ready, the Finns would be encouraged to make a public appeal to Norway and Sweden to allow Allied troops to pass through their territories. The Allies would urge the two neutrals to grant this request, and offer them military support in the event of a German attack.[78] Ambitious plans were quickly drawn up to dispatch an Anglo-French expeditionary force roughly one hundred thousand strong to the region to occupy key ports, including Narvik, Stavanger, Bergen, and Trondheim, to secure the Gällivare ore fields and the port of Luleå, and to provide support to the Finns.[79]

This development was welcomed by Churchill, who was eager to seize any opportunity to place Allied troops in Scandinavia, even if it increased the risk of hostilities with the Soviet Union. Allied forces might not be able to prevent a Soviet victory in Finland, but he believed that when these forces withdrew, they could occupy and secure the Gällivare ore fields.[80] But despite his support for this project, Churchill seems to have remained convinced that naval action against the Narvik iron-ore shipments remained the best means to further Allied interests in the region. In mid-February he attempted to exploit widespread indignation against Norway for its role in the *Altmark* episode, when a German ship carrying British prisoners was intercepted by the Royal Navy in Norwegian waters. Churchill pressed the War Cabinet to reconsider its views about violating Norway's neutrality. 'Strike while the iron is hot!' he urged his colleagues on 14 February.[81]

The French government also believed this incident provided a convenient pretext for the Allies to seize Stavanger and other Norwegian ports. But when the Narvik scheme was taken up by the War Cabinet on 23 February, Churchill's hopes for action were again dashed by the Foreign Secretary. Halifax accepted that a legal case existed for violating Norwegian neutrality, but warned that this risked turning public opinion in neutral states, including the United States, against Britain. There was, moreover, no certainty that Germany's imports of Swedish iron ore would in fact be diminished by the stoppage of the Narvik trade. Norway and Sweden might respond, he observed, by reducing their trade with Britain and increasing iron-ore shipments to Germany via the Baltic. The prime minister was ambivalent. Britain, Chamberlain observed, had 'entered the war on moral grounds', and had to be 'careful not to undermine our position, else we might lose the support of the world'. He claimed that his 'instincts were in favour of taking action', but he preferred to delay a decision until he could consult with the Dominions and the opposition parties.[82]

The War Cabinet soon refocused on the question of aiding Finland. The details of an appeal to Norway and Sweden to allow the passage of Allied troops to Finland were worked out on 1 March, but it was decided on the 4th that no action could be taken until the Finns had appealed for assistance.[83] Churchill, who was concerned that the Germans would move to secure the Swedish ore fields when the ice in the Baltic broke up in the spring, remained eager to see Allied troops introduced into the region as soon as possible. The Allies, he argued, should be prepared to send an expedition even if the Swedes and Norwegians declined to cooperate. If necessary, he stated, British forces could be landed at Narvik to secure control of the port. 'We should not be turned from our purpose,' he maintained on 6 March, 'by mere protests extorted by German intimidation.'[84]

This position was endorsed by Chamberlain at the War Cabinet on 11 March. If the Allies abandoned the operation in the face of Scandinavian protests, the prime minister feared that it 'would be said that we had never meant business at all and that our offer of assistance [to the Finns] had been a mere sham'.[85] Discussion now turned to the details of the expedition, and the question of whether to occupy other Norwegian ports in addition to Narvik. The Chief of the Air Staff (CAS) wanted to secure Stavenger in order to deny its aerodrome to the Germans, but Churchill insisted that the simultaneous seizure of additional Norwegian ports 'would savour too much of a general attack with the object of occupying all the strategic points'. Their ostensible goal, he reminded them on 12 March, was to provide aid to the Finns. Stavanger and Bergen were important objectives, but they were 'not on the way to Finland'. The War Cabinet concluded that a landing would initially be made only at Narvik, but that forces should be ready to depart for Trondheim once this operation was successfully completed. Forces for Stavanger and Bergen would be kept ready to depart at short notice. The expedition's naval and military commanders received their instructions directly from Chamberlain and other members of the War Cabinet later that day.[86]

These plans were disrupted by the sudden end of the Russo-Finnish war on 13 March. Churchill insisted that this unexpected development should not affect the decision to send an expedition to Narvik, as the provision of aid to Finland had only been 'cover' for Britain to secure the Gällivare ore fields. With this pretext now gone, Churchill argued that preparations should continue on the ostensible grounds that a Soviet advance through Scandinavia to the Atlantic would threaten British security.[87] But Chamberlain and Halifax were both opposed. The prime minister thought that with the fighting in Finland now over, Britain had an opportunity to improve relations with Norway and Sweden. If this could be achieved, he believed Sweden would willingly reduce its exports of iron ore to Germany. The Foreign Secretary was also concerned that Allied forces would meet active resistance in Norway and Sweden now that the pretext of aiding Finland was gone. Like Chamberlain, he hoped that by increasing British influence in Sweden, ore shipments to Germany could be reduced. With opinion in the War Cabinet hardening against him, Churchill reminded his colleagues that the real goal all along had been to secure the ore fields, thereby 'shortening the length of the war, and perhaps...obviating the slaughter which would otherwise inevitably ensue on the Western Front'. But the War Cabinet was not swayed: it decided that the forces gathered for an expedition should be dispersed.[88]

Deeply frustrated by this turn of events, Churchill had good cause to complain to Halifax about the lack of drive in the government's decision-making machinery. 'There is no possibility,' he lamented, 'of any positive project to gain the initiative, and acquire direction of events, getting through the critical and obstructive apparatus which covers up on every side.'[89] Churchill was also disturbed by the difficulties his other offensive scheme, the mining of German rivers, had run into. After months of preparation, the navy was ready to begin laying mines any time after 12 March. The air force would not be ready until mid-April, however, and Churchill favoured delaying the operation—code-named 'Royal Marine'—so that both means of delivery could be employed simultaneously.[90] The War Cabinet accepted this proposal, but the French government insisted on delaying the operation by two months in order to protect their aircraft factories from German reprisals.[91]

Undeterred by these difficulties, Churchill wasted no time looking for other means to strike at the Germans. On the day the Narvik scheme was rejected, he questioned Pound about the possibility of dispatching fast merchant ships equipped with strengthened bows and rams to search out and 'accidentally' ram German merchant ships carrying ore along the Norwegian coast.[92] A few days later he informed the War Cabinet that the Naval Staff was examining a new project to stop shipments of iron ore from Luleå when they resumed in the spring. The navy would use aircraft launched from a carrier along Norway's Atlantic coast to lay mines in the approaches to Luleå and to bomb ships in the port.[93] While these plans were being investigated, Churchill also attempted to revive 'Catherine'. He renewed Cork's appointment on 20 March, and three days later wrote to Pound instructing him to continue the modification of warships so that a Baltic expedition would be possible in 1941. Britain must be ready, he insisted, 'and have all our tackle prepared to take advantage of any political situation which may arise in this theatre. Only in this way can we acquire the power to guide the war as we desire.'[94]

Operations in the Baltic were soon overshadowed, however, by new proposals from Paris. Eager to seize the initiative from Germany and invigorate the Allied war effort, a new French government under Paul Reynaud pressed the British in late March to undertake offensive operations in the Caucasus, the Black Sea, the Caspian, and Scandinavia.[95] This development was not

welcomed by either Halifax or Chamberlain, who preferred that any operations should strike at Germany directly rather than through neutral states.
They therefore hoped to convince the French to support the project for
mining the Rhine. In the meantime, the British leaders proposed to issue a
strong warning to Norway and Sweden that would provide justification for
Allied measures to interrupt the iron-ore trade should it eventually became
necessary. Churchill, who still hoped to lay mines off the Norwegian coast,
suggested to the War Cabinet that Britain should accept French requests to
take action against Swedish ore shipments in return for French acquies-
cence in 'Royal Marine'.[96] This is the position Chamberlain adopted when
the Supreme War Council met on 28 March. The British prime minister
tried to reassure the French regarding the merits of a long war strategy, but
also voiced support for the French view that opportunities should be seized
for offensive action whenever possible. To this end, he restated Britain's case
for the execution of 'Royal Marine'. Reynaud agreed to press the scheme
on the French War Committee provided the British were prepared to take
action to stop the flow of iron ore through Narvik and Luleå. This proved
acceptable to both sides, and the Council agreed on a timetable for carrying
out both operations: a note would be delivered to the governments of
Sweden and Norway on 1 April; the mining of the Rhine would begin on
the evening of 4 April; and the Norwegian mine-laying operation would
commence the next day.[97]

The British moved rapidly to carry out these decisions, but the French soon
had second thoughts. On 31 March a 'gloomy and apologetic' French ambassador informed Chamberlain that Edouard Daladier, the French Minister of
National Defence, was so alarmed by the possibility of German reprisals
that he had compelled his government to request a three-month delay to
'Royal Marine' so that critical French factories could be dispersed. Chamberlain
immediately pressed the French to reconsider this decision, and warned that
if they did not adhere to the original plan, the British would have to reconsider their support for the Norway project. 'No mines—no Narvik,' he
stated.[98] The War Cabinet postponed the delivery of a warning to Norway,
but still assumed that the operation would be carried out and hoped that the
French could be persuaded to change their position on 'Royal Marine'.
Churchill, however, did not want to take any chances. He wrote to Chamberlain
on 1 April to persuade him that the two operations should not be linked.[99]
Two days later, Churchill argued that the War Cabinet should lay a minefield
in Norwegian waters irrespective of the French decision on 'Royal Marine'.

His colleagues agreed. 'Matters had now gone too far for us not to take action,' Chamberlain remarked. A warning telegram would now be sent to Norway and Sweden on 5 April, with the laying of mines to take place three days later.[100]

Churchill's persistence had at last paid off. On the evening of 6 April naval forces departed to begin laying mines. There was no certainty in London as to the enemy's reaction, but it had always been assumed that the Germans might retaliate by moving forces into southern Norway or Sweden. Intelligence reports indicated that the enemy had assembled troops and shipping that could be employed for this purpose. The British hastily assembled troops to be held in readiness for pre-emptive landings if the Germans sent forces into the region. Plan R4, approved by the War Cabinet on 6 April, called for the dispatch of two separate Allied forces. The first would occupy Narvik and secure the railway lines (as far as the Swedish frontier) leading to the Gällivare ore fields. The second would be divided between the ports of Stavanger, Bergen, and Trondheim.[101] Nothing went according to plan, however. British decision-makers, including Churchill, had always assumed that Germany would only move into Scandinavia after Britain had violated Norway's neutrality by laying mines. But Hitler, fearing that the Allies would attempt to interfere with his supplies of Scandinavian iron ore, had decided in late March to launch a major operation to seize control of all of Norway. Despite mounting evidence of German preparations for an invasion, no serious thought was given to the possibility that the enemy might move first. On the morning of 9 April, as German land forces invaded Denmark, the War Cabinet learned that enemy warships had reached Oslo Fiord, Stavanger, Bergen, and Trondheim.

The German invasion of Norway was a daring, almost reckless, operation that took the British completely by surprise.[102] The belief that Germany would not dare launch an assault on Norway in the face of vastly superior Allied sea power was so entrenched that when intelligence began to reveal unusual German ship movements on 7 and 8 April, the Admiralty at first assumed the Germans must be preparing to launch heavy raiders into the Atlantic. This miscalculation had unfortunate consequences for the British. The Home Fleet, which might have intercepted German ships heading for central Norway, was sent instead to block the exits from the North Sea. To make matters worse, on the evening of 7 April the troops loaded on cruisers at Rosyth in the Firth of Forth to implement Plan R4 were disembarked.[103] These ships, together with those assigned to cover the movement of troops from the Clyde to Narvik and Trondheim, were ordered to sea to support the Home Fleet. By the time German intentions were clear, it was too late to prevent enemy forces from reaching their initial objectives.

Even though the Germans had stolen the initiative, Churchill was optimistic that the extension of the war into Scandinavia would ultimately favour the Allies. He confidently predicted that German warships would soon be either destroyed or driven away by Britain's far-superior navy. 'The German forces which had been landed were commitments for them,' he pronounced, 'but potential prizes for us.'[104] Allied leaders now faced the problem of where to concentrate Britain's limited resources. On the morning of 9 April, Churchill and Ironside proposed to send troops to secure Narvik, which did not yet appear to be a German objective, and to begin preparations to recapture Trondheim and Bergen.[105] The situation became more complicated, however, as news began to arrive in the afternoon that the Germans had also landed troops at Narvik. At a meeting of the Supreme War Council later that day, French leaders urged the British 'not to lose sight of the Allies' essential aim of cutting off Germany's supply of iron ore from Scandinavia'. In their view, it was essential to concentrate on capturing Narvik.[106]

This opinion was shared by Churchill and other members of the Military Coordination Committee, which met later that evening. With large-scale operations now under way, this body began to assume a more prominent role in the direction of British strategy. Chatfield had resigned his office as Minister for the Coordination of Defence in early April, and Churchill began to chair the MCC's meetings shortly before the Norwegian campaign began. He would later complain that this new position gave him 'an exceptional measure of responsibility but no power of effective direction'. Decisions taken by the MCC still had to be approved by the War Cabinet, and rapid decisions on important matters were seldom possible.[107] But at the outset of the Norwegian campaign, Churchill and the service chiefs found themselves substantially in agreement as to the right course to take. Ironside advised that the Allies possessed only enough forces to retake one of the occupied ports. Since the capture of Narvik would allow the Allies to extend their control over the Gällivare ore fields in northern Sweden, operations there seemed to offer the best chance of success, as Narvik was far removed from German air bases in southern and central Norway. The recapture of Narvik was therefore given priority, a decision endorsed by the War Cabinet the following day.[108]

The first elements of the Allied expedition to recapture Narvik—a small force of around three hundred men under the command of General Pierse Mackesy—were scheduled to depart on 11 April. Their immediate goal was to secure a forward base at Harstad, a small Norwegian town about 25 miles northwest of Narvik. Four battalions of British troops would be dispatched two days later, with additional British and French forces to follow. That same morning Churchill informed his colleagues that the recapture of Narvik might take as long as two weeks, and that until then 'no serious operations could be undertaken against Bergen or Trondhjem'. These priorities were accepted by both the War Cabinet and the French government.[109] Thus, despite having lost the initiative to the Germans, the initial British response to the invasion demonstrated a sound appreciation of what could realistically be accomplished and which objectives were most important.

While preparations were under way for retaking Narvik, planners also began to study the requirements for an expedition to recapture Trondheim. It was clear that this would be a difficult undertaking, and when the MCC met on the evening of 11 April, Ironside emphasized that the terrain in the area would present a serious obstacle. Churchill supported the general consensus in the committee that such operations should be studied, but he stipulated that 'no action should be taken' until it was clear what would be required to recapture Narvik.[110] After this meeting, Churchill instructed Admiralty officials to continue their own investigation into the recapture of Trondheim. 'After Narvik is cleared up, and we are established there,' he wrote, 'very good forces will be available for other enterprises.' He predicted that it might take as many as twenty thousand men to take Trondheim, making it a much bigger operation than Narvik, but he hoped that it would be possible if operations in the north could be wrapped up quickly. Rather than prepare for a direct assault on Trondheim, he assumed that British forces would advance overland from a forward base at Namsos, about a hundred miles to the north.[111]

When members of the Air and Naval Staffs discussed the subject later that evening at the Admiralty, the importance of securing Namsos as a base for later operations was recognized. At the end of the meeting, an informal delegation consisting of Churchill, Pound, Phillips, Air Chief Marshal Sir Cyril Newall (Chief of the Air Staff), and Air Chief Marshal Sir Philip Joubert de la Ferté, headed to the War Office to persuade Ironside to allocate a portion of the Narvik force to Namsos, 'with a view to "staking out a claim"…for Trondheim'. This meeting went badly. Ironside recorded in his diary that he lost his temper 'and banged the table' after learning of delays in receiving important information from the Admiralty. Another observer, Captain Ralph Edwards, noted in his diary that everything 'was going well when Winston lost his temper and spoilt the whole show'.[112] In the event, no decision appears to have been reached that evening regarding the movement of a small advance force to Namsos.

Churchill obtained the War Cabinet's consent to begin studying the problem of occupying Namsos on the morning of 12 April, being careful to stress that the recapture of Trondheim itself would be a difficult undertaking. When ministers assembled again later that afternoon, discussion was dominated by Trondheim. The strategy established by Churchill and the MCC now began to derail. The governments of Norway and Sweden were both pressing the Allies to focus their efforts on Trondheim, and the political arguments for doing so were accepted by the Foreign Office and Lord Halifax. The Foreign Secretary urged his colleagues to reconsider the priorities they had accepted earlier. Focusing on Narvik might be sound from 'the military point of view,' he remarked, but 'would have very much less political effect than an attempt to clear the Germans out of the Southern part of Norway'.[113] Retaking Trondheim would help to sustain Norwegian resistance and keep open vital rail communications with Sweden, as Halifax noted, but the German position there was much stronger than at Narvik. Churchill understood the danger of dividing Britain's limited resources between two distinct objectives, and was determined not to embark on any additional major operations until the success of the first expedition was certain. He reassured his colleagues that the Military Coordination Committee appreciated the desirability of recapturing Trondheim, and were already investigating the possibility of staging a landing at Namsos.[114]

The instructions Churchill subsequently issued to the COS's Joint Planning Committee were clearly designed to satisfy the War Cabinet's newfound interest in Trondheim without endangering operations to recapture Narvik. After emphasizing the 'very high political importance' of action in central Norway, Churchill accepted that 'major risks on a small scale' would be justifiable. However, he insisted that large forces would not be available for this region until Narvik had been taken, and that any operations 'must be in the nature of a demonstration, a diversion and bluff'. Churchill still wished to occupy Namsos in order to secure a base for later operations, but this operation was now packaged as a feint to 'give the impression of an attack' on Trondheim. This would be combined with constant naval action along the Norwegian coast designed to 'rouse the population and puzzle the enemy'. Churchill claimed that these actions would encourage both Norway and Sweden and, by 'menacing' Trondheim, draw large German reinforcements into the region. If this happened before an Allied expedition could be mounted, the Allies could attack Bergen instead when resources became available. 'The use of flexible amphibious power may give remarkable rewards,' he asserted.[115]

This was not enough for his colleagues, however. When the War Cabinet reconvened the following day, Halifax continued to press for a major change in strategy. '[E]arly action against Trondhjem [sic] was imperative from the political point of view,' he maintained, 'while it seemed that, if necessary, the operation at Narvik could wait.' Chamberlain threw his weight behind the Foreign Secretary. Trondheim was important, he maintained, 'from the political point of view. If at the moment we merely concentrated on Narvik, there was a danger lest the Norwegians and Swedes would feel that our only interest was the iron ore.' Chamberlain and Halifax hoped to increase the size and scope of a Trondheim expedition, if necessary by withdrawing British troops from France or by employing France's Chasseurs Alpins division, which had been earmarked for the recapture of Narvik.

None of this was to Churchill's liking. According to the minutes, he opposed 'any proposals which might tend to weaken our intention to seize Narvik':

> Nothing must be allowed to deflect us from making the capture of this place as certain as possible. Our plans against Narvik had been very carefully laid, and there seemed every chance that they would be successful if they were allowed to proceed without being tampered with. Trondhjem [sic] was, on the other hand, a much more speculative affair, and he deprecated any suggestion which might lead to the diversion of the Chasseurs Alpins until we had definitely established ourselves at Narvik. Otherwise, there was a grave danger that we should find ourselves committed to a number of ineffectual operations along the Norwegian coast, none of which would succeed.[116]

This was sound advice, but Churchill was unable to sway his colleagues. The War Cabinet decided that priority should be given jointly to Narvik and Trondheim, and that an approach would be made to the French government for permission to divert French troops, already en route to Narvik, to Trondheim if this became necessary.[117]

Despite his reservations, Churchill loyally supported the War Cabinet's decision and immediately threw himself into ensuring the success of the new operation. His frustration over the change in strategy appears to have been offset by the Second Battle of Narvik on 13 April. This was an outstanding success for the British, and resulted in the destruction of the German warships and transports at Narvik. Unfortunately, mistaken reports soon followed indicating that the enemy had withdrawn from the town entirely. When the Military Coordination Committee met that evening, Churchill predicted that British forces would not face serious opposition when they arrived, in which event he was willing to bolster the forces for Trondheim by diverting one of the British brigades intended for Narvik to Namsos. With optimism running high, the Chiefs of Staff were instructed to investigate the possibility of landing forces at Trondheim itself.[118] The 146th Territorial Brigade, already at sea, was accordingly diverted.

Debate now shifted to where Allied forces should land. When the French indicated their willingness to add the Chasseurs Alpins division to the Trondheim project, it was calculated that the Allies would be able to assemble 23,000 troops against a force of approximately 3,500 Germans. This figure was soon increased to 25,000 Allied troops plus three battalions of Norwegians.[119] In these circumstances, Churchill and the service advisers were initially optimistic about the prospect of launching a direct assault on Trondheim itself, rather than concentrating troops at Namsos. But even the latter course began to pose difficulties when a naval landing party reported that the area was 'under four feet of snow and offered no concealment from the air'. When the War Cabinet met on 15 April, Halifax and Chamberlain were both disappointed that the COS had decided to delay the landing of troops at Namsos owing to the unfavourable conditions reported there.[120]

At a meeting of the MCC the next day, Chamberlain again stressed the importance of acting quickly to recapture Trondheim. Churchill shared this desire for speed, but he was concerned that the COS's preliminary plans devoted too many troops to Namsos, including elements of the French division, and not enough for the assault on Trondheim from the sea.[121] While the Admiralty and Admiral Forbes investigated the requirements for landing forces near Trondheim under naval cover, Churchill drafted a memorandum for the MCC describing his own views on how such an operation should develop. Small-scale landings at Namsos and Aandalesnes, a port to the south of Trondheim, would serve as diversions to confuse the Germans and provide immediate encouragement to the Norwegians. A fleet would then force its way into

Trondheim harbour, where it would suppress or destroy the local aerodrome and support the landing of up to eight thousand Allied troops.[122]

These calculations were soon complicated, however, by unexpected delays at Narvik. General Mackesy reported that he intended to wait until the snow melted and reinforcements arrived before attempting to recapture the port. Churchill was greatly perturbed by this development, which threatened to delay the opening of an assault until the end of April. Confident of the navy's ability to dominate northern Norway, Churchill had come to expect a quick and easy victory at Narvik. He pressed the hapless Mackesy to take immediate action with forces that were ill-equipped for the task, and was indignant when the general turned the Narvik operation, in Churchill's words, into 'a damaging deadlock' and 'a kind of siege'.[123] But while Churchill and the COS agreed that Narvik was ultimately their most important objective, they were determined that delay there should not undermine preparations for the recapture of Trondheim.[124] Despite earlier concerns about conditions at Namsos, the 146th brigade was landed there on 16 and 17 April. This was followed by the landing of troops at Aandelsnes. Mackesy was informed that the Chasseurs Alpins would not be put at his disposal after all, and the first of these troops were also directed to Namsos.

While these movements were taking place, the Joint Planning Committee and Admiral Forbes developed strong doubts about the feasibility of a frontal assault on Trondheim (operation 'Hammer'). Nevertheless, the COS were reluctant to abandon the plan. When Churchill reported to the War Cabinet on 17 April that the assault on Trondheim might begin around 22 April, Newall, the CAS, reported that the Chiefs approved the project. 'The operation was of course attended by considerable risks,' he noted, but these 'were not out of proportion to value of success if achieved.' Newall reminded the politicians, however, that the project had originated with them: 'The Military value of a success should not perhaps be rated too highly,' he warned, even though 'the political and moral advantages which would result from the capture of Trondhjem [sic] would be very great.'[125] This confidence did not last long, however. By 19 April the COS had concluded that a frontal assault was unlikely to succeed. They now proposed instead to continue the landing of troops at Namsos and Aandalesnes, which was proceeding well, and to begin preparations for a more cautious 'pincer' operation to take Trondheim by land.

Churchill later recorded that he was 'indignant' about this sudden 'right-about-turn', but he was unable to overcome the united opposition of the three services and grudgingly assented to the new plan.[126] In the event, even this more-cautious scheme proved to be overly ambitious. Heavy air attack on the Allied positions at Namsos and Aandalesnes virtually halted the arrival of reinforcements and prevented any rapid movement towards Trondheim. By 21 April the Allies were struggling just to hold onto their lodgments in the face of German land and air attacks. With the situation in central Norway deteriorating, Churchill's attention swung back to Narvik. He assumed that the Germans would try to reinforce this position via Luleå once the Gulf of Bothnia was free of ice, and he proposed to reinforce Mackesy with at least three thousand troops as soon as possible. This, he hoped, would enable the Allies to capture the town and its garrison, and secure the railway up to the Swedish border. It was 'of the utmost importance,' he reminded the War Cabinet on 20 April, 'not to have our attention diverted by operations elsewhere from our principal objective, which had always from the very start been the control of the Gallivare ore-fields'.[127] He repeated this argument in a letter to Chamberlain later that day. He now proposed that a demi-brigade of the French Chasseurs Alpins should be immediately diverted to Narvik, while British forces around Trondheim would be converted to a 'holding force' pending the arrival of two divisions of reinforcements promised by the French.[128]

Britain's ally also wished to concentrate on operations in the north, and when the Supreme War Council met in Paris on 22 April, Churchill had little difficulty persuading French leaders to divert the Chasseurs Alpins to Narvik.[129] Two days later, with the 'pincer' movement on Trondheim having clearly failed, Churchill suggested that consideration should be given to reviving operation 'Hammer', a direct assault on Trondheim. This was supported by Admiral Phillips, but rejected by the Joint Planners, who did not believe the Allies possessed sufficient anti-aircraft resources to hold the port even if they succeeded in capturing it.[130] When the MCC met on the morning of 26 April, Chamberlain, who was now regularly chairing its meetings, advocated the eventual evacuation of Allied forces from central Norway, despite the negative impact this action would have on both neutral opinion and the British public. Churchill, who was eager to reinforce Narvik, readily agreed. 'Our policy,' he advised, 'should be to withdraw from the Trondhjem [sic] area, after giving the Germans as hard a knock as we could with the Regular troops which had been put in on that front.' The Committee agreed in principle to the evacuation of central Norway. Britain's primary objective was now to be the 'capture of Narvik and subsequent advance to the Swedish border'.[131] The first of these goals was eventually accomplished. On 28 May, after Churchill had become prime minister (10 May), a combination of British, French, Norwegian, and Polish troops drove the last German defenders out of Narvik. But the situation on the Western Front had so badly deteriorated by this time that the War Cabinet had already decided to withdraw from Norway entirely.

The Norwegian campaign bears many similarities to the Dardanelles, and like that episode it highlights Churchill's strengths and weakness in almost equal measure. His shortcomings are most evident, on this occasion, at the operational level. The First Lord was still impatient and domineering; and he remained predisposed to meddle in naval operations. In the official history of British naval operations, Stephen Roskill noted, with complete accuracy, that 'Mr Churchill used, during critical periods of naval operations, to spend long hours in the Admiralty Operational Intelligence Centre.'[132] There is no doubt that he and the senior naval officers present issued operational orders to commanders at sea. The frequency and extent of these intrusions was the subject of a famous debate between Roskill and Arther Marder, another prominent and highly respected historian of the Royal Navy.[133] Roskill argued that Churchill dominated his naval advisers, particularly Pound, and on occasion assumed personal control of operations.[134] Marder, on the other hand, maintained that as First Lord, Churchill 'leaned over backwards...not to lay down the law upon strategy or operational matters to the sailors', and that Pound was both able and willing to stand up to him.[135] While both historians were inclined to overstate their case, the evidence tends to favour Marder's interpretation. The Dardanelles had made a deep impression on Churchill. He continued to be a difficult and demanding master, but he was more willing during the Second World War to accept views that did not accord with his own, and less inclined to overrule his professional advisers.

While responsibility for all operational orders emanating from the Admiralty during the Norwegian campaign is now commonly assigned to Churchill alone, Pound was also inclined to interfere in operations at sea and may bear at least as much responsibility as Churchill, if not more.[136] Captain Ralph Edwards, the Deputy Director of Operations (Home), was closely involved in the decision-making process at this time and, while critical of Churchill's propensity to meddle, later admitted to Roskill that 'in retrospect he regarded Churchill's interventions in naval operations as insignificant compared to those initiated by Pound.'[137] It is virtually impossible now to determine which signals originated with Pound, which with Churchill, and which were genuinely joint efforts. But in a sense it does not really matter: Churchill was closely involved in the operational decision-making process throughout the Norwegian campaign and must accept at least a share of the blame for the mistakes that were made.

The impact of the Admiralty's meddling in operational matters is difficult to judge. To be sure, this interference seldom had beneficial results, and undoubtedly contributed to the general confusion that prevailed at the time and the frustrations of senior officers at sea. But Churchill's willingness to interfere in the movement of warships did not fundamentally alter the outcome of the Norwegian campaign. The Royal Navy would probably have achieved better results if Churchill had abstained from meddling, but the campaign was virtually unwinnable once the Germans had established a foothold in Norway. In other words, operational miscalculations at sea, whether the fault of Churchill, Pound, or the Admiralty, were not the cause of strategic defeat.

To make the case that Churchill was the main cause of this embarrassing failure, his critics have sometimes claimed that he intervened in the *strategic* direction of the campaign as frequently as he did in naval operations, and with even more disastrous results. It has been argued, for example, that Churchill was unable to settle on a single strategic objective during the campaign and recklessly shifted resources back and forth between Narvik and Trondheim. In Correlli Barnett's words, Churchill was 'puffed this way and that by the shifting breezes of opportunity'. There is also a tendency to assume that Churchill had no trouble imposing his will on the War Cabinet. A recent appraisal by Carlo d'Este, for example, states that Churchill, 'who hardly ever seemed able to make up his mind', acted 'as if he were the commander in chief'.[138] The reality was much different. When it came to shaping the broad outlines of British strategy during the Norwegian campaign, Churchill's influence was largely positive. He correctly identified the most important strategic objective—the denial of Swedish iron ore to Germany— and he resisted efforts to disperse British resources. It was the War Cabinet's inability to settle on a single objective that undermined Churchill's efforts, not the other way round. Chamberlain and Halifax were responsible for altering the basis of Allied strategy in Scandinavia and spreading Britain's limited resources between multiple objectives. Churchill was the only member of the War Cabinet to keep his eyes on the prize—Sweden's iron ore—once it was realized that the Germans had launched a full-scale invasion of Norway. His initial instincts, moreover, were correct. The Allies were incapable of recapturing Trondheim once the Germans were established there, but they could and did occupy Narvik once sufficient resources were committed to the enterprise.

Churchill's political career might have been irreparably harmed if he had been generally perceived in May 1940 as the cause of Britain's humiliating setbacks in Scandinavia. There was no shortage of observers in Whitehall who questioned his judgement and were predisposed to see the Norwegian campaign as a new Gallipoli. But Churchill's reputation survived the Norway fiasco, in large part because attention had become focused on Chamberlain's shortcomings as a war leader. After eight months of war, concerns about Churchill's share of responsibility for Norway were eclipsed by a consensus that Chamberlain had proven himself ineffective and uninspiring, and that the machinery he had put into place for the direction of the nation's war effort had failed. Churchill was an obvious beneficiary of the general dissatisfaction with the decision-making apparatus by the end of the Norwegian campaign. At the end of April, Chamberlain had initiated a major restructuring that would make Churchill responsible to the MCC 'for giving guidance and direction to the Chiefs of Staff Committee'. In this new role Churchill was to have a small central organization under a senior staff officer (Major General Hastings Ismay), who would also serve as his representative on the COS committee. In effect, Churchill was to assume the role of de facto Minister of Defence in addition to his duties as First Lord of the Admiralty.[139]

This new machinery was never tested. The decision to evacuate Allied forces from central Norway had greater political consequences than either Chamberlain or his government colleagues expected. For many, the supreme irony of this episode is that Churchill was not driven from the Admiralty in disgrace, but instead elevated to the prime minister's office. A fierce debate on the conduct of the Norwegian campaign in the House of Commons on 7 and 8 May resulted in a political crisis that ended with the First Lord becoming the head of a new coalition government. Churchill, who loyally defended the Chamberlain administration's record throughout the crucial debate, later remarked that it was 'a marvel that I survived and maintained my position in public esteem and Parliamentary confidence'.[140] He was indeed fortunate. When the dust settled, Churchill had gained the one thing he had hitherto always lacked: a position of supreme power.

7

The War Against Germany
and Italy, 1940–1

Winston Churchill became prime minister of Great Britain and Minister of Defence in May 1940 just as Germany launched its long-awaited offensive through the Low Countries and into France. Despite months of preparations, the Allies proved to be no match for the powerful German army. The British Expeditionary Force and the French army advanced into Belgium to meet the enemy, but from the outset they were caught wrong-footed. The Germans' northern assault was only intended to draw the Allies into Belgium: the main weight of their attack unexpectedly fell further south. Within days the German army had broken through the French lines near Sedan, and armoured spearheads were soon racing towards the Channel coast. Allied forces never recovered from the speed and audacity of the initial German attack. Within six weeks, the Netherlands, Belgium, and France had all fallen. Britain's battered expeditionary force was lucky to survive the disaster. Against expectations, nearly two hundred thousand British troops were evacuated from the beaches and harbour at Dunkirk between 26 May and 4 June, although their weapons and equipment had to be left behind.

Hitler's rapid victory in the west dramatically altered the strategic balance. Britain lost its only major European ally, its cities were now within range of German air bases, and its small army was incapable of repelling an invasion. Germany's position, on the other hand, was immeasurably strengthened: it could now draw upon the resources of vast occupied territories, as well as those of Italy—which entered the war shortly before the French collapse—and the Soviet Union. It also gained new bases along the coast of Europe from France all the way to Norway. To most observers, Britain's position seemed hopeless. Churchill fully appreciated the magnitude of the disaster, but also understood the consequences of compromising with Hitler. Rather than seek peace terms, as many expected, he was determined to continue the struggle.[1]

This was undoubtedly a gamble, as his colleagues realized. Churchill was nevertheless able to persuade the War Cabinet and the nation that Britain should keep fighting. In the short term, he was confident that Britain could withstand German air attacks and, if necessary, repel an invasion. But he also believed that victory over Germany was ultimately possible. Churchill pinned his hopes on the United States throwing its industrial power behind the British war effort, and eventually entering the war as a full belligerent. He also remained optimistic that Nazi Germany, despite its dominating position in continental Europe, was still vulnerable to economic pressure.[2] This calculation was completely unfounded, but Churchill was not alone: both the COS and the Ministry of Economic Warfare believed that attacks on Germany's oil supplies, communications, and industry would have a devastating impact on the Nazi war economy.[3]

These developments strengthened Churchill's view that air power would provide Britain's main offensive weapon. 'The Navy can lose us the war,' he wrote in September 1940, 'but only the Air Force can win it.'[4] Even before the Battle of Britain had begun in early July, Churchill professed that he could see 'only one sure path' to victory. 'We have no continental army which can defeat the German military power,' he wrote to a colleague:

> The blockade is broken and Hitler has Asia and probably Africa to draw from. Should he be repulsed here or not try invasion, he will recoil eastward, and we have nothing to stop him. But there is one thing that will bring him back and bring him down, and that is an absolutely devastating, exterminating attack by very heavy bombers from this country upon the Nazi homeland. We must be able to overwhelm them by this means, without which I do not see a way through.[5]

By September, Churchill and the COS had agreed on the outlines of a new grand strategy. As before, the central assumption was that German strength and morale must be worn down in a protracted war of attrition. In the short term, Britain would remain on the defensive and concentrate on building up its strength. With the French army removed from the equation, there was no hope of competing with Germany in land forces. The government continued to aim at fifty-five divisions, but offensive plans now centred on the strategic air offensive. 'Bombers alone provide the means of victory,' Churchill told the War Cabinet. 'We must therefore develop the power to carry an ever-increasing volume of explosives to Germany, so as to pulverise the entire industry and scientific structure on which the war effort and economic life of the enemy depends.'[6] The navy would continue to protect Britain's maritime communications, while seizing every opportunity to take offensive action, either by assaulting the enemy's coastline or launching amphibious raids against occupied territories. These measures would be supplemented by subversion and propaganda aimed at weakening German morale and promoting resistance in occupied Europe. As Britain's strength grew, its superior sea power would allow it to adopt a peripheral strategy. Offensive operations would focus first on Italy, the weaker of Britain's opponents. Eventually, the balance of strength would swing in Britain's favour, and its forces would return to the Continent to inflict the final blow against Germany.[7]

These long-term plans were overshadowed in the summer of 1940 by a more pressing problem: survival. One of the first questions facing the government after the fall of France was the fate of the French fleet. The armistice between Germany and France allowed the Vichy government to retain control of French warships, but the British were understandably worried that these vessels might still fall under German control. Italy's entry into the war imposed major new commitments on the Royal Navy in the Mediterranean (Map 4), and if the French fleet were also hostile Britain's margin in capital ships would be perilously low. Churchill was particularly alarmed about the fate of the modern battleships *Richelieu* and *Jean Bart*. In German hands, he warned, these powerful vessels 'might alter the whole course of the war'.[8]

On 27 June the War Cabinet agreed that French warships must be neutralized, if necessary by force. This involved serious risk. The Joint Planning Committee advised against taking action, warning that the danger of bringing France into the war against Britain outweighed the advantages of destroying French warships. The COS, however, supported the government's decision.[9] On 3 July 1940 French commanders at Alexandria and Mers-el-Kébir, a French port in Algeria, were given the choice of continuing the fight against Germany or disarming their ships. Admiral Andrew Cunningham, the Commander-in-Chief of Britain's Mediterranean fleet, negotiated the disarming of the French squadron at Alexandria, but the French force at Mers-el-Kébir was unwilling to comply with British demands. Under pressure from Churchill, the warships of Britain's Force H, under Admiral James Somerville, fired on the French ships, destroying the battleship *Bretagne* and badly damaging *Provence* and *Dunkerque*.[10]

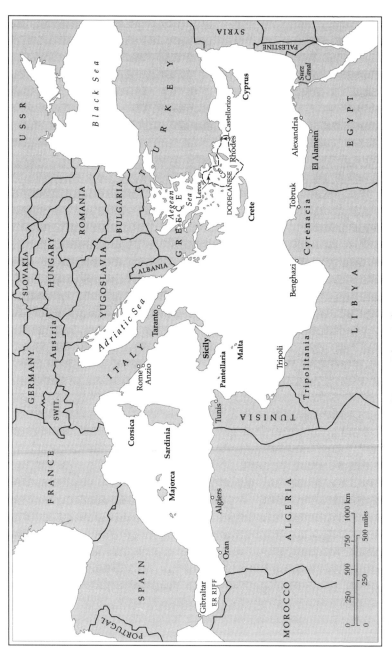

Map 4. The Mediterranean

The other, and more serious, threat to Britain's survival in the months after the fall of France was a full-scale German invasion. The British army was in no state to defeat a large enemy force on British soil, and it seemed unlikely that the navy could prevent an invasion indefinitely if Germany obtained a clear advantage in the skies. 'The crux of the matter,' the COS concluded, 'is air superiority.'[11] British production priorities were rearranged to ensure that the immediate needs of the RAF would be met. At the end of May the Admiralty did its bit to free up resources by suspending work on most of the capital ships then under construction, in addition to an aircraft carrier and various smaller ships.[12] To counter a German invasion, the Admiralty, with Churchill's backing, decided to maintain a large force of small warships around the southeast coast of England. The necessary vessels were provided by stripping the Home Fleet and the Atlantic convoys of cruisers, destroyers, corvettes, and other light craft.

These redispositions naturally came at a cost. The mobility of the Home Fleet was restricted, and losses in merchant shipping to U-boats increased significantly. Admiral Forbes, Commander-in-Chief of the Home Fleet, protested at having so many ships tied down in static roles.[13] The navy, he complained, 'should be freed to carry out its proper function—offensively against the enemy and in defence of our trade—and not be tied down to provide passive defence to our country, which had now become a fortress'.[14] These were legitimate concerns, but Churchill supported the Admiralty's anti-invasion patrols. In early July he expressed his confidence that there was no possibility of a large German force reaching Britain's shores undetected. '[I]t would be a most hazardous and even suicidal operation,' he remarked, 'to commit a large army to the accidents of the sea in the teeth of our very numerous patrolling vessels, of which two or three hundred are always at sea.'[15]

The need to augment Britain's strength in smaller warships prompted Churchill to ask President Franklin Roosevelt for the loan of forty to fifty First World War-vintage US destroyers.[16] The president initially sent a discouraging reply, noting the difficulty of gaining Congressional approval, but Churchill was not ready to abandon the idea. When several more appeals to Roosevelt met with no encouragement, Churchill queried Admiralty officials about the desirability of exchanging one of Britain's battleships for thirty-five American destroyers.[17] This unorthodox proposal was immediately dismissed by Pound and Churchill's successor as First Lord of the Admiralty, the Labour politician A. V. Alexander.[18] The prime minister continued to press the United States for the transfer of destroyers over the summer of 1940. Progress was slow, but in mid-August Roosevelt agreed to provide fifty of these ships in exchange for the right to maintain American bases in British possessions in the western hemisphere.[19] This promised to alleviate Britain's urgent need for light warships, but it would take time for the deal to be finalized and for the vessels to be reconditioned and transferred. In the meantime, Churchill urged Alexander to maintain a large and steady construction programme of smaller warships.

Churchill was less enthusiastic about the resumption of battleship construction. These ships tied up considerable resources, but would take years to complete. He wanted ships that could be used immediately, and he urged the Admiralty to concentrate on converting the old Royal Sovereign-class battleships 'into properly armoured and bulged bombarding vessels with heavy deck armour'.[20] The Naval Staff took a different view of shipbuilding priorities. Italy's entry into the war convinced the Admiralty that its full construction programme must be resumed if Britain was not to fall behind its enemies in heavy ships. Britain expected to have a total of eighteen capital ships in service by the end of 1941, but this figure included seven unmodernized older ships. Only four of the navy's new King George Vs would be ready by that date. The completion of *Bismarck* and *Tirpitz* during the same period would give Germany a fleet of four modern capital ships, while Italy had recently added two more battleships to the four it already possessed. Britain was therefore falling behind in new battleship construction, and the gap appeared likely to widen. The final ship of the King George V-class, HMS *Howe*, might be completed in 1942, but this would be quickly followed by two new Italian battleships. Germany's construction programme was less certain. The Admiralty assumed that new battleships would eventually be built on the slips vacated by *Tirpitz* and *Bismarck*, but aerial reconnaissance indicated that one of these was still vacant, and the other was occupied by a new vessel of a smaller class. It was thought that Germany had probably suspended work on its capital-ship programme, but if new ships had been started in secrecy they might enter service in 1942–3. Britain's position was worse still if Japanese construction were taken into account. The Naval Staff calculated that Japan would possess thirteen new or modernized battleships and three small battlecruisers by the end of 1941, and would add two more battleships and two small battlecruisers in 1942–3. To ensure rough parity with Germany and Italy in 1945–6, Pound concluded that all the battleships previously authorized must be completed.[21]

The COS supported the Admiralty's position, but Churchill continued to urge priority for the reconstruction of the Royal Sovereigns. Initially, the only battleship he would consider resuming work on was *Howe*, which could be completed by mid-1942.[22] The Admiralty argued that it could not afford to take the Royal Sovereigns out of service for the eighteen months needed to complete their transformation.[23] Faced with firm opposition from the navy, and with the Destroyers-for-Bases deal with the United States now concluded, Churchill relented. He informed the First Lord on 15 September that since much of the plant and labour needed for battleship construction was not useful for other purposes, he was prepared in principle to resume the programme. But he urged that two of the older battleships should be reconstructed as soon as possible, and that no additional aircraft carriers or cruisers should be started until the following year.[24]

Churchill was clearly inclined to share the view of his naval advisers that capital ships were still the ultimate expression of a nation's naval power. The value of aircraft carriers was clearly recognized, but their potential to revolutionize naval warfare was not yet grasped. When construction priorities came before the War Cabinet in late October, Churchill threw his weight behind the Admiralty's proposals. 'At the end of the war,' he remarked, 'we should be faced with the formidable task of clearing up the situation in the Far East, and we should be unequal to that task if we fell behind Japan in capital ship construction.' Despite the reservations of some ministers, the War Cabinet accepted Churchill's recommendation and approved the Admiralty's programme, subject to the understanding that delays would have to be expected if resources were more urgently needed elsewhere.[25]

The German air offensive against Britain and the threat of invasion did not prevent Churchill from seizing every opportunity to take the offensive, even if it meant accepting serious risks. The most promising opportunities to strike at the Axis powers in 1940 were in the Mediterranean theatre. In the summer of 1939, Churchill had been confident that a vigorous naval offensive against Italy would quickly establish British dominance in the region, leaving Italian forces in Africa isolated and removing any threat to Egypt and the Suez Canal.[26] The COS tended to be more cautious. Even before the German invasion of France, they warned that if Italy entered the war they would have to adopt a primarily defensive strategy in the Mediterranean.[27] Admiral Cunningham took a similar view. His plans at this time focused on retaining control of communications in the Aegean and the eastern Mediterranean. Churchill expected more. 'Unless it is found that the fighting qualities of the Italians are high,' he admonished the COS, 'it will be much better that the Fleet at Alexandria should sally forth and run some risks than that it should remain in a posture so markedly defensive. Risks must be run at this juncture in all theatres.'[28] Cunningham, regarded by many as Britain's greatest fighting admiral of the Second World War, did not need to be lectured by Churchill. He had every intention of sending the fleet into the central Mediterranean to interrupt Italian communications and attack the Italian coast, and he immediately reassured London that 'all in the Fleet are imbued with a burning desire to get at the Italian Fleet'.[29]

Cunningham also shared Churchill's disdain for the Admiralty's suggestion that the Mediterranean fleet, based at Alexandria, might have to move to a less exposed position at Gibraltar.[30] Experience soon proved that the fleet was in fact able to operate from Alexandria, and, after the Italian invasion of Greece in October 1940, it gained the use of Suda Bay in Crete as well. Churchill's concerns that Cunningham would remain inactive were unfounded. The island of Malta, a British possession in the central Mediterranean, was too weakly defended and too close to Italian air bases to be of any use as a base for the British Mediterranean fleet. Cunningham could only challenge Italy's dominance in the central Mediterranean by periodically conducting offensive sweeps from Alexandria. The results were nevertheless encouraging. Italy's larger surface forces avoided battle with Cunningham's fleet, and Italian air power was much less effective than expected. Only Churchill was dissatisfied with the results. Cunningham's ability to operate in the central Mediterranean only served to raise the prime minister's expectations, and foster his concerns that naval authorities were excessively cautious in the face of Italian air attacks. He was particularly frustrated by Pound and Cunningham's reluctance to pass convoys for Egypt through the Mediterranean, rather than send them by the much longer route round the Cape.[31] 'Naturally,' he complained, 'they [i.e. admirals] all stand together like doctors in a case which has gone wrong. The fact remains that an exaggerated fear of Italian aircraft has been allowed to hamper operations.'[32] By September 1940, he was certain that opportunities were being lost in this theatre, and began to press for stronger defences at Malta so that Cunningham might station light craft on the island and use it as a temporary fleet base.[33]

Britain's naval position in the Mediterranean improved steadily during the final months of 1940, and by November Malta's defences were nearing full strength. The aircraft stationed there were able to attack Italian shipping, and the dispatch of the aircraft carrier *Illustrious* to join the Mediterranean fleet allowed Cunningham to launch a successful air strike against the Italian fleet at Taranto on 11 November.[34] This attack crippled half the Italian battle fleet and drove the other half to a more remote base at Naples. By the end of the month, Cunningham considered that 'our control of the Mediterranean was close on being re-established'.[35] This was an impressive achievement, but it still did not provide the sort of dramatic victories Churchill wanted. For these, he looked to the army. From the moment General Wavell opened his offensive against the Italians in December 1940, Churchill was mesmerized by land operations in North Africa. Large Italian forces had advanced from Libya into Egypt in September, but these were rapidly driven back by Wavell's much smaller army, first to the frontier, and then beyond. By February 1941, British and Commonwealth forces had achieved far more than anyone had expected, taking all of the Libyan province of Cyrenaica and capturing around 130,000 Italian prisoners.

This campaign was a triumph for Churchill, who had run considerable risks in dispatching soldiers and tanks to the Middle East in the autumn of 1940 when Britain's home defences were still badly deficient. But before the Italian presence in Libya could be eliminated, Churchill and his advisers, confident that these gains were secure, diverted a large portion of their forces to assist in the defence of Greece. This action coincided with the arrival of German forces in North Africa to bolster their flagging ally. The movement of the Luftwaffe to Sicily in January had already devastated Malta's defences and threatened the navy's ability to operate in the central Mediterranean. The presence of the German army in Libya and, later, in Greece further transformed the situation in the Mediterranean. By mid-April the British had been expelled from all of Libya except Tobruk. Shortly afterwards, resistance in Greece collapsed and Allied forces there had to be evacuated.

The deteriorating situation on land did not prevent Cunningham scoring an impressive victory over the Italian navy at the end of March. The battle of Cape Matapan in late March 1941 saw the destruction of three modern Italian cruisers and two destroyers. For once, Churchill was elated. 'The tearing up of the paper fleet of Italy,' he remarked.[36] But any goodwill Cunningham earned was short-lived. As the threat to Egypt and the Suez Canal grew, Churchill expected the navy to run exceptional risks and accept heavy losses if it would help to avert disaster on land. One means to impede the Axis advance, he suggested, was to launch commandos along the coast of Libya. The loss of their landing craft and specially modified 'Glen' ships would be justified, he maintained, 'if the result was an appreciable delay in the enemy's advance'.[37] But the best chance of retrieving the situation was to deprive Field Marshall Erwin Rommel's forces of supplies. Churchill demanded that Cunningham stop Axis convoys from reaching the port of Tripoli, but the admiral was naturally reluctant to endanger his ships in a region where Germany possessed control of the air. When he suggested that bombers could neutralize the port more effectively than battleships, Churchill was incensed. 'At the present time,' he wrote to Pound, 'the whole situation in the Nile Valley is compromised by the failure of the Navy to close the passage from Italy to Libya, or to break up the port facilities at Tripoli....We must be prepared to face some losses at sea, instead of the Navy sitting passive and leaving it to the Air.'[38] After learning on 14 April that an Axis convoy had reached North Africa, Churchill again rebuked the Admiralty. 'This is a serious Naval failure,' he complained. 'Another deadly convoy has got through. We have a right to ask why did not the Navy stop them. It is the duty of the Navy to stop them.'[39]

As prime minister, Churchill was less inclined than he had been while First Lord to monitor naval movements, but he was also in a stronger position to intervene when he believed that the navy should be doing more to support operations on land. With the backing of the War Cabinet, Churchill now issued a new directive for commanders in the Middle East, making it clear that Cunningham's first priority was to deny the use of the harbour at Tripoli to the enemy. To achieve this, he expected the fleet to bombard the harbour at every opportunity. '[U]ndue fears' of German dive bombers 'must not be entertained', he insisted, and 'heavy losses in battleships, cruisers and destroyers, must if necessary be accepted'.[40] Churchill was also attracted to the idea of using ships to block the harbour. Pound thought that the old battleship *Centurion*, which had been converted into a target ship in the 1920s, might be suitable as a blockship.[41] Churchill, however, was so alarmed by the threat to Egypt that he was willing to sacrifice one of the battleships in Cunningham's fleet for this purpose. The following day the Admiralty instructed Cunningham to use the battleship *Barham* and a light cruiser for a blocking operation. The admiral immediately protested against the pointless sacrifice of these two ships and their crews. It would be almost impossible to position the vessels correctly, he warned, and even if the operation were successful, the Germans could keep their forces supplied through

Tunisian ports. Moreover, so many supplies had already been landed at Tripoli that its loss would have little immediate impact on the Axis offensive.[42]

Cunningham was able to persuade the Admiralty to drop the blocking operation, but only by agreeing to use his fleet to bombard the harbour. This was done on 21 April 1941. The German air force was fully engaged elsewhere at the time and the fleet was able to escape undamaged. Cunningham probably assumed that the success of this operation would bring demands for another bombardment, and immediately warned Pound that they could not count on being so lucky a second time. He also made clear his resentment at being forced to take such serious risks with the fleet when heavy bombers operating from Egypt could inflict the same damage more efficiently. The Air Ministry, he complained, 'are trying to lay their responsibilities on Navy's shoulders and are not helping us out here on [the] Naval side of [the] war as they should'.[43] Pound now accepted that a blocking operation would be futile and proposed instead to maintain a battleship at Malta in order to disrupt Axis convoys. Churchill was also accommodating. He rebuked Cunningham for his complaints about insufficient air support in the theatre, but he did not insist on another bombardment by the fleet. He could not resist pointing out, however, that he had been right to disregard the air threat on this occasion, and asserted that the blocking operation would have succeeded.[44]

Cunningham wisely chose not to debate this point, but he continued to insist that the fleet was greatly hindered by inadequate air support. The 'Navy alone can only interrupt and can't stop communications particularly in the case of Libya.' He warned Churchill that unless the RAF was considerably strengthened in the Middle East, they might lose Egypt and a large part of the Mediterranean fleet.[45] Churchill was conciliatory, writing to the admiral on 1 May to inform him that additional aircraft were on their way, and congratulating him on the navy's outstanding performance during the evacuation of Greece.[46] However, he still had concerns about Cunningham being too timid. When the Germans began their assault on Crete later that month, one of Churchill's private secretaries noted that the prime minister 'deprecates the navy's way of treating ships as if they were too precious ever to risk. What do you think we build the ships for?' A few days later he noted again that Churchill felt the Mediterranean fleet had 'a tendency to shirk its task of preventing a seaborne landing in Crete since Cunningham fears severe losses from bombing. The P.M.'s line is that Cunningham must be made to take every risk: the loss of half the Mediterranean fleet would be worthwhile in order to save Crete.'[47]

These complaints were unjustified. Cunningham *was* willing to run risks over Crete, but he was not prepared to incur losses that would cripple his fleet and endanger Britain's control of the eastern Mediterranean.[48] Heavier losses would not have made any difference to the outcome of the battle. As it was, the navy suffered heavily in operations around Crete: three cruisers and six destroyers were sunk, and two battleships, an aircraft carrier, six cruisers, and seven destroyers were damaged. This was a serious setback. Lacking an aircraft carrier, and with most of his destroyers tied up supplying the besieged Allied garrison at Tobruk, Cunningham had no choice but to adopt a more defensive strategy during the latter half of 1941. Somerville's Force H, based at Gibraltar, assumed the main burden of bringing supplies into Malta. In this respect, the British were fortunate. The German invasion of Russia in June 1941 led to the withdrawal of the Luftwaffe from Sicily. By September, British aircraft and submarines were able to operate from Malta again, and soon began to achieve considerable success against Axis shipping. The situation improved so much that the following month a striking force of light cruisers and destroyers, known as Force K, was also based at Malta.

Churchill welcomed these developments, but continued to feel that the navy could be doing more to disrupt enemy shipping. 'Cunningham,' he complained in October, 'seems to be laying very low since Crete.'[49] However, his criticisms now became relatively minor and infrequent. Operations in the Mediterranean over the course of 1940–1 had undoubtedly led to a better appreciation of the navy's limitations. By the autumn of 1941, Churchill's attention was focused on preparations for a new land offensive in North Africa, operation 'Crusader', which opened in November. He expected victory in the Middle East to be won on land, not at sea.

While operations in North Africa and the Mediterranean were Churchill's main preoccupation in the months after the fall of France, he was also eager to strike at Germany. Even as Britain's fortunes reached their lowest point in the summer of 1940, Churchill was unwilling to adopt a purely defensive posture. Amphibious raids along the coast of occupied Europe offered one of the few means to hit back, and Churchill was eager to develop Britain's capabilities in this area. The successful evacuation of the BEF from Dunkirk in the face of heavy German opposition suggested that specially trained and equipped formations might be transported to and from enemy-held territory.

'[I]f it is so easy for the Germans to invade us in spite of [our superior] sea-power,' he remarked, 'some may feel inclined to ask the same question—why should it be thought impossible for us to do anything of the same kind to them.' In early June 1940, Churchill proposed that special raiding forces, organized into units of one thousand men, should be prepared for raids along the coast of occupied Europe. 'We have got to get out of our minds the idea that the Channel ports and all the country between them are enemy territory,' he wrote:

> Enterprises must be prepared, with specially trained troops of the hunter class, who can develop a reign of terror down these coasts, first of all on the 'butcher and bolt' policy, but later on, or perhaps as soon as we are organized, we should surprise Calais or Boulogne, kill or capture the Hun garrison and hold the place until all the preparations to reduce it by siege or heavy storm have been made, and then away.[50]

The Chiefs of Staff were receptive to the idea. They appointed Lieutenant General Alan Bourne, the Adjutant General of the Royal Marines, as Director of Combined Operations (DCO), and gave him control of new commando units in the process of being formed by the War Office, and of six independent army companies that had been raised earlier for irregular operations in Norway. The first British coastal raid, employing just 115 commandos, was launched on Boulogne on 23 June. Little was achieved, but Churchill was nevertheless eager to launch another operation.[51] In early July his attention turned to the Channel Islands, which had recently been occupied by the Germans. He had high hopes for a raid on Guernsey, and expected commandos to eliminate the entire German garrison there.[52] The results were a considerable disappointment. When the assault was launched on 14 July, one landing party was deposited on the wrong island altogether, and another had to turn back due to mechanical problems. The one group to reach Guernsey contained only forty men, and they were unable even to locate the German garrison. When they withdrew, three men had to be left behind because they could not swim.[53]

Despite these unimpressive results, the War Office continued to support the idea of small raids, arguing that until Britain had the resources for more substantial operations, these 'mosquito raids' were a valuable opportunity to develop new techniques and give troops experience.[54] Churchill disagreed. He informed the Secretary of State for War, Anthony Eden, that there must be no more 'silly fiascos' like the raids on Boulogne and Guernsey. 'The idea of working all these coasts up against us by pin-prick raids and fulsome communiqués is,' he concluded, 'one to be strictly avoided.'[55] In his view, the solution was larger raids. On 17 July 1940, Churchill appointed Admiral of the Fleet Sir Roger Keyes as the new Director of Combined Operations. Keyes, the hero of the daring raid on Zeebrugge in 1918, lost no opportunity to impress upon Churchill his determination to take the war to the enemy. He seemed to possess not just the aggressive drive that Churchill admired, but also the authority and prestige that would be needed if the new organization were to achieve meaningful results. Churchill instructed Keyes to begin planning 'medium-sized actions' employing between five and ten thousand troops.[56] At this time, Churchill hoped to launch several such raids along the French coast before the end of 1940. These were to be followed in 1941 by 'large armoured irruptions' into the Continent.[57] Privately, he speculated about eventually landing one hundred thousand or more troops for a 'destructive raid into the Ruhr', the seizure of the Cherbourg Peninsula, or the invasion of Italy.[58]

The 'butcher and bolt' policy Churchill had outlined in June was thus remarkably short-lived. He continued to give the commandos his strong support, but he increasingly viewed them as the basis of an elite striking force comparable to the storm troops Germany had employed on the Western Front in 1918, or to the 'incredibly small number of highly equipped elite who, while the dull mass of the German Army came on behind, made good the conquest' of France in 1940. On 25 August he explained to Eden that any offensive in 1941 'must be amphibious in its character and there will certainly be many opportunities of minor operations all of which will depend on surprise landings of lightly equipped nimble forces accustomed to work like a pack of hounds instead of being moved about in the ponderous manner which is appropriate to the regular formations'.[59]

While Keyes set to work expanding Britain's amphibious capabilities, Churchill threw his support behind plans for landing General Charles de Gaulle's Free French forces at Dakar in French West Africa. There was, in theory, much to be said for this operation. If successful, it would prevent German U-boats ever operating from this port; French warships located there, including the battleship *Richelieu*, would be neutralized; and de Gaulle's movement would obtain a base from which to extend control over other French African colonies. The likelihood of success, moreover, appeared to be high, particularly as there was a chance that de Gaulle would be welcomed by the colonial authorities, making force unnecessary.

PLATE I Churchill and Lord Fisher leaving a meeting of the Committee of Imperial Defence, 1913.

PLATE 2 Churchill (second from right) on the conning tower of Submarine D2, Portsmouth harbour, 6 November 1911.

PLATE 3 Churchill boarding a Maurice Farman seaplane in August 1913 at Calshot Naval Air Station. The pilot, Lt Spenser Grey, RN, was one of Churchill's regular flying instructors.

PLATE 4 Sir Robert Borden, Prime Minister of Canada, and Churchill leaving the Admiralty, 1912. Churchill hoped that Canada would supply the additional dreadnoughts the Royal Navy needed to maintain a strong presence in the Mediterranean.

PLATE 5 Churchill at the Yarrow shipyard for the launch of HMS *Marlborough*, November 1911. He is flanked by Lord Fisher (left) and Rear-Admiral Ernest Troubridge, his Naval Secretary (right).

The MEN who are DIRECTING BRITAIN'S NAVY.

THE FIRST LORD WITH HIS TWO HIGHEST EXECUTIVE OFFICERS

DRAWN BY F. MATANIA

RIGHT HON. WINSTON CHURCHILL—Mr. Churchill is not quite forty years old yet, but he is known throughout the world as a most capable administrator of English affairs. He was first elected for Parliament in 1900 as a Conservative member, but in the year 1906 he was returned for N.W. Manchester as a Liberal. He has been First Lord of the Admiralty since 1911

REAR-ADMIRAL CHARLES MADDEN (second in command) has just relinquished the command of the 3rd Cruiser Squadron of the Home Fleets. He entered the Navy in 1875. He was in command of one of the earliest flotillas of torpedo-boat destroyers in the Mediterranean. He became captain of the original "Dreadnought" in 1907. He has gained a high reputation

ADMIRAL SIR JOHN JELLICOE—Vice-Admiral Jellicoe has just been appointed Commander-in-Chief of the Home Fleet in place of Admiral Callaghan. Admiral Jellicoe has acted since 1912 as Second Sea Lord of the Admiralty. He saw service in China from 1898-1901, when he commanded the Naval Brigade there. He was commander of the Atlantic Fleet during 1910-11

PLATE 6   Wartime illustration depicting Churchill, as First Lord of the Admiralty, discussing strategy with Admiral Sir John Jellicoe, Commander-in-Chief of the Grand Fleet (right), and Admiral Charles Madden, Jellicoe's chief of staff (centre).

PLATE 7 The Board of Admiralty, 6 December 1939. Around the table, left to right: Geoffrey Shakespeare (Parliamentary and Financial Secretary); Rear-Admiral H. M. Burough (Assistant Chief of the Naval Staff); Vice-Admiral Sir Alexander R. Ramsey (Fifth Sea Lord); Rear-Admiral T. S. V. Phillips (Deputy Chief of Naval Staff); Admiral of the Fleet Sir Dudley Pound (First Sea Lord); Sir J. Sidney Barnes (Deputy Secretary); Churchill (First Lord of the Admiralty); Sir Archibald Carter (Secretary); Admiral Sir Charles Little (Second Sea Lord); Rear-Admiral Bruce Fraser (Third Sea Lord); Rear-Admiral G. S. Arbuthnot (Fourth Sea Lord); and Captain A. U. M. Hudson (Civil Lord).

PLATE 8 Churchill as First Lord of the Admiralty, with Admiral Sir Alfred Dudley Pound, First Sea Lord from 1939–1943.

PLATE 9 Churchill addressing the company of HMS *Exeter* on 14 February 1940 upon its return to Plymouth following the Battle of the River Plate.

PLATE 10   Churchill signs autographs for men of HMS *Ajax* and HMS *Exeter*, 23 February 1940, following a banquet in their honour at the Guildhall, London.

PLATE 11   The combination of air cover and surface escorts eventually proved effective in neutralizing the U-boat threat in the mid-Atlantic. Churchill is seen here inspecting personnel from the RAF's Coastal Command in Reykjavík, Iceland, August 1941. A Royal Canadian Navy escort, the destroyer HMCS *Assiniboine*, is in the background.

PLATE 12   The sinking of HMS *Prince of Wales* and HMS *Repulse* by Japanese aircraft on 10 December 1941. Crew members of HMS *Prince of Wales* shown here scrambling over the side into life boats.

PLATE 13   Churchill on deck of the aircraft carrier HMS *Victorious* during a visit to the Royal Navy's Home Fleet on 11 October 1942. Left to right: Captain Henry Bovell, Churchill, Rear-Admiral Arthur Lumley Lyster, Sir Stafford Cripps.

PLATE 14   Churchill, Admiral Sir Bruce Fraser, Admiral Sir John Tovey
(Commander-in-Chief of the Home Fleet), and Randolph Churchill on HMS *King
George V*, 11 October 1942.

PLATE 15 (*opposite*)   The Board of the Admiralty entertained Churchill and US
government and naval officials in the painted hall at Greenwich, London, on 25
July 1942. Left to right: John Winant (US Ambassador); A. V. Alexander (First
Lord of the Admiralty); Churchill; William Bullitt (Special Assistant to the
Secretary of the Navy); Admiral Ernest J. King (Commander-in-Chief of the US
Fleet and Chief of Naval Operations); Harry Hopkins (adviser to President
Roosevelt); Admiral Harold Stark (Commander of US Naval forces in Europe);
and Admiral of the Fleet Sir Dudley Pound (First Sea Lord).

PLATE 16   A Hawker Sea Hurricane being catapulted from a Catapult Armed Merchant (CAM) ship at Greenock (note the flame from the rocket assistors). Churchill was initially enthusiastic about using these ships for trade protection in the mid-Atlantic, but they fell short of expectations.

PLATE 17   Churchill talking to General Sir Alan Brooke, the Chief of the Imperial General Staff, while traveling to France on the destroyer HMS *Kelvin*, 12 June 1944.

PLATE 18 Leading protagonists in the "Battle of the Air", the fierce debate in Whitehall over the allocation of aircraft between the Battle of the Atlantic and the strategic bombing campaign against Germany. Left to right: Lord Cherwell, Air Chief Marshal Sir Charles Portal, Admiral Pound, and Churchill. They are photographed watching a display of anti-aircraft gunnery.

PLATE 19 Churchill crossing the Rhine River in an amphibious Landing Vehicle Tracked ("Buffalo") crewed by British soldiers, 26 March 1945. The shortage of landing craft was the source of much frustration for Churchill in 1943–44. 'How it is that the plans of two great empires like Britain and the United States should be so much hamstrung and limited by a hundred or two of these particular vessels will never be understood by history' (Churchill to General George Marshall, April 1944).

The operation, codenamed 'Menace', was another fiasco.[60] A squadron of Vichy warships reached Dakar shortly before the operation began on 14 September. This nearly resulted in its cancellation, but the expedition's commanders successfully pressed London for permission to continue. When Allied forces arrived on the 23rd, the French garrison remained loyal to the Vichy government. Free French troops landed near Dakar came under heavy fire and withdrew the same day. British warships bombarded the French defences and warships until the 25th, sinking two Vichy submarines but inflicting negligible damage on *Richelieu*. By the end of the action several British ships had themselves been damaged, including the battleship *Resolution*, which was put out of action for several months.

The failure at Dakar did nothing to diminish Churchill's interest in combined operations. However, a shortage of resources made the larger operations he wanted impossible, while his injunction against 'pin prick' raids precluded most of the operations the Combined Operations Headquarters (COHQ) considered feasible. Churchill dismissed most proposals out of hand. When the COS suggested using Moroccan troops for a raid on the French coast, for example, he commented that it 'would be most undesirable for it to appear that the only people who dared raid the occupied coasts of France were black troops from Morocco. Moreover I do not think the course of the war will be materially affected by a petty affair of 40 men.'[61]

With few suitable targets within range of Britain, his attention naturally shifted to the increasingly active Mediterranean theatre. Churchill was strongly attracted to a proposal from Keyes in November 1940 to use commandos to capture Pantelleria, a small island approximately 150 miles north-west of Malta between Sicily and Tunisia.[62] In British hands, Churchill believed it would provide a base from which to contest Italian communications with North Africa and protect British convoys passing through the central Mediterranean. Keyes was confident that the island could be captured and held, but members of the Defence Committee, which had replaced the Military Coordination Committee as the main body in which ministers and the Chiefs of Staff met to oversee military operations, were sceptical. The Committee only agreed to begin planning for this operation, codenamed 'Workshop', when Churchill threw his weight behind the project.

Opposition soon began to mount, however. The COS and Admiral Cunningham agreed that the island could probably be captured, but they did not feel that sufficient resources were available to hold it.[63] Furthermore, Cunningham considered the Dodecanese Islands in the Aegean a more valuable objective.[64] Churchill remained firm. On 9 December 1940 he persuaded the Defence Committee to allow preparations to continue, with the understanding that they could be called off at any time if conditions changed.[65] Two days later he informed Cunningham that the operation was going forward. It was 'no doubt a hazard', he admitted, but it might also 'be surprisingly easy'.[66] Despite Churchill's determination to push it through, the operation was suspended within a week. The great success of the British offensive against Italian forces in North Africa raised concerns in London that Germany might undertake some bold move to bolster its faltering ally. The British had been concerned about Spanish and Portuguese islands in the Atlantic since the fall of France, and they now worried that the Germans might attempt to seize the Canary Islands. In mid-July the COS had taken the precaution of assembling an expeditionary force, comprised primarily of Royal Marines, to be held in readiness in the event it became necessary to seize the Azores and Cape Verde Islands.[67] With the danger of German action now increased, the decision was taken to hold the troops and shipping earmarked for the Pantelleria expedition for possible use in the Atlantic.[68]

Churchill soon had second thoughts about the wisdom of delaying 'Workshop'. In late December he pressed for the operation to be launched when conditions were right in January. He agreed to postpone action until February when the COS objected, but he soon regarded this as a mistake as well.[69] 'I flinched,' he told one of his secretaries, 'and now I have cause to regret it.'[70] The establishment of German air bases in Sicily in early January 1941 completely transformed the situation in the central Mediterranean. The occupation of Pantelleria was now, in Churchill's view, more urgent.[71] Service leaders, on the other hand, doubted that the operation was still feasible in view of the German air threat, and noted that the Germans could dominate the region just as easily from Sicily. But Churchill was not interested in seizing the Dodecanese, as Cunningham and the COS desired. Capturing the smaller islands in this group would accomplish little, he warned, other than to 'stir up the area without destroying the danger'. And while he was not opposed in principle to taking one of the large islands, this would require longer preparation, and he urged that 'Workshop' be given priority.[72]

The matter was settled by the Defence Committee on 20 January. The Chiefs of Staff insisted that their main objective must be the security of Britain's position in the eastern Mediterranean. Churchill grudgingly agreed to support an assault on the Dodecanese, code-named 'Mandibles', which would at least help to secure Britain's communications with Greece and Turkey.[73] A large portion of the specialized shipping, landing craft, and commandos that had been built up in Britain was therefore dispatched to the Middle East, where it would no longer come under the direct control of the Defence Committee in London.[74] This was a serious setback for Keyes, but Churchill, who still had high hopes for combined operations, threw his support behind the admiral's efforts to rebuild his organization. The two men did not always agree, however, on suitable targets. In early January 1941, Churchill rejected a plan for a raid to destroy the Jøssingfjord power station in Norway. The COHQ believed this was a soft target from which their organization could gain valuable experience, but Churchill declared that he 'did not wish to disturb the Norwegian coast for a trifle like this'.[75] A number of relatively small operations were conducted, however. The first involved dropping thirty-six troops by air into southern Italy to destroy an important aqueduct.[76] A few days later around two hundred commandos raised from Wavell's forces in the Middle East were landed on the island of Castellorizo in the Dodecanese. This operation went badly. A supporting force of Royal Marines was prematurely withdrawn from the island, and reinforcements were not landed immediately to help hold it. Italian troops landed two days later, retaking the island and capturing many of the commandos. As Cunningham remarked, the operation 'was a rotten business and reflected little credit on anyone'.[77]

The only successful British combined operation in this period was an amphibious raid on Norway's Lofoten islands. On 3 March 1941 approximately one thousand troops were landed there unopposed. They destroyed the islands' eleven fish-oil factories and stores of oil and glycerine, sank five ships of approximately 18,000 tons, and returned with more than two hundred German prisoners and over three hundred Norwegian volunteers.[78] Churchill was delighted. 'This admirable raid has done serious injury to the enemy and has given an immense amount of innocent pleasure at home.'[79] But he still hoped for action on a larger scale. In mid-February, he had revived the idea of a raid on the Channel Islands. It was 'most desirable,' he wrote, 'that some offensive action be undertaken to force the Germans to fight and to inflict military losses on them at an early date'. Even if British and German losses in such a raid were about even, he believed 'we would be able to count the moral effect an important gain'.[80] This proposal was rejected by the Joint Planners, who recommended instead a series of small raids on the French coast to obtain information about German invasion preparations. This scheme obtained the backing of both the COS and Keyes.[81] Churchill, however, came out strongly against it. The capture of a handful of German soldiers 'seemed a very small prize', he informed the COS, particularly as the same information could probably be obtained by aerial reconnaissance.[82] The operation was cancelled, and Keyes' efforts were soon diverted to preparations for operations in the Atlantic.

The COS, alarmed by British setbacks in North Africa and Greece in the spring of 1941, wanted an expedition ready to sail to the Canary Islands in the event that German pressure on Spain resulted in the loss of Gibraltar, which would be a devastating blow to Britain's ability to control the western Mediterranean. Churchill approved this operation, codenamed 'Puma', on 24 April. Forces were also held in readiness for a descent on the Azores ('Thruster') and Madeira ('Springboard'). Operation 'Puma' was ready to go in mid-May, but Churchill was unable to obtain President Roosevelt's support for the expedition, and the Defence Committee decided to postpone it. The forces assembled were initially kept at seven days' notice, but in June 1941 they were stood down until July.[83] There was no intention of dispersing them, however. The loss of Gibraltar would have such serious repercussions that the Joint Planners advised that 'we must at all times be prepared to act instantly' if it appeared the Germans were about to move.[84] Keyes was irritated by this ongoing commitment, which immobilized around twenty-four thousand men and nearly the entire available fleet of landing craft and assault shipping. He urged Churchill and Eden to seize the Atlantic islands as soon as possible, even if it meant Spanish hostility and the loss of Gibraltar.[85]

The German invasion of the Soviet Union on 22 June led to a diversion of German resources eastwards and stimulated fresh interest in London in combined operations along the northern coast of France. The next day Churchill instructed the COS to investigate the possibility of a major raid within range of British fighter cover. He was thinking of 'something of the scale of 25 to 30 thousand men—perhaps the Commandos plus one of the Canadian divisions.'[86] Anthony Eden, now serving as Foreign Secretary, also believed that the reduction of German fighter aircraft in France presented opportunities for bold action. 'From the political point of view,' he wrote in early July, 'a few successful raids would be most valuable.' Not only would they 'encourage the Russians in their grim struggle', they would also dispel 'old doubts' in Europe 'of our ability to give knocks on land'.[87] The COS were themselves eager to take advantage of Germany's distractions in the east, but they recognized that an operation on the scale proposed by Churchill was not possible with the resources at hand. They instructed Keyes to begin planning something more manageable, but until forces earmarked for Atlantic operations were released there was little his organization could do. On 4 July he presented plans for a raid on Le Touquet in northern France, although he could only muster 320 men and 6 tanks for the operation. Churchill was firmly opposed to a raid on this scale. He derided Keyes' proposal as 'most inadequate and out of proportion in the general war situation':

> The results would be very small and might be achieved with disproportionate loss. The enemy would claim to have repulsed an attack and the general attitude throughout the world would probably be ridicule at the feeble efforts which were all that we could achieve to help the Russians. The whole affair would appear as a fiasco.

The Defence Committee agreed with Churchill that combined operations must be designed on a scale that would ensure 'useful results'.[88] An operation on the scale Churchill wanted was not yet feasible, however, as even he soon realized. 'The Germans have forty divisions in France alone,' he explained to Joseph Stalin later that month, 'and the whole coast has been fortified with German diligence for more than a year....To attempt a landing in force would be to encounter a bloody repulse, and petty raids would only lead to fiascos'. No amphibious operation Britain could mount was likely to divert German forces from the Soviet front.[89]

The COS and Keyes chafed at Churchill's restriction on small raids, and in July they were given permission to launch minor reconnaissance raids along the French coast.[90] Churchill still wanted something bigger, however, and urged Keyes to prepare another assault in northern Norway, this time employing three to four thousand men and remaining three or four nights before evacuation.[91] Keyes continued to be constrained by preparations for the seizure of the Atlantic islands. On 23 July operations 'Puma', 'Thruster', and 'Springboard' were merged into a single expanded scheme, christened 'Pilgrim', for the simultaneous seizure of all the islands. Churchill initially planned to launch this operation in September, but when American support was not forthcoming the operation was put on hold until it was clear that the Germans were themselves preparing to act.[92] Keyes was dismayed. He was becoming increasingly sceptical about the prospects of 'Pilgrim', and preferred to use these resources for large cross-Channel raids or the capture of Sardinia. He held out the prospect of achieving the sort of results Churchill had long hoped for, such as the seizure of the Cherbourg Peninsula and the permanent occupation of the Channel Islands.[93] But Churchill and the COS remained committed to preparations for 'Pilgrim', which was not formally cancelled until February 1942. At all events, Keyes' tenure as DCO was nearing its end. During his fourteen months in this position he had frequently clashed with the COS, and by October 1941 their relationship had deteriorated to the point that Churchill reluctantly accepted that Keyes must be relieved.[94]

Combined operations had thus failed to produce anything like the results Churchill had expected when he embraced the concept in June 1940. Only a handful of minor raids had been launched, and nearly all were embarrassing failures. The only unqualified success was the assault on the Lofoten Islands, but the destruction of remote Norwegian fish-oil factories was, by itself, of no strategic value. Churchill instinctively disliked small raids, declaring on one occasion that it was 'unworthy of such a large entity as the British Empire to send over a few cut-throats'.[95] But he still saw a useful role for amphibious operations, provided they were launched on a scale that would allow for real strategic gains. When Captain Lord Louis Mountbatten of the Royal Navy was appointed to replace Keyes, Churchill instructed him to 'start a programme of raids of ever-increasing intensity, so as to keep the whole of the enemy coastline on the alert from the North Cape to the Bay of Biscay'. However, by late 1941 he no longer regarded combined operations primarily as a means to tie down and disperse German resources: his attention was increasingly drawn towards the problem of returning to the Continent in force. Churchill therefore used this change in leadership to insist on a major shift in emphasis for the Combined Operations Headquarters. Your *main object,* he informed Mountbatten, '*must be the re-invasion of France.* You must create the machine which will make it possible for us to beat Hitler on land. You must devise the appurtenances and appliances which will make the invasion possible.'[96]

Churchill's offensive instincts were also constrained by the heavy defensive obligations forced on the navy during this phase of the war. The German conquest of France and Norway dramatically improved their ability to attack Britain's seaborne trade. U-boats no longer had to run the British blockade to escape from the North Sea; they could remain on station much longer; and they could penetrate further into the Atlantic. Germany's surface ships also continued to prey on shipping. In the spring of 1940 the Germans began using converted merchant ships as commerce raiders. By the end of 1941 these 'ghost cruisers' had sunk or captured nearly half a million tons of unescorted merchant shipping worldwide.[97] At the same time, heavy units of the German fleet presented a constant threat to Allied convoys. The pocket battleship *Scheer* roamed the sea lanes between October 1940 and March 1941, sinking sixteen merchant ships of nearly 100,000 tons. A sortie by the battlecruisers *Scharnhorst* and *Gneisenau* from January to March 1941 accounted for another twenty-two ships of over 115,000 tons. The heavy cruiser *Hipper* was also employed as a raider, sinking slightly more than 40,000 tons during its two cruises.[98] These ships all avoided destruction on the high seas. The battleship *Bismarck* was less fortunate. This ship embarked on its first cruise in May 1941, and soon became the subject of a massive hunt by units of the Home Fleet and Somerville's Force H. *Bismarck* was destroyed before it could reach safety at the French port of Brest, but only after sinking the battlecruiser *Hood* and damaging the *Prince of Wales*.

The destruction of the *Bismarck* marked the end of Germany's use of heavy warships as commerce raiders in the Atlantic Ocean, but the Admiralty still kept heavy ships in home waters in the event of another breakout attempt. The U-boat threat proved far more difficult to eliminate. In August 1940 Hitler declared a total blockade of the British Isles, and soon afterwards the U-boats began to employ deadly new 'wolf-pack' tactics for coordinated night-time attacks on convoys. As a defensive measure, merchant shipping was routed through the North West Approaches, but the redeployment of escort vessels to anti-invasion duties left convoys dangerously exposed. The British were fortunate that Hitler was not in a better position to capitalize on this vulnerability. U-boat production during the 'phoney war' had not kept pace with losses, and German strength had actually declined slightly since the beginning of the war. Nevertheless, even with fewer than thirty operational U-boats available to the Germans during the latter half of 1940, the British suffered heavy losses. German submariners would later refer to this period of plentiful targets and weak defences as the 'Happy Time'.

Churchill was not alarmed at first by the sudden surge in shipping losses during the summer of 1940. Britain's merchant fleet was still the largest in the world, and its strength had been augmented by nearly 2 million tons of shipping acquired from continental states that had been overrun by the Germans. There seemed to be little danger of an immediate shipping shortage developing. A more serious threat appeared to be the congestion in Britain's western ports, which struggled to handle the sudden surge of shipping being diverted from more vulnerable areas.[99] Import levels declined more rapidly during the latter half of 1940 than authorities expected, however. In part this was the result of the mounting losses being inflicted on British shipping, but it also stemmed from the heavy logistical demands created by Churchill's decision to build up forces in the Middle East. As historian Kevin Smith notes, between June 1940 and January 1942 nearly a quarter of British-controlled shipping tonnage was employed either full- or part-time in meeting military needs in this theatre.[100]

By October 1940 the shipping situation was starting to become serious. In that month alone over 350,000 tons of merchant shipping were sunk by U-boats, and another 90,000 tons were lost to other causes.[101] As losses mounted and the danger of invasion seemed to recede, the Admiralty began to press for the release of escort vessels from anti-invasion patrols. The Defence Committee, chaired by Churchill, was initially reluctant to do so. Britain could continue to suffer heavy shipping losses for some time without risking a collapse, but a successful invasion would be immediately fatal. And with troops and tanks being dispatched from Britain to the Middle East, it seemed essential that the navy be able to prevent German forces getting ashore. Thus, given a choice between two strictly defensive roles for the navy's light ships, Churchill opted for the one that would enable him to take the offensive elsewhere.[102] The COS secured only a modest transfer of ships—four destroyers and ten anti-submarine trawlers—on 3 October.[103] Churchill hoped the escorts could gradually be strengthened with new construction and American destroyers as they became available, and he continued to oppose the release of ships from the southeast coast until the end of October, by which time intelligence indicated that the German invasion had been postponed till the following year.[104]

The transfer of resources back to trade defence coincided with warnings from Ronald Cross, the Minister of Shipping, that continued heavy losses would have grave long-term repercussions. Britain's annual imports stood at 43.5 million tons in the first year of the war, but officials at the Ministry of Shipping estimated that this would drop to around 32 million tons by the third year of war if the present rate of loss were not reduced. This calculation assumed, moreover, that demands on British shipping for the Middle East would remain stable. If operations in this theatre expanded, as Churchill wanted, Britain's imports would be further reduced.[105] This message was reinforced a week later by Arthur Greenwood, Minister without Portfolio, who reported that imports might also be drastically curtailed by the continuing congestion in Britain's western ports.[106]

Churchill took this problem seriously and in January 1941 created the Import Executive, under the chairmanship of the Minster of Supply, to ensure that optimal use was being made of the available shipping.[107] While this was a sensible step, Churchill stopped short of another measure that would have had an immediate impact on the U-boat campaign: the diversion of aircraft to the protection of shipping. In early November 1940 the First Lord of the Admiralty proposed that the RAF's Coastal Command, whose aircraft cooperated with the navy in the defence of trade, should be increased from around three hundred planes to nearly one thousand.[108] This expansion could only come at the expense of the strategic air offensive, however, and Churchill was determined not to divert resources to what he regarded as a strictly defensive task. When the matter was discussed by the Defence Committee, he criticized the Admiralty for putting forward 'extravagant demands…which could not possibly be met at a time when we were engaged on the task of increasing our power to bomb Germany'. He noted that the RAF was 'forming itself into the leading element in bringing about our victory', and recalled how the Royal Naval Air Service, the predecessor of the Fleet Air Arm, had absorbed 'great quantities of men and material' during the First World War. 'The result,' he complained, 'was that at a time when the Royal Flying Corps was fighting for its life in France, large resources stood comparatively idle in this country. Such a thing must never be allowed to happen again.'[109]

Churchill later employed this same logic to reject a proposal from Cunningham to establish a Mediterranean Coastal Command to provide dedicated support to his fleet. This request, Churchill complained in July 1941, 'would practically ruin our Air Force in the Middle East'. In his view, the fleet should only expect air support for relatively brief periods, 'when engaged on important operations'.[110] To ensure that the air resources devoted to defensive tasks were being used effectively, Churchill recommended an investigation into means to improve the efficiency of Coastal Command, including the possibility that it be taken over by the Admiralty.[111] But he stipulated that any proposals must avoid 'an undue diversion of resources to defensive duties owing to the desire of the F.A.A. [Fleet Air Arm] to ensure its requirements being met on an over-generous scale'.[112] The Air Ministry and the Admiralty worked out a plan for a small increase to Coastal

Command's numbers, but despite the backing of Lord Beaverbrook, Minister of Supply, the navy was unable to obtain full control. Churchill was sympathetic to the idea in principle when it was discussed on 4 December, but he was not prepared to initiate such a disruptive and controversial change in wartime. The Defence Committee agreed to place Coastal Command under the Admiralty's operational control, although it would remain an integral part of the Royal Air Force.[113]

Churchill was more receptive to ideas that did not involve weakening bomber command. In November 1940 the lowest speed for independently sailed merchant ships was reduced from 16 to 13 knots, in hopes that releasing faster vessels from the constraints of convoy would increase shipping capacity without incurring heavier losses.[114] The following month Churchill urged the Admiralty to consider equipping merchant ships with catapults for launching fighter aircraft in order to provide convoys with protection against long-range German aircraft.[115] Continued heavy losses in the first months of 1941 compelled him to take an active interest in the work of the Import Executive. Churchill was confident that the tonnage available for imports could be increased by repairing merchant ships more quickly, and that greater efficiency could be achieved by reducing the time ships spent on their voyages and in port. Under Churchill's direction, the Import Executive instructed the Admiralty to consider a scheme whereby workers could be diverted from naval construction to the repair of merchant ships. This body also considered a variety of other measures, including a further decrease in speed for independently sailed ships to 12 knots.[116] The heavy losses inflicted by the wolf packs on ships under escort had clearly raised doubts about the continued viability of convoy. Churchill reassured the Admiralty that he remained 'personally convinced of the soundness of the convoy system', but he instructed Pound that 'it should be continually subjected to unprejudiced judgement in the light of ascertained facts'.[117]

After reporting another devastating convoy attack to the War Cabinet on 27 February, Churchill grudgingly accepted that trade defence 'must for the moment, be our supreme exertion'.[118] He pressed the COS to give higher priority to the provision of anti-aircraft guns to merchant vessels and the development of new bases for Coastal Command in Northern Ireland and Scotland. He also made it clear that Bomber Command would have to provide some assistance. Air Marshal Sir Charles Portal, the CAS, warned Air Chief Marshal Sir Richard Peirse, the head of Bomber Command, on 1 March that 'A very high proportion of bomber effort will inevitably be required to pull the Admiralty out of the mess they have got into.'[119] A few days later Churchill issued a new directive proclaiming the onset of the 'Battle of the Atlantic'. This, he subsequently remarked, was meant 'to focus the extreme attention and energies of all concerned upon this struggle for life'.[120] Typically, he began by stressing the importance of offensive measures. 'The U-boat at sea must be hunted,' he declared, 'the U-boat in the building yard or in dock must be bombed. The Fokke Wulf, and other bombers…must be attacked in the air and in their nests'. To achieve this, he called for 'extreme priority' to be given to fitting out merchant ships to launch fighter aircraft. In addition, greater effort would be made to concentrate Coastal Command's resources on the North-Western Approaches, to allocate more defensive weapons to merchant ships, and to improve the anti-aircraft defences at Britain's main western ports. Churchill's directive also demanded a drastic reduction in the amount of shipping awaiting repair, a faster turnaround time for ships in port at home and abroad, and a possible further reduction in the lower speed for ships allowed to sail outside convoy.[121]

To oversee the progress of these schemes, Churchill created the high-level Battle of the Atlantic Committee, which he chaired himself.[122] This body consisted of ministers concerned with various aspects of shipping and supply situation, including the three service chiefs, and was regularly attended by the First Sea Lord, members of the Naval Staff, and representatives of the other services, including the head of Coastal Command. When it began meeting in late March 1941, most of its efforts were dedicated to increasing the efficiency of British shipping and ports. Its first achievement was a reduction in the amount of shipping awaiting or undergoing repair. In late February, when the figure stood at nearly 2.6 million tons, the Import Executive had hoped to increase the monthly repair rate by at least 100,000 tons.[123] Considerable success was achieved. By July 1941 the amount of shipping requiring repair had been reduced by nearly a million tons. As historian Max Schoenfeld has noted, this was not due entirely to the efforts of the Battle of the Atlantic Committee. Improved weather conditions during the summer, a decrease in German air attacks beginning in May, and the transfer of some repair work to American shipyards under the provisions of lend-lease aid from the United States, all contributed to the reduction of this backlog. But the Committee's efforts to transfer workers from other tasks undoubtedly made a valuable contribution.[124]

The main casualty of this diversion of labour was the navy. When its new construction programme came up for consideration in March 1941,

Churchill maintained that the transfer of dockyard labour to repair work would rule out the commencement of any new fleet aircraft carriers once the three then under construction were completed. As any new carriers could not be completed until 1944, Churchill probably did not regard this as a sacrifice. He was still intent on getting new ships into service promptly, and once again insisted on priority for small craft and heavy units that could be completed quickly, which included the three remaining King George V-class battleships and *Vanguard*, which had been authorized in March 1940. Work on the first two Lion-class battleships was suspended, and the two that were to follow were cancelled.[125]

The Battle of the Atlantic Committee was also successful in reducing the turnaround time of merchant ships. The problem of congestion in British ports had been largely resolved by the spring of 1941, but Churchill believed that greater efficiency was still possible.[126] He noted in May that cargo liners took an average of thirty-nine days to complete a round trip to North America in peacetime, but in early 1941 that figure had stood at eighty-six days. The time these same ships spent in port or moving coastwise had similarly increased from fourteen to forty-three days.[127] At the first meeting of the Battle of the Atlantic Committee, Churchill called for a reduction in turnaround time by fifteen days.[128] This goal was nearly achieved. By July 1941 Schoenfeld calculates that ships were spending around twenty days fewer in British west coast ports and coastal waters. Increased efficiency in British ports was partially responsible for this improvement, but American Lend-Lease aid was also an important factor. The British could now safely reduce their level of exports—and hence the time ships spent loading cargoes in British ports—without endangering their ability to pay for American imports.[129] The result of these efforts was a net improvement of thirteen days in turnaround time, even though ships in convoy were now spending more time at sea.[130]

The Committee did not fare as well when it came to providing convoys with merchant ships capable of launching fighter aircraft at sea, known as Catapult Aircraft Merchantmen (CAM). Churchill was optimistic at first that these vessels would greatly reduce the amount of shipping lost to long-range German aircraft, but he was soon disillusioned. The first ships to be equipped with catapults entered service at the end of April 1941, by which time serious disagreement had emerged as to whether their cargo-carrying capacity should be sacrificed so that they might perform their new military role more efficiently. Churchill observed that if the ships continued to transport goods, as most members of the Committee expected, they would spend only about thirty days each year in waters beyond the range of land-based air cover. 'This,' he complained, 'would be a very uneconomical use of specially fitted ships and Hurricane aircraft.' He therefore insisted that the first ten ships to enter service should be used solely for patrolling in the areas where convoys were at greatest risk of air attack, even though this would preclude their use as 'ordinary freighters'. If this experiment proved successful, he conceded that it would be necessary to begin equipping smaller merchant ships with catapults, so as to reduce the amount of carrying capacity that was lost. But Churchill was clearly beginning to doubt that a large fleet of catapult-equipped merchant ships would be an efficient use of resources, and at the end of April he decided that plans for converting as many as two hundred vessels must be abandoned.[131] Under pressure from the Committee, Churchill later agreed that the thirty-five catapult-equipped merchant ships that were expected to enter service by August should all be employed 'on ordinary cargo service on the Canadian and Sierra Leone routes'. Until experience was gained with these ships, he recommended that no more be fitted with catapults.[132] In the event, these ships had little impact on the Battle of the Atlantic and were eventually replaced with naval 'escort carriers'—small aircraft carriers (about a third the size of the navy's 'fleet' carriers) capable of being built relatively quickly and suitable for service on the trade routes.[133]

The decision to reduce the upper speed for ships in convoy proved to be a more serious mistake. The Admiralty opposed pressure from Churchill and the Import Executive to exclude ships capable of 12 knots from convoy, but this measure was nevertheless adopted on an experimental basis in March 1941.[134] By May, statistics compiled by the Admiralty clearly showed that the speed reduction had led to greater losses. Between mid-November 1940 and early May 1941, independently routed ships travelling between 13 and 15 knots had suffered 12.8 per cent losses, Alexander reported, while the rate for ships in convoy had been only 5.7 per cent.[135] Churchill was not pleased. He complained that it was 'unreasonable to discontinue the experiment so quickly', and proposed that the First Lord should submit another report after discussing his figures with Lord Cherwell, a close associate who ran a special statistical branch within the government. But there was little Churchill could do at this point to prevent a reversal of policy. On 19 June the War Cabinet decided that ships travelling between 12 and 15 knots should once again sail in convoy.[136]

The Battle of the Atlantic directive had made no reference to the United States, but Churchill was eager to secure as much American assistance as possible. The most pressing need was for merchant ships, and Churchill hoped that the American shipbuilding programme could be doubled.[137] Just prior to the passage of Lend-Lease by the US Congress in mid-March, a merchant shipping mission under Sir Arthur Salter was dispatched to bring home to the Roosevelt administration the seriousness of the import situation and to secure as much American shipping as possible. Churchill anticipated American assistance two weeks later by reducing Britain's own shipbuilding programme in order to accelerate repairs to existing ships. '[W]e should not at the present time proceed with any merchant vessels which cannot be completed by the end of 1941,' he directed. 'It is to the United States building that we must look for relief in 1942.'[138]

Around the same time, the possibility of American naval assistance also seemed to open up. Churchill reported to the War Cabinet on 17 March that John Winant, the US ambassador, and Averell Harriman, Roosevelt's special envoy, were 'longing for Germany to commit some overt act', and that they had raised the possibility of the United States expanding its role in the protection of convoys. Churchill was naturally eager to seize this opportunity. The steady improvement of British defences in the North West Approaches during the previous months had pushed U-boat operations further into the North Atlantic, where air cover was unavailable and convoys were still without escort. Churchill hoped that the Americans might fill this gap by escorting ships west of 30° longitude, but he hesitated to ask the president to take such a blatantly un-neutral step (Map 5).[139] Instead, he proposed on 19 March that American warships and aircraft should maintain a presence in the central Atlantic, 'as they have a perfect right to do without any prejudice to neutrality'. He refrained from asking that American forces report the location of German raiders to the British, although he suggested that their 'mere presence might be decisive as the enemy would fear that they might report what they saw and we could then despatch an adequate force to try to engage them'.[140]

Churchill kept Roosevelt informed of the difficulties Britain was encountering in the central Atlantic, and his efforts were soon rewarded. The president informed him on 11 April that the United States would extend its patrol areas in the North Atlantic to approximately 25° and actively seek out and report any Axis raiders operating west of this line.[141] This measure would ease Britain's difficulties along the trade routes, but more importantly, it

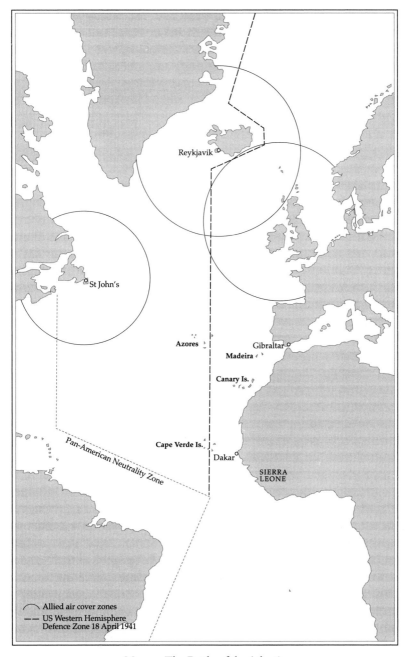

Reykjavik

St John's

Azores

Gibraltar

Madeira

Canary Is.

Cape Verde Is.

Dakar

SIERRA
LEONE

Pan-American Neutrality Zone

⌒ Allied air cover zones
-- US Western Hemisphere
Defence Zone 18 April 1941

Map 5. The Battle of the Atlantic

represented a significant move towards American belligerency. Churchill was elated. 'Have no doubts that 25th Meridian is a long step towards salvation,' he cabled to Roosevelt.[142] American involvement in the Atlantic war took another step forward in May when Roosevelt offered to send American troops to relieve the British forces occupying Iceland, which was developing into a vital base for British aircraft and escort vessels protecting the mid-Atlantic convoy routes.

On 25 June 1941 Churchill outlined the progress that had been made thus far in the Battle of the Atlantic to a secret session of the House of Commons. His directive of 6 March had predicted that victory could be obtained within four months, but this was proving more difficult than expected. Allied and neutral merchant ships were still being sunk at an alarming rate. Total losses to all causes in April 1941 exceeded 687,000 tons, the highest level so far. That figure had dropped to 511,000 tons in May, and would decline to 432,000 tons in June, but even this was still no better than the average rate for most months in 1940.[143] The only real improvement Churchill could report was that losses in the North Atlantic to German aircraft had decreased substantially since the beginning of the year. But even though Britain appeared to have made little concrete progress in mastering the U-boats, Churchill was optimistic about the future. British imports were on track to exceed the minimum levels set for 1941, and the United States was increasing its production of merchant ships. British and American shipyards would eventually be in a position to replace future losses even if the rate of sinking did not significantly decline.[144] Churchill was therefore confident that shipping shortages would not become serious enough to undermine Britain's ability to take the offensive in 1942. This, in his opinion, represented a successful bottom line in the Battle of the Atlantic.

Churchill's optimism was briefly shaken at the beginning of July when Pound informed him that the Admiralty had underestimated the number of new U-boats being built. Admiral Doenitz's operational strength had remained relatively stable at around thirty boats during the previous year, but increased production now meant that, for the first time since the beginning of the war, the Germans were able to do more than just make good their losses. The number of operational U-boats doubled to around sixty-five in July 1941, and was expected to be as high as one hundred by the end of the year.[145] Greater numbers portended proportionately heavier losses, which threatened to undermine all of Churchill's previous calculations.

'I had been reassured' by the Admiralty's predictions, he wrote to Pound on 5 July, 'but now feel very anxious indeed, especially if there are going to be any more surprises of this kind.'[146] It soon became apparent, however, that more U-boats would not automatically translate into heavier losses. On the contrary, in July 1941 the situation at sea took a sudden turn for the better. Losses to all causes for this month dropped sharply, to slightly under 121,000 tons, and were only slightly higher the following month.[147]

There were several reasons for this improvement. First, there were more escorts than ever before: in July 1941 the number available was roughly double what it had been at the beginning of the war.[148] Nearly all the destroyers acquired from the United States in 1940 were now in service, and British and Canadian shipyards were producing a large and steady flow of new ships. As a result, more vessels could be allocated to individual convoys, and continuous protection was for the first time available across the entire North Atlantic. In addition, escorts were becoming better equipped and their crews better trained. Intelligence was also making a significant contribution. The British began decrypting U-boat signals for the first time in the spring of 1941, which allowed, at least temporarily, the evasive routing of convoys. The decision to increase the speed for ships in convoy also had immediate benefits, as losses to independently sailed ships declined sharply. At the same time, the increasing effectiveness of Coastal Command aircraft along the North West Approaches forced U-boats to operate further from their bases, which reduced their operational efficiency.

Churchill assumed—incorrectly—that the long-term shipping situation was now secure. With the victory he had predicted in March now seemingly within grasp, his interest in the Battle of the Atlantic waned. He pressed ahead with plans for Allied operations in North Africa, which would involve a huge commitment of Anglo-American shipping resources. He also began to shift long-range aircraft from trade defence to the strategic bombing offensive against Germany. The Air Ministry had been never been happy about the diversion of its resources for attacks on U-boat bases, heavy surface ships, and the airfields used by German bombers to operate over the sea lanes.[149] At the time, Churchill had insisted that these diversions were necessary. 'Naturally,' he wrote to Portal, 'I sympathize with the desire to attack Germany, to use the heaviest bombs and to give Berlin a severe dose', but he held that attacks on warships would have to continue.[150] In mid-July the situation at sea had improved to the point that Bomber Command was permitted to devote the full weight of its resources to attacks on Germany.

Churchill also began to reconsider Coastal Command's requirements. He informed Portal on 21 July that the Battle of the Atlantic had been 'very much eased by recent developments', and asked whether Coastal Command's long-range B-24 Liberators, which he considered 'ideal bombers for Berlin', should be transferred to Bomber Command. The same day he told the Defence Committee that he 'deplored the fact that Liberators received from America had been allocated to Coastal Command; now was the time for every heavy bomber to concentrate on Germany.'[151] Churchill received no encouragement from the Air Ministry, however. The Liberators were not considered suitable for strategic bombing, and Portal preferred to leave them with Coastal Command.[152]

Churchill nevertheless continued to worry that long-range aircraft were being squandered on defensive tasks. By August he was confident 'that the corner had been turned in the Battle of the Atlantic', and he instructed the CAS to consider whether resources could be redirected from Coastal Command to Bomber Command. According to Ismay, Churchill was thinking of not only diverting new aircraft coming into service but also of transferring entire squadrons.[153] The Admiralty immediately protested. 'Any suggestion that the Battle of the Atlantic has turned the corner in our favour is not supported by facts,' remarked Captain A. J. Power, an Assistant Chief of Naval Staff. 'We have not yet even felt the full weight of [Germany's] offensive against our trade,' he continued. 'To relax our preparations at the present moment is courting disaster.' Coastal Command aircraft had clearly played a critical role in driving U-boats away from British shores, and Admiralty officials were understandably reluctant to see their numbers—already considered inadequate—reduced further. 'We require every single surface ship and every long-range aircraft we can possibly muster if we are to even hope to keep our losses within reason,' Power warned.[154]

This was a realistic assessment, and the Admiralty's fears seemed to be borne out by a surge in shipping losses during September. But Churchill remained optimistic that the U-boat threat had been reduced to manageable proportions. His confidence was bolstered by growing American involvement in the Battle of the Atlantic. At the beginning of September the United States navy began escorting Allied convoys as far as Iceland, which lay within the area designated as a war zone by Germany. This eased the strain on the British and Canadian navies in the North Atlantic, and brought the United States even closer to open belligerency. On 4 September a U-boat attacked the USS *Greer*, an American destroyer, and was promptly counter-attacked.

This effectively marked the beginning of an undeclared naval war in the North Atlantic between Germany and the United States.

When shipping losses declined again in October 1941, Churchill proposed to transfer Whitley and Wellington bombers from Coastal Command to Bomber Command. Alexander immediately protested, complaining that it would reduce Coastal Command's long-range aircraft by half. He was supported again by Portal, who assured Churchill that these aircraft would be a major loss to Coastal Command, but only a relatively small gain for Bomber Command.[155] The German decision in late 1941 to transfer a large portion of its operational U-boat fleet to the Mediterranean led to additional improvements in the Battle of the Atlantic during November, but Churchill was by now becoming alarmed by evidence of a growing gap between the number of U-boats being sunk and the number being built. After receiving a report from the head of the Secret Service that the disparity might be even greater than the Admiralty was reporting, Churchill's confidence in the navy's anti-submarine capabilities was badly shaken. 'I am much disquieted by these facts,' he reproved Alexander and Pound. 'The failure of our methods about which so much was proclaimed by the Admiralty before the war, is painfully apparent.'[156]

This criticism was not entirely fair. To be sure, asdic had failed to live up to the Naval Staff's optimistic pre-war predictions. The use of massed U-boats for night-time surface attacks had also exposed the limitations of the convoy system. But by mid-1941 the navy had demonstrated that if given sufficient resources it could create an effective system for the defence of British trade. The organization of merchant shipping into convoy, the provision of escorts equipped with both asdic and radar, and the use of long-range aircraft to provide air cover had all been effective in reducing the U-boat threat to manageable proportions around the British Isles by mid-1941. The Germans were thereafter only able to inflict heavy losses on Allied shipping in areas where this defensive system did not exist. The problem facing the Admiralty was to secure adequate resources to extend its system to other threatened areas, particularly the vital supply routes across the North Atlantic.

Pound set to work on preparing the Admiralty's case immediately after receiving Churchill's rebuke. He admitted to the VCNS that 'this Battle of the Atlantic business' had not been taken 'sufficiently seriously', and complained that inadequate resources had been allocated to trade defence, particularly in the air. The navy's first requirement, he concluded, was an increased bombing effort against U-boat construction yards and bases, and against German surface ships. Pound also wanted more long-range aircraft for Coastal Command, more destroyers and corvettes for escort duty, and auxiliary aircraft carriers to provide air cover to convoys beyond the range of land-based aircraft.[157] The first such ship, HMS *Audacity*, had entered service in September 1941 and provided valuable service in the Bay of Biscay before being lost to a U-boat in December. The Admiralty hoped to have no fewer than fifteen of these carriers in service by the following year, and another fifteen the year after. But there were growing concerns that there would not be enough fighter aircraft for these ships and for the new armoured fleet carriers that would soon be entering service. Alexander informed Churchill on 4 December that 'drastic steps' were needed to ensure an adequate supply of fleet fighters, but this was a difficult proposition to sell. The First Lord admitted that increased production would have to come at the expense of aircraft for the RAF. The Admiralty calculated that its needs could largely be met if the production of heavy bombers was reduced by around twenty per month.[158]

There was every reason for naval leaders to assume that this request would be denounced as further extravagance, but Churchill's confidence in the bomber offensive had been wavering since August 1941, when a detailed study, known as the Butt report, cast serious doubts on the ability of British aircraft to locate targets inside Germany. This investigation, initiated by Cherwell, Churchill's chief scientific adviser, suggested that only around 5 per cent of bombers managed to drop their bombs within five miles of their target. Precision bombing clearly was not working, and the Air Ministry began to develop plans for a new campaign directed against German cities. For this to be effective in destroying German morale, Portal informed Churchill on 25 September that as many as four thousand bombers would be required, which represented a roughly tenfold increase in the number of machines available.[159] This proposal, coming so soon after the Butt report, received a frosty reception. 'It is very disputable,' Churchill told Portal, 'whether bombing by itself will be a decisive factor in the present war.' Rather than giving Bomber Command more aircraft, Churchill proposed that its results could be improved by achieving greater accuracy in locating targets. 'The most we can say' about strategic bombing, he charged, 'is that it will be a heavy and, I trust, a seriously increasing annoyance'.[160]

In a lengthy minute to Portal on 7 October, Churchill elaborated on these views. He admitted that the bomber offensive would have to continue, as it constituted the only effective means then available to damage German morale. But he was now sceptical of the Air Ministry's claims that bombing alone could achieve decisive results. 'One has to do the best one can,' he wrote, 'but he is an unwise man who thinks there is any *certain* method of winning this war, or indeed any other war between equals in strength.'[161] By the autumn of 1941, Churchill had concluded that land forces would eventually have to be employed on the Continent to ensure Germany's defeat. His confidence in Bomber Command was again shaken by the heavy losses it suffered in November 1941, which finally convinced him that a more cautious strategy would have to be adopted in the short term. 'In battle, heavy losses must be faced,' he remarked, 'but it was undesirable to expose our aircraft to extreme hazards in the course of routine operations.' The Air Ministry was instructed to conserve its strength for the spring of 1942.[162]

The Admiralty therefore had reason to hope that its request for an increased share of resources at the expense of Bomber Command would not be dismissed out of hand. Churchill replied on 6 December that he was prepared to help the Admiralty 'get all that you require for the Armoured [i.e. "fleet"] carriers, even in priority over the Bomber Command'. But he expressed reservations about the proposed 'multiplication of improvised [i.e. light "auxiliary"] Carriers which, though I like it, I cannot feel stands on the same level'.[163] Thus encouraged, Alexander warned Churchill that the recent reduction in shipping losses had 'perhaps induced a false sense of security', and he forwarded an Admiralty memorandum outlining all the navy's requirements.[164] Churchill was thus presented with an accurate appraisal of what it would take to defeat the U-boats, and could have been left with no doubt that this would involve some reduction in the British bombing campaign against German cities. But before a new debate over the allocation of resources between the services could begin, both the U-boat threat and the strategic air campaign were temporarily eclipsed by the failure of British policy in the Far East.

8

'Courting Disaster': The Deterrence of Japan and the Dispatch of Force Z

Japan's neutrality at the beginning of the Second World War allowed Churchill and the COS to avoid a divisive debate over the allocation of resources for a three-front war against Germany, Italy, and Japan simultaneously. It was only in 1941, when tensions in the Pacific had escalated to the point that the issue could no longer be ignored, that the problem had to be addressed head-on. Prior to this, the only ones eager to discuss Far Eastern issues were the Australians. When he became First Lord of the Admiralty, Churchill was confronted almost immediately by demands from Canberra that Britain reaffirm its pre-war pledges to send a fleet to Singapore in the event of war with Japan. Until then, the Australian government naturally hesitated to release its forces for the war against Germany.[1] In November 1939, Australia's High Commissioner in London reminded Churchill that his predecessor as First Lord of the Admiralty, Lord Stanhope, had 'specifically stated that a Fleet of a definite strength i.e. containing 7 capital ships would be sent to the Far East if Japan entered the war against us'.[2] This was true, although in March 1939 Neville Chamberlain had hedged on this commitment. In the event of war with Germany, Italy, and Japan, a 'combination never envisaged in our earlier plan', Chamberlain warned that the size of the fleet sent to Singapore could not be guaranteed.[3] After the outbreak of war, Richard Casey, an Australian Cabinet minister, explained to British leaders that his government believed that Britain was still pledged to dispatch a fleet to Singapore 'almost immediately after the outbreak of war with Japan and quite irrespective of any direct threat of invasion of Australia'.[4]

Churchill had not been a party to pre-war discussions with the Australians, and he had no desire to see British resources diverted to the Far East if, in his opinion, they would be better employed elsewhere. It would be a 'false strategy', he told representatives of the Australian and New Zealand governments in November 1939, 'to undertake to keep a Fleet at Singapore without regard to the actual naval situation. Any such undertaking would be crippling to the operation of our sea power, and would give to Japan the power to immobilise half our Fleet by a mere paper declaration of war.'[5] In the event of war with Germany, Italy, and Japan simultaneously, Churchill pledged that the defence of the Pacific dominions would rank 'next to the mastering of the principal [i.e. German] fleet to which we are opposed, and that if the choice were presented of defending them against a serious attack, or sacrificing British interests in the Mediterranean, our duty to our kith and kin would take precedence'.[6] But this promise came with an important caveat: British forces would only be sent in the event of a *serious* attempt by Japan either to capture Singapore or invade Australia; Churchill did not intend to be drawn off by raids or feints. Until such time as a major threat developed, he believed the right strategy was to concentrate naval forces in the Mediterranean to knock Italy out of the war as quickly as possible.[7]

Churchill was eager to secure the release of Australian forces for the European theatre, but there is nothing to suggest that to accomplish this he misrepresented his intentions or deliberately underestimated the Japanese threat. The arguments he presented to Dominion representatives in November 1939 were the same ones he had rehearsed at length before the war, and differed little from the opinions he had expressed as Chancellor during the 1920s. When the war in Europe began, there was good reason to think that if things went well, Britain would never have to make good its pledges to Australia. Singapore, Churchill wrote, was 'a fortress armed with five 15-inch guns, and garrisoned by nearly 20,000 men. It could only be taken after a siege by an army of at least 50,000 men, who would have to be landed in the marshes and jungle of the Isthmus which connects it with the mainland.' Japan would be unwise, he argued, to attempt an operation on this scale so far from its bases. If at any time Britain dispatched a fleet to relieve Singapore 'the besieging army would become prisoners of war. It is not considered possible,' he concluded, 'that the Japanese, who are a prudent people … would embark upon such a mad enterprise.' And if the capture of Singapore was an imposing prospect, an invasion of Australia or New Zealand was even more so. The distances were even greater in this case, and the Japanese would have to expect the intervention of a British fleet. The most Australia had to fear, Churchill insisted, was a 'tip-and-run raid'.[8]

The fall of France in the summer of 1940 transformed the strategic landscape in the Far East just as it did in Europe. With Britain's survival in doubt, little could be spared to defend imperial interests in the Pacific. The only bright spot was that the Japanese appeared content to bide their time. During the summer of 1940 the COS concluded that Japan would probably pursue a cautious policy and avoid an open clash with Britain until the European situation became clearer. Rather than risking a direct attack on British possessions, Japan would set about strengthening its position in South East Asia. As there was no possibility of sending a powerful British fleet to the Far East in the near future, Britain would have to go to great lengths to avoid open confrontation with Japan. British policy, the service chiefs advised, 'should be to play for time; to cede nothing until we must; and to build up our defences as soon as we can.'[9]

This was the line Churchill's new government adopted in July 1940 when Japan began pressing London to close the Burma Road, the principal supply route to Chiang Kai-shek's Nationalist government in China. The strongest voice against this concession came not from Churchill but from Lord Halifax, who advised that this action would undermine Britain's standing in China and the United States, and lead to even more humiliating demands.[10] When the matter was discussed by the War Cabinet on 5 July, Halifax, a leading advocate of appeasement during the 1930s, advised that there was 'a big element of bluff' in Japan's attitude, and that Britain 'should lose less by standing up to Japanese blackmail than by relinquishing our principles'. Churchill, on the other hand, was willing to make concessions. Given Britain's current weakness, the prime minister 'did not think that we ought to incur Japanese hostility for reasons mainly of prestige'.[11] The government therefore agreed to a temporary closure of the Burma Road.

The best deterrent to Japanese aggression, Churchill maintained, was the improvement of Britain's position in Europe. Resources were therefore to be concentrated in the decisive theatre. If Japan did enter the war, Churchill wanted only minimal forces sent to the Far East until it was certain that either Singapore or Australia was directly threatened.[12] As long as Japan's intentions were unclear, the fleet would remain concentrated in the Mediterranean and the Admiralty would dispatch only a modest force to eastern waters, including the battlecruiser *Hood* and two of the Ramillies-class battleships, which dated from the First World War.[13] Pound was even less optimistic about Britain's ability to respond to Japanese aggression. At the time, he proposed to allocate only the battlecruiser *Renown* and the carrier *Ark Royal* in the event of war. In his view, Britain could hope to do no more in the short term than defend British trade in the Indian Ocean, for which purpose Trincomalee in Ceylon would probably make a better base than Singapore (Map 6).

Churchill approved the First Sea Lord's proposal, although even as Britain's fortunes ebbed he never despaired about the situation in the Far East.[14] Japan's energies were still seemingly absorbed in China, and it would always have to worry about the intervention of either the United States or the Soviet Union if it embarked on new adventures in South East Asia or beyond. Churchill doubted that Japan's leaders would launch an expedition against Singapore unless Britain could no longer put up serious resistance.[15] If Japan did attack Singapore or attempt to invade Australia, Churchill hoped that the United States would come to Britain's aid. But, if US support did not materialize, he still maintained that 'our course was clear':

> We could never stand by and see a British Dominion overwhelmed by a yellow race, and we should at once come to the assistance of that Dominion with all the forces we could make available. For this purpose we should be prepared, if necessary, to abandon our position in the Mediterranean and the Middle East.[16]

Australian leaders accepted Churchill's assurances and continued to send troops to fight in the Middle East, but they remained uneasy about Singapore's weak defences and the lack of a firm commitment from London to dispatch naval forces. In December 1940, following the successful air attack on the Italian fleet at Taranto, Robert Menzies, the Australian prime minister, pressed Churchill for the transfer of three or four capital ships to Singapore from the Mediterranean fleet. This appeal was renewed when Menzies visited London in March 1941, and again in August of the same year.[17] The idea of employing a squadron of capital ships to deter Japan also found adherents in Whitehall. In November 1940, for example, R. A. Butler, the parliamentary under-secretary at the Foreign Office, suggested immediately stationing a battlecruiser and an aircraft carrier at Ceylon to bolster British prestige in the region, 'hearten Australia and New Zealand', and help deter Japan.[18] Churchill, however, remained firm. He had no intention of letting capital ships sit idle at Singapore while Britain was fighting for its life against Germany and Italy. As he informed Menzies in December 1940, Britain

Map 6. The Indian Ocean

could only transfer capital ships to the Far East 'by ruining the Mediterranean situation. This I am sure you would not want to do unless or until the Japanese danger becomes far more menacing than at present.'[19]

Churchill took the same position on the critical question of air and ground reinforcements for Malaya. In 1940 British commanders in the Far East calculated that 566 aircraft were necessary to defend Singapore from a determined Japanese attack.[20] The Chiefs of Staff hoped that a lesser figure would suffice. They informed Sir Robert Brooke-Popham, the Commander-in-Chief, Far East, that 'a very fair degree of security' could be achieved with only 336 aircraft, a figure they hoped to attain by the end of 1941. But even this was too much for Churchill, who denounced any large-scale 'diversions of force' to Malaya. In January 1941 he informed the COS that the 'political situation in the Far East does not seem to require, and the strength of our Air Force by no means warrants, the maintenance of such large forces in the Far East at this time'.[21] In December 1941, Malaya Command could count on only 158 aircraft, and these were mostly obsolescent models.[22]

A proposal from Brooke-Popham to reinforce the small British garrison at Hong Kong was also dismissed. 'If Japan goes to war with us,' Churchill observed, 'there is not the slightest chance of holding Hong Kong or relieving it':

> It is most unwise to increase the loss we shall suffer there. Instead of increasing the garrison it ought to be reduced to a symbolical scale. Any trouble arising there must be dealt with at the Peace Conference after the war. We must avoid frittering away our resources on untenable positions. Japan will think long before declaring war on the British Empire, and whether there are two or six battalions at Hong Kong will make no difference to her choice.[23]

The United States' attitude towards Britain and the Pacific was an increasingly important factor in Churchill's calculations during the winter of 1940–1. American leaders shared British concerns about Japanese intentions, which raised the possibility that British security in the Far East might eventually be improved by enlisting US military and diplomatic support in the region. This would obviate the need to divert British forces from the war against Germany and Italy, and Churchill pursued this goal with determination. The willingness of Roosevelt and his top advisers to enter into secret staff talks with the British at this time was an encouraging sign, but the president was determined not to enter into any binding agreements or to commit American resources directly to the protection of British colonial interests. This made it difficult to prepare joint plans for an Anglo-American war on two fronts. Churchill's preferred strategy for this eventuality was to concentrate first on the defeat of Germany and Italy while adopting a strictly defensive posture in the Pacific. Japan could always be dealt with later, he reasoned; Germany could not. Fortunately, the Americans agreed. In November 1940 a memorandum by the USN's Chief of Naval Operations, Admiral Harold Stark, recommended that the European theatre of operations be given priority, even if it meant that US political and military influence in the Far East was temporarily effaced.[24] This document, known as 'Plan D', became the basis of US grand strategy.

Churchill was delighted by this development. 'Plan D,' he wrote, 'is strategically sound and also most highly adapted to our interests.' If sacrifices had to be made, he preferred to make them in a secondary theatre, especially since the possibility of active US support made the dangers in this area appear negligible. 'Should Japan enter the war on one side and the United States on ours,' Churchill informed the First Sea Lord, 'ample naval forces will be available to contain Japan by long-range controls in the Pacific':

> The Japanese Navy is not likely to venture far from its home bases so long as the superior battle-fleet is maintained at Singapore or Honolulu. The Japanese would never attempt a siege of Singapore with a hostile, superior American Fleet in the Pacific. The balance of the American Fleet, after providing the necessary force for the Pacific, would be sufficient, with our Navy, to exercise in a very high degree the command of all the seas and oceans except those within the immediate Japanese regions. A strict defensive in the Far East and the acceptance of its consequences is also our policy. Once the Germans are beaten the Japanese would be at the mercy of the combined fleets.[25]

Churchill shared his naval advisers' hopes that the Americans could be persuaded to base a powerful fleet at Singapore rather than Pearl Harbor in Hawaii, but in his mind a US fleet would be capable of containing Japan from either location. The Admiralty, however, was determined to see the Americans use Singapore as a base. In October 1940 the COS concluded that the US should, if possible, be persuaded to take the Royal Navy's pre-war plans against Japan 'as the basis of their strategy, the United States fleet taking the place of the British fleet in this plan'.[26] Pound and his colleagues urged this course on US naval representatives in London over the next two months. Singapore, they insisted, was the 'only main fleet base available for the Allies in the Far East'. It security was therefore vital 'to the position both of the British Empire and of the United States of America in that area.

If Singapore were lost, it would not be possible,' they asserted, 'to re-establish the position in the Far East.'[27] Admiralty officials calculated that British and US interests could both be adequately protected if the Americans allocated ten capital ships to Singapore, five to the Atlantic, and none to Hawaii.[28] The west coast of the United States had nothing greater to fear, they insisted, than 'tip and run' raids.[29]

The Americans made no secret of their aversion to these ideas. In December 1940, as both sides were preparing for secret staff conversations in Washington, Admiral Stark informed the British that their requests for a US fleet at Singapore were 'unacceptable', as this would not provide for the full protection of US interests.[30] Having decided that the Atlantic would be the primary theatre, US naval leaders prepared to base their main eastern fleet at Pearl Harbor and accept the possible loss of the Philippines. The British and Dutch would be left to defend their interests in South East Asia as best they could. The Admiralty was unhappy, but Churchill did not want to quibble with the Americans over what he regarded as a secondary issue. 'There is no use in putting before them a naval policy which they will not accept,' he insisted, 'and which will only offend them and make it more difficult to bring them into the war. If they prefer Hawaii to Singapore there is no more to be said.'[31]

The Admiralty began to show a more flexible attitude on this matter, but naval leaders still hoped to convince the Americans of the wisdom of their strategy. At the ABC (American-British-Canadian) Staff Conference in Washington in January–March 1941, British delegates tried once again to persuade their hosts to fall in with their plans. Admiral Roger Bellairs, the head of the British delegation, insisted that the loss of Singapore would be 'a disaster of the first magnitude, second only to the loss of the British Isles'. It was essential, therefore, to 'retain a card of re-entry' into the Far East. The British did not think that the Americans fully appreciated the consequences of abandoning South East Asia. Japan, they warned, would 'become the undisputed master of East Asia, of the East Indies and of the Western Pacific'. This would not only deprive the Allies of important resources, but also make Japan economically self-sufficient. Furthermore, the prestige of the Western powers would suffer a devastating blow, especially in Asia; Chinese resistance would collapse; and Russia, 'faced with a Japan supreme in the Orient, might well throw in her lot definitely with the Axis'. If the Americans would not base a fleet at Singapore, the only other sensible course, according to the British, was to strengthen the US Asiatic Fleet, based on the Philippines.[32]

This proposal met with a cool reception. The Americans were unwilling to divide their forces in such a manner and were annoyed that the British would not let the matter drop. The most they were prepared to do was strengthen US naval forces in the Atlantic and Mediterranean in order to release British ships for the Far East. When news of these continuing disagreements made their way back to London, Churchill was justifiably angry with the navy. 'What has been the use of all this battling?' he asked the First Lord in February 1941. 'Anyone could have seen that the United States would not base a battle-fleet on Singapore and divide their naval forces.' Britain's first object, he insisted, was to get the United States to enter the war. Once this had been accomplished, he was confident that 'the proper strategic dispositions' would eventually emerge. The Americans, he suggested, would probably come around to the British view 'when they are up against reality, and not trying to enter into hypothetical paper accords beforehand'. In the meantime, Britain should not make difficulties. Churchill instructed the staff mission in Washington to tell the Americans that they 'loyally accept the United States Navy dispositions for the Pacific'. His closing remarks were surprisingly candid: 'I do not see why, even if Singapore were captured, we could not protect Australia by basing a fleet on Australian ports. This would effectively prevent invasion.'[33]

Faced with the prime minister's displeasure and firm opposition from the US military, the British delegation dropped the matter. The ABC agreement of March 1941 confirmed the 'Germany first' strategy that both sides favoured, but deferred to US views on Far Eastern dispositions. With the passage of the Lend-Lease Act the same month, Churchill had ample grounds for optimism about the course of Anglo-American relations. Roosevelt seemed determined to throw his country's resources behind the British war effort and, if possible, to enter the war on Britain's side. This strengthened Churchill's conviction that British and imperial forces should be concentrated on the war against Germany and Italy. In April 1941 he informed the COS that it was 'very unlikely' that 'Japan will enter the war either if the United States have come in, or if Japan thinks they would come in, consequent on a Japanese declaration of war'. In his opinion, it could now be 'taken *as almost certain* that the entry of Japan into the war would be followed by the immediate entry of the United States on our side'. Churchill probably hoped that this assurance would stifle any debate over the division of resources between theatres. 'These conditions are to be accepted by the Service Departments as a guide for all plans and actions,' he insisted. 'Should they cease to hold good, it will be the responsibility of Ministers to notify the Service Chiefs in good time.'[34]

The service chiefs were less confident than Churchill of US support, and more worried about Britain's growing vulnerability in the Far East. In May 1941 the CIGS, General Sir John Dill, challenged Churchill's views and reasserted the priorities that had been approved by the COS before the war. In his opinion, the loss of the Middle East would not spell disaster for Britain, and the defence of Singapore should have a higher priority. 'Egypt is not even second in order of priority,' he argued, 'for it has been an accepted principle in our strategy that in the last resort the security of Singapore comes before that of Egypt. Yet the defences of Singapore are still considerably below standard.' It was necessary, he insisted, to 'look well ahead. If we wait till emergency arises in the Far East, we shall be too late.'[35]

Churchill brusquely rejected these arguments. 'I gather you would be prepared to face the loss of Egypt and the Nile Valley,' he charged, 'together with the surrender or ruin of the army of half a million we have concentrated there, rather than lose Singapore. I do not take that view, nor do I think the alternative is likely to present itself.' Japan, he argued, would 'not be likely to besiege Singapore' at the beginning of a war, 'as this would be an operation far more dangerous to her and less harmful to us than spreading her cruisers and battle-cruisers on the Eastern trade routes'.[36] Until the defeat of Germany and Italy was certain, Churchill insisted that Britain rely on the United States both to deter Japan and to protect British interests if deterrence failed. This involved running serious risks, and Churchill was prepared to relieve his military advisers of responsibility for the consequences. In return, he made it clear that the Chiefs of Staff must accept political direction on this issue.[37]

Hitler's invasion of the Soviet Union in June 1941 provided Britain with a major ally capable of engaging the full weight of the German army on land, although it would take several months for British leaders to gain much confidence that the Soviet war effort would last out the year. Churchill was eager to provide his new ally with all the support he could. With no possibility of an offensive in France to divert German troops from the Eastern Front, Churchill and the War Cabinet accepted the necessity of providing military aid to the Soviets on the largest possible scale, even at the expense of Britain's own military operations. The service departments, acutely aware of their deficiencies in modern weapons and equipment, were not enthusiastic about undertaking this major new commitment.[38] The dispatch of aircraft, tanks, and other supplies to Russia in the latter half of 1941 diverted resources from British forces in North Africa, and pushed Malaya even further down Churchill's list of priorities. This left Britain's position in the Far East more dependent than ever on the United States. Throughout 1941, London carefully followed Washington's lead in the Pacific in hopes of averting a new war. US leaders were determined to take a hard line with Japan, however, and their policies, though intended to prevent conflict, were increasingly provocative. The tightening of Anglo-American economic sanctions against Japan after its occupation of French Indochina in July 1941 led to a sharp decline in relations between Japan and the Anglo-Saxon powers, and finally set Japan on the path to war.

The deteriorating situation in the Far East during the summer of 1941 compelled Churchill to alter course. Unwilling still to divert resources to the Far East on a large scale, he sought other means to demonstrate solidarity with the United States and impress Japan with Britain's growing strength. In these changing circumstances, the transfer of naval reinforcements to Singapore might at last serve a useful purpose. On 25 August 1941, Churchill informed the Admiralty that he wanted to dispatch one of the new King George V-class battleships to serve as the nucleus of a 'formidable, fast, high-class squadron', which he hoped to have operating in the Indian Ocean as early as October 1941. This, he suggested, would provide a powerful deterrent to Japan. 'We have only to remember all the preoccupations which are caused us by the *Tirpitz*,' he remarked, 'to see what an effect would be produced upon the Japanese Admiralty by the presence of a small but very powerful and fast force in Eastern waters.'[39]

The Admiralty had different plans at this time. The American refusal to send capital ships to Singapore or reinforce the Asiatic Fleet meant that Britain had to protect its own interests in South East Asia. Before the ABC Conference had concluded, the Admiralty began to consider schemes for building up a modest fleet in the Far East once US capital ships were moved into European waters.[40] By August 1941 its plans were well advanced. When Churchill raised the idea of sending a fast squadron of capital ships to eastern waters, Pound informed him that the Admiralty hoped to build up a balanced fleet in the region by March 1942. Four of the navy's unmodernized 'R'-class battleships would be sent to the Indian Ocean between mid-September 1941 and early January 1942, where they would initially serve as troop convoy escorts. Between November 1941 and mid-January 1942, the battleships *Nelson* and *Rodney* and the battlecruiser *Renown* would move to either Trincomalee or Singapore. With the addition of an aircraft carrier, cruisers, and destroyers, these vessels would ultimately form a balanced fleet that could be stationed at Singapore.[41] In the meantime, Pound hoped that the presence of heavy ships in the Indian Ocean would placate the Australians and deter Japan from sending battleships or large cruisers into the Indian Ocean in the event of war. He was strongly opposed, however, to sending any of Britain's modern battleships to the region, claiming that they were all needed in home waters in the event of a breakout by the German battleship *Tirpitz*.

There was much to be said for these proposals, but Churchill swept them aside. 'It is surely a faulty disposition,' he complained on 29 August, 'to create in the Indian Ocean a fleet considerable in numbers, costly in maintenance and man-power, but consisting entirely of slow, obsolescent, or unmodernized ships which can neither fight a fleet action with the main Japanese force nor act as a deterrent upon his modern fast, heavy ships, if used singly or in pairs as raiders.' There was also much to be said for these objections. Political considerations, however, were clearly foremost in Churchill's mind. Japan, he argued, would be unwilling to contemplate war with the 'combination now forming against her of the United States, Great Britain, and Russia, while already occupied in China'. It was very likely, he claimed, that Japan 'will negotiate with the United States for at least three months without making any further aggressive move or joining the Axis actively. Nothing would increase her hesitation more than the appearance of the force I mentioned, and above all of a K.G.V. [King George V-class battleship] This might indeed be a decisive deterrent.'[42]

Speed was therefore critical to the prime minister's plans, but the Admiralty was working to a different timetable. Churchill did not necessarily object to the navy's goal of creating a formidable battle fleet in eastern waters. His criticisms at this time focused on Pound's immediate plans to employ the four 'R'-class battleships as convoy escorts in the Indian Ocean. Once these ships were reinforced, they would have formed the backbone of a fleet that might have been able to engage a large Japanese force under favourable conditions, but this mattered little to Churchill. If the critical decisions about peace and war would be made in Tokyo before 1942, as he expected, capital ships were needed in the Far East immediately if they were to serve any purpose. Churchill did not reject the goal of a large eastern fleet in 1942, he simply ignored it in order to achieve his immediate objectives. And since Britain could spare only a small force in 1941, a fast, new battleship would be far more likely to impress observers than a squadron of old, slow vessels which had nearly been consigned to the scrapheap only two years before.

The Admiralty's firm opposition deflected Churchill on this occasion, but the idea was taken up again in September by Anthony Eden, now Foreign Secretary. Eden and the Foreign Office were optimistic that Japan could be deterred from war by a display of strength. On 12 September the Foreign Secretary advised Churchill that Japan's leaders were 'hesitating', but that their 'better mood has only been brought about by the contemplation of the forces that may confront them':

> Russia, the United States, China and the British Empire, to say nothing of the Dutch, is more than this probably over-valued military power is prepared to challenge. Our right policy is, therefore, clearly to keep up the pressure....We want the Japanese to feel that we are in a position to play our hand from strength.[43]

Eden and Churchill discussed the Far Eastern situation that day over lunch. According to Eden's diary, 'Winston insisted that we could now put pressure on Japs':

> I agree in the sense that they are beginning to understand their isolation, but process must take a little longer. Nothing could help it more than arrival of modern battleship or two at Singapore. We agreed that 'R' ships such as Admiralty propose is a weak compromise. I told him that politically I had rather not have them. Modern battleship, Carrier and Battle Cruiser or nothing we agreed.[44]

This enthusiasm for naval reinforcements was reinforced by an awareness that the defensive position of the Anglo-Saxon powers in the Far East was increasing. The transfer of American B-17 bombers to the Philippines at this time, together with the gradual increase of British air strength in Malaya, were themselves seen as significant deterrents to Japanese aggression. In early October 1941 the desirability of impressing the Japanese by a further show of force was backed up by leading civilian and military figures in the Far East, who emphasized the 'propaganda value of even one or two battleships at Singapore'.[45]

The fall of the Konoye government in Japan put the dispatch of capital ships back on the agenda. Eden warned Churchill on 16 October that the new Japanese government would probably be under the influence of 'extreme elements', but that it should still be possible to deter them. 'There is nothing yet to show in which direction they will move, if any,' he concluded. 'But it is no doubt true that the stronger the joint front the A.B.C.D. [America, Britain, China, Dutch] powers can show, the greater the deterrent to Japanese action.' The 'possibility of capital ship reinforcements to the Far East' was, he claimed, now 'more urgent, and I should be glad if it could be discussed at the Defence Committee'.[46]

When the question was taken up by this committee the following day, Churchill criticized the Admiralty's plans to transfer six of its older and slower capital ships to the Far East. According to Sir Tom Phillips, the VCNS, Churchill was 'scathing in his comments on the Admiralty attitude to this matter'.[47] A large force of old, unmodernized battleships could not engage the full weight of the Japanese fleet, he maintained, nor run away from a superior force. It would also be too slow to catch Japanese raiders in the Indian Ocean. A fast, modern capital ship like the *Prince of Wales*, on the other hand, could hunt down and destroy such vessels, and, by its mere presence in the Far East, tie down a much larger number of Japanese battleships. The *Tirpitz*, Churchill noted, compelled the Admiralty to retain no fewer than three British capital ships in home waters, 'in addition to the United States forces patrolling in the Atlantic'. The presence of one of Britain's most modern ships in the Far East, he argued, would 'have a similar effect on the Japanese Naval Authorities, and thereby on Japanese foreign policy'.[48]

A. V. Alexander, the First Lord, contested the *Tirpitz* analogy. The German ship was dangerous, he observed, because it threatened Britain's Atlantic convoys. In the Far East, British dispositions would be 'governed more by the need to protect our own trade routes than to raid Japanese shipping'. Another 'strong reason' for keeping all the King George Vs in home waters, he maintained, was to have them available for operations in the western Mediterranean, an argument Churchill himself might have employed earlier in the year. The Foreign Secretary now intervened to shift the discussion towards the larger problem of averting war in the Far East altogether. The dispatch of one 'modern ship, such as the PRINCE OF WALES, to the Far East would have a far greater effect politically,' he claimed, 'than the presence in those waters of a number of the last war's battleships. If the PRINCE OF WALES were to call at Cape Town on her way to the Far East, news of her movements would quickly reach Japan and the deterrent effect would begin from that date.'

Phillips, standing in for the absent Pound, disagreed. The only credible deterrent, he insisted, would be the large, balanced fleet that the Admiralty planned for 1942. In his view, a force of seven older capital ships should 'be a match for any forces the Japanese were likely to bring against them', as long as it was operating near its own bases and within range of shore-based air cover.[49] With the First Sea Lord absent from the meeting, Churchill was not prepared to press for a decision and the discussion was deferred. When the Committee reassembled on 20 October, Pound attempted to counter the prime minister's arguments by reminding those present that the Admiralty had to worry not only about a breakout by the *Tirpitz* but also the battlecruisers *Scharnhorst* and *Gneisenau*. Any one of these ships had the ability to inflict great losses on British shipping. The dispatch of the *Prince of Wales* to the Far East, he insisted, would increase the risks in the Atlantic and do little to avert war, as Japan 'could easily afford to put four modern ships with any big convoy destined for an attack in Southern Waters'. The only real deterrent, he claimed, would be a fleet at Singapore large enough to compel the Japanese to 'detach the greater part of their Fleet' to cover any southward expedition, which would expose Japan to attack by the American fleet at Pearl Harbor.

Churchill expressed surprise that the 'R's were eventually to form part of a battle fleet at Singapore, even though Pound rightly pointed out that this had always been the Admiralty's goal. Churchill continued, however, to focus on the objections to using the 'R's as convoy escorts in the Indian Ocean in the short term. 'The only thing,' he maintained, that 'would induce caution in the Japanese would be the presence in Eastern Waters of a fast striking force. This would be still more true before war had actually begun.'[50] He clearly overestimated the impact of a few fast capital ships on Japanese naval strategy, but his arguments were primarily intended to discredit the Admiralty's short-term dispositions. The real issue at stake was whether the Admiralty would send an older battleship like the *Rodney* or *Nelson* to Singapore in the coming weeks, or whether it would substitute the *Prince of Wales*.

Eden was firmly on Churchill's side: from the 'political point of view,' he observed, 'there was no doubt as to the value of our sending...a really modern ship.' Churchill even conceded that the *Prince of Wales* might eventually be replaced in the Far East by the *Nelson* once that ship had been fully repaired. The important thing for the prime minister and his Foreign Secretary was that a modern capital ship proceed to Singapore immediately. Unable to deflect them from this goal, Pound suggested a compromise: the *Prince of Wales* would be sent to Cape Town, and only then would a final decision be taken on its ultimate destination. This was accepted by the Defence Committee, although there was probably never any doubt that the ship would sail on to Singapore.[51]

Churchill's belief that Japan was still hesitating had also played a role in the decision the previous month to dispatch two battalions of reinforcements to Hong Kong.[52] The COS had rejected earlier proposals from Brooke-Popham to reinforce this exposed outpost 'because they considered that it would only have been to throw good money after bad'. In September 1941 they were pressed again for additional forces, this time by a former General Officer Commanding, Hong Kong, who indicated that the Canadian government would be willing to supply the troops if asked.[53] The Chiefs, reversing their earlier position, supported this request. The 'position in the Far East has now changed,' they told the prime minister:

> Our defences in Malaya have been improved and Japan has latterly shown a certain weakness in her attitude towards Great Britain and the United States.
>
> A small reinforcement of one or two battalions would increase the strength of the garrison out of all proportion to the actual numbers involved, and it would provide a strong stimulus to the garrison and the Colony. Further it would have a very great moral effect in the whole of the Far East and it would show Chiang Kai Shek that we really intend to fight it out at Hong Kong.

Their final argument probably carried the most weight with the prime minister: the United States, they noted, 'have recently dispatched a small reinforcement to the Philippines and a similar move by Canada would be in line with the present United States Policy of greater interest in the Far East'.[54]

Churchill replied that he had 'no objection to the approach being made as proposed'.[55] Like his service advisers, he was eager to act in unison with the United States. As he remarked a few weeks later, the 'Far Eastern situation had undoubtedly changed' in recent months, and 'the United States Government was nearer to a commitment than they had been in the past'. Britain, he insisted, must 'regard the United State as having taken charge in the Far East. It was for them to take the lead in this area, and we would support them'.[56] The Canadian government agreed to release two infantry battalions for garrison duty at Hong Kong, and these forces, like the *Prince of Wales* and the battlecruiser *Repulse*, arrived in the Far East shortly before the outbreak of war.

These movements were part of the attempt to create an impression of growing British strength and resolve in the Far East, but it is important to understand that they were conceived as part of a broader strategy of deterrence. Neither Churchill nor the Chiefs of Staff believed that two additional battalions would enable them to hold Hong Kong indefinitely, or that a small squadron of capital ships could halt a determined invasion of Malaya.[57] Nor did they think that these forces would be sufficient in themselves to instil caution in Japanese leaders. The decisions to dispatch these token forces to the Far East in late 1941 are only explicable as part of Churchill's long-standing policy of aligning British and American policies so closely that both the Americans and the Japanese would take Anglo-American co-belligerency for granted. British capital ships and Canadian infantrymen were symbols of resolve and determination, warnings that Britain still possessed considerable latent strength despite its preoccupations in Europe and the Middle East, and, most importantly, gestures of solidarity with the United States.

Churchill may have hoped in the autumn of 1941 that British strength would be sufficient to restrain Japan, but he ultimately counted on the combined power of Britain *and* the United States to avert war. His deterrent strategy was designed to convince Japanese leaders that Britain and America were *deliberately* coordinating their actions, and that they would act together in wartime as well. Churchill hoped to deter an attack on British interests by persuading Japan's leaders that this would automatically mean war with the United States. It seemed inconceivable to him that the Japanese, who were still regarded as inherently cautious individuals, would risk certain defeat by challenging the United States. They might be able to shrug off two British capital ships at Singapore—which in fact they did—but Churchill knew they had to take the threat of war with the United States seriously.

This strategy involved a strong element of risk, as Churchill could not be certain that the Americans *would* automatically support Britain. The worst-case scenario always in the back of British minds was that the Japanese would attack only British interests, and that the United States would remain neutral. Churchill was also eager, therefore, to send the right signals to leaders in the United States. His speech of 10 November 1941 at the Guildhall in London, which promised immediate British support for the United States in the event of a Japanese attack, was part of this attempt to form a common front with the Americans.[58] These efforts were not lost on decision-makers in Washington. In November 1941, for example, Roosevelt suggested to Churchill that Japan might still be deterred by the 'continuing [American] efforts to strengthen our defenses in the Philippine Islands, parallelled by similar efforts by you in the Singapore area, which will tend to increase Japan's distant hesitation'.[59] Churchill was determined to persuade Roosevelt that the two powers were acting in unison, and that a real partnership existed, not just because it would induce caution in Tokyo, but because he desperately needed the United States to bail Britain out if deterrence failed. If Japan attacked Britain because it had faithfully followed the American lead, Britain would at the very least have a moral claim to American support.

Churchill's deterrent strategy was a failure, since it failed to prevent war with Japan. But the underlying logic was mostly sound. Churchill rightly judged that the Americans were serious about standing up to the Japanese, that Roosevelt wanted to support Britain in the event of war, that Japan could be crushed by the enormous military potential of the United States, and that the Japanese were aware of these things. His only real mistake was thinking that Japanese leaders would give in to American pressure rather than begin a war they could not hope to win. In Tokyo, a different cost-benefit calculation took place: once Anglo-American pressure became intolerable, confrontation was preferred to compromise, even though the prospects of a Japanese victory were small. Churchill, who had kept Britain in the war in the summer of 1940 despite seemingly insurmountable odds, should have known better than to assume that foreign statesmen would not gamble if backed into a corner. But it is worth emphasizing that Churchill's deterrent strategy was successful in its secondary goal: convincing Japanese leaders that an attack on Britain would bring the United States into the war. Churchill may not have created that expectation in Tokyo, but he certainly did everything in his power to *reinforce* it. When Japan's leaders contemplated their options in late 1941, they could not be certain that the United States would stand aside if they attacked easy targets like the Malaya, Thailand, and the Netherlands East Indies, which is why the Pacific War began with a pre-emptive strike against the United States navy.

Churchill was, of course, enormously relieved when the Japanese onslaught started with attacks on both Britain and the United States. As he recorded in his memoirs, 'to have the United States at our side was to me the greatest joy'. Britain's survival and ultimate victory now appeared certain. 'I went to bed,' he recalled, 'and slept the sleep of the saved and thankful'.[60] In the short term, however, Britain's strategic position took a dramatic turn for the worse. Japan's surprise attack on the United States Pacific Fleet at Pearl Harbor on the morning of 7 December was far more destructive than Churchill had at first realized. With no fewer than eight American battleships destroyed or damaged in the attack, the main obstacle to Japanese expansion in South East Asia was eliminated, and all Churchill's strategic calculations rapidly fell apart. Japan no longer had to fear American naval intervention if it sent a major expedition south to attack British possessions. The deterrent forces Churchill had sent to the region now found themselves caught up in the conflict they were meant to avert, and with disastrous results.

The Admiralty plans to form a balanced eastern fleet by early 1942 were still far from completion when the Pacific war began. To make matters worse, the aircraft carrier *Indomitable*, which was to have joined the two capital ships at Singapore, ran aground in the West Indies and had to be sent to the United States for repairs. On the evening of 8 December, Admiral Phillips, the commander of Britain's nascent eastern fleet, decided to use the *Prince of Wales* and *Repulse* to disrupt Japanese landings in Malaya and Thailand. These ships, with their escort of four destroyers, were code-named Force Z. The decision to seek out enemy forces was a calculated gamble. As the Royal Air Force could not guarantee continuous air cover for these ships as they traversed the South China Sea, Phillips had to count on speed and surprise for protection. The gamble did not pay off. On the morning of 10 December, Force Z, having abandoned its mission, was caught off the coast of Malaya by Japanese land-based aircraft operating from Indochina. Within hours, both the *Prince of Wales* and *Repulse* had been sunk, with the loss of 840 lives.

Their loss was a tremendous blow to wartime Britain. Churchill later claimed that 'In all the war I never received a more direct shock.'[61] The intrinsic superiority of the Royal Navy was a matter of faith for the British public and elites alike: a naval disaster of this magnitude was as unexpected as it was distressing. More bad news followed. The remnants of the two Canadian battalions surrendered at Hong Kong, along with the rest of the garrison, on Christmas Day. The greatest and most humiliating disaster, however, was yet to come. Britain's defences in Malaya collapsed with astonishing speed. On 15 February 1942, Singapore's garrison capitulated to a numerically smaller Japanese force: 139,000 British and imperial troops were either killed or marched into captivity.

Britain's deterrent strategy not only failed to prevent war, it needlessly sacrificed two Canadian battalions and placed British capital ships in harm's way at the worst possible moment. Blame for the destruction of Force Z has

increasingly been directed at Churchill. It is often argued that he misunderstood what these ships could accomplish in wartime; that he did not
yet appreciate the danger to warships from aircraft; and that he badly underestimated Japanese fighting capabilities. There is some truth in these
charges, but they are not sufficient to explain what the ships were doing at
Singapore when the war began. Moreover, most criticisms of Churchill are
based on the mistaken assumption that disaster became inevitable the
moment the decision was taken to dispatch capital ships to the Far East. In
other words, the debate between Churchill and his advisers over *wartime*
naval strategy has tended to obscure the fact that these ships were sent as
part of a *peacetime* deterrent. When decision-makers in London moved the
Prince of Wales eastward, peace still reigned in the Pacific: war with Japan,
naval disasters, and the loss of empire appeared anything but inevitable. The
origins of Force Z lie in Churchill's overly optimistic assumptions about
the symbolic value of capital ships and the willingness of Japan's leaders to
resort to war, rather than his mistaken views about what a small squadron
of British capital ships might accomplish if deterrence failed.

The assignment of blame over the loss of these ships has also been complicated by the fact that they arrived in the Far East less than a week before
the Japanese onslaught began. London's decision to send them *to* Singapore
is thus often conflated with Phillip's to sail them *from* Singapore in search of
enemy forces. By moving these ships to Singapore in a time of crisis,
Churchill undeniably made their destruction possible, even probable, but
not necessarily inevitable. Churchill was unrealistic about the ability of such
a small squadron to protect British interests in wartime, but this had nothing
to do with Phillips' decision to seek out enemy targets on 8 December. The
recently promoted Phillips lacked first-hand war experience and was well
known for underestimating the vulnerability of capital ships to aircraft. A
different commander might not have endangered his ships on such a reckless mission—one that had never been discussed by the Defence Committee in London, as Phillips would have known. Force Z was destroyed in
circumstances that could have been avoided, and in pursuit of objectives
that neither the Admiralty nor Churchill had explicitly approved. On two
occasions prior to the outbreak of war Pound even suggested to Phillips that
he consider taking his ships safely away from Singapore. A clear distinction
should therefore be drawn between Churchill's decision to place two capital
ships at Singapore on the eve of war, and the subsequent decision, taken
thousands of miles away, that resulted in these ships being caught in the

open and without air cover off the coast of Malaya on the morning of 10 December 1941.[62] There may have been little else that Phillips could have done in the circumstances, but his role in the disaster should not be underestimated.

Although he did not say so publicly, Churchill himself was disposed to blame Phillips for the loss of Force Z. 'The last thing in the world that the Defence Committee wished,' he wrote in 1953 in response to criticisms by Stephen Roskill, 'was that anything like the movement which Admiral Phillips thought it right to make to intercept a Japanese invasion force should have been made by his two vessels without even air cover.'[63] Churchill was perfectly willing to urge admirals to take bold and reckless actions when he felt it would achieve some useful purpose, but he notably refrained from urging reckless action on Phillips in December 1941, as he had, for example, on Cunningham when Egypt appeared to be threatened earlier in the year. However, if Churchill had different ideas from Phillips about the deployment of these ships, he failed to make his wishes clear in time to avert a catastrophe.

What Churchill wanted to see happen is, in fact, uncertain. He subsequently maintained that he had always intended the ships to move out of harm's way. His memoirs record that on the night of 9 December, a meeting, 'mostly Admiralty', was convened in the Cabinet war room to consider the naval situation in the Far East. According to Churchill, there was general agreement that these ships 'must go to sea and vanish among the innumerable islands':

> I thought myself that they should go across the Pacific to join what was left of the American Fleet. It would be a proud gesture at this moment, and would knit the English-speaking world together....We were all much attracted to this line of thought. But as the hour was late we decided to sleep on it, and settle the next morning what to do with the *Prince of Wales* and the *Repulse*. Within a couple of hours they were at the bottom of the sea.[64]

He repeated this claim in 1953, insisting that his goal had been for the ships of Force Z to 'go to Singapore, should be known to have arrived at Singapore, and should then disappear into the immense archipelago which lies within a thousand miles of it. Thus they would have exerted all the deterrent effects upon the Japanese in any moment to attack which the TIRPITZ and at other times other vessels have brought to bear upon us.'[65] There are no contemporary documents to support these claims, however. After searching the official records of the COS and Defence Committee, Roskill concluded 'they never discussed the "disappearing strategy"'. It is perhaps surprising, therefore, that he mentions this plan in the *War at Sea*, even though he is careful to attribute it to Churchill's memoirs.[66]

But Churchill's interest in sending the *Prince of Wales* to Pearl Harbor is not actually contradicted by the official record, and it is corroborated by the diary of one of the participants at the meeting. General Alan Brooke, soon to become CIGS, noted that Churchill was upset that the Japanese attack on Pearl Harbor had 'entirely upset the balance in the Pacific and leaves Japs masters of the ocean until we can assemble some forces there. We therefore examined possibility of sending British battleship to restore situation. Finally left matter to be thought over and broke up.'[67] This suggests that Churchill, despite his reputation for recklessness, was inclined on this occasion to be cautious, and that he continued to think about these particular warships primarily in terms of their political and symbolic value.

Two months after the loss of Force Z, Britain suffered its greatest disaster in the Far East, the fall of Singapore. This defeat is also controversial. Churchill never attempted to deny his ultimate responsibility for this disaster. 'If we have handled our resources wrongly, no one is so much to blame as me,' he told Parliament in January 1942. 'If we have not got large modern air forces and tanks in Burma and Malaya tonight, no one is more accountable than I am.'[68] He also never regretted the low priority assigned to the defence of Malaya. 'I would do exactly the same again,' he told one colleague.[69] 'The decision was taken,' he explained, 'to make our contribution to Russia, to try to beat Rommel, and to form a stronger front from the Levant to the Caspian. It followed from that decision that it was in our power only to make a moderate and partial provision in the Far East against the hypothetical danger of a Japanese onslaught.'[70]

Churchill deliberately ran risks in the Far East in 1940–1 in part because he underestimated the likelihood of war with Japan, but also, and more importantly, because after the fall of France he had little choice but to concentrate resources in the main and decisive theatre. The logic behind his priorities is difficult to fault. Britain's survival was now at stake: its resources were dangerously overstretched, and risks were being run everywhere. Further defeats in Europe and the Middle East would have had serious and immediate repercussions for Britain. Investing in the survival of the Soviet Union was also a far-sighted decision, and one that would ultimately pay huge dividends. The resources Stalin received from Britain in 1941 may not have been decisive in ensuring that the USSR did not collapse, but recent scholarship has shown that British aid played an important role during this critical period.[71] It only made sense to concentrate resources in the Middle East and Russia. The Far East, in contrast, remained calm. 'In war one only has to compare one evil with another,' Churchill wrote before the war, 'and the lesser evil ranks as a blessing.'[72] So it was in 1941. Japan had not yet attacked British interests, and there was no certainty that it would. The choice for Churchill was therefore an easy one: forces sitting idle in Malaya and Singapore would do nothing to stave off disaster in Europe. The Chiefs of Staff were also prepared to gamble in this region, because there was no other reasonable choice, but they would have hedged their bets by diverting at least modest reinforcements to Malaya. In this respect Churchill's intervention was decisive. The prime minister was accustomed to differences with his service advisers and was willing to change course when he encountered firm resistance, but throughout 1941 he was not prepared to tolerate opposition to his Far Eastern policies. This was not, in his view, a strictly military decision. Political considerations, which were best judged by civilian leaders, had to take precedence. Consequently, Dill and Pound both saw their arguments for caution in this theatre either dismissed or belittled. In the end, they decided to save their strength for other battles.

Churchill's uncompromising position grew from the conviction that the risks Britain was running in the Far East were small. His reasons went beyond a simple underestimation of Japanese strength and fighting capabilities, although these were also factors. In the decades leading up to war, Churchill's approach to the problem of British security in the Far East was generally both realistic and pragmatic. Unlike Britain's service leaders, who had overly ambitious plans for waging a protracted total war in the Far East, Churchill rightly concluded that Britain alone did not possess sufficient strength to inflict a decisive defeat on Japan. He was also more willing to sacrifice secondary British interests if they were not worth the cost of defending. These considerations dictated a defensive strategy in the Far East. Britain would have to defend Singapore, but solely as a means of protecting its only truly vital interests in the region, Australia and New Zealand. Anything more ambitious than this would depend on American support.

It was clear to Churchill at an early date that Britain's position in the Far East ultimately rested on the ability and willingness of the United States to contain Japanese expansion. As prime minister, he was ready to assume a supporting role for Britain in the region. The steady improvement of Anglo-American relations in 1940–1 raised his hopes that Japan could be deterred from war, and provided a safety net in case he was wrong. If Britain could depend on US support, which seemed increasingly likely in 1941, Japan's ultimate defeat was assured. Britain could make good its losses when the fighting was over, and, most importantly, the security of Australia and New Zealand would be assured. US belligerency would transform Britain's strategic position, and make even Singapore expendable. Churchill does not seem to have realized how vulnerable this possession had become by December 1941, but his propensity to run risks with its security was strengthened by his expectations of US support. *That* gamble, at least, paid off.

9

The Battle of the Atlantic,
the Imports Crisis, and the
Closing of the 'Air Gap'

The loss of British territories in the Far East was more than offset, in Churchill's view, by the entry of the United States into the Second World War. The devastating success of the Japanese surprise attack on the US Pacific fleet at Pearl Harbor left the Allies far more vulnerable in this theatre than Churchill could have foreseen, but he never doubted that American belligerency marked a decisive turning point in the conflict. The immediate challenge facing the Allies was to ensure that their combined resources were employed as efficiently as possible in the new global conflict. For the British, this meant adhering to the Germany-first strategy that the Americans had agreed to in pre-war discussions. Churchill and the COS always regarded Germany as the greatest threat to Allied security. Germany's downfall would make Japan's defeat all but inevitable, but if Germany over-came Soviet resistance and consolidated its conquest of Europe, its position would become virtually insurmountable. The Americans had accepted this logic before their entry into the war, but the British knew that Roosevelt was under strong domestic pressure after Pearl Harbor to retaliate against Japan.

Churchill and his military advisers departed for Washington in mid-December 1941 for discussions with their American counterparts. During their trans-Atlantic journey, Churchill outlined his views on grand strategy in a series of memoranda for the British Chiefs of Staff. As before, he assumed that German strength and morale must be substantially worn down before a final blow could be struck on land. It now seemed safe to assume that much of the wearing-down would be done by the Soviet Union.

The Wehrmacht had failed to crush the Red Army in a single campaign, as Hitler had intended, and the renewal of fighting on the Eastern Front in 1942 would impose a heavy burden on Germany's resources. 'Neither Great Britain nor the United States have any part to play in this event,' Churchill noted in a memorandum, 'except to make sure that we send, without fail and punctually, the supplies we have promised.' While the Soviets tied down the bulk of Germany's forces, British and American troops would undertake operations to wear down German strength, beginning with the clearance of North Africa. Churchill was optimistic that General Auchinleck's 'Crusader' offensive in the western desert would drive German and Italian forces to the French frontier at Tunisia, and he hoped that these victories, together with the United States' entry into the war, would persuade Vichy France to throw in its lot with the Allies. In this event, British and American formations would immediately be poured into French North Africa. If the Germans fought to maintain a presence in the region, they would do so at a serious disadvantage. 'The North-West African theatre is one most favourable for Anglo-American operations,' he claimed, 'our approaches being direct and convenient across the Atlantic, while the enemy's passage of the Mediterranean would be severely obstructed'.[1]

These efforts would be supplemented by strategic bombing. 'It must be remembered,' Churchill wrote in the same memorandum, 'that we place great hopes of affecting German production and German morale by ever more severe and more accurate bombing of their cities and harbours, and that this, combined with their Russian defeats, may produce important effects upon the will to fight of the German people, with consequential internal reactions upon the German Government.'[2] Churchill admitted that the strategic air offensive had 'so far fallen short of our hopes', but he assumed that the addition of American bomber squadrons would produce better results. These efforts to wear down German strength from the air might eventually achieve decisive results, he hoped, by creating 'internal convulsions in Germany', although he assumed that final victory would require the decisive defeat of the German army. This could be accomplished, he proposed, by landing Anglo-American forces throughout occupied Europe in order to spark a general uprising against Nazi rule. The 'conquered populations' would never be able to revolt on their own, he maintained:

> owing to the ruthless counter-measures that will be employed, but if adequate and suitably equipped forces were landed in several of the following countries, namely, Norway, Denmark, Holland, Belgium, the French Channel coasts and

the French Atlantic coasts, as well as in Italy and possibly the Balkans, the German garrisons would prove insufficient to cope both with the strength of the liberating forces and the fury of the revolting peoples. It is impossible for the Germans, while we retain the sea-power necessary to choose the place or places of attack to have sufficient troops in each of these countries for effective resistance. In particular, they cannot move their armour about laterally from north to south or west to east; either they must divide it between the various conquered countries—in which case it will become hopelessly dispersed—or they must hold it back in a central position in Germany, in which case it will not arrive until large and important lodgements have been made by us from overseas.[3]

Churchill calculated that around forty armoured divisions, specially trained and equipped for amphibious operations, would be sufficient to spearhead an invasion of Europe in the summer of 1943. These forces, half British, half American, would be followed by additional Allied formations—'another million men of all arms'—but he expected the people of Europe, once armed by the Allies, also to play a major part in the final destruction of the German army. Victory might be achieved, he concluded, by the end of 1943 or sometime in 1944.[4]

While the exploitation of Allied sea power was central to Churchill's plans for the war in Europe, the navy's main role in this theatre was to enable offensive operations by land and air forces. Navies still had important battles to win in the Far East, and would be necessary to bring decisive pressure against Japan, but in the Atlantic and Mediterranean, which Churchill regarded as the most important theatres, their role was a supporting one. They would keep open the sea lanes essential to Britain's survival, allow the build-up of American forces in the European theatre, and protect Anglo-American armies operating overseas. But the experiences of 1940 and 1941 had impressed upon Churchill that naval power alone was incapable of inflicting significant damage on either Germany or Italy. Mediterranean operations had shown that the navy could not inflict a decisive blow against Italy, or even sever its communications with North Africa. Germany's conquests in Europe meant that economic pressure now depended on air power. Churchill's outline of Anglo-American grand strategy in December 1941 did not contain even a token reference to maritime blockade as a means of wearing down German strength. The navy, in his eyes, had become a predominantly defensive weapon, at least in the European war.

Churchill's military advisers shared his broad views on the future development of grand strategy. By the time they arrived in Washington, they had agreed that German strength would be worn down over the course of 1942 by a combination of Anglo-American operations in North Africa, strategic bombing, blockade, propaganda, and subversion on the Continent. This, it was hoped, would allow a final assault to be launched against Germany in 1943.[5] The British were relieved to discover that American leaders still accorded priority to the European war, and agreement was easily reached that 'only the minimum of force necessary for the safeguarding of vital interests in other theatres should be diverted from operations against Germany'. The Americans also accepted, with only a minimum of discussion, the general outline of Allied grand strategy sketched out by the British, although they were unwilling to commit American forces to operations in North Africa and expressed reservations about the idea of launching 'simultaneous landings in several of the occupied countries' in 1943.[6]

The first wartime meeting of British and American leaders, known as the Arcadia Conference, did little, therefore, to prepare either side for the disagreements that would emerge over when and where Anglo-American armies would be employed against Germany and Italy. But before this issue became contentious, Churchill's calculations were upset by two unexpected developments: the failure of the 'Crusader' offensive to drive back Axis forces in North Africa; and the growing U-boat threat to Allied shipping.

The entry of the United States into the war allowed Germany to begin operating U-boats for the first time along the east coast of the United States (see Map 5). Despite having ample time and opportunity to prepare against this threat, the Americans were not ready for an attack in their own waters. In January 1942 the first U-boat commanders to arrive were amazed to find that merchant ships were running along the coast unescorted, and many were not taking even basic precautions against attack such as running without lights or zig-zagging. To make matters worse, American coastal cities were still brightly lit up at night, leaving ships clearly silhouetted for U-boats laying offshore. As in 1940, the Allies were probably fortunate that the carnage was not greater. The Germans had nearly one hundred operational U-boats available at the beginning of 1942, but Hitler insisted on keeping most of them in the Mediterranean and off Norway. Nevertheless, even with only about a dozen U-boats operating at any time in the western Atlantic, the Germans inflicted heavy losses: over a million and a half tons of Allied shipping were sunk during the first four months of 1942.[7]

The Admiralty was appalled by these heavy—and mostly unnecessary—losses, and urged the Americans to set up at least a rudimentary convoy system. Churchill was sufficiently alarmed by the destruction along the American seaboard that he tactfully drew Roosevelt's attention to the problem in February. The following month he cabled Harry Hopkins, one of Roosevelt's close advisers, to suggest the temporary release of American destroyers from the Pacific theatre to allow for the introduction of convoy in the western Atlantic and Carribean.[8] But Admiral Ernest J. King, the Commander-in-Chief of the US Fleet, was slow to take action, believing that ships would be safer sailing independently than in weakly defended convoys. Until more escorts were available, he suggested to Roosevelt that the British might help by stepping up their air attacks on U-boat bases and building yards, 'thus checking submarine activities at their source'.[9]

The allocation of British bomber forces was already the subject of heated debate in London. The decision in November 1941 to conserve bomber strength for the spring had resulted in a substantial diversion of resources over the winter to attacks on Germany's heavy surface ships at Brest. The Air Ministry remained committed to strategic bombing, however, and in early February 1942 it proposed that Bomber Command should once again concentrate the greatest possible effort against German cities.[10] A change of targets became unavoidable on 12 February, when the ships Bomber Command had been targeting—*Scharnhorst*, *Gneisenau*, and the heavy cruiser *Prinz Eugen*—made their 'Channel Dash' from Brest to Germany. Two days later, Churchill minuted that he was now 'entirely in favour of the resumption of the full bombing of Germany'. On the basis of this minute, the Air Ministry issued a new directive to Bomber Command authorizing the resumption of attacks on the German civilian population.[11]

From the Admiralty's perspective, this was a move in the wrong direction. Naval leaders wanted more rather than fewer air resources dedicated to naval needs. Alexander immediately informed the Defence Committee that his service could not support the RAF's bombing policy until the navy's air requirements were adequately met. To deal with the U-boat threat, he maintained that Coastal Command needed a significant increase in strength: six and a half Wellington squadrons from bomber command, and eighty-one new B-17 'Flying Fortresses' or Liberators from the United States. These aircraft would enable Coastal Command to provide additional land-based air cover for convoys in the north Atlantic, and allow for continuous patrols over the Bay of Biscay, through which U-boats travelled to and from their bases in France. In addition, the Admiralty proposed to send another two squadrons from Bomber Command to protect communications in the Indian Ocean.[12]

This was the opening shot in what Admiral Pound later dubbed the 'Battle of the Air', a year-long struggle between the Admiralty and the Air Ministry over the allocation of air resources and, ultimately, the basis of British grand strategy. To reinforce the navy's case for more aircraft, the First Sea Lord decided it would be necessary to submit a second memorandum to the Defence Committee. On 24 February he invited members of the Naval Staff to offer suggestions on how to present the navy's case.[13] He soon received a flood of memoranda revealing just how frustrated staff members and senior officers had become with the RAF. There was a clear consensus that unless more aircraft were allocated to supporting the navy, Britain risked losing the war. The most immediate danger was to the Atlantic trade routes, but lack of air support had created serious problems for the service everywhere. 'The Navy is fighting a losing battle,' Admiral Max Horton wrote, 'owing to the continually increasing risks it has been compelled to undertake in every theatre of war.'[14] Nor was there any confidence that the strategic bombing offensive favoured by the Air Ministry could produce either rapid or decisive results. 'It is no longer necessary,' wrote the Director of Plans, 'to buoy ourselves up with exaggerated hopes of the success of our bombing policy.'[15] There was general agreement within the upper ranks of the navy that air raids on Germany should continue, but not on a scale that would deprive the other services of vital air support, and primarily as a means to tie down German resources and provide relief to the Russians.

The navy had a strong case for more air support, and with the strain on naval resources greater than ever the upper ranks of the service were ready for a showdown. As Admiral Geoffrey Blake observed, 'the question is whether the essential air support to our Naval operations is to have a higher degree of priority than bombing Germany'. In his opinion, the 'answer cannot be in doubt but it will require <u>someone</u> to say so'.[16] With naval opinion solidly behind him, Pound laid out the Admiralty's requirements to the Defence Committee in a new memorandum dated 5 March. 'If we lose the war at sea,' he began, 'we lose the war.' To prevent this, he insisted that more aircraft were urgently needed to protect shipping in the Atlantic and to support naval forces in other theatres. The Admiralty now estimated that Coastal Command would have to be increased to over 1,900 aircraft, more than double its current strength.[17] Pound also urged that the Coastal Command organization be replicated abroad, with operational control and training for this branch being taken over entirely by the navy.

The Air Ministry was opposed to such a substantial modification of the existing system, which it feared would mean the virtual loss of Coastal Command by the RAF. Nor was it enthused about diverting long-range bombers to support the other services.[18] Senior air force officers continued to argue that Bomber Command could make a greater contribution to the defence of trade by offensive means, such as attacking industrial targets and naval dockyards inside Germany. A memorandum for the Defence Committee on 8 March by the Secretary of State for Air, Sir Archibald Sinclair, maintained that diverting bombers 'to an uneconomical defensive role would be unsound at any time':

> It would be doubly so now when we are about to launch a bombing offensive with the aid of a new technique [the navigational aid 'Gee'] of which we have high expectations and which will enable us to deliver a heavy and concentrated blow against Germany at a moment when German morale is low and when the Russians are in great need of our assistance.

The Air Ministry nevertheless offered to allocate new Catalina flying boats and Flying Fortresses to Coastal Command as they became available. These aircraft would meet most of the navy's requirements by the end of 1942, but Sinclair claimed that little could be done to improve the situation during the first half of the year. To provide immediate relief in the Battle of the Atlantic, the Air Ministry would agree only to loan Coastal Command a single squadron of Whitley bombers equipped with air-to-surface vessel (ASV) radar.[19]

The Defence Committee was thus confronted with two distinct visions of Britain's future strategy. One entailed the use of air resources primarily for cooperation with the other two services, and would ensure, among other things, that Britain did not lose the war by having its maritime communications severed. The other involved running risks at sea and on land in the short term in hopes of crippling Germany through strategic bombing. Given the fundamental divergence of opinion between the Air Ministry and the Admiralty, no immediate decision was possible.[20] Churchill generally shared the air marshals' view that offensive measures should have priority, and that trade protection was an intrinsically defensive task. But he hesitated to come down entirely in favour of the Air Ministry. Strategic bombing was already becoming controversial, and its critics were not restricted to the army and navy. Churchill's room to manoeuvre was further restricted by a request from Roosevelt for a greater bombing effort against the U-boat bases and building yards, which reached him on 20 March. Meeting with Pound and Charles Portal, Chief of the Air Staff, that evening, he described the competing needs of strategic bombing and the disruption of submarine yards and bases as 'acute', especially as the latter had 'been emphasized in importance by the request of the President'.[21] Churchill's first reaction was to look to the Americans to solve the problem for him. He explained to Roosevelt on 29 March that the Admiralty was eager to begin continuous patrolling over the Bay of Biscay, but that this would come at the expense of the bombing campaign against Germany. The only way to meet both obligations, he suggested, would be to expedite the dispatch of American bomber squadrons to Britain to ensure that the strategic offensive was not unduly weakened.[22]

Churchill's instinctive preference for strategic bombing was strengthened by a minute he received the next day from his scientific adviser, Lord Cherwell, laying out in detail how many bombs an expanded bomber fleet might be expected to drop on German towns. By concentrating its resources on the strategic campaign, Cherwell predicted that Bomber Command could render roughly a third of the German population homeless by the middle of 1943. 'There seems little doubt,' he concluded, 'that this would break the spirit of the people.'[23] Churchill forwarded this minute to the Air Ministry, which agreed that these results were attainable, provided that all unnecessary diversion of bombers away from the strategic offensive could be avoided.[24]

Cherwell's intervention in this debate seems to have made a strong impression on Churchill, who became increasingly vocal in his support for the air force. When the army also requested greater air support for its forces, Churchill summarily rejected its demands on the grounds that they 'would be destructive of the principle of an independent Royal Air Force'. As with the proposal to expand the Coastal Command organization, one of his concerns was that aircraft assigned to army cooperation would be idle for lengthy periods when they might otherwise be engaged in bombing the Germans. 'There would be enormous dangers in tethering an immense proportion of our Air Force to Army units,' he wrote, 'most of which will be waiting about for months, and perhaps years, without becoming engaged with the enemy.'[25] Churchill also lashed out at critics of the bomber offensive in a minute to Clement Attlee, the leader of the Labour Party and deputy prime minister. 'It is no use flying out squadrons [to India and the Middle East] which sit helpless and useless when they arrive', he complained. 'We have built up a great plant here for bombing Germany, which is the only way in our power of helping Russia. From every side people want to break it up. One has to be sure that one does not ruin our punch here without getting any proportionate advantage elsewhere.'[26]

The Admiralty's request for additional air support fared only slightly better than the army's. A compromise was reached in mid-April by which four squadrons (two Wellingtons, two Whitleys) would be transferred to Coastal Command for anti-submarine duties. The Air Ministry hoped this would end the dispute, but the Admiralty was still far from satisfied. Alexander complained again to the prime minister on 19 April about the shortage of air support. 'If I could get for our outer [Biscay] patrols the number of heavy bombers we lose [over Germany] in a few days,' he wrote, 'we could make a great start.'[27] He followed this up with another minute on 1 May requesting the loan of four squadrons from Bomber Command for Biscay patrols to bridge the gap until American-built Flying Fortresses began to arrive. Churchill rejected this new proposal out of hand next day: 'I cannot agree to this further inroad upon the only offensive against Germany now in progress.'[28]

Pound found himself under mounting pressure from his subordinates to press the navy's claims for aircraft against the Air Ministry. A meeting of the naval Commanders-in-Chief at the Admiralty on 1 June left the First Sea Lord with little doubt as to the strength of feelings within the upper ranks of the service. 'Whatever the results of the bombing of cities might be,' argued Admiral Tovey, Commander-in-Chief of Home Fleet, on 7 June, 'it could not of itself win the war, whereas the failure of our sea communications would assuredly lose it.' He therefore proposed a reduction of the bomber offensive to ensure that the needs of the army and navy were met. 'It was difficult,' he maintained, 'to believe that the population of Cologne would notice much difference between a raid of 1,000 bombers and one by 750':

> I realised [he continued] that Their Lordships [of the Admiralty] had for a long time been pressing for increased air support; but it had not materialised, and I informed Their Lordships that in my opinion the situation at sea was now so grave that the time had come for a stand to be made, even if this led to Their Lordships taking the extreme step of resignation. I was supported in my contentions by Admiral of the Fleet Sir Charles Forbes and Admiral Sir Andrew Cunningham.[29]

Pound returned to the offensive on 16 June with a memorandum for the COS casting doubt on the RAF's ability to achieve greater accuracy with new navigational aids and emphasizing the very high level of losses still being inflicted on Allied shipping. He reported that an average of over 677,000 tons of shipping had been lost each month from March till May, more than Allied shipyards had built during the same period. The need for more aircraft to operate with the navy was therefore a matter of 'supreme urgency', and he recommended that the problem be investigated by the Joint Planning Staff.[30] This idea was supported by General Alan Brooke, the CIGS, but Portal objected and the issue was sent instead for study by representatives of the Admiralty and Air Ministry.[31]

Behind the scenes, Air Marshal Sir Arthur Harris, the Air Officer Commanding-in-Chief (AOC-in-C), Bomber Command, wrote directly to Churchill on 17 June seeking priority for the bomber offensive. In a personal minute to the prime minister, he insisted that Germany could be knocked 'out of the War in a matter of months' if only British air power were concentrated on the strategic offensive. Coastal Command, in his view, was 'merely an obstacle to victory'; its long-range bombers, along with those assigned to cooperate with the army, should be reassigned to Bomber Command.[32] While Churchill did not subscribe to this extreme viewpoint, he was determined to strengthen the bombing campaign and was willing to give Harris an opportunity to present his case. The Air Marshal needed little encouragement. A second memorandum, dated 28 June, did not pull any punches. 'The purely defensive use of air power is grossly wasteful,' Harris charged:

> The Naval employment of aircraft consists of picking at the fringes of enemy power, of waiting for opportunities that may never occur, and indeed probably never will occur, of looking for needles in a haystack. They attempt to sever each capillary vein, one by one, when they could, with much less effort, cut the artery. Bomber Command attacks the sources of all Naval power, rather than the fringes of the one type of enemy Naval operation which obviously menaces us – the submarine.

'Bomber Command,' he concluded, 'provides our only offensive action yet pressed home directly against Germany.'[33]

Harris' arguments would have appealed strongly to Churchill's offensive predilections. The Admiralty was fortunate that the Chief of the Air Staff was prepared to be more accommodating. Portal conceded to Pound that a 'very real need' did indeed exist for an immediate increase in air support for trade protection. In mid-July an agreement was reached by which Lancaster bombers belonging to Bomber Command would assist Coastal Command until it could be brought up to its approved strength with new Flying Fortresses and Liberators.[34] This fell short of what the Admiralty wanted, but Pound was eager to put a positive spin on it. He claimed that there had been 'a real change in heart on the part of the Air Ministry', and suggested this had probably 'been brought about by the general feeling that the sea war was not getting its fair share. However, whatever may be the reason, I feel that it is genuine.'[35]

Churchill's prejudices, meanwhile, had been further strengthened by Lord Cherwell, who charged that Coastal Command was not carrying out as many sorties as it was capable of. Until greater efficiency was achieved, he denied that there was any need to transfer additional squadrons from Bomber Command. Churchill endorsed the deal Portal and Pound had worked out to use Lancasters to supplement Coastal Command's strength, but he continued to have misgivings. These were outlined in a memorandum he submitted to the War Cabinet on 21 July. With the United States now an ally, Churchill made it clear that the bomber was no longer Britain's primary means to defeat Germany. 'We look forward to mass invasion of the Continent by liberating armies,' he wrote, 'and general revolt of the populations against the Hitler tyranny.' But this did not mean the bomber no longer had a central role to play. It 'would be a mistake,' he wrote, 'to cast aside our original thought which, it may be mentioned, is also strong in American minds, namely, that the severe, ruthless bombing of Germany on an ever-increasing scale will not only cripple her war effort, including U-boat and aircraft production, but will also create conditions intolerable to the mass of the German population'. The strategic air campaign was therefore still a valuable tool, 'second only to the largest military operations which can be conducted on the Continent'.

Churchill observed 'with sorrow and alarm the woeful shrinkage of our plans for Bomber expansion'. He insisted that the strategic air campaign must continue on the largest possible scale, although he conceded that it might be temporarily interrupted at some point to provide air support for military operations on the Continent. This fell short of the absolute priority Harris had called for, but Churchill also implicitly rejected the Admiralty's demands for a greater share of air resources. He acknowledged that Germany's attack on shipping was bound to have an impact on British imports, and that this might result in additional rationing. But he did not believe that shortages would become critical. On the contrary, he expected the import situation to improve in 1943, by which time the United States would be producing enough new ships to replace losses, even if they continued at their current high rate. Stocks could be allowed to run down in the short term, he maintained, as long as it was certain they could be made good before a crisis point was reached. Churchill was thus willing to bear heavy shipping losses at sea in order to bring the maximum pressure to bear on Germany. 'It might,' he wrote, 'be true to say that the issue of the war depends on whether Hitler's U-boat attack on Allied tonnage, or the increase and application of Allied Air power, reach their full fruition first.'[36]

Churchill's strategy deliberately deprived the navy of air support that would have reduced losses in the Battle of the Atlantic during the remainder of 1942 and early 1943. This was a calculated gamble on his part. He assumed that strategic bombing would be far more effective than it actually was, and, more importantly, that the United States would be both able and willing to supply enough new merchant shipping tonnage to meet both American and British needs. Churchill was confident on both points, although he recognized that the allocation of new merchant ships to Britain depended entirely on American goodwill. It was therefore important, he wrote, to obtain 'a solemn compact, almost a treaty, with the United States about the share of their new building we are to get in 1943 and 1944'.[37] There were grounds for optimism on this point. At the Arcadia conference in December 1941, agreement was reached in principle that all Allied shipping should be pooled and allocated according to need by a Combined Shipping Adjustment Board.[38] Roosevelt had been sympathetic to British needs in 1941, and had willingly taken steps to increase the availability of American shipping before the US entered the war. British requests for American tankers in 1942 were met generously and promptly by Roosevelt—over the course of 1942, the United States provided over 1.24 million deadweight tons of tankers to keep up Britain's oil reserves.[39] Churchill therefore had reason to think that the United States would make good British non-tanker shipping losses, even if the U-boat threat was not mastered.

In March 1942 the prime minister had outlined the import situation to Roosevelt, noting that 'very substantial additions to our shipping resources' were necessary not just to keep the British people fed and the war economy functioning, but also to sustain British operations in the Middle East and elsewhere.[40] By mid-1942 there was less room for optimism, as it became increasingly clear that the United States' armed forces were making such heavy demands on American shipping, most of it for the war in the Pacific, that British needs were not being met. To monitor this situation, the Import Executive was replaced with a new inter-departmental Shipping Committee. This body calculated that Britain was headed for a shortfall of 8.4 million tons in non-tanker imports between January 1942 and the end of June 1943. Around half of this deficit could be met, it predicted, by running down existing stocks and effecting various economies, but the balance would require additional shipping from the United States.[41] If this were not obtained, British stocks, it predicted, might be exhausted by mid-1943.

The War Cabinet discussed this problem on 28 July. Churchill insisted that Britain's import program must have first call on the Allied shipping, even if this interfered with the build-up of American troops and supplies in Britain (Operation 'Bolero') for the invasion of Europe. The nation's 'irreducible minima' for imports were pegged at 25 million tons in 1942, and 27 million tons the following year. British authorities felt that the immediate cause of shipping shortages was the excessive demands being made by the American armed services, particularly for the Pacific. The Americans would therefore have to be persuaded to cut back their commitments outside the European theatre, and even, if possible, to reduce the equipment being transported for Bolero, which appeared to be greater than required. Oliver Lyttelton, the Minister of Production, suggested that this would be easier if Britain took steps to reduce the demands made by its own armed services. Churchill, who believed that British forces overseas were being provided for on an overly lavish scale, agreed. It was essential, he remarked, that the British army 'should learn to travel light'. Measures should therefore be taken 'to cut down to the bare minimum the establishments of the rearward formations'.[42]

The most vocal opposition to Churchill's efforts to reorient British grand strategy came not from the Admiralty, however, but from Stanley Bruce, the Australian High Commissioner. Bruce had sided with the navy during the debates in June over bomber allocation, and he was not satisfied that the agreement between Pound and Portal did enough to meet the service's air requirements. The subject was taken up by the War Cabinet, in Churchill's absence, on 12 August. Bruce insisted that the Bomber offensive should not be allowed to endanger Britain's safety at sea, particularly in the Indian Ocean. 'Surely,' he argued, 'more than a bare minimum should be provided for a task of such paramount importance as preserving our sea communications.'[43] He received no support, however, from Pound, who loyally defended the agreement he had hammered out with Portal. Nor were ministers eager to open the question of strategic priorities. The discussion of the subject was thus deferred.

In the weeks that followed, Churchill circulated to the War Cabinet two documents that were clearly calculated to bolster support for the bomber offensive. The first was Harris' memorandum of 28 June calling for absolute priority to be given to Bomber Command. The second was a note by Lord Trenchard, the influential former CAS. Trenchard, a fervent believer in the value of strategic bombing, forcefully presented the case for concentrating resources on Bomber Command. 'We have in our possession,' he wrote in August, 'the opportunity of producing decisive effects if we realise now that air power has already been proved to be the dominant deciding and final power in the warfare of to-day and the future.' Dispersion of aircraft for other purposes, in his view, would mean 'dissipating our present decisive superiority in support of long-drawn-out campaigns of costly battles which can only give us victory at the cost of hundreds of thousands of human lives'.[44] Churchill informed his colleagues in September that he did not himself 'adopt or endorse the views expressed, which I think fall into the error of spoiling a good case by overstatement'. But he claimed that these documents would 'serve as a considerable answer to those who attack the usefulness of our Bombing policy'.[45]

The Admiralty's efforts to obtain additional aircraft continued to be blocked by Churchill. In mid-August, Alexander had reported that steps were being taken to increase the number of sorties flown by Coastal Command, but he explained that this would result in greater wear on aircraft and reduce the numbers available at short notice to serve as a striking force. He also warned that squadrons loaned by Bomber Command were seldom available quickly and lacked the training necessary to operate effectively at sea.[46] Churchill was unsympathetic. 'You must not trench so heavily upon the resources of the RAF,' he told Pound on 24 August. 'I do not sustain the impression that the costly Biscay patrol has justified its inroads on our Bombing resources.'[47]

Pound replied with statistics to show that the Biscay patrols had in fact been 'a highly profitable operation'. But he maintained that forces loaned by Bomber Command, 'though very keen were amateurs and not properly equipped'. Better results could be obtained, he argued, with aircraft permanently assigned to Coastal Command.[48] Churchill also frustrated the Admiralty's efforts to build up reserves of fighter aircraft for the Fleet Air Arm.

'There can be no question of taking machines which will be used in action by the R.A.F. in order to build up inordinate reserves for the Admiralty,' Churchill minuted on 28 August. 'The Admiralty always want not only to win the game, but to go to bed with the ace. This tendency must be strongly resisted.'[49]

The Admiralty naturally took a different view. In late September, Pound again found himself being pressed by his subordinates, this time to present the navy's case for air support directly to the War Cabinet. 'To get the air-craft required is an eternal battle,' the Deputy First Sea Lord wrote. 'I know that the feeling throughout the Navy is that we are not getting a fair deal and that without this we may well lose the war.'[50] This opinion was shared by Air Chief Marshal Sir Philip Joubert de la Ferté, the AOC-in-C, Coastal Command. Joubert warned Pound on 21 September that the anti-U-boat war was not going well. The Germans were building three new U-boats for every one the Allies sank; tankers were being lost faster than they could be replaced; and merchant-ship construction was barely keeping up with losses.[51] On 5 October Pound submitted a memorandum to the Defence Committee (Supply) outlining the navy's deficiencies and demanding a greater share of the nation's manpower and industrial resources. The most critical requirements, he insisted, were more long-range aircraft and replace-ment aircraft capable of greater distances.[52]

Churchill, however, was already moving in a different direction. Cherwell continued to advise him that Coastal Command could improve its effi-ciency by flying more sorties rather than by taking aircraft away from Bomber Command. On 15 September he suggested that since operations were less dangerous over the sea than over Germany, it would not 'be unfair to ask Coastal Command for an increased rate of effort if more sorties are required'. Churchill forwarded this minute to Sinclair. 'We must have more Bomber Squadrons,' he commented. 'You must arm me to get them.'[53] Two days later, he asked the Air Ministry to prepare plans to increase Bomber Command from thirty-two operational squadrons to fifty by the end of the year. Two of these new squadrons, he suggested, might be taken from Coastal Command.[54]

Pound agreed to return to Bomber Command two of the four medium bomber squadrons previously loaned, but the Naval Staff was upset by this latest attempt to bolster Bomber Command at the expense of the other services.[55] The First Sea Lord attempted to impress upon Churchill the extent of the Admiralty's concerns. '[T]he situation generally at sea is so serious,' he warned, 'that the Cabinet should be informed and the urgency of the Navy's needs re-assessed.' It was essential, he maintained, for the government to issue a directive giving priority to the provision of aircraft for the war at sea and the construction of new ships.[56] This plea came too late: Churchill had already submitted a new memorandum to the War Cabinet reasserting the primacy of Bomber Command over the navy. 'There preys upon us,' he wrote on 24 October, 'as the greatest danger to the United Nations, and particularly to our Island, the U-boat attack':

> The Navy call for greater assistance from the Air. I am proposing to my colleagues that we try for the present to obtain this extra assistance mainly from the United States, and that we encroach as little as possible upon our Bomber effort against Germany, which is of peculiar importance during these winter months. I have, on the contrary, asked for an increase in the Bomber effort, rising to 50 squadrons by the end of the year. Thereafter our bombing power will increase through the maturing of production. It may be that early in 1943 we shall have to damp down the Bomber offensive against Germany in order to meet the stress and peril of the U-boat war. I hope and trust not, but by then it will be possible at any rate to peg our bomber offensive at a higher level than at present. The issue is not one of principle, but of emphasis. At present, in spite of U-boat losses, the Bomber offensive should have first place in our air effort.[57]

This was a clear defeat for the Admiralty, but the situation at sea had deteriorated so much by the autumn of 1942 that Churchill found it difficult to adhere to his preferred strategy. The implementation of convoy in the western Atlantic had led to a sharp drop in shipping losses in American waters by midyear, but the U-boats had simply shifted their main effort back to the North Atlantic, where they continued to inflict heavy losses on Allied shipping. Coastal Command's shortage of very long-range (VLR) aircraft left a long stretch south of Greenland, known as the 'Air Gap', in which U-boats could operate with little threat of being detected or destroyed from the skies. For once, Admiral Dönitz was in an excellent position to capitalize on this weakness. In October 1942 he had nearly two hundred operational U-boats at his disposal, and new vessels were being built faster than the Allies could sink them. The mid-Atlantic convoy routes were soon infested with wolf packs. To make matters worse, Ultra intelligence had not been available to the Allies since February, and the evasive routing of convoys was becoming increasingly difficult. Over 619,000 tons of shipping were lost to U-boats alone in October, and in November the figure reached 729,000 tons.[58] Most alarmingly, nearly half the ships sunk during this period were sailing in convoy.[59]

Continued losses on this scale would eventually reduce British imports below the levels deemed essential. The amount of merchant shipping under British control had declined by nearly 650,000 tons between January and September 1942, and the gap between losses and gains was widening at an alarming rate. In the final three months of the year the net loss to British shipping would be an additional 708,000 tons.[60] At the end of October the Shipping Committee advised the War Cabinet that the import situation was becoming critical: even if stocks were run down by four million tons in the first half of 1943 as planned, Britain would still need the Americans to provide an additional 3.5 million tons of shipping during this period, and probably another 4 million over the latter part of the year.[61] The Anglo-American invasion of North Africa in November 1942—Operation 'Torch'—placed a heavy additional burden on British shipping and further exacerbated the import situation. But British diplomats in Washington had not yet been able to secure a firm commitment from the United States to meet Britain's minimum import requirements.[62] The need for a 'solemn compact' with the United States over shipping was becoming critical, and in early November the War Cabinet dispatched Lord Lyttelton to Washington to obtain, among other things, a greater allocation of merchant shipping and escort vessels for Britain.

Before his departure, Lyttelton questioned whether the Allies should be relying so heavily on replacing lost ships rather than on preserving them. 'To accept a loss of 6 or 7 hundred thousand tons a month of ships with their invaluable cargoes as a basis for Anglo-American war effort would be a most melancholy conclusion,' he asserted at the end of October. 'A ship which survives a year is worth two ordered to be built. A diminution in the losses at sea is far more valuable even than the increased volume of new construction.'[63] Churchill was evidently impressed by this argument. Writing to Roosevelt on the eve of Lyttelton's departure, he remarked that it was 'horrible to me that we should be budgeting jointly for a balance of shipping on the basis of 700,000 tons a month loss':

> True, it is not yet as bad as that. But the spectacle of all these splendid ships being built, sent to sea crammed with priceless food and munitions, and being sunk—three or four every day—torments me day and night. Not only does this attack cripple our war energies and threaten our life, but it arbitrarily limits the might of the United States coming into the struggle. The Oceans which were your shields, threaten to become your cage.

Following Lyttelton's arguments, he remarked that 'A ship not sunk in 1943 is worth two built for 1944'. But in the short term, replacement ships were essential. Churchill explained that Britain urgently needed its 'fair share' of new American construction, and reminded Roosevelt that an agreement had already been reached in principle that shipping should be allocated to a common pool for use according to strategic requirements. Britain, he warned, was fast approaching a position in which military commitments would have to be cut in order to maintain essential food supplies.[64]

The growing seriousness of the import situation and the uncertainty of American aid now threatened to undermine the priorities Churchill had laid down in July, and he had little choice but to give greater attention to the reduction of shipping losses. In the first week of November he resurrected the Battle of the Atlantic Committee, which had ceased to meet the previous year, in order to stimulate efforts to improve the situation at sea. This body, now called the Anti-U-Boat Warfare Committee, began meeting weekly, with Churchill in the chair, on 4 November. The decision to concentrate on the Battle of the Atlantic was long overdue, although it did not represent 'an abrupt about-face' on Churchill's part, as one historian has suggested.[65] The prime minister made it clear at the Committee's first meeting that Bomber Command's aircraft were off limits. Any additional air support for trade defence would have to be provided by American-built long-range aircraft deemed 'unsuitable for night-bombing'.[66] The Anti-U-Boat Warfare Committee was thus intended to operate within the strategic framework outlined by Churchill between July and October 1942. But the prime minister was otherwise open-minded when it came to countering the U-boat threat, and was prepared, if necessary, to begin putting fast merchant ships into convoy for added protection.

The Anti-U-Boat Committee immediately identified the mid-Atlantic 'air gap' as the most pressing problem. Two solutions were considered. The first was to increase the number of land-based aircraft capable of operating over this area. Britain produced no suitable aircraft with the necessary range, but the American-built B-24 Liberator offered a potential solution. Nine VLR Liberator Mark Is, with a cruising range of around 2500 miles, had been allocated to 120 Squadron of Coastal Command in mid-1941, but these were too few to close the air gap on their own. The Admiralty's attempts to increase these numbers had been largely unsuccessful, as the RAF, backed by Churchill, had insisted that new Liberators must go to Bomber Command. An additional eight Liberators were allocated to trade defence in April 1942, but these were Mark IIs and IIIs, which possessed a considerably shorter range than the Mark I. Coastal Command began receiving more of these models in July, but they were employed on the Biscay patrols and not modified to VLR standards for use in the mid-Atlantic, where they were more urgently needed.[67] At the first meeting of the Anti-U-Boat Warfare Committee, Joubert estimated that only 40 VLR aircraft were needed to close the 'air gap' for good. The critical decision was now taken to increase the supply of modified Liberators to Coastal Command.

The other means to provide air support to convoys in mid-ocean were sea-based aircraft. The Admiralty had already put in hand a construction program of small, rapidly built 'escort carriers' (CVEs), suitable for trade-protection duties, which would be ready around mid-1943. The gap before these arrived might have been filled by the four American-built CVEs already in service with the Royal Navy, but these were used instead to support Allied landings in North Africa. New CVEs being supplied under lend-lease would also be delayed because the Admiralty decided to modify the ships so they were capable of more than just anti-submarine work. The immediate needs of the Battle of the Atlantic were thus neglected in order, as Correlli Barnett remarks, to turn these vessels into 'poor man's fleet carriers'.[68]

To fill the gap, the Admiralty and the Ministry of War Transport had decided to modify some merchant ships to carry four or five Swordfish aircraft each.[69] These ships, designated Merchant Aircraft Carriers (MACs), represented an improvement on the catapult-equipped merchant ships of 1941. Their Swordfishes would be capable of destroying U-boats (unlike the CAM's Hurricanes, which were intended for use against German long-range aircraft), and they could retrieve and reuse their aircraft (again, unlike the catapult-launched Hurricanes, which had to be ditched at the end of their flight). Despite concerns that Britain could not afford to lose the services of these merchant ships during the time it would take for their conversion, the decision was taken at the Committee's first meeting to investigate the possibility of modifying twelve vessels.[70]

Additional concerns were later raised about the vulnerability of MACs to attack by U-boats when the Committee reassembled the following week, and priority was finally given to the development of land-based aircraft. This need would be met by modifying thirty-three Liberators then being used to patrol the Bay of Biscay.[71] To fill the gap in the Biscay offensive, the Air Ministry proposed that Coastal Command retain two squadrons of

Halifax bombers already on loan from Bomber Command, with the latter being compensated with new aircraft. Churchill was willing to accept this proposal, even though it might mean a delay in his plan to expand Bomber Command to fifty squadrons.[72] But he hoped to avoid this by persuading the Americans to allocate some of their bombers to the Bay offensive. He wrote to Roosevelt on 20 November explaining that he was 'most reluctant to reduce the weight of bombs we are able to drop on Germany'. If the United States could provide thirty Liberators equipped with the new centimetric ASV, he promised that they could be utilized immediately and would make a direct contribution to the American War Effort.[73]

Hopkins informed Churchill on 1 December that this request could not be met, but that twenty-one Liberators were being assigned to General Dwight Eisenhower, the Commander of US forces in the European theatre, and these might temporarily be made available for anti-U-boat operations.[74] Whatever disappointment this generated was probably balanced by the apparent success of Lyttelton's mission to Washington. Roosevelt informed Churchill on 30 November that the United States would further increase its shipbuilding program and that Britain could count on receiving enough tonnage to meet its minimum import requirements.[75] The British were aware, however, that the shipping they required might still not be forthcoming, and that even if the president's assurances were fulfilled, they could not alleviate the import situation in the short term. Planning was also complicated by a growing manpower crisis at home. By November 1942 Britain had reached the point where there were no additional sources of labour to draw on to meet the needs of both the armed services and the munitions industry.[76] Drastic cuts were unavoidable, but Churchill was now so alarmed by the situation in the Atlantic that the navy was not hit as hard as the other services. 'The greatest danger which now confronts us,' he informed the War Cabinet, 'is the U-boat peril':

> We must expect attack by increasingly large numbers and spread over wider areas. The highest priority must therefore be accorded to vessels and weapons for use against the U-boat. No construction of merchant shipbuilding below 1,100,000 tons or slowing down of repair work can be accepted.

But the decision to concentrate on the needs of the Battle of the Atlantic required the navy to make sacrifices in other areas. Churchill insisted that the construction of larger warships would have to be curtailed, and that some of Britain's older battleships might have to go into reserve.[77]

Churchill's growing concerns about an import crisis did not reduce his commitment to the bomber offensive. He reminded the War Cabinet in mid-December of the plan to raise Bomber Command to fifty squadrons by the end of the year, and insisted that the bombing campaign must still 'be regarded as our prime effort in the Air'. To reduce strain on the import situation, Churchill agreed that Britain would have to reduce its imports of raw materials and accept a reduction in munitions production. He also looked to economize on shipping in the Indian Ocean. The British victory at the Battle of el Alamein in October–November 1942 had greatly reduced the dangers in the Middle East, and Churchill believed that the British army could cut back substantially on reserves and supplies in this theatre. He was also prepared to shift some of the burden of shipping shortages from Britain to its colonies. 'There is no reason,' he wrote, 'why all parts of the British Empire should not feel the pinch in the same way as the Mother Country has done.'[78] In fact, some colonies would end up feeling the pinch rather worse. India was already experiencing food shortages at the end of 1942, but Lord Cherwell, determined to keep up Britain's stockpiles at any cost, was not concerned about the possible repercussions of a reduction in shipping in the region east of Suez. He informed the prime minister that halving the number of ships employed in the eastern theatres would allow an increase of around 3.5 million tons in imports to Britain during the first half of 1943. Churchill, with little thought for the consequences in the eastern empire, jumped at the opportunity: in early January 1943 he instructed that sailings to the Indian Ocean area should be limited to forty a month, less than half the current amount.[79]

At the Casablanca Conference, which opened on 14 January 1943, American service leaders accepted the British argument that the war against the U-boats must 'remain a first charge on our resources'.[80] To address this problem, the Combined Chiefs of Staff agreed that eighty VLR aircraft— twice the number Joubert had asked for in November—should be provided to fill the air gap. This resulted in more American-built Liberators being allocated to Britain, but delays in converting these aircraft to VLR standards in Britain prevented any immediate relief in the North Atlantic. By the beginning of February 1943, only two of the thirty-three Liberators designated for modification in November had become operational. Coastal Command did its best to plug the air gap in February, but with an average of only fourteen VLR aircraft available on any given day, the U-boats continued to enjoy considerable freedom in the mid-Atlantic.[81] The flow of

Ultra intelligence resumed in December 1942, but even this provided little relief. There were now so many U-boats operating in the mid-Atlantic that evasive routing was almost impossible. Convoy escorts began to find themselves outnumbered, as wolf packs now regularly totalled in the double digits, and sometimes exceeded twenty in number. A total of 359,000 tons of shipping were lost to U-boats during the course of February 1943. In March the rate increased sharply, ultimately reaching a total of 627,000 tons. Around 82 per cent of these losses were sailing in convoy.[82]

Heavy losses in the North Atlantic, combined with heavier than expected demands on shipping to support Allied operations in North Africa, increased anxiety in London over imports. Roosevelt's promise to ensure that Britain's minimum requirement of 27 million tons was met did not result in any immediate improvement in the shipping situation. The president had warned Churchill that American assistance was likely to be slow at first, but the British worried that current shortfalls would not be made up quickly enough to avert a crisis. Their concerns were well founded. The president had made his pledge without consulting his advisers, and the relevant military and civilian agencies were not even informed of this new commitment until January. Roosevelt probably hoped that his promise to the British could be fulfilled from increased shipbuilding output in 1943, but the American military continued to make huge demands on American shipping resources and had no interest in relinquishing vessels for Britain. On the contrary, American military planners pressed the British at the Casablanca Conference to make more of their shipping available for the build-up of American strength in Britain.[83] The War Shipping Administration (WSA), the civilian agency responsible for overseeing American shipping, virtually repudiated Roosevelt's promise on 18 January. The British were informed that the shipping figures promised by the president were being 'taken as estimate only, and not as commitment to allocate a precise amount of shipping'.[84]

Churchill was optimistic, however, that Roosevelt would ultimately make good on his commitment. At the end of December 1942, he informed the president that British imports between November 1942 and March 1943 would likely be at a level equivalent to only 17 million tons a year, far below Britain's minimum requirement. 'This,' he remarked, 'is indeed a grim prospect, and one which means for us dangerous and difficult decisions between military operations, food and raw materials.'[85] The Shipping Committee noted on 17 January that additional American assistance had so far amounted to around 100,000 deadweight tons (DWT). For Britain to meet its import target for the first half of 1943, American assistance would have to be maintained at between 500,000 and 600,000 DWT per month from March until June.[86] By early March it was clear that these figures would not be met. The COS concluded that only increased assistance from the United States would enable Britain to meet all the commitments undertaken at the Casablanca Conference, including Bolero, the invasion of Sicily, and the reconquest of Burma.

News that the British might have to scale back their military commitments was not well received in Washington, and US military authorities remained reluctant to divert merchant shipping away from their own needs.[87] To break the deadlock over shipping, Churchill finally appealed directly to Roosevelt. He instructed Cherwell to prepare a paper outlining Britain's difficulties for use by Eden, who was due to travel to Washington for meetings with the president. This document predicted that British stocks would be nearly 1 million tons below the 'the minimum safety level' by April. This would not immediately bring industry to a standstill, it stated, but 'we shall be living from hand to mouth. Any further drop and the wheels would cease to turn and rations would be jeopardised.'

The most frustrating aspect of the problem for British leaders was that while the shipping available to Britain continued to decline, American tonnage was steadily increasing. According to Cherwell, new construction in the United States had exceeded losses in 1942 by 2.7 million tons, but British shipping had declined by 2 million tons during the same period. 'Our tonnage constantly dwindles,' he complained, 'the American increases.' The problem, he concluded, is that Allied merchant shipping was still 'not treated as freely interchangeable and distributed according to needs'.[88] Eden was instructed 'to bring home to our friends in the United States that our minimum imports must be considered an absolute first charge on Allied shipping; that they are as vital to the war effort as supplies to the various theatres':

> North-West Africa has recently been receiving about three-quarters as much cargo shipping each month as the whole of the United Kingdom; one-eighth of the Allied fleet is not a great fraction to reserve for United Kingdom imports, to maintain a great munitions output, as well as 44 million civilians, and 3 millions in the Services. Our own [merchant] fleet is diminished by operating before and after America came into the war, in the most dangerous waters. We have undertaken arduous and essential operations encouraged by

the belief that we could rely on American shipbuilding to see us through. But we must know where we stand. We cannot live from hand to mouth on promises limited by provisos. This not only prevents planning and makes the use of ships less economical, it may, in the long run, even imperil good relations. Unless we can get a satisfactory long-term settlement, British ships will have to be withdrawn from their present military service even though our agreed operations are crippled or prejudiced.[89]

Churchill followed this up with a personal appeal to Roosevelt on 24 March warning that an increased provision of shipping from the United States had become an 'urgent and immediate necessity'. British imports in 1943 had so far 'been at such a low rate,' he observed, 'that even with increasing allocations already notified for forward months, it is going to be extremely difficult to make up leeway'.[90]

While Churchill attempted to avert an import crisis by securing additional American shipping, the Admiralty continued its efforts to obtain more aircraft for the war at sea. There was little more that could be done to hasten the conversion of Liberators to VLR standards, but long- and medium-range aircraft from Bomber Command could potentially be employed for patrols in the Bay of Biscay. Admiralty officials were naturally attracted to 'offensive' operations to hunt down the U-boats in their transit areas. The failure to obtain additional aircraft from the Americans for the Bay offensive in November 1942 had resulted in the diversion of twenty Halifax bombers, with Churchill's reluctant consent, to Coastal Command, but this did not produce significantly better results.[91] In March 1943 the Admiralty requested more aircraft to strengthen the Biscay patrols. Pound informed the Anti-U-Boat Warfare Committee at the end of the month that the concentration of U-boats in this area 'afforded us a great opportunity to initiate attacks', and that the provision of additional aircraft should be treated as 'an absolute necessity and not a luxury in the anti-U-boat campaign'. The Air Ministry was strongly opposed. Sinclair rehearsed the argument that the bomber offensive against Germany was still the 'most valuable contribution we could make to helping Russia', and both he and Portal expressed reasonable doubt as to whether more aircraft would produce better results in the Bay of Biscay. The CAS suggested that any increase in the offensive would have to wait for the arrival of new aircraft from the United States in June.[92]

Cherwell shared the Air Ministry's doubts about the value of additional aircraft for the Biscay patrols. Churchill had previously expressed his own reservations about the effectiveness of the Bay offensive, but he now proclaimed that even a slight increase in the number of U-boats destroyed in this region 'must be regarded as a very important objective'. The continuing heavy losses inflicted by U-boats that month, and the lingering uncertainty about the supply of American shipping, meant that Churchill was faced with the very real prospect of an import crisis and the collapse of Allied offensive plans for 1943. He was therefore unusually receptive to the Admiralty's latest plea for additional air support. The transfer of aircraft from Bomber Command, he noted, 'would mean a reduction in the bomber offensive at...an extremely critical moment'. But he concluded that 'something more could...be done to provide additional aircraft for the Bay patrols, without impairing the effectiveness of the bomber offensive'.[93]

Churchill's alarm about the Battle of the Atlantic is also evident in his change of heart over the bombing of U-boat bases in France, a measure he had previously opposed. Although the U-boats themselves were now well protected by reinforced concrete pens, the United States Eighth Air Force had undertaken ten precision raids on the main U-boat bases in the Bay of Biscay between October 1942 and early January 1943. These had no evident impact on the U-boat offensive, and the Admiralty began to press for larger-scale and less-discriminate area attacks on the bases and surrounding cities.[94] Churchill and the War Cabinet had hesitated to take this step when the idea was first broached, fearing heavy French civilian casualties, but on 11 January they accepted the Admiralty's argument—which turned out to be mistaken—that heavy and sustained bombing attacks could impede U-boat operations.[95]

This diversion of bombers was strongly opposed by Harris, who complained to the Anti-U-Boat Warfare Committee on 31 March that his forces would be much more effectively employed against U-boat construction yards and supporting factories in Germany. 'There was continuous confirmation,' he claimed, 'that the U-boat construction programme was being considerably interfered with by these attacks and if they were stopped he was certain that the output of U-boats per month would increase'. This was not true, although Harris was right to question the effectiveness of air attacks on the U-boat bases, which caused massive destruction to French cities but had a negligible impact on the German submarine offensive.[96] Churchill was nevertheless determined to give the bombers a chance. '[W]e must work to dislocate the U-boats as much as possible and check them coming in and out of their bases,' he informed the Committee.[97] Even Portal was sufficiently alarmed by the deteriorating situation at sea to suggest that Bomber Command could employ some of its less experienced bomber crews on these attacks, as the German defences would not be very strong. This compromise was approved by the Committee.[98]

While these measures were being debated in London, Roosevelt was finally persuaded that he would have to intervene to ensure that his promise to the British was upheld. In late March 1943 the president gave British imports top priority, despite protests from his military leaders.[99] He also threw his weight behind efforts to close the air gap. An inter-Allied (British-American-Canadian) conference in Washington in early March had resulted in a decision to transfer forty-eight American VLR aircraft to the Royal Canadian Air Force (RCAF) to operate over the air gap from the western side of the Atlantic.[100] The USAAF was reluctant to give up these aircraft, however, and Roosevelt had to intervene personally to ensure their release.[101] Not all the promised aircraft were transferred, but fifteen VLR Liberators were established in Newfoundland between April and June. The increased flow of American aircraft to Britain for trade defence, together with the gradual conversion of aircraft already under British control, allowed the Allies to operate forty-one VLR aircraft over the mid-Atlantic by mid-May, effectively closing the air gap.

By the end of May 1943 the turning point had been reached in the Battle of the Atlantic. The closing of the air gap and the ability to read U-boat communications made an important contribution to the defeat of Germany's attack on shipping, although other factors also contributed to the Allied victory. Probably the most important was the increasing number of escort vessels, which allowed the creation of special escort support groups capable of rapidly reinforcing convoys under attack in the mid-Atlantic. By May 1943 six such groups had been formed. Three of these included an escort carrier, which began to enter service in the North Atlantic in February. Additional air support was also being provided by the first converted merchant aircraft carrier.[102] These factors, in conjunction with steady improvements in the efficiency of aircraft and convoy escorts and their equipment, swung the tactical balance at sea decisively in favour of the Allies. Convoys were now able to fight their way through the mid-Atlantic wolf packs and inflict a heavy toll on their adversaries. The amount of shipping lost to U-boats during May dropped to 264,000 tons, while the number of U-boats destroyed rose to forty-one. Dönitz was unwilling to go on sustaining losses at such high levels. At the end of May he decided to reduce attacks on the critical North Atlantic convoys in order to seek out easier targets elsewhere and allow his U-boat fleet time to re-equip.

Allied shipping losses declined dramatically in the months that followed. Between 1 June and 18 September 1943 only fifteen ships were lost to U-boats in the entire North Atlantic, whereas thirty-one U-boats were destroyed.[103] When the Germans attempted to concentrate again on the Atlantic convoys later in the year, it quickly became clear that the U-boats could not breach the Allied defences. The sharp drop in shipping losses was accompanied by increased American shipbuilding efforts. The Allied victory was complete: Germany was never again able to threaten Britain's vital lifelines.

Churchill's role in the Battle of the Atlantic has generated less controversy than might be expected. Historians have sometimes noted his neglect of Coastal Command in favour of Bomber Command, but they have generally not censured him for unnecessarily prolonging the Battle of the Atlantic. In part this is because the 'bomber barons' of the RAF offer more satisfying villains. But it also stems from the tendency of naval historians to concentrate on the operational aspects of the campaign rather than its strategic direction. The Battle of the Atlantic is typically treated as a back-and-forth struggle between U-boats and naval escorts for dominance at sea, with little attention paid to the influence of decision-makers in London, and virtually none to what historian Kevin Smith calls the 'managerial' aspects of the campaign—the employment of organizational, industrial, and diplomatic measures to help ensure the safe and timely arrival of an adequate number of cargo ships in ports.[104]

The navy's response to the U-boat threat was to focus first on the destruction of enemy submarines, and secondly on the avoidance of merchant-ship losses. But Churchill had a wider range of tools at his disposal to ensure that Britain's essential import needs were being met. Shipping requirements could be reduced by additional rationing, the depletion of stocks, or improvements in Britain's transportation infrastructure; shipping tonnage could be increased by diverting industrial resources to Britain's own shipbuilding programme, by prising more ships out of the Americans, or the curtailment of overseas operational commitments. For Churchill, the Battle of the Atlantic was never just a question of achieving tactical superiority at sea—the challenge, as he saw it, was to ensure an adequate level of imports with the least possible commitment of resources to the Royal Navy and

Coastal Command. He was therefore prepared to suffer heavier-than-necessary shipping losses if this freed up resources for other critical purposes, whether the dispatch of ground forces to North Africa or, later, the strategic bombing campaign.

Churchill sought to strike a very delicate balance between the resources devoted to the Battle of the Atlantic and to strategic bombing. Bomber Command usually came out the winner, but Churchill, it must be noted, took a more realistic view of Britain's needs than those like Harris who advocated absolute priority for the strategic air offensive and ignored the potential consequences at sea. The full extent of Churchill's influence over the Atlantic campaign is seldom appreciated, however. Part of the reason lies in the influence of his Second World War memoirs, which created the impression that Churchill gave the defence of trade his constant attention and a consistently high priority. 'The only thing that ever really frightened me during the war,' he remarked in the second volume, 'was the U-boat peril.'[105] Frequently quoted statements like this give a misleading impression. Churchill clearly was alarmed by the losses the U-boats inflicted on British and Allied shipping, but his concerns were sporadic rather than constant, and were, to some extent, the result of his own actions. There were only two periods during which Churchill appears to have been truly alarmed by the German attack on trade: December 1940 to June 1941, and November 1942 to May 1943. In the months prior to the first crisis, Churchill showed little alarm at the damage being inflicted on British shipping. He was confident that Britain's large merchant fleet could absorb heavy losses in the short term, and was willing to run risks in this area so that he might take offensive action in the Middle East. The second crisis was also preceded by a long period of complacency towards the U-boat threat. Throughout most of 1942 Churchill was again willing to accept heavy losses at sea, this time because he believed that American industry could build enough new ships to avert a decisive defeat, and because he was determined to maximize Britain's offensive efforts—now embodied by the bomber offensive—by ruthlessly limiting the resources committed to defensive tasks.

Churchill's memoirs do not attempt to conceal the importance he attached to strategic bombing, but they do gloss over the fact that the grand strategy he championed during 1942 deliberately deprived the navy of much-needed air support, led to avoidable losses in merchant ships and their crews, and may have ultimately delayed victory in the Battle of the Atlantic. But while Churchill's decision to starve Coastal Command of aircraft during

1942 contributed to the navy's problems in a variety of ways, it was not necessarily the main cause of the delay in closing the critical 'air gap'. The long-range aircraft the Admiralty called for—and that Churchill repeatedly denied—in 1942 were earmarked for 'offensive' patrols in the Bay of Biscay. Churchill's reservations about the effectiveness of the Bay offensive were, in fact, entirely justified. These operations tied up considerable resources, but produced only meagre results. A post-war Naval Staff study noted that from June 1942 until the end of February 1943 this campaign involved an average of 3,500 patrol hours per month, but accounted for the destruction of only seven U-boats—less than one per month. This contrasted poorly with the aircraft employed on trade-protection duties in the northeast Atlantic, which had only one-third as much flying time but prevented countless attacks on convoys and destroyed seventeen U-boats.[106] Coastal Command did not need more aircraft in 1942 so much as it needed the right kind of aircraft. Churchill was responsible for keeping numbers down, but not for decisions over how these machines were employed. Neither Coastal Command nor the Admiralty pressed the prime minister for more VLR aircraft in mid-1942, and when they began to receive new Liberators later in the year, they were responsible for the decision not to modify them for use over the mid-Atlantic, where they would have been most effective. Some credit is due to Churchill, therefore: it was his Anti-U-Boat Warfare Committee that correctly identified the importance of VLR aircraft to the Battle of the Atlantic, and ensured that steps were taken to provide the relatively small numbers that were required.

IO

The Defeat of the Axis Powers

While shipping shortages acted as the main brake on Anglo-American operations against Germany in 1942, Allied strategy was also complicated by the demands of the war in the Pacific. Allied leaders had agreed in December 1941 that operations against Japan should be restricted as much as possible, but this was easier said than done. British and American resources had to be poured into this theatre just to stem the tide of the Japanese advance. In the early months of the Pacific war, the Japanese drove British, American, and Dutch forces out of China and South East Asia. By the spring of 1942 they were in a position to threaten both India and Australia. After the fall of Singapore in February, the British still had to worry about the Japanese army's advance through Burma towards the Indian frontier, and the possibility of a seaborne attack on India or raids on British shipping in the Indian Ocean, particularly the critical supply route from the Cape to Egypt (see Map 6). Churchill, who had briefly considered sending Force Z to join with the remnants of the United States fleet at Pearl Harbor, now rejected the idea of using British ships to reinforce the Americans in the Pacific. The devastation of the US Pacific Fleet had removed the main deterrent to the Japanese navy entering the Indian Ocean in force, and both Churchill and Pound believed a strong naval presence had to be built up to protect Britain's vital interests in the region.[1]

By the end of March 1942 the Commander-in-Chief of Britain's new eastern fleet, Admiral Sir James Somerville, had three aircraft carriers and five battleships at his disposal, but this force, which included the old light carrier *Hermes* and four of the antiquated 'R'-class battleships, was no match for the Japanese forces that entered the Indian Ocean in early April. A powerful fleet under Admiral Nagumo, who had commanded the air attack on Pearl Harbor, now devastated the ports at Colombo and Trincomalee in Ceylon and sank several British warships, including two cruisers and the carrier *Hermes*. At the same time, a smaller Japanese force raided shipping along the Indian coast, sinking over 112,000 tons of merchant shipping and bringing trade in the region to a standstill. Churchill appealed to Roosevelt in April for a demonstration by American forces in the Pacific to draw the Japanese away from the Indian Ocean, but no assistance was forthcoming.[2] Somerville's fleet was lucky to escape destruction. Fortunately for the British, the Japanese never intended to remain in the region. When they withdrew, Britain's weakness in the east had been clearly demonstrated. The R-class battleships were withdrawn for their own safety to Kilindini in Kenya, whence they could provide protection to convoys passing between Egypt and the Cape. The rest of the eastern fleet took refuge at Bombay, while efforts were made to strengthen the defences in Ceylon and to find modern capital ships to reinforce Somerville. Preparations were also set in motion for an amphibious operation—successfully launched the following month—to seize Diego Suarez in Madagascar from Vichy forces and ensure that the port could not be used by the Japanese.[3]

The heavy losses suffered by the Japanese navy in the Battles of the Coral Sea and Midway in May and June 1942 improved Britain's position in the east and made another Japanese incursion into the Indian Ocean unlikely. Pound was content to see Somerville maintain a defensive strategy in the region, and even Churchill was disinclined to run risks.[4] He rejected American requests in mid-1942 for a British naval strike to support an offensive by Douglas MacArthur in the South West Pacific theatre, noting that this would be a 'very dangerous action'. He confessed to Pound in July 'great anxieties' about committing the Eastern Fleet 'to waters where the Japanese shore-based aircraft may be found too powerful'.[5] The destruction of Force Z had clearly made an impression, but he was still unwilling to accept a purely defensive posture in the region. 'Admiral Somerville has two first-class carriers and [the battleship] Warspite,' Churchill complained to the First Sea Lord in July. 'He has been doing nothing for several months and we really cannot keep his fleet idle indefinitely.'[6] The Admiralty defended Somerville's actions, but this seems to have made little impression on the impatient prime minister. If Somerville did not intend to use his heavy ships more aggressively, Churchill wanted them moved to the eastern Mediterranean, where Britain's maritime communications were inadequately defended at the time by light craft and air power.[7] The Admiralty was against this measure, pointing out that the movement would be immediately known to the enemy and might entice the Japanese to send surface raiders back into the Indian Ocean. Churchill allowed the matter to drop, but made it clear to Pound that he did not accept his arguments for keeping capital ships in the Indian Ocean. 'Idle ships,' he admonished, 'are a reproach.'[8]

The US navy's victories in the Pacific and the heavy commitment of American resources to the Pacific theatre not only eased the pressure on Britain in the Indian Ocean; it also relieved Britain of the need to divert resources to the defence of Australia. This now became an American responsibility. For Churchill, the eastern theatre was soon reduced to a strategic backwater: his main preoccupation throughout 1942 was the struggle with Germany. The entry of the United States into the war and the continued resistance of the Soviet Union offered British leaders a wider range of strategic options in the European theatre than they had hitherto enjoyed. Churchill and the COS were already turning their attention to the problem of reintroducing the British army into Europe even before the attack on Pearl Harbor, and as opportunities to do so began to open up, the small-scale raids that had provided the original rationale for the Combined Operations organization receded in importance.

Only a handful of amphibious raids were mounted in the months after Louis Mountbatten replaced Keyes as the Director of Combined Operations. The first of these, launched in late December 1941 against targets in Norway, demonstrated that considerable progress was being made in coordinating operations by the three services. Hitler was sufficiently alarmed by these attacks to begin moving troops and heavy warships to Norway. Mountbatten's next two raids were conceived with specific purposes in mind. In February 1942 commandos seized new German radar equipment at Bruneval, and the following month a successful raid was launched to destroy the dry dock at St Nazaire, the only one along the French Atlantic coast large enough to accommodate the new German battleship *Tirpitz*.

Despite the success of these raids, Churchill was now interested in combined operations primarily as a means to establish large Anglo-American armies on the Continent. He was conscious, however, of Germany's far superior strength and the dangers inherent in launching amphibious attacks against strong defences. He and the British Chiefs of Staff preferred to adopt a peripheral strategy. Rather than striking in a theatre where the enemy possessed superior forces and could reinforce a threatened position quickly, British leaders wanted to exploit the mobility conferred by superior sea power to hit the Germans where they would be forced to fight at a disadvantage. This preference was increasingly the cause of tension with the

Americans, who favoured a more direct approach and resisted what they regarded as British efforts to disperse Allied resources in attacks on secondary objectives. In the spring of 1942 both parties could agree on the desirability of building up resources in Britain for a major Anglo-American invasion of France in 1943 (Operation Round-up), but the employment of Allied resources in 1942 proved to be a more contentious subject. American military leaders hoped to launch a major cross-Channel attack that year (Operation Sledgehammer). After giving this project careful consideration, Churchill and his advisers decided against any major landings on the Continent that did not aim to establish a permanent presence.[9] The most ambitious operation they were prepared to undertake at this time was a raid on Dieppe, which was expected to employ as many as seven thousand men. Churchill himself described this as a 'butcher and bolt' operation, and an assault of this size seems to have been in line with what he intended when he first used this expression in 1940. But he was unwilling to consider anything more ambitious unless the German army was nearing the point of collapse.

As the majority of forces available for Sledgehammer were British, their veto on a cross-Channel invasion in 1942 was decisive. Churchill's own preference for that year continued to be the invasion of French North Africa (Operation Gymnast), although he was also attracted to the possibility of a major landing in northern Norway (Operation Jupiter). This, he suggested, would allow the Allies 'to start to unroll Hitler's map of Europe from the top'.[10] Churchill frequently returned to this proposal, but operations in Norway held little appeal, now or later, to either British or American planners, who rightly saw it as a strategic dead end. Once it became clear that the British would not budge over Sledgehammer, General George Marshall, the US army's Chief of Staff, grudgingly agreed, under pressure from Roosevelt, to the option the US army found the least distasteful: an invasion of French North Africa, now re-christened Operation Torch. Marshal foresaw that North African operations would tie up so many Allied resources that Round-up would likely have to be abandoned. The British COS also acknowledged that this was the case, although Churchill was reluctant to do so, and stubbornly clung to plans for a 1943 cross-Channel invasion right up to the end of December 1942, by which time there was little room left for doubt that the second front would have to be delayed until 1944.[11]

American armies landed in Morocco and Algeria in November 1942 and quickly overcame French resistance, but despite the British victory at the

Battle of el Alamein the same month, German opposition in North Africa proved more formidable than expected, especially as Hitler unwisely decided to pour in reinforcements. With Round-up now an impossibility, the Allies were left to consider what to do in 1943 after the Axis had been driven from Africa. Churchill, supported by the British COS, always felt that Allied victories in Africa should be exploited in the Mediterranean theatre. 'I never meant the Anglo-American Army to be stuck in North Africa,' he wrote. 'It is a springboard and not a sofa.'[12] At the end of November 1942, while he still clung to hopes for Round-up in 1943, Churchill proposed that Allied forces assembled in North Africa should 'strike at the under-belly of the Axis in effective strength and in the shortest time'. The first objective would be the invasion of either Sardinia or Sicily, with the goal of intensifying Allied pressure on Italy.[13] The subsequent postponement of Round-up made it even more important in Churchill's eyes to strike a major blow in the Mediterranean that year. This did not hold much appeal for the Americans, however, who had seen the invasion of France pushed back once and did not want to become committed to additional operations in the Mediterranean, which might mean further delays. But the prospect of Allied land forces remaining idle in 1943 while the Soviet Union continued to engage the full weight of the German army was unthinkable. At the Casablanca Conference in January 1943, the Americans agreed to the invasion of Sicily.

The decision at Casablanca to make the defeat of the German attack on shipping the Allies' first priority was an acknowledgement that the timing and scale of future offensive operations would be determined by the availability of shipping. What was not yet fully appreciated was how far shortages of specialized landing craft for amphibious operations would also restrict the Allies' strategic options. This was especially true for the British, who were dependent on American generosity to make up their deficit in landing craft. One of the first casualties of Operation Torch in 1942 had been British plans for amphibious operations along the Arakan coast of Burma (Operation Anakim) (Map 7). In June 1942 Churchill hoped to regain the initiative in this theatre by launching a seaborne expedition that year to recapture Rangoon, to be followed by an attack on Bangkok.[14] These plans were overly ambitious and had to be abandoned the following month, but the demise of Round-up later that year appeared to free up shipping and landing craft for use in the Burma theatre in 1943. At the Casablanca Conference the British agreed to undertake amphibious operations in the Bay of Bengal later that year. This was soon ruled out, however, by the shipping

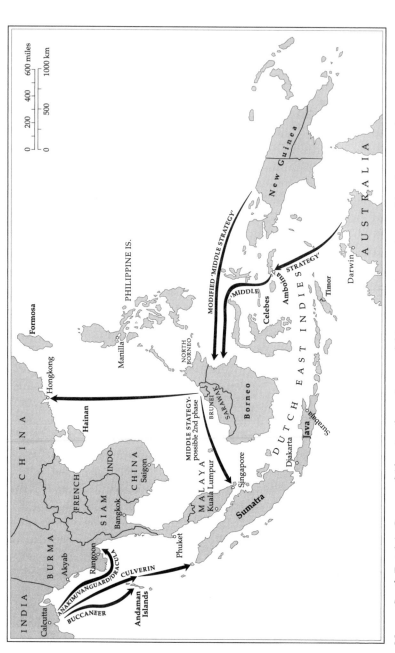

Map 7. South East Asia Command (showing the various amphibious operations under consideration, 1942–5)

crisis in early 1943.[15] By this time, Churchill's attention had shifted: if resources were available for this sort of amphibious operation, he preferred to launch it in the more important Mediterranean theatre. The capture of Sicily, he wrote in April 1943, was 'only a stepping stone'. No one, he informed the COS 'could rest content with such a modest and even petty objective for our armies in 1943'.[16]

Churchill hoped to follow the conquest of Sicily with an invasion of mainland Italy, which offered the prospect of knocking Italy out of the war and imposing heavy new commitments on the Germans in southern Europe. These opportunities appeared too good to pass up, and Churchill was determined to use the substantial forces already assembled in the Mediterranean for further operations in this region even if it meant delaying—or potentially even cancelling—the cross-Channel invasion of France (Operation Overlord), now scheduled for May 1944. 'I will in no circumstances allow the powerful British and British-controlled armies in the Mediterranean to stand idle,' he informed Field Marshal Smuts in July 1943. 'Not only must we take Rome and march as far north as possible in Italy, but our right hand must give succour to the Balkan patriots....I shall go to all lengths to procure the agreement of our Allies. If not, we have ample forces to act by ourselves.'[17]

In the event that the expansion of Allied commitments in the Mediterranean precluded Operation Overlord, Churchill suggested to the COS that 'Jupiter'—the invasion of Norway—offered a viable alternative.[18] None of this went over well with the Americans, however, who were determined not to allow Mediterranean sideshows to prevent a major cross-Channel attack in 1944. At the Quadrant Conference in Quebec in August 1943, they agreed to the invasion of Italy the following month, but this did not mean they shared British hopes for major strategic gains in this theatre: their main goal was to keep Allied land forces actively engaged with the enemy during the remaining months of 1943, and they made it clear that they would only support an Italian campaign to the extent that it did not detract from preparations for the invasion of France.

This compromise did not resolve the underlying divergence in British and American strategic views, and fresh tensions emerged soon after Anglo-American forces landed in Italy in early September. Churchill was eager to exploit Italy's surrender by securing control of the Dodecanese Islands in the Aegean, which he believed would allow Britain to project its power into the Balkans and, it was hoped, induce Turkey to join the war on the

Allied side. A shortage of resources prevented the British from mounting an expedition against these islands to coincide with the invasion of the Italian mainland, and on 9 September the Germans moved rapidly to seize control of Rhodes, the largest of the islands and strategically the most important. British troops occupied several other islands, including Cos and Leros, without difficulty the following week. Their ability to hold these positions depended, however, on eliminating the Germans' hold on Rhodes. Churchill succeeded in obtaining the release of some resources from Eisenhower, the Supreme Allied Commander in the Mediterranean, to support operations in the Aegean, but when the Germans took the island of Cos from the British on 4 October, it became clear that a more substantial effort would be required if Britain were to hold the other islands in the region *and* effect the capture of Rhodes.[19]

Churchill wanted some of the landing craft in the theatre used for the capture of Rhodes, but the Americans planned to send them all to Britain for Overlord. He complained to Roosevelt on 7 October that enough assault craft for a full division could be retained in the eastern Mediterranean for several weeks without jeopardizing the date for Overlord, but his appeals met with a flat refusal.[20] The president did not share Churchill's fascination with military matters, and he had little interest in taking part in the formulation of Allied strategy unless important political or diplomatic considerations were also involved. On the advice of the US Joint Chiefs of Staff, he now refused to allow any diversions that might prejudice Overlord or drain resources from the main campaign in Italy.[21] Churchill and the COS nevertheless supported the decision of the local British commander, General Maitland Wilson, to attempt to hold Leros and other islands with the forces already at his disposal. Another appeal to Roosevelt in early November succeeded in delaying the withdrawal of some landing craft from the Mediterranean theatre, but German command of the air made the British position in the Aegean untenable. Leros fell on 16 November, and other islands held by the British were soon captured or evacuated.

While this was a decisive and embarrassing defeat, Churchill did not give up his Aegean ambitions easily. He continued to hope for several weeks that if Turkey joined the Allied cause an amphibious operation might still be launched to capture Rhodes in early 1944.[22] But even if the Turks had been cooperative, there still would have been intense competition for the necessary landing craft. The British were being pressed by the Americans to undertake amphibious operations in the Indian Ocean; they had agreed to an assault on the south coast of France to coincide with Overlord; and commanders in Italy hoped to speed up the capture of Rome by landing Allied forces along the Italian coast behind German lines. The shortage of landing craft made it impossible to contemplate all these operations and still adhere to the agreed date for the invasion of France.

The British were frustrated by the Americans' insistence on the sanctity of Overlord, which severely limited the gains that might be made in the Mediterranean theatre. Churchill was also irritated that the Americans could veto operations they disliked by withholding landing craft, and even more by the 'absurd shortage' of specialized assault craft that created so many limitations on Anglo-American strategy in the first place. 'How it is,' he later complained to Marshall, 'that the plans of two great empires like Britain and the United States should be so much hamstrung and limited by a hundred or two of these particular vessels will never be understood by history.'[23]

To alleviate this problem, Churchill and the British Chiefs of Staff decided to postpone amphibious operations in the Indian Ocean. This promised to allow greater flexibility in the Mediterranean. In late December they agreed that the assault on Rhodes should be dropped in favour of an amphibious assault along the coast of Italy at Anzio (Operation Shingle). This, it was hoped, would break the deadlock that had emerged in the Italian campaign. With the support of Eisenhower, who believed the operation could be staged by 20 January 1944, Churchill appealed to Roosevelt in late December 1943 for another three weeks' delay in removing landing craft from the Mediterranean for Overlord. Having kept the vessels in the theatre this long, he maintained that it seemed:

> irrational to remove them for the very week when they can render decisive service. What also can be more dangerous than to let the Italian battle stagnate and fester on for another three months thus certainly gnawing into all preparations for and thus again affecting OVERLORD. We cannot afford to go forward [in France] leaving [this] vast half-finished job behind us.[24]

Roosevelt agreed to this delay, but the Anzio landings failed to produce a decisive breakthrough. Churchill continued nevertheless to believe that major strategic gains could still be made in the Mediterranean, and he was frustrated during the early months of 1944 by his ally's determination to deprive this theatre of resources in favour of Overlord. But American opposition was decisive. Troops and landing craft were diverted from the Mediterranean, leaving Allied commanders in Italy presiding over a stagnating campaign with no strategic goals other than to hold down German forces that might otherwise be employed in France.

Churchill's peripheral strategy in Europe began running out of steam just as new maritime opportunities were opening up in the war against Japan. Italy's defeat greatly eased the strain on Allied—and especially British—naval resources. As Churchill remarked in October 1943, 'we are in the position of a man who has suddenly succeeded to two fortunes, the Italian Fleet and the British Fleet which has been containing it so long'.[25] The challenge now was to decide where and how these additional resources should be employed against Japan. The Americans preferred to see the British launch an amphibious assault along the Arakan coast of Burma (Operation Anakim), an operation that would help to reopen the Burma Road and enable the Allies to increase their support for China. The British, however, had considerably less faith than the Americans in China's potential, either as an ally or as a base for operations against Japan's home islands, and they were resistant to the idea of waging a difficult and costly land campaign to reconquer Burma solely as a means to pass supplies to Chiang Kai-shek.

The cancellation of Anakim in April 1943 allowed the British to consider other options in this theatre. Churchill, whose enthusiasm for amphibious operations was undiminished, had been among the first to disparage the logic underlying Anakim, which he likened to 'a man attacking a hedgehog by pulling out its bristles one by one'.[26] If Britain had the resources to mount an amphibious assault to capture Rangoon, he preferred to use them for objectives of greater strategic value in the region. Prior to the Trident Conference in May 1943, Churchill outlined his views on eastern strategy for the Chiefs of Staff. 'Going into swampy jungles [in Burma] to fight the Japanese is like going into the water to fight a shark,' he maintained:

> It is better to entice him into a trap or catch him on a hook and then demolish him with axes after hauling him out on to dry land. How then to deceive and entrap the shark?
> The strategic virtues of 'Torch' compelled or induced the enemy to fight in a theatre most costly to himself....Can we not seize in [South East Asia] some strategic point or points which will force the Japanese to counter-attack under conditions favourable to us? For this purpose the naval command of the Bay of Bengal must be secured. It will next be necessary to establish effective shore-based air command radiating from the key point captured. Thus protected, comparatively small numbers of troops can maintain

themselves, unless the enemy brings a disproportionate army to bear, in which case our people can either be reinforced or withdrawn, according to our general plans.

He went on to explain that the 'seizure of even one key point intolerable to the enemy would impose upon him not only operations to recapture it, but a dispersion of his forces over the immense coastline exposed to the menace of sea-power'.[27]

Over the next few months Churchill became increasingly attracted to the idea of landing British and Indian forces either at Penang in Malaya or on the western tip of Sumatra (Operation Culverin) in the Dutch East Indies. At the Quadrant Conference in August 1943, he proposed to the COS that such an operation could be launched in 1944 in conjunction with a limited land campaign in northern Burma. He was not in favour, however, of attempting to retake Singapore, which would entail, he warned, 'the painful process of labouring through jungles and hundreds of miles of difficult country, apart from the sea distances, in order to attack the enemy at his strongest point'. Singapore, he predicted, would more likely be 'recovered at the peace table than during the war'.[28]

The difficulty with Culverin, the COS pointed out, was that Britain did not have the resources to carry it out in 1944 without substantial American support. By October service planners were examining less ambitious plans to capture the Andaman Islands (Operation Buccaneer). But this threatened to tie up scarce landing craft that Churchill now wanted for the Mediterranean, and his commitment to the operation was never strong. 'The capture of the Andamans,' he remarked in November 1943, 'is a trivial prize compared with Rhodes.'[29] His support for Buccaneer collapsed the following month when he discovered how costly the operation would be. Planners working for Mountbatten, who had become the Supreme Allied Commander in the Allies' new South East Asia Command (SEAC), estimated that fifty thousand British and Indian troops would be required to capture the islands. Churchill was appalled by the proposed scale of the attack, which seemed entirely out of proportion to the approximately five thousand Japanese troops on the islands. 'Nothing is more futile,' he lectured the COS in early December, 'than to try to win battles by crowding mobs of low-grade soldiery up against an enemy armed with modern weapons.' If that many troops were available, it would be better, he suggested, to 'pick the 10,000 bravest for the assault and let the other 40,000 be put to work on the roads'.[30]

Buccaneer was cancelled the following month and the landing craft allocated to it were transferred to the Mediterranean. The British were also able to persuade Roosevelt to renounce the pledge he made to Chiang Kai-shek at the Cairo Conference that a substantial amphibious operation would be launched in the Bay of Bengal early in 1944. This cleared the way for the assault on Anzio, but Churchill was not willing to give up on the idea of capturing the northern tip of Sumatra. He informed Mountbatten privately in January 1944 that his first priority should be to launch Culverin later that year after the monsoon season had ended. 'This,' he explained, 'I am determined to press to the very utmost, day in day out':

> I am counting on you to present good solid plans laid out for this in October or November [1944]. I trust by then there will be plenty of landing craft and seaborne aircraft. Here is your great chance. Do not allow anything to take your eye off it. Here alone will you have opportunity of opening new fields in the world war, and here alone in the amphibious sphere will you have my aid.[31]

When it became clear that Mountbatten was also enthusiastic about Culverin, Churchill informed the COS that he was 'more convinced than ever' that this was 'incomparably the most effective operation open in 1944 in this theatre and I am resolved to do everything in my power to render it possible in October'.[32]

The COS, however, were already committed to a different course. In November 1943 they had agreed with their American counterparts to dispatch a large British naval force to the Pacific to operate with the Americans, using Australia as a base. British and Indian land forces were to remain concentrated in the South East Asia theatre, but after the defeat of Germany four additional British divisions would be dispatched to Australia for operations in the Pacific.[33] These commitments had, rather surprisingly, escaped Churchill's notice when they were formalized by the Anglo-American Combined Chiefs of Staff at the Cairo Conference. When they were brought to his attention in January 1944 he immediately objected, fearing that the dispatch of a fleet to Australia would preclude amphibious operations against Sumatra. He explained to the COS on the 24th that he had no objection to sending a modest British squadron to join with the US fleet in the Pacific, but only as long as it did not interfere with Culverin. The large British forces already assembled in the SEAC theatre could not be left idle for the entire year, he argued, and no other operation offered the same opportunity to divert Japanese forces from other theatres and seize valuable bases for future offensive operations.[34]

By February, however, it was clear to the COS that Britain did not have the resources to launch Culverin in 1944 *and* dispatch a fleet to the Pacific.[35] The stage was therefore set for a heated debate between Churchill and his military advisers when Mountbatten's Chief of Staff, General Albert Wedemeyer, arrived in London in mid-February to gather support for SEAC's plans for operations in Sumatra. Wedemeyer met with the chiefs of staff on 14 February, but they continued to harbour doubts that Culverin would contribute much to the ultimate defeat of Japan or provide an outlet for the surplus naval forces now at Britain's disposal. It was also clear by this time that Culverin would, as the Joint Planners noted, 'draw off from the Pacific more of our forces...than those of the enemy, and for a much longer period'.[36] Churchill, however, warmly supported the SEAC proposals. Culverin, he insisted, would draw Japanese forces into South East Asia and was therefore the best means available to assist the American advance in the Pacific. He also doubted whether Admiral King actually wanted British naval forces to operate in the Pacific, a view supported by Wedemeyer.[37]

The movement of the main Japanese fleet to Singapore in late February provided Churchill with additional ammunition for Culverin. Britain could no longer count on maintaining command of the Bay of Bengal, and he argued that it would be unwise to leave the Indian Ocean at the mercy of a powerful enemy fleet by sending British ships to the Pacific. At the same time, Churchill began to emphasize the political arguments for his strategy. Employing the Royal Navy as a 'subsidiary force under the Americans in the Pacific' would threaten Britain's claims to Malaya and Singapore after the war, he asserted:

> If the Japanese should withdraw from them or make peace as the result of the main American thrust, the United States Government would after the victory feel greatly strengthened in its view that all possessions in the East Indian Archipelago should be placed under some international body upon which the United States would exercise a decisive control. They would feel with conviction: 'We won the victory and liberated these places, and we must have the dominating say in their future and derive full profit from their produce, especially oil.'[38]

Political considerations also weighed heavily in the calculations of Churchill's ministerial colleagues. Eden, for example, warned that leaving colonial possessions under Japanese occupation would increase the difficulties in re-establishing British control after the war. A campaign to liberate these areas, on the other hand, would 'have immediate psychological and political effects which in themselves will contribute materially to the defeat of Japan. It will also do more than the Pacific strategy to discredit the Japanese Army, which is vitally important.'[39]

To bolster his position, Churchill insisted on determining whether the United States actually wanted a British fleet in the Pacific. He wrote to Roosevelt on 10 March asking whether there was any specific operation planned by the Americans in the Pacific in 1945 that would be hindered or prevented by the absence of a British fleet.[40] He made no attempt to conceal from the president his own preference for keeping British resources in the Indian Ocean in order to develop an amphibious strategy there. Roosevelt promptly assured Churchill that there was, in fact, no urgent need of British naval reinforcements in the Pacific.[41] But this did not necessarily translate into American support for Culverin. On the contrary, Roosevelt had urged the prime minister several weeks earlier to abandon the idea of operations in Sumatra or Malaya and to concentrate British resources for 'an all-out drive into Upper Burma so that we can build up our air strength in China and ensure the essential support for our westward advance to the Formosa-China-Luzon area'.[42]

This did little to deter Churchill, who also sought to undermine his military advisers by inviting the Minister of War Transport to report on the difficulties that would be encountered in lengthening British lines of communications by operating in the Pacific from Australian bases. The COS, however, remained firmly opposed to Culverin. This operation could not be mounted, they argued, until additional resources had been released by the defeat of Germany. The land forces already allocated to SEAC would be fully employed in Burma and India, and any surplus could be used in South West Asia. Nor were they swayed by political considerations. The United States would get most of the credit for the defeat of Japan no matter where British forces were deployed. The advantage of a Pacific strategy, in their view, was that it offered the best means to hasten the defeat of Japan by strengthening the main and decisive thrust in the central Pacific. They were confident, moreover, that the movement of the Japanese fleet to Singapore was a purely defensive measure, and that a major incursion into the Indian Ocean was unlikely.[43]

Ismay warned Churchill on 4 March that the COS were unlikely to give way on this question and that their resignations could not be ruled out. 'A breach of this kind,' he warned, 'undesirable at any time, would be little short of catastrophic at the present juncture', with Overlord just two months away.[44] A special meeting was therefore held four days later to resolve the differences between the politicians and the service chiefs over eastern strategy. Churchill ensured that several Cabinet ministers, including Attlee and Eden, were there to support him. It was not an easy meeting. Brooke recorded in his diary that Admiral Cunningham was 'so wild with rage that he hardly dared let himself speak!! I therefore had to do most of the arguing and for 2½ hours . . . I went at it hard arguing with the PM and 4 Cabinet Ministers. The arguments of the latter were so puerile that it made me ashamed to think they were Cabinet Ministers!'[45] By the end of the meeting Brooke believed he had made some progress in convincing his chief that capturing the tip of Sumatra would do little to further the Allies' long-term strategic goals, but it was also clear that shipping shortages and logistical difficulties posed a serious obstacle to the Pacific strategy. Churchill did make a significant concession in agreeing to launch an investigation into the capacity of Australian bases and their ability to sustain British naval operations in the Pacific. But the minutes of the meeting record that, in the meantime, preparations were to continue for launching Culverin in the spring of 1945 from bases in India.[46]

Less than two weeks later, Churchill, now armed with Roosevelt's assurance that British naval forces were not essential to American plans in the Pacific, informed each of the Chiefs of Staff individually that since he and the ministers on the Defence Committee were in favour of the Bay of Bengal strategy, he was ruling, in his capacity as prime minister and Minister of Defence, that British naval forces should be built up in the Indian Ocean and preparations were to begin for amphibious operations in the Bay of Bengal. To counter Brooke's objection that he had given insufficient attention to developing a long-term strategy for the defeat of Japan, Churchill maintained that Britain's ultimate objective in the region was the reconquest of Singapore. The only concession he would make to the service chiefs was that a mission would still be dispatched to examine bases and facilities in Australia.[47] To expedite preparations for Culverin, Churchill attempted to bypass the Chiefs of Staff by directing the work of the Joint Planning Staff himself.[48]

The COS remained unconvinced of the merits of Culverin, and were doubtful that Britain would have the resources to mount major amphibious operations in the Indian Ocean even after the defeat of Germany.[49] They were also faced, however, with growing evidence that Admiral King viewed a British fleet in the Pacific as 'more of an embarrassment than a help'.[50]

They therefore began in early April to explore a new option: an Anglo-Australian advance from Australian bases through the South West Pacific towards Borneo. This line of attack, soon dubbed 'the Middle Strategy' (see Map 7), offered the British an opportunity to run, as Brooke put it, 'an entirely British Imperial campaign, instead of just furnishing reinforcements for American operations'.[51] The historian H. P. Willmott suggests that the plan may have been advanced less on its merits than as a means to induce Churchill to abandon his commitment to the Indian Ocean.[52] In any event, Cunningham reported on 8 April that Churchill was 'favourably inclined' towards this proposal, since it did not involve the 'long haul round Australia' that he disliked in the Pacific strategy.[53] But within a few weeks the prime minister had returned to Culverin as the best means to use the large forces in SEAC to strike at the Japanese before the defeat of Germany.[54] The COS nevertheless began to flesh out the details of the new strategy. By mid-May they were agreed that Anglo-Australian forces should prepare to launch the Middle Strategy in late 1944 or early 1945 with an assault on the island of Amboina in the Dutch East Indies. An alternative plan also emerged, known as the 'Modified Middle Strategy', for an assault on Borneo using bases in New Guinea and eastern Australia.

To make the Middle Strategy more appealing to Churchill, Brooke claimed that this advance would lead to the recapture of Borneo, which would open the possibility of striking towards either Singapore or Hong Kong.[55] The COS had some success in persuading Eden and Attlee to support their proposals, but Churchill, even while accepting that resources were not available for Culverin, remained sceptical. The Americans were also unenthusiastic: the rapid progress of their operations in the Pacific meant that the proposed Middle Strategy would no longer contribute anything to the main offensive against Japan. By late June, Churchill was again determined to keep Britain's efforts focused on the Indian Ocean. As before, he relied on political considerations to justify his position. 'The political importance of making some effort to recover British territory must not be underrated,' he informed Ismay on 24 June:

> Rangoon and Singapore are great names in the British eastern world, and it will be an ill day for Britain if the War ends without our having made a stroke to regain these places and having let the whole Malay Peninsula down until it is eventually evacuated as the result of an American-dictated peace at Tokio, even though there is a very small British force in the American Armies.[56]

There was no reason, he suggested to the COS in July, why Britain could not send some of its surplus naval forces to the Pacific to work with the Americans while concentrating the bulk of its resources for operations in the Bay of Bengal.[57]

After eastern strategy was debated at length on 14 July, Cunningham complained in his diary that the politicians' 'attitude of mind about this question is astonishing':

> They are obviously afraid of the Americans laying down the law as to what is to happen when Japan is defeated to the various islands, ports and other territories. This appears to be quite likely if the Americans are left to fight the Japanese by themselves. But they [i.e. Churchill and his political colleagues] will not lift a finger to get a force into the Pacific; they prefer to hang about outside and recapture our own rubber trees.[58]

To the consternation of the COS, Churchill refused to make a final decision on eastern strategy until Mountbatten could be brought back to London for further consultation. As a result, the matter was allowed to drift for another three weeks. During this time, Churchill grudgingly accepted that the shortage of landing craft and other resources for this theatre might in fact rule out large-scale amphibious operations against Sumatra until late 1945. He informed the COS on 24 July that if Culverin could not be launched, he was willing—'with very great sorrow'—to support plans that had been drawn up by SEAC for the recapture of Rangoon, 'which at least gives us back one of our own capital cities'. He also conceded that if this less ambitious operation were accepted in the Indian Ocean, a British fleet might be detached for operations on MacArthur's flank.[59]

These concessions brought the two sides closer to an agreement, but important differences still had to be overcome. The debate resumed with the arrival of Mountbatten and his deputy in London in August. On the 8th they outlined to the COS, Churchill, and several members of the War Cabinet two alternatives for operation in the SEAC theatre. The first involved a land offensive into Upper Burma, something Churchill had made clear he would not contemplate under any circumstances. The COS were also unenthusiastic about this idea, and support quickly coalesced around the second proposal, an amphibious assault to capture Rangoon (Operation Vanguard). But opinion soon diverged over the rationale for this operation. Brooke saw Vanguard as the prelude to operations to clear the rest of Burma of Japanese troops, while Churchill regarded it as the first step in an advance eastward, towards Bangkok, the Kra Isthmus, or the Malay Peninsula. After capturing

Rangoon, the prime minister insisted that Japanese forces remaining in Burma should be left 'to rot away'. The best course, he maintained, was 'to reduce to the smallest possible limits British forces operating in the swamps of Burma'.[60]

When discussion resumed later that day, Churchill continued to argue that the capture of Rangoon should be followed by some version of Culverin. He conceded, however, that without American support, this operation could not be contemplated until after Germany's collapse.[61] But Brooke refused to give way. He did not believe the Japanese could simply be bypassed, as Churchill advocated, and it was clear that the Americans, who preferred the British to concentrate on operations in northern Burma, would be unlikely to support Culverin. The employment of British naval resources was more easily resolved. A large naval presence was no longer required in the Bay of Bengal, and Brooke recommended that surplus naval forces be combined with the Australian army to create a British Empire Task Force in the South West Pacific under MacArthur.[62] Eden, on the other hand, suggested that if Australian forces were available, they would be better employed in Burma. British resources released by the defeat of Germany could then be used later for an assault on Malaya or Sumatra. It was preferable, in his view, to 'recapture our own territory than to play a minor role in the Pacific'. Churchill, however, came out in favour of using surplus naval strength to bolster the American offensive in the central Pacific. He now proposed that Britain should offer naval assistance to the United States on the largest scale possible. If a British fleet was not wanted or needed for the main thrust, he recommended that it should 'participate in the recapture of some of those areas where we had been so humiliated'. The important thing, he maintained, was to put the British offer on record. 'We should then have a valuable argument,' he stated, 'which might be produced if we were at any time accused of not fulfilling our part as an Ally in the Pacific operations.'[63]

By the end of the day all parties agreed that Rangoon would be the first objective in the South East Asia theatre. But no consensus could be reached on the question of where to strike next, and the issue was simply left unresolved.[64] These decisions were confirmed the next day. Churchill did not conceal that he intended to press for Culverin after Rangoon was taken, and Brooke was equally determined on further operations to eliminate the Japanese presence in Burma.[65] Cunningham also had doubts about the sincerity of Churchill's commitment to sending a British fleet to the Pacific, predicting in his diary that the prime minister would be 'bitterly disappointed' if the Americans accepted the offer.[66] But even Brooke conceded that the compromise, though 'not ideal', had much in its favour.[67] The COS had, in fact, obtained most of what they had been after since the beginning of the year: a major deployment of British naval forces to the Pacific and an immediate commitment of SEAC resources to the campaign in Burma. In return, Churchill had succeeded in keeping open the option for some version of Culverin at a later date—a hollow victory, given that the chronic shortage of resources for this theatre and the early end of the Pacific war ultimately precluded this option being exercised. In any event, it was agreed on 9 August that plans would continue for the recapture of Malaya and for the transfer of troops from the European theatre as soon as possible after Germany's defeat. In the event of an early German collapse, provision was also made for the possibility that Culverin might supercede Vanguard.[68]

The role assigned to the British fleet was ultimately decided by the Americans. Churchill's offer of a large and balanced naval force to participate in the main operations against Japan was accepted by Roosevelt at the first plenary meeting of the second Quebec Conference on 13 September 1944. The British Pacific Fleet was formed in the Indian Ocean two months later. This force, commanded by Admiral Sir Bruce Fraser, arrived at Sydney, its main base, in February 1945, and subsequently cooperated with the USN in operations against Japan. The Americans also agreed to British plans for Burma, although by this time Churchill and his military advisers had developed doubts as to the feasibility of an operation (now renamed Dracula) to recapture Rangoon in March 1945. With German resistance showing no sign of collapsing in 1944, the British had to accept that they could not afford to transfer troops or landing craft from Europe in time to meet their timetable. Nor were the Americans willing to make good British deficiencies. On 2 October, Churchill and the COS admitted that Dracula would have to be delayed until November 1945. In the meantime, Mountbatten was instructed to concentrate on operations in northern Burma.[69]

Thus, by October 1944 the main outlines of British naval strategy for the war against Japan were settled. Despite Churchill's best efforts, Britain was committed to what he had earlier termed the 'laborious reconquest of Burma, swamp by swamp'. His plans for amphibious operations in South East Asia had grown out of an instinctive desire to avoid just such a costly and protracted campaign. Once the Japanese advance on India had been decisively halted and Japanese naval power worn down by the USN in the

Pacific, Churchill was eager to exploit the opportunities sea power offered to recover lost territories and restore British prestige in this region. This would utilize British naval resources and Anglo-Indian land forces already in the theatre. But specialized landing craft and other necessary resources were never available to allow such ambitious plans in a subsidiary theatre. In the end, Churchill had to accept that, for the immediate future, at least, he would have to abandon the idea of an amphibious campaign across the Bay of Bengal culminating in the recapture of Singapore. A land campaign in Burma was the only realistic use for the armies already in the region, and a naval commitment to the Pacific campaign offered the only means to employ Britain's surplus naval power in a meaningful way and achieve worthwhile, though less tangible, political goals.

While the navy had for the last two decades justified its most extravagant shipbuilding programs on the basis of its needs in a Far Eastern conflict, the extension of the war to the Pacific in December 1941 did not help it to prise additional ships from the government. Until late 1944, Britain's ship-building resources were allocated entirely according to the needs of the European war. Churchill continued to insist, as he had in 1939–41, that priority must be given to the warships that could be completed most rapidly. This preference, and the unrelenting demand for convoy escorts, landing craft, and other light ships, ensured that new construction was skewed towards smaller vessels for the duration of the war. Britain's battleship programme was the main casualty of these priorities. The last ships of the King George V class, *Anson* and *Howe*, were completed in 1942, but the only other battleship under construction at this time was *Vanguard*, which had been authorized in 1940. The four battleships of the projected Lion class were unlikely to be ready in time to take part in the current war, and in 1942 even the Admiralty accepted that there was no urgency in proceeding with these vessels. The new construction programme for that year included provision for gun mountings and guns for *Lion*, but no other work on this ship was to be done until the following year.

There was a stronger case for beginning new aircraft carriers. By mid-war these ships had supplanted the battleship as the most powerful warships afloat. The problem facing the navy was that the most desirable vessel of this class—the large armoured 'fleet' carrier—took nearly as long to build as a battleship. Britain had two such ships under construction in 1942, and the Admiralty proposed to include another two in that year's program, even though it was not certain they would be finished before the end of the war. To bolster the fleet's carrier strength as soon as possible, the Admiralty proposed to begin four smaller ('intermediate') fleet carriers, which could be finished more rapidly but were still capable of operating with the fleet.[70] In September 1942 the need for aircraft carriers was so pressing that the War Cabinet agreed to include an additional nine intermediate carriers in the 1942 program.[71]

The battleship *Lion* was suspended again in 1943, but the Admiralty's appetite for aircraft carriers was undiminished. Its new construction programme for that year included four fleet carriers and eight intermediate carriers.[72] This was an ambitious programme, and naval leaders could not conceal that they were now beginning to look beyond the defeat of Japan to the needs of the post-war period. Alexander, however, had reservations about proceeding with the new batch of intermediate carriers, which were more elaborate than their predecessors and would require longer to build. He informed Churchill in October 1943 that since the first of the new carriers could not enter service until 1947, he could endorse only two of the eight ships his advisers wanted. This would allow Britain to shift resources to building liners, which would be useful, he observed, 'not merely for post war commercial purposes but also for the large trooping movements that will be necessary both for the war against Japan and for the final demobilisation'.[73]

Churchill was developing doubts of his own about the navy's long-term construction projects. He warned Alexander later that month that with the German and Italian fleets both 'practically extinct', the navy's future programs would 'be subjected to a very strict scrutiny'.[74] His main concern at this time was manpower. With Britain's population now fully mobilized there was no possibility of meeting all the demands of the armed services and industry in 1944.[75] Looking to make cuts, Churchill wrote to the First Lord on 1 November questioning the Admiralty's increased manpower claims for the coming year. Britain had defeated the U-boat threat, he observed; the *Tirpitz* had been neutralized; the Italian fleet had surrendered; France had joined the Allies; and the United States possessed a 2:1 advantage over Japan in warships. He therefore asserted that the navy should be considering ways to reduce its manpower requirements, if necessary by laying up older vessels. 'The Admiralty,' in his view, 'would not render the best service to the country at this [manpower] crisis if it kept in commission a single vessel not needed against the enemy.'[76]

A few days later Churchill proposed to allocate only enough new manpower to the navy in 1944 to maintain its current strength, although a small addition to its numbers was sanctioned later that month.[77] The programme of intermediate carriers was not settled until the end of January 1944. Churchill approved a compromise between Alexander and the Sea Lords to retain four of the eight ships authorized the previous year, although he stipulated that the first two vessels should be given priority. By this time, however, it was becoming clear that the heavy ships in the navy's 1943 programme were falling far behind schedule. The main reason was the continuing demand for smaller vessels. Victory over the U-boats in 1943 substantially decreased the need for new escorts, but this coincided with a sharp surge in demand for small landing craft and larger landing ships for amphibious operations. In December the War Cabinet approved a crash programme designed to produce an additional eighty landing ships by April 1945.[78] This new programme would inevitably cause further delays in carrier construction.

The Admiralty began considering the implications for its 1944 new construction programme early in the New Year. Post-war needs were an increasingly important consideration, and attention now swung from aircraft carriers back to battleships.[79] Naval leaders no longer had any doubts as to the vital importance of the aircraft carrier, but they were equally convinced that these vessels, which could not operate their aircraft in all weathers or at night, required the protection of ships mounting guns big enough to neutralize the surface ships of an enemy fleet. 'Battleships and Aircraft Carriers are complementary,' declared one Admiralty memorandum, 'and the enthusiast for one arm or the other must not be allowed to upset the balance.'[80] The slow pace of battleship construction since 1940 meant that Britain would emerge from the war with a relatively modest force of seven modern or modernized battleships. Naval leaders calculated that twelve battleships were required for a balanced post-war fleet, and they proposed to use two of the building slips previously allocated to fleet carriers for *Lion* and *Temeraire*, the first of the new 16-inch-gun battleships. Work would begin on the gun turrets in 1944, and the ships themselves would be included in the 1945 programme.[81]

The Admiralty was relieved to find that Churchill was sympathetic to these proposals. He had told Alexander in January that he wanted to see all four Lion-class battleships completed.[82] When the Admiralty's new construction programme for 1944 came before the War Cabinet in May,

Churchill expressed his confidence that 'the sovereignty of the battleship was still maintained':

> The submarine was not regarded as a real risk to a battleship with an appropriate escort. No doubt the battleship was exposed to great risks if within the range of shore-based air forces. But in the big open spaces, if attended by an aircraft carrier, the battleship still held its sway.

The only dissenting voices belonged to Sinclair and Cherwell, who maintained that air power would soon make the battleship obsolete. Churchill maintained, however, that he 'saw no reason to lose faith in the battleship at the present time,' although he conceded that 'the position would have to be reviewed in the light of experience'.[83] Admiral Cunningham, for once, was delighted with the prime minister's intervention. 'The PM carried the whole thing through on his own,' he recorded in his diary. 'He is very sound on the battleship question and had evidently been reading the Staff memorandum on the post-war fleet.'[84]

The future of the battleship remained a contentious subject, although not, at this stage of the war, a particularly pressing one. Cherwell complained to Churchill in July 1944 that 'The laws of nature put the battleship at such a disadvantage compared with the aircraft that I fear it will not survive in the evolutionary race.'[85] He prepared a lengthy memorandum outlining his arguments, but Churchill was presumably not eager to reopen this debate before a final decision was necessary, and the document was not circulated to the War Cabinet until December.[86] Having already secured Churchill's support, Admiralty officials were not in any hurry to reopen the debate either. They were clearly annoyed by Cherwell's intervention, but they did not respond to his challenge until July 1945, shortly after submitting their proposed new construction programme for that year. The Admiralty's case rested on the belief that aircraft carriers still required the protection of powerful ships capable of operating in any weather and light conditions, and that new designs would evolve to meet new threats. 'The "battleship" of the future will bear little resemblance to the battleship as we know it now,' the Admiralty predicted. If, for example, 'the rocket weapon replaces the gun it may be possible to build a smaller ship which will still fulfil the essential requirement of the "battleship"—i.e., the ability under all conditions to seek out and destroy the most powerful ships of the enemy.'[87] The Admiralty now asked for permission to lay down *Lion* and *Temeraire* as soon as possible, and hopefully in 1946, which would allow for their completion by 1952. *Conqueror* and *Thunderer*, the final two ships of the class, would continue to be deferred.[88]

The 1945 new construction programme attempted to balance the immediate operational requirements for the Far East with the navy's plans to begin building a modern and balanced post-war fleet, but the Admiralty recognized that short-term needs must prevail. In late 1944, with Germany's defeat seemingly imminent, priority was given to ships that could be in service in time to take part in the war against Japan, which at the time was expected to last until the end of 1946.[89] The proposed new construction programme was therefore a modest affair. A start would be made on the two new battleships, but shipyards would continue to concentrate on landing ships and various small craft. No addition would be made to Britain's carrier programme, and some of the intermediate carriers approved in earlier years were now deferred.[90]

The Admiralty plans for the post-war period were nevertheless ambitious, if not very realistic. In May 1944 the Board envisioned a peacetime fleet including twelve battleships, twenty-four aircraft carriers, fifty cruisers, and large numbers of smaller warships and support vessels. It was calculated that 220,000 men would be required from the empire for this fleet, of which 170,000 would be provided by Great Britain.[91] Churchill, however, was not inclined to look this far ahead. In January 1944 he had speculated that the post-war fleet would include just ten battleships, including the four Lion-class ones.[92] But his own preference was to defer post-war considerations for as long as possible. And with the Pacific war expected to drag on for another year after the defeat of Germany, the size and shape of the peacetime navy never made its way onto the War Cabinet's agenda.

Churchill himself seems to have given the matter little consideration, although he clearly believed that wartime developments in air power meant a reduced role for the navy in Britain's post-war defence requirements. He warned the Admiralty in July 1944 that its personnel numbers after the war would 'have to resort to at least pre-war strength'.[93] This would have reduced the navy to, at best, around 135,000 men, far below the figure the Admiralty believed was necessary.[94] Churchill commented on the navy's post-war requirements on two other occasions before the end of the war, both times suggesting a reduced role for it. The first remark was prompted by a statement from the Civil Lord of the Admiralty suggesting that the navy was planning to enlarge the royal dockyards. Churchill immediately demanded an explanation. 'You must realize,' he wrote to Alexander the next day, 'that after the war the Air will take a very large part of the duties hitherto discharged by the Royal Navy.'[95] Writing to the Chancellor of the Exchequer a month later, Churchill indicated his approval for the two battleships in the 1945 programme, but he acknowledged that the question would have to 'come up for consideration after the war, in the light of the increase of the power of the Air'. But the time had not yet come, in his view, for a far-reaching examination of post-war defence requirements. 'The whole question of the Navy, Army and Air, in relation to one another,' he wrote, 'will of course be one of the largest problems that will have to be settled after the war by any Government that is responsible.'[96] Churchill undoubtedly assumed that he would be the one presiding over these deliberations, but the general election of July 1945 resulted in a landslide victory for the Labour Party. He resigned as prime minister and Minister of Defence on 26 July, immediately after the election results were announced.

II

Churchill's Last Naval Battle

While Churchill had the satisfaction of presiding over Nazi Germany's unconditional surrender in May 1945, the unexpected triumph of the Labour Party abruptly removed him from office just weeks before Japan's surrender brought the Second World War to a close. Although stung by his party's electoral defeat, the former prime minister, now approaching his seventy-first birthday, never seriously considered retirement: quitting was not in his nature. He was determined to lead the Conservative Party back to power, and quickly settled into his new roles as Leader of the Opposition and distinguished elder statesman.

The strategic landscape confronting British leaders at the end of the war was vastly different from what it had been just a few years earlier. Europe, devastated by years of total war, had now ceased to be the centre of the international system. The resulting power vacuum was filled by the United States and the Soviet Union, whose enormous economic and military potential had been unlocked by the unprecedented demands of the Second World War. Britain remained a global power, with its vast network of overseas commitments undiminished, but its decline into second-rank status was now painfully evident. It simply did not possess the resources to compete with the new 'superpowers' in the post-war world, and was hard pressed to preserve its global interests and revive its failing economy.

Churchill's perspective on British security in this new era was shaped by two overriding considerations: the emerging Cold War with the Soviet Union, and the development of atomic weapons. The key to meeting the Soviet military threat, in his view, was the maintenance of a unified front by a well-armed bloc of Western powers. Above all, Churchill wanted to see the preservation of close Anglo-American relations, Franco-German reconciliation, a unified Europe, and the maintenance of American nuclear supremacy. As long as the Soviets were confronted by a strong and united coalition,

Churchill was confident that Stalin and his successors would avoid direct confrontation with the West. The cornerstone of this deterrent strategy was the American nuclear arsenal, which offered the most effective counter-weight to the Soviet Union's massive superiority in conventional forces.

For a statesman whose military career had started during the reign of Queen Victoria, Churchill grasped the strategic implications of atomic weapons with remarkable speed.[1] He had recognized the potential of nuclear energy to revolutionize warfare as early as 1924, when he had written about the possibility that 'a bomb no bigger than an orange [might] be found to possess a secret power to destroy a whole block of buildings—nay, to con-centrate the force of a thousand tons of cordite and blast a township at a stroke'.[2] He returned to this subject a few years later, noting in 1931 that nuclear energy would be 'incomparably greater than the molecular energy which we use to-day'. All that was missing, he observed, 'is the match to set the bonfire alight, or it may be the detonator to cause the dynamite to explode. The Scientists,' he warned, 'are looking for this.'[3] Churchill was therefore an early and enthusiastic supporter of British—and later Anglo-American—efforts to develop an atomic bomb, and he never questioned President Harry Truman's decision to use this weapon against Japan once it was ready.

Churchill's views on the utility of nuclear weapons went through sev-eral major shifts in the decade after 1945. That the proliferation of atomic weapons would one day make a major war too destructive to contemplate was never in doubt. 'The bomb brought peace,' he told the House of Commons on 16 August 1945, just a week after the bombing of Nagasaki, 'but men alone can keep that peace, and henceforward they will keep it under penalties which threaten the survival, not only of civilization but of humanity itself.'[4] And yet Churchill did not immediately regard the bomb as unusable. For nuclear weapons to fulfil their primary role as a deterrent, Churchill insisted that the threat must be credible: Soviet leaders had to believe that the United States was prepared to pull the trigger. As he told an American audience in 1949, the Soviets must be 'convinced that you will use—you will not hesitate to use—these forces, if necessary, in the most ruthless manner'. They must 'be convinced', he continued, that 'they are confronted by superior force—but [also] that you are not restrained by any moral consideration if the case arose from using that force with complete material ruthlessness'.[5] And as long as the United States held a monopoly on atomic weapons, Churchill believed that they offered a means to extract concessions from the Soviet Union. On numerous occasions in the late 1940s he spoke of the desirability of forcing a 'showdown' with the Soviets in order to achieve a 'settlement' of outstanding differences on terms favourable to the West.

Even after the Soviets had developed their own atomic bomb, Churchill assumed that the much larger supply of these weapons in American hands would temporarily continue to give the West a diplomatic advantage—a 'lever', as he put it on one occasion, 'by which we can hope to obtain reasonable consideration in any attempt to make a peaceful settlement with Soviet Russia'.[6] But this hope faded with the development of the far more destructive hydrogen bomb in 1952, together with the steady expansion of the Soviet atomic arsenal. Churchill was quick to grasp that a numerical advantage in nuclear weapons would eventually cease to provide either side with 'strategic superiority' in any meaningful sense. A 'saturation' point will inevitably be reached, he warned on 1 March 1955, in his last great speech to the House of Commons. Both sides would soon possess enough weapons to ensure the other's annihilation. The greatest danger, in these circumstances, was that the Soviets, being at a disadvantage, would have an incentive to launch a surprise attack. The only counter to this, he concluded, was the development of what would later be called a second-strike capability: the United States must be able to launch an immediate and overwhelming nuclear counter-attack in the event of a Soviet first strike. In time, the USSR would acquire the same assured retaliatory capabilities. But this, paradoxically, would lead to a more stable and peaceful world, as 'both sides will then realise that global war would result in mutual annihilation'. Nuclear weapons would soon make war too dangerous for either side to contemplate. 'Safety,' he concluded in a speech in March 1955, 'will be the sturdy child of terror, and survival the twin brother of annihilation.'[7]

Churchill's fascination with nuclear weapons did not blind him to the need for conventional forces. These were clearly still necessary for Britain—which did not conduct its first atomic test until 1952—to meet Soviet encroachments that did not warrant a nuclear response, and to defend British interests against other challengers. As Leader of the Opposition during the 1940s, Churchill had continued to pay generous tributes to the Royal Navy. In war, he declared in March 1948, the navy was 'our means of safety; in peace it sustains the prestige, repute, and influence of this small island; and it is a major factor in the cohesion of the British Empire and Commonwealth.'[8] But he continued to take a pragmatic view of the navy's role in any future conflict. As long as bombers remained the sole means of delivering nuclear weapons to their targets, Churchill would favour the air force over the other services. 'For good or ill,' he told an audience at the Massachusetts Institute of Technology in March 1949, 'Air mastery is today the supreme expression of military power, and fleets and armies, however necessary, must accept a subordinate rank.'[9] Nuclear weapons were the best means of either deterring or fighting a major war. Naval forces, on the other hand, contributed little to Britain's deterrent capabilities at this time, and would play only a minor role in the critical early stages of a global conflict. Churchill was also impressed in the immediate post-war years by the absence of any serious challenger at sea. He was consequently more concerned about how the Labour government managed the reduction of British naval strength than by the fact that the navy was being run down, a development he regarded as natural and inevitable. What most irritated him was Labour's willingness to scrap many warships—particularly battleships—that could help to maintain British prestige in peacetime and provide valuable reserves in wartime, but he did not otherwise take much interest in naval developments during his years in opposition.

This lack of interest continued when Churchill, now nearing his seventy-seventh birthday, returned to power in the general election of October 1951. The new prime minister was pleased to discover that the previous administration had made substantial progress towards developing a British atomic bomb, and he was determined that further research on this weapon should be 'pursued energetically'.[10] He was less certain, however, about the fate of the large rearmament programme that Labour had launched after the outbreak of the Korean War in June 1950. The new Conservative government inherited a huge balance of payments deficit, and drastic measures appeared necessary to avert an economic crisis. Politicians were particularly eager to divert resources from armaments to the nation's 'metal-using industries' in order to bolster this critical sector of the export trade. It was also becoming clear, however, that careful thought had to be given to the level of forces Britain could afford to maintain after the current economic difficulties had passed. The Cold War was clearly not going to pass quickly, and, as historian Eric Grove has noted, politicians were now coming to grips with the realization that Britain needed a defence policy that was affordable over the 'long haul'. Peacetime forces had to be adequate to deter attacks on vital interests, but not so expensive that they would overburden the economy.[11]

Churchill shared the general conviction that defence expenditure would have to be cut, and therefore in mid-December 1951 he recommended a reduction of £250 million in spending for all three services in the coming year from an overall budget of £1,547 million. The largest share of this would be borne by the army, but naval spending was expected to drop substantially as well, from £402 million to £330 million.[12] Under strong pressure to economize, the fighting services were forced to rely more heavily on the deterrent power of atomic weapons. A new Global Strategy paper by the COS in mid-1952 called for forces to meet the nation's peacetime commitments and to fight a global war, but emphasis now began to shift to forces that would deter conflict in the first place. In the event that a major war did break out, the COS concluded that priority should be given to preparations for surviving the 'first few intense weeks' of the conflict, with 'little provision being made for more long-term requirements'.[13]

This order of priorities was potentially problematic for the navy, which would be able to contribute little during the opening stages of a global nuclear war. Its primary wartime role would be the protection of maritime communications during the extended period of 'broken-backed' warfare that was expected to follow an initial nuclear exchange.[14] The navy's commitment to a predominantly defensive mission was never going to inspire Churchill's enthusiasm, however. The prime minister was alarmed to discover shortly after returning to office that the newest generation of enemy submarines would be virtually impossible to detect from the air, and he immediately appreciated that offensive mining and submarine attacks by the Soviet Union posed a 'potentially mortal danger' to maritime communications during an extended conflict.[15] But the emergence of a genuine naval threat did not automatically translate into support for larger British naval forces. Churchill's first instinct was to find offensive means to deal with the danger, and, in his eyes, this meant Allied air attacks on Soviet naval bases.[16]

The fighting services accepted heavy cuts to their programmes over the course of 1952, but the politicians were still not satisfied that the right balance had been struck. Defence expenditure for 1953–4 was finally set at £1,610 million, a much higher figure than the Chancellor of the Exchequer wanted, but only on the understanding that a 'radical review' of defence policy would be undertaken to consider more drastic measures to bring defence spending into line with economic and financial considerations.[17] This marked an important turning point in the navy's fortunes. Churchill had shown little inclination since becoming prime minister again to single the Admiralty out for economies, or to dictate how the service cut its spending, but the government's 'radical review' took on a momentum of its own and gradually developed into a serious assault on the navy's core programmes. The initial driving force behind these attacks was not Churchill, however, but his son-in-law, Duncan Sandys, the Minister of Supply.

Sandys was a member of the government's new Ministerial Committee on Defence Policy, which was established in June 1953 after early investigations by civil servants and defence officials failed to produce any useful, let alone radical, proposals.[18] Political oversight was clearly necessary to effect major changes, and Churchill chaired the new Committee himself. When ministers met for the first time, however, the prime minister expressed his concern that large cuts in defence spending might undermine his ongoing efforts to open high-level discussions aimed at achieving some form of détente with the Soviet Union. It 'would be fatal,' he warned, 'if it became known that we were about to reduce the level of our defence expenditure'. A wide range of potential economies were discussed, but the most important proposal came from Sandys, who suggested that no major savings were possible until Britain's defence priorities were redefined. In his view, the most dangerous period would be the first six weeks of a major global conflict: if Britain could not survive this, he argued, preparations for the subsequent phase would be irrelevant. He therefore proposed that the nation's defence posture should be heavily geared towards a nuclear war of relatively short duration. 'Anything which did not come within this definition,' he proposed, 'would have to wait if necessary.'[19] This would permit large savings by cutting back on forces intended primarily for a lengthy 'broken-backed' war.

Churchill and the Committee supported this proposal, which left the navy dangerously exposed in the coming months. The attack was led by Sandys, who immediately targeted naval aviation for major cuts. In his view, the offensive duties envisioned for naval aircraft could be performed more economically by the land-based aircraft of the RAF. Moreover, any NATO striking fleet would be amply provided with naval aircraft by the United States navy, so there was no need for Britain to duplicate its ally's capabilities. Britain could therefore afford, he maintained, to dispense with its two heavy 'fleet' carriers.[20] The junior minister found two important allies in his anti-navy campaign: Lord Swinton, the Commonwealth Secretary, who had served as Secretary of State for Air during the 1930s, and Sir Norman Brook, the Cabinet Secretary. Churchill initially took no part in the debate over the restructuring of British defence policy—he suffered a major stroke on 27 June 1953 and was effectively sidelined for several months. During this period, the Chancellor, R. A. Butler, insisted on a cap of £1,650 million for defence spending in 1955, and serious consideration was given to scrapping the navy's heavy carriers, as Sandys proposed.

When Viscount Alexander of Tunis, the Minister of Defence, alerted Churchill to these developments in October 1953, the prime minister was at first non-committal. 'It may well be that the increasing range of shore-based aircraft and the approaching development of guided missiles will affect the recent short-lived pre-eminence of the heavy aircraft-carrier,' he minuted, 'but considering how much money we have put into them and the large part they play in British and American Naval strength it would indeed be foolish to write them off in public as of no value.'[21]

A more serious concern for Churchill as he began to take up his duties again was the Admiralty's plans to scrap major reserve warships, including the four remaining King George V-class battleships. Despite the earlier decision to concentrate on preparations for the initial six weeks of war, Churchill insisted in October 1953 that these vessels 'would probably be able to fulfil a valuable rôle' in 'the "broken-backed" warfare which was likely to succeed the first atomic phase of a future war'.[22] The prime minister's apparent endorsement of preparations for a prolonged war did nothing to relieve pressure on the navy, however. The First Lord of the Admiralty, J. P. L. Thomas, and First Sea Lord, Admiral Sir Rhoderick McGrigor, vigorously presented the Admiralty's case, but were unable to convince ministers that heavy carriers were indispensable. In mid-November the navy suffered another setback when the Minister of Defence also expressed his doubts. Aircraft carriers were undoubtedly necessary for the protection of British warships and convoys in the open seas, he informed the committee, but light carriers would be adequate for this purpose. Heavy carriers equipped for a strike role were, he suggested, a luxury Britain could not afford.[23]

Behind the scenes, Brook pressed the same views on the prime minister. The effects of age were already showing when Churchill returned to office in 1951, and his once-formidable powers of concentration declined even further after his stroke. During his final year and a half in power, he became heavily reliant on the Cabinet Secretary to keep him abreast of developments and brief him for important meetings. Like Sandys, Brook believed that the navy offered the best scope for large economies. By late November, Churchill had come around to their view. The aircraft carrier would have an important role to play for another decade at least, the prime minister predicted, but he now warned his colleagues that 'the range of shore-based aircraft and development of flying aircraft [i.e. guided missiles] continually increases':

> The reign of aircraft carriers is over. They will die out surely and swiftly as a factor. This is because, first, the aircraft maintained upon them are much more costly to maintain and keep afloat than shore-based aircraft, and secondly, they are themselves an increasingly vulnerable target for shore-based bombing and guided missiles. One hit may be fatal. The concentrated vulnerability is a deadly factor.
>
> On land there is hardly any limit for dispersion and camouflage [of aircraft]. Ten sham can be produced for one reality. Two or three miles can nearly always be found for dispersion. Here, where power is growing and so many solid advantages repose lies the future. These tendencies, however unwelcome, affect all ships at sea in wartime. The battleships and cruisers of our former glory will increasingly become floating bull's-eyes. This must wring our hearts, but most not hide the truth.[24]

But Churchill hesitated to dispose of these vessels prematurely. On 27 November he suggested that rather than scrapping the navy's two heavy carriers, consideration should be given instead to how they would be employed.[25] Following this lead, Alexander suggested a compromise in January 1954 by which the ships would both be retained, but 'manned and equipped for a light carrier role only'. The carriers would thus still be available for fleet or trade protection on the open seas, but they would not need to be supplied with aircraft necessary for a strike role, whether attacks at source or the support of land operations—these duties could be left to the United States. This would produce a savings of around £10 million.[26]

The Admiralty's case for its heavy carriers was a strong one, however. Most criticisms of these ships were based on the mistaken premise that they were intended primarily for a strike role against land targets, and therefore duplicated capabilities provided more cheaply by the air force. But the navy wanted these ships primarily to provide cover to naval forces operating at sea, a role performed in earlier times by Britain's main battle fleets. The fact that heavy carriers, suitably equipped, could also strike at land targets was purely incidental, Thomas informed Churchill in February 1954, but no less valuable for that. 'Carriers known to be capable of operating aircraft carrying the atomic bomb are essential to the Navy in the coming decade,' the First Lord insisted. These ships provided access to targets beyond the reach of land-based aircraft, and were more difficult than air bases for the enemy to locate and destroy. Fleet carriers would therefore lessen Britain's reliance on strategic bombers and provide a more robust nuclear deterrent. The First Lord also pointed out that fleet carriers were needed to meet Britain's naval commitments to NATO. Abandoning them would result in a loss of influence with the United States, and strike a heavy blow to the navy's prestige and morale.[27]

Thomas warned Churchill that the Board of Admiralty 'had strong feelings' on this issue, a veiled threat of resignations. The prime minister was unmoved, however. When the matter was discussed by the Ministerial Committee on 26 February 1954, Churchill supported the compromise proposed by the Minister of Defence. But with Sandys absent from the critical meeting, the prime minister was not disposed to press the issue. The Committee therefore agreed to a new compromise suggested by the First Lord: the navy would be allowed to keep its heavy carriers as long as the Admiralty met the Chancellor's financial demands by cutting an equivalent amount from other parts of its budget.[28]

This was a deft move on the Admiralty's part, but the respite it brought was short lived. Within a few months, the Chancellor was calling for another drastic reduction in defence expenditure, this time to £1,500 million. A new ministerial committee, chaired again by the prime minister, was established in the spring of 1954 to reexamine defence expenditure in light of the continuing pressures on government finances and the development of the hydrogen bomb by both the United States and the Soviet Union. Churchill immediately pressed the case for Britain to develop its own hydrogen bomb. Failure to possess 'the latest types of atomic weapon,' he warned his colleagues in May 1954, would deprive Britain of its 'voice in determining the major issue of peace or war'. He also assumed that this development would allow 'some reduction in our production of the so-called "conventional" weapons'.[29]

The COS also attempted to chart a path forward with a new strategic assessment at the end of May. They concluded that the advent of the hydrogen bomb had made a major war less likely, and that Britain should therefore give priority to meeting its Cold War commitments in peacetime, preventing the spread of communism, and deterring a major conflict. This was best achieved, they suggested, by strengthening Britain's influence as a world power and maintaining its alliance with the United States. Such a shift in priorities was potentially advantageous for the navy, which proposed to downgrade preparations for the control of maritime communications in a 'broken-backed' war in favour of maintaining a balanced fleet to support 'foreign and commonwealth policy' in peacetime.[30] The Admiralty proposed a variety of measures that would achieve savings of £25 million in the coming year, including reductions in minesweepers, manpower levels, and the reserve fleet.

While these were large and significant cuts, the navy, like the other fighting services, failed to produce anything like the savings demanded by the Chancellor. On 27 July 1954 the full Cabinet endorsed the new priorities recommended by the COS, but only accepted the services' proposed cuts as a first instalment towards the larger reductions that were deemed necessary. Churchill, urged on by Brook, now proposed that further savings should be investigated by a small ministerial committee.[31] This new body, formally known as the Cabinet Committee on the Defence Review, appears to have been deliberately constructed to ensure that additional cuts would fall most heavily on the navy. Following Brook's advice, its chairman was Lord Swinton, the former Air Minister and a persistent critic of the navy throughout the earlier stages of the 'radical review'. The only other members were Sandys and Alexander.[32] Unfortunately for the navy, the Swinton Committee, as it became known, worked quickly in late July and early August 1954, holding no fewer than five meetings and drafting its report while the Minister of Defence, who was becoming sympathetic to the Admiralty's position on heavy carriers, was out of the country.[33]

Predictably, Swinton and Sandys concentrated their attacks on naval aviation. As before, their case rested on the erroneous claim that the Admiralty wanted heavy carriers in order to attack targets ashore. They therefore resurrected the proposal that Britain's two heavy carriers should be downgraded to light carriers for the protection of maritime communications, and that air attacks on land targets should be left entirely to the RAF. The navy was fortunate to find an ally at this critical juncture in the Minister of Defence. Alexander, who was clearly irritated that the Committee's deliberations had been rushed through in his absence, immediately noted that the heavy carriers were actually intended for the protection of communications at sea. The fact that they might also be employed for strategic strikes ashore was simply a bonus. He therefore declined to support the proposed cuts to naval aviation, and warned the prime minister that the navy could not be singled out for further heavy reductions unless a deliberate decision was taken to reduce it to a lesser status than the other two services. Alexander maintained that this course would be 'entirely wrong', but some decision-makers *were* prepared to take this step.[34]

Privately, Brook urged the prime minister to reject the Defence Minister's advice. It would be a 'novel doctrine', he complained, 'that, regardless of our strategic needs, we must bow to a political necessity that the three services must remain more or less equal in status. We never did so in former times when our safety rested on sea power.' The Cabinet Secretary's minute went on to disparage the navy's motives. 'The Navy have put their faith in Naval Air,' he wrote, 'partly because of the bitter lessons of Norway and Singapore, and partly because they see that air-power is displacing sea-power and they want, for self preservation, to have their share of it.' He therefore advised Churchill to stand by his view that carriers were becoming obsolescent.[35] The prime minister probably needed little prompting: he had always been willing to shift resources between the services according to the strategic circumstances of the day, and he had already gone on record favouring the air force over the army and navy.

In response to Brook's minute, Churchill outlined his own thoughts. 'The three Services are equal in status and honour,' he pronounced in early September 1954, 'but vary in size and character with technical and world events':

> There can be no question of having a larger Navy than we need or can afford in order to gratify those serving in it or public opinion. We must make the best use of existing material. Thus the two heavy carriers now allocated to the allied striking fleet should, as proposed in [the Swinton Committee's draft report], be diverted to Atlantic escorts and their complement of aircraft reduced to that of light carriers.

Churchill also echoed Brook's concerns that the navy's interest in naval aviation was motivated by the fact that 'Air power is displacing sea power.' It was only 'natural that the Navy should wish to have their share of it,' he remarked, but the cost was clearly beyond Britain's means. 'Moreover,' he continued:

> if the carrier is becoming more obsolescent through the ever-increasing range of shore-based aircraft, the help naval air can give to the strength and status of the Admiralty will be short-lived. Sir Norman Brook has pointed out to me that in terms of the long run future the days of the manned aircraft are numbered and naval strength will probably rest on the development of guided missiles—ship to ship, ship to air, and perhaps even ship to shore. Certainly this is not the time to make a great development of manned aircraft for the Navy when guided missiles are obviously their most suitable weapon.[36]

Churchill presented these views to the Swinton Committee the following day.[37] Despite Alexander's dissent, the prime minister's anti-navy remarks were subsequently added verbatim to the draft report. The revised version pronounced that 'the relative importance of sea power in our defences is evidently diminishing and there is no sign that this trend will be arrested'.[38] Sandys and Swinton were clearly determined to bear down on the Defence Minister's resistance. Brook also continued to work in the background to maintain Churchill's support. On 20 September he submitted a lengthy minute to the prime minister to prepare him for a meeting of the committee the following day. Once again he appealed to his chief's conviction that the nation's air power must have priority. 'If money is limited (as it is),' he wrote, 'the only way of maintaining an up-to-date Air Force is to cut back on the Navy. If reductions have to be made in the Navy, it is in Naval Air that the economy can be made with least damage to our sea-power.'[39] This had the desired effect. Churchill swept aside the navy's objections when deliberations resumed next day, commenting that nothing in the committee's discussions had 'led him to modify his view that expenditure on the scale planned for the Fleet Air Arm was the most fruitful field for the further economies which must be secured in our defence expenditure'.[40]

The Admiralty's chances of preserving its heavy carriers appeared to be crumbling fast, but the strong opposition it put up, together with Alexander's firm support, seems to have given Churchill and Brook second thoughts. The Cabinet Secretary suggested a few days later that the navy might be allowed to find other places to economize, and Churchill, whose heart was probably never wholly in the battle, minuted that the Admiralty should be allowed to decide for itself how many heavy and light carriers it required, and what aircraft they should be equipped with. More importantly, he agreed that the next meeting of the Swinton Committee could go ahead without Sandys, who was travelling abroad.[41] When ministers reassembled on 28 September without the Minister of Supply, the navy's fortunes dramatically improved. Alexander made it clear that he was unable to accept the draft report as it stood, and warned that if it went forward for consideration by the Cabinet he would have to oppose it. The sections of the document relating to naval aviation, he complained, 'betrayed some signs of bias.' Swinton was unwilling to back down, but Churchill was. The prime minister reaffirmed his view that the importance of the navy had declined in relation to air power, but admitted that he did not regard the 'terms of the draft report as sacrosanct.' The Committee therefore decided that the future expenditure on naval aviation should be investigated jointly not, as hitherto, by Swinton and Sandys, but by the Minister of Defence and the First Lord of the Admiralty.[42]

Alexander was succeeded as Minister of Defence shortly afterward by Harold Macmillan, who was also eager to secure a compromise that would preserve the navy's heavy carriers. Surprisingly, however, when defence policy was referred to the Cabinet for a decision in early November, Churchill circulated, with his endorsement, a report from Swinton that included the recommendation that the navy's heavy carriers should only be maintained as light carriers.[43] The Admiralty immediately mounted a full counter-attack, including a new threat of resignations from the Board, but there was no danger that the campaign against the navy's carriers would be revived. Even within the Admiralty, it was recognized that the 'whole object of plugging the half-empty carrier in the Defence Review Report may be to make certain that the Admiralty accept everything else and feel thankful they are to be spared the last straw'. One member of the Admiralty secretariat predicted that while 'Fireworks from the Prime Minister may be expected', there was in fact little to fear from him.[44]

This proved to be an accurate prediction. Churchill informed the Cabinet on 5 November that he was 'not convinced that the large and increasing resources which would be absorbed by the Fleet Air Arm were justified by the contribution which it would make to our defences', but he immediately made it clear that he was happy to allow Macmillan and the Admiralty to examine 'alternative means of securing savings in naval expenditure'.[45] With these words, the threat to the navy's heavy carriers finally disappeared. Churchill, who would finally retire in April 1955, made no more significant contributions to the formulation of British naval policy.

Epilogue: The Verdict of History

Churchill's post-war years were not entirely dominated by current politics: he was also determined to protect his place in history and ensure that his pre-war career and wartime leadership were presented to the public in the most favourable light. He was fortunate to find a receptive audience. The Conservative Party's unexpected defeat in the 1945 general election did little harm, if any, to Churchill's reputation as war leader. British defeats early in his premiership had given rise to some grumbling in the press and Parliament, but at the end of the Second World War all that mattered was that Britain had survived and that Nazi Germany was decisively defeated. It was a personal triumph for Churchill. His inspirational leadership had sustained the British people during the lowest points in the war; he had refused to negotiate with Hitler despite the seemingly insurmountable odds against victory; and he had helped to forge the alliance and the grand strategy that ensured Britain would prevail. In the first flush of victory, there was little desire to question, much less to undermine, the foundations of his legacy. On the contrary, Churchill's triumph during the Second World War helped to rehabilitate his reputation from the First World War.

Churchill had campaigned tirelessly during the interwar years to vindicate the Dardanelles campaign of 1915, and he achieved some measure of success. He was greatly assisted in this by the public's growing revulsion at the slaughter on the Western Front and disillusionment with Britain's First World War generals. By the 1930s, the British people were open to the idea that the naval assault on Turkey in 1915 had been a worthwhile endeavour that might have dramatically altered the course of the war. Converts to this view included the popular military writer Sir Basil Liddell Hart.[1] In *The World Crisis* and other works, Churchill chipped away at the idea that the

naval assault had been doomed to fail. He also argued that the campaign on
the Gallipoli Peninsula might have turned out differently if only local commanders had acted more forcefully at a number of key turning points. His
view that the fleet had been on the verge of success in March 1915 when
the naval offensive was called off found a receptive audience, and was
endorsed by no less a naval authority than Admiral Roger Keyes, de Robeck's
Chief of Staff during the campaign. After the Second World War, the
Churchillian view of the Dardanelles as a brilliant design poorly executed
gained many new supporters. In November 1954, for example, Clement
Attlee declared in Parliament that the attack had been 'the only imaginative
strategic idea of the war. I only wish you had had full power to carry it to
success.'[2] Opinion on this campaign was and remains sharply divided, but
given how low Churchill's reputation had sunk in 1915, and the overwhelming consensus for many years that he was personally responsible for this
disaster, even partial rehabilitation was a victory.

The remarkable prestige Churchill enjoyed after the Second World War
served to deflect much early criticism of his wartime leadership. The case
for Churchill as a poor naval strategist only developed gradually. The first
naval controversy to emerge after 1945 involved Churchill's impact on the
fleet, and on the armed forces generally, as Chancellor of the Exchequer
during the 1920s. There had been some complaints during the 1930s about
the naval cuts Churchill had championed and the impact of the ten-year
rule on British rearmament, but after 1940 Churchill's record at the Treasury
was overshadowed in the public mind by his vigorous campaign for rearmament, opposition to appeasement, and dynamic wartime leadership. Events
confirmed that he had been right about Hitler all along. The evacuation of
the BEF at Dunkirk dramatically highlighted the shortcomings in Britain's
preparations for war, but Churchill, who had been kept out of office after
1931, escaped censure. 'Winston is about the only person who has an absolutely clean sheet,' Lord Halifax noted in 1940.[3] This view gained strength
over time. Churchill emerged in popular memory as the unheeded prophet
of the 1930s whose inspirational leadership saved the nation from the disastrous path his predecessors had set it upon. Blame for Britain's discredited
pre-war policies fell on Baldwin, Chamberlain, and other prominent members of the Conservative Party.[4]

There was little interest during the Second World War in searching for
scapegoats among the leaders of the 1920s. The authors of *Guilty Men*, the
best-known and most influential attack on Britain's pre-war policies, charged

that things began to go wrong for Britain with the appearance of the first National government, which took office in August 1931, a month before Japan's attack on Manchuria.[5] Only one significant figure at this time challenged this view: Lord Chatfield, the former First Sea Lord and Minister for the Coordination of Defence. Chatfield's memoirs, written during the early years of the war, drew attention to the continuities between the policies of the 1920s and 1930s. The retired admiral denounced the 'crushing, soul-destroying influence' of the ten-year rule, which he described as 'the dangerous law which laid down for the guidance of the Services, and all indeed in Whitehall, that it was to be assumed that there would be no great war for ten years'. He was especially critical of the decision in 1928 to extend the rule indefinitely. 'Protest was unavailing,' he complained. 'Gagged and bound hand and foot, they [the fighting services] were handed over to the Treasury Gestapo. Never has there been such a successful attempt to hamstring the security of an Empire.'[6] These charges had no immediate impact, however, as the War Cabinet denied Chatfield permission to publish the controversial sections of his memoirs during wartime.[7] A volume of memoirs covering his early life and seagoing appointments was published in 1942, but his attacks on the ten-year rule and criticism of the machinery of government were not made public until a second volume appeared in 1947.

Churchill addressed the origins of the war and the impact of the ten-year rule in *The Gathering Storm*, the first volume of his highly influential and widely read Second World War memoirs (1948–53).[8] The Second World War, he maintained, was an 'unnecessary war': Hitler could have been stopped at an early stage if only British leaders had acted promptly when clear threats to peace began to emerge in the early 1930s. Churchill maintained that he was willing to accept his share of the blame for his policies as Chancellor, although he denied that his actions contributed significantly to Britain's later problems. An early draft of his memoirs allowed that there 'may be some substance' to claims that the ten-year rule had 'lulled the fighting departments into a false sense of security, that Research was neglected, and only short term views prevailed'.[9] But this concession was excised before publication. Churchill also amended his account of the rule's origin. Early drafts stated that it had been 'laid down' by Churchill during his years at the Treasury. The published version, however, distanced him from the rule by noting its origins under Lloyd George's leadership in 1919, and emphasizing that its subsequent renewals were collectively sanctioned by the Cabinet and the CID.

Churchill defended himself on the grounds that his position had been reasonable given the international situation at the time. 'Up till the time when I left office in 1929,' he wrote, 'I felt so hopeful that the peace of the world would be maintained that I saw no reason to take any new decision [regarding the ten-year rule]; nor in the event was I proved wrong':

> War did not break out till the autumn of 1939. Ten years is a long time in this fugitive world. The ten-year rule with its day-to-day advance remained in force until 1932 when... MacDonald's Government rightly decided that its abandonment could be assumed.
>
> At this time the Allies possessed the strength, and the right, to prevent any visible or tangible German rearmament, and Germany must have obeyed a strong united demand from Britain, France and Italy to bring her actions into conformity with what the Peace Treaties had prescribed. In reviewing again the history of the eight years from 1930 to 1938, we can see how much time we had. Up till 1934 at least, German rearmament could have been prevented without the loss of a single life. It was not time that was lacking.[10]

Churchill's memoirs skirted around inconsistencies in his positions during the 1930s, and exaggerated his differences with the politicians in office at this time, but this did little to limit their appeal. His case against the leaders of the 1930s was so persuasive and seemingly authoritative that few were initially inclined to question it.[11] Even those who defended the National governments of the 1930s did not challenge the popular view that Churchill's pre-war record was unblemished. Nevertheless, the establishment of the ten-year rule constituted a potential chink in Churchill's formidable armour. Chatfield's memoirs did not make an explicit connection between the rule and the former Chancellor, but Hankey, the former Cabinet Secretary, attempted to do so in November 1948 in response to the first volume of Churchill's memoirs.

Writing to *The Times*, Hankey maintained that British rearmament after 1933 had been severely constrained by the 'dangerous and demoralizing' impact of the ten-year rule, which had badly damaged not just the fighting services but the arms industry that supported it. Churchill, in his opinion, could not 'escape some responsibility for our misfortunes', and he wondered 'whether Mr Churchill would have been any more successful in overcoming the consequences of his own Ten Years Rule than those whom he pillories'.[12] In a covering letter to *The Times*, Hankey claimed that 'Several Service people and ex-Ministers have begged me to write on the subject.' The 'whole official world' knew that Churchill was responsible for the ten-year rule, Hankey asserted, 'and the Services—higher ranks at any rate—have never forgiven him'.[13]

These criticisms drew an immediate response from General Ismay, Churchill's wartime Chief of Staff, who wrote to *The Times* to make the obvious point that Churchill could hardly be held responsible for the actions of governments he did not belong to.[14] The ten-year rule was not binding on any of them, Ismay noted, and it could have been abandoned at any time. Blame for Britain's deficiencies rested, in his opinion, with those who waited over eighteen months after the rule's abandonment to begin planning for rearmament. Hankey was unwilling to let the matter drop, but his next letter did nothing to strengthen his case. He conceded that Churchill was not *directly* responsible for the retention of the rule after 1929, but was unwilling to absolve him of blame, claiming that Germany could have been recognized as a potential aggressor in the 1920s. He also asserted that the ten-year rule was not as easy to abandon as Ismay implied because the MacDonald government, with its commitment to disarmament, could not have been expected to overturn 'a financial rule to stop rearmament imposed by a Conservative Government of which Mr Churchill, of all men, was Chancellor'.[15]

This dubious argument prompted another letter from Ismay, who argued that his former chief should not be blamed because 'those who came after him continued to observe a rule which was no longer in relation to the conditions which it was drawn up to meet'.[16] Hankey nevertheless continued to insist that Churchill's perpetuation of the ten-year rule had created enormous difficulties for his successors. Cabinet decisions could always be changed at short notice, he conceded, but a 'Treasury rule sponsored by a powerful Chancellor of the Exchequer . . . is always hard and . . . sometimes impossible' to change. This was a considerable distortion of the truth, but Hankey was supported by Lord Stanhope, Churchill's predecessor as First Lord of the Admiralty in 1938–9. Stanhope also wrote to *The Times*, recalling a letter he had received in 1939 from Sir Oswyn Murray, a long-serving Secretary of the Admiralty, which asserted that Churchill had 'pulled down so much of the building while in office (as Chancellor of the Exchequer) that he [Churchill] will find it difficult to shore it up again.'[17]

The Times declined to publish an additional letter from Hankey openly challenging the value of Churchill's public campaign in the 1930s for more vigorous rearmament. The result of Churchill's efforts, he insisted, 'was to discredit British Governments in the thirties, to reduce public confidence in rearmament, to hamper our foreign policy, to <u>discourage</u> our own people, the Empire, our Allies and friendly neutrals, and to encourage <u>Hitler</u>. How far these tendencies may have been set off by a possible spur to rearmament and public opinion can be left to posterity.'[18] The following year, Hankey began preparing a more sustained indictment of Churchill's record on defence matters during the interwar period. This was never completed, but in 1951 Hankey supplied copies of his correspondence with *The Times* to Viscount Templewood (Samuel Hoare), one of the leading members of the National governments of the 1930s.[19] Hoare's memoirs, published in 1954, drew attention to Churchill's activities as Chancellor, and suggested that he was 'misguided in withdrawing the time limit that had previously restricted the formula to a single ten years period'. Hoare may have wished to take his criticisms further, but as a member of Baldwin's government in 1924–9 he was clearly conscious of his share in the Cabinet's collective responsibility for these policies.[20]

The public controversy over the ten-year rule in the letter columns of *The Times* prompted Churchill to draft a long letter defending his record. He repeated here the basic arguments from his memoirs: that responsibility for the ten-year rule was ultimately a collective one, and that it proved to be a reasonable estimate. Hankey's and Stanhope's criticisms were attributed to 'the uneasy consciences of some ex-ministers and former high officials'. Hankey, Churchill suggested, was 'no doubt' distressed by his own record during the 1920s, during which he 'never formally or informally raised the slightest protest to the prolongation of the Ten Years' Rule under a day to day scrutiny':

> Of what he did afterwards during the ten-and-a-half years I was out of office, and the eight years which he continued to serve in his key position, I did not know at the time and have not sought to examine fully. As however the passage of time will reveal the records of the Committee of Imperial Defence to history he would do well to consider whether he is wise to become prominent in this controversy. Certainly in what Sir Thomas Inskip called 'The Locust Years' few had more influence and none more knowledge.

In response to Stanhope, Churchill noted that during his time at the Treasury naval expenditure was not in fact reduced. 'Indeed,' he remarked, 'it rose slightly from £56,505,000 in 1924 to £56,569,000 in 1929. The heavy reductions were made in the more dangerous years after I had left office. To pretend,' he concluded, 'that my administration of the Exchequer ending ten-and-a-half years before war, produced irreparable damage to our naval strength . . . only shows the hard straits to which his Lordship is reduced'.[21]

After having this letter checked by Ismay and Major General Sir Leslie Hollis, the deputy military secretary to the Cabinet, Churchill decided not to send it, probably deciding, as historian David Reynolds suggests, that it would be more dignified to remain silent.[22] In the event, he had little need to worry: Hankey's criticisms had no immediate impact on Churchill's reputation. The Churchillian critique of appeasement, including the assumption that the path to war began in 1931, was already well entrenched by this time, and would remain so until the 1960s, when the opening of the official records to historians revealed the full extent of Churchill's attacks on the defence services as Chancellor. It was only at this time that scholars really began to grapple with the incongruity between Churchill's stinginess in the 1920s and his reputation as the far-sighted advocate of Britain's military preparedness.

The opinion of J. C. C. Davidson, who had served as the Parliamentary and Financial Secretary to the Admiralty in Baldwin's second government, proved to be particularly influential. Davidson attributed Churchill's attacks on the services to his tendency to 'put the whole of his energy into what he believed to be the right policy of the Department over which he presided. When he was at the Exchequer he believed that he was the keeper of the public purse and must keep a most severe control over all spending departments.'[23] This emphasis on departmental concerns was adopted by several prominent historians during the late 1960s.[24] Vice Admiral Sir Peter Gretton, for example, wrote that:

> Explanations of the apparent inconsistency of his policies towards the services in general and the Navy in particular are difficult to find. We have already seen the pattern. Economy in the defence departments in 1910 to help the schemes for social security, immediately followed in 1912 by a large expansion of shipbuilding. Now we have savage cuts in 1925 to be followed by demands for rearmament in the 1930s. One explanation must be that Churchill became absorbed in his task, whatever it was, and fitted himself with mental blinkers which allowed him to appreciate no one else's point of view. He then pursued his policies regardless of opposition and focused every energy on the task to be done . . . .
>
> Out of office in 1930, with blinkers discarded, he saw the danger at once and started to preach rearmament.[25]

Churchill's determination to cut the services and extend the ten-year rule during the 1920s was thus rationalized as a 'paradox of this remarkable man's personality'.[26] This explanation quickly gained popularity, although others have been suggested.[27]

A link was thus re-established in the 1960s between Churchill's period as Chancellor and Britain's later defence problems, although most early revisionists went no further than the observation that Churchill must take a share of the blame, even if a relatively minor one, for Britain's weakness in the 1930s. However, Churchill's tenure at the Treasury has provided ample ammunition for scholars looking to undermine what they regard as a grossly inflated reputation. His attacks on defence spending during the 1920s have been cited as evidence of hypocrisy, opportunism, and recklessness. It has been argued that Churchill's cuts were so serious that he must be considered one of the leading causes of the services' deficiencies during the 1930s and the early years of the Second World War.

This argument rests, of course, on the doubtful assumption that British defence expenditure in general, and naval spending in particular, would have been significantly higher in 1925–9 under a different Chancellor. But it is also clearly linked to the erroneous claim, first advanced by Hankey, that Churchill was responsible not just for the cuts implemented while he was Chancellor but also for those imposed by his successors.[28] This distortion allowed critics to burden Churchill with sole blame for the deficiencies accumulated during the period after 1929, when the deepest cuts were made in Britain's interwar defence budgets. Similarly, by labelling Churchill as the principal instigator of the original 'ten-year rule' in 1919, he can be blamed for virtually all the problems and deficiencies accumulated by the armed services during the entire period from 1919 until at least 1932, if not later.[29] Some scholars have also been quick to represent Churchill's optimism about the stability of the international situation in the 1920s, and his underestimation of the long-term dangers posed by Japan, as evidence that his strategic judgement was seriously flawed throughout his career, particularly with respect to the Far East.[30] In this manner, a direct causal relationship is sometimes implied between Churchill's policies in the 1920s and Britain's two great defeats at the beginning of the Pacific war, the loss of Force Z and the fall of Singapore.[31]

The next naval controversy to emerge after the war concerned the Norwegian campaign of 1940. This embarrassing disaster for British arms, and Churchill's role in it, were overshadowed for over a decade by the momentous events that immediately followed—Hitler's rapid conquest of Western

Europe in May–June 1940 and the Battle of Britain. Serious criticisms of
Churchill's influence during this episode did not emerge until the 1950s.
His first critic, and ultimately the most influential, was Captain Stephen
Roskill, the retired naval officer selected by the Cabinet Office's Historical
Section to produce the government's official history of naval operations
during the Second World War.[32]

Roskill's account of the Norwegian campaign stated that the Admiralty
had interfered too often in the operations of the Home Fleet. After noting
that Pound had expressed the view on more than one occasion that naval
commanders-in-chief should be left free to conduct operations as they saw
fit, Roskill suggested that Admiralty interventions were largely the result of
'the powerful personality of the First Lord':

> Mr. Churchill used, during critical periods of naval operations, to spend long
> hours in the Admiralty Operational Intelligence Centre and the tendency for
> him to assume direct control therefrom is easily to be understood. Many of
> the signals sent during such periods bear the unmistakable imprint of his
> language and personality and, admirable though their purpose and intention
> were, it now appears plain that they sometimes confused the conduct of oper-
> ations and increased the difficulties of the Commander-in-Chief.[33]

The charge that the Admiralty had interfered more often than warranted
was not necessarily damaging to Churchill personally. In *The Gathering
Storm*, Churchill admitted that the Admiralty had been wrong to cancel an
attack Admiral Forbes intended to launch against the Germans at Bergen
shortly after the German invasion. 'Looking back on this affair,' he wrote,
'I consider that the Admiralty kept too close a control upon the Commander-in-Chief, and, after learning his original intention to force the
passage into Bergen, we should have confined ourselves to sending him
information.'[34] The important aspect of Roskill's account of the Norwegian campaign is that it shifted responsibility for *all* Admiralty interference
directly onto Churchill. This was evident even before the book was published. Churchill was again prime minister in 1953, when the first volume
of *The War at Sea* was being readied for publication. When Cabinet officials brought these critical passages to his attention, he defended the
Admiralty's right to intervene in operations, and complained that Roskill's
goal was 'to show that everything that went wrong was due to civilian
interference'.[35] Privately, Churchill complained to his wife Clementine
that Roskill 'belongs to the type of retired Naval Officers who think that
politicians should only be in the Admiralty in time of War to take the

blame for naval failures and provide Naval Officers with rewards in the cases of their successes, if any'.[36] But despite his strong feelings on the subject, he accepted the advice of Norman Brook, the Cabinet Secretary, and Commodore Allen, the naval adviser for his memoirs, that he should not press for changes.[37]

Churchill was upset when the publication of Roskill's official history the following year led, as he had feared, to claims in the press that he had 'assumed personal control of Naval operations and sent operational signals on his own authority'.[38] This may have been more than Roskill himself had intended. The historian's main goal, it appears, was to highlight the general principle that naval commanders at sea should not be subjected to unnecessary interference from superiors ashore. He actually had little to say concerning the effects of Churchill's interference, noting only that it had contributed to the 'difficulties and uncertainties' that plagued the Norwegian campaign.[39] This was a fair comment, insofar as the purely naval aspects of the campaign were concerned. As First Lord of the Admiralty, Churchill *did* sometimes interfere in the conduct of naval operations. But the extent of his meddling has become increasingly prone to exaggeration. Roskill himself is partly to blame for this. In *Churchill and the Admirals*, published in 1977, the former official historian offered a far more critical account of the First Lord's interference during the campaign. This strengthened the view, already widely held, that Admiralty interference was almost exclusively Churchill's responsibility.

In this new work, Roskill subtly manipulated the evidence to create a more damning picture of Churchill's personal involvement. This is best illustrated by his treatment of operation R4, the plan to land British troops to occupy key points in Norway prior to the arrival of the Germans. This scheme, which offered the best chance of altering the course of the subsequent land campaign, was abruptly cancelled so that the ships involved could support the Grand Fleet's mistaken efforts to counter a breakout attempt by Germany's heavy ships. Roskill now blamed this decision entirely on Churchill, although to make his case he had to omit key evidence from the wartime diary of Captain Ralph Edwards, who served alongside Churchill and Pound in the War Room during the critical early stages of the campaign. Roskill drew extensively on Edwards' recollections in this book, but the excerpts he published left out Edwards' description of the cancellation of R4. According to the typescript copy in Roskill's papers, Edwards recalled that:

At a meeting in the Board Room in the evening [of 7 April] at which were present all the senior members of the Naval Staff, I tried to get across the theory that this fleet movement [by the Germans] was all part of an attack upon Norway and not a break out into the Atlantic. I remember Winston remarking 'I believe the boy is right' and for a short while plans for dispositions to meet the possible Norwegian attack were in process of preparation. The First Sea Lord was away down at Broadlands fishing for salmon and arrived back rather late in the evening. He sent for me and went for me like a pick-pocket for—as he put it—trying to lead the Naval Staff away from the main objective which was the defence of the Atlantic convoy routes. He would not listen to my arguments that all the evidence tended to suggest that Norway was to be the victim.[40]

Roskill's omission of the passage is surprising. Edwards is the only participant in these events to leave a written account. If it is accurate—as it probably is—Churchill emerges from this incident in a very different light from the one Roskill suggests. In this instance, it certainly appears that it was Pound who overrode Churchill!

Churchill's role in the Norwegian campaign has also been distorted over the years by the assumption that his interference at the operational level was replicated at the strategic level. It is now an article of faith for many historians that the First Lord interfered just as eagerly in the strategic direction of the campaign, recklessly shifting resources back and forth between different objectives on his own authority. The influential historian Arthur Marder, for example, wrongly claims that Churchill and the Admiralty were responsible for the sudden shift in priorities from Narvik to Trondheim, and that they were acting *against* the expressed wishes of the War Cabinet, which had given priority to Narvik. Marder was less critical than Roskill on the question of Churchill's personal interference in naval operations, but he nevertheless judged the First Lord to be a 'strong influence on the inept overall strategy of the campaign, including the constant changes of plan'.[41] Liddell Hart described Churchill as 'the main contributor' to the Norway 'fiasco'.[42] Correlli Barnett's popular history of the wartime Royal Navy labels the entire campaign 'a Churchillian disaster'.[43]

The mistaken claim that Churchill was solely responsible for shifting Britain's efforts back and forth between Narvik and Trondheim is almost invariably backed by only a single source: a volume of General Ironside's diaries published in 1962. This book describes a colourful scene in which Churchill unexpectedly appeared at the War Office in the early hours of 14 April and ordered a reluctant Ironside to divert the rear half of the

Narvik-bound convoy to Namsos. However, this account was not written by Ironside shortly after the incident occurred: it was reconstructed, as the editors make clear, from a description Ironside 'approved some years afterward, and which accords with the clear recollection of his Military Assistant with whom he discussed the matter the next day'.[44] While the accuracy of this account is open to doubt, the real damage was done by the book's editors, who mistakenly claimed that when this episode took place the Military Coordination Committee had agreed that the capture of Trondheim should only be studied, and that no troops would be allocated for it. Thus, it is made to appear that Churchill was acting entirely on his own initiative, and that he greatly exceeded his authority. In fact, the decision to commit troops— both British and French—for an assault on Trondheim had already been taken by the War Cabinet on 13 April.[45] And, as noted, that body had acted *against* Churchill's advice not to spread Britain's limited resources between multiple objectives. The editors are also wrong about the state of deliberations within the Military Coordination Committee. When that body met on the evening of 13 April to discuss Scandinavian operations, it agreed in principle that the Narvik-bound convoy could be split, provided that the optimistic accounts of the situation at Narvik were judged to be accurate. In this event, Churchill was authorized 'without further reference to the Committee' to make 'arrangements for diverting the second brigade of the Narvik force to Namsos'.[46]

Most historians have followed this lead. Correlli Barnett, for example, also blames Churchill for the decision to shift Britain's efforts from Narvik to Trondheim, although his claim rests on a misreading of the official records.[47] Barnett's account of strategic planning in Whitehall notes that Churchill argued in favour of concentrating British efforts on Narvik on 10 and 13 April, and that on the latter date the War Cabinet overruled him. Barnett nevertheless attributes *all* the consequences of the Cabinet's decision to Churchillian irresolution. To support this case, Barnett makes two misleading claims. First, he implies that on 11 April Churchill was wavering in his support of Narvik and wanted a major diversion of effort to Trondheim. But, as noted above, Churchill was only thinking in terms of a small operation in central Norway to secure a forward base for later operations. He consistently emphasized around this time that nothing should be done to detract from the main attack on Narvik. Second, Barnett asserts that Churchill 'changed his mind again' on 14 April when he threw his weight behind an early assault on Trondheim. By this date, however, Churchill cannot be blamed for unilaterally altering British priorities. On the contrary, his actions, for good or ill, conformed to the new strategy laid down by the government the day before.

One of the key assumptions underlying much of the criticism of Churchill as a strategist during this campaign is that he virtually dictated British strategy, and that he is therefore responsible for every bad decision and change of plan that emanated from London. As First Lord of the Admiralty, Churchill did have considerable freedom to direct naval operations. And as a member of Chamberlain's War Cabinet, he enjoyed growing influence over the strategic direction of the war effort. His position in this respect was strengthened in early April 1940 when Chamberlain appointed him chairman of the Military Coordination Committee. But even then, Churchill could not dominate the strategic decision-making process to the extent that many assume. He could be blocked from below by the united resistance of the Chiefs of Staff, as in the case of Operation Hammer. And on major questions of strategy he was ultimately at the mercy of his ministerial colleagues, who usually took their cue from the more cautious Chamberlain and Halifax. This is best illustrated by the War Cabinet's decision of 13 April to recapture Trondheim, which was taken against the wishes not only of Churchill but also of the armed services and the French.[48]

The destruction of Force Z has received similar treatment by historians. Once again, Churchill's earliest and most influential critic was Roskill, whose official history contained the first detailed account of the decision-making process that led to the dispatch of the *Prince of Wales* to Singapore. Roskill was certain that blame for the disaster rested entirely with Churchill, and he was determined that the official history should reflect this. But he was also critical of Pound for not taking a stronger stand on this issue. In a letter to J. R. M. Butler, the editor of the government's official histories, Roskill maintained that 'Sea Lords should resign rather than allow the country's battle fleet...to be juggled hither and tither for political purposes, & against their own professional judgement & advice'.[49] In an early draft of *The War At Sea*, Roskill glossed over the political considerations that had motivated the Defence Committee in October 1941, and highlighted instead Churchill's shortcomings as a naval strategist. 'The proposal to use part of the fleet for political ends is nothing new,' he wrote, 'but the fact that, in this case, it was a bluff which would all to [*sic*] easily be called appears to have been overlooked. Nowhere in the discussion does the soundness or unsoundness of the move from the point of view of maritime <u>strategy</u> appear to have been given much weight.'[50]

This opinion did not pass unchallenged. When an early draft reached Commodore Allen, he complained that Roskill had 'overweighted' the 'strategical argument' and failed to pay sufficient attention to 'the supreme responsibility of Ministers'.[51] Sir Norman Brook agreed that 'in the original text of this chapter, "political" reasons were written down and too much emphasis laid on the strategic proprieties'. Allen and Brook both pressed Roskill to make changes to his text.[52] As a result, the most explicit criticisms of the prime minister were dropped from the published version. However, Roskill's narrative still revolved around the debate between Churchill and the Admiralty over naval strategy rather than the overarching political considerations. 'I have toned down the truth,' he informed Butler, 'which is that Pound allowed himself to be overridden. I hope, none the less, that the reader will realise that was the truth. I can go no further.'[53]

As with the Norwegian campaign, Roskill set the tone for subsequent studies. Churchill's memoirs, the relevant volume of which had been published three years earlier, did little to help his case. The political factors that had motivated the Defence Committee in the autumn of 1941 were not emphasized in this account, although the prime minister's correspondence with Pound in August 1941 was published in an appendix. This has provided ammunition to those who have argued that Churchill was motivated principally by his views on naval strategy rather than the broader diplomatic situation; that he knew that these ships would have to fight the Japanese; that he had pressed his views on the Admiralty for months before finally wearing down Pound's opposition; and that the role of other decision-makers—Eden in particular—was insignificant. The popular view now is that the dispatch of Force Z to Singapore was a poorly conceived bluff—that Churchill assumed the mere presence of two capital ships would be sufficient to overawe the Japanese, and that the ships' destruction was inevitable once the fighting began.

Churchill clearly failed to anticipate the charges that would be raised by Roskill and later historians. When the critical passages in the official history were brought to his attention in 1953, he complained, with some cause, that this work was 'very misleading' and 'devised with the intention or at least with the effect of throwing the blame upon civilian interference with the Naval Staff's wisdom for political or diplomatic reasons'. However, even at this date the prime minister was not prepared to concede that his views on naval strategy had been mistaken. 'When one has lived through the anxieties which a couple of first class ships can produce as long as their whereabouts at the moment are not known, one does not underrate the fact that similar reactions may be excited from the enemy.'[54]

While the trend has been for early criticisms of Churchill to become harsher and more elaborate over time, he has received less criticism over his role in the Battle of the Atlantic than might have been expected. In this instance, Churchill's memoirs were probably instrumental in preserving his reputation. The dispute between the Admiralty and the Air Ministry over the allocation of long-range aircraft was outlined in the British official histories, but Churchill emerged from these volumes relatively unscathed. Post-war investigations revealed that the bomber offensive was far less effective in 1942 than its supporters claimed at the time, and that Bomber Command could have relinquished aircraft for trade protection without significantly diminishing the impact of its strategic campaign against Germany. Sir James Butler concluded that it was 'difficult not to agree with those who believed that in the shipping emergency of [1942] increased assistance to the war at sea would have been worth a slight reduction in the strength of the strategic air offensive'.[55] Sir Michael Howard, another official historian, endorsed this view, although he was implicitly critical of Churchill, noting that the prime minister had actively sided with the Air Ministry and used his position to ensure priority for the bomber offensive.[56]

Roskill, however, was more circumspect. The drawn-out struggle with the prime minister's office over his treatment of the Norwegian campaign and the dispatch of the *Prince of Wales* to Singapore may have diminished his appetite for controversy by the time he came to writing about the Battle of the Atlantic. The second volume of *The War at Sea*, published after Churchill had left office, observed that 'in the early spring of 1943 we had a very narrow escape from defeat in the Atlantic; and that, had we suffered such a defeat, history would have judged that the main cause had been the lack of two more squadrons of very long range aircraft for convoy escort duties'. But he does not explicitly criticize either Churchill or the Air Ministry for giving priority to Bomber Command, noting only that the question of whether the Battle of the Atlantic might have be won sooner if aircraft had been allocated differently was 'likely to be a subject of dispute'.[57]

In January 1954, Roskill proposed to Butler that he might expand on his criticisms of Churchill in a confidential annex to the first volume of

The War at Sea.[58] The draft he submitted at this time dealt primarily with
subjects covered in that volume, which only went up to December 1941,
but when he came to discuss Churchill's preference for offensive operations,
Roskill included a reference to the controversies of 1942. 'The priority
given to the bombing of North-West Germany,' he wrote, 'at a time when
lack of long-range aircraft was causing great losses in the Atlantic seems to
have been largely attributable to the prime minister's insistence on this
"offensive" measure against the enemy. The historian, on the other hand,
can see that the relatively small numbers of aircraft needed at sea would have
(and ultimately did) exert an influence far beyond the loss of offensive
capacity caused by their diversion from bombing.'[59] The second volume of
Roskill's official history contained little in the way of criticism, however. It
noted Churchill's support for the bomber campaign, but the 'Battle of the
Air' in 1942 was represented as an inter-departmental dispute between the
Admiralty and the Air Ministry. Roskill largely ignored Churchill's involvement in the controversy, although he does credit him with bringing the
conflict to conclusion through the establishment of the Anti-U-Boat Warfare Committee in November 1942.[60]

Roskill's later treatment of the Battle of the Atlantic in *Churchill and the
Admirals* suggests that he was not entirely comfortable blaming Churchill
for the delays in winning this campaign. He was no longer reticent, however, about proclaiming the general rightness of the Admiralty's case. The
U-boats might have been defeated 'at least six months earlier', he claimed,
if the navy's views had prevailed. Churchill's neglect of Coastal Command
was probably, in his opinion, 'the most far-reaching and tragic strategic error
which can, at any rate in part, be laid at Churchill's door, since it was shortage of shipping that delayed every offensive by the United Nations in every
theatre up to mid-1944, and so prolonged the struggle at the cost of inestimable suffering to the peoples of the occupied countries'. But he was seemingly inclined to regard the rigid views of air force leaders about the utility
of strategic bombing—which he privately derided as 'the gospel according
to St. Trenchard'— and their persistent obstructionism as the fundamental
cause of the Admiralty's problems.[61] The Air Ministry now emerged as the
real villain in the dispute, while Churchill was treated more as the victim of
bad advice than a fundamental cause of the Admiralty's difficulties. From
Roskill's perspective, the problem was not just that the offensive-minded
Churchill was overly susceptible to the arguments of bombing advocates
such as Portal, Harris, and Cherwell, but that the other side of the case was

not presented with equal force by the Admiralty. '[I]t is reasonable,' Roskill asserted, 'to feel that a stronger stand by Alexander and Pound [in mid-1942] would have brought Churchill to see what lay ahead at that time.'[62]

Roskill also felt compelled to acknowledge that the Admiralty had made mistakes of its own over the allocation of aircraft, the most serious being its demands for attacks on U-boat bases in France and its preference for strengthening the Biscay patrols at the expense of the Atlantic convoy routes.[63] But what is most significant here is that the official historian never singled Churchill out for criticism over the Battle of the Atlantic the way he had with Norway and Force Z. Without a firm lead from Roskill, later historians of the anti-U-boat campaign have accepted at face value Churchill's statements about the high priority and close attention he gave to the Battle of the Atlantic throughout the war.[64]

Historians today are probably further than ever from a consensus on Churchill's record as the custodian of British sea power, although it is likely safe to say that there is general agreement on some things. Few would now dispute Churchill's shortcomings when it came to the actual conduct of operations at sea. Both as First Lord and as prime minister, Churchill could be impatient and overbearing: he was too quick to second-guess commanders on the spot and meddle in matters best left to naval professionals, and these efforts were seldom rewarded with success. There is also general acknowledgement that Churchill's strategic judgement was, at best, inconsistent; that he possessed a brilliant and fertile imagination, tremendous courage, and unbounded optimism, but that these qualities were marred by his restlessness and offensive spirit, which sometimes led him to champion reckless and impracticable schemes. What divides historians is how much these shortcomings matter. Opinion on this varies widely.

To his most ardent critics, Churchill's acknowledged deficiencies overshadow everything else. His strategic judgement was severely flawed, in their view, and he was solely responsible for the worst naval disasters Britain suffered during both world wars. This rather extreme view is far from universal, but the trend of historical scholarship over the last sixty years has undoubtedly been towards a negative verdict of Churchill as a naval strategist. Unfortunately, broad judgements on this subject have become stuck in well-worn grooves established by Stephen Roskill in the 1950s. The official historian's criticisms of Churchill, though not always well founded, have been regarded as definitive by later generations of naval historians, who have repeated and elaborated on them so often that they frequently bear little resemblance to the original. The urge to debunk the myth of Churchill's unblemished greatness has always been strong, even long after he ceased to enjoy anything like universal acclaim. But the largely negative image this process has produced rests rather uncomfortably, where the navy is concerned, on a body of assumptions that are often either inaccurate or unfounded.

One of the first assumptions that needs to be discarded is that easy generalizations can be drawn from a few high-profile incidents like the Norwegian campaign and the loss of Force Z. The former seems to confirm what was first revealed by the Dardanelles campaign: that Churchill routinely issued ill-conceived orders to naval commanders at sea on his own authority, and that he could not be controlled even by his ministerial colleagues. Similarly, the dispatch of the *Prince of Wales* to Singapore has come to embody Churchill's willingness as prime minister to ride roughshod over his uniformed advisers in pursuit of his own unrealistic objectives. But neither episode offers such simple or convenient conclusions, and they should not be treated as representative of his interactions with the navy during the entire course of the Second World War. After he became prime minister, Churchill did sometimes urge naval commanders to take a more offensive stance, but he did not directly interfere again in operations at sea as he had during the Norwegian campaign. It was also rare for him to overrule the Admiralty on questions of naval strategy. The movement of the *Prince of Wales* to Singapore against naval protests was an exception rather than the rule, and in this instance Churchill was acting on the basis of mainly *political* calculations, in which he had strong support from Eden and other civilian members of the Defence Committee.

Churchill's meddling was not nearly as widespread as some critics allege, nor were the consequences usually serious. A more representative incident, in most respects, was his proposal in 1941 to sacrifice a battleship to block Tripoli harbour. This action was undeniably reckless and pointless. But Churchill was not lightly demanding that extraordinary risks be run. Rather, he hoped that a dramatic move by the navy would help to avert a major crisis in the land war. Most importantly, he was stopped from taking this course by the firm opposition of his naval advisers, and no more was heard of the idea.

It would also be wrong to assume that Churchill had virtually limitless power, even as prime minister, to impose his views on submissive colleagues and uncooperative subordinates. Churchill's strong will, forceful manner, and persuasiveness made him a formidable colleague and a demanding master, but his wishes could be, and were, regularly thwarted by firm opposition. Standing up to Churchill could not have been an enjoyable experience, but the necessity for doing so was widely appreciated, even at an early stage of his career. As Lloyd George remarked in his First World War memoirs, men of Churchill's 'ardent temperament and powerful mentality need exceptionally strong brakes' to check their 'more erratic impulses...before plunging into action'.[65] Admiral Beatty made a similar observation in 1915: 'the First Lord is obstinate when set on a thing, but really it only requires firm treatment to make him realize when he goes off the rails, but indeed it must be astonishingly firm'.[66]

Britain was fortunate during the Second World War in having admirals such as Pound and Cunningham in office, and generals such as Brooke. These men applied the necessary brakes on numerous occasions, and more than once deflected Churchill from ideas that would have needlessly increased the navy's losses. This led to tensions and frustration on both sides, but the relationship between the prime minister and his COS was hardly one of unrelieved discord. John Ehrman, one of the official historians of British grand strategy in the Second World War, offers a perceptive and balanced appreciation:

> Probably only those who have experienced [Churchill's] exceptional powers of interference and obstinacy can appreciate exactly how difficult he could be. But that must not blind us to the fact that he always kept those powers within limits—even of his own choosing....However exasperating he might be—and it must not be overlooked that very often he had good cause—the Chiefs of Staff knew that he would not intrigue, that he would not abandon them in secret, and that in the last resort he would listen to their opinion.[67]

That such a high standard of civil-military relations was maintained during the war—in distinct contrast to Lloyd George's experiences in the First World War—is due in no small measure to Churchill's respect for his advisers and his willingness to compromise. It also reflects the fact that he and the service chiefs were usually in agreement over the broad principles of British strategy. Time after time they were able to present a united front in discussions with their American counterparts. The decision-making machinery undoubtedly creaked from time to time under the strain Churchill put on it. Time was wasted debating all manner of reckless and impracticable schemes, but out of this process there ultimately emerged a coherent and reasonably effective strategy.

In terms of grand strategy, there was also a broad consensus between Churchill and his advisers over the allocation of resources between the three fighting services. When Pound sought higher priority for the navy in 1942 his real concern was not so much to shift resources from the RAF to the navy, but to force the Air Ministry to switch more of its resources from Bomber Command to Coastal Command. Churchill clearly made a mistake in supporting the diversion of so many aircraft from trade protection (and army cooperation) to strategic bombing, which consistently fell short of expectation. But he otherwise struck a sensible balance between the three services. Churchill was never an extreme partisan of one branch of the armed forces. He rejected arguments for the absolute primacy of the navy in the First World War, even when he was First Lord, and he rejected similar arguments for Bomber Command in the next conflict, even as he came to regard it as the most effective weapon at his disposal. As a civilian leader, Churchill had to—and did—take a broad perspective of Britain's strategic needs. Despite his early attraction to the idea of the army as the lesser of Britain's fighting forces, he soon came to appreciate that it would also play a vital role in a major European war. The challenge, in peace and war alike, was to strike the best possible balance between Britain's two (and later three) fighting services.

Churchill's record here is impressive. In the Great War he was one of the few to protest the priority allocation of resources to the navy during the latter stages of the conflict—by which time Britain was massively over-insured at sea—at the expense of the army on the decisive Western Front. He wisely promoted the expansion of air forces between the wars, and just as wisely reined in the RAF when it claimed that air power alone could be decisive. The navy was kept short of resources during the war, but so were the other services, even the air force. In the end, the navy got enough to win the Battle of the Atlantic and achieve its most important goals. The army, also deprived of resources, was still built up to a continental scale and was able to take part in the final destruction of German fighting power on land. The navy could only have obtained a greater share of the nation's resources at the expense of the other services, and Churchill correctly foresaw that this would unduly weaken Britain in other critical areas.

Although Churchill often opposed the allocation of money and resources to the navy, he was never in any real sense 'anti-navy'. His respect and admiration for the service was genuine and deep-rooted. But he was never dogmatic about the navy's place in Britain's defence structure. His views on sea power were both utilitarian and pragmatic. What the navy had done in the past meant less than what it was doing now, and still less than what it could do in the future. In a great European war, Churchill realized at an early date that sea power would play only a supporting role. The navy could ensure that Britain was not defeated at sea, but he was never optimistic about its ability to inflict decisive pressure on a continental enemy through economic pressure alone. To prevail, Britain also needed an army (and later an air force) and powerful allies. Sea power would also allow Britain to fight campaigns overseas, but not, in his opinion, to inflict decisive pressure on a non-European great power like Japan. Given these limitations, hard choices had to be made about priorities, and Churchill was not afraid to make them. As First Lord in 1911–14 he correctly prioritized the North Sea over the Mediterranean, and the Mediterranean over the Pacific. During the Great War he rightly focused on Germany, his temporary preoccupation with eastern sideshows in 1915 notwithstanding. He was prepared, from the 1920s onward, to write off most of Britain's interests east of Suez if it was necessary to meet a mortal threat closer to home, and he ensured that the European theatre retained primacy throughout the Second World War. These were the right decisions, even though they meant that Churchill often had to deny the navy everything it wanted.

During the first half of the twentieth century air power gradually eclipsed sea power as Britain's most potent and valuable weapon, and would have done so whether Churchill was in power or not. But even when the nation's sea power was being deliberately neglected and its naval resources run down, Churchill ensured that the navy's most important needs were met, and that its long-term interests were protected as well as possible. He was better equipped than any other civilian statesman of this period to understand how Britain's strategic needs were changing in a world dominated by major technological and geopolitical shifts, and to make reasonable and informed choices about national priorities in a period defined by inadequate and declining resources. Winston Churchill understood the navy's capabilities and its limitations better than probably any other politician of this period. The nation was fortunate that he was so frequently and prominently involved in managing its naval affairs.

Notes

LIST OF ABBREVIATIONS

AU   Anti-U-Boat Warfare Committee

BA   Battle of the Atlantic Committee

C   Cabinet Paper

CA   Confidential Annex

CC   Cabinet Conclusions

CP   Cabinet Paper

CWP   *The Churchill War Papers*, ed. Martin Gilbert, 3 vols (New York: Norton, 1993–2001)

DBFP   *Documents on British Foreign Policy 1919–1939*

DMV   Visits of Ministers from Dominions

DO   Defence Committee (Operations)

DP   Defence Policy Committee

FDR   Franklin Delano Roosevelt

LNA   Committee on Further Reduction of Naval Armaments

NP   Naval Programme Committee

NSC   CID Sub-Committee on the Question of the Capital Ship in the Navy

SWC   Supreme War Council

SWW   Winston S. Churchill, *The Second World War*, 6 vols (Boston: Houghton Mifflin, 1948–53)

WM   War Cabinet minutes

WP   War Cabinet paper

WSC   Winston S. Churchill

WSC   Randolph S. Churchill and Martin Gilbert, *Winston S. Churchill*, 8 volumes and 13 companion books (London: Heinemann, 1969–88)

INTRODUCTION

1. Admiral Sir William James, 'Churchill and the Navy', *Churchill by his Contemporaries*, ed. Charles Eade (London: Hutchinson, 1953), 141.

2. The most reliable attribution to Churchill comes from the politician and writer Sir Harold Nicolson, who recorded in his diary on 17 August 1950

that 'Paddy Leigh Fermor tells me [that] when Winston was at the Admiralty, the Board objected to some suggestion of his on the grounds that it would not be in accord with naval tradition. "Naval tradition? Naval tradition?" said Winston. "Monstrous. Nothing but rum, sodomy, prayers and the lash."' However, Anthony Montague Browne, Churchill's last Private Secretary, later told Richard Langworth that he had asked Churchill about this statement around 1955. 'I never said it,' Churchill replied. 'I wish I had.' *Harold Nicolson: Diaries and Letters*, ed. Nigel Nicolson, 3 vols (London: Collins 1966–8), III:193; Richard M. Langworth, *Churchill by Himself* (New York: Public Affairs, 2008), 577.

3. Patrick Beesly, *Room 40* (London: Hamish Hamilton, 1982), 135.

4. Brock to Edmond Slade, 28 December 1911, Slade papers, MRF/39/1, National Maritime Museum, Greenwich (NMM).

5. *The Jellicoe Papers*, ed. A. Temple Patterson, 2 vols (London: Navy Records Society, 1966–8), I:26–7.

6. Pound to Cunningham, 20 September 1940, and Cunningham to Pound, 10 December 1941, *The Cunningham Papers*, ed. Michael Simpson, 2 vols (Aldershot: Ashgate for the Navy Records Society, 1999 and 2006), I:150, 546; Stephen Roskill, *Churchill and the Admirals* (London: Collins, 1977), 130; Davis to Roskill, 20 October 1961, ROSK (Roskill papers, Churchill College Archives Centre, Cambridge) 5/124.

7. Pound to Cunningham, 20 September 1940, in Simpson, *Cunningham Papers*, I:150; Cunningham diary, 29 August 1944, Cunningham papers, British Library, Add Ms 52577.

8. Davis to Roskill, 20 October 1961, ROSK 5/124; Roskill, *Churchill and the Admirals*, 130; Drax, unpublished memoir, February 1966, DRAX (Drax papers, Churchill College Archives Centre, Cambridge) 6/8.

9. Winston S. Churchill, *The World Crisis*, 6 vols (New York: Scribners, 1963–4), and *idem.*, *The Second World War* (cited hereafter as *SWW*), 6 vols (Boston: Houghton Mifflin, 1948–53).

10. David Reynolds, *In Command of History* (London: Allen Lane, 2004), and John Ramsden, *Man of the Century: Winston Churchill and his Legend since 1945* (New York: Columbia University Press, 2003).

11. Stephen Roskill, *The War at Sea*, 3 vols (London: HMSO, 1954–61).

12. Nicholas Lambert, *Sir John Fisher's Naval Revolution* (Columbia, SC: University of South Carolina Press, 1999), 204–11; *idem.*, 'British Naval Policy, 1913–1914: Financial Limitation and Strategic Revolution', *Journal of Modern History*, 67, no. 3 (September 1995), 595–626; Jon Sumida, 'Churchill and British Sea Power, 1908–29', *Winston Churchill: Studies in Statesmanship*, ed. R. A. C. Parker (London: Brassey's, 1995).

13. The classic study of Britain's naval decline is Paul Kennedy, *The Rise and Fall of British Naval Mastery* (London: Fontana Press, 1983). For a thoughtful and penetrating critique of Kennedy's arguments, see the articles by Gordon Martel, Keith Neilson, John Ferris, and B. J. C. McKercher in the November 1991 issue of *The International History Review*.

CHAPTER 1

1. Speech of 12 May 1901, House of Commons, *Winston S. Churchill: His Complete Speeches*, ed. Robert Rhodes James, 8 vols (New York: Chelsea House, 1974) (hereafter cited as *Complete Speeches*), I:83.

2. Winston S. Churchill, *Mr. Brodrick's Army* (Sacramento, CA: The Churchilliana Co., 1977), 6.

3. Speech of 12 February 1903, Wallsend, North Tyneside, ibid., 80.

4. Ibid.

5. Speech of 18 March 1912, *Complete Speeches*, II:1,928.

6. Andrew Lambert, 'The Royal Navy, 1856–1914: Deterrence and the Strategy of World Power', in *Navies and Global Defense*, ed. Keith Neilson and Elizabeth Errington (Westport, CN: Praeger, 1995), 73; Arthur J. Marder, *The Anatomy of British Sea Power* (New York: Alfred Knopf, 1940), 13–16.

7. Speech of 26 March 1913, *Complete Speeches*, II:2,094.

8. Speech of 17 March 1914, *Complete Speeches*, II:2,261.

9. Matthew Seligmann, 'Switching Horses: The Admiralty's Recognition of the Threat from Germany, 1900–1905', *International History Review*, XXX (June 2008), 239–58.

10. Speech of 14 August 1908, Swansea, *Complete Speeches*, II:1,085. See also speech of 17 July 1909, Scottish Liberal Club, Edinburgh. Ibid., II:1,288–9.

11. Cabinet paper, 2 February 1909, Randolph S. Churchill and Martin Gilbert, *Winston S. Churchill* (the Official Biography, hereafter cited as *WSC*) (8 volumes and 13 companion books, London: Heinemann, 1969–88), II, companion book 2:939–42.

12. WSC to Lloyd George, 31 August 1911, and undated WSC memorandum, *WSC*, II/2:1,105, 1,118–19.

13. CID 114th mtg, 23 August 1911, CAB 2/2; Lambert, *Fisher's Naval Revolution*, 204–11.

14. *Jellicoe Papers*, I:26–7.

15. Alfred Gollin, *The Impact of Air Power on the British People and their Government, 1909–14* (Stanford, CA: Stanford University Press, 1989); Eric Grove, 'Seamen or Airmen? The Early Days of British Naval Flying', in *British Naval Aviation: The First 100 Years*, ed. Tim Benbow (Aldershot: Ashgate, 2011), 7–26.

16. *Jellicoe Papers*, I:26–7.

17. Earl of Oxford and Asquith, *Memories and Reflections 1852–1927*, 2 vols (Toronto: McClelland and Stewart, 1928), II:67.

18. Arthur Marder, *From the Dreadnought to Scapa Flow*, 5 vols (Oxford: Oxford University Press, 1961–71), I:260–2; Vice-Admiral Sir Peter Gretton, *Former Naval Person* (London: Cassell, 1968), 89–92.

19. Speech of 9 November 1911, Guildhall, *Complete Speeches*, II:1,892.

20. J. Sumida, *In Defence of Naval Supremacy* (Boston: Unwin Hyman, 1989), 258–9.

21. Churchill, *World Crisis*, I:76–7.

22. Sumida, *In Defence of Naval Supremacy*.

23. WSC memorandum, 'Naval Programme 1912/13', n.d., CAB 1/32; Lambert, *Fisher's Naval Revolution*, 247–8.

24. WSC to Sir Edward Grey, 31 January 1912, *WSC*, II/3:1,503–4.

25. Speech of 18 March 1912, House of Commons, *Complete Speeches*, II:1,919–35.

26. John H. Maurer, 'Churchill's Naval Holiday: Arms Control and the Anglo-German Naval Race, 1912–1914', *Journal of Strategic Studies*, 15:1 (March 1992), 102–27.

27. For Churchill's assessment of the new German navy law, see his memoranda of 14 and 15 February 1912, ADM 116/3099; *WSC*, II/3:1,517–19.

28. Speech of 18 March 1912, House of Commons, *Complete Speeches*, II:1,929.

29. Undated note by WSC (*c*.9 January 1912), *WSC*, II/3:1,494.

30. WSC to Viscount Haldane, 6 May 1912, *WSC*, II/3:1,549.

31. WSC Troubridge, 1 February 1912, ADM 116/3099; Lambert, *Naval Revolution*, 250–1.

32. Nicholas A. Lambert, 'Admiral Sir John Fisher and the Concept of Flotilla Defence, 1904–1909', *Journal of Military History*, 59:4 (October 1995), 639–60.

33. Lambert, *Naval Revolution*, 250–1.

34. WSC Cabinet memorandum, 15 June 1912, ADM 116/1294B; *WSC*, II/3:1,564–9. Emphasis in original.

35. Ibid.

36. CID 117th mtg, 4 July 1912, CAB 2/2.

37. Marder, *Dreadnought to Scapa Flow*, I:294–5.

38. Sir Charles Hobhouse diary, 10 July 1912, *Inside Asquith's Cabinet*, ed. Edward David (London: John Murray, 1977), 117.

39. Speech of 22 July 1912, *Complete Speeches*, II:1,994. Also his speech of 24 July, ibid., II:2,004.

40. CID 118th mtg, 11 July 1912, CAB 2/2.

41. WSC memorandum of 15 July 1910, CAB 37/103/32.

42. WSC to Asquith, 14 April 1912, ADM 116/3485; *WSC*, II/3:1,538.

43. Borden to WSC, 28 August 1912, Borden papers, Library and Archives Canada, microfilm reel C4349, ff. 67313–16; *WSC*, II/3:1,641–2.

44. WSC to Borden, 29 August 1912, Borden papers, ff. 67319–20.

45. WSC to Harcourt, 13 September 1912, CHAR (Churchill papers, Churchill College Archives Centre, Cambridge) 13/10.

46. Secret Admiralty memorandum for the Canadian government, 20 September 1912, CAB 37/112/105; Gilbert Norman Tucker, *The Naval Service of Canada*, 2 vols (Ottawa: King's Printer, 1952), II:406.

47. WSC to Borden, 4 November 1912, Borden papers, ff. 57400–1; *The Collective Naval Defence of the Empire, 1900–1940*, ed. Nicholas Tracy (Aldershot: Ashgate for the Navy Records Society, 1997), 174.

48. Speech of 31 March 1913, House of Commons, *Complete Speeches*, II:2,108; see also Churchill's note on this speech, *WSC*, II/3:1,807.

49. Marder, *Dreadnought to Scapa Flow*, I:304–5.

50. WSC memorandum, 23 September 1913, *WSC*, II/3:1,784.

51. WSC to Grey and Asquith, 22 October 1912, Cab 1/34.

52. Ballard memorandum, 'Considerations as to the Best Composition of the Mediterranean Fleet in 1915', 20 November 1912, ADM 116/3099.

53. WSC Cabinet memorandum, 'The Three Canadian Ships', 3 June 1913, CAB 37/113/128; *WSC*, II/3:1,808–10.

54. Borden to WSC, 1 June 1913, Tracy, *Collective Naval Defence*, 203; Hobhouse diary, 6 June 1913, *Inside Asquith's Cabinet*, 137.

55. WSC to Borden, 30 June 1913, Tracy, *Collective Naval Defence*, 207–11.

56. 'Submarine Construction—1914–15: Precis of Papers', Keyes papers, British Library, Add Ms 82455; Lambert, *Naval Revolution*, 278–84.

57. WSC to Borden, 30 June 1913, Borden papers, ff. 67776–85.

58. WSC memorandum, 'Navy Estimates, 1914–15', 5 December 1913, *WSC*, II/3:1,818–24.

59. Lloyd George memorandum, December 1913, CAB 37/117/97; Friedrich Wilhelm Wiemann, 'Lloyd George and the Struggle for the Navy Estimates of 1914', *Lloyd George: Twelve Essays*, ed. A. J. P. Taylor (New York: Atheneum, 1971), 71–91.

60. Wiemann, 'Navy Estimates of 1914', 79.

61. WSC memorandum, 13 December 1913; WSC to Asquith, 18 December 1913; WSC to Grey, 25 December 1913; *WSC*, II/3:1,825–7, 1,834–5, 1,836–8.

62. WSC to Asquith, 18 December 1913, *WSC*, II/3:1,835.

63. Undated [but 1913 based on internal evidence] WSC memorandum, CHAR 13/6A.

64. WSC to Borden, 19 December 1913, Borden papers, ff. 67896–7.

65. Borden to WSC, 31 December 1913, Borden papers, ff. 67914–15.

66. WSC minute to Battenberg and Jackson, CHAR 13/6A.

67. Asquith to King George V, 29 January 1914, CAB 41/35/1.

68. WSC Cabinet memorandum, 6 February 1914, CAB 37/119/25; *WSC*, II/3:1,863–6.

69. Asquith to King George V, 11 February 1914, CAB 41/35/3.

70. WSC to DID, 26 February 1914, CHAR 13/25.

71. WSC memorandum, 'Italian and Austrian building programmes', 26 April 1914, CAB 37/119/57.

72. WSC to Battenberg, 13 May 1914, *WSC*, II/3:1,977.

73. WSC to Masterton-Smith, 23 May 1914, CAB 1/34. See also Geoffrey Miller, *The Millstone* (Hull: University of Hull Press, 1999), ch. 16.

74. WSC minute, 30 May 1914, CAB 1/33.

75. WSC to Asquith, 4 July 1914, *The Submarine Service, 1900–1918*, ed. Nicholas A. Lambert (Aldershot, Hants: Ashgate for the Navy Records Society, 2001), 259.

76. Speech of 7 July 1914, *Complete Speeches*, III:2,323.

77. CHAR 8/61. See also Churchill's speech of 26 March 1913 on the Navy Estimates, *Complete Speeches*, II:2,080.

78. *Complete Speeches*, II:2,183.

79. WSC minute, 'Notes on Submarines', 20 August 1913, DEY (Sir Eustace Tennyson d'Eyncourt papers, NMM); Lambert, *Submarine Service*, 207–9; see also WSC to Fisher, 30 August 1913, FISR (Fisher papers, Churchill College Archives Centre, Cambridge), 1/13.

80. WSC to King George V, 9 March 1910, *WSC*, II/2:991; speech of 9 March 1910, *Complete Speeches*, II:1,510.

81. Marder, *Dreadnought to Scapa Flow*, I:348–51.

82. 'Notes on the Manoeuvres: Prepared for the Prime Minister by the First Lord', 17 October 1912, ADM 116/3381; Marder, *Dreadnought to Scapa Flow*, I:352–3.

83. Lambert, *Fisher's Naval Revolution*, 261–8; Shawn T. Grimes, *Strategy and War Planning in the British Navy, 1887–1918* (Woodbridge, Suffolk: Boydell Press, 2012), 176–7.

84. War Orders, Home Fleet, 16 December 1912, ADM 116/3412; Grimes, *Strategy and War Planning*, 178–81.

85. Lambert, *Fisher's Naval Revolution*, 263–8.

86. WSC to Battenberg, 17 February 1913, ADM 116/3412.

87. Admiralty to Bayly, 31 January 1913, ADM 137/452. Grimes, *Strategy and War Planning*, 181–5; Nicholas Black, *The British Naval Staff in the First World War* (Woodbridge: Boydell Press, 2009), 71–3; Lambert, *Fisher's Naval Revolution*, 270–2.

88. WSC, 'The Time Table of a Nightmare', 16 April 1913, *WSC*, II:613–27.

89. WSC to Sir Henry Jackson, 18 April 1913, *WSC*, II/3:1,725–7.

90. Jellicoe autobiographical notes, *Jellicoe Papers*, I:29; Marder, *Dreadnought to Scapa Flow*, I:353–4; Churchill, *World Crisis*, I:154.

91. Lambert, *Fisher's Naval Revolution*, 272.

92. WSC memorandum, 21 August 1913, and WSC to Asquith, 8 September 1913, *WSC*, II/3:1,770–7. The Admiralty's plans to protect British trade during this period are well covered in Matthew Seligmann, *The Royal Navy and the German Threat 1901–1914* (Oxford: Oxford University Press, 2012). I am grateful to Dr Seligmann for allowing me to have an advance look at his important new book.

93. Seligmann, *Royal Navy and the German Threat*, 134–6.

94. WSC memorandum, 21 August 1913, *WSC*, II/3:1,772–3.

95. WSC to Grey, 15 November 1911, CAB 1/34; Seligmann, *Royal Navy and the German Threat*, 40, 133.

96. WSC memorandum, 21 August 1913, *WSC*, II/3:1,772–3.

97. Seligmann, *Royal Navy and the German Threat*, 136–53.

98. Speech of 26 March 1913, House of Commons, *Complete Speeches*, II:2,085; WSC to Battenberg, 18 September 1913, *WSC*, II/3:1,779.

99. WSC to Battenberg, 18 September 1913, *WSC*, II/3:1,779–80.

100. WSC memorandum, 21 August 1913, *WSC*, II/3:1,772–3.

101. Seligmann, *Royal Navy and the German Threat*, 158–62.

102. WSC to Battenberg, 18 September 1913, *WSC*, II/3:1,779–80.

103. WSC minute, 14 April 1914, ADM 116/3381; Seligmann, *Royal Navy and the German Threat*, 159–61.

104. Marder, *Dreadnought to Scapa Flow*, I:360–2; Bryan Ranft, 'The Protection of British Seaborne Trade and the Development of Systematic Planning for War, 1860–1906', *Technical Change and British Naval Policy 1860–1939*, ed. Bryan Ranft (London: Hodder and Stoughton, 1977), 1–23.

105. WSC memorandum, 21 August 1913, *WSC*, II/3:1,777.

106. WSC to Fisher, 1 January 1914, FISR 1/14.

107. WSC to the First, Second, and Third Sea Lords, 25 December 1913, CHAR 13/22B.

108. On navalist views of economic warfare during this period, see in particular Lord Hankey, *The Supreme Command* (London: George Allen and Unwin, 1961); A. C. Bell, *A History of the Blockade of Germany and the Countries Associated with her in the Great War, Austria-Hungary, Bulgaria and Turkey* (London: Historical Section, Committee of Imperial Defence, 1937); Avner Offer, *The First World War: An Agrarian Interpretation* (Oxford: Clarendon Press, 1991); and Nicholas Lambert, *Planning Armageddon: British Economic Warfare and the First World War* (Cambridge, MA: Harvard University Press, 2012).

109. CID 120th mtg, 6 December 1912, CAB 2/3.

110. CID 121st mtg, 7 January 1913, CAB 2/3.

111. CID 121st mtg, 7 January 1913, CAB 2/3. Nicholas Lambert attaches greater significance to the revised conclusion than appears warranted, and seems not to realize that this represented a significant retreat by Asquith rather than a firm commitment by the prime minister and senior Cabinet ministers to the ruthless prosecution of economic warfare. N. Lambert, *Planning Armageddon*, 178.

112. Bell, *Blockade of Germany*, 31–2; Lambert, *Armageddon*, 174–81, 210–11.

113. Draft War Plans (War with Germany), [June] 1914, ADM 116/3096.

114. Lambert, *Planning Armageddon*.

115. WSC to Battenberg, 17 February 1913, ADM 116/3412. Emphasis added.

116. Bell, *Blockade of Germany*, 23.

117. Ballard memorandum, 'Proposals Regarding the Use of Mines in an Offensive Strategic Policy', 6 February 1913, ADM 116/3412; Lambert, *Fisher's Naval Revolution*, 270–2; Lambert, *Planning Armageddon*, 180–1; Grimes, *Strategy and War Planning*, 185–6. Notably, when the idea of mining was raised in August 1914, Asquith, who was generally in favour of strong measures to inflict economic pressure, declared that he was 'all against this provocative & rather barbarous mode of procedure'. Asquith to Venetia Stanley, 17 August 1914, in *H. H. Asquith: Letters to Venetia Stanley*, ed. Michael and Eleanor Brock (Oxford: Oxford University Press, 1982), 171.

118. Bell, *Blockade of Germany*, 32.

119. WSC memorandum, 21 August 1913, *WSC*, II/3:1,773.

120. 'Record of Conference held in First Lord's Room on 9th December', Keyes papers, Add Ms 82455.

121. WSC First, Second, and Third Sea Lords, 25 December 1913, CHAR 13/22B.

122. Lambert, *Fisher's Naval Revolution*, 296.

123. CHAR 8/61.

124. WSC minute to Moore and d'Eyncourt, 1 June 1914, ADM 138/428A (ship's cover, Polyphemus), Brass Foundry, Woolwich.

125. WSC to Greene and Battenberg, 12 July 1914, Cab 1/34; see also the undated memorandum by the Second Sea Lord, HTN/124, Admiral Sir Frederick Tower Hamilton papers, NMM.

126. WSC to Battenberg, 12 July 1914, Cab 1/34.

127. Sturdee memoranda, 'What is the Strategic and Tactical Value of a Polyphemus?' and 'What is the *Raison D'Être* of a Polyphemus at the Present Time', MB1/T37/361–2, Prince Louis of Battenberg papers, University of Southampton Library, Archives and Manuscripts. These deliberations were uncovered by Nicholas Lambert, and are examined at length in his book *Fisher's Naval Revolution*, ch. 9. A different interpretation was subsequently developed by the present author in 'Sir John Fisher's Naval Revolution Reconsidered: Winston Churchill at the Admiralty, 1911–14', *War in History*, 18, no. 3 (July 2011), 350–4.

128. Bell, 'Fisher's Naval Revolution Reconsidered', 353–4.

129. Battenberg to Jackson, 11 May 1914, ADM 116/3096.

130. WSC to Battenberg, 11 June 1914, and Jackson to Callaghan, 15 June 1914, ADM 116/3096; extract from Jellicoe's autobiographical notes, *Jellicoe Papers*, I:36.

131. WSC minute of 25 July 1914, ADM 1/8386/213.

CHAPTER 2

1. On the employment of the British fleet as a deterrent, see Lambert, 'The Royal Navy, 1856–1914'.

2. Richmond diary, 5 August 1914, *Portrait of an Admiral*, ed. Arthur J. Marder (Cambridge, MA: Harvard University Press, 1952), 92.

3. Bell, *Blockade of Germany*, 31–2; Lambert, *Armageddon*, 174–81, 210–11.

4. Letter by J. A. Pease, 28 August 1914, cited in David French, *British Strategy and War Aims 1914–1916* (London: Allen & Unwin, 1984), 27; and Lambert, *Armageddon*, 204–5.

5. The best source on British strategy during this period is French, *British Strategy*.

6. This is implicitly the argument made in Lambert, *Armageddon*.

7. WSC (endorsed by Battenberg and Oliver) to Grey and Asquith, *WSC*, III/1:12–14.

8. WSC to Battenberg and Sturdee, 9 August 1914, *WSC*, III/1:24–6.

9. WSC to Asquith, Grey, and Kitchener, 7 September 1914, *WSC*, III/1:97–9.

10. Hobhouse diary, 8 September 14, *Inside Asquith's Cabinet*, 189.

11. Lambert, *Armageddon*, 216–26, provides a good summary of these deliberations.

12. Churchill, *World Crisis*, I:253; see also Viscount Grey, *Twenty-Five Years: 1892–1916*, 2 vols (Toronto: Ryerson Press, 1925), II:68–70.

13. Speech of 11 September 1914, National Liberal Club, London, *Complete Speeches*, III:2,331.

14. Speech of 9 November 1914, *Complete Speeches*, III:2,340–1.

15. Clementine Churchill to WSC, *c.*19 September 1914, in *Speaking for Themselves*, ed. Mary Soames (Toronto: Stoddart, 1998), 104–5.

16. Richmond diary, 24 October 1914, *Portrait*, 121; *WSC*, III/1:216.

17. Asquith to Venetia Stanley, 7 October 1914, in *Asquith Letters*, 266; Asquith, *Memories and Reflections*, 54–5.

18. Quoted in Lambert, *Armageddon*, 286.

19. *Jellicoe Papers*, I:36–41; WSC to Asquith, 31 July 1914, ADM 137/452; *WSC*, III/1:6–7; Black, *Naval Staff*, 95–8.

20. WSC to Battenberg and Admiral Sturdee, 9 August 1914, *WSC*, III/1:24–6. See also WSC to Asquith, 31 July 1914, ADM 137/452; Black, *Naval Staff*, 96–103; Grimes, *Strategy and War Planning*, 193–4.

21. WSC memorandum, 19 August 1914, *WSC*, III/1:45–6.

22. Wilson to WSC, 10 September 1914, ADM 137/452.

23. Richmond diary, 12 August 1914, *Portrait*, 96–8; Black, *Naval Staff*, 96–103.

24. *Jellicoe Papers*, I:69.

25. WSC to Jellicoe, 8 October 1914, *WSC*, III/1:180–2.

26. WSC to Asquith, 29 December 1914, *WSC*, III/1:345.

27. War Council, 28 January 1915, *WSC*, III/1:464–5; also Hankey, *Supreme Command*, I:272, where the wording differs slightly.

28. Undated (but pre-November 1914) memorandum, CHAR 13/27.

29. Wilson to WSC, 10 December 1914, CHAR 13/27/44; *WSC*, III/1:304.

30. 21 September 1914, *Complete Speeches*, III:2,337.

31. WSC to Fisher, 11 December 1914, FISR 1/16; also WSC to Fisher, 21 December 1914, *Fear God and Dread Nought*, ed. Arthur J. Marder, 3 vols (London: Jonathan Cape, 1952–9), III:105. Graham Clews, *Churchill's Dilemma: The Real Story Behind the Origins of the 1915 Dardanelles Campaign* (Santa Barbara, CA: Praeger, 2010), 26–8.

32. War Council minutes, 1 December 1914, *WSC*, III/1:290–1.

33. Robin Prior, *Churchill's 'World Crisis' as History* (London: Croom Helm, 1983), 47.

34. For example, Rear Admiral Cecil Burney to WSC, 8 November 1914, FISR 1/16; Clews, *Churchill's Dilemma*, 27–8.

35. WSC to Fisher, 21 December 1914, *Fear God and Dread Nought*, III:105; *WSC*, III/1:323–4; WSC to Fisher, 22 December 1914, *WSC*, III/1:325–6; Black, *Naval Staff*, 112–14.

36. On Fisher and the Baltic, see Churchill, *Great Contemporaries* (London: Odhams, 1948), 266–7; Ruddock F. Mackay, *Fisher of Kilverstone* (Oxford: Clarendon Press, 1973), 468, 472–3; Andrew Lambert, 'The German North Sea Islands, the Kiel Canal and the Danish Narrows in Royal Navy Thinking and Planning, 1905–1918', in *The Danish Straits and German Naval Power 1905–1918*, ed. Michael Epkenhans and Gerhard P. Gross (Potsdam: Militärgeschichtliches Forschungsamt, 2010), 35–62; Grimes, *Strategy and War Planning*, 204–11.

37. Lambert, *Armageddon*, 296–300.

38. For Churchill's views on mining, see his memorandum of October 1914 in *World Crisis*, I:566–9.

39. Lambert, 'German North Sea Islands', 52–8.

40. On Fisher's views, see his memorandum 'On the possibility of using our Command of the Sea to influence more drastically the Military Situation on the Continent,' *WSC*, III/1:284–7; Mackay, *Fisher*, 456–72; Black, *Naval Staff*, 116–19. For Churchill, see WSC to Fisher, 22 December 1914, *WSC*, III/1:325–6.

41. WSC to Asquith, 29 December 1914, and memorandum, 31 December 1914, *WSC*, III/1:343–5, 347–9.

42. Hankey memorandum, 28 December 1914; Lloyd George memorandum, 31 December 1914, *WSC*, III/1:337–43, 350–6; Hankey, *Supreme Command*, I:244–52.

43. Fisher to WSC, 3 and 4 January 1915, Marder, *Fear God*, III:117–18; *WSC*, III/1:367, 371–2. Arthur Balfour, the former Conservative prime minister, also preferred a northern offensive against Germany to an attack on Turkey. Stephen Roskill, *Hankey: Man of Secrets*, 3 vols (London: Collins, 1970–4), I:150–1.

44. Asquith to Stanley, 17 August 1914, *Asquith Letters*, 171; WSC to Grey, 6 September 1914; WSC to Fisher, 30 October 1914, *WSC*, III/1:40, 95, 236.

45. E.g. Robert Rhodes James, *Gallipoli* (London: Macmillan, 1989), 31; Geoffrey Best, *Churchill and War* (London: Hambledon & London, 2005), 56. For a valuable corrective, see Clews, *Churchill's Dilemma*.

46. Fisher to Hankey, 2 January 1915, CAB 63/4; Robin Prior, *Gallipoli* (New Haven, CT: Yale University Press, 2009), 12.

47. WSC to Fisher, 4 January 1915, *WSC*, III/1:371.

48. See in particular Clews, *Churchill's Dilemma*.

49. WSC to Fisher, Wilson, and Oliver, 3 January 1915; WSC to Jellicoe, 4 January 1915, *WSC*, III/1:365–6, 367–8.

50. War Council, 7 January 1915, *WSC*, III/1:384–90.

51. WSC to Sir John French, 11 January 1915, *WSC*, III/1:401.

52. Kitchener to WSC, 2 January 1915, *WSC*, III/1:360–1.

53. Clews, *Churchill's Dilemma*.

54. CHAR 8/134; cited in Prior, *Churchill's 'World Crisis'*, 47.

55. WSC to Carden, 3 January 1915, and Carden to WSC, 5 January 1915, *WSC*, III/1:367, 380.

56. Bayly to Admiralty, 8 January 1915, ADM 137/1089.
57. Jackson memorandum, 'Note on forcing the passage of the Dardanelles and Bosphorus by the Allied Fleets, in order to destroy the Turko-German Squadron and threaten Constantinople without military co-operation', 5 January 1915, ADM 137/1089; Black, *Naval War Staff*, 120–2.
58. Carden to WSC, 11 January 1915, *WSC*, III/1:405–6.
59. Prior, *'World Crisis'*, 55, 58–60; Clews, *Churchill's Dilemma*, ch. 8.
60. See, for example, his comments to the French Minister of Marine: George H. Cassar, *The French and the Dardanelles* (London: Allen and Unwin, 1971), 57–8, 66.
61. War Council, 13 January 1915, *WSC*, III/1:409–11; Grey, *Twenty-Five Years*, II:75–6. There was never, Grey recalled, any possibility that the Dardanelles operation would have been planned from the outset as a joint military and naval operation. '[I]f this had been proposed the operation would never have been agreed to.'
62. David French, 'The Origins of the Dardanelles Campaign Reconsidered', *History*, 68, no. 233 (June 1983), 210–24.
63. Hankey, *Supreme Command*, I:265–6.
64. War Council, 13 January 1915, *WSC*, III/1:409–11.
65. Hobhouse diary, 16 February 1915, *Inside Asquith's Cabinet*, 222.
66. Jackson to Oliver, 15 January 1915, *WSC*, III/1:419–21.
67. WSC to Fisher and Oliver, 20 January 1915, and WSC to Kitchener, 20 January 1915, *World Crisis*, II:114–19, *WSC*, III/1:432–3.
68. 'Memorandum by the First Sea Lord on the Position of the British Fleet and its Policy of Steady Pressure', 25 January 1915, *WSC*, III/1:452–4.
69. WSC memorandum, 27 January 1915, *World Crisis*, II:157. See also WSC to Beatty, 30 November 1914, *Beatty Papers*, ed. B. Ranft, 2 vols (Aldershot: Ashgate for the Navy Records Society, 1989–93), I:169: 'You must all get the 60 per cent standard out of your minds. No one has any ground for complaint at fighting on equal terms.'
70. WSC to Fisher, 26 January 1915, *WSC*, III/1:458.
71. Lambert, *Armageddon*, 335–6.
72. Jackson memorandum, 'Attack on Constantinople', 13 February 1915, *WSC*, III/1:506–12.
73. Asquith to Venetia Stanley, 13 February 1915, *Asquith Letters*, 429–30.
74. Hankey to Balfour, 10 February 1915, *WSC*, III/1:500; Asquith to Venetia Stanley, 13 February 1915, *Asquith Letters*; Clews, *Churchill's Dilemma*, ch. 14.
75. War Council, 16 February 1915, *WSC*, III/1:516.
76. WSC to Kitchener, 18 February 1915, *WSC*, III/1:518–19.
77. WSC memoranda of 23 and 25 February 1915, *WSC*, III/1:547, 563–4.
78. WSC to Carden, 24 February 1915, *WSC*, III/1:550.
79. War Council, 26 February 1915, *WSC*, III/1:567–77; Clews, *Churchill's Dilemma*, ch. 18.

80. Prior, *Gallipoli*, 48.
81. WSC to Kitchener, 4 March 1915, *World Crisis*, II:195.
82. War Council minutes, 3 March 1915, *WSC*, III/1:610.
83. WSC to Jellicoe, 9 March 1915, *WSC*, III/1:656.
84. WSC to Carden, 11 March 1915, *World Crisis*, II:220; *WSC*, III/1:677.
85. War Council, 24 February 1915, *WSC*, III/1:555–61; Hankey, *Supreme Command*, I:283. Writing to Jellicoe on 1 June, Churchill was quite candid about this. 'The Dardanelles has run on like a Greek tragedy,' he remarked. 'Our early successes converting what was originally launched only as an experiment into an undertaking from wh[ich] it was impossible to recede . . .' *WSC*, III/2:976.
86. Prior, *Gallipoli*, 54–7.
87. De Robeck to Admiralty, 23 March 1915, *World Crisis*, II:236; Prior, *Gallipoli*, 65–9.
88. WSC telegrams and draft telegram to de Robeck, 23 and 24 March 1915, *World Crisis*, II:237–8, *WSC*, III/1:724–8.
89. WSC memorandum, 24 March 1915, *WSC*, III/1:732–8.
90. War Council, 14 May 1915, *WSC*, III/2:873–80.
91. WSC to Sir Archibald Sinclair, 30 July 1915, *WSC*, IV:7.
92. WSC to Asquith, Arthur Balfour, Andrew Bonar Law, and Lord Curzon, 11 June 1915, *WSC*, III/2:1,003–8.
93. WSC to Asquith and Balfour, 21 August 1915; WSC to Balfour, 6 October 1915, *WSC*, III/2:1,151–5, 1,204.
94. WSC to Asquith, 4 October 1915, *WSC*, III/2:1,193–6.
95. E.g. WSC memorandum, 'Dardanelles', 15 October 1915, *WSC*, III/2:1,220–4.
96. Prior, *Gallipoli*, 242.
97. Hankey, *Supreme Command*, I:185.
98. Speech of 15 November 1915, House of Commons, *Complete Speeches*, III:2,400.
99. Edward J. Erickson, 'One More Push; Forcing the Dardanelles in March 1915', *Journal of Strategic Studies*, 24, no. 3 (September 2001), 158–76.
100. WSC draft statement, 8 September 1916, *WSC*, III/2:1,554–5. See also Churchill's resignation speech of 15 November 1915: 'Naval operations did not necessarily involve military operations. This was a separate decision, which did not rest with me or the Admiralty.' *Complete Speeches*, III:2,390–403.
101. WSC to Hankey, 2 June 1915, *WSC*, III/2:984.
102. Churchill, *SWW*, II:15.
103. 'The Great Amphibian', *Sunday Pictorial*, 23 July 1916, *Winston S. Churchill: The Collected Essays*, ed. Michael Wolff, 4 vols (London: Library of Imperial History, 1976), I:100–4.
104. Speech of 23 May 1916, *Complete Speeches*, III:2,430.
105. WSC statement, 3 June 1916, *WSC*, III/2:1,511–12.

106. 'The War by Land and Sea', *London Magazine*, October 1916, in *Collected Essays*, I:113–19.

107. WSC to Sinclair, 23 August 1916, *WSC*, IV/1:25.

108. Julian S. Corbett, *Some Principles of Maritime Strategy* (London: Brassey's, 1998); Donald M. Schurman, *Julian S. Corbett, 1854–1922* (London: Royal Historical Society, 1981).

109. Sydenham, 'Sea Heresy: Mr Churchill and Naval Strategy', *The Times*, 4 October 1916, 6; Custance, 'Decisive Victory at Sea', *The Times*, 9 October 1916, 6; Schurman, *Corbett*, 167–9.

110. 'The War by Land and Sea', *London Magazine*, December 1916, in *Collected Essays*, I:131–40.

111. 'The War by Land and Sea', *London Magazine*, January 1917, in *Collected Essays*, I:140–50. Churchill repeated this argument in the House of Commons on 21 February 1917, *Complete Speeches*, III:2,510.

112. Sturdee memorandum, 'Remarks on the Main Naval Strategy of the War', 24 November 1916, *Jellicoe Papers*, II:98–100.

113. WSC to Jellicoe, 2 December 1916, *Jellicoe Papers*, II:108. Emphasis in original.

114. 'The War by Land and Sea', *London Magazine*, January 1917, *Collected Essays*, I:140–50.

115. Ibid.

116. Paul G. Halpern, *A Naval History of World War I* (Annapolis, MD: Naval Institute Press, 1995), 341.

117. WSC to Admiralty, March 1917, *World Crisis*, IV:81–2.

118. 'The Real Need of the British Navy', *Sunday Pictorial*, 24 June 1917, *Collected Essays*, I:201–4.

119. E.g. Marder, *Dreadnought*, IV:168–9; Barry Hunt, *Sailor–Scholar: Admiral Sir Herbert Richmond, 1871–1946* (Waterloo, ON: Wilfrid Laurier University Press, 1982), 58–9.

120. GT 1397: WSC memorandum, 'Naval War Policy, 1917', 7 July 1917, CAB 24/19; *WSC*, IV/1:77–99.

121. Jellicoe memorandum, July 1917, *Jellicoe Papers*, II:174–8; A. Temple Patterson, *Jellicoe* (London: Macmillan, 1969), 192–3; Marder, *Dreadnought*, IV:229–30; Grimes, *Strategy and War Planning*, 215–20.

122. Patterson, *Jellicoe*, 194–7; Marder, *Dreadnought*, IV:231–6; Grimes, *Strategy and War Planning*, 215–20.

123. On this period of Churchill's career, see in particular Eugene Edward Beireger, *Churchill, Munitions and Mechanical Warfare: The Politics of Supply and Strategy* (New York: Peter Lang, 1997).

124. Speech of 5 March 1917, House of Commons, *Complete Speeches*, III:2,522.

125. WSC memorandum, 1 November 1917, *WSC*, IV/1:185.

126. WSC to Fisher, 19 May 1918, *Fear God*, III:536; *WSC*, IV/1:318.

127. WSC to Geddes, unsent draft, 13 December 1917, *WSC*, IV/1:213.

CHAPTER 3

1. Wemyss to Beatty, 7 January 1919, cited in Marder, *Dreadnought*, V:200.
2. See in particular John R. Ferris, *Men, Money, and Diplomacy* (Ithaca, NY: Cornell University Press, 1989), 63–75.
3. WSC departmental note, 12 January 1919, *WSC*, IV/1:452.
4. Ferris, *Men, Money, and Diplomacy*, 65–86.
5. WSC to Lloyd George, 1 May 1919, *Beatty Papers*, II:35–7; *WSC*, IV/1:633–7.
6. Speech of 26 November 1918, Dundee, *Complete Speeches*, III:2,642.
7. WSC to Long, 13 November 1919, CHAR 2/106.
8. WSC to Lloyd George, 1 May 1919, *Beatty Papers*, II:35–7; *WSC*, IV/1:633–7.
9. 'Our Armaments After the War', 29 June 1919, *Weekly Dispatch*, in *Collected Essays*, I:218–20.
10. WSC memorandum, 1 August 1919, *WSC*, IV/2:782–3.
11. WSC to Lloyd George, 4 August 1919, *WSC*, IV/2:792.
12. Hankey memorandum, 'Towards a National Policy', 17 July 1919, CAB 21/159.
13. G-257: 'Memorandum by the Treasury on the Financial Position and Future Prospects of this Country', 18 July 1919, CAB 24/15; GT 7646: Austen Chamberlain Cabinet memorandum, 'Navy Votes', 8 July 1919, CAB 24/83.
14. Undated Board of Admiralty memorandum, 'Suggested Memorandum for War Cabinet: Naval Policy', ADM 167/59.
15. 'Naval Policy and Expenditure', 24 October 1919, ADM 167/56.
16. Naval attitudes towards the US are outlined in Christopher M. Bell, 'Thinking the Unthinkable: American and British Naval Strategies for an Anglo-American War, 1918–31', *International History Review*, XIX, no. 4 (November 1997), 789–808. See also B. J. C. McKercher, '"The Deep and Latent Distrust": The British Official Mind and the United States, 1919–1929', in *Anglo-American Relations in the 1920s*, ed. B. J. C. McKercher (Edmonton, AB: University of Alberta Press, 1990), 209–38; D. C. Watt, *Personalities and Policies* (Notre Dame, IL: University of Notre Dame Press, 1965), ch. 2.
17. WC 616A, 15 August 1919, CAB 23/15; on the origins and impact of the ten-year rule during this period, see John R. Ferris, 'Treasury Control, the Ten Year Rule and British Service Policies, 1919–1924', *Historical Journal*, 30, no. 4 (December 1987), 859–83.
18. E.g. Correlli Barnett, *The Collapse of British Power* (London: Eyre Methuen, 1972), 277; David MacGregor, 'Former Naval Cheapskate: Chancellor of the Exchequer Winston Churchill and the Royal Navy, 1924–29', *Armed Forces and Society*, 19, no. 3 (Spring 1993), 319–20; Robert Rhodes James, *Churchill: A Study in Failure* (London: Weidenfeld and Nicolson, 1970), 124, 165.
19. On the origins and development of the one-power standard, see Christopher M. Bell, *The Royal Navy: Seapower and Strategy between the Wars* (Stanford, CA: Stanford University Press, 2000), ch. 1.

20. Walter Long memorandum, 'Naval Estimates and Naval Policy', 13 February 1920, ADM 167/61.
21. *Parliamentary Debates*, Commons, 5th ser., vol. 126, cols 2300–1: 17 March 1920.
22. Bell, *Royal Navy*, 8–11; Beatty memorandum, 'Naval Policy and Construction', 8 July 1920, ADM 167/60.
23. CID 134th mtg, 14 December 1920, CAB 2/3.
24. Ibid.
25. Ibid.
26. CID 135th mtg, 23 December 1920, CAB 2/3.
27. NSC 27: Richmond memorandum, 9 February 1921, CAB 16/37/2; see also Christopher Bell, '"How are we going to make war?": Admiral Sir Herbert Richmond and British Far Eastern War Plans', *Journal of Strategic Studies*, 20, 4 (September 1997), 126–7.
28. CID Sub-Committee on the Question of the Capital Ship in the Navy [NSC], 2nd mtg, 3 January 1921, CAB 16/37/1; NSC 2 and NSC 9, CAB 16/37/2.
29. NSC 22: Air Staff memorandum, 'The Big Ship Controversy from the Air Point of View', January 1921; see also NSC 24: memorandum by Major General Frederick Sykes, 'Notes on Naval Armaments as Affected by Aircraft Development', 26 January 21, CAB 16/37/2.
30. NSC 9th mtg, 26 January 1921, CAB 16/37/1.
31. Ibid.
32. NSC 5th mtg, 11 January 1921, CAB 16/37/1.
33. WSC to Balfour, 26 February 1921, *WSC*, IV/2:1,379.
34. Bell, 'Thinking the Unthinkable'. Roskill was evidently uncomfortable with the navy's willingness to consider war with the United States as a possibility, however remote. His account of the Capital Ship Committee's work ignores its lengthy discussions relating to strategy for an Anglo-American war and the anti-American sentiment expressed by some officers. Stephen Roskill, *Naval Policy Between the Wars*, 2 vols (London: Collins, 1968–76), I:223–5.
35. N-11: 'Report of the Sub-Committee on the Question of the Capital Ship in the Navy 1920–21', 2 March 1921, CAB 16/37/1.
36. Cabinet minutes, 30 May 1921, CAB 23/25; *WSC*, IV/3:1,479.
37. Roskill, *Naval Policy*, I:292–8; John Ferris, 'The Symbol and Substance of Seapower: Britain, the United States and the One-Power Standard, 1919–1921', in McKercher, *Anglo-American Relations in the 1920s*, 55–80.
38. Cabinet memorandum, 4 July 1921; see also his earlier memorandum, CP 3048: 'The Anglo-Japanese Alliance', 17 June 1921, CAB 24/125; *WSC*, IV/3:1,512–13, 1,539–42.
39. Erik Goldstein, 'The Evolution of British Diplomatic Strategy for the Washington Conference', *The Washington Conference, 1921–22: Naval Rivalry, East*

Asian Stability and the Road to Pearl Harbor, ed. Erik Goldstein and John Maurer (London: Frank Cass, 1994).

40. WSC to the Prince of Wales, 2 January 1922, *WSC*, IV/3:1,710.

41. The other committee members were Lord Birkenhead, Edwin Montagu, and Stanley Baldwin.

42. Undated Board of Admiralty memorandum, 'Admiralty Proposals for Reduction in Expenditure', ADM 167/66.

43. CID 244-C, 'Naval Policy: The Development of Imperial Defence Policy in the Far East', 24 March 1925, CAB 5/5.

44. 'Admiralty Memorandum in reply to Paragraph 101 of Questionnaire [from the Geddes Committee]', n.d., ADM 1/8615/200.

45. Ibid.

46. GRC (DD) [Committee Appointed to Examine Part I (Defence Departments) of the Report of the Geddes Committee on National Expenditure], 3rd mtg, 21 January 1922, CAB 27/164.

47. CP-3692, 'Report of Committee Appointed to Examine Part I (Defence Departments) of the Report of the Geddes Committee on National Expenditure', 4 February 1922, CAB 24/133.

48. Memorandum by Barstow, 20 February 1922, 'Reports of the Geddes Committee and Churchill Committee', T 172/1228.

49. WSC to Sir Robert Horne, 11 February 1922, T 172/1228.

50. CP 2957: memorandum by the First Lord, 'Anglo-Japanese Alliance', 21 May 1921, CAB 24/123.

51. Ibid.

52. Keyes to WSC, 24 March 1925, *The Keyes Papers*, ed. Paul G. Halpern, 3 vols (London: Navy Records Society, 1979–81), II:112.

53. On the history of the Singapore Naval Base, see in particular James Neidpath, *The Singapore Naval Base and the Defence of Britain's Eastern Empire, 1919–1941* (Oxford: Clarendon Press, 1981), and W. David McIntyre, *The Rise and Fall of the Singapore Naval Base, 1919–1942* (London: Macmillan, 1979). The oil question is examined in Orest Babij, 'The Royal Navy and Inter-war Plans for War against Japan: The Problem of Oil Supply', *The International Marine in International Affairs, 1850–1950*, ed. Greg Kennedy (London: Frank Cass, 2000).

54. CP-3692, CAB 24/133.

55. 'The Case for Singapore', *Sunday Chronicle*, 30 March 1924, *Collected Essays*, 1:256–9.

56. *The Navy*, May 1924, 132–9.

57. Speech of 28 March 1924, *The Navy*, May 1924, 138; *Complete Speeches*, IV:3,450–1.

CHAPTER 4

1. WSC to Baldwin, 15 December 1924, T 161/243/S25613/ANNEX/5; *WSC*, V/1:304.

2. Bell, *Royal Navy*, ch. 3.

3. RS (Committee on Replacement of Fleet Units other than Capital Ships and Singapore), (24) 5: memorandum by the First Lord, 'Ten Year Building Programme', 9 April 1924, CAB 27/236; draft plans division memorandum, '10 Year Building Programme', 6 March 1925, ADM 1/8685/152.

4. WSC to Baldwin, 15 December 1924, T 161/243/S25613/ANNEX/5.

5. Ibid.

6. Cabinet 64 (24), 26 November 1924, cited in CID 1055-B, 'The Basis of Service Estimates', 23 June 1931, CAB 4/21.

7. WSC to Baldwin, 15 December 1924, T 161/243/S25613/ANNEX/5. Emphasis added.

8. CID 193rd mtg, 5 January 1925, CAB 2/4.

9. Ibid.; see also CP 139/25: Admiralty memorandum, 'Political Outlook in the Far East', 5 March 1925, CAB 24/172, and NP (25) 5, CAB 27/273.

10. WSC to Bridgeman, 23 January 1925, T 161/243/S25613/ANNEX/5.

11. CP 39 (25): 'Navy Estimates', 29 January 1925, CAB 24/171.

12. Beatty to his wife, 2 February 1925, *Beatty Papers*, II:282–3; WSC to Beatty, 4 February 1925, *WSC*, V/1:373–6.

13. Board of Admiralty minute 2005, 11 February 1925, ADM 167/71.

14. Bridgeman to Baldwin, 11 February 1925, *The Modernisation of Conservative Politics: The Diaries and Letters of William Bridgeman, 1904–1935*, ed. Philip Williamson (London: Historians' Press, 1988), 180.

15. Cecil to WSC, 12 February 1925, *WSC*, V/1:390; Roskill, *Naval Policy*, I:447–8.

16. Cabinet 8 (25), 12 February 1925, CAB 23/49.

17. NP (Naval Programme Committee) (25) 1st mtg, 2 March 1925, CAB 27/273.

18. NP (25) 2nd mtg, 5 March 1925, CAB 27/273.

19. Ibid.

20. WSC to Birkenhead, 8 March 1925, *WSC*, V/1:426; CID 198th and 199th mtgs, 30 March and 2 April 1925, CAB 2/4.

21. CID 199th mtg, 2 April 1925, CAB 2/4.

22. Ibid. This definition of the one-power standard was approved by the Cabinet in May.

23. NP (25) 8th mtg, 30 June 1925, CAB 27/273.

24. Ibid.

25. See Keith Middlemas and John Barnes, *Baldwin: A Biography* (London: Weidenfeld and Nicolson, 1969), 336–9; Robert Rhodes James, *Memoirs of a Conservative: J. C .C. Davidson's Memoirs and Papers, 1910–37* (London: Macmillan, 1969), 213–16.

26. John R. Ferris, '"It is our Business in the Navy to Command the Seas": The Last Decade of British Maritime Supremacy, 1919–1929', *Far Flung Lines*, ed. Keith Neilson, and Greg Kennedy (London: Frank Cass, 1996), 124–70.

27. Thomas Jones, *Whitehall Diary*, ed. Keith Middlemass (London: Oxford University Press, 1969), I:315; see also P. J. Grigg, *Prejudice and Judgment* (London: Jonathan Cape, 1948), 175–7.

28. On the Treasury's strategic views, see Bell, *Royal Navy*, 13–24; Ferris, *Men, Money, and Diplomacy*, 4–5, 15–20; G. C. Peden, *British Rearmament and the Treasury, 1932–1939* (Edinburgh: Scottish Academic Press, 1979).

29. See, for example, Barstow minute, 1 October 1923, T 161/800/S18917/2; Barstow to Philip Snowden, 26 February 1924, T 161/800/S18917/2.

30. CID 193rd mtg, 5 January 1925, CAB 2/4.

31. CID 215th mtg, 22 July 1926, CAB 2/4.

32. Barnett, *Collapse*, 281; Ian Hamill, 'Winston Churchill and the Singapore Naval Base, 1924–1929', *Journal of Southeast Asian Studies* (September 1980); idem., *The Strategic Illusion* (Singapore: Singapore University Press, 1981), 108–10.

33. Barstow to WSC, 25 May 1927, and WSC minute, 26 May 1927, T 161/295/S34442.

34. CID 193rd mtg, 5 January 1925, CAB 2/4.

35. Churchill began encouraging the Air Ministry to press its claims in December 1924. WSC to Hoare, 12 December 1924, T 172/1440.

36. Egerton minute, 16 April 1926, and Beatty to Bridgeman, 28 April 1926, ADM 116/2416; Enclosure A to Admiralty to CID, 16 July 1926, CID 275-C, 'Third Interim Report of the Sub-Committee on Singapore', appendix II, CAB 16/63.

37. CID 215th mtg, 22 July 1926, CAB 2/4.

38. CID 209th mtg, 18 February 1926, CAB 2/4.

39. WSC to Bridgeman, 22 December 1926, *WSC*, V/1:901.

40. Ibid.

41. On British policy and the Geneva naval conference, see in particular Dick Richardson, *The Evolution of British Disarmament Policy in the 1920s* (New York: St. Martin's Press, 1989), ch. 9; B. J. C. McKercher, *The Second Baldwin Government and the United States, 1924–1929* (Cambridge: Cambridge University Press, 1984), ch. 3. Churchill's influence on the Geneva conference is examined in Tadashi Kuramatsu, 'Viscount Cecil, Winston Churchill and the Geneva Naval Conference of 1927: *si vis pacem para pacem* versus *si vis pacem para bellum*', *Personalities, War and Diplomacy: Essays in International History*, ed. T. G. Otte and Constantine A. Pagedas (London: Frank Cass, 1997), and Phillips O'Brien, 'Churchill and the US Navy', *Winston Churchill: Studies in Statesmanship*, ed. R. A. C. Parker (London: Brassey's, 1995). Roskill's account of the Geneva conference does not mention the role played by Churchill, while Churchill's official biography by Martin Gilbert does not mention the Geneva conference.

42. Undated memorandum by the Sea Lords for the Board of Admiralty, 'Limitation of Armaments', ADM 167/76.

43. Pound to Keyes, 17 June 1927, Halpern, *Keyes Papers*, II:221.

44. CID 227th mtg, 20 May 1927, CAB 2/4; CID 808-B: plans division memorandum, 'Further Limitation of Naval Armaments', 14 April 1927, CAB 4/16; Roskill, *Naval Policy*, I:498–503.

45. CID 227th mtg, 20 May 1927, CAB 2/4.

46. WSC memorandum, 'Three fallacies', 25 June 1927, T 161/295/S34442.

47. Baldwin to Bridgeman, 29 June 1927, *Documents on British Foreign Policy 1919–1939* (hereafter cited as *DBFP*), ed. W. N. Medlicott, Douglas Dakin, and M. E. Lambert (London: HMSO, 1970), series IA, III:627.

48. CP 189 (27): WSC memorandum, 29 June 1927, CAB 24/187; *DBFP*, series IA, III:627–8.

49. Kuramatsu, 'Geneva Naval Conference', 115; Bridgeman, *Modernisation of Conservative Politics*, 218; Beatty to his wife, 21 June 1927, *Beatty Papers*, II:350.

50. Austen Chamberlain to Esme Howard, *DBFP*, IA, III:634–5.

51. Roskill, *Naval Policy*, I:505–6.

52. CID 228th mtg, 7 July 1927, CAB 2/4.

53. CID 818-B: memorandum by Beatty, 'Reduction and Limitation of Armaments: Cruisers', 7 July 1927, CAB 4/16.

54. For the instructions sent to Bridgeman, see CID 228th mtg, 7 July 1927, CAB 2/4; CID 816-B (Revise): 'Reduction and Limitation of Armaments', 7 July 1927, CAB 4/16; *DBFP*, series IA, III:648–53.

55. WSC memorandum, 'Cruisers and Parity', 20 July 1927, T 161/295/S34442/2; *WSC*, V/1:1,030–5.

56. CID 229th mtg, 14 July 1927, CAB 2/4.

57. Barstow memorandum, 15 July 1927, T 161/295/S34442.

58. LNA (Committee on Further Reduction of Naval Armaments) (27) 3rd mtg, 19 July 1927, CAB 27/350.

59. LNA (27) 1st mtg, 15 July 1927, CAB 27/350.

60. Baldwin to Bridgeman, 15 July 1927, *DBFP*, series IA, III:683–4.

61. LNA (27) 1st and 2nd mtgs, 15 and 18 July 1927, CAB 27/350.

62. *DBFP*, series IA, III:691–5.

63. For the final British proposals see Roskill, *Naval Policy*, I:511–12.

64. WSC to Cecil, 14 September 1927, *WSC*, V/1:1,048–9.

65. William Bridgeman to M. R. Bridgeman, 10 August 1927, *Modernisation of Conservative Politics*, 210; Beatty to Bridgeman, 6 August 1927, *Beatty Papers*, II:355.

66. WSC to Bridgeman, 18 August 1927, T 161/281/S32700/1; *WSC*, V/1: 1,044–5; Cabinet 48 (27), 4 August 1927; Cabinet 49 (27), 25 August 1927, CAB 23/55.

67. R. V. N. Hopkins to WSC, 14 October 1927; P. J. Grigg memorandum recording a discussion between Churchill and Bridgeman, 19 October 1927; WSC to Baldwin, 19 October 1927, T 161/281/S32700/1; *WSC*, V/1:1,062–3.

68. Bridgeman to Baldwin, 21 October 1927, *Modernisation of Conservative Politics*, 211.

69. WSC to Bridgeman, 4 November 1927, T 161/281/S32700/1; *WSC*, V/1:1,088–9.

70. NP (27) 1st mtg, 10 November 1927, CAB 27/355.

71. Ibid. Churchill also noted privately that there was not even any certainty that battleship construction *would* be resumed in 1931. In fact, no new battleships

were laid down before 1937. WSC to Birkenhead, 30 November 1927, *WSC*, V/1:1,120.

72. NP (27) 3rd mtg, 22 November 1927, CAB 27/355.

73. Barstow, for example, wrote that the Admiralty's claim to 45 cruisers for trade defence 'apparently means that if the British Empire had the only fleet in the world she would nevertheless require 45 cruisers for the protection of her trade. Does it also mean that if the United States or Japan have a thousand cruisers the figure for the British Empire is 45?' Memorandum of 15 July 1927, T 161/295/ S34442.

74. NP (27) 3rd mtg, 22 November 1927, CAB 27/355.

75. NP (27) 4th mtg, 1 December 1927, CAB 27/355.

76. CP 305 (27), 'Naval Programme Committee: Report on Cruisers', 14 December 1927, CAB 24/190. Roskill, *Naval Policy*, I:555–6, provides a misleading and inaccurate account of these events.

77. WSC to Bridgeman, 16 January 1928, T 161/285/S33101/2; *WSC*, V/1:1, 182–5.

78. Bridgeman to WSC, 21 January 1928, T 161/285/S33101/2.

79. Undated Admiralty memorandum, 'Answers to questions asked by Colwyn Committee', ADM 116/2282; minute by Fraser (supply department, Treasury), 8 February 1928, T 161/285/S33101/2.

80. Fraser minute, 29 December 1927, T 161/285/S33101/3; Upcott minute, 17 February 1928, T 161/285/S33101/4.

81. Fraser minute, 17 February 1928, T 161/285/S33101/4.

82. CP 207 (27), Laming Worthington-Evans memorandum, 'The Preparation of the Army for War', 19 July 1927, CAB 24; CID 1055-B, 'The Basis of Service Estimates: Note by the Secretary', 23 June 1931, CAB 4/21; Gibbs, *Grand Strategy*, 54–5; Cab 45 (27), 28 July 1927, CAB 23/55.

83. Waterfield minute, 6 January 1928, T 161/285/S33101/3.

84. Waterfield memorandum, 'Navy Estimates 1928', 27 January 1928, T 161/285/ S33101/3; see also Fraser's minute of 24 January 1928, T 161/285/S33101/3.

85. NP (27) 6th mtg, 2 February 1928, CAB 27/355.

86. CP 47 (28), 'Naval Programme Committee: Report on Naval Oil Fuel Reserve', 20 February 1928, CAB 24/192.

87. WSC to Bridgeman, 20 February 1928, T 161/285/S33101/4.

88. Minute by Fraser (Treasury), 8 February 1928, T 161/285/S33101/2.

89. Treasury to Admiralty, 13 March 1928, T 161/285/S33101/4.

90. CID 236th mtg, 5 July 1928, CAB 2/5; Cabinet 39 (28), 18 July 1928, CAB 23/58.

91. Warren Fisher minute, 21 November 1928, T 161/292/S34216.

92. WSC to Bridgeman, 31 July 1928, ADM 116/3388.

93. Bridgeman to WSC, 29 November 1928, ADM 167/78.

94. WSC to Bridgeman, 14 February 1929, ADM 116/3388; *WSC*, V/1:1,424.

95. Minute of 15 January 1928, T 161/285/S33101/3.

96. On the Belligerent Rights subcommittee, see B. J. C. McKercher, 'Belligerent Rights in 1927–1929: Foreign Policy versus Naval Policy in the Second Baldwin Government', *Historical Journal*, 29 (1986), 963–74; Roskill, *Hankey*, II:451–9.

97. Christopher Bell, 'The Royal Navy, War Planning and Intelligence Assessments of Japan between the Wars', *Intelligence and Statecraft*, ed. Jennifer Siegel and Peter Jackson (Westport, CN: Praegar, 2005).

98. WSC memorandum, 10 February 1928, HNKY (Hankey papers, Churchill College Archives Centre) 5/1.

99. Ibid.

100. Hankey memorandum, 14 February 1928, HNKY 5/1. Hankey insisted that this memorandum was not to be shown to anyone other than the Chancellor.

101. Christopher Hall, *Britain, America and Arms Control, 1921–37* (New York: St Martin's Press, 1987); David Carlton, 'The Anglo-French Compromise on Arms Limitation, 1928', *Journal of British Studies*, 8, no. 2 (May 1969), 141–62; McKercher, *Second Baldwin Government*.

102. WSC to Baldwin, 30 September 1928, PREM 21/321; *WSC*, V/1:1,352.

103. 'Synopsis of Suggested Reply', 30 September 1928, PREM 21/321; *WSC*, V/1:1,353–5; Hankey to Salisbury, 13 November 1928, PREM 21/321; McKercher, *Second Baldwin Government*, 185.

104. Cabinet memorandum, 19 November 1928, CP 358 (28), CAB 24/199; *WSC*, V/1:1,380–2. The phrase 'New England backwoodsman' was borrowed from an editorial in the *New Statesman* of 17 November 1928.

105. CP 394/28, 'The Cruiser Programme, 1928–9,' December 1928, CAB 24/199.

106. Cabinet 57 (28), 19 December 1928, CAB 23/59.

107. Cabinet 5 (29), 7 February 1929, CAB 23/59.

108. CID 943-B and CID 944-B: First and Second Reports dealing with Maritime Belligerent Rights, 13 February and 6 March 1929, CAB 4/18; *DBFP*, series IA.

109. The minority proposed that if belligerent rights were included in an arbitration treaty, Britain should insist on defining clearly what those rights were. *DBFP*, series IA, vol. VI:851.

110. Eg. Rhodes James, *Churchill*, 164; Middlemas and Barnes, *Baldwin*, 326; Gretton, *Former Naval Person*, 244–5.

111. Eg. Barnett, *Collapse of British Power*, 275–8; MacGregor, 'Former Naval Cheapskate'; Gordon Corrigan, *Blood, Sweat and Arrogance and the Myth of Churchill's War* (London: Orion Publishing Co., 2006), 86, 152; A. J. P. Taylor, 'The Statesman', *Churchill: Four Faces and the Man*, 22; Robert O'Neill, 'Churchill, Japan, and British Security in the Pacific 1904–1942', *Churchill*, ed. Robert Blake and William Roger Louis (New York: W. W. Norton, 1993), 288–9; B. J. C. McKercher, 'The Limitations of the Politician-Strategist: Winston Churchill and the German Threat, 1933–39', *Churchill and Strategic Dilemmas before the World Wars*, ed. John H. Maurer (London: Frank Cass, 2003), 94.

112. Ferris, 'Last Decade'; G. A. H. Gordon, *British Seapower and Procurement Between the Wars* (Annapolis, MD: Naval Institute Press, 1988).

113. Bell, *Royal Navy*, 93–8.

114. E.g. Taylor, 'Statesman'; 22; McKercher, 'Churchill and the German Threat', 94.

115. Barnett, *Collapse of British Power*, 277; *idem.*, *Britain and her Army 1509–1970* (London: Allen Lane, 1970) 411, 415; MacGregor, 'Former Naval Cheapskate', 319–20; Rhodes James, *Churchill*, 124, 165.

CHAPTER 5

1. Speech of 16 August 1929, Canadian Club, Empire Club, and Board of Trade Luncheon, Toronto, *Empire Club of Canada: Addresses Delivered to the Members During the Year 1929* (Toronto: T. H. Best, 1930), 203–14. See also Churchill's speech in Ottawa the day before: *Complete Speeches*, V:4,670.

2. David Marquand, *Ramsay MacDonald* (London: Jonathan Cape, 1977), 466–74; David Carlton, *MacDonald versus Henderson* (London: Macmillan, 1970), ch. 5.

3. Robert Craigie minute, 26 March 1929, FO 371/13520; Cabinet Conclusions 16 (29), 1, 11 April 1929, CAB 23/60.

4. For a recent overview of the first London Conference and the Anglo-American discussions preceding it, see Christopher M. Bell, 'Britain and the London Conference, 1930', in *At the Crossroads between Peace and War: Naval Rivalries and Arms Control between the World Wars*, ed. John H. Maurer and Christopher M. Bell (Annapolis, MD: Naval Institute Press, forthcoming).

5. Orest Babij, 'The Second Labour Government and British Maritime Security, 1929–1931', *Diplomacy and Statecraft*, 6 (November 1995): 645–71; Keith Neilson, '"Unbroken Thread": Japan, Maritime Power and British Imperial Defence, 1920–32', *British Naval Strategy East of Suez 1900–2000*, ed. Greg Kennedy (London: Frank Cass, 2005), 79; Bell, 'London Conference'.

6. Jones to Baldwin, 14 September 1929, in *Whitehall Diary*, II: 210–11.

7. Babij, 'Second Labour Government'.

8. Ferris, 'Last Decade', Gordon, *British Seapower and Procurement*.

9. Speech of 2 June 1930, House of Commons, *Complete Speeches*, V:4,814–22; these themes were repeated in his speech on the 1930 navy estimates, 21 July 1930, ibid., 4,893–8.

10. WSC to Baldwin, 17 May 1930, *WSC*, V/2:156–7.

11. Ibid.; WSC to Richmond, 24 May 1930, RIC/7/2, Richmond papers, NMM.

12. Speech of 23 November 1932, House of Commons, *Complete Speeches*, V:5, 199–200.

13. Speech of 13 May 1932, House of Commons, *Complete Speeches*, V:5,173–4.

14. Speech of 17 February 1933, Anti-Socialist and Anti-Communist Union Meeting, Queen's Hall, London, *Complete Speeches*, V:5,219–20.

15. R. A. C. Parker, *Churchill and Appeasement* (London: Macmillan, 2000), 28–45.

16. Speech of 28 November 1934, House of Commons, *Complete Speeches*, V:5,441.

17. E.g. Speech of 28 November 1934, House of Commons, *Complete Speeches*, V:5,441; also speech of 14 March 1933, ibid., 5,234.

18. Speech of 14 March 1933, House of Commons, *Complete Speeches*, V:5,234.

19. E.g. CID 1084-B: 'Imperial Defence Policy: Annual Review for 1932 by the COS Committee', 3 March 1932, CAB 4/21.

20. DRC 14: 'Report of the DRC', 28 January 1934, CAB 16/109.

21. The classic study of British grand strategy during this period is N. H. Gibbs, *Grand Strategy*, I (London: HMSO, 1976). More recent works on the subject include Peter Bell, *Chamberlain, Germany and Japan, 1933–4* (London: Macmillan, 1996); Keith Neilson 'The Defence Requirements Sub-Committee, British Strategic Foreign Policy, Neville Chamberlain and the Path to Appeasement', *English Historical Review*, cxviii (June 2003), 651–84.

22. DRC 14: 'Report of the DRC', 28 January 1934, CAB 16/109.

23. DC(M)(32) 120: 'Note by the Chancellor of the Exchequer on the Report of the D.R.C.', 20 June 1934, CAB 16/111.

24. Ibid.

25. Neilson, 'DRC', 677–8; CP 205 (34): 'Defence Requirements: Report', 31 July 1934, CAB 24/250.

26. This theme is explored in George Peden, 'Winston Churchill, Neville Chamberlain and the Defence of Empire,' *The Limitations of Military Power*, ed. John B. Hattendorf and Malcolm Murfett (Basingstoke: Macmillan, 1990), 160–72.

27. 'Organise our Supplies', 29 May 1936, in Winston S. Churchill, *Step by Step 1936–1939* (London: Odhams, 1948), 21.

28. Parker, *Churchill and Appeasement*, ch. 6.

29. Speech of 5 October 1938, House of Commons, *Complete Speeches*, 6:6,011.

30. Joseph Maiolo, *The Royal Navy and Nazi Germany, 1933–39* (London: Macmillan, 1998); Clare Scammell, 'The Royal Navy and the Strategic Origins of the Anglo-German Naval Agreement of 1935', *Journal of Strategic Studies*, 20, no. 2 (June 1997), 92–118.

31. Speeches of 11 and 22 July 1935, House of Commons, *Complete Speeches*, VI:5,652–6, 5,661–4.

32. Speech of 22 July 1935, House of Commons, ibid., 5,663.

33. Speech of 22 May 1935, House of Commons, ibid., 5,612; see also his speech of 24 July 1935 at Harlow, ibid., 5,665.

34. 'Our Navy Must be Stronger', 15 May 1936, *Step by Step*, 17–20.

35. 'The Mission of Japan', *Collier's*, 20 February 1937, *Collected Essays*, I:365–72.

36. 'Germany and Japan', 27 November 1936, in Churchill, *Step by Step*, 71–4.

37. 'What Japan Thinks of Us', 21 January 1938, *Step by Step*, 194.

38. WSC to his wife, 15 January 1936, *WSC*, V/3:16.

39. Speech of 16 March 1936, House of Commons, *Complete Speeches*, VI:5,706; see also 'Defending the Empire', 13 May 1937, *Step by Step*, 119.

40. Speech of 17 March 1938, House of Commons, *Complete Speeches*, VI:5,933.

41. Speech of 11 March 1937, House of Commons, *Complete Speeches*, VI: 5,837; 'Rebuilding the Battle Fleet', 22 March 1937, *Step by Step*, 102–5.
42. Speech of 18 February 1937, House of Commons, *Complete Speeches*, VI: 5,837. See also his speeches of 4 and 11 March 1937; 'Future Safeguards of National Defence', *News of the World*, 1 May 1938, *Collected Essays*, I: 400–1.
43. Chatfield to WSC, 5 May 1936, CHT/4/3; *WSC*, V/3:139; see also R. G. Henderson to WSC, 23 November 1936, CHAR 2/272.
44. Roskill, *Naval Policy*, II: 221, 330; Joseph Moretz, *The Royal Navy and the Capital Ship in the Interwar Period: An Operational Perspective* (London: Frank Cass, 2002), 54–5; CID 1258-B: 'Vulnerability of Capital Ships to Air Attack', report by the Sub-Committee, 30 July 1936, CAB 4/24.
45. Moretz, *Capital Ship*, 197–9; speech of 11 March 1937, House of Commons, *Complete Speeches*, VI: 5,840; Churchill, 'Is Air Power Decisive?', 1 September 1938, *Step By Step*, 263–4.
46. 'Is Air Power Decisive?', 1 September 1938, *Step By Step*, 263–4.
47. 'Future Safeguards of National Defence', *News of the World*, 1 May 1938, *Collected Essays*, I: 401.
48. Speech of 17 March 1938, House of Commons, *Complete Speeches*, VI: 5,933.
49. Geoffrey Till, *Air Power and the Royal Navy* (London: Jane's, 1979).
50. Speech of 4 May 1936, House of Commons, *Complete Speeches*, VI: 5,742–3. Churchill estimated that the US and Japanese navies already possessed around 1,000 and 800 naval aircraft respectively. Britain, he claimed, would not even reach 217 until the aircraft provided in the 1936 estimates were completed. Notably, it did not occur to Churchill that Japan might also be developing a *qualitative* lead over Britain in this area.
51. 'Fleet Air Arm', draft memorandum, 15 April 1937, *WSC*, V/3:646–8; reprinted in Churchill, *SWW*, I: 675–8, where it is dated 1936.
52. E.g. WSC to Air Commodore J. A. Chamier, 19 November 1936, *WSC*, V/3:419; speech of 4 May 1936, House of Commons, *Complete Speeches*, VI: 5,744.
53. Chatfield to WSC, 5 May 1936, CHT/4/3; *WSC*, V/3:137.
54. Lord Chatfield, *It Might Happen Again* (London: Heinemann, 1947), 139; Churchill, *SWW*, III: 163–4.
55. WSC to Chatfield, 18 June 1938, CHT/4/3; *WSC*, V/3:1,064–5; Churchill, *SWW*, I: 164.
56. 'Defending the Empire', 13 May 1937, *Step by Step*, 121; speeches of 4 March 1937 and 1 February 1939, House of Commons, *Complete Speeches*, VI.
57. WSC unsent letter to Hoare, 1 August 1936, *WSC*, V/3:303; Churchill, *SWW*, I: 160–2; speech of 17 March 1938, House of Commons, *Complete Speeches*, VI: 5,929.
58. The minutes in ADM 116/3735 illustrate this concern. See also Chatfield, *It Might Happen Again*, ch. 17; Roskill, *Naval Policy*, II: 220–1, 279–80, 328.
59. Hoare to WSC, July 1936, CHAR 2/272.
60. Bell, *Royal Navy*, 36–8.

61. Eg. speeches of 17 March 1938, House of Commons, and 28 June 1939, City Carlton Club, London, *Complete Speeches*, VI; 'Future Safeguards of National Defence', *News of the World*, 1 May 1938, *Collected Essays*, I:400.

62. 'The Anglo-German Naval Agreement', 12 January 1939, *Step by Step*, 307.

63. Ibid.

64. 'Future Safeguards of National Defence', *Collected Essays*, I:401. On the navy's concerns regarding a potential 'knock-out blow' against Britain's import system, see Maiolo, *Royal Navy*, ch. 3.

65. 'Future Safeguards of National Defence', *Collected Essays*, I:398.

66. Speech of 17 March 1938, House of Commons, *Complete Speeches*, VI:5,932.

67. For the navy's response to the problems posed by a two-hemisphere war, see Bell, *Royal Navy*, 26–44, 99–111.

68. DRC 37: 'Third Report of Defence Requirements Sub-Committee', 21 November 1935, CAB 16/112. For the Admiralty's pursuit of the 'new standard', see Bell, *Royal Navy*, 27–44.

69. In contrast, the navy estimates for 1935/36 stood at slightly over £60 million. 'Board Memorandum on a New Standard of Naval Strength', 26 April 1937, ADM 1/9081.

70. DP(P) 3, 'A New Standard of Naval Strength,' memorandum by the Board of Admiralty, 26 April 1937, CAB 16/181.

71. Ibid.

72. Admiralty war plans during this period are examined in Bell, *Royal Navy*, 78–90.

73. War Memorandum (Eastern), ADM 116/4393.

74. Bell, *Royal Navy*.

75. Remarks at a meeting of the 1922 Committee of the House of Commons, 7 December 1936: report to the Cabinet. *WSC*, V/3:467. See also 'Japan Guesses Wrong', *Collier's*, 30 July 1938, *Collected Essays*, I:410–11.

76. 'Memorandum on Sea-Power, 1939,' 27 March 1939, PREM 1/345; FO 371/23982; *WSC*, V/3:1,414–17.

77. Ibid., 1,416.

78. Ibid., 1,415. 'One can take it as quite certain,' he wrote, 'that Japan would not run such a risk [of an attack on Australia]. They are an extremely sensible people.'

79. 'Japan Entangled', 26 May 1938, *Step by Step*, 233–6. Churchill returned to this theme in 'A Word to Japan!', *Daily Mirror*, 11 August 1939, *Collected Essays*, I:468, and his speech of 28 June 1939, City Carlton Club, London, *Complete Speeches*, 6:6,144.

80. 'Japan Entangled', *Step by Step*, 233–6.

81. Speech of 26 October 1937, Waltham Abbey, *Complete Speeches*, VI:5,898.

82. Bell, *Royal Navy*, 81–90.

83. SAC 4: 'Note by the First Sea Lord,' 28 February 1939, CAB 16/209.

84. Ibid.; see also Backhouse's minute of 24 March 1939, ADM 1/9909.

85. 'Composition of the Far Eastern Fleet in War', 15 March 1939, DRAX 2/9, Drax papers.

86. The Mediterranean in British defence planning during this period is covered in Lawrence Pratt, *East of Malta, West of Suez* (Cambridge: Cambridge University Press, 1975).

87. SAC 6th mtg, 17 April 1939, CAB 16/209.

88. SAC 1st and 2nd mtgs, 1 and 13 March 1939, CAB 16/209.

89. 'Memorandum on Sea-Power, 1939', 27 March 1939.

90. Ibid. The importance of striking first against Italy was also emphasized in Churchill's 16 March 1939 speech on the annual navy estimates, *Complete Speeches*, VI:6,088–9. On naval planning against Italy and the problems of inflicting a knock-out blow, see Bell, *Royal Navy*, ch. 5.

91. Ibid., VI:6,088; 'Memorandum on Sea-Power, 1939'.

92. *WSC*, V/3:1,414.

93. Ironside diary, 25 July 1939, *WSC*, V/3:1,576–7.

94. Cadogan to Lindsay, 17 April 1939, FO 371/23982. I am grateful to Trevor Checkley for bringing this file to my attention.

95. Chatfield to Chamberlain, 29 March 1939, PREM 1/345.

96. Minute by Tom Phillips, 5 July 1939, ADM 1/9767.

97. War Memorandum (Eastern), Section XVI, July 1939, ADM 1/9767.

98. See COS 928, 'The Situation in the Far East', 18 June 1939, CAB 53/50.

CHAPTER 6

1. J. M. Butler, *Grand Strategy* (London: HMSO, 1957), II: 9–21; Talbot Imlay, *Facing the Second World War* (Oxford: Oxford University Press, 2003); Nick Smart, *British Strategy and Politics During the Phony War* (Westport, CT: Praeger, 2003).

2. WSC to Chamberlain, 18 September 1939, *The Churchill War Papers*, ed. Martin Gilbert, 3 vols (New York: Norton, 1993–2001) (cited hereafter as *CWP*), I:111–12.

3. WP [War Cabinet paper] (39) 14: 'Report by the Land Forces Committee', 8 September 1939, CAB 66/1/14; WP (39) 21: 'Report of the Land Forces Committee', 9 September 1939, CAB 66/1/21; *CWP*, I:43–6, 54–5; Churchill, *SWW*, I:355; Michael Howard, *The Continental Commitment* (Harmondsworth: Penguin, 1974), 127–31; Butler, *Grand Strategy*, II:32.

4. WP (39) 41, 'Discussion on Second Report of the Land Forces Committee', 22 September 1939, CAB 66/1/41.

5. Chamberlain to WSC, 16 September 1939, *CWP*, I:101.

6. WM [War Cabinet minutes] (39) 20, confidential annex [hereafter CA], 19 September 1939, CAB 65/3/10.

7. WSC to Chamberlain, 18 September 1939, *CWP*, I:111; Churchill, *SWW*, I:360.

8. WP (39) 37, 'Second Report by the Land Forces Committee', 19 September 1939, CAB 66/1/37; WM (39) 23, 22 September 1939, CAB 65/1/23.

9. WSC to Chamberlain, 18 September 1939, *CWP*, I:111–12; Churchill, *SWW*, I:360.

10. WSC to Neville Chamberlain, 10 September 1939, *CWP*, I:60–2; WSC to Pound et al., 11 September 1939, *CWP*, I:73–5.

11. WSC to Pound et al., 11 September 1939, ADM 205/2; *CWP*, I:73–5.

12. Pound memorandum, *c.*22 September 1939, ADM 167/105.

13. Undated memorandum, 'Conclusions of Meeting in 1st Lord's Room 12th September', ADM 205/2.

14. Board of Admiralty minutes, 28 September 1939, ADM 167/103; *CWP*, I:167.

15. WSC to Pound et al., 8 October 1939, ADM 205/2; *CWP*, I:223–4.

16. Report by C-in-C, China, 'Japanese Building Programme', 5 November 1939; Naval Attaché, Tokyo to DNI, 21 December 1939, ADM 116/5757.

17. DNI memorandum, 'Japanese Building Programme', 18 January 1940, ADM 116/5757.

18. WSC to Pound et al., 'Japanese strength', 11 February 1940, ADM 116/5757; *CWP*, I:746.

19. DNI minute, 22 February 1940, ADM 116/5757. On British naval intelligence assessments of Japan, see Bell, 'The Royal Navy, War Planning and Intelligence Assessments of Japan'; Wesley K. Wark, 'In Search of a Suitable Japan: British Naval Intelligence in the Pacific before the Second World War', *Intelligence and National Security*, I, no. 2 (May 1986), 189–211.

20. Desmond Morton to Eric Seal, 16 February 1940, ADM 116/5757.

21. DNI minute, 22 February 1940, ADM 116/5757.

22. WM (40) 67, 13 March 1940, CAB 65/6/12; *CWP*, I:876. They also insisted that the decision be reviewed before the end of the calendar year.

23. WP (40) 53: WSC memorandum, 'Naval Programme 1940–41', 2 March 1940, CAB 66/5/33.

24. WP (40) 95: Naval Staff memorandum, 'Comparison of British and Japanese Fleets', 12 March 1940, CAB 66/6.

25. Quoted in Butler, *Grand Strategy*, II:81.

26. James Levy, 'Ready or Not?: The Home Fleet at the Outset of World War II', *Naval War College Review* (Autumn 1999).

27. Quoted in Stephen Roskill, *The Navy at War* (London: Collins, 1960), 34.

28. Andrew Lambert, 'Seapower 1939–1940: Churchill and the Strategic Origins of the Battle of the Atlantic', *Journal of Strategic Studies*, 17, no. 1 (March 1994), 98–100.

29. Butler, *Grand Strategy*, II:84.

30. WSC to Pound et al., 20 November 1939, *CWP*, I:397.

31. Lambert, 'Seapower 1939–1940', 100–2.

32. For the composition of these groups and their dispositions, see Churchill, *SWW*, I:403–5.

33. WSC to Pound, 20 September 1939, ADM 205/4; *CWP*, I:127.

34. WSC memorandum, 'Catherine', 12 September 1939, ADM 205/4; *CWP*, I:82–4.
35. Prior, *Churchill's 'World Crisis'*, 270–1; Keyes to WSC, 23 November 1926, *WSC*, V/1:886–7.
36. WSC memorandum, 'Catherine', 12 September 1939, ADM 205/4; *CWP*, I:82–4.
37. Cork memorandum, 'Catherine', 26 September 1939, ADM 205/4.
38. Pound memorandum, 'Notes on "C"', 20 September 1939, ADM 205/4; *CWP*, I:126.
39. Admiralty memorandum, 'Catherine: precis of stages of planning', 17 February 1940, ADM 205/4.
40. Pound to WSC, 3 December 1939, ADM 199/1929; *CWP*, I:456–7.
41. WSC to Pound, Phillips and Sir Archibald Carter, 11 December 1939, ADM 199/1928; *CWP*, I:496–7.
42. See Drax to Admiralty, 7 December 1939, ADM 199/1929.
43. WSC to Pound, Phillips, and Sir Archibald Carter, 11 December 1939, ADM 199/1928; *CWP*, I:496–7.
44. WSC letters to Admiral Fraser and Captain Boyd, and to Pound and Philips, both 19 November 1939, *CWP*, I:387–9; ADM 205/2; Churchill, *SWW*, I:399–400.
45. Air Ministry memorandum, 'Mining the Rhine', 7 December 1939, *CWP*, I:482–5; ADM 116/4239; WM (39) 110, 10 December 1939, CAB 65/2/44; *CWP*, I:491–2.
46. Patrick Salmon, 'British Plans for Economic Warfare against Germany 1937–1939: The Problem of Swedish Iron Ore', *The Second World War: Essays in Military and Political History*, ed. Walter Laqueur (London: Sage, 1982).
47. Salmon, 'British Plans', 37.
48. Ibid., 40–5.
49. WP (39) 57: WSC memorandum, 'Norway and Sweden', 29 September 1939, CAB 66/2/7.
50. WSC to Pound et al., 19 September 1939, ADM 199/892.
51. Cross to WSC, 9 November 1939, ADM 199/892.
52. Morton to Cross, 27 November 1939, FO 837/24; MEW memorandum I/81/1, 27 November 1939, FO 837/802, and ADM 116/4471.
53. WM (39) 99, 30 November 1939, CAB 65/2/33.
54. MEW draft paper, 12 December 1939, FO 837/24. For background see Talbot Imlay, 'Allied Economic Intelligence and Strategy during the "Phoney War"', *Intelligence and National Security*, 13, 4 (Winter 1998), 123.
55. WM (39)116, 15 December 1939, CAB 65/2/50.
56. WP (39) 162: WSC memorandum, 'Norway—Iron-Ore Traffic', 16 December 1939, CAB 66/4/12; *CWP*, I: 522–4; Churchill, *SWW*, I:431–3.
57. WM (39) 118, 18 December 1939, CAB 65/2/52; *CWP*, I:532–3.

58. *The Ironside Diaries, 1937–40*, ed. Roderick Macleod and Dennis Kelly (London: Constable, 1962), 174–88; MCC (39)10, 20 December 1939, CAB 83/1; *CWP*, I, 547–8.

59. WM (39)122, CA, 22 December 1939, CAB 65/4/29; *CWP*, I:553–6.

60. Halifax memorandum, 'The German Iron-Ore Traffic', 20 December 1939, CAB 66/4/18; *CWP*, I:546–7; WM (39)122, CA, 22 December 1939, CAB 65/4/29; *CWP*, I:555.

61. WSC memorandum, 'A Note on the War in 1940', 25 December 1939, *CWP*, I:568–70.

62. Pound to WSC, 25 December 1939, ADM 199/1929.

63. Pound to WSC, 31 December 1939, ADM 205/4; *CWP*, I:589–91.

64. WSC to Pound, 1 January 1940, ADM 205/4; *CWP*, I:592–3.

65. Pound to WSC, 10 January 1940, ADM 205/4.

66. WSC to Pound, 15 January 1940, ADM 205/4; *CWP*, I:644–6.

67. Pound to WSC, 25 December 1939, ADM 199/1929.

68. Ironside diary, 28 and 30 December 1939, in Macleod and Kelly, *Ironside Diaries*, 173–6, 189–90; WP (39) 179: Report by the COS, 'Military Implications of a Policy Aimed at Stopping the Export of Swedish Iron Ore to Germany', 31 December 1939, CAB 66/3.

69. WP (39) 180: Report by the COS, 'Stoppage of the Export of Iron Ore to Germany: Balance of Advantage between the Major and Minor Projects', 31 December 1939, CAB 66/3.

70. WP (40) 3: WSC memorandum, 'Swedish Iron Ore', 31 December 1939, CAB 66/3; *CWP*, I:587–8.

71. WM (40) 1 and 2, CA, 2 and 3 January 1940, CAB 65/11; *CWP*, I:597–8, 600–2.

72. WM (40) 2, CA, 3 January 1940, CAB 65/11/2; *CWP*, 600–2.

73. WM (40) 8, CA, 10 January 1940, CAB 65/11/8, 10 January 1940, *CWP*, I:618–20.

74. WM (40) 9, CA, 11 January 1940, CAB 65/11/9; *CWP*, I:624–6.

75. WM (40) 16, CA, 17 January 1940, CAB 65/11/16.

76. WM (40) 10, CA, 12 January 1940, CAB 65/11/10; *CWP*, I:629–31.

77. WP (40) 35: COS report, 'Intervention in Scandinavia: Plans and Implications', 28 January 1940, Cab 66/5.

78. SWC (Supreme War Council minutes) (39/40) 5, 5 February 1940, CAB 99/3; *CWP*, I:719; on French interest in opening a Scandinavia theatre, see Imlay, *Facing the Second World War*, 63–8.

79. WM (40) 35, CA, 7 February 1940, CAB 65/11/25; *CWP*, I:723; WP (40) 51: COS report, 'The Employment of Allied Land Forces in Scandinavia and Finland', 14 February 1940, CAB 66/5; Salmon, 'Great Britain, the Soviet Union and Finland', 121.

80. WM (40) 45, CA, 18 February 1940, CAB 65/11/32; *CWP*, I:778.

81. WP (40) 60: WSC memorandum, 'Stoppage of traffic in Norwegian territorial waters', 14 February 1940, CAB 66/5; *CWP*, I:761–2.

82. WM (40) 50, 23 February 1940, CAB 65/5/50; *CWP*, I:795–6.

83. WM (40) 56, CA, 1 March 1940, CAB 65/12/1; WM (40) 59, CA, 4 March 1940, CAB 65/12/4; *CWP*, I:839–40, 846.

84. Churchill: note for Pound, 6 March 1940, ADM 116/4471; *CWP*, I:853–4.

85. WM (40) 65, CA, 11 March 1940, CAB 65/12/10; *CWP*, I:868–9.

86. WM (40) 66, CA, 12 March 1940, CAB 65/12/11; *CWP*, I:872–3; John Kennedy, *The Business of War* (London: Hutchinson, 1957), 46–51.

87. WM (40) 68, CA, 14 March 1940, CAB 65/12/12; WP (40) 96: Naval Staff memorandum, 'Effect of the Russian-Finnish Treaty on our Naval Situation', 14 March 1940, CAB 66/6/26; *CWP*, I:878–80.

88. WM (40) 68, CA, 14 March 1940, CAB 65/12/12; *CWP*, I:879–80.

89. WSC to Halifax, 14 March 1940, *CWP*, I:883–4. Churchill had expressed similar concerns, in more muted terms, at the War Cabinet meeting of 12 January 1940, WM (40) 10, CA, CAB 65/11/10; *CWP*, I:630.

90. WP (40) 84: WSC memorandum, 'Royal Marine Operation', 4 March 1940, CAB 66/6/14; *CWP*, I:844–5.

91. WM (40) 66, CA, 12 March 1940, CAB 65/12/11; WM (40) 67, 13 March 1940, CAB 65/6/12; *CWP*, I:872–5.

92. WSC to Pound et al., 14 March 1940, *CWP*, I:881; Marder, *From the Dardanelles to Oran* (London: Clarendon Press, 1974), 153.

93. WM (40) 71, CA, 18 March 1940, CAB 65/12/13; WM (40) 72, 19 March 1940, CAB 65/6/17; *CWP*, I:898, 902.

94. WSC to Pound, 23 March 1940, *CWP*, I:911.

95. WP (40) 109: Paul Reynaud, 'French Government's Views on the Future Conduct of the War', 25 May 1940, CAB 66/6/39.

96. WM (40) 76, 27 March 1940, CAB 65/6/21; *CWP*, I:920–1; WP (40) 107: Halifax memorandum, 'Policy to Be Adopted Towards Norway and Sweden in Consequence of their Attitude During the Finnish War', CAB 66/6/37.

97. SWC (39/40) 6, 28 March 1940, CAB 99/3; *CWP*, I:925–6; Churchill, *SWW*, I:455–7.

98. Note by Chamberlain, 31 March 1940, *CWP*, I:944; WM (40) 78, 1 April 1940, CAB 65/6/23; *CWP*, I:946; Churchill, *SWW*, I:459–60.

99. WSC to Chamberlain, 1 April 1940, *CWP*, I:948.

100. WM (40) 80, CA, 3 April 1940, CAB 65/12/15; *CWP*, I:951–3.

101. WP (40) 122: COS memorandum, 'Plan R.4: Instructions to Commanders', 4 April 1940, CAB 66/7/2; WM (40) 83, 6 April 1940, CAB 65/12/17.

102. F. H. Hinsley, et al., *British Intelligence in the Second World War* (London: HMSO, 1979), I:115–25, Olav Riste, 'Intelligence and the "Mindset": The German Invasion of Norway in 1940', *Intelligence and National Security*, 22, 4 (August 2007), 521–36; Wesley Wark, 'Beyond Intelligence: The Study of British Strategy and the Norway Campaign, 1940', *Power, Personalities and Policies*, ed. Michael Graham Fry (London: Frank Cass, 1992).

103. The order was given by Pound, although it is not entirely certain whether the decision was his alone, Churchill's, or was taken by the First Lord and First Sea Lord jointly. The diary of Captain Ralph Edwards, then Deputy Director of Operations (Home), seems to point conclusively to Pound as the driving force. Edwards diary typescript, ROSK 4/75.

104. WM (40) 86, 9 April 1940, CAB 65/6/31; *CWP*, I:988–91.

105. WM (40) 85, 9 April 1940, CAB 65/6/30.

106. SWC (39/40) 7, 9 April 1940, Cab 99/3; François Kersaudy, *Norway 1940* (Lincoln, NB: University of Nebraska Press, 1998), 85.

107. *SWW*, I:586–9; Lord Ismay, *The Memoirs of Lord Ismay* (London: Heinemann, 1960), 108–12.

108. MCC (40) 17, 9 April 1940, CAB 83/3; *CWP*, I:997–9; WM (40) 87, CA, 10 April 1940, CAB 65/12/19.

109. Notes of an informal meeting at 10 Downing Street, 11 April 1940, ADM 205/4; *CWP*, I:1,007; WM (40) 88, CA, 11 April 1940, CAB 65/12/20.

110. MCC (40) 19, 11 April 1940, CAB 83/3; *CWP*, I:1,029.

111. WSC to Pound et al., 11 April 1940, *CWP*, I:1,031.

112. Ralph Edwards' diary, 11 April 1940, Edwards papers, Churchill College Archives Centre, REDW 1/2; Roskill, *Churchill and the Admirals*, 102; Ironside diary, 11 April 1940, in Macleod and Kelly, *Ironside Diaries*, 253. Much confusion has subsequently been caused by the mistaken assertion by Macleod and Kelly that the Admiralty was preparing at this time to launch a naval assault directly on Trondheim, and that forces were needed at Namsos to support it.

113. WM (40) 90, CA, 12 April 1940, CAB 65/12/22; *CWP*, I:1,039; *The Diaries of Sir Alexander Cadogan*, 269–70.

114. WM (40) 90, CA, 12 April 1940, CAB 65/12/23.

115. WSC memorandum, 'Notes by the Chairman of the Military Co-ordination Committee for the Joint Planning Staff', 12 April 1940, *CWP*, I:1,043–4.

116. WM (40) 91, CA, 13 April 1940, CAB 65/12/23; *CWP*, I:1,048; Churchill, *SWW*, I:614, where the wording of the minutes is altered slightly and is wrongly described as coming from a meeting of the Military Co-ordination Committee.

117. *The Diaries of Sir Alexander Cadogan, 1938–1945*, ed. David Dilks (New York: G. P. Putnam's Sons, 1972), 270; WM (40) 91, CA, 13 April 1940, CAB 65/12/23; *CWP*, I:1,048–50; WSC to Reynaud and Daladier (draft), CAB 21/1388.

118. MCC (40) 22, 13 April 1940, CAB 83/3; *CWP*, I:1,054–5.

119. WM (40) 92, CA, 14 April 1940, CAB 65/12/24; *CWP*, I:1,059; MCC (40) 25, 15 April 1940, CAB 83/3.

120. MCC (40) 23, 14 April 1940, CAB 83/3; WM (40) 93, CA, 15 April 1940, CAB 65/12/25.

121. MCC (40) 26, 16 April 1940, CAB 83/3; *CWP*, I:1,073–4. On the background to this meeting and Chamberlain's decision to take the chair, see *CWP* I:1,071–3.

122. WSC memorandum, 'Military Coordination Committee: Note by the Chairman', 16 April 1940, ADM 199/1929; *CWP*, I:1,076–7.

123. WSC to Cork and Mackesy, 17 April 1940, *CWP*, I:1,083; WSC to Forbes, 17 April 1940, *CWP*, I:1,084. Mackesy's son, the historian Piers Mackesy, offers an impassioned defence of his father in 'Churchill as Chronicler: The Narvik Episode', *History Today*, 35 (March 1985), 14–20.

124. MCC (40) 77: WSC memorandum, 'Operation "Rupert"', 17 April 1940, *CWP*, I:1,078–9; WSC to Cork and Mackesy, 17 April 1940, *CWP*, I:1,083. WM (40) 95, CA, 17 April 1940, CAB 65/12/26; *CWP*, I: 1,081–3.

125. WM (40) 95, CA, 17 April 1940, CAB 65/12/26.

126. Churchill, *SWW*, I:628; MCC (40) 30, 19 April 1940, CAB 83/3.

127. WM (40) 98, CA, 20 April 1940, CAB 65/12/29; MCC (40) 82: Churchill memorandum, 'Operation "Rupert"', 20 April 1940, *CWP*, I:1,104–5.

128. WSC to Chamberlain, 21 April 1940, ADM 116/4471; *CWP*, I:1,116–17.

129. SWC (39/40) 8, 22 April 1940, CAB 99/3; *CWP*, I:1,118–20; Churchill, *SWW*, I:640–1; Butler, *Grand Strategy*, II:137–8.

130. Phillips memorandum, 25 April 1940, ADM 199/1929; Butler, *Grand Strategy*, II:139; MCC (40) 34, 26 April 1940, CAB 83/3; *CWP*, I:1,139–40.

131. MCC (40) 30, 26 April 1940, CAB 83/3; *CWP*, I:1,140.

132. Roskill, *War at Sea*, I:202; see also Marder, *Dardanelles to Oran*, 137–40.

133. Barry Gough, *Historical Dreadnoughts* (Barnsley: Seaforth Publishing, 2010).

134. Roskill, *War at Sea*, I:202; idem., *Churchill and the Admirals*, 285–91.

135. Marder, *Dardanelles to Oran*, ch. 4.

136. A good example of the tendency to shift blame entirely onto Churchill is David Brown, 'Norway 1940: The Balance of Interference', *Britain and Norway in the Second World War*, ed. Patrick Salmon (London: HMSO, 1995), 26–31.

137. Marder, *Dardanelles to Oran*, 171; Roskill, 'Marder, Churchill and the Admiralty, 1939–42', *Journal of the Royal United Services Institute* (January 1973).

138. Carlo d'Este, *Warlord: A Life of Winston Churchill at War, 1874–1945* (New York: Harper, 2008), 364–5.

139. *SWW*, I:641–5; *Memoirs of Lord Ismay*, 112–14.

140. Churchill, *SWW*, I:511. An unpublished draft of his memoirs read: 'it was a marvel—I really do not know how—I survived and maintained my position in public esteem while all the blame was thrown on poor Mr Chamberlain'. Reynolds, *In Command of History*, 126.

CHAPTER 7

1. David Reynolds, *From World War to Cold War: Churchill, Roosevelt, and the International History of the 1940s* (Oxford: Oxford University Press, 2006), 75–98; Reynolds, *In Command of History*, ch. 11; John Lukacs, *Five Days in London, May 1940* (New Haven, CT: Yale University Press, 1999).

2. Reynolds, *From World War to Cold War*, 75–98.

3. WP (40) 168: COS memorandum, 'British Strategy in a Certain Eventuality', 25 May 1940, CAB 66/7/48; WP (40) 362: COS memorandum, 'Future Strategy', 4 September 1940, CAB 65/11/42.

4. WP (40) 352: WSC memorandum, 'The Munitions Situation', 3 September 1940, CAB 66/11/32; *CWP*, II:762.

5. WSC to Beaverbrook, 8 July 1940, Kenneth Young, *Churchill and Beaverbrook* (London: Eyre & Spottiswoode, 1966), 154; *CWP*, II:492–3. See also WSC to Jan Smuts, 27 June 1940, and WSC to Lindemann, 29 June 1940, *CWP*, II:429, 441.

6. WP (40) 352: WSC memorandum, 'The Munitions Situation', 3 September 1940, CAB 66/11/32; *CWP*, II:762–4.

7. Ibid.; WP (40) 362: COS memorandum, 'Future Strategy', 4 September 1940, CAB 65/11/42.

8. WM (40) 176, CA, 22 June 1940, CAB/65/13/47; *CWP*, II:396.

9. Marder, *Dardanelles to Oran*, 222–6.

10. David Brown, *The Road to Oran: Anglo-French Naval Relations, September 1939–July 1940* (London: Frank Cass, 2004); Marder, *Dardanelles to Oran*, ch. 5.

11. WP (40) 169: COS memorandum, 26 May 1940, CAB 66/7/49.

12. WM (40) 144, 28 May 1940, CAB 65/7/39.

13. WSC to Ismay, 1 July 1940, and WSC to Alexander and Pound, 4 August 1940, Churchill, *SWW*, II:207, 531; Roskill, *War at Sea*, I:253–4; James Levy, *The Royal Navy's Home Fleet in World War II* (Basingstoke: Palgrave, 2003), 69–72.

14. Roskill, *War at Sea*, II:257.

15. WSC to Ironside and General Dill, 10 July 1940, ADM 205/6; Churchill, *SWW*, II:252–3.

16. WSC to FDR, 15 May 1940, *Churchill and Roosevelt: The Complete Correspondence*, ed. Warren Kimball, 3 vols (Princeton, NJ: Princeton University Press, 1984), I:37; Philip Goodhart, *Fifty Ships that Saved the World* (London: Heinemann, 1965), 1–11.

17. 'Minutes of Meeting held in Upper War Room, Admiralty', 21 June 1940, ADM 205/7.

18. WSC to FDR, 15 June 1940, in Kimball, *Churchill and Roosevelt*, I:49–51; WSC to Lord Lothian, 17 June 1940, in Kimball, *Churchill and Roosevelt*, I:52; Goodhart, *Fifty Ships*, 69–77.

19. FDR to WSC, 13 August 1940, in Kimball, *Churchill and Roosevelt*, I:57–9; Goodhart, *Fifty Ships*, 144–66.

20. WSC to Alexander, 22 August 1940, *CWP*, II:705–6.

21. Pound memorandum, 25 August 1940, ADM 205/5.

22. WP (40) 362: COS memorandum, 4 September 1940, CAB 65/11/42; WSC to Alexander, 9 September 1940, *CWP*, II:792–3.

23. WP (40) 349: Alexander memorandum. 7 September 1940, CAB 66/11/29.

24. WSC to Alexander, 15 September 1940, ADM 205/5; *CWP*, II:811–13.

25. WM (40) 277, 25 October 1940, CAB 65/9/39.

26. WSC to Eden, 18 October 1938; 'Memorandum on Sea-Power, 1939', 27 March 1939, *WSC*, V/3:1,231, 1,414–17.

27. WP (40) 134: COS memorandum, 'Implications of Possible Italian Action in the Mediterranean', 21 April 1940, CAB 66/7/14.

28. COS (40) 404: WSC to Ismay, 'Policy in the Mediterranean', 28 May 1940, CAB 80/12; Defence Committee (Operations) minutes, 25 May 1940, *CWP*, II:146, 175–6.

29. Cunningham to Pound, 7 June 1940, in Simpson, *Cunningham Papers*, I:49–50.

30. Pound to Cunningham, 16 June 1940, and Cunningham to Pound, 18 and 27 June 1940, Add Ms 52560, in Simpson, *Cunningham Papers*, I:74–6, 84; COS (40) 469 (JP), 17 June 1940, CAB 80/13; WSC to Alexander, 17 June 1940, and WSC to Alexander and Pound, 15 July 1940, ADM 199/1930.

31. Churchill, *SWW*, II:395–401.

32. WSC to Alexander, 7 September 1940, *CWP*, II:785.

33. WSC to Cunningham, 8 September 1940, in Simpson, *Cunningham Papers*, I:146; Churchill, *SWW*, II:400; *CWP*, II:791–2; WP (40) 421: WSC to COS, 15 October 1940, CAB 66/13/1.

34. Michael Simpson, *A Life of Admiral of the Fleet Viscount Cunningham of Hyndhope* (London: Routledge, 2004), 75–7.

35. Simpson, *Cunningham Papers*, I:195.

36. Colville diary, 30 March 1941, John Colville, *The Fringes of Power: 10 Downing Street Diaries 1939–55* (New York: W. W. Norton, 1985), 369.

37. DO (41) 13, 13 April 1941, CAB 69/2; WSC directive, 14 April 1941, *CWP*, III:488, 497.

38. WSC to Pound, 12 April 1941, *CWP*, III:484.

39. WSC to Alexander and Pound, 14 April 1941, ADM 199/1933; *CWP*, III:492.

40. WSC directive, 14 April 1941, *CWP*, III:496–8.

41. Pound to Cunningham, 8 and 11 April 1941, in Simpson, *Cunningham Papers*, I:336, 339.

42. Admiralty to Cunningham, and Cunningham to Admiralty, 15 April 1941, in Simpson, *Cunningham Papers*, I:341–4.

43. Cunningham to Pound, 22 April 1941, in Simpson, *Cunningham Papers*, I:353.

44. Pound to Cunningham, 23 April 1941, in Simpson, *Cunningham Papers*, I:354; WSC to Cunningham, 26 April 1941, *CWP*, III:545–6.

45. Cunningham to WSC, 29 April 1941, in Simpson, *Cunningham Papers*, I:361–2.

46. WSC to Cunningham, 1 May 1941, in Simpson, *Cunningham Papers*, I:395–6; *CWP*, III:588.

47. Colville diary, 22 and 25 May 1941, *Fringes of Power*, 389, 391.

48. For Cunningham's views, see Simpson, *Cunningham Papers*, I:411–12.

49. WSC to Admiralty, 7 October 1941, ADM 178/322.

50. WSC to Ismay, 3 June 1940, PREM 3/330/5; WSC to Ismay, 5 June 1940, PREM 3/330/5; *CWP* II:251 and Churchill, *SWW*, II:217–18. Churchill's views on combined operations during this period are discussed in Bernard Ferguson, *The*

Watery Maze (London: Collins, 1961), ch. 2; Glen St. J. Barclay, '"Butcher and Bolt": Admiral Roger Keyes and British Combined Operations, 1940–1941', *Naval War College Review*, 35, 1 (March 1982), 18–29; Howard Steers, 'Raiding the Continent: The Origins of British Special Service Forces' (Master of Military Art and Science thesis, US Army Command and General Staff College, 1980).

51. Ferguson, *Watery Maze*, 48–9; Barclay, 'Butcher and Bolt', 19–20.

52. WM (40) 191, CA, 2 July 1940, CAB 65/14/12; WSC to Ismay, 2 and 10 July 1940, PREM 3/330/9; *CWP* II:457, 499–500; Churchill, *SWW*, II:566.

53. Ferguson, *Watery Maze*, 49.

54. Undated War Office memorandum, PREM 3/330/9.

55. WSC to Eden, 23 July 1940, PREM 3/330/9; *CWP*, II:559; Churchill, *SWW*, II:572.

56. WSC to Keyes, 25 July 1940, *CWP*, II:568.

57. WSC to Eden, 23 July 1940, *SWW*, II:572; *CWP*, II:559.

58. John Colville diary, 9 and 30 August 1940, *Fringes of Power*, 214, 233.

59. WSC to Eden, 25 August 1940, *CWP*, II:721–2.

60. Churchill, *SWW*, ch. 24; Arthur Marder, *Operation Menace* (London: Oxford University Press, 1976); Tim Benbow, '"Menace" to "Ironclad": The British Operations against Dakar (1940) and Madagascar (1942)', *Journal of Military History*, 75, no. 3 (July 2011), 769–809.

61. WSC to Ismay, 23 November 1940, PREM 3/330/9; Steers, 'Raiding the Continent', 57.

62. Halpern, *Keyes Papers*, III:97–101.

63. Ibid., III:80.

64. Cunningham to Pound, 21 November 1940, in Simpson, *Cunningham Papers*, I:191; Cunningham to Admiralty, 9 December 1940, DO [Defence Committee (Operations) minutes] (40) 49, Annex I, CAB 69/1.

65. DO (40) 49, 9 December 1940, CAB 69/1; *CWP*, II:1,205–7; Keyes, 'Diary of 19 November to 9 December relating to Operation "Workshop"', Halpern, *Keyes Papers*, III:110–12.

66. WSC to Cunningham, 11 December 1940, in Simpson, *Cunningham Papers*, I:205–7; *CWP*, II:1,173–4, and Churchill, *SWW*, II:618–19, where it is dated 3 December 1940.

67. WP (40) 265: COS memorandum, 16 July 1940, CAB 66/9/45; WM (40) 209, CA, 22 July 1940, CAB 65/14/13; Butler, *Grand Strategy*, II:238–9.

68. Pound to Cunningham, 15 December 1940, Halpern, *Keyes Papers*, III:127; Simpson, *Cunningham Papers*, I:209.

69. WSC to Ismay, 26 December 1940, *CWP*, II:1,294; COS to WSC, 31 December 1940, Halpern, *Keyes Papers*, III:137.

70. Colville diary, 12 January 1941, *Fringes of Power*, 335.

71. WSC to Ismay for the COS, 13 January 1941, *CWP*, III:82.

72. Defence Committee (Operations) minutes, 13 January 1941, CAB 69/2; *CWP*, III:85; WSC to Ismay for COS, 13 January 1941, *CWP*, III:81.

73. David Brown (ed), *The Royal Navy and the Mediterranean* (London: Frank Cass, 2002), II:253–5; DO (41) 6; Defence Committee (Operations) minutes, 20 January 1941, CAB 69/2; *CWP*, III:101–4.

74. Defence Committee (Operations) minutes, 20 January 1941, CAB 69/2; *CWP*, III:101–4; WSC to Ismay for COS, 21 January 1941, CAB 69/2; *CWP*, III:105–6.

75. Christopher Mann, 'Combined Operations, the Commandos, and Norway, 1941–1944', *Journal of Military History*, 73, 2 (April 2009), 471–95; WSC to Pound, 3 January 1941, CAB 120/655; *CWP*, III:17.

76. Barclay, 'Butcher and Bolt', 24.

77. Cunningham to Pound, 11 March 1941, in Simpson, *Cunningham Papers*, I:299.

78. Ferguson, *Watery Maze*, 78.

79. WSC to Tovey, 7 March 1941, *CWP*, III:328.

80. Steers, 'Raiding the Continent', 76.

81. Ibid., 78.

82. Ibid., 79.

83. DO (41) 29, 14 May 1941, and DO (41) 40, 10 June 1940, CAB 69/2.

84. J. M. A. Gwyer and J. R. M. Butler, *Grand Strategy* (London: HMSO, 1964), III:7–8.

85. Keyes to WSC, 9 May 1940; Keyes to Eden, 12 May 1941; Captain Herbert Woolley to Keyes, 26 July 1941, Halpern, *Keyes Papers*, III:166–70, 177–8; Butler, *Grand Strategy*, III:8.

86. WSC to Ismay for COS, 23 June 1941, PREM 3/330/9; *CWP*, III:841.

87. Eden to WSC, 2 July 1941, PREM 3/330/9.

88. DO (41) 46, 4 July 1941, CAB 69/2.

89. Joan Beaumont, *Comrades in Arms: British Aid to Russia 1941–1945* (London: Davis-Poynter, 1980), 30.

90. COS (41) 235, 7 July 1941, CAB 79/12; Steers, 'Raiding the Continent', 107–8.

91. WSC to Keyes, 7 March 1941, PREM 3/328/7; Barclay, 'Butcher and Bolt', 25; WSC to Ismay, 8 July 1941, PREM 3/330/9; *CWP*, III:911.

92. WSC to FDR, 28 August 1941, in Kimball, *Churchill and Roosevelt*, I:234.

93. Keyes memoranda, 6 and 27 August 1941, Halpern, *Keyes Papers*, III:183–6.

94. On Keyes' relief, see Halpern, *Keyes Papers*, III:83–5.

95. Interview with Major General O. M. Lund, 8 May 1942, DEFE 2/699.

96. Ferguson, *Watery Maze*, 87–8.

97. Frederick Barley and David Waters, *The Defeat of the Enemy Attack on Shipping, 1939–1945*, ed. Eric Grove (Aldershot: Ashgate, 1997), 1B, table 27; Terry Hughes and John Costello, *The Battle of the Atlantic* (New York: The Dial Press, 1977), 111.

98. Barley and Waters, *Enemy Attack on Shipping*, 1B, table 27.

99. WSC to Sir John Reith, 11 August 1940, *CWP*, II:648; Kevin Smith, *Conflict Over Convoys: Anglo-American Logistics Diplomacy in the Second World War* (Cambridge: Cambridge University Press, 1996), 10–11.

100. Smith, *Conflict over Convoys*, 28–30, 37.

101. Butler, *Grand Strategy*, II:571.

102. Levy, *Royal Navy's Home Fleet*, 70.

103. DO (40) 33, 3 October 1940, CAB 69/1; WM (40) 266, 4 October 1940, CAB 65/9/28; *CWP*, II:899.

104. WM (40) 271, 15 October 1940, CAB 65/9/33; *CWP*, II:950; DO (40) 39, 31 October 1940, CAB 69/1; Hinsley, *British Intelligence*, I:188–90.

105. WP (40) 411: Cross memorandum, 30 October 1940, CAB 66/12/41.

106. WP (G) (40) 289, Greenwood memorandum, 5 November 1940, CAB 67/8/89.

107. Churchill, *SWW*, II:532–4, III:98–102.

108. WP (40) 434: Alexander memorandum, 4 November 1940, CAB 66/13/14.

109. DO (40) 40, 5 November 1940, CAB 69/1; *CWP*, II:1,051–2.

110. WSC to Alexander, 3 July 1941, ADM 199/1934; *CWP* III:894.

111. DO (40) 40, 5 November 1940, CAB 69/1; *CWP*, II:1,051–2.

112. WP (40) 458: 'Coastal Command', 23 November 1940, CAB 66/13/38.

113. DO (40) 47, 4 December 1940, CAB 69/1; John Buckley, *The RAF and Trade Defence, 1919–1945: Constant Endeavour* (Keele: Ryburn Publishing, Keele University Press, 1995), 122.

114. Roskill, *War at Sea*, I:457; Max Schoenfeld, 'Winston Churchill as War Manager: The Battle of the Atlantic Committee, 1941', *Military Affairs*, 52 (1988), 125.

115. WSC to Alexander and Pound, 27 December 1940, Churchill, *SWW*, II:534.

116. Import Executive minutes, 26 and 28 February 1941, CAB 86/1; *CWP*, III:267–8, 290–1.

117. WSC to Alexander and Pound, 28 February 1941, *CWP*, III:289.

118. WM (41) 21, 27 February 1941, CAB 65/17/21.

119. Charles Webster and Noble Frankland, *The Strategic Air Offensive Against Germany 1939–1945*, 4 vols (London: HMSO, 1961), I:164–5.

120. Secret session speech, House of Commons, 25 June 1941, *Complete Speeches*, VI:6,434.

121. WSC directive, 'The Battle of the Atlantic', 6 March 1941, CAB 86/1; Churchill, *SWW*, III:107–9; Roskill, *War at Sea*, I:609–11.

122. Schoenfeld, 'Churchill as War Manager'; W. J. R. Gardner, 'An Allied Perspective', in *The Battle of the Atlantic 1939–1945*, ed. Stephen Howarth and Derek Law (London: Greenhill, 1994), 516–37.

123. Import Executive minutes, 26 February 1941, CAB 86/1; Churchill, *SWW*, III:100.

124. Schoenfeld, 'Churchill as War Manager', 125–6; C. B. A. Behrens, *Merchant Shipping and the Demands of War* (London: HMSO and Longmans, Green and Co., 1955), 143–5.

125. WP (41) 69, WSC memoranda, 26 March 1941 and 27 March 1941, CAB 66/15/42; *CWP*, III:400–1, 413–14; WP (41) 88: Alexander memorandum, 20 April 1941, CAB 66/16/11.

126. Behrens, *Merchant Shipping*, 130–8; Smith, *Conflict over Convoys*, 48–55.
127. BA (Battle of the Atlantic Committee) (41) 9th mtg, 22 May 1941, CAB 86/1.
128. BA (41) 1st mtg, 19 March 1941, CAB 86/1.
129. Smith, *Conflict Over Convoys*, 55–7.
130. Schoenfeld, 'Churchill as War Manager', 125–6.
131. BA (41) 6th mtg, 23 April 1941, CAB 86/1; WSC to Bridges, Ismay et al., 28 April 1941; Churchill, *SWW*, III:128–9.
132. BA (41) 8th mtg, 8 May 1941, CAB 86/1.
133. Schoenfeld, 'Churchill as War Manager', 123–5.
134. Ibid., 125.
135. BA (41) 10th mtg, 5 June 1941, CAB 86/1; Barley and Waters, *Enemy Attack on Shipping*, 304–5; Roskill, *War at Sea*, 457–8.
136. WM (41) 61, 19 June 1941, CAB 65/18/40.
137. *WSC*, VI:1,032.
138. WP (41) 69: WSC memorandum, 'Naval Programme 1941', 27 March 1941, CAB 66/15/42.
139. WM (41) 29, 17 March 1941, CAB 65/18/8.
140. WSC to FDR, 19 March 1941, in Kimball, *Churchill and Roosevelt*, I:149–50.
141. FDR to WSC, 11 April 1941, in ibid., I:166–7.
142. WSC to FDR, 13 April 1941, in ibid., I:169.
143. Roskill, *War at Sea*, I:616.
144. BA (41) 10th mtg, 5 June 1941, CAB 86/1; *Complete Speeches*, VI:6,444; WSC to Wendell Wilkie (unsent), 19 May 1941, in Kimball, *Churchill and Roosevelt*, I:189–90.
145. Pound to WSC, 2 July 1941, ADM 205/10; Roskill, *War at Sea*, I:614; Butler, *Grand Strategy*, III:10; Hinsley, *British Intelligence*, II:147–8, 167.
146. WSC to Pound, 5 July 1941, ADM 205/10; *CWP*, III:899.
147. Roskill, *War at Sea*, I:616.
148. Barley and Waters, *Enemy Attack on Shipping*, 1B, plans 9–10.
149. Webster and Frankland, *Strategic Air Offensive*, I:168.
150. WSC to Portal, 17 April 41, *CWP*, III:510.
151. WSC to Portal, 21 July 1941, PREM 3/97/2; Defence Committee (Operations) minutes, 21 July 1941, *CWP*, III:968.
152. Portal to WSC, 23 July 1941, PREM 3/97/2.
153. Ismay to Portal, 20 August 1941, ADM 205/8.
154. Power to Pound, 21 August 1941, ADM 205/8; Roskill, *War at Sea*, I:467.
155. WSC to Alexander and Pound, 8 October 1941; Alexander to WSC, 16 October 1941; Portal to WSC, n.d., PREM 3/97.
156. WSC to Pound, 9 November 1941, ADM 199/1934; WSC to Pound and Alexander, 14 November 1941, ADM 199/1934; Churchill, *SWW*, III:749; *CWP*, III:1,454.
157. Pound to HR Moore, 19 November 1941, and undated memorandum, ADM 205/13.

158. Alexander to WSC, 4 December 1941, PREM 3/171/3.

159. Webster and Frankland, *Strategic Air Offensive*, I:179–82.

160. WSC to Portal, 27 September 1941, *CWP*, III:1270.

161. WSC to Portal, 7 October 1941, *CWP*, III:1313–14; Webster and Frankland, *Strategic Air Offensive*, I:184–5; Gwyer and Butler, *Grand Strategy*, III:37–8.

162. WM (41) 111, 11 November 1941, CAB 65/20/4; WSC to Archibald Sinclair and Portal, 11 November 1941, *CWP*, III:1,436; Webster and Frankland, *Strategic Air Offensive*, I:185–7.

163. WSC to Alexander, 6 December 1941, PREM 3/171/3.

164. Alexander to WSC, 8 December 1941, ADM 205/13.

CHAPTER 8

1. For Australia's position, see David Day, *The Great Betrayal* (New York: Norton, 1989), ch. 2.

2. DMV (Visits of Ministers from Dominions) (39) 8th Mtg, 20 November 1939, ADM 1/11062.

3. Chamberlain to J. A. Lyons, Prime Minister of Australia, 20 March 1939, *Documents on Australian Foreign Policy 1937–49,* ed. R. G. Neale et al. (Canberra: Australian Government Publishing Service, 1976–82), II:75.

4. DMV (39) 8, 20 November 1939, ADM 1/11062.

5. Ibid.

6. Ibid.; WP (39) 135: WSC memorandum, 'Australian and New Zealand Naval Defence,' 21 November 1939, CAB 66/3/5; *CWP*, I:401–3.

7. Ibid.

8. WM (39) 68, 2 November 1939, CAB 65/2/2; Day, *Great Betrayal*, 24.

9. COS (40) 592 (Revise), 'Far Eastern Appreciation', 15 August 1940, CAB 80/15.

10. WP (40) 234, Halifax memorandum, 'Policy in the Far East', 29 June 1940, CAB 66/9/14; WP (40) 263, Halifax memorandum, 'Policy in the Far East', 12 July 1940, CAB 66/9/43.

11. WM (40) 194, 5 July 1940, CAB 65/8/6; *CWP*, II:478–9.

12. WM (40) 222, CA, 8 August 1940, CAB 65/14/20; *CWP*, II:634. Two weeks earlier, Churchill thought that Britain would have to rely 'mainly on submarines and a few fast cruisers at the outset'. WSC to Ismay, 25 July 1940, ibid., II:570.

13. WSC to Alexander and Pound, 1 August 1940, ADM 199/1930; *CWP*, II:597.

14. Pound memorandum for Alexander, 1 August 1940, 'Redistribution of the Fleet in the event of war with Japan', ADM 205/6; Robin Brodhurst, *Churchill's Anchor* (Barnsley: Leo Cooper, 2000), 193–4; WSC to Alexander and Pound, 2 August 1940, ADM 199/1930; *CWP*, II:599.

15. COS minutes, 19 September 1940, CAB 79/6; *CWP*, II:836. Also WSC to Ismay, 10 September 1940, ibid., 796: 'The presence of the United States Fleet in the

Pacific must always be a main pre-occupation to Japan. They are not at all likely to gamble. They are usually most cautious, and now have real need to be, since they are involved in China so deeply.'

16. WM (40) 222, CA, 8 August 1940, CAB 65/14/20; *CWP*, II:634.

17. COS (41) 80 (O), 'Despatch of a Fleet to the Far East', 18 May 1941; Menzies to WSC, 11 August 1941, PREM 3/156/1; *Documents on Australian Foreign Policy 1937–49*, V:65–6.

18. FE (Far East Committee) (40) 65, 'Far Eastern Situation', 23 November 1940, CAB 96/1. For Whitehall's views on the employment of capital ships as a deterrent, see Christopher M. Bell, 'The "Singapore Strategy" and the Deterrence of Japan: Winston Churchill, the Admiralty, and the Dispatch of Force Z', *English Historical Review*, 116, 467 (June 2001), 617–19.

19. WSC to Menzies, 8 December 1940, *CWP*, II:1,187–8.

20. COS (40) 1053: 'Tactical Appreciation of Defence Situation in Malaya', report by Far Eastern Cs-in-C, 16 October 1940, CAB 80/24; S. Woodburn Kirby, *The War Against Japan* (London: HMSO, 1957), I:48–9.

21. WSC to COS, 13 January 1941, COS (41) 33, CAB 80/24; Butler, *Grand Strategy*, II:495; see also WSC to Lord Cranborne, 15 December 1940, *CWP*, II:1,237–8.

22. On British deficiencies in Malaya see in particular John R. Ferris, 'The Singapore Grip: Preparing Defeat in Malaya, 1939–1941', paper prepared for Anglo-Japanese conference at Hayama, September 2000.

23. WSC to Ismay, 7 January 1941, PREM 3/157/1; Churchill, *SWW*, III:177; Christopher M. Bell, '"Our Most Exposed Outpost": Hong Kong and British Far Eastern Strategy', *Journal of Military History*, 60, 1 (January 1996), 76–81.

24. Stark to Secretary of the Navy, 12 November 1940, *Strategic Planning in the U.S. Navy: Its Evolution and Execution 1891–1945* (Wilmington, DE: Scholarly Resources Inc., n.d.), roll 5.

25. WSC to Pound and Alexander, 22 November 1940, *CWP*, II:1,126–7; James Leutze, *Bargaining for Supremacy: Anglo-American Naval Collaboration, 1937–1941* (Chapel Hill, NC: University of North Carolina Press, 1977), 200.

26. COS (40) 807 JP, 7 October 1940, CAB 80/20; Admiralty to C-in-C, China, 15 October 1940, ADM 1/11183.

27. Leutze, *Bargaining for Supremacy*, 198–9, 201–2, 206; Record of a meeting held at the Admiralty, 22 November 1940, *Strategic Planning in the U.S. Navy*, roll 5; Ghormley to Stark, 14 November 1940, ibid., roll 6.

28. Record of a meeting held at the Admiralty, 22 November 1940, *Strategic Planning in the U.S. Navy*, roll 5.

29. Notes by Captain A. G. Kirk, USN, on meeting of US naval representatives with Pound, 19 November 1940, *Strategic Planning in the U.S. Navy*, roll 6. According to Pound, the 'distances in the Pacific were so vast that it did not appear likely the Japanese would dare risk vital units. It was assumed the force necessary for such an operation would be one carrier plus probably one heavy

cruiser. The danger to such a force of air attack by U.S. shore based aircraft was estimated as too great to justify the hazard.'

30. Leutze, *Bargaining for Supremacy*, 206; Ian Cowman, *Dominion or Decline* (Oxford: Berg, 1996), 190.

31. WSC to Ismay, 9 December 1940, *CWP*, II:1,209.

32. BUS (J) [British-United States Staff Conversations] (41) 13: 'The Far East: Appreciation by the United Kingdom Delegation', 11 February 1941; BUS (J) (41) 3, 3 February 1941; BUS (J) (41) 4, 5 February 1941; BUS (J) (41) 6, 10 February 1941, *Strategic Planning in the U.S. Navy*, roll 5.

33. WSC to Pound and Alexander, 17 February 1941, ADM 199/1932; *CWP*, III:234–6.

34. WSC to COS, 28 April 1941, PREM 3/156/6; DO (Defence Committee (Operations) (41) 20, 29 April 1941, CAB 69/2; *CWP*, III:556, 575 COS (41) 139(O), 16 July 1941, CAB 80/58. Emphasis added.

35. Dill memorandum, 'The Relation of the Middle East to the Security of the United Kingdom', 6 May 1941, Churchill, *SWW*, III:421–2; Dill to WSC, 15 May 1941, Butler, *Grand Strategy*, II:581; Ong Chit Chung, *Operation Matador: Britain's War Plans Against the Japanese 1918–1941* (Singapore: Times Academic Press, 1997), 164–6.

36. WSC to Dill, 13 May 1941, Churchill, *SWW*, III:422–3.

37. Ibid., p. 423. 'I have already given you the political data upon which the military arrangements for the defence of Singapore should be based,' he informed Dill, 'namely that should Japan enter the war the United States will in all probability come in on our side . . .'

38. Beaumont, *Comrades in Arms*, 31–58.

39. WSC to Pound and Alexander, 25 August 1941, ADM 205/10; Churchill, *SWW*, III:854–5.

40. Pound to WSC, 13 February 1941, ADM 205/10; Cowman, *Dominion or Decline*, 208–9.

41. Director of Plans to Pound, 25 August 1941; Pound to WSC, 28 August 1941, ADM 205/10; Churchill, *SWW*, III:855–8.

42. WSC to Pound, 29 August 1941, ADM 205/10; Churchill, *SWW*, III:858–9.

43. Eden to WSC, 12 September 1941, FO 371/27981; Eden Diary, 12 September 1941, Papers of the first Earl of Avon, Special Collections Department, University of Birmingham; Antony Best, *Britain, Japan, and Pearl Harbor* (London: Routledge, 1995), 172.

44. Eden Diary, 12 September 1941.

45. JP (41) 816, 'Japan: Our Future Policy', 7 October 1941, annex I, CAB 84/35.

46. Eden to WSC, 16 October 1941, DO (41) 21, CAB 69/3.

47. Phillips to Pound, 17 October 1941, ADM 178/322; *CWP*, III:1,346.

48. DO (41) 65, 17 October 1941, CAB 69/2; *CWP*, III:1,344–5.

49. DO (41) 65, 17 October 1941, CAB 69/2.

50 DO (41) 66, 20 October 1941, CAB 69/8.
51. DO (41) 66, 20 October 1941, CAB 69/8. Prior to the publication of his official history, Roskill searched in vain for any record that the final destination of these ships was formally approved. The absence of any official decision on this matter later fuelled an elaborate conspiracy theory by Ian Cowman. Cowman, 'Main Fleet to Singapore? Churchill, the Admiralty, and Force Z', *Journal of Strategic Studies*, 18, 2 (March 1995), 79–93. For a refutation, see Christopher M. Bell, 'Singapore Strategy'.
52. The reasons for this decision are explored in Bell, 'Our Most Exposed Outpost', 75–88.
53. COS minutes, 3 September 1941, CAB 79/14.
54. Hollis to WSC, 10 September 1941, PREM 3/157/1; also War Office to Brooke-Popham, 6 November 1941, WO 106/2409.
55. WO 106/2409.
56. WM (41) 103, CA, 16 October 1941, CAB 65/23.
57. Japanese decision-makers agreed. On 1 December 1941, Admiral Nagano, the Chief of the Japanese Naval Staff, noted Britain's last-minute manoeuvring, but concluded that these measures did 'not call for changes in the deployment of our forces. It will have no effect on our operations.' Nobutaka Ike (ed.), *Japan's Decision for War* (Stanford, CA: Stanford University Press, 1967), 280–1.
58. *Complete Speeches*, VI:6,504. Churchill had made this promise to Roosevelt privately on 20 October 1941. Kimball, *Churchill and Roosevelt*, 20 October 1941, I:256–7.
59. Roosevelt to WSC, 7 November 1941, in Kimball, *Churchill and Roosevelt*, I:267.
60 Churchill, *SWW*, III:606–8.
61. Churchill, *SWW*, III:620.
62. On 1 and 3 December. See Barnett, *Engage the Enemy More Closely*, 405–6.
63. WSC to Allen, 11 August 1953, CAB 103/327.
64. WSC, *SWW*, III:547–8.
65. WSC to Commodore G. R. G. Allen, 11 August 1953, CAB 103/327.
66. Roskill to Butler, 20 and 27 August 1953, CAB 140/109; Roskill, *War at Sea*, I:559.
67. Brooke diary, 9 December 1941, *War Diaries 1939–1945: Field Marshal Lord Alanbrooke*, ed. Alex Danchev and Daniel Todman (London: Weidenfeld and Nicolson, 2001), 209.
68. Speech of 27 January 1942, *Complete Speeches*, VI:6,561.
69. WSC to Attlee, 30 December 1941, *CWP*, III:1,718; Churchill, *SWW*, IV:9.
70. Speech of 27 January 1942, *Complete Speeches*, VI:6,561.
71. Alexander Hill, 'British Lend-Lease Aid and the Soviet War Effort, June 1941–June 1942', *Journal of Military History*, 71, no. 3 (July 2007), 773–808.
72. 'Memorandum on Sea-Power, 1939', 27 March 1939, *WSC*, V/3:1,414–17.

CHAPTER 9

1. 'Memorandum on the Conduct of the War: Part I—The Atlantic Front', 16 December 1941, *CWP*, III:1,633–7.
2. Ibid.
3. 'Memorandum on the Future Conduct of the War: Part III—1943', 18 December 41, *CWP*, III:1,642–4.
4. Ibid.
5. Gwyer, *Grand Strategy*, III/1, 339–48.
6. Ibid., III/2:669.
7. Michael Howard, *Grand Strategy*, 6 vols (London: HMSO, 1972), 4:17.
8. WSC to Hopkins, 12 March 1942, Churchill, *SWW*, IV:103–4.
9. Roosevelt to WSC, 19 March 1942, *Churchill and Roosevelt*, I:424; Churchill, *SWW*, IV:105; Clay Blair, *Hitler's U-boat War*, 2 vols (New York: Random House, 1996 and 1998), I:523.
10. DO (42) 14: Sinclair memorandum, 'Bombing Policy', 9 February 1942, CAB 69/4; Barnett, *Engage the Enemy*, 459; Webster and Frankland, *Strategic Air Offensive*, I:320–1.
11. Webster and Frankland, *Strategic Air Offensive*, I:322–3; Butler, *Grand Strategy*, III/2:525.
12. DO (42) 15: Admiralty memorandum, 'Bombing Policy', 14 February 1942, CAB 69/4; Webster and Frankland, *Strategic Air Offensive*, I:325; Barnett, *Engage the Enemy*, 459.
13. Pound to VCNS et al., 24 February 1942, ADM 205/15.
14. Horton memorandum, 'R.A.F. and Sea Power', 26 February 1942, ADM 205/15.
15. Director of Plans memorandum, 'Sea and Air Power in Future Developments', 27 February 1942, ADM 205/15.
16. Blake memorandum, 'Air Support for Naval Operations', 27 February 1942, ADM 205/15.
17. DO (42) 23: Pound memorandum, 'Air Requirements for the Successful Prosecution of the War at Sea', 5 March 1942, CAB 69/4; Barnett, *Engage the Enemy*, 460; Roskill, *War at Sea*, II:79–81; Webster and Frankland, *Strategic Air Offensive*, I:326.
18. Duncan Redford, 'Inter- and Intra-Service Rivalries in the Battle of the Atlantic', *Journal of Strategic Studies*, 32, no. 6 (December 2009), 918–24.
19. DO (42) 24: Sinclair memorandum, 8 March 1942, CAB 69/4, cited in Barnett, *Engage the Enemy*, 460–1; Webster and Frankland, *Strategic Air Offensive*, I:326; Butler, *Grand Strategy*, III/2:535.
20. DO (42) 8, 18 March 1942, CAB 69/4, cited in Barnett, *Engage the Enemy*.
21. WSC minute to Ismay for COS, 21 March 1942, PREM 3/97/1.
22. WSC to Roosevelt, 29 March 1942, Kimball, *Churchill and Roosevelt*, I:434–5.
23. Cherwell to WSC, 30 March 1942, PREM 3/11/4; Webster and Frankland, *Strategic Air Offensive*, I:331–2.

24. Sinclair to WSC, 6 April 1942, PREM 3/11/4.

25. WSC to Ismay for COS, 7 April 1942, Churchill, *SWW*, IV:760–1.

26. WSC to Attlee, 16 April 1942, cited in Butler, *Grand Strategy*, III/2:528–9.

27. Alexander to WSC, 19 April 1942, PREM 3/171/3.

28. Alexander to WSC, 1 May 1942, and WSC to Alexander, 2 May 1942, PREM 3/97.

29. Barley and Waters, *Enemy Attack on Shipping*, 354; Roskill, *War at Sea*, II:85; see also Tovey to Pound, 7 June 1942, ROSK 7/210.

30. COS (42) 171(O): Pound memorandum, 'The Bombing of Germany', 16 June 1942, copy in PREM 3/11/4.

31. COS 180 and 188, 16 and 24 June 1942, CAB 79/21; Butler, *Grand Strategy*, III/2:536–8.

32. Harris to WSC, 17 June 1942, cited in Webster and Frankland, *Strategic Air Offensive*, I:340–1.

33. WP (42) 374: 'Note by Air Marshal Sir Arthur Harris, K.C.B., O.B.E., A.F.C., on the Role and Work of Bomber Command', 28 June 1942, CAB 66/28/4.

34. Portal draft memorandum, 'Provision of Long Range Aircraft for Anti-Submarine Patrols', 9 July 1942, Pound to Portal, 13 July 1942, and Portal to Pound, 14 July 1942, ADM 205/24; WP (42) 302: COS report, 'Provision of Aircraft for the War at Sea', 18 July 1942, CAB 66/26/32; Butler, *Grand Strategy*, III/2:537–8.

35. Pound to Drax, 21 July 1942, ADM 205/22A.

36. WP (42) 311: WSC memorandum, 'A Review of the War Position', 21 July 1942, CAB 66/26/41; Churchill, *SWW*, IV:781–4.

37. Ibid.

38. Smith, *Conflict over Convoys*, 68–70; Behrens, *Merchant Shipping*, 287–8.

39. Blair, *Hitler's U-boat War*, I:591–2; Kimball, *Churchill and Roosevelt*, I:491.

40. WSC to FDR, 4 March 1942, Kimball, *Churchill and Roosevelt*, I:379–80.

41. Behrens, *Merchant Shipping*, 304–6.

42. WM (42) 98, 28 July 1942, CAB 65/27/14.

43. WM (42) 111, CA, 12 August 1942, CAB 65/31/15; WP (42) 325: Bruce memorandum, 'Provision of Aircraft for the War at Sea', 31 July 1942, CAB 66/27/6.

44. WP (42) 399: 'Note by Lord Trenchard on our War Policy—August 1942', 29 August 1942, CAB 66/28/29.

45. WP (42) 405: WSC memorandum, 'Air Policy', 9 September 1942, CAB 66/28/35.

46. Alexander to WSC, 13 August 1942, PREM 3/97/1.

47. WSC to Alexander, 24 August 1942, PREM 3/97/1.

48. Pound to WSC, 28 August 1942, PREM 3/97/1.

49. WSC to Ismay and Bridges, 28 August 1942, Churchill, *SWW*, IV:788.

50. Draft memorandum by Admiral Sir Charles Kennedy-Purvis, 28 September 1942, ADM 205/15.

51. Joubert memorandum, 'The Anti-Submarine War', 21 September 1942, ADM 205/24.

52. DO (S) (42) 88: Pound memorandum, 'The Needs of the Navy', 5 October 1942, CAB 70/5; Barnett, *Engage the Enemy*, 471.

53. Cherwell to WSC, 15 September 1942, and WSC to Sinclair, 16 September 1942, PREM 3/97/1.

54. WSC to Sinclair and Portal, 17 September 1942, WP (42) 481, CAB 66/30/11; Churchill, *SWW*, IV:793.

55. Sinclair to WSC, 9 October 1942, WP (42) 481, CAB 66/30/11.

56. Pound to WSC, 25 October 1942, ADM 205/15.

57. WSC memorandum, 'Policy for the Conduct of the War', 24 October 1942, CAB 66/30/13.

58. Roskill, *War at Sea*, II:485.

59. Barley and Waters, *Enemy Attack on Shipping*, 302.

60. Behrens, *Merchant Shipping*, 293.

61. WP (42) 497: 'Third Report by the Shipping Committee', 31 October 1942, CAB 66/30/27.

62. Smith, *Conflict over Convoys*, 91–6.

63. WP (42) 486 Revise: Lyttelton memorandum, 'Visit of the Minister of Production to America', 29 October 1942, CAB 66/30/16; Howard, *Grand Strategy*, IV:8–9.

64. WSC to FDR, 31 October 1942, in Kimball, *Churchill and Roosevelt*, I:648–50.

65. Richard Goette, 'Britain and the Delay in Closing the Mid-Atlantic "Air Gap" during the Battle of the Atlantic', *Northern Mariner*, 15, 4 (October 2005), 32.

66. AU [Anti-U-Boat Warfare Committee] (42) 1, 4 November 1942, CAB 86/2.

67. Goette, 'Closing the Mid-Atlantic Air Gap', 29–30; Redford, 'Inter- and Intra-Service Rivalries', 909–12.

68. Barnett, *Engage the Enemy*, 583–4.

69. WP (42) 485: joint memorandum by Alexander and Lord Leathers, 'Construction of Merchant Ship Aircraft Carriers', 27 October 1942, CAB 66/30/15.

70. AU (42) 1, 4 November 1942, CAB 86/2.

71. AU (42) 2, 13 November 1942, CAB 86/2.

72. AU (42) 3, 18 November 1942, CAB 86/2.

73. WSC to FDR via Hopkins, 20 November 1942, CAB 86/4; Churchill, *SWW*, IV:284–5; Kimball, *Churchill and Roosevelt*, II:27.

74. Hopkins to WSC, CAB 86/4; Kimball, *Churchill and Roosevelt*, II:26; Howard, *Grand Strategy*, IV:306.

75. FDR to WSC, 30 November 1942, in Kimball, *Churchill and Roosevelt*, II:44–5.

76. Howard, *Grand Strategy*, IV:6–7.

77. WP (42) 556: WSC memorandum, 'Manpower', 28 November 1942, CAB 66/31/66.

78. Madhusree Mukerjee, *Churchill's Secret War* (New York: Basic Books, 2010), 191.

79. Behrens, *Merchant Shipping*, 319–20; Smith, *Conflict over Convoys*, 122–31; Mukerjee, ch. 5.

80. COS memorandum, Howard, *Grand Strategy*, IV:215.
81. Goette, 'Air Gap', 36; Howard, *Grand Strategy*, IV:310.
82. Roskill, II:485; Gardner, *Decoding History*, 182–3.
83. Smith, *Conflict over Convoys*, 109, 133–51.
84. Ibid., 113–14.
85. WSC to FDR, 30 December 1942, in Kimball, *Churchill and Roosevelt*, II:95.
86. WP (43) 28: 'Fourth Report by the Shipping Committee', 17 January 1943, CAB 66/33/28.
87. Howard, *Grand Strategy*, IV:295–7.
88. WP (43) 100: Cherwell memorandum, 'The Shipping Position', 7 March 1943, CAB 66/34/50.
89. Ibid.
90. WSC to FDR, 24 March 1943, in Kimball, *Churchill and Roosevelt*, II:167.
91. AU (43) 5, 2 December 1942, CAB 86/2.
92. AU (43) 13, 31 March 1943, CAB 86/2.
93. Ibid.
94. Josef W. Konvitz, 'Bombs, Cities, and Submarines: Allied Bombing of the French Ports, 1942–1943', *International History Review*, 14, no. 1 (February 1992), 28–30; WP (43) 11: Alexander memorandum, 'U-Boat Bases in the Bay of Biscay', 7 January 1943, CAB 66/33/11.
95. WM (43) 6 CA, CAB 65/37/1; Redford, 'Inter- and Intra-Service Rivalries', 904–5.
96. Konvitz, 'Bombs, Cities and Submarines', 43.
97. AU (43) 13, 31 March 1943, CAB 86/2.
98. Ibid.
99. Howard, *Grand Strategy*, IV:297–8; Smith, *Conflict over Convoys*, 173–6.
100. Howard, *Grand Strategy*, IV:305; Goette, 'Air Gap', 37–8.
101. Buckley, 153–4; Goette, 'Air Gap', 38.
102. Barley and Waters, *Enemy Attack on Shipping*, 95; Roskill, *War at Sea*, II:201, 366–7.
103. Barley and Waters, *Enemy Attack on Shipping*, 99.
104. Kevin Smith, 'Maritime War: Combat, Management, and Memory', in *A Companion to the Second World War*, ed. Thomas Zeiler (Malden, MA: Wiley-Blackwell Publishing, 2012). I am grateful to Professor Smith for providing me with a copy of this article prior to publication.
105. Churchill, *SWW*, II:529.
106. Barley and Waters, *Enemy Attack on Shipping*, 106.

CHAPTER 10

1. Pound to WSC, 8 March 1942, ADM 205/13.
2. WSC to FDR, 7 April 1942, in Kimball, *Churchill and Roosevelt*, I:442–3.
3. Benbow, '"Menace" to "Ironclad"'.

4. Pound to WSC, 10 June 1942, ADM 205/14.

5. WSC to Alexander and Pound, 4 July 1942, ADM 199/1935.

6. WSC to Pound, (c. 12 July 1942), ADM 205/14; *The Somerville Papers*, ed. Michael Simpson (Aldershot: Scolar Press for the Navy Records Society, 1995), 432.

7. WSC to Alexander and Pound, 4 July 1942, ADM 199/1935; WSC to Pound, 15 October 1942, ADM 205/14.

8. WSC to Pound, 16 October 1942, ADM 205/14.

9. WM (42) 73, CA, 11 June 1942, CAB 65/30/20; WSC to FDR, 20 June 1942, Churchill, *SWW*, IV:342–3.

10. WM (42) 73, CA, 11 June 1942, CAB 65/30/20; WSC to Ismay for COS, 1 May 1942, Churchill, *SWW*, IV:312–13; WSC to Ismay for COS, 13 June 1942, WP (42) 286, CAB 66/26/16.

11. Howard, *Grand Strategy*, IV:207–16.

12. WSC to COS, 18 November 1942, Churchill, *SWW*, IV:582–3.

13. WP (42) 543: WSC memorandum, 'Plans and Operations in the Mediterranean, Middle East and near East', 25 November 1942, CAB 66/31/23.

14. Howard, *Grand Strategy*, IV:85.

15. Ibid., IV:398–404.

16. WSC to Ismay/COS, 2 April 1943, Churchill, *SWW*, IV:838.

17. WSC to Smuts, 15 July 1943, cited in Howard, *Grand Strategy*, IV:503.

18. WSC to COS, 19 July 1943, cited in Howard, *Grand Strategy*, IV:564.

19. John Ehrman, *Grand Strategy*, 6 vols (London: HMSO, 1956), V:92–5.

20. WSC to FDR, 7 and 8 October 1943, in Kimball, *Churchill and Roosevelt*, II:498–9, 504.

21. Kimball, *Churchill and Roosevelt*, II:504–6.

22. WSC to Ismay and COS, 21 November and 6 December 1943, Churchill, *SWW*, V:368, 598–9; Ehrman, *Grand Strategy*, V:103; remarks at Plenary Session, Teheran Conference, 28 November 1943, Ehrman, *Grand Strategy*, V:174–6. WSC minute, 10 December 1943, Ehrman, *Grand Strategy*, V:195.

23. WSC to Marshall, 16 April 1944, Churchill, *SWW*, V:454.

24. WSC to FDR, 26 December 1943, in Kimball, *Churchill and Roosevelt*, II:632–3; see also Churchill, *SWW*, V:386.

25. Admiral Percy Noble to Cunningham, 1 October 1943, in Simpson, *Cunningham Papers*, II:151.

26. Howard, *Grand Strategy*, IV:404.

27. WSC memorandum, 'Notes on "Anakim"', 8 May 1943, PREM 3/443/7; Churchill, *SWW*, IV:702–5.

28. WSC to Ismay/COS, 17 August 1943, PREM 3/147/3.

29. WSC to Ismay/COS, 21 November 1943; Churchill, *SWW*, V:598–9.

30. WSC to Ismay/COS, 6 December 1943, PREM 3/147/7.

31. WSC to Mountbatten, marked 'Most personal, secret and private. Copies should not be circulated to anyone', 10 January 1944, PREM 3/147/7.

32. Mountbatten to COS and WSC, 10 January 1944 and WSC to COS, 11 January 1944, PREM 3/147/8.

33. Ehrman, *Grand Strategy*, V:421–6.
34. WSC to Ismay/COS, 24 January 1944, CAB 120/704; Churchill, *SWW*, V:505.
35. JP 44 (32) (Final), 2 February 1944, Cab 84/60.
36. H. P. Willmott, *Grave of a Dozen Schemes* (Annapolis, MD: Naval Institute Press, 1996), 49–54.
37. COS (44) 48th Mtg, 14 February 1944, PREM 3/160/7.
38. WSC memorandum, proof copy, 29 February 1944, PREM 3/160/7; Ehrman, *Grand Strategy*, V:441–4.
39. Ehrman, *Grand Strategy*, V:439.
40. WSC to FDR, 10 March 1944, Churchill, *SWW*, V:509–10.
41. FDR to WSC, 13 March 1944, Churchill, *SWW*, V:510–11.
42. FDR to WSC, 25 February 1944, Ehrman, *Grand Strategy*, V:455.
43. COS to WSC, 8 March 1944, PREM 3/160/7; Alexander memorandum, 1 March 1944, ADM 205/35; Cunningham to WSC, 18 March 1944, in Simpson, *Cunningham Papers*, II:309–10; Ehrman, *Grand Strategy*, V:444–8.
44. Ismay to WSC, 4 March 1944, PREM 3/160/7; see also Brooke diary, 3 March 1944, *War Diaries*, 528.
45. Brooke diary, 8 March 1944, *War Diaries*, 530.
46. COS (44) 79th Mtg (O), 8 March 1944, PREM 3/160/7.
47. WSC to Cunningham, Brooke, and Portal, 20 March 1944, Churchill, *SWW*, V:511–12.
48. Ehrman, *Grand Strategy*, V:457–8; Willmott, *Grave*, 72.
49. Willmott, *Grave*, 76–7.
50. Noble to Cunningham 2 April 1944, in Simpson, *Cunningham Papers*, II:312.
51. Brooke diary, 14 April 1944, 540.
52. Willmott, *Grave*, 93–5.
53. Cunningham to Noble, 8 April 1944, in Simpson, *Cunningham Papers*, II:314.
54. WSC to Ismay/COS, 21 April 1944, PREM 3/160/7.
55. COS (44) 236th mtg (O), 15 July 1944, PREM 3/160/5.
56. WSC to Ismay, 24 June 1944, PREM 3/160/5.
57. COS (44) 236th mtg (O), 15 July 1944, PREM 3/160/5.
58. Cunningham diary, 14 July 1944, in Simpson, *Cunningham Papers*, II:320.
59. WSC to Ismay/COS, 24 July 1944, CAB 120/707.
60. COS (44) 264th mtg (O), 8 August 1944, PREM 3/160/6.
61. COS (44) 265th mtg (O), 8 August 1944, PREM 3/160/6.
62. COS (44) 264th mtg (O), 8 August 1944, PREM 3/160/6.
63. COS (44) 266th mtg (O), 8 August 1944, PREM 3/160/6.
64. Ibid.
65. COS (44) 267th mtg (O), 9 August 1944, PREM 3/160/6; Brooke diary, 9 August and 5 September 1944, 579, 587–8.
66. Cunningham diary, 10 August 1944, in Simpson, *Cunningham Papers*, II:322.
67. Brooke diary, 9 August 1944, 579.

68. COS (44) 269th mtg (O), 9 August 1944, PREM 3/160/6; Ehrman, *Grand Strategy*, V:493–8.
69. Cunningham diary, 2 October 1944, in Simpson, *Cunningham Papers*, II:326; WSC to Mountbatten, 5 October 1944, Churchill, *SWW*, VI:147–8; Ehrman, *Grand Strategy*, V:532–3; Willmott, *Grave*, 131–3.
70. WP (42) 173: Alexander memorandum, 'New Construction Programme, 1942', 21 April 1942, CAB 66/24/3.
71. WM (42) 128, 22 September 1942, CAB 65/27/44.
72. WP (43) 122: Alexander memorandum, 'New Construction Programme, 1943', 26 March 1943, CAB 66/35/22.
73. Alexander to WSC, 7 October 1943, PREM 3/322/5/6; George Moore, *Building for Victory: The Warship Building Programmes of the Royal Navy 1939–1945* (Gravesend, Kent: World Ship Society, 2003), 87–90.
74. WSC to Alexander, 24 October 1943, Churchill, *SWW*, V:593.
75. WP (43) 490: WSC memorandum, 'Man-power', 1 November 1943, CAB 66/42/40; W. K. Hancock and M. M. Gowing, *British War Economy* (London: HMSO, 1949), 448–52.
76. WSC to Alexander, 1 November 1943, PREM 3/322/5/6; Churchill, *SWW*, V:595.
77. WP (43) 539: Anderson memorandum, 'Man-power Policy for 1944', 27 November 1943, 66/43/39; WP (43) 534: Alexander memorandum: 'Man-power for the Navy in 1944', 25 November 1943, CAB 66/43/34.
78. WP (43) 549: Alexander memorandum: 'Production of New Type Landing Ships and Other Changes in New Construction Programme, 1943', 2 December 1943, CAB 66/43/49; WM (43) 171, 16 December 1943, CAB 65/36/39; Moore, *Building for Victory*, 92–8.
79. Moore, *Building for Victory*, 98–106.
80. Memorandum by First Sea Lord's office, 'The Empire's Post-War Fleet', 4 May 1944, ADM 167/122.
81. WP (44) 245: Alexander memorandum, 'New Construction Programme, 1944', 1 May 1944, CAB 66/49/45.
82. WSC to Alexander and Cunningham, 31 January 1944, PREM 3/322/5/6; Churchill, *SWW*, V:604.
83. WM (44) 65, 18 May 1944, CAB/65/42/23.
84. Cunningham diary, 18 May 44, in Simpson, *Cunningham Papers*, II:379.
85. Cherwell to WSC, 5 July 1944, PREM 3/322/5/6.
86. WP (44) 764: Cherwell memorandum, 'Battleships *versus* Aircraft', 29 December 1944, CAB 66/60/14.
87. CP (45) 57: Admiralty memorandum, 'Battleships *versus* Aircraft', 2 July 1945, CAB 66/67/7; see also plans division memorandum, 6 February 1945, ADM 205/53.
88. CP (45) 54: Bracken memorandum, 'The New Construction Programme, 1945', 29 June 1945, CAB 66/67/4.

89. Board minute 3983, 22 November 1944, ADM 167/120; Moore, *Building for Victory*, 109–10.

90. CP (45) 54: Bracken memorandum, 'The New Construction Programme, 1945', 29 June 1945, CAB 66/67/4.

91. D of P memorandum, 'State of Planning for the Post-War Fleet', 5 March 1945, ADM 205/53; memorandum by First Sea Lord's office, 'The Empire's Post-War Fleet', 4 May 1944, ADM 167/122; board minute 3954, 19 May 1944, ADM 167/120.

92. WSC to Alexander and Cunningham, 31 January 1944, PREM 3/322/5/6; Churchill, *SWW*, V:604.

93. WSC to Alexander and Cunningham, 17 July 1944, Churchill, *SWW*, VI:599.

94. Eric Grove, *Vanguard to Trident* (Annapolis, MD: Naval Institute Press, 1987), 20.

95. WSC to Alexander, 10 March 1945, ADM 1/19056; ADM 205/43; Simpson, *Cunningham Papers*, 384.

96. WSC to Anderson, 9 April 1945, PREM 3/322/7.

CHAPTER 11

1. See Jonathan Rosenberg, 'Before the Bomb and After: Winston Churchill and the Use of Force', *Cold War Statesmen Confront the Bomb: Nuclear Diplomacy since 1945*, ed. John Lewis Gaddis, Philip H. Gordon, Ernest R. May, and Jonathan Rosenberg (Oxford: Oxford University Press, 1999).

2. 'Shall We All Commit Suicide?', originally published September 1924 in *Nash's Pall Mall*, reprinted in *Thoughts and Adventures* (London: Thornton Butterworth, 1932).

3. 'Fifty Years Hence', published December 1931 in *The Strand*, reprinted in *Thoughts and Adventures*.

4. Speech of 16 August 1945, House of Commons, *Complete Speeches*, VII:7,211.

5. Speech of 25 March 1949, New York City, *Complete Speeches*, VII:7,799.

6. Speech of 14 December 1950, House of Commons, *Complete Speeches*, VIII:8,143.

7. Speech of 1 March 1955, House of Commons, *Complete Speeches*, VIII:8,629.

8. Speech of 8 March 1948, House of Commons, *Complete Speeches*, VII:7,603–4.

9. Speech of 31 March 1949, Massachusetts Institute of Technology, *Complete Speeches*, VII:7,805.

10. WSC to Cherwell, 15 November 1951, PREM 11/292.

11. Grove, *Vanguard to Trident*, 79–82.

12. PDP/P/51/1: WSC memorandum, 'Progress of Defence Programmes: Service Estimates', 17 December 1951, PREM 11/270.

13. D (52) 41: COS Report: 'The Defence Programme', 29 September 1952, CAB 131/12.

14. Richard Moore, *The Royal Navy and Nuclear Weapons* (London: Frank Cass, 2001), ch. 2.

15. WSC to Henry Tizard, 27 December 1951, PREM 11/609; WSC to COS, 28 November 1951, PREM 11/74A.

16. WSC to Harold Alexander, 13 May 1952, PREM 11/369; WSC to Tizard, 27 December 1951, PREM 11/609.

17. Sir Norman Brook minute, 7 November 1952, PREM 11/616; Grove, *Vanguard*, 88–90.

18. For an excellent account of these deliberations, see Tim Benbow, 'British Naval Aviation and the "Radical Review", 1953–55', in *British Naval Aviation*, 125–50; also Grove, *Vanguard*, 90–115.

19. DP(M) (53) 1st mtg, 18 June 1953, CAB 134/809.

20. Benbow, 'British Naval Aviation', 131–2.

21. Alexander to WSC, 'The problem of the Fleet Carrier', 12 October 1953; WSC to Alexander, 16 October 1953, PREM 11/614.

22. D (53) 13th mtg, 14 October 1953, CAB 131/13.

23. DP (M) (53) 13: Alexander memorandum: 'Naval Air', 16 November 1953, CAB 134/809.

24. Unsigned memorandum, 23 November 1953, PREM 11/614; Churchill presented these views to the Ministerial Committee the same day: DP (M) (53) 5th mtg, 23 November 1953, CAB 134/809.

25. DP (M) (53) 6th mtg, 27 November 1953, CAB 134/809.

26. Alexander memorandum of 26 January 1954, cited in Benbow, 'British Naval Aviation', 134.

27. Thomas to WSC, 22 February 1954, PREM 11/614.

28. DP (M) (54), 2nd mtg, 26 February 1954, CAB 134/809.

29. DP (54) 1st mtg, 4 May 1954, CAB 134/808.

30. DP (54) 6: COS memorandum, 'UK Defence Policy', 1 June 1954, CAB 134/808.

31. CC (54) 54th Conclusions, 27 July 1954, CAB/128/27; Benbow, 'British Naval Aviation', 138–9.

32. Brook to WSC, 26 July 1954, CAB 21/4440.

33. On the Swinton Committee and its deliberations see in particular Benbow, 'British Naval Aviation', 139–47.

34. Alexander to WSC, 25 August 1954, PREM 11/617.

35. Brook to WSC, 6 September 1954, PREM 11/617.

36. WSC 'Notes', 7 September 1954, PREM 11/617.

37. DR (54) 6th mtg, 8 September 1954, CAB 134/811.

38. Draft Report (Third Revise), CAB 134/811.

39. Brook to WSC, 'Defence Review', 20 September 1954, PREM 11/617.

40. DR (54) 8th mtg, 21 September 1954, CAB 134/811.

41. WSC to Brook, 26 and 27 September 1954, PREM 11/1501 and CAB 21/3507.

42. DR (54) 9th mtg, 28 September 1954, CAB 134/811.

43. C (54) 329: 'Defence Policy', 3 November 1954, CAB 129/71.
44. Minute by Philip Newell, head of the Admiralty's military branch, quoted in Grove, *Vanguard*, 113.
45. CC (54) 73, 5 November 1954, CAB 128/27.

EPILOGUE

1. Edward Spiers, 'Gallipoli', in *The First World War and British Military History*, ed. Brian Bond (Oxford: Oxford University Press, 1991), 165–88.
2. Glibert, *WSC*, VIII:1,074.
3. Cited in David Dutton, *Neville Chamberlain* (London: Arnold, 2001), 103.
4. This process is nicely outlined in Dutton, *Chamberlain*, ch. 4.
5. 'Cato' (Michael Foot, Peter Howard, and Frank Owen), *Guilty Men* (London: Gollancz, 1940).
6. Chatfield, *It Might Happen Again*, 10–11.
7. WM 118 (41), 24 November 1941, CAB 65/20. Chatfield did air some of his criticisms in the House of Lords in 1944: 'The ten-year rule . . . gave power to the Lords of the Treasury to refuse all demands by the Service Departments which might lead to an unpopular Budget. Samson had his locks cut off by Delilah, but Britannia cut off her own.' Speech of 28 March 1944, *Parliamentary Debates*, Lords, vol. 131, col. 276.
8. Churchill, *SWW*, vol. 1.
9. CHUR 4/76 A.
10. Churchill, *SWW*, I:40.
11. Reynolds, *In Command of History*, and Ramsden, *Man of the Century*.
12. *The Times*, 2 November 1948, 5.
13. Hankey to the editor, *The Times*, 31 October 1948, HNKY 24/4.
14. *The Times*, 5 November 1948, 5.
15. *The Times*, 9 November 1948, 5.
16. *The Times*, 11 November 1948, 5.
17. *The Times*, 15 November 1948, 5.
18. Hankey, unpublished letter to *The Times*, 20 November 1948, HNKY 24/4.
19. Hoare to Hankey, 1 and 14 August 1951; Hankey to Hoare, 17 August 1951, HNKY 24/4.
20. Viscount Templewood, *Nine Troubled Years* (London: Collins, 1954), 112–13.
21. CHUR 2/157.
22. Reynolds, *In Command of History*, 141–2.
23. Rhodes James, *Memoirs of a Conservative*, 209–10.
24. Robert Rhodes James, 'The Politician', *Churchill: Four Faces and the Man*, 91–2; idem., *Churchill*, 164; Middlemas and Barnes, *Baldwin*, 326.
25. Gretton, *Former Naval Person*, 244–5.
26. Ibid., 242; Basil Liddell Hart, 'The Military Strategist', *Churchill: Four Faces and the Man*; Roskill, *Churchill and the Admirals*, 77.

27. E.g. MacGregor, 'Former Naval Cheapskate', 319–33; John Charmley, *Churchill: The End of Glory* (London: Hodder and Stoughton, 1993), 207; Sumida, 'Churchill and British Sea Power', 5–21.

28. E.g. A. J. P. Taylor, 'The Statesman', *Churchill: Four Faces and the Man*, 22; B. J. C. McKercher, 'The Limitations of the Politician-Strategist: Winston Churchill and the German Threat, 1933–39', *Churchill and Strategic Dilemmas*, 94.

29. Barnett, *Collapse of British Power*, 277; idem., *Britain and her Army 1509–1970* (London: Allen Lane, 1970), 411, 415; MacGregor, 'Former Naval Cheapskate', 319–20; Rhodes James, *Churchill*, 124, 165.

30. Barnett, *Collapse*, 275–8; MacGregor, 'Former Naval Cheapskate'; Corrigan, *Blood, Sweat and Arrogance*, 86, 152.

31. Robert O'Neill, 'Churchill, Japan, and British Security in the Pacific 1904–1942', in Blake and Louis, *Churchill*, 288–9.

32. For background, see Barry Gough, *Historical Dreadnoughts*.

33. Roskill, *War at Sea*, I:202.

34. Churchill, *SWW*, I:470.

35. WSC to Allen, 11 August 1953, CAB 103/327.

36. WSC to Clementine Churchill, 25 May 1954, in Soames, *Speaking for Themselves*, 579.

37. Allen to WSC, 24 August 1953, and Brook to WSC, 2 September 1953, CAB 103/327.

38. Brook to Acheson, 28 June 1954, CAB 103/327.

39. Roskill, *War at Sea*, I:201.

40. ROSK 4/75; cf. Roskill, *Churchill and the Admirals*, 102.

41. Arthur J. Marder, *From the Dardanelles to Oran*.

42. Basil Liddell Hart, 'The Military Strategist', *Churchill: Four Faces and the Man*, 187.

43. Barnett, *Engage the Enemy*, 120–1; Levy, *Royal Navy's Home Fleet*, 63. Barnett's verdict is echoed by Levy, whose chapter on the Norway is subtitled 'A Man-Made Disaster'.

44. Macleod and Kelly, *Ironside Diaries*, 256–7.

45. WM (40) 91, CA, 13 April 1940, CAB 65/12/23; *CWP*, I:1,048; *SWW*, I:484, where the wording of the minutes is altered slightly and is wrongly described as coming from a meeting of the Military Co-ordination Committee.

46. MCC (40) 22, 13 April 1940, CAB 83/3; *CWP*, I:1,054–5.

47. Barnett, *Engage the Enemy*, 120.

48. Curiously, some historians *have* noted Churchill's consistent preference for Narvik, but still insist on depicting it as evidence of poor judgement. See Smart, *British Strategy and Politics*, 210–11; John D. Fair, 'The Norwegian Campaign and Winston Churchill's Rise to Power in 1940: A Study of Perception and Attribution', *International History Review*, IX, no. 3 (1987), 423.

49. Roskill to Butler, 31 July 1953, CAB 140/109.

50. CAB 103/327.

51. Minute by Allen to WSC, 24 August 1953, CAB 103/327.
52. Norman Brook to WSC, 2 September 1953, CAB 103/327; also see Brook to Acheson, 23 July 1953, CAB 103/326.
53. Roskill to Butler, 31 July 1953, CAB 140/109.
54. WSC to Commodore GRG Allen, 11 August 1953, CAB 103/327.
55. Butler, *Grand Strategy*, III/2:544.
56. Howard, *Grand Strategy*, IV:24–5.
57. Roskill, *War at Sea*, II:370–1.
58. Roskill to Butler, 20 January 1954, CAB 140/109.
59. 'Mr Churchill's views on Maritime Strategy and his Relations with Prominent Sea Officers in the War of 1939–45', draft of a proposed 'confidential appendix' to Roskill, *The War at Sea*, vol. I, CAB 140/109.
60. Roskill, *War at Sea*, II:89–90; Roskill's opinion is repeated in Butler, *Grand Strategy*, III/2:544.
61. Roskill to Admiral Sir William Davis, 12 November 1979, ROSK 5/10.
62. Roskill, *Churchill and the Admirals*, 229–30.
63. Ibid., 139.
64. Clay Blair is the only authority I have come across who expresses any scepticism about Churchill's claims concerning his anxiety about the Battle of the Atlantic. Blair, *Hitler's U-boat War*, I:319, 427.
65. David Lloyd George, *War Memoirs of David Lloyd George*, 6 vols (London: Ivor Nicholson & Watson, 1933–6), III:25–6.
66. Beatty to Hamilton, 17 February 1915, *Beatty Papers*, I:249.
67. Alex Danchev, 'Waltzing with Winston: Civil-Military Relations in Britain in the Second World War,' *War in History*, 2, no. 2 (1995), 229.

Select Bibliography

Unpublished Documents

The National Archives, Kew, London

ADM 1	Admiralty and Secretariat papers
ADM 116	Admiralty and Secretariat cases
ADM 137	Historical Section: Records used for Official History, First World War
ADM 167	Board of Admiralty minutes and memoranda
ADM 178	Admiralty: papers and cases, supplementary series
ADM 199	Admiralty: war history cases and papers, Second World War
ADM 205	First Sea Lord papers
CAB 1	Cabinet Office: Miscellaneous Records
CAB 2	Committee of Imperial Defence, minutes
CAB 4	Committee of Imperial Defence, imperial defence memoranda
CAB 5	Committee of Imperial Defence, colonial defence memoranda
CAB 16	Committee of Imperial Defence, ad hoc subcommittees
CAB 21	Cabinet Office, registered files
CAB 23	Cabinet minutes
CAB 24	Cabinet memoranda
CAB 27	Cabinet committees, general series
CAB 37	Cabinet Papers
CAB 41	Cabinet letters in the Royal Archives
CAB 53	Chiefs of Staff Committee
CAB 55	Joint Planning Committee
CAB 65	War Cabinet minutes
CAB 66	War Cabinet memoranda
CAB 69	Defence Committee
CAB 79	Chiefs of Staff Committee, minutes
CAB 80	Chiefs of Staff Committee, memoranda
CAB 81	Chiefs of Staff Committee, minutes and memoranda

CAB 83   Military Coordination Committee, minutes and memoranda
CAB 84   Joint Planning Committee
CAB 86   Battle of the Atlantic Committee and Anti-U-Boat Warfare Committee, minutes and memoranda
CAB 96   Far Eastern Committee
CAB 99   Supreme War Council, 1939–40
CAB 103   Official Histories
CAB 120   Minister of Defence Secretariat: Records
CAB 128   Cabinet minutes
CAB 129   Cabinet memoranda
CAB 131   Defence Committee, minutes and memoranda
CAB 134   Cabinet committees
DEFE 4   Chiefs of Staff Committee meetings
FO 371   Foreign Office, general correspondence, political
FO 954   Avon papers
PREM 1   Prime Minister's Office
PREM 3   Prime Minister's Office, confidential papers
PREM 4   Prime Minister's Office, operational papers
PREM 11   Prime Minister's Office
T 161   Supply files
T 172   Chancellor of the Exchequer's Office, miscellaneous papers

Personal Papers

Alexander, A.V. (1st Earl Alexander of Hillsborough). *Churchill College Archives Centre*
Battenberg, Admiral of the Fleet Prince Louis. *University of Southampton Library, Archives and Manuscripts*
Beatty, Admiral of the Fleet David (1st Earl Beatty). *National Maritime Museum*
Borden, Sir Robert. *Library and Archives Canada*
Butler, J. R. M. *Churchill College Archives Centre*
Chatfield, Admiral of the Fleet Ernle (1st Baron Chatfield). *National Maritime Museum*
Churchill, Sir Winston S. *Churchill College Archives Centre*
Cunningham, Admiral of the Fleet Andrew Brown (1st Viscount Cunningham of Hyndhope). *British Museum*
D'Eyncourt, Sir Eustace Tennyson. *National Maritime Museum*
Davis, Admiral Sir William. *Churchill College Archives Centre*
Drax, Admiral Sir Reginald Plunkett-Ernle-Erle Drax. *Churchill College Archives Centre*
Dreyer, Admiral Sir Frederic Charles. *Churchill College Archives Centre*
Edwards, Ralph. *Churchill College Archives Centre*
Fisher, Admiral of the Fleet John (1st Baron Fisher of Kilverstone). *Churchill College Archives Centre*

Hamilton, Admiral Sir Frederick Tower. *National Maritime Museum*
Hankey, Maurice (1st Baron Hankey). *Churchill College Archives Centre*
Ismay, Hastings (1st Baron Ismay). *Liddell Hart Centre for Military Archives*
Keyes, Admiral of the Fleet Roger (Lord Keyes of Zeebrugge). *British Museum*
King, Admiral Ernest J. King. *Naval Historical Collection, Naval War College*
Liddell Hart, Sir Basil. *Liddell Hart Centre for Military Archives*
Pound, Admiral of the Fleet Sir Alfred Dudley. *Churchill College Archives Centre*
Richmond, Admiral Sir Herbert. *National Maritime Museum*
Roskill, Captain Stephen S. *Churchill College Archives Centre*
Troubridge, Admiral Sir Ernest Charles Thomas. *National Maritime Museum*
Wemyss, Admiral of the Fleet Rosslyn Erskine (1st Baron Wester Wemyss of Wemyss).
     Churchill College Archives Centre

Published Primary Sources

Churchill's writings, speeches, and correspondence

Thoughts and Adventures. London: Thornton Butterworth, 1932.
Great Contemporaries. London: Odhams, 1948.
Step by Step, 1936–1939. London: Odhams, 1948.
The Second World War, 6 vols. Boston, MA: Houghton Mifflin, 1948–53.
Memoirs of the Second World War. Boston, MA: Houghton-Mifflin, 1959.
The World Crisis, 5 vols. New York: Scribners, 1963–4.
Mr. Brodrick's Army. Sacramento, CA: The Churchilliana Co., 1977.
Boyle, Peter G. (ed.). *The Churchill-Eisenhower Correspondence*. Chapel Hill, NC:
     University of North Carolina Press, 1990.
Gilbert, Martin (ed.). *The Churchill War Papers*, 3 vols. New York: Norton,
     1993–2001.
Kimball, Warren (ed.). *Churchill and Roosevelt: The Complete Correspondence*, 3 vols.
     Princeton, NJ: Princeton University Press, 1984.
Rhodes James, Robert (ed.). *Winston S. Churchill: His Complete Speeches*, 8 vols. New
     York: Chelsea House Publishers, 1974.
Sand, G. W. (ed.). *Defending the West: The Truman-Churchill Correspondence, 1945–1960*.
     Westport, CT: Praeger, 2004.
Soames, Mary (ed). *Speaking for Themselves*. Toronto: Stoddart, 1998.
Wolff, Michael (ed.). *Winston S. Churchill: The Collected Essays*, 4 vols. London:
     Library of Imperial History, 1976.

Other published primary sources

Brock, Michael and Eleanor (eds). *H. H. Asquith: Letters to Venetia Stanley*. Oxford:
     Oxford University Press, 1982.
Colville, John. *The Fringes of Power: 10 Downing Street Diaries 1939–55*. New York:
     W. W. Norton, 1985.
Danchev, Alex and Daniel Todman (eds). *War Diaries 1939–1945: Field Marshal Lord
     Alanbrooke*. London: Weidenfeld and Nicolson, 2001.

David, Edward (ed.). *Inside Asquith's Cabinet*. London: John Murray, 1977.

Dilks, David (ed.). *The Diaries of Sir Alexander Cadogan 1938–1945*. New York: G. P. Putnam's Sons, 1972.

Esher, Viscount (ed.). *Journals and Letters of Reginal Viscount Esher*, 4 vols. London: Ivor Nicholson and Watson, 1938.

Halpern, Paul G. (ed.). *The Keyes Papers*, 3 vols. London: Navy Records Society, 1979–81.

Hattendorf, John B et al. (eds). *British Naval Documents 1204–1960*. Aldershot: Ashgate for the Navy Records Society, 1993.

Lambert, Nicholas A. *The Submarine Service, 1900–1918*. Aldershot: Ashgate for the Navy Records Society, 2001.

Lumby, E. W. R. (ed.). *Policy and Operations in the Mediterranean, 1912–14*. London: Navy Records Society, 1970.

Macleod, Roderick and Dennis Kelly (eds). *The Ironside Diaries, 1937–40*. London: Constable, 1962.

Marder, Arthur J. (ed.). *Portrait of an Admiral*. Cambridge, MA: Harvard University Press, 1952.

——(ed.). *Fear God and Dread Nought*, 3 vols. London: Jonathan Cape, 1952–9.

Middlemass, Keith (ed.). *Whitehall Diary*. Oxford: Oxford University Press, 1969.

Neale, R. G. et al. (eds). *Documents on Australian Foreign Policy 1937–49*, vols II–V. Canberra: Australian Government Publishing Service, 1976–82.

Patterson, A. Temple (ed.). *The Jellicoe Papers*, 2 vols. London: Navy Records Society, 1966–8.

Ranft, B. McL. (ed.). *The Beatty Papers*, 2 vols. Aldershot: Ashgate for the Navy Records Society, 1989–93.

Simpson, Michael (ed.). *Anglo-American Naval Relations 1917–1919*. Aldershot: Ashgate for the Navy Records Society, 1991.

——(ed.). *The Somerville Papers*. Aldershot: Scolar Press for the Navy Records Society, 1995.

——(ed.). *The Cunningham Papers*, 2 vols. Aldershot: Ashgate for the Navy Records Society, 1999 and 2006.

——(ed.). *Anglo-American Naval Relations, 1919–1939*. Aldershot: Ashgate for the Navy Records Society, 2010.

Strategic Planning in the U.S. Navy: Its Evolution and Execution 1891–1945. Wilmington, DE: Scholarly Resources, n.d., roll 5.

Tracy, Nicholas (ed.). *The Collective Naval Defence of the Empire, 1900–1940*. Aldershot: Ashgate for the Navy Records Society, 1997.

Williamson, Philip (ed.). *The Modernisation of Conservative Politics: The Diaries and Letters of William Bridgeman, 1904–1935*. London: Historian's Press, 1988.

Wilson, Keith (ed.). *The Cabinet Diary of J. A. Pease, 24 July–5 August 1914*. Leeds: Leeds Philosophical and Literary Society, 1983.

Woodward, E. L. et al. *Documents on British Foreign Policy 1919–1939*. 4 Series, London: HMSO, 1946–77.

Memoirs

Bayly, Lewis. *Pull Together: The Memoirs of Admiral Sir Lewis Bayly*. London: Harrap, 1939.

Chatfield, Lord. *The Navy and Defence*. London: William Heinemann Ltd., 1942.

—— *It Might Happen Again*. London: William Heinemann Ltd., 1947.

Cunningham of Hyndhope, *A Sailor's Odyssey*. London: Hutchinson, 1951.

Dewar, Kenneth. *The Navy From Within*. London: Gollancz, 1939.

Fisher, Lord. *Memories* and *Records*. London: Hodder and Stoughton, 1919.

Grey, Viscount. *Twenty-Five Years: 1892–1916*. Toronto: Ryerson Press, 1925.

Grigg, P. J. *Prejudice and Judgement*. London: Jonathan Cape, 1948.

Hankey, Lord. *The Supreme Command*. London: George Allen and Unwin, 1961.

Ismay, Lord. *The Memoirs of Lord Ismay*. London: Heinemann, 1960.

Jellicoe, Admiral Viscount. *The Grand Fleet*. New York: George H. Doran Co., 1919.

Joubert de la Ferté, P. B. *Birds and Fishes*. London: Huchinson, 1960.

Kennedy, John. *The Business of War*. London: Hutchinson, 1957.

Keyes, Roger. *The Naval Memoirs of Admiral of the Fleet Sir Roger Keyes*. London: Thornton Butterworth, 1934.

Macmillan, Harold. *Tides of Fortune: 1945–1955*. New York: Harper and Row, 1969.

Maund, L. E. H. *Assault from the Sea*. London: Methuen and Co., 1949.

Oxford and Asquith, Earl of. *Memories and Reflections 1852–1927*. Toronto: McClelland and Stewart, 1928.

Rhodes James, Robert (ed.). *Memoirs of a Conservative: J. C. C. Davidson's Memoirs and Papers, 1910–37*. London: Macmillan, 1969.

Shakespeare, Geoffrey. *Let Candles Be Brought In*. London: MacDonald, 1949.

Slessor, John. *The Central Blue*. London: Cassell, 1956.

Templewood, Viscount. *Nine Troubled Years*. London: Collins, 1954.

Books

Allen, Louis. *Singapore 1941–1942*. London: Davis-Poynter, 1977.

Ash, Bernard. *Someone Had Blundered: The Story of the Repulse and the Prince of Wales*. New York: Doubleday, 1960.

Austin, Douglas. *Churchill and Malta*. Stroud: Spellmount, 2006.

Bacon, Admiral Sir R. H. *The Life of Lord Fisher of Kilverstone*, 2 vols. Garden City, NY: Doubleday, Doran and Co., 1929.

Baer, George W. *One Hundred Years of Sea Power: The U.S. Navy 1890–1990*. Stanford, CA: Stanford University Press, 1993.

Barley, Frederick and David Waters. *The Defeat of the Enemy Attack on Shipping, 1939–1945*, ed. Eric Grove. Aldershot: Ashgate, 1997.

Barnett, Correlli. *The Collapse of British Power*. London: Eyre Methuen, 1972.

—— *Engage the Enemy More Closely*. New York: Norton, 1991.

Bath, Alan Harris. *Tracking the Axis Enemy*. Lawrence, KS: University Press of Kansas, 1998.

Beaumont, Joan. *Comrades in Arms: British Aid to Russia 1941–1945*. London: Davis-Poynter, 1980.

Beesly, Patrick. *Very Special Intelligence*. London: Hamish Hamilton, 1977.

—— *Very Special Admiral*. London: Hamish Hamilton, 1980.

—— *Room 40*. London: Hamish Hamilton, 1982.

Behrens, C. B. A. *Merchant Shipping and the Demands of War*. London: HMSO and Longmans, Green and Co., 1955.

Beireger, Eugene Edward. *Churchill, Munitions and Mechanical Warfare: The Politics of Supply and Strategy*. New York: Peter Lang, 1997.

Bell, A. C. *A History of the Blockade of Germany and the Countries Associated with her in the Great War, Austria-Hungary, Bulgaria and Turkey*. London: Historical Section, Committee of Imperial Defence, 1937.

Bell, Christopher M. *The Royal Navy, Seapower and Strategy Between the Wars*. Stanford, CA: Stanford University Press, 2000.

Bell, Peter. *Chamberlain, Germany and Japan, 1933–4*. London: Macmillan, 1996.

Ben-Moshe, Tuvia. *Churchill: Strategy and History*. Boulder, CO: Lynne Rienner Publishers, 1991.

Benbow, Tim (ed.). *British Naval Aviation: The First 100 Years*. Aldershot: Ashgate, 2011.

Best, Antony. *Britain, Japan and Pearl Harbor: Avoiding War in East Asia, 1936–41*. London: Routledge, 1995.

—— *British Intelligence and the Japanese Challenge in Asia, 1914–41*. London: Palgrave, 2003.

Best, Geoffrey. *Churchill: A Study in Greatness*. London: Hambledon and London, 2001.

—— *Churchill and War*. London: Hambledon and London, 2005.

Black, Nicholas. *The British Naval Staff in the First World War*. Woodbridge: Boydell Press, 2009.

Blair, Clay. *Hitler's U-boat War*, 2 vols. New York: Random House, 1996 and 1998.

Blake, Robert and William Roger Louis (eds). *Churchill*. New York: Norton, 1993.

Brodhurst, Robin. *Churchill's Anchor*. Barnsley: Leo Cooper, 2000.

Brown, David (ed.). *The Royal Navy and the Mediterranean*, vol. II. London: Frank Cass, 2002.

—— *The Road to Oran: Anglo-French Naval Relations, September 1939–July 1940*. London: Frank Cass, 2004.

Buckley, John. *The RAF and Trade Defence, 1919–1945: Constant Endeavour*. Keele: Ryburn Publishing, 1995.

Butler, J. R. M. *Grand Strategy*, vol. II. London: HMSO, 1957.

Callahan, Raymond. *The Worst Disaster: The Fall of Singapore*. Newark, DE: University of Delaware Press, 1977.

Carlton, David. *MacDonald versus Henderson*. London: Macmillan, 1970.

Cassar, George H. *The French and the Dardanelles*. London: Allen and Unwin, 1971.

'Cato' (Michael Foot, Peter Howard, and Frank Owen). *Guilty Men*. London: Gollancz, 1940.

Chalmers, W. S. *The Life and Letters of David, Earl Beatty*. London: Hodder and Stoughton, 1951.

Charmley, John. *Churchill: The End of Glory*. London: Hodder and Stoughton, 1993.

Chung, Ong Chit. *Operation Matador: Britain's War Plans Against the Japanese 1918–1941*. Singapore: Times Academic Press, 1997.

Churchill, Randolph S. and Martin Gilbert. *Winston S. Churchill*, 8 vols and 13 companion books. London: Heinemann, 1966–88.

Clews, Graham. *Churchill's Dilemma: The Real Story Behind the Origins of the 1915 Dardanelles Campaign*. Santa Barbara, CA: Praeger, 2010.

Coates, Tim (ed.). *Lord Kitchener and Winston Churchill: The Dardanelles Commission Part I, 1914–15*. London: The Stationery Office, 2000.

Corbett, Julian S. *Naval Operations*. London: Longmans, 1920.

Corrigan, Gordon. *Blood, Sweat and Arrogance and the Myth of Churchill's War*. London: Orion Publishing Co., 2006.

Cosgrave, Patrick. *Churchill at War: Alone 1939–40*. London: Collins, 1974.

Cowman, Ian. *Dominion or Decline*. Oxford: Berg, 1996.

Cumpston, I. M. *Lord Bruce of Melbourne*. Melbourne: Longman Cheshire, 1989.

D'Este, Carlo. *Decision in Normandy*. New York: Harper Perennial, 1994.

—— *Warlord: A Life of Winston Churchill at War, 1874–1945*. New York: Harper, 2008.

Day, David. *The Great Betrayal*. New York: Norton, 1989.

Derry, T. K. *The Campaign in Norway*. London: HMSO, 1952.

Dutton, David. *Neville Chamberlain*. London: Arnold, 2001.

Eade, Charles (ed.). *Churchill by his Contemporaries*. London: Hutchinson, 1953.

Ferguson, Bernard. *The Watery Maze*. London: Collins, 1961.

Ferris, John. *Men, Money, and Diplomacy*. Ithaca, NY: Cornell University Press, 1989.

Freedman, Lawrence, Paul Hayes, and Robert O'Neill. *War, Strategy and International Politics*. Oxford: Oxford University Press, 1992.

French, David. *British Economic and Strategic Planning 1905–1915*. London: Allen and Unwin, 1982.

—— *British Strategy and War Aims 1914–1916*. London: Allen and Unwin, 1984.

—— *The Strategy of the Lloyd George Coalition*. Oxford: Clarendon Press, 1995.

Gardner, W. J. R. *Decoding History: The Battle of the Atlantic and Ultra*. Annapolis, MD: Naval Institute Press, 1999.

Gibbs, N. H. *Grand Strategy*, vol. I. London: HMSO, 1976.

Goldrick, James. *The King's Ships Were at Sea*. Annapolis, MD: Naval Institute Press, 1984.

Goldstein, Erik and John Maurer. *The Washington Conference, 1921–22*. London: Frank Cass, 1994.

Gollin, Alfred. *The Impact of Air Power on the British People and their Government, 1909–14*. Stanford, CA: Stanford University Press, 1989.

Goodhart, Philip. *Fifty Ships that Saved the World*. London: Heinemann, 1965.

Gordon, G. A. H. *British Seapower and Procurement Between The Wars*. Annapolis, MD: Naval Institute Press, 1988.

Gough, Barry. *Historical Dreadnoughts*. Barnsley: Seaforth Publishing, 2010.

Gow, Ian and Yoichi Hirama. *The History of Anglo-Japanese Relations, 1600–2001*, vol. III: *The Military Dimension*. London: Palgrave, 2002.

Grenfell, Russell. *Main Fleet to Singapore*. London: Faber, 1951.

Gretton, Vice Admiral Sir Peter. *Former Naval Person*. London: Cassell, 1968.

Grimes, Shawn T. *Strategy and War Planning in the British Navy, 1887–1918*. Woodbridge, Suffolk: Boydell Press, 2012.

Grove, Eric. *Vanguard to Trident*. Annapolis, MD: Naval Institute Press, 1987.

—— *The Royal Navy*. New York: Palgrave Macmillan, 2005.

Gwyer, J. M. A. and J. R. M. Butler. *Grand Strategy*, vol. III. London: HMSO, 1964.

Haggie, Paul. *Britannia At Bay*. Oxford: Clarendon Press, 1981.

Hall, Christopher. *Britain, America and Arms Control, 1921–37*. New York: St. Martin's Press, 1987.

Halpern, Paul G. *The Mediterranean Naval Situation 1908–1914*. Cambridge, MA: Harvard University Press, 1971.

—— *A Naval History of World War I*. Annapolis, MD: Naval Institute Press, 1995.

Hamill, Ian. *The Strategic Illusion*. Singapore: Singapore University Press, 1981.

Hamilton, Keith A. and Edward Johnson (eds). *Arms and Disarmament in Diplomacy*. London: Vallentine Mitchell, 2008.

Hancock, W. K. and M. M. Gowing. *The British War Economy*. London: HMSO, 1949.

Harding, Richard. *The Royal Navy 1930–2000: Innovation and Defence*. London: Routledge, 2004.

Harvey, Maurice. *Scandinavian Misadventure*. Tunbridge Wells: Spellmount, 1990.

Hastings, Max. *Finest Years: Churchill as Warlord 1940–45*. New York: HarperPress, 2009.

Hattendorf, John and Robert Jordan (eds). *Maritime Strategy and the Balance of Power*. London: Macmillan, 1989.

Higgins, Trumbull. *Winston Churchill and the Second Front*. New York: Oxford University Press, 1957.

—— *Churchill and the Dardanelles*. London: Heinemann, 1963.

Hill, J. R. *The Oxford Illustrated History of the Royal Navy*. Oxford: Oxford University Press, 1995.

Hinsley, F. H. et al. *British Intelligence in the Second World War*, vols 1–3. London: HMSO, 1979–88.

Hough, Richard. *Former Naval Person*. London: Weidenfeld and Nicolson, 1985.

Howard, Michael. *Grand Strategy*, vol. IV. London: HMSO, 1972.

—— *The Continental Commitment*. Harmondsworth: Penguin, 1974.

Howarth, Stephen and Derek Law (eds). *The Battle of the Atlantic 1939–1945*. London: Greenhill, 1994.

Hughes, Terry and John Costello. *The Battle of the Atlantic*. New York: The Dial Press, 1977.

Hunt, Barry. *Sailor–Scholar: Admiral Sir Herbert Richmond, 1871–1946*. Waterloo: Wilfrid Laurier University Press, 1982.

Imlay, Talbot. *Facing the Second World War*. Oxford: Oxford University Press, 2003.

Jablonsky, David. *Churchill, The Great Game and Total War*. London: Frank Cass, 1991.

Jordan, Gerald. *Naval Warfare in the Twentieth Century*. London: Croom Helm, 1977.

Kennedy, Greg (ed). *British Naval Strategy East of Suez 1900–2000: Influences and Actions*. London: Frank Cass, 2004.

Kennedy, Paul. *The Rise and Fall of British Naval Mastery*. London: Fontana, 1983.

—— *The Realities Behind Diplomacy*. London: Fontana, 1989.

Kersaudy, François. *Norway 1940*. Lincoln, NB: University of Nebraska Press, 1998.

Kirby, S. Woodburn. *Singapore: Chain of Disaster*. New York: Macmillan, 1971.

Lamb, Richard. *Churchill as War Leader: Right or Wrong?* London: Bloomsbury, 1991.

Lambert, Nicholas. *Sir John Fisher's Naval Revolution*. Columbia, SC: University of South Carolina Press, 1999.

—— *Planning Armageddon: British Economic Warfare and the First World War*. Cambridge, MA: Harvard University Press, 2012.

Larres, Klaus. *Churchill's Cold War*. New Haven, CT: Yale University Press, 2002.

Leutze, James. *Bargaining for Supremacy: Anglo-American Naval Collaboration, 1937–1941*. Chapel Hill, NC: University of North Carolina Press, 1977.

Levy, James. *The Royal Navy's Home Fleet in World War II*. Basingstoke: Palgrave, 2003.

Lukacs, John. *Five Days in London, May 1940*. New Haven, CT: Yale University Press, 1999.

—— *Blood, Toil, Tears and Sweat*. New York: Basic Books, 2008.

Mackay, Ruddock F. *Fisher of Kilverstone*. Oxford: Clarendon Press, 1973.

Maiolo, Joseph. *The Royal Navy and Nazi Germany, 1933–39*. Basingstoke: Macmillan, 1998.

Marder, Arthur J. *From the Dreadnought to Scapa Flow*, 5 vols. Oxford: Oxford University Press, 1961–1971.

—— *From the Dardanelles to Oran*. London: Clarendon Press, 1974.

—— *Operation Menace*. London: Oxford University Press, 1976.

—— et al. *Old Friends, New Enemies*, 2 vols. Oxford: Oxford University Press, 1981–90.

Marquand, David. *Ramsay MacDonald*. London: Jonathan Cape, 1977.

Maurer, John H. (ed.). *Churchill and Strategic Dilemmas before the World Wars*. London: Frank Cass, 2003.

May, Ernest (ed.). *Knowing One's Enemies*. Princeton, NJ: Princeton University Press, 1986.

McIntyre, W. David. *The Rise and Fall of the Singapore Naval Base, 1919–1942*. London: Macmillan, 1979.

McKercher, B. J. C. *The Second Baldwin Government and the United States, 1924–1929*. Cambridge: Cambridge University Press, 1984.

—— *Transition of Power: Britain's Loss of Global Pre-eminence to the United States 1930–1945.* Cambridge: Cambridge University Press, 1999.

Medlicott, W. N. *The Economic Blockade*, 2 vols. London: HMSO, 1952–9.

Middlebrook, Martin and Patrick Mahoney. *Battleship*. Harmondsworth: Penguin Books, 1977.

Middlemas, Keith and John Barnes. *Baldwin: A Biography*. London: Weidenfeld and Nicolson, 1969.

Miller, Geoffrey. *The Millstone*. Hull: University of Hull Press, 1999.

Milner, Marc. *Battle of the Atlantic*. St Catherines, ON: Vanwell, 2003.

Moore, George. *Building for Victory: The Warship Building Programmes of the Royal Navy 1939–1945.* Gravesend, Kent: World Ship Society, 2003.

Moore, Richard. *The Royal Navy and Nuclear Weapons*. London: Frank Cass, 2001.

Moorehead, Alan. *Gallipoli*. London: Hamish Hamilton, 1958.

Moretz, Joseph. *The Royal Navy and the Capital Ship in the Interwar Period: An Operational Perspective*. London: Frank Cass, 2002.

Moulton, J. L. *The Norwegian Campaign of 1940*. London: Eyre and Spottiswoode, 1966.

Mukerjee, Madhusree. *Churchill's Secret War*. New York: Basic Books, 2010.

Murfett, Malcolm H. (ed.). *The First Sea Lords: From Fisher to Mountbatten*. Westport, CT: Praeger, 1995.

—— *Naval Warfare 1919–1945*. London: Routledge, 2009.

Murray, Williamson and Alan Millett (eds). *Military Innovation in the Interwar Period*. Cambridge: Cambridge University Press, 1996.

Neidpath, James. *The Singapore Naval Base and the Defence of Britain's Eastern Empire, 1919–1941.* Oxford: Oxford University Press, 1981.

Neilson, Keith. *Britain, Soviet Russia and the Collapse of the Versailles Order, 1919–1939.* Cambridge: Cambridge University Press, 2006.

Neilson, Keith and Elizabeth Jane Errington (eds). *Navies and Global Defense*. Westport, CT: Praeger, 1995.

Neilson, Keith and Greg Kennedy (eds). *Far-Flung Lines*. London: Frank Cass, 1996.

O'Brien, Phillips Payson (ed.). *Technology and Naval Combat in the Twentieth Century and Beyond*. London: Frank Cass, 2001.

Offer, Avner. *The First World War: An Agrarian Interpretation*. Oxford: Clarendon Press, 1991.

Orde, Anne. *The Eclipse of Great Britain: The United States and British Imperial Decline, 1895–1956.* London: Macmillan, 1996.

Osborne, Eric W. *Britain's Economic Blockade of Germany 1914–1919*. London: Frank Cass, 2004.

Parker, R. A. C. *Chamberlain and Appeasement*. London: Macmillan, 1993.

—— (ed.). *Winston Churchill: Studies in Statesmanship*. London: Brassey's, 1995.

—— *Churchill and Appeasement*. London: Macmillan, 2000.

Patterson, A. Temple. *Jellicoe*. London: Macmillan, 1969.

Peden, G. C. *British Rearmament and the Treasury: 1932–1939.* Edinburgh: Scottish Academic Press, 1979.

—— *Arms, Economics and British Strategy: From Dreadnoughts to Hydrogen Bombs.* Cambridge: Cambridge University Press, 2007.

Postan, M. M. *British War Production.* London: HMSO, 1952.

Pratt, Lawrence R. *East of Malta, West of Suez: Britain's Mediterranean Crisis, 1936–1939.* Cambridge: Cambridge University Press, 1975.

Prior, Robin. *Churchill's 'World Crisis' as History.* London: Croom Helm, 1983.

—— *Gallipoli.* New Haven, CT, and London: Yale University Press, 2009.

Ramsden, John. *Man of the Century: Winston Churchill and his Legend since 1945.* New York: Columbia University Press, 2003.

Ranft, Bryan (ed.). *Technical Change and British Naval Policy, 1860–1939.* London: Hodder and Stoughton, 1977.

Reynolds, David. *The Creation of the Anglo-American Alliance 1937–41.* London: Europa Publications Ltd., 1981.

—— *In Command of History.* London: Allen Lane, 2004.

—— *From World War to Cold War: Churchill, Roosevelt, and the International History of the 1940s.* Oxford: Oxford University Press, 2006.

Rhodes James, Robert. *Gallipoli.* New York: Batsford, 1965.

—— *Churchill: A Study in Failure.* London: Weidenfeld and Nicolson, 1970.

Rhys-Jones, Graham. *Churchill and the Norway Campaign 1940.* London: Pen and Sword, 2008.

Richardson, Dick. *The Evolution of British Disarmament Policy in the 1920s.* New York: St. Martin's Press, 1989.

Richmond, Admiral Sir Herbert. *Statesmen and Sea Power.* Oxford: Oxford University Press, 1947.

—— *National Policy and Naval Strength.* Aldershot: Gregg, 1993.

Rodger, N. A. M. *Naval Power in the Twentieth Century.* London: Macmillan, 1996.

Roskill, Stephen. *The War at Sea,* 3 vols. London: HMSO, 1954–61.

—— *The Navy at War 1939–1945.* London: Collins, 1960.

—— *Naval Policy Between the Wars,* 2 vols. London: Collins, 1968–76.

—— *Hankey: Man of Secrets,* 3 vols. London: Collins, 1970–4.

—— *Churchill and the Admirals.* London: Collins, 1977.

—— *Admiral of the Fleet Earl Beatty.* London: Collins, 1980.

Runyan, Timothy and Jan Copes (eds). *To Die Gallantly: The Battle of the Atlantic.* Boulder, CO: Westview Press, 1994.

Salmon, Patrick (ed.). *Britain and Norway in the Second World War.* London: HMSO, 1995.

—— *Scandinavia and the Great Powers.* Cambridge: Cambridge University Press, 1997.

Sarantakes, Nicholas Evan. *Allies against the Rising Sun.* Lawrence, KS: University Press of Kansas, 2009.

Schurman, Donald M. *Julian S. Corbett, 1854–1922*. London: Royal Historical Society, 1981.

Seldon, Anthony. *Churchill's Indian Summer*. London: Hodder and Stoughton, 1981.

Seligmann, Matthew. *The Royal Navy and the German Threat 1901–1914*. Oxford: Oxford University Press, 2012.

Simpson, Michael, *A Life of Admiral of the Fleet Viscount Cunningham of Hyndhope*. London: Routledge, 2004.

Siney, Marion C. *The Allied Blockade of Germany 1914–1916*. Ann Arbor, MI: University of Michigan Press, 1957.

Smart, Nick. *British Strategy and Politics During the Phony War*. Westport, CT: Praeger, 2003.

Smith, Kevin. *Conflict Over Convoys: Anglo-American Logistics Diplomacy in the Second World War*. Cambridge: Cambridge University Press, 1996.

Smith, Malcolm. *British Air Strategy between the Wars*. Oxford: Clarendon Press, 1984.

Steiner, Zara and Keith Nielson. *Britain and the Origins of the First World War*, 2nd edn. Basingstoke: Palgrave, 2003.

Sumida, Jon. *In Defence of Naval Supremacy*. Boston, MA: Unwin Hyman, 1989.

Taylor, A. J. P. et al. *Churchill: Four Faces and the Man*. London: Book Club Associates, 1969.

Thompson, Neville. *The Anti-Appeasers: Conservative Opposition to Appeasement in the 1930s*. Oxford: Clarendon Press, 1971.

Thorne, Christopher. *Allies of a Kind*. London: Hamish Hamilton, 1978.

Till, Geoffrey. *Air Power and the Royal Navy*. London: Jane's, 1979.

——— (ed.). *The Development of British Naval Thinking*. London: Routledge, 2006.

Tucker, Gilbert Norman. *The Naval Service of Canada*, 2 vols. Ottawa: King's Printer, 1952.

Van der Vat, Dan. *The Atlantic Campaign*. Edinburgh: Birlinn, 2001.

——— *The Dardanelles Disaster*. London: Duckworth Overlook, 2009.

Wallin, Jeffrey D. *By Ships Alone: Churchill and the Dardanelles*. Durham, NC: Carolina Academic Press, 1981.

Watt, D. C. *Personalities and Policies*. Notre Dame, IL: University of Notre Dame Press, 1965.

——— *Too Serious A Business*. London: Temple Smith, 1975.

Webster, Charles and Noble Frankland. *The Strategic Air Offensive Against Germany 1939–1945*, 4 vols. London: HMSO, 1961.

Willmott, H. P. *Grave of a Dozen Schemes*. Annapolis, MD: Naval Institute Press, 1996.

Wilson, Thomas. *Churchill and the Prof*. London: Cassell, 1995.

Winton, John. *Cunningham*. London: John Murray, 1998.

Wood, Derek (ed.). *Seek and Sink: A Symposium on the Battle of the Atlantic*. London: Royal Air Force Historical Society, 1992.

Young, Kenneth. *Churchill and Beaverbrook*. London: Eyre and Spottiswoode, 1966.

Ziegler, Philip. *Mountbatten*. New York: Knopf, 1985.

Articles

Andrew, Christopher. 'Churchill and Intelligence', *Intelligence and National Security*, 3, no. 3 (July 1988), 181–93.

Babij, Orest. 'The Second Labour Government and British Maritime Security, 1929–1931', *Diplomacy and Statecraft*, 6, no. 4 (November 1995), 645–71.

—— 'The Royal Navy and Inter-war Plans for War against Japan: The Problem of Oil Supply', *The Merchant Marine in International Affairs, 1850–1950*, ed. Greg Kennedy. London: Frank Cass, 2000, 84–106.

Barclay, Glen St. J. '"Butcher and Bolt": Admiral Roger Keyes and British Combined Operations, 1940–1941', *Naval War College Review*, 35, no. 1 (March 1982), 18–29.

Baxter, Colin F. 'Winston Churchill: Military Strategist', *Military Affairs*, 47, no. 1 (February 1983), 7–10.

Bell, Christopher M. '"Our Most Exposed Outpost": Hong Kong and British Far Eastern Strategy, 1921–1941', *Journal of Military History*, 60, no. 1 (January 1996), 61–88.

—— '"How are we going to make war?": Admiral Sir Herbert Richmond and British Far Eastern War Plans', *Journal of Strategic Studies*, 20, no. 3 (September 1997), 123–41.

—— 'Thinking the Unthinkable: American and British Naval Strategies for an Anglo-American War, 1918–31', *International History Review*, XIX, no. 4 (November 1997), 789–808.

—— 'The "Singapore Strategy" and the Deterrence of Japan: Churchill, the Admiralty and the Dispatch of Force Z', *English Historical Review*, CXVI, no. 467 (June 2001), 604–34.

—— 'The Royal Navy, War Planning and Intelligence Assessments of Japan between the Wars', *Intelligence and Statecraft: The Use and Limits of Intelligence in International Society*, ed. Peter Jackson and Jennifer Siegel. Westport, CT: Praeger, 2005.

—— 'Winston Churchill and the Ten-Year Rule', *Journal of Military History*, 74, no. 4 (October 2010), 523–56.

—— 'Sir John Fisher's Naval Revolution Reconsidered: Winston Churchill at the Admiralty, 1911–14', *War in History*, 18, no. 3 (July 2011), 333–56.

—— 'Britain and the London Naval Conference, 1930', *At the Crossroads between Peace and War: Naval Rivalries and Arms Control between the World War*, ed. John H. Maurer and Christopher M. Bell. Annapolis, MD: Naval Institute Press, 2013.

Benbow, Tim. '"Menace" to "Ironclad": The British Operations against Dakar (1940) and Madagascar (1942)', *Journal of Military History*, 75, no. 3 (July 2011), 769–809.

Best, Antony. 'Constructing an Image: British Intelligence and Whitehall's Perception of Japan, 1931–1939', *Intelligence and National Security*, 11, no. 3 (July 1996), 403–23.

—— '"This Probably Over-Valued Military Power": British Intelligence and Whitehall's Perception of Japan, 1939–41', *Intelligence and National Security*, 12, no. 3 (July 1997), 67–94.

Bond, Brian. 'British War Planning for Operations in the Baltic before the First and Second World Wars', *In Quest of Trade and Security: The Baltic in Power Politics,*

1500–1990, ed. Göran Rystad, Klaus-R. Böhme, and Wilhelm M. Carlgren. Lund, Sweden: Lund University Press, 1995, II, 107–35.

Booth, Ken. 'The Ten-Year Rule: An Unfinished Debate', *Journal of the Royal United Services Institute*, 116 (September 1971), 58–63.

Brooks, John. '*Dreadnought*: Blunder, or Stroke of Genius?', *War In History*, 14, no. 2 (April 2007), 157–78.

Brown, David. 'Norway 1940: The Balance of Interference', *Britain and Norway in the Second World War*, ed. Patrick Salmon. London: HMSO, 1995, 26–31.

Buckley, John. 'Air Power and the Battle of the Atlantic 1939–45', *Journal of Contemporary History*, 28 (1993), 143–61.

—— 'Contradictions in British Defence Policy 1937–1939: The RAF and the Defence of Trade', *Twentieth Century British History*, 5, no. 1 (1994), 100–13.

Carlton, David. 'Great Britain and the Coolidge Naval Disarmament Conference of 1927', *Political Science Quarterly*, 83, no. 4 (December 1968), 573–98.

—— 'The Anglo-French Compromise on Arms Limitation, 1928', *Journal of British Studies*, 8 (1969), 141–62.

Coles, Michael. 'Ernest King and the British Pacific Fleet: The Conference at Quebec, 1944 ("Octagon")', *Journal of Military History*, 65, no. 1 (January 2001), 105–30.

Cowman, Ian. 'An Admiralty "Myth": The Search for an Advanced Far Eastern Fleet Base before the Second World War', *Journal of Strategic Studies*, 8, no. 3 (September 1985), 317–26.

—— 'Main Fleet to Singapore? Churchill, the Admiralty, and Force Z', *Journal of Strategic Studies*, 18, no. 2 (March 1995), 79–93.

Curran, Tom. 'Who was Responsible for the Dardanelles Naval Fiasco?', *Australian Journal of Politics & History*, 57, no. 1 (March 2011), 17–33.

D'Ombrain, Nicholas J. 'Churchill at the Admiralty and the Committee of Imperial Defence, 1911–14', *Journal of the Royal United Services Institution*, 115, no. 657 (1970), 38–41.

Danchev, Alex. 'Waltzing with Winston: Civil-Military Relations in Britain in the Second World War', *War in History*, 2, no. 2 (1995), 202–30.

Dawson, R. MacGregor. 'The Cabinet Minister and Administration: Winston S. Churchill at the Admiralty, 1911–15', *Canadian Journal of Economics and Political Science*, 6, no. 3 (August 1940), 325–58.

Day, David. 'Churchill's Pacific Strategy', *Pacific and American Studies*, 8 (March 2008), 87–98.

Dilks, David. 'Great Britain and Scandinavia in the "Phony War"', *Scandinavian Journal of History*, 2, (1997), 29–51.

Douglas, W. A. B. and David Syrett, 'Die Wende in der Schlacht im Atlantik: Die Schliessung des "Gronland-Luftlochs" 1942–3', *Marine Rundschau*, 83, 1–3 (1986), 2–11, 70–3, 147–9.

Erickson, Edward J. 'One More Push; Forcing the Dardanelles in March 1915', *Journal of Strategic Studies*, 24, no. 3 (September 2001), 158–76.

Fair, John D. 'The Norwegian Campaign and Winston Churchill's Rise to Power in 1940: A Study of Perception and Attribution', *International History Review*, IX, no. 3 (1987), 410–37.

Fairbanks, Jr., Charles H. 'The Origins of the Dreadnought Revolution: A Historiographical Essay', *International History Review*, XIII, no. 2 (May 1991), 246–72.

Farrell, Brian. 'Yes, Prime Minister: Barbarossa, Whipcord and the Basis of British Grand Strategy, Autumn 1941', *Journal of Military History*, 57, no. 4 (October 1993), 599–625.

Ferris, John R. 'Treasury Control, the Ten-Year Rule and British Service Policies, 1919–1924', *Historical Journal*, 30, no. 4 (December 1987), 859–83.

—— 'The Symbol and Substance of Seapower: Britain, the United States and the One-Power Standard, 1919–1921', *Anglo-American Relations in the 1920s*, ed. B. J. C. McKercher. Edmonton: University of Alberta Press, 1990, 55–80.

—— '"The Greatest Power on Earth": Great Britain in the 1920s', *International History Review*, XIII, no. 4 (November 1991), 726–50.

—— '"Worthy of Some Better Enemy?": The British Estimate of the Imperial Japanese Army 1919–41, and the Fall of Singapore', *Canadian Journal of History*, XXVIII, no. 3 (August 1993), 223–56.

Ford, Douglas. 'Planning for an Unpredictable War: British Intelligence Assessments and the War Against Japan, 1937–45', *Journal of Strategic Studies*, 27, no. 1 (March 2004), 136–67.

French, David. 'The Origins of the Dardanelles Campaign Reconsidered', *History*, 68, no. 233 (June 1983), 210–24.

Gardner, Jock. 'The Battle of the Atlantic, 1941—the First Turning Point?', *Journal of Strategic Studies*, 17, no. 1 (March 1994), 109–23.

Gilbert, Martin. 'Churchill and Gallipoli', in *Gallipoli: Making History*, ed. Jenny Macleod. London: Frank Cass, 2004, 14–43.

Goette, Richard. 'Britain and the Delay in Closing the Mid-Atlantic "Air Gap" during the Battle of the Atlantic', *Northern Mariner*, 15, no. 4 (October 2005), 19–41.

Gordon, Andrew, 'The Admiralty and Imperial Overstretch, 1902–41', *Journal of Strategic Studies*, 17, no. 1 (March 1994), 63–85.

Grove, Philip. 'Vaagso and Lofoten Island (Operation Claymore, Gauntlet, Archery and Anklet, 1941)', in *Amphibious Assault: Manoeuvre from the Sea*, ed. T. Lovering. Portsmouth: Royal Navy, 2005, 95–106.

Haggie, Paul. 'The Royal Navy and War Planning in the Fisher Era', *The War Plans of the Great Powers 1880–1914*, ed. Paul Kennedy. Boston, MA: Allen and Unwin, 1979.

Hamill, Ian. 'Winston Churchill and the Singapore Naval Base, 1924–1929', *Journal of Southeast Asian Studies*, 11, no. 2 (September 1980), 277–86.

Hamilton, C. I. 'British Naval Policy, Policy-Makers and Financial Control, 1860–1945', *War in History*, 12, no. 4 (November 2005), 371–95.

Hill, Alexander A. 'British Lend-Lease Aid and the Soviet War Effort, June 1941–June 1942', *Journal of Military History*, 71, no. 3 (July 2007), 773–808.

Imlay, Talbot. 'Allied Economic Intelligence and Strategy during the "Phoney War"', *Intelligence and National Security*, 13, no. 4 (Winter 1998), 107–32.

——, 'A Reassessment of Anglo-French Strategy During the Phony War, 1939–1941', *English Historical Review*, CXIX, no. 481 (April 2004), 362–70.

Jacobsen, Mark. 'Winston Churchill and the Third Front', *Journal of Strategic Studies*, 14, no. 3 (September 1991), 337–62.

Kelly, Bernard. 'Drifting Towards War: The British Chiefs of Staff, the USSR and the Winter War, November 1939–March 1940', *Contemporary British History*, 23, no. 3 (September 2009), 267–91.

Kennedy, Paul. 'The Influence and Limitations of Sea Power', *International History Review*, X, no. 1 (February 1988), 2–17.

——, 'British "Net Assessment" and the Coming of the Second World War', *Calculations: Net Assessments and the Coming of World War II*, ed. A. R. Millett and W. Murray. New York: The Free Press, 1992.

Konvitz, Josef W. 'Bombs, Cities, and Submarines: Allied Bombing of the French Ports, 1942–1943', *International History Review*, XIV, no. 1 (February 1992), 23–44.

Kuramatsu, Tadashi. 'The Geneva Naval Conference of 1927: The British Preparation for the Conference, December 1926 to June 1927', *Journal of Strategic Studies*, 19, no. 1 (March 1996), 104–21.

—— 'Viscount Cecil, Winston Churchill and the Geneva Naval Conference of 1927: *si vis pacem para pacem* versus *si vis pacem para bellum*', in *Personalities, War and Diplomacy: Essays in International History*, ed. T. G. Otte and Constantine A. Pagedas. London: Frank Cass, 1997.

Lambert, Andrew. 'Seapower 1939–1940: Churchill and the Strategic Origins of the Battle of the Atlantic', *Journal of Strategic Studies*, 17, no. 1 (March 1994), 86–108.

—— '"This Is All We Want": Great Britain and the Baltic Approaches 1815–1914', in *Britain and Denmark: Political, Economic and Cultural Relations in the 19th and 20th Centuries*, ed. J. Sevaldsen. Copenhagen: Museum Tusculanum Press, 2003, 147–69.

—— '"The Possibility of Ultimate Action in the Baltic": Die Royal Navy im Krieg, 1914–1916', *Skagerrakschlacht: Vorgeschichte—Ereignis—Verarbeitung*, ed. Michael Epkenhans, J. Hillman, and F. Nägler. Munich: Oldenbourg, 2009.

—— 'The German North Sea Islands, the Kiel Canal and the Danish Narrows in Royal Navy Thinking and Planning, 1905–1918', *The Danish Straits and German Naval Power 1905–1918*, ed. Michael Epkenhans and Gerhard P. Gross. Potsdam: Militärgeschichtliches Forschungsamt, 2010, 35–62.

Lambert, Nicholas A. 'British Naval Policy, 1913–1914: Financial Limitation and Strategic Revolution', *Journal of Modern History*, 67, no. 3 (September 1995), 595–626.

—— 'Admiral Sir John Fisher and the Concept of Flotilla Defence, 1904–1909', *Journal of Military History*, 59, 4 (October 1995), 639–60.

Langdon, Jeremy. '"Too Old or Too Bold" The Removal of Sir Roger Keyes as Churchill's First Director of Combined Operations', *Imperial War Museum Review*, 8 (1993), 72–84.

Larew, Karl G. 'The Royal Navy in the Battle of Britain', *Historian*, 52, no. 2 (Winter 1992), 243–54.

Lautenschläger, Karl. 'Plan "Catherine": The British Baltic Operation, 1940', *Journal of Baltic Studies*, 5 (1974), 211–21.

Levy, James. 'Ready or Not? The Home Fleet at the Outset of World War II', *Naval War College Review*, vol. LII, no. 4 (Autumn 1999), 90–108.

—— 'Lost Leader: Admiral of the Fleet Sir Charles Forbes and the Second World War', *Mariner's Mirror*, 88, no. 2 (May 2002), 186–95.

—— 'The Needs of Political Policy versus the Reality of Military Operations: Royal Navy Opposition to the Arctic Convoys, 1942', *Journal of Strategic Studies*, 26, no. 1 (March 2003), 36–52.

MacGregor, David. 'The Use, Misuse, and Non-Use of History: The Royal Navy and the Operational Lessons of the First World War', *Journal of Military History*, 56, no. 4 (October 1992), 603–15.

—— 'Former Naval Cheapskate: Chancellor of the Exchequer Winston Churchill and the Royal Navy, 1924–29', *Armed Forces and Society*, vol. 19, no. 3 (Spring 1993), 319–33.

Mackesy, Piers. 'Churchill on Narvik', *RUSI Journal*, CXV, no. 670 (December 1970), 28–33.

—— 'Churchill as Chronicler: The Narvik Episode', *History Today*, 35 (March 1985), 14–20.

Maiolo, Joseph. 'Deception and Intelligence Failure: Anglo-German Preparations for U-boat Warfare in the 1930s', *Journal of Strategic Studies*, 22, no. 4 (December 1999), 55–76.

Mann, Christopher, 'Combined Operations, the Commandos, and Norway, 1941–1944', *Journal of Military History*, 73, no. 2 (April 2009), 471–95.

Martin, Christopher. 'The Complexity of Strategy: "Jackie" Fisher and the Trouble with Submarines', *Journal of Military History*, 75, no. 2 (April 2011), 441–70.

Maurer, John H. 'Churchill's Naval Holiday: Arms Control and the Anglo-German Naval Race, 1912–1914', *Journal of Strategic Studies*, 15, no. 1 (March 1992), 102–27.

—— 'The Anglo-German Naval Rivalry and Informal Arms Control, 1912–1914', *Journal of Conflict Resolution*, 36, no. 2 (June 1992), 284–308.

McDonald, J. Kenneth. 'Lloyd George and the Search for a Postwar Naval Policy, 1919', *Lloyd George: Twelve Essays*, ed. A. J. P. Taylor. New York: Atheneum, 1971, 191–222.

McKay, C. G. 'Iron Ore and Section D: The Oxelosund Operation', *Historical Journal*, 29, no. 4 (December 1986), 975–8.

McKercher, B. J. C. 'Belligerent Rights in 1927–1929: Foreign Policy *versus* Naval Policy in the Second Baldwin Government', *Historical Journal*, 29 (1986), 963–74.

—— 'A Sane and Sensible Diplomacy: Austen Chamberlain, Japan and the Naval Balance of Power in the Pacific Ocean, 1924–1929', *Canadian Journal of History*, XXI (1986), 187–213.

—— '"Our Most Dangerous Enemy": Great Britain Pre-Eminent in the 1930s', *International History Review*, XIII, no. 4 (November 1991), 751–83.

—— 'From Enmity to Cooperation: The Second Baldwin Government and the Improvement of Anglo-American Relations, November 1928–June 1929', *Albion*, 24, no. 1 (Spring 1992), 65–88.

—— 'No Eternal Friends or Enemies: British Defence Policy and the Problem of the United States, 1919–1939', *Canadian Journal of History*, 28, no. 2 (August 1993), 257–93.

—— 'From Disarmament to Rearmament: British Civil-Military Relations and Policy Making, 1933–1934', *Defence Studies*, I, no. 1 (Spring 2001), 21–48.

—— 'Deterrence and the European Balance of Power: The Field Force and British Grand Strategy, 1934–1938', *English Historical Review*, CXXIII, no. 500 (2008), 98–131.

Morewood, Steven. 'The Chiefs of Staff, the "Men on the Spot" and the Italo-Abyssinian Emergency, 1935–36', *Decisions and Diplomacy*, ed. Dick Richardson and Glyn Stone. London: Routledge, 1985.

—— 'Protecting the Jugular Vein of Empire: The Suez Canal and British Defence Strategy, 1919–1941', *War and Society*, 10, no 1 (May 1992), 81–107.

Mount, Ferdinand, 'Churchill Capsized: The Dardanelles Campaign was Fatally Misjudged', *The Spectator*, 264 (14 April 1990), 8–11.

Murfett, Malcolm H. '"Living in the Past": A Critical Re-examination of the Singapore Naval Strategy, 1918–1941', *War and Society*, XI, no. 1 (May 1993), 73–103.

Neilson, Keith. '"Greatly Exaggerated": The Myth of the Decline and Fall of Great Britain', *International History Review*, XIII, no. 4 (November 1991), 695–725.

—— 'The Defence Requirements Sub-Committee, British Strategic Foreign Policy, Neville Chamberlain and the Path to Appeasement', *English Historical Review*, CXVIII, no. 477 (June 2003), 651–84.

—— '"Unbroken Thread": Japan, Maritime Power and British Imperial Defence, 1920–32', *British Naval Strategy East of Suez 1900–2000*, ed. Greg Kennedy. London: Frank Cass, 2005.

Parker, R. A. C. 'Britain, France and Scandinavia', *History*, 61 (1976), 369–87.

Peden, George. 'Winston Churchill, Neville Chamberlain and the Defence of Empire', *The Limitations of Military Power*, ed. John B. Hattendorf and Malcom Murfett. London: Macmillan, 1990.

Pritchard, John. 'Winston Churchill, the Military, and Imperial Defence in East Asia', *From Pearl Harbor to Hiroshima*, ed. Saki Dockrill. New York: St Martin's Press, 1994.

Quinault, Roland. 'Churchill and Australia: The Military Relationship, 1899–1945', *War and Society*, 6, no. 1 (May 1988), 41–64.

—— 'Churchill and Russia', *War and Society*, 9, no. 1 (May 1991), 99–120.

Redford, Duncan. 'The March 1943 Crisis in the Battle of the Atlantic: Myth and Reality', *History*, 92, no. 305 (January 2007), 64–83.

—— 'Inter- and Intra-Service Rivalries in the Battle of the Atlantic', *Journal of Strategic Studies*, 32, no. 6 (December 2009), 899–928.

Reguer, Sara. 'Churchill's Role in the Dardanelles Campaign', *British Army Review*, no. 108 (December 1994), 70–80.

Reynolds, David. 'Churchill's Writing of History: Appeasement, Autobiography and *The Gathering Storm*', *Transactions of the Royal Historical Society*, sixth series, XI (2001), 221–47.

—— 'Churchill's Memoirs and Australia's War: Imperial Defence and "Inexcusable Betrayal"', *War & Society*, 24, no. 2 (2005), 35–52.

Richmond, Admiral Sir Herbert, 'Singapore', *Fortnightly Review*, vol. CXLXI (March 1942), 240–3.

Riste, Olav. 'Intelligence and the "Mindset": The German Invasion of Norway in 1940', *Intelligence and National Security*, 22, no. 4 (August 2007), 521–36.

Rosenberg, Jonathan. 'Before the Bomb and After: Winston Churchill and the Use of Force', *Cold War Statesmen Confront the Bomb: Nuclear Diplomacy since 1945*, ed. John Lewis Gaddis, Philip H. Gordon, Ernest R. May, and Jonathan Rosenberg. Oxford: Oxford University Press, 1999.

Roskill, Stephen W. 'The Ten-Year Rule: The Historical Facts', *Journal of the Royal United Services Institute*, 117 (March 1972), 69–71.

—— 'Marder, Churchill and the Admiralty, 1939–42', *Journal of the Royal United Services Institute*, 117 (January 1973), 49–53.

Salmon, Patrick. 'Churchill, the Admiralty and the Narvik Traffic, September–November 1939', *Scandinavian Journal of History*, 4 (1979), 305–26.

—— 'British Plans for Economic Warfare against Germany 1937–1939: The Problem of Swedish Iron Ore', *The Second World War: Essays in Military and Political History*, ed. Walter Laqueur. London: Sage, 1982.

—— 'Great Britain, the Soviet Union and Finland at the Beginning of the Second World War', *The Baltic and the Outbreak of the Second World War*, ed. John Hiden and Thomas Lane. Cambridge: Cambridge University Press, 1992.

Sarantakes, Nicholas Evan. 'One Last Crusade: The British Pacific Fleet and its Impact on the Anglo-American Alliance', *English Historical Review*, 121, no. 491 (April 2006), 429–66.

Scammell, Clare. 'The Royal Navy and the Strategic Origins of the Anglo-German Naval Agreement of 1935', *Journal of Strategic Studies*, 20, no. 2 (June 1997), 92–118.

Schoenfeld, Max. 'Winston Churchill as War Manager: The Battle of the Atlantic Committee, 1941', *Military Affairs*, 52 (1988), 122–7.

Seligmann, Matthew. 'New Weapons for New Targets: Sir John Fisher, the Threat from Germany, and the Building of H.M.S. *Dreadnought* and H.M.S. *Invincible*, 1902–1907', *International History Review*, XXX, no. 2 (June 2008), 303–31.

—— 'Switching Horses: The Admiralty's Recognition of the Threat from Germany, 1900–1905', International History Review, XXX, no. 2 (June 2008), 239–58.

Silverman, Peter G. 'The Ten-Year Rule', *Journal of the Royal United Services Institute*, 116 (March 1971), 42–5.

Simpson, Michael. 'Force H and British Strategy in the Western Mediterranean 1939–42', *Mariner's Mirror*, 83 (1997), 62–75.

Smith, Kevin. 'Maritime War: Combat, Management, and Memory', in *A Companion to the Second World War*, ed. Thomas Zeiler. Malden, MA: Wiley-Blackwell Publishing, 2012.

Spiers, Edward. 'Gallipoli', *The First World War and British Military History*, ed. Brian Bond. Oxford: Oxford University Press, 1991, 165–88.

Strachan, Hew. 'The British Army, its General Staff and the Continental Commitment, 1904–14', *The British General Staff*, ed. David French and Brian Holden Reid. London: Frank Cass, 2002, 75–94.

Sumida, Jon. '"The Best-Laid Plans": The Development of British Battle-Fleet Tactics, 1919–42', *International History Review*, XIV, no. 4 (November 1992), 681–700.

—— 'Churchill and British Sea Power, 1908–29', *Winston Churchill: Studies in Statesmanship*, ed. R. A. C. Parker. London: Brassey's, 1995.

—— 'Sir John Fisher and the *Dreadnought*: The Sources of Naval Mythology', *Journal of Military History*, 59, 4 (October 1995), 619–38.

—— 'Sir John Fisher's Naval Revolution', *Naval History*, 10, no. 4 (July/August 1996), 20–6.

—— 'Demythologizing the Fisher Era: the Role of Change in Historical Method', *Militärgeschichtliche Zeitschrift*, 59 (2000), 171–81.

—— 'British Preparations for Global Naval War, 1904–1914', *The Fog of Peace and War Planning: Military and Strategic Planning under Uncertainty*, ed. Monica Toft and Talbot Imlay. London: Routledge, 2006.

—— 'Geography, Technology, and British Naval Strategy in the Dreadnought Era', *Naval War College Review*, 59 (Summer 2006), 89–102.

Till, Geoffrey, 'Perceptions of Naval Power Between the Wars: The British Case', *Estimating Foreign Military Power*, ed. Peter Towle. London: Croom Helm, 1982.

Towle, Philip. 'Winston Churchill and British Disarmament Policy', *Journal of Strategic Studies*, 2, no. 3 (September 1979), 335–47.

Wallin, Jeffrey D. 'Politics and Strategy in the Dardanelles Operation', *Statesmanship*, ed. Harry V. Jaffa. Durham, NC: Carolina Academic Press, 1981, 131–55.

Wark, Wesley 'In Search of a Suitable Japan: British Naval Intelligence in the Pacific before the Second World War', *Intelligence and National Security*, vol. 1, no. 2 (May 1986), 189–211.

—— 'Beyond Intelligence: The Study of British Strategy and the Norway Campaign, 1940', *Power, Personalities and Policies: Essays in Honour of Donald Cameron Watt*, ed. Michael Graham Fry. London: Frank Cass, 1992.

Wilt, A. F. 'The Significance of the Casablanca Decisions, January 1943', *Journal of Military History*, 55, no. 1 (January 1991), 517–29.

Young, Robert J. 'Spokesmen for Economic Warfare: The Industrial Intelligence Centre in the 1930s', *European Studies Review*, 6 (1976), 473–87.

Dissertations

Babij, Orest. 'The Making of Imperial Defence Policy in Britain, 1926–1934', DPhil. thesis, Oxford University, 2003.

Steers, Howard J. 'Raiding the Continent: The Origins of British Special Service Forces', Master of Military Art and Science thesis, US Army Command and General Staff College, Fort Leavenworth, Kansas, 1980.

Photographic Acknowledgements

© Trinity Mirror/Mirrorpix/Alamy: **5, 15**; Australian War Memorial (P02018.055): **12**; Churchill Archives Centre, Other Deposited Collections Relating to Sir Winston Churchill (WCHL 4/36): **13**; © Corbis: **8**; © Hulton Archive/Corbis: **7**; Dept. of National Defence/Library and Archives Canada (PA-190794): **11**; Mary Evans Picture Library: **6**; © Fleet Air Arm Museum, Stephen Cribb Collection: **3**; © Hulton Archive/Getty Images: **9, 10**; © Time & Life Pictures/Getty Images: **19**; By permission of The Imperial War Museum: **16** (A 9423), **18** (H 10306); www.maritimequest.com: **14**; Library and Archives Canada (C-002082): **4**; © PA/PA Archive/Press Association Images: **1**; © TopFoto: **2**; U. S. National Archives and Records Administration: **17**

Index

Aandalesnes 189–91
Achilles, HMS 167
Admiralty, *see* Royal Navy
Adriatic Sea 26, 57
Agadir crisis 14
Ajax, HMS 167
Alamein, Battle of El 274, 287
Alexander, A.V. 199–201, 217, 221,
        227–9, 238, 243, 258, 262, 267,
        303, 306–7, 337
Alexander of Tunis, Viscount 314–20
Alexandretta 65
Alexandria 19, 197, 202
Allen, Commodore Gordon 330, 334
Altmark 180
Ameland 54
American-British-Canadian Staff
        Conference 237, 240
Amery, Leopold 128, 130
'Anakim' 287, 292
Andaman islands 293–4
Anglo-French compromise 128
Anglo-German Naval Agreement 144, 150
Anglo-Japanese Alliance 95, 97, 99, 129
Anson, HMS 302
Anti-U-Boat Warfare Committee 271–2,
        277–9, 282, 336; *see also* Battle of
        the Atlantic Committee
Antwerp 51, 54
Anzio 291, 294
Arcadia Conference 257, 265
Ark Royal, HMS 233
army 39, 63, 70, 89, 133–4, 143, 196, 261,
        266, 285, 294
        29th Division 67–8
        146th Territorial Brigade 189–90
        British Expeditionary Force 14–15,
        38–9, 50, 53, 71, 89, 161, 195,
        206, 322

Asquith, H. Henry 15, 23, 26, 29, 32, 34,
        37, 46, 49, 54, 56, 59, 71–2,
        75–6, 82
    and Dardanelles 66–7, 75
    and economic warfare 43, 51, 348 n. 117
    forms coalition 71
Attlee, Clement 261, 297–8, 322
Auchinleck, General Claude 255
Audacity, HMS 228
Australia 22–3, 95–6, 101, 105, 156–7,
        230–1, 233, 252, 285, 294,
        296–8, 301
    army 72, 300
    navy 22–3
Australia, HMAS 23
Austria-Hungary 14, 21, 26, 28,
        33, 67–8
Azores 210, 212–13

Backhouse, Admiral Sir Roger
        155–6, 158
Baldwin, Stanley 101, 103–5, 107, 109,
        112, 115, 118, 124, 128, 130, 137–8,
        140–1, 322
Balfour, Arthur J. 77, 94, 118–19,
        351
Ballard, Captain George 26
Baltic Sea 56–9, 61–2, 69, 81, 157–8,
        168–76, 180, 182
Bangkok 287, 299
Barham, HMS 204
Barnett, Correlli 193, 272, 331–2
Barstow, Sir George 99, 118,
        361 n. 73
Bartolomé, Commodore
        Charles de 54, 92
Battenberg, Admiral Prince
        Louis of 31, 33, 38, 41, 47–8,
        51, 54, 57

Battle of the Atlantic 221–9, 257–82, 340
　'air gap' 269, 271–2, 274, 279, 282
　air resources 217–19, 225–8, 258–60,
　　262–74, 277–9, 281–2, 335–6
　Biscay offensive 228, 259, 261–2, 267,
　　272–3, 277–8, 282, 337
　and Churchill's reputation 335–7
　directive 219, 222
Battle of the Atlantic Committee
　　219–21, 271; see also Anti-U-Boat
　　Warfare Committee
Bayly, Rear-Admiral Sir Lewis 38, 48,
　　54, 62
Beatty, Admiral David 92–4, 106, 109,
　　112–13, 115–16, 118–21, 123, 339
Beaverbrook, Lord 218
Belgium 43, 49, 51, 97, 195, 255
Bellairs, Admiral Roger 237
Belligerent Rights subcommittee 126,
　　128, 130
Bergen 177, 179, 181, 184–6, 188, 329
Birkenhead, Lord 107, 120, 122
Birkenhead committees, see Naval
　　Programme Committees
Biscay offensive, see Battle of the Atlantic
Bismarck 162–3, 200, 215
Black Sea 63, 65–6, 182
Blake, Admiral Geoffrey 259
Blockade 42–4, 49–52, 79, 84, 160,
　　162, 168
'Bolero' 266, 276
Bombay 284
Bomber Command, see Royal Air Force
Bonar Law, Andrew 92, 94
Borden, Sir Robert 22–4, 26–7, 29–30, 32
Borkum 58, 61–2, 64, 69–71, 81, 169
Borneo 298
Bosphorus 59
Bothnia, Gulf of 172–3, 191
Boulogne 207
Bourne, Lieutenant-General Alan 207
Bretagne 197
Bridgeman, William 106–7, 112–15,
　　117–20, 122–5, 128, 130
Britain, Battle of 196, 329
Brock, Captain Osmond de Beauvoir 2, 93
Brook, Sir Norman 313–14, 317–19, 330
Brooke, General Alan 251, 263, 339
　and eastern strategy 297–301

Brooke-Popham, Sir Robert 235, 245
Browne, Anthony Montague 343 n. 2
Bruce, Stanley 266
Bruneval raid 285
'Buccaneer' 293–4
Bulgaria 59, 62
Burma 283, 287, 292–3, 296, 299–302
Burma Road 232, 292
Butler, James R. M. 333–5
Butler, R. A. 233, 312, 314, 316–17
Butt report 228

Cabinet Committee on the Defence
　　Review, see Swinton Committee
Cadogan, Sir Alexander 158
Cairo Conference 294
Callaghan, Admiral Sir George 48
Canada 22–4, 26–9, 31–2, 95, 135, 245
　air force 279
　army 212
　and Hong Kong 245, 248
　naval policy 22–5, 30–1
　navy 226
Canary Islands 210, 212–13
Cape Matapan, battle of 203
Cape Verde islands 210
capital-ship subcommittee 92–5,
　　356 n. 34
Carden, Vice-Admiral Sir Sackville 62–6,
　　68–9
Casablanca Conference 274–6, 287
Casey, Richard 230
Castellorizo 211
Catapult Aircraft Merchantmen
　　218–21, 272
'Catherine' 169–71, 175–6, 182
Cecil, Lord 107, 114, 118–19
Centurion, HMS 204
Ceylon 158, 233, 283–4
Chamberlain, Sir Austen 88, 105, 108,
　　116, 118, 124–5, 130
Chamberlain, Neville 4, 6, 122, 142–4,
　　152, 156, 158, 160–2, 175, 177–8,
　　180–1, 183–4, 322, 333
　and appeasement 144
　and Japan 142–3, 152, 230
　and Norwegian campaign 188–94
　and rearmament 142–3, 152,
　　158–9, 161

and Swedish iron-ore 175, 177–8, 180–1, 183–4
Channel Islands 207, 211
Chatfield Admiral Ernle 124, 323–4, 393 n. 7
  as First Sea Lord 147–9, 155–6
  as Minister for the Coordination of Defence 156, 158, 174, 185
Cherwell, Lord 221, 228, 261, 264, 268, 274, 276–7, 305, 336
Chiang Kai-shek 232, 245, 292, 294
Chiefs of Staff Committee (COS) 141, 155, 194, 196, 199, 201–2, 263, 285, 292, 339
  and Cold War strategy 312, 316–17
  and combined operations 209–10, 212–14
    in Bay of Bengal 287, 291, 293, 295–7, 301
    in Mediterranean 209–10, 291
  and Far East 232, 235, 238, 245–6, 252
  and 'Middle Strategy' 298
  and Pacific fleet 295–7, 299–301
  and Scandinavian strategy 175–7, 179, 189–90
  and second front 286, 291
  and U-boats 216
China 97, 105, 140, 145, 154, 156, 164, 232–3, 241–3, 283, 292, 296
Churchill and the Admirals (Roskill) 5, 330, 336
Churchill Committee (1922) 97–101
Churchill, Clementine 53, 329
Churchill, Lord Randolph 11
Churchill, Winston S.
  and aircraft carriers 220, 229, 302, 304, 314–15, 318–20
  and air power 85–6, 141, 151, 158, 161, 196, 265, 306–7, 311, 318–19, 340–1
  and Anglo-Japanese alliance 91, 95–6, 115–16, 129
  and appeasement 144, 322, 327
  and army 11–12, 53, 67–8, 76, 85–6, 340
  and Australia 96, 101, 105, 154, 157, 231–3, 238, 252–3, 366
  and Baltic Sea 56–9, 81, 157, 168
    'Catherine' 169–71, 175–6, 182
and battleships 35–6, 47, 94, 147–50, 159, 163, 200–1, 273, 302, 304, 306, 311
and belligerent rights 126–7
and Canadian dreadnoughts 22–3, 26–7, 29, 32–3
becomes Chancellor of the Duchy of Lancaster (1915) 71
becomes Chancellor of the Exchequer (1924) 101
becomes Colonial Secretary (1921) 95
and combined operations 56, 67, 204, 206–14, 292
  in Bay of Bengal 287–9, 291–7, 299–302
  in Mediterranean 209–14, 285, 289–91, 293
and convoy 41, 80, 114, 122, 218–19, 221, 258
and cruiser requirements 108–9, 114, 116–17, 121–2, 129–30, 138
and deterrence
  of Japan 232, 240–7
  of Soviet Union 308–9
and economic pressure 9, 37–8, 42–4, 50–3, 58, 79, 84, 126, 168, 171, 196, 256, 341
appointed First Lord of the Admiralty
  (1914) 15
  (1939) 160
and imports 216, 224, 264–5, 274–5, 277–8
and interference in naval operations 192–3, 204, 329–33, 337
and invasion 12, 36–8, 151, 199, 216
and Italian threat 140, 151, 157–8, 165
and Japanese threat 100–1, 104–5, 107–8, 132, 146, 153–4, 165, 231–47, 249–52
and landing craft, 290–1, 293, 299
and mechanization 82–3, 85–6
Mediterranean strategy
  (pre-1914) 19, 25, 29–30, 34–5
  (WWII) 151, 157–8, 201–6, 209–10, 231, 233, 235, 256, 287–9, 291–2
and merchant shipping 8, 39–40, 42, 80, 215–16, 222–4, 265, 270, 276–7, 277, 280–1

Churchill, Winston S. (*cont.*)
  and mines 57–8, 71
  becomes Minister of Munitions
      (1917) 82
  and monitors 57, 62, 69–71, 165
  and naval aviation 149, 159, 267,
      318, 320
  and 'naval holiday' 17–18, 29
  and North Sea 18–19, 33–4, 36, 171
    forward strategy in 38, 45, 47–8, 50,
      54, 56–9, 64, 68–70, 80–1, 168–9
  and nuclear weapons 308–11,
      314, 316
  and Pacific fleet 22–3, 294–301
  and post WWII fleet 303–4
  becomes Prime Minister
      (1940) 194–5
      (1951) 311
  and rearmament (1930s) 1, 140, 143,
      146, 150–1, 322
  and relative importance of the armed
      services 11–12, 307, 311, 318–20,
      340–1
  reputation 2–8, 131, 280, 321–39
  and RN's contribution in WWI
      84, 86
  and RN as a defensive weapon 9–10,
      12, 151, 256
  and sea power 9, 11–12, 52, 256
  and second front 256–7, 285–9, 291
  becomes Secretary of State for War
      and Air (1919)
  and shipbuilding industry 87–8,
      132, 143
  and shipping insurance scheme 39–40
  and Singapore 100, 105, 132, 153–4,
      157, 231, 233, 236–9, 244, 249–53
  and Singapore naval base 100–1,
      106–8, 110–11, 131, 153, 157
  and Soviet Union 140, 154–5,
      308–10, 313
  and strategic bombing 225, 228–9,
      255, 258, 260–1, 264–5, 267, 269,
      273, 281
  and strategy for a Far Eastern
      war 100–1, 104–5, 132, 153–4,
      158, 230, 251–2
  and submarines 26–7, 31–6, 42, 45–6
  and trade defence 39–42, 48, 280

  and U-boats 149–51, 162–3, 166–7,
      171, 215–16, 226, 271–3,
      278–81
  and US as Cold War ally 308–10
  and US collaboration in the Far
      East 96, 146, 155–7, 233, 235–40,
      246–7, 252–3
  and US naval competition 87–8, 91–2,
      94–5, 112, 114–17, 119–20, 127,
      129, 132, 135, 146–7
  and Western Front 59, 61, 76, 82,
      84, 340
Coastal Command, *see* Royal Air Force
Combined Chiefs of Staff 274, 294
Combined Operations
      Headquarters 209, 211, 214
Combined Shipping Adjustment
      Board 265
Committee of Imperial Defence
      (CID) 15, 48, 113, 117
  and capital ship 148
  and economic pressure 42–4, 51
  and Geneva Conference 116–17
  and invasion 37–9
  and Japanese threat, 105, 108
  and Mediterranean 20–1
  and Singapore naval base
      100, 111
  and ten-year rule 124–5
  and US naval challenge 90–2
Conference on Limitation and
      Reduction of Armaments 139
Conqueror, HMS 164, 306
Conservative Party 103, 130, 136, 140,
      308, 321–2
Cork and Orrery, Admiral of the Fleet
      the Earl of 169–70, 182
Constantinople 59, 63–4, 68
Convoy 41–2, 80, 114, 122, 218–19, 218,
      221, 258, 269
Coolidge, Calvin 129
Coral Sea, Battle of 284
Corbett, Sir Julian 77–8
Cos 290
Courageous, HMS 167
Crete 202, 205–6
Cross, Ronald 173, 216–17
'Crusader' 206, 255, 257
'Culverin' 293–301

Cunningham, Admiral Sir Andrew 3, 197, 202–6, 209–11, 217, 262, 339
  Churchill's frustration with 202, 204–6
  eastern strategy 297–301
  strategy in Mediterranean 201–3
Custance, Admiral Sir Reginald 77–8

Dakar 208–9
Daladier, Edouard 183
Dardanelles 59, 61, 63, 74; see also Gallipoli
  campaign 62, 68–70, 192
  and Churchill's reputation 1, 3–4, 73–4, 321–2, 338
Dardanelles Committee 71–2
Davidson, J. C. C. 327
Davis, Admiral Sir William 3
Declaration of London (1909) 42, 52
Declaration of Paris (1856) 42
Defence Committee 268
  and air resources 259–60
  and Battle of the Atlantic 217, 258
  and combined operations 209–13
  and eastern strategy (1944–45) 297
  and movement of ships to the Far East 243–5, 249, 333–4, 338
Defence Requirements Committee 142–3, 152
Denmark 59, 81, 184, 255
Deutschland 167
Dieppe raid 286
Dill, General Sir John 239, 252
Dodecanese islands 209–11, 289–91, 293
Dönitz, Karl 166, 269, 279
Drax, Admiral Sir Reginald 3, 156, 171
Dreadnought, HMS 13
Dunkerque 197
Dunkirk evacuation 195, 206, 322

economic pressure 37, 42–4, 49–50, 127, 153, 160, 168, 196
Eden, Anthony 178, 207–8, 212, 276
  and capital ship movement to Far East 242–4, 334, 338
  and eastern strategy (1944–45) 295, 297–8, 300
Edwards, Captain Ralph 187, 192–3, 330–1

Egypt 19, 201–5, 239, 250
Ehrman, John 339
Eisenhower, General Dwight 273, 290–1
Elbe river 54, 56
Entente Cordiale 13
Esher, Lord 42
  d'Este, Carlo 193
  Exeter, HMS 167
  d'Eyncourt, Sir Eustace Tennyson 45

Federated Malay States, see Malaya
Fermor, Paddy Leigh 343 n. 2
Finance Committee 89
Finland 174–5, 179–81
Fisher, Admiral Sir John ('Jacky') 8, 14, 16–17, 42, 57–9, 61, 77–8, 83
  and Baltic 58, 169
  and Dardanelles 59–66, 70–1
  and 'flotilla defence' 8, 19, 48
  resignation 71
  and submarines 8, 42, 80
Fisher, Sir Warren 125, 142
Fleet Air Arm 148–9, 159, 217, 267, 319–20
'flotilla defence' 8, 19, 48
  in Mediterranean 19–20, 26, 29, 33–4, 46
Forbes, Admiral Sir Charles 165, 189–90, 199, 262, 329
Foreign Office 51–2, 105, 108, 125, 128, 130, 133, 135–6, 142, 158, 160, 187, 242
France 14–15, 18, 25, 49–50, 87, 89, 97, 128, 138–40, 144, 146, 179, 182, 182, 195, 197, 212–14, 232, 255, 303, 324
  army 14–15, 72, 139, 171, 192, 195–6
  Chasseurs Alpins division 188–9, 191–2
  Free French 208–9
  naval agreement with Britain 20, 25, 28
  navy 20, 25, 34, 57, 68–70, 75, 82, 157, 165, 197, 208–9
Fraser, Admiral Sir Bruce 301

Gallipoli peninsula 61, 66–8
  campaign 70–2, 75
  casualties 72–3

Gaulle, General Charles de 208
Geddes, Sir Eric 83, 92, 94, 97
Geneva Conference 112–14, 118–19, 122, 125, 136
Germany 86, 139
  air force 168, 203, 206, 212, 219–20, 224
  army 195, 203, 208, 255
  navy 13, 53, 165
    High Seas Fleet 36 , 40, 53, 56–7, 77, 87
    U-boats 150, 167, 214–5, 224, 227, 257, 274, 278–80
    'pocket battleships' 130, 162, 166
    U-boat production 215, 224, 268–9, 278
Gibraltar 19, 202, 206, 212
Gneisenau 162, 215, 244, 258
Godfrey, Rear-Admiral John 164
Goeben 61
Graf Spee 167
Greece 59, 61–2, 67, 72, 202–3, 211–12
Greenwood, Arthur 217
Greer, USS 226
Gretton, Vice-Admiral Sir Peter 327
Grey, Sir Edward 14, 21, 26, 29, 49, 51, 61, 64, 69, 352 n. 352
Grigg, P. J. 110
Grove, Eric 311
Guilty Men 322
'Gymnast', *see* 'Torch'

Haldane, Viscount 18
Halifax, Lord 156, 161, 175, 177–8, 180–3, 187–9, 193, 232, 322, 333
Hall, Admiral Sir Reginald 'Blinker' 2
Hall, Admiral S. S. 92
Hamilton, General Sir Ian 70
'Hammer' 190–1, 333
Hankey Maurice 42, 59, 61, 64, 67, 73, 88, 115, 126–8, 324–8
Harcourt, Sir Lewis 24
Harriman, Averell 222
Harris, Air Marshal Sir Arthur 263–4, 267, 278, 281, 336
Harstad 186
Heligoland 15, 56, 58, 81
Heligoland Bight 48, 54, 81
Henderson, Admiral R. 149

Hermes, HMS 284
Hipper 215
Hitler, Adolf 141–2, 150, 160, 165–6, 184, 196, 215, 255, 285, 287, 323, 326
Hoare, Sir Samuel 150, 326
Hobhouse, Sir Charles 65
Hollis, Major-General Sir Leslie 327
Hong Kong 153, 235, 245–6, 248, 298
Hood, HMS 232
Hoover, Herbert 129, 136–7
Hopkins, Harry 258, 273
Horne, Robert 92, 94, 99, 110
Horton, Admiral Max 259
Howard, Sir Michael 335
Howe, HMS 200–1, 302

Iceland 224, 226
Illustrious, HMS 203
Imperial Conferences
  (1909) 22
  (1921) 98
Import Executive 217–19, 221, 266
India 283–4, 296
  army 62, 293–4, 302
Indomitable, HMS 23, 248
Industrial Intelligence Centre 164, 171
Inskip, Sir Thomas 326
Ireland 86
Ironside, General Sir Edmund 157, 174, 176–7, 185–7, 331–2
Ismay, Major-General Hastings 194, 226, 296, 298, 325, 327
Istanbul *see* Constantinople
Italy 87, 97, 146, 162, 195, 197, 287
  air force 202
  army 203
  campaign in 289, 291–2
  navy 14, 33, 57, 82, 203, 292

Jackson, Admiral Sir Henry 31, 63–6
Japan 87, 95–6, 99, 145; *see also* Anglo-Japanese Alliance
  army 283, 296
  navy 82, 283–4, 295–6, 301
Jean Bart 197
Jellicoe, Admiral Sir John 2, 15–16, 39, 48, 53–4, 56, 61, 66, 69, 100
  as First Sea Lord 79–81

Joint Planning Committee 187, 191, 197, 211–12, 263, 295, 297
Jones, Thomas 136–7
Joubert de la Ferté, Air Chief Marshal Sir Philip 186, 268, 272, 274
'Jupiter' 286, 289
Jutland, Battle of 76–7

Kellog-Briand Pact 125
Kenya 284
Keyes, Admiral Roger 100, 169, 208–9, 211–14, 285, 322
Kiel Canal 54, 56–7, 59
King George V, HMS 149
King George V-class battleships 162–3, 200, 220, 240–1, 243, 302, 314
King, Admiral Ernest J. 258, 295, 297
Kitchener, Field Marshal Lord 51–2, 58–9, 62, 64, 67–70, 75
Korean War 311

Labour Party 103, 307–8
Land Forces Committee 161
League of Nations 139, 140, 144–5
League of Nations Preparatory Commission 128
Leros 290
Liberal Party 17, 46
Liberator aircraft 226, 258, 264, 271–4, 277, 279, 282
Libya 203–4
Liddell Hart, Sir Basil 321, 331
Lion-class battleships 162–5, 220, 302–4, 306
Lion, HMS 165, 302–4
Lloyd George, David 339
  as Chancellor 13, 28, 31, 43, 46, 49, 59
  as Prime Minister 82, 87–92, 116, 133, 323, 339
  and US naval challenge 90–2, 116
London Magazine 77–8
London Naval Conference and Treaty
  (1930) 137–8, 145, 147
  (1935) 145–6, 150
Long, Walter 86, 90, 94
Luleå 173, 179, 182–3, 191
Lyttelton, Oliver 266, 270–1, 273

MacArthur, Douglas 284, 300
MacDonald, J. Ramsay 101, 135, 137

Mackesy, General Pierse 186, 190
McGrigor, Admiral Sir Rhoderick 314
Macmillan, Harold 320
Madden, Admiral Sir Charles 121, 124
Madeira 212–13
Mahan, Alfred Thayer viii
Malaya 111, 235, 240, 242, 245, 248, 251–2, 293, 295–6, 299–301
Malta 20–1, 28, 34, 202–3, 205–6
Manchuria 140
Marder, Arther J. 192, 331
Marmara, Sea of 66–8, 70
Marshal, General George C. 286, 291
Menzies, Robert 233
Merchant Aircraft Carriers 272, 279
Mers-el-Kébir 197
'Middle Strategy' 298
Midway, Battle of 284
Military Coordination Committee 174, 185, 187, 189, 191, 194, 209, 332–3
Ministerial Committee on Defence Policy 313, 316
Ministry of Economic Warfare 164, 168, 173, 176
Ministry of Shipping 216
Ministry of Supply 143
Ministry of War Transport 272
Morton, Desmond 164, 173
Mountbatten, Lord Louis
  combined operations 214, 285
  SEAC 293–4, 299, 301
Munich Conference 144
Murray, Sir Oswyn 325

Nagumo, Admiral 283, 383 n. 57
Namsos 186–7, 189–91, 332
Naples 203
Napoleon 76
Narvik 172–3, 175, 177–9, 181, 183–5, 331–2
  recapture of 185–8, 190–4
  second battle of 189
Nautilus, HMS 45
naval holiday 17–18, 29
naval programme committees
  (1925) 107–9, 118
  (1927) 120–3

naval standards 21, 32–3, 88–90,
  138, 151–2
  50% over Germany in North Sea 32–3
  60% over Germany 18–21, 28–9, 31–3,
    352 n. 69
  new standard (1930s) 152
  one-power standard
    (Mediterranean) 21–3, 25–34, 46
  one-power standard (interwar) 90, 92,
    95, 97–9, 106–9, 111–12, 117, 124,
    137–8, 152
  two-power standard 18
navy estimates
  (1909–10) 13
  (1911–12) 28
  (1912–13) 16–18, 31
  (1913–14) 24, 26
  (1914–15) 27–32, 45–6
  (1915–16) 31–2
  (1920–1) 89–90
  (1925–6) 106–7
  (1926–7) 112
  (1927–8) 103, 112, 120, 122
  (1928–9) 122–4, 129
  (1929–30) 123, 125
  (1936–7) 149
  (1938–9) 150
  (1940–1) 164–5
Navy League 101
Nazi-Soviet pact 168
Nelson, HMS 168, 240, 244
Netherlands 43, 51–2, 69, 81, 97, 195
Netherlands East Indies 247, 293–5, 300;
    see also 'Culverin'
Newall, Sir Cyril 181, 186, 190
Newfoundland 279
New Guinea 298
New Zealand 22–3, 72, 95–6, 100–1, 105,
    156, 231, 233, 252–3
New Zealand, HMS 23
northern barrage 82, 166
Norway 48, 51, 56, 181, 183, 191, 211,
    214, 285
  army 192
  Churchill's plans to invade
    ('Jupiter') 286, 289
Norwegian campaign 184–94
  and Churchill's reputation 3, 5–6,
    192–4, 328–30

Octagon Conference 301
Oil Fuel Board 111
Oliver, Admiral Henry 58, 63
one-power standard see naval standards
Operational Intelligence Centre 192
Ottley, Sir Charles 42
Ottoman Empire, see Turkey
'Overlord' 286–7, 289–91
Oxelösund 172

Pantellaria 209–10
Paris Peace Conference 126
Passchendaele, Battle of 82
Pearl Harbor 236–7, 244, 247, 251, 254,
    283, 285
Peel, Lord 130
Philippines 237, 242
Phillips, Admiral Sir Tom 164, 169–70,
    186, 191, 227, 243
  and Force Z 248–50
Pierse, Air Chief Marshal Sir
    Richard 218
'Pilgrim' 213–14
Poland 161, 165, 170
Polyphemus-class cruiser 46–7
Portal, Air Marshal Sir Charles 218–19,
    225–8, 261, 263–4, 266–7,
    277–8, 336
Portugal 97
Pound, Admiral Sir Dudley 3, 81, 113,
    158, 163–5, 167, 182, 186, 192,
    199–200 , 202, 204–5, 225, 235,
    252, 283–5, 337, 339
  and Baltic 169–70, 175–6
  and 'Battle of the Air' 259–64, 266–8, 340
  and Battle of the Atlantic 218,
    227–8, 267
  and capital ship for Far East 232,
    240–1, 244, 249
  interference in operations 192–3, 331
Power, Captain A. J. 226
Prince of Wales, HMS 149, 243, 244–5,
    250–1, 335, 338
  loss of 3, 5, 248, 328, 333–4
Prinz Eugen 258
Provence 197

Quadrant conference (Quebec) 289, 293
Queen Elizabeth, HMS 63, 71

'R4' 184, 330–1
Radical Review 312–13, 317
Raeder, Admiral Erich 165
Rangoon 287, 292, 298–9, 301
'R'-class battleships 165, 169–70, 200–1, 232, 240, 242, 244, 283–4
Renown, HMS 233
Repulse, HMS 245, 248, 250
Resolution, HMS 209
Reynaud, Paul 182–3
Reynolds, David 327
Rhine river 171
Rhodes 290–1, 293
Richelieu 197
Richmond, Captain Herbert 49, 54, 56, 92, 138
Robeck, Vice-Admiral John de 69–71
Rodney, HMS 240, 244
Rommel, Field Marshall Erwin 204
Roosevelt, Franklin D. 199, 212, 222–4, 235, 246–7, 254, 258, 261, 265, 284, 286, 294, 296–7
    and landing craft 290–1
    and shipping 270–1, 273, 275, 279
'Round-up', *see* Overlord
Roskill, Captain Stephen 5–6, 192, 250, 329–31, 333–7, 356 n. 34, 383
Royal Air Force 82, 86, 92–3, 133, 143, 148, 161, 171, 182, 199, 217, 226, 248, 258, 272, 277, 313
    and Battle of the Atlantic 228, 280, 335–6
    Bomber Command 218, 227, 229, 258–62, 264, 267–8, 271, 273, 279–81, 335–6, 340
    Coastal Command 217–19, 225–7, 258, 260, 264, 267–8, 271, 280–2, 336, 340
        120 Squadron 271–2
    and strategic bombing 196–7, 225–6, 228, 258, 261
'Royal Marine' 171, 182–3
Royal Marines 66, 68–9, 210–11
Royal Naval Air Service *see* Fleet Air Arm
Royal Navy
    auxiliary aircraft carriers 228–9
    and blockade 37–8, 45
    and 'broken-backed' war 312–14, 317

British Pacific Fleet 301
    competition with Ministry of Munitions 83
    defensive arming of merchant ships 40–1
    escort carriers 221, 272, 279
    fleet carriers 229, 302–3, 313–17, 319–20
    Force H 215
    Force K 206
    Force Z 248–50, 283–4, 328, 333–4
    Home Fleet 165, 167, 184–5, 199, 215
    manoeuvres
        (1912) 37
        (1913) 39
    Mediterranean fleet 167, 201–2, 205–6
    Naval Intelligence Division 40, 164
    and postwar requirements 303–4, 306
    prize manual 44
    and US naval challenge 88–9
    war plans 37, 104, 152–3, 155–6, 158, 236–7, 252
Rumania 59, 171
'Rum, Sodomy and the Lash' 2, 343
Russia 61, 63, 86; *see also* Soviet Union
    army 56, 61
    navy 13, 57
Russo-Finnish war 181
Russo-Japanese war 13

Salonica 67
Salter, Sir Arthur 222
Sandys, Duncan 313–14, 316–17, 319–20
Sardinia 287
St Nazaire raid 285
Scapa Flow 87, 165
Scharnhorst 162, 215, 244, 258
Scheer 215
Schleswig-Holstein 59
Schoenfeld, Max 219–20
Second World War, The (Churchill) 75, 250–1, 281, 323–4, 329, 334, 373 n. 140
Serbia 59, 67
Shipping Committee 266, 270, 275
Sicily 287–9

Sinclair, Sir Archibald 72, 77, 260, 268,
    277, 305
Singapore 237, 295
  fall of 248, 251, 283
  Japanese fleet at 295–6
  naval base 100–1, 104, 106–8, 110–11,
    141, 143
  proposed recapture of 293, 297–8, 302
  'Sledgehammer' 286
Smith, Kevin 216, 280
Smuts, Field Marshal Jan 289
Somerville, Admiral Sir James
    197, 284
  Churchill's frustration with 284
Somme, Battle of 82
Snowden, Philip 110
South Africa 23
South East Asia Command 293–6,
    298–9, 301
Soviet Union 124, 140, 162, 170–1, 174,
    179, 195, 212, 233, 254–5, 285, 308
  British aid to 239–40, 251–2, 255
  naval threat from 312
Spanish Civil War 148
Spee, Admiral Graf von 53
Stalin, Josef 213, 309
standards, see naval standards
Stanhope, Lord 230, 325–7
Stark, Admiral Harold 236–7
Stavanger 48, 177, 179–81, 184
Strategic Appreciation Committee
    156, 158
Sturdee, Admiral Sir Doveton 47,
    51, 78
Suez Canal 201, 203
Sumatra, see Netherlands East Indies
Sunday Chronicle 101
Sunday Pictorial 76, 80
Supreme War Council 179, 183, 185
Suvla Bay 72
Sweden 56, 170, 181
  iron ore 171, 173–4, 179, 181, 185,
    191, 193
Swinton Committee 317, 319–20
Swinton, Lord 313, 317, 319–20
Swordfish HMS 45
Sydenham of Combe, Lord 77–8
Sykes, Major-General Sir Frederick 93
Syria 59, 65

Temeraire, HMS 165, 304
Ten Year Rule 4, 89, 97–8, 105, 108–9,
    111, 122–5, 133–4, 141, 322–8,
    393 n. 7
Thomas, J. P. L. 314–16, 320
Thunderer, HMS 164, 306
Times, The (London) 77, 92, 324–6
Tirpitz 162–3, 200, 240–1, 243–4, 250,
    285, 303
Tobruk 203, 206
'Torch' 270, 272, 286–7
Tovey, Admiral John 3, 262
Treasury 88, 98–9, 101, 103, 105–6,
    109–12, 123–5, 131, 133–4, 142,
    150, 152
Treaty of Versailles 141, 145
Trenchard, Hugh 93, 267
Trident conference 292
Tripoli 204–5, 338
Trondheim 177, 179, 184–5, 331–2
  plans to recapture 186–94, 333
Troubridge, Admiral 19
Truman, Harry 309
Tunisia 205
Turkey 59, 61, 84, 86, 211, 289–90
  army 66
  navy 63
two-power standard, see naval standards

Ultra intelligence 225, 269, 275
United States 43, 51, 80, 88–92, 94–5, 97,
    146, 227, 308
  aid to Britain 200–1, 219–20, 222, 225,
    233, 238, 265
  air force 278–9
  army 286
  Civil War 76
  Joint Chiefs of Staff 290
  and landing craft 287, 290–1
  and merchant shipbuilding 224, 265,
    270, 273, 275–7
  and naval limitations 96–7, 115–16,
    136–7, 146
  navy 82, 88–9, 106, 222, 226, 236, 238,
    247–8, 283, 301, 313
  nuclear weapons 308–10, 316
  and second front 290–1
  staff talks with British 235–8
  U-boat offensive against 257–8, 269

Vanguard, HMS 164–5, 220, 302
Vulnerability of Capital Ships
          committee 148

War at Sea, The (Roskill) 5, 251, 329,
          333–56
War Cabinet (WWI) 80, 82, 89
War Cabinet (WWII) 160–1, 171, 173–5,
          177–84, 196–7, 201, 204, 222, 239,
          278, 323
     and Battle of the Atlantic 218, 221,
          266, 273, 278
     and imports 266, 270
     and Japan 232
     and naval construction 162, 201, 303–5
     and Norwegian campaign 181, 185–9,
          191–3, 331–3
     and strategic bombing 264, 267,
          269, 274
War Committee 72
War Council 57–8, 61, 64–5, 67–71, 73–5

War Shipping Administration 275
Warspite, HMS 284
Washington Conference and Treaty
          (1921–2) 97, 99, 104, 137
Waterfield, A. C. 123
Wavell, General A. 203
Wedemeyer, General Albert 295, 299
Weekly Dispatch 87
Wemyss, Admiral Sir Rossyln 85
Western Front (1914–18) 71, 73, 83
Wilson, Admiral Sir Arthur K. 14–15,
          37–8, 56–8
Wilson, General Sir Henry 15
Wilson, General Maitland 290
Wilson, Woodrow 126
Winant, John 222
'Workshop', *see* Pantelleria
World Crisis, The (Churchill) 34, 46, 62,
          121, 321

Zeebrugge raid 83, 208